Seeing Ourselves

Classic, Contemporary, and Cross-Cultural Readings in Sociology

EDITED BY

John J. Macionis
Kenyon College

Nijole V. Benokraitis
University of Baltimore

Peter Urmetzer
University of British Columbia

Fourth Canadian Edition

PEARSON

Toronto

Vice-President, Editorial Director: Gary Bennett
Editor-in-Chief: Michelle Sartor
Acquisitions Editor: Matthew Christian
Marketing Manager: Lisa Gillis
Developmental Editor: Karen Townsend
Project Manager: Kimberley Blakey
Production Editor: Maheswari PonSaravanan (Jouve India)
Copy Editor: Karen Alliston
Proofreader: Ruth Chernia
Compositor: Jouve India
Permissions Researcher: Rachel Irwin
Art Director: Julia Hall
Cover Designer: Miriam Blier
Cover Image: Getty Images/Lorie Slater

6 18

Library and Archives Canada Cataloguing in Publication

Seeing ourselves : classic, contemporary, and cross-cultural readings in
sociology / edited by John J. Macionis, Nijole V. Benokraitis, Peter Urmetzer.—4th Canadian ed.

Includes bibliographical references.
ISBN 978-0-13-281900-8

  1. Sociology—Textbooks. 2. Sociology—Cross-cultural studies—Textbooks.
3. Canada—Social conditions—Textbooks. I. Macionis, John J
II. Benokraitis, Nijole V. (Nijole Vaicaitis) III. Urmetzer, Peter, 1955–

HM586.S44 2013   301   C2012-908326-7

ISBN 978-0-13-281900-8

Annotated Table of Contents

Preface

Two of the many advantages that sociology offers are its variety and its overlap with other disciplines. Think of any topic and sociologists will likely have studied it: sexual behaviour, food, language, music, and organized crime are just a few examples. These topics can be approached through a variety of sociological perspectives, from the motives of the individual to the architecture of global systems. Such variety is reflected in the readings in this book. *Seeing Ourselves*, Fourth Canadian Edition, examines subjects as diverse as serial killers, skater girls, self-identity through ringtones, drug-takers, the economic elite, and how work is organized in strip clubs. In terms of interdisciplinarity, the topics covered overlap with, among others, demographics, economics, political science, anthropology, political economy, and women's studies.

One does not necessarily have to be a sociologist, or for that matter an academic, to make insightful sociological observations. Thus, several readings in this text are written by people who are not professional sociologists; they include a pollster (Adams), a public intellectual (Wright), a journalist (Condon), a union economist (Stanford), and a health economist (Deber). Significant sociological issues (e.g., health care, aging population, assisted suicide) are summarized in a way that is both informative and easy for introductory students to understand. These articles also suggest that students need not rely exclusively on academic journals for sociological analysis; good sociology can be found in a variety of sources. For this reason, we suggest that students read widely and supplement their academic readings with newspapers, magazines, and online sources in order to keep abreast of what is going on in the world. Sociological theory can serve as a guide for putting current events into

perspective—for example, the next time you read or hear something about the health care debate in Canada, try to analyze it through the perspective of Deber's article on health care funding.

This reader provides excellent material for use in a wide range of courses. *Seeing Ourselves* is most widely used in introductory sociology, but it's also well suited for courses in social problems, cultural anthropology, social theory, social stratification, Canadian society, women's studies, and marriage and the family. The fourth edition offers sixty-eight readings that represent the broadest range of material found in any similar text.

THE THREE C'S: CLASSIC, CONTEMPORARY, AND CROSS-CULTURAL

Seeing Ourselves is the only reader that systematically weaves together three types of selections. For each general topic typically covered in a sociology course, three types of articles are included: classic, contemporary, and cross-cultural.

Classic articles—twenty-two in all—are sociological statements of recognized importance and lasting significance. Included here are the ideas of sociology's founders and shakers—including Emile Durkheim, Karl Marx, Max Weber, and Georg Simmel, as well as Margaret Mead, W. E. B. Du Bois, George Herbert Mead, and Thomas Robert Malthus. Also included are more recent contributions by such luminaries as Alfred Kinsey, John Porter, Erving Goffman, C. Wright Mills, and Jo Freeman.

We realize that not everyone will agree about precisely which selections should be called "classics." But we hope that instructors will be pleased to see the work of so many outstanding women and men—carefully edited with undergraduate students in mind—available in a single, affordable source.

Twenty-eight contemporary selections focus on current sociological issues, controversies, and applications. These articles show sociologists at work and demonstrate the importance of ongoing research. They address many of the issues that concern today's students, providing solid data and reasoned analysis. Among the contemporary selections in *Seeing Ourselves* are Bruce Ravelli on Canadian sociology; Michael Adams on Canadian and American value differences; George Ritzer on McDonaldization and jobs; Jacqueline Lewis on the organization of strip clubs; David Ross, Katherine Scott, and Peter Smith from the Canadian Council on Social Development on the prevalence of poverty in Canada; Chris Schneider on identity and cell phones; Russel D. Ogden on assisted suicide, Brenda Beagan and Scott Davies in two separate readings on social class; James Overboe on disability and genetics; Raisa Deber on the Canadian health care system; Donald Clairmont and Dennis Magill on Africville, a black community in Nova Scotia; and Ronald Wright on the importance of taking care of our environment.

The eighteen cross-cultural selections offer sociological insights about the striking cultural diversity of Canada and the larger world. Included are such well-known works as "Body Ritual Among the Nacirema" by Horace Miner, "India's Sacred Cow" by Marvin Harris, "The Amish: A Small Society" by John Hostetler, and "Homosexuality in Cross-Cultural Perspective" by J. M. Carrier. Other articles focus on such topics as Arab women and social research, the ways in which global inequality benefits rich countries, including Canada, how courtship and marriage differ around the world, and how the right-to-die cause has become an international social movement. Cross-cultural selections broaden

students' understanding of other cultures and, in the process, sharpen their understanding of our own society.

ORGANIZATION OF THE READER

This reader parallels the chapter sequence common to textbooks used in introductory sociology. Instructors can easily and effectively use these articles in a host of other courses and can assign articles in whatever order they wish. For each of the twenty-three general topics, we present a cluster of two to five articles, wherever possible including one classic, one contemporary, and one cross-cultural selection. The expansive coverage of these sixty-eight articles ensures that instructors can choose readings well suited to their own classes, and at the lowest cost.

The first grouping of articles describes the distinctive sociological perspective, brings to life the promise and pitfalls of sociological research, and demonstrates the discipline's applications to a variety of issues. The selections that follow emphasize key concepts: culture, society, socialization, social interaction, groups and organizations, deviance, and the importance of sexuality to our society. The focus then turns to various dimensions of social inequality, with attention to class, gender, race and ethnicity, and aging. The major social institutions are covered next, including the economy and work; politics, government, and the military; families; religion; education; and health and medicine. The final sets of articles explore dimensions of global transformation—including population growth, urbanization, the natural environment, social movements, and social change.

A NOTE ON LANGUAGE

One of the advantages of using this reader is that students are able to read the exact words of dozens of notable sociologists. The editors have assembled their selections from the sources in their original form; although we have edited some readings for length, we have not altered any author's language. At the same time, we want students and instructors to know that some of the older selections—especially the classics—use male pronouns rather than more contemporary gender-neutral terminology, and that one article employs the term "Negro." We have not changed the language in any article, wishing not to violate the historical authenticity of any document. That said, we urge faculty and students to consider the importance of language and how it has changed.

TEACHING FEATURES

Seeing Ourselves, Fourth Canadian Edition, has two features that enhance student learning. First, a brief introduction, placed at the beginning of each selection, summarizes the main argument and highlights important issues to keep in mind while reading the article. Second, at the end of each article are three critical-thinking questions that develop the significance of the reading, help students evaluate their own learning, and stimulate class discussion.

CHANGES TO THE FOURTH CANADIAN EDITION

We are grateful to our colleagues at colleges and universities across Canada who have made *Seeing Ourselves* a part of their courses. In response to this unparalleled reception, the editors have worked especially hard this time around to prepare what we believe is the best and strongest reader available for our discipline. Here are the key changes:

1. Fifteen new articles appear in the Fourth Canadian Edition.
2. We have added one classic selection: "The Second Shift: Marriage in the Stalled Revolution" by Arlie Russell Hochschild. Most

of the changes in this edition are new contemporary selections and reflect recent scholarship that has attracted a lot of attention both within and beyond the field of sociology. These new and popular selections include "The Promise of a Sociology Degree in Canadian Higher Education" by Antony Puddephatt and Randle W. Nelsen; "Discomforting Comfort Foods: Stirring the Pot on Kraft Dinner and Social Inequality in Canada" by Melanie Rock, Lynn McIntyre, and Krista Rondeau; "Is Biotechnology the Answer? The Evidence from NAFTA" by Gerardo Otero and Gabriela Pechlaner; "'It's Like They Have Two Parents': Consequences of Inconsistent Socialisation of Inuit Children" by Anne S. Douglas; "The Music Ringtone as an Identity Management Device" by Christopher J. Schneider; "Hunting Humans: A Historical Overview" by Elliot Leyton; "Why Is Our Educational System Still Guilty of Whiteness?" by Patrina Duhaney; "Aging in Contemporary Canada" by Neena Chappell, Lynn McDonald, and Michael Stones; "The Economy and Society" by Jim Stanford; "Do You Know Left from Right?" by Peter Urmetzer; "'Bringing Up' and 'Growing Up': Parents, Children, and Family Life" by Gillian Ranson; and "Facebook: Friend or Foe?" by Daniel Trottier.

In addition, this Canadian edition of *Seeing Ourselves* offers two new cross-cultural selections, enriching the anthology's multicultural and global content. The new selections in this category are Russel D. Ogden's "Suicide, Canadian Law, and Exit International's 'Peaceful Pill'" and Sarah S. Mosko's "How Many Energy Servants Are Supporting Your Lifestyle?"

3. A greater emphasis on race, class, and gender. Because so much of the research carried out in sociology deals with the causes, character, and consequences of social inequality, this new edition of *Seeing Ourselves* offers more on these vital issues than ever before.

SUPPLEMENTS FOR THE INSTRUCTOR

peerScholar

Firmly grounded in published research, peer-Scholar is a powerful online pedagogical tool that helps develop your students' critical and creative thinking skills. peerScholar facilitates this through the process of creation, evaluation, and reflection. Working in stages, students begin by submitting a written assignment. peerScholar then circulates their work for others to review, a process that can be anonymous or not depending on your preference. Students receive peer feedback and evaluations immediately, reinforcing their learning and driving the development of higher-order thinking skills. Students can then re-submit revised work, again depending on your preference. Contact your Pearson representative to learn more about peerScholar and the research behind it.

MyTest and Test Item File

MyTest from Pearson Canada is a powerful assessment generation program that helps instructors easily create and print quizzes, tests, exams, as well as homework or practice handouts. Questions and tests can all be authored online, allowing instructors ultimate flexibility and the ability to efficiently manage assessments at any time, from anywhere. MyTest for the Fourth Canadian Edition of *Seeing Ourselves* includes six multiple-choice questions and four essay questions for all sixty-eight readings. The MyTest for *Seeing Ourselves* is available at www.pearsonmytest.com. A Test Item File (in Microsoft Word) is also available for download from a password-protected section of Pearson Canada's Instructor Resource Central (http://catalogue.pearsoned.ca). Navigate to your book's catalogue page to view a list of supplements that are available. See your local sales representative for details and access. These questions are also available in Microsoft Word format on Instructor's Resource Central.

We welcome comments and suggestions by faculty, students, and whoever else may happen to read this book. The contact information for the Canadian editor is peter.urmetzer@ubc.ca or Peter Urmetzer, Sociology, Unit 6, University of British Columbia Okanagan, 3333 University Way, Kelowna, British Columbia.

ACKNOWLEDGMENTS

First I would like to thank Katie McWhirter from Pearson Canada for introducing me to the editorial board and making my participation in this project possible. I would also like to thank Lisa Rahn, Karen Townsend, Maheswari PonSaravanan, and Karen Alliston at Pearson for working with me on this project, answering my endless questions and making this an enjoyable experience. Amanda Davison, my very capable research assistant, helped me with the selection of articles and editing; the equally accomplished Bethany Wade assisted with the final editing process. Thanks must also go to the authors and publishers of the readings included here. Much thought and work has gone into each one of these articles, and a text such as this would not be possible without the ongoing research that is conducted on a daily basis by academics across the country. Thanks must also go to my students for always asking interesting questions and engaging me in sociological issues. Shelley Pacholok and Mary Ann Murphy recommended readings that are included here, and I thank them for their suggestions. I would also like to thank Barb Wilke for helping to prepare this document and Christopher Schneider and Jessica Stites Mor for academic advice and musical support. A word of appreciation must also go to Rowen Siemens for emphatic sartorial advice and technical expertise. And last, I would like to thank my partner, Ann McKinnon, for all her support, encouragement, and joy she brings into my life.

Peter Urmetzer

About the Editors

John J. Macionis is Professor and Distinguished Scholar of Sociology at Kenyon College in Gambier, Ohio. Born and raised in Philadelphia, he earned a bachelor's degree from Cornell University and a doctorate in sociology from the University of Pennsylvania. Macionis has authored a number of best-selling sociology textbooks, including *Sociology,* the leading comprehensive text; *Society: The Basics,* the leading brief textbook; and *Social Problems,* the leading text for that course. Professor Macionis has been active in academic programs in other countries, having traveled to more than fifty nations. In 2002, the American Sociological Association honored Macionis for his work with textbooks and for pioneering the use of new technology in sociology by bestowing on him the major Award for Distinguished Contributions to Teaching. At Kenyon, Macionis offers a wide range of upper-level courses, but his favorite course is Introduction to Sociology, which he teaches every year. He enjoys extensive contact with students, making an occasional appearance on campus to play oldies rock and roll, and each term inviting his students to enjoy a home-cooked meal. The Macionis family—John, Amy, and children McLean and Whitney—live on a farm in rural Ohio. In his free time, Macionis enjoys playing the Scottish bagpipes, working for environmental organizations, and sharing an adventure with his two children.

Nijole V. Benokraitis is Professor of Sociology at the University of Baltimore. She earned a B.A. at Emmanuel College (Boston), an M.A. at the University of Illinois at Urbana-Champaign, and a doctorate at the University of Texas at Austin. Professor Benokraitis, who immigrated to the United States from Lithuania with her family when she was 6 years old, is bilingual and bicultural, and is very empathetic of students who try to balance two cultural worlds. She is the author, co-author, editor, and co-editor of seven books, including *Marriages and Families: Changes, Choices, and Constraints.* Benokraitis has published numerous articles and book chapters on topics such as sexism and institutional racism, has received grants and fellowships from many institutions—including the Ford Foundation and the Administration on Aging—and has made numerous appearances on local radio and television shows. She currently serves on the editorial board of *Women & Criminal Justice* and reviews international fellowship applications for the American Association of University Women's Educational Foundation. Benokraitis and her husband, Vitalius, have two adult children, Gema and Andrius. If she had free time, Benokraitis would read mystery novels, expand her mug collection, have more lunches with her past students, garden, and watch at least two movies every day.

Peter Urmetzer is head of history and sociology and associate professor of sociology at the University of British Columbia, Okanagan Campus. He has a B.A. and M.A. from Carleton University in Ottawa and a Ph.D. from the University of British Columbia—all degrees are in sociology. Peter Urmetzer teaches introductory sociology, survey methods, and Canadian society. He is currently conducting research on how values inform economic decision-making. Over the years, his academic interests have consistently leaned toward the distribution of income and wealth. His most recent book, *Globalization Unplugged* (University of Toronto Press), looks at the consequences of globalization for Canada. *From Free Trade to Forced Trade* (Penguin Canada) directly speaks to some of the concerns that Canadians have about free trade, in particular the WTO (World Trade Organization). Urmetzer's other academic interests include research methods and what constitutes good evidence.

1

The Sociological Imagination

C. WRIGHT MILLS

To C. Wright Mills, the sociological imagination is a special way to engage the world. To think sociologically is to realize that what we experience as personal problems are often widely shared by others like ourselves. Thus, many personal problems are actually social issues. For Mills, one of sociology's most outspoken activists, the sociological imagination encourages collective action to change the world in some way.

Nowadays men often feel that their private lives are a series of traps. They sense that within their everyday worlds, they cannot overcome their troubles, and in this feeling, they are often quite correct: What ordinary men are directly aware of and what they try to do are bounded by the private orbits in which they live; their visions and their powers are limited to the close-up scenes of job, family, neighborhood; in other milieux, they move vicariously and remain spectators. And the more aware they become, however vaguely, of ambitions and of threats which transcend their immediate locales, the more trapped they seem to feel.

Underlying this sense of being trapped are seemingly impersonal changes in the very structure of continent-wide societies. The facts of

contemporary history are also facts about the success and the failure of individual men and women. When a society is industrialized, a peasant becomes a worker; a feudal lord is liquidated or becomes a businessman. When classes rise or fall, a man is employed or unemployed; when the rate of investment goes up or down, a man takes new heart or goes broke. When wars happen, an insurance salesman becomes a rocket launcher; a store clerk, a radar man; a wife lives alone; a child grows up without a father. Neither the life of an individual nor the history of a society can be understood without understanding both.

Yet men do not usually define the troubles they endure in terms of historical change and institutional contradiction. The well-being they enjoy, they do not usually impute to the big ups and downs of the societies in which they live. Seldom aware of the intricate connection between the patterns of their own lives and the course of world history, ordinary men do not usually know what this connection means for the kinds of men they are becoming and for the kinds of history-making in which they might take part. They do not possess the quality of mind essential to grasp the interplay of man and society, of biography and history, of self and world. They cannot cope with their personal troubles in such ways as to control the structural transformations that usually lie behind them.

Surely it is no wonder. In what period have so many men been so totally exposed at so fast a pace to such earthquakes of change? That Americans have not known such catastrophic changes as have the men and women of other societies is due to historical facts that are now quickly becoming "merely history." The history that now affects every man is world history. Within this scene and this period, in the course of a single generation, one-sixth of mankind is transformed from all that is feudal and backward into all that is modern, advanced, and fearful. Political colonies are freed; new and less visible forms of imperialism installed. Revolutions occur; men feel the intimate grip of new kinds of authority. Totalitarian societies rise, and are smashed to bits—or succeed fabulously. After two centuries of ascendancy, capitalism is shown up as only one way to make society into an industrial apparatus. After two centuries of hope, even formal democracy is restricted to a quite small portion of mankind. Everywhere in the underdeveloped world, ancient ways of life are broken up and vague expectations become urgent demands. Everywhere in the overdeveloped world, the means of authority and of violence become total in scope and bureaucratic in form. Humanity itself now lies before us, the super-nation at either pole concentrating its most coordinated and massive efforts upon the preparation of World War III.

The very shaping of history now outpaces the ability of men to orient themselves in accordance with cherished values. And which values? Even when they do not panic, men often sense that older ways of feeling and thinking have collapsed and that newer beginnings are ambiguous to the point of moral stasis. Is it any wonder that ordinary men feel they cannot cope with the larger worlds with which they are so suddenly confronted? That they cannot understand the meaning of their epoch for their own lives? That—in defense of selfhood—they become morally insensible, trying to remain altogether private men? Is it any wonder that they come to be possessed by a sense of the trap?

It is not only information that they need—in this Age of Fact, information often dominates their attention and overwhelms their capacities to assimilate it. It is not only the skills of reason that they need—although their struggles to acquire these often exhaust their limited moral energy.

What they need, and what they feel they need, is a quality of mind that will help them to use information and to develop reason in order to achieve lucid summations of what is going on in the world and of what may be happening within themselves. It is this quality, I am going to contend, that journalists and scholars, artists and publics, scientists and editors are coming to expect of what may be called the sociological imagination.

The sociological imagination enables its possessor to understand the larger historical scene in terms of its meaning for the inner life and the external career of a variety of individuals. It enables him to take into account how individuals, in the welter of their daily experience, often become falsely conscious of their social positions. Within that welter, the framework of modern society is sought, and within that framework the psychologies of a variety of men and women are formulated. By such means the personal uneasiness of individuals is focused upon explicit troubles and the indifference of publics is transformed into involvement with public issues.

The first fruit of this imagination—and the first lesson of the social science that embodies it—is the idea that the individual can understand his own experience and gauge his own fate only by locating himself within his period, that he can know his own chances in life by becoming aware of those of all individuals in his circumstances. In many ways it is a terrible lesson; in many ways a magnificent one. We do not know the limits of man's capacities for supreme effort or willing degradation, for agony or glee, for pleasurable brutality or the sweetness of reason. But in our time we have come to know that the limits of "human nature" are frighteningly broad. We have come to know that every individual lives, from one generation to the next, in some society; that he lives out a biography, and that he lives it out within some historical sequence. By the fact of his living he contributes, however minutely, to the shaping of this society and to the course of its history, even as he is made by society and by its historical push and shove.

The sociological imagination enables us to grasp history and biography and the relations between the two within society. That is its task and its promise. To recognize this task and this promise is the mark of the classic social analyst. It is characteristic of Herbert Spencer—turgid, polysyllabic, comprehensive; of E. A. Ross—graceful, muckraking, upright; of Auguste Comte and Emile Durkheim; of the intricate and subtle Karl Mannheim. It is the quality of all that is intellectually excellent in Karl Marx; it is the clue to Thorstein Veblen's brilliant and ironic insight, to Joseph Schumpeter's many-sided constructions of reality; it is the basis of the psychological sweep of W. E. H. Lecky no less than of the profundity and clarity of Max Weber. And it is the signal of what is best in contemporary studies of man and society.

No social study that does not come back to the problems of biography, of history, and of their intersections within a society has completed its intellectual journey. Whatever the specific problems of the classic social analysts, however limited or however broad the features of social reality they have examined, those who have been imaginatively aware of the promise of their work have consistently asked three sorts of questions:

1. What is the structure of this particular society as a whole? What are its essential components, and how are they related to one another? How does it differ from other varieties of social order? Within it, what is the meaning of any particular feature for its continuance and for its change?

2. Where does this society stand in human history? What are the mechanics by which it is changing? What is its place within and its meaning for the development of humanity as a whole? How does any particular feature we are examining affect, and how is it affected by, the historical period in which it moves? And this period—what are its essential features? How does it differ from other periods? What are its characteristic ways of history-making?

3. What varieties of men and women now prevail in this society and in this period? And what varieties are coming to prevail? In what ways are they selected and formed, liberated and repressed, made sensitive and blunted? What kinds of "human nature" are revealed in the conduct and character we observe in this society in this period? And what is the meaning for "human nature" of each and every feature of the society we are examining?

Whether the point of interest is a great power state or a minor literary mood, a family, a prison, a creed—these are the kinds of questions the best social analysts have asked. They are the intellectual pivots of classic studies of man in society—and they are the questions inevitably raised by any mind possessing the sociological imagination. For that imagination is the capacity to shift from one perspective to another—from the political to the psychological; from examination of a single family to comparative assessment of the national budgets of the world; from the theological school to the military establishment; from considerations of an oil industry to studies of contemporary poetry. It is the capacity to range from the most impersonal and remote transformations to the most intimate features of the human self—and to see the relations between the two. [At the] back of its use there is always the urge to know the social and historical meaning of the individual in the society and in the period in which he has his quality and his being.

That, in brief, is why it is by means of the sociological imagination that men now hope to grasp what is going on in the world, and to understand what is happening in themselves as minute points of the intersections of biography and history within society. In large part, contemporary man's self-conscious view of himself as at least an outsider, if not a permanent stranger, rests upon an absorbed realization of social relativity and of the transformative power of history. The sociological imagination is the most fruitful form of this self-consciousness. By its use men whose mentalities have swept only a series of limited orbits often come to feel as if suddenly awakened in a house with which they had only supposed themselves to be familiar. Correctly or incorrectly, they often come to feel that they can now provide themselves with adequate summations, cohesive assessments, comprehensive orientations. Older decisions that once appeared sound now seem to them products of a mind unaccountably dense. Their capacity for astonishment is made lively again. They acquire a new way of thinking, they experience a transvaluation of values: In a word, by their reflection and by their sensibility, they realize the cultural meaning of the social sciences.

Perhaps the most fruitful distinction with which the sociological imagination works is between "the personal troubles of milieu" and "the public issues of social structure." This distinction is an essential tool of the sociological imagination and a feature of all classic work in social science.

Troubles occur within the character of the individual and within the range of his immediate relations with others; they have to do with his self and with those limited areas of social life of which he is directly and personally aware. Accordingly, the statement and the resolution of troubles properly lie within the individual as a biographical entity and within the scope of his immediate milieu—the social setting that is directly open to his personal experience and to some extent his willful activity. A trouble is a private matter: Values cherished by an individual are felt by him to be threatened.

Issues have to do with matters that transcend these local environments of the individual and the range of his inner life. They have to do with the organization of many such milieux into the institutions of an historical society as a whole, with the ways in which various milieux overlap and interpenetrate to form the larger structure of social and historical life. An issue is a public matter: Some value cherished by publics is felt to be threatened. Often there is a debate about what that value really is and about what it is that really threatens it. This debate is often without focus if only because it is the very nature of an issue, unlike even widespread trouble, that it cannot very well be defined in terms of the immediate and everyday environments of ordinary men. An issue, in fact, often involves a crisis in institutional arrangements, and often too it involves what Marxists call "contradictions" or "antagonisms."

In these terms, consider unemployment. When, in a city of 100,000, only one man is unemployed, that is his personal trouble, and for its relief we properly look to the character of the man, his skills, and his immediate opportunities. But when in a nation of 50 million employees, 15 million men are unemployed, that is an issue, and we may not hope to find its solution within the range of opportunities open to any one individual. The very structure of opportunities has collapsed. Both the correct statement of the problem and the range of possible solutions require us to consider the economic and political institutions of the society, and not merely the personal situation and character of a scatter of individuals.

Consider war. The personal problem of war, when it occurs, may be how to survive it or how to die in it with honor; how to make money out of it; how to climb into the higher safety of the military apparatus; or how to contribute to the war's termination. In short, according to one's values, to find a set of milieux and within it to survive the war or make one's death in it meaningful. But the structural issues of war have to do with its causes; with what types of men it throws up into command; with its effects upon economic and political, family and religious institutions; with the unorganized irresponsibility of a world of nation-states.

Consider marriage. Inside a marriage a man and a woman may experience personal troubles, but when the divorce rate during the first four years of marriage is 250 out of every 1,000 attempts, this is an indication of a structural issue having to do with the institutions of marriage and the family and other institutions that bear upon them.

Or consider the metropolis—the horrible, beautiful, ugly, magnificent sprawl of the great city. For many upper-class people, the personal solution to "the problem of the city" is to have an apartment with private garage under it in the heart of the city and, forty miles out, a house by Henry Hill, garden by Garrett Eckbo, on a hundred acres of private land. In these two controlled environments—with a small staff at each end and a private helicopter connection—most people could solve many of the problems of personal milieux caused by the facts of the city. But all this, however splendid, does not solve the public issues that the structural fact of the city poses. What should be done with this wonderful monstrosity? Break it up into scattered units, combining residence and work? Refurbish it as it stands? Or, after evacuation, dynamite it and build new cities according to new plans in new places? What should those plans be? And who is to decide and to accomplish whatever choice is made? These are structural issues; to confront them and to solve them requires us to consider political and economic issues that affect innumerable milieux.

Insofar as an economy is so arranged that slumps occur, the problem of unemployment becomes incapable of personal solution. Insofar as war is inherent in the nation-state system and in the uneven industrialization of the world, the ordinary individual in his restricted milieu will be powerless—with or without psychiatric aid—to solve the troubles this system or lack of system imposes upon him. Insofar as the family as an institution turns women into darling little slaves and men into their chief providers and unweaned dependents, the problem of a satisfactory marriage remains incapable of purely private solution. Insofar as the overdeveloped megalopolis and the overdeveloped automobile are built-in features of the overdeveloped society, the issues of urban living will not be solved by personal ingenuity and private wealth.

What we experience in various and specific milieux, I have noted, is often caused by structural changes. Accordingly, to understand the changes of many personal milieux we are required to look beyond them. And the number and variety of such structural changes increase as the institutions within which we live become more embracing and more intricately connected with one another. To be aware of the idea of social structure and to use it with sensibility is to be capable of tracing such linkages among a great variety of milieux. To be able to do that is to possess the sociological imagination.

CRITICAL THINKING QUESTIONS

1. Why do people tend to think of the operation of society in personal terms?
2. What are the practical benefits of the sociological perspective? Are there liabilities?
3. What does Mills have in mind in suggesting that, by developing the sociological imagination, we learn to assemble *facts* into *social analysis*?

2

The Promise of a Sociology Degree in Higher Education

ANTONY PUDDEPHATT AND RANDLE W. NELSEN

Sociology is a popular program in universities and colleges across the country. This reading examines how various departments in Canada attempt to promote the idea of sociology.

<table>
The Sociological Imagination
CLASSIC
CONTEMPORARY
CROSS-CULTURAL
</table>

METHODS AND DATA

The purpose of this paper is to assess the various promotional messages Canadian sociology departments make in their efforts to recruit students, as evidence for the perceived benefits of sociology for educating students in higher education. To accomplish this, we conducted a content analysis of undergraduate program descriptions from the webpages for all English-speaking sociology departments in Canada, taken from the CAUT listing of Canadian universities (Association of Universities and Colleges of Canada 2008). As such, a total of 54 program descriptions were collected to assess what the expressed purpose of a sociology degree is, and why students ought to enroll.[1]

Using NVivo qualitative analysis software, we undertook a textual analysis of the program descriptions, coding the text as we went along, until a number of categories emerged. What began as a large number of free nodes were eventually split or compiled with each other and were then organized into broader categories. Thirty plus free nodes eventually boiled down to three central themes, holding a total of eight discrete categories altogether. Thus, the analysis is partly grounded in the data, and partly guided by our own theoretical interests (Charmaz 2006; Strauss and Corbin 1998). We inevitably privileged some issues over others, and made choices based on the frequency with which an issue appeared, as well as how relevant it was to our research questions. These constructed categories are not meant to be mutually exclusive, and it is possible for one department to draw on two seemingly contradictory rhetorical themes at once.

Source: From *Canadian Review of Sociology*: 47. 4, pp. 405–430. Copyright © 2010, Canadian Sociological Association.

We were also interested in how these analytical themes were distributed according to the research emphasis and overall prestige of the university. As such, we compared the counts of each category between classes of university; more specifically, medical-doctoral, comprehensive, and primarily undergraduate. . . . The final count had 31 as primarily undergraduate, 11 comprehensive, and 12 medical-doctoral universities. Since we believed that the comprehensive and medical-doctoral programs in sociology are similar based on our coding, and the reputational prestige of sociology departments, and in order to give a larger sample of cases for comparison, we merged comprehensive and medical-doctoral into one category with 23 cases, to compare against the 31 primarily undergraduate programs. This split between doctoral-comprehensive and primarily undergraduate is useful as a comparison variable for certain aspects of the content analysis, to see how certain types of emphases vary by the prestige and research emphasis of the university. In order to make comparisons, we calculated the percentage of departments in each grouping that made use of a particular theme at least

once in their promotional message. This yielded interesting differences, and allowed for a clear presentation of our findings.

FINDINGS

The analysis described above led us to create three sections that represent the most frequently cited promises of what sociology offers prospective undergraduate students. We found variation among three key themes: (1) the central promise of the degree for undergraduate students; (2) the skills promised to the students; and (3) the overall learning experience offered. The following chart (see Table 1) shows how themes differed by whether the department is in a doctoral-comprehensive versus a primarily undergraduate university. The numbers in the chart below reflect the percentage of departments from each grouping that drew on a theme at least once.

We consider the qualitative descriptions of each category, as well as offer a discussion based upon the relative counts. The analysis to follow is primarily qualitative in nature, and thus, these numbers are meant only to be indicative of how the themes we observe in our

TABLE 2.1 Promotional Themes in Sociology Program Descriptions: Percentage Use by Doctoral-Comprehensive and Primarily Undergraduate

	Doctoral-Comprehensive (N = 23) (%)	Primarily Undergraduate (N = 31) (%)
Promise of degree		
Liberal arts education	9	35
Career pathway	52	48
Improve social conditions	17	35
Skills to be acquired		
Critical thinking	30	55
Market based	26	13
Learning experience		
Elite program	35	13
Accessible learning	30	29
Intellectual stimulation	13	16

textual analysis are distributed. As such, we will be referring back to the distributions listed in Table 2.1 throughout our discussion.

The Promise of the Sociology Degree

The purpose of the degree seemed to take three general forms across the program descriptions analyzed. Students were either told that they would (1) receive a broad, liberal arts education that would ensure a well-rounded learning experience; (2) achieve a clear pathway to particular careers as a result of the credential; or (3) enhance their ability to improve the world around them through critical analysis as well as the mobilization of particular social values. We consider these three themes in turn.

Sociology as liberal arts degree. Traditionally, liberal arts universities and colleges in Canada and the United States have focused upon the study of the social sciences and humanities. Even in the modern day university, where professional schools overshadow the liberal arts, students must make at least a symbolic bow to diversity, usually being required to sample some of the offerings from both the humanities and social sciences. In addition to these diversity requirements, a liberal arts education is often characterized not only by the orientation but also the size of the institution offering it. It is small enough to feature both introductory classes and upper-level seminars taught by veteran full-time faculty, rather than inexperienced instructors and graduate teaching assistants. The goal is to encourage a good deal of teacher-student interaction in both the classroom as well as more informal settings. Promises to provide a broad and diverse liberal arts program through sociology varied dramatically depending on the tier of the university. Departments in primarily undergraduate universities mentioned this benefit frequently, in about 35 percent of cases. In contrast, departments in the doctoral-comprehensive category mentioned a broad liberal arts curriculum only 9 percent of the time, perhaps reflecting the devaluation of this

form of education as perceived preparation for the labor market. The following three quotes from our data are exemplary of statements that espouse a broad-based liberal arts education: "First, arts courses are meant to broaden our minds and help us appreciate the workings of our world"; "Rooted in the liberal arts tradition, we cover a wide and diverse range of courses . . ."; "Liberal studies courses aimed at broadening the student's perspective and enriching the educational experience." These statements tend to highlight the romantic ideal of a university education; a broad, diverse knowledge base that allows for students to pursue the ideas they are most passionate about, while gaining a stronger insight into the workings of the world around them. These messages would not usually stop here, however, as the perceived need for positive market assets would often lead to another rhetorical step. Departments would often pitch these broad-based skills as advantageous over disciplinary rigidity, being well suited to jobs in an ever-changing, knowledge-based information society.

As such, university promoters have discovered the wisdom of advertising the practical economic benefits that can result from studying the liberal arts, another theme we found in examining the mission statements. Here are two examples: "Moreover, students have found that a sociological perspective is relevant to almost any other area of study"; "Sociology, the study of human society, is a broadly based liberal arts and research discipline—one of the most diversified, interesting, and practical disciplines there is (we think!)." Students are aware that they are not merely purchasing a particular skill set or mastery of a subject, but are gaining skills that can apply to any job or subject matter they may encounter, leading to an image of "limitless possibilities." As disciplines move further toward providing students with instrumental skills for success in the market, it should not be surprising that departments often lean toward "proper" intellectual and political positions appropriate to the white collar careers that follow (Nelsen 2006). Roughly translated, in terms of knowledge for knowledge's sake and knowledge as a practical asset, maybe you can have your cake and eat it too.

Sociology as career pathway. Many programs went beyond the assurance that the general skills gained from a liberal arts education would help their career in an indirect way, and pushed the fact that specific career pathways would become available as a result of completing the degree. The direct relation between an undergraduate degree in sociology and specific career pathways is questionable, but it is no surprise that students want reassurance in this regard. It seems that the pressure to satisfy student anxiety in relation to future career paths is felt equally across sociology departments in both the doctoral-comprehensive (52 percent) and primarily undergraduate (48 percent) universities. In contrast to describing a more broad-based liberal arts degree with various indirect benefits for advancement in the world, these statements would push the particular applicability of the sociology degree to a number of specific and concrete career opportunities for students.

Some make broad promises for direct career paths: "Our department offers a broad range of courses that equip students theoretically, methodologically and substantively for graduate work, professional programs, and careers in media, management, the non-profit sector including international development and social, health and personal services," while others reference particular job sites by name: ". . . careers in federal government departments and agencies such as Statistics Canada, Justice Canada, Human Resources and Social Development Canada, Industry Canada, Health Canada, Public Safety Canada, among others." Other ways to promote the use of a sociology degree are to mention advanced educational opportunities available: "Our graduates move into a variety of fields, such as law, social work and teacher education, as well as pursue further education in graduate school." Such descriptions fail to mention that

almost any general arts degree would set up the same postgraduate opportunities, and would undermine the message of the unique employment potential of a sociology degree. Finally, other pitches emphasize the moral virtues of the unique employment opportunities afforded by one trained with the sociological imagination. One description asks, "What role do you wish to play in our global society?" The answer, "Community planner, youth worker, research associate, health researcher, recreation supervisor, human rights educator/activist, data analyst, police officer, journalist, educator, the possibilities are endless."

In sum, many program descriptions attempt to position the sociology degree as a major asset that will launch numerous possibilities for positive and fulfilling career trajectories. Of course departments must defend their relevance to some extent and relieve students of the worry that sociology is not a marketable degree. Nonetheless, to the extent that these promises are overblown, or hide similarities to other disciplines in the social sciences and liberal arts, they can undermine the faculty's intellectual integrity, uncovering the role of the university as a business rather than a trusted source of information and knowledge (Nelsen 2002; Schafer 2005).

Sociology to improve social conditions. Beyond offering a foundation for life after university and career specialization, sociology is touted as an excellent foundation from which to challenge enduring social problems. Not only does it transform students, but it also has the potential to provide them with the knowledge and will to improve social conditions. As Mills (1961) put it, the sociological imagination carries with it the wisdom of knowing how to distinguish between private troubles and public issues in order to best foster community change. Such a promise to improve social conditions was twice as likely to be made by departments in primarily undergraduate (35 percent) as compared with doctoral-comprehensive (17 percent) universities. The lower number of mentions in doctoral-comprehensive schools may reflect the perception that prospective students to upper-tier universities are more career oriented than those aiming for a liberal arts college, and are thus less interested in improving the world. Conversely, the higher percentage in primarily undergraduate departments may reflect the perception that students aiming for a liberal arts college are less set on gaining esteemed credentials, and are more open to thinking about agendas for change, both within themselves as well as in their community.

The charge to improve or better social conditions was made in several ways. The great majority of departments making use of this social improvement pitch emphasized the practical applications of a sociological approach, and stressed the value of critical thought. Typical is the following: "By paying attention to 'real world' applications, we also hope to make it clear that sociology is more than a set of ideas—it is an activity or practice." Another similar statement reads: "We also share a strong commitment to critical scholarship that is engaged with real world issues of power and inequality in their diverse local and global manifestations. We believe that sociology and social anthropology can make both academic and practical contributions."

Many statements about improving social conditions go further in defining their value orientations, usually including empathy and tolerance, social justice, and an opposition to inequality and imbalances of power: "We draw strength and purpose from various value positions: empowerment of women, social justice, and modes of inquiry affirming the freedom and dignity of the person." In other instances, departments claim to teach students "to explore the possibilities for progressive social change" and that "students interested in social justice issues will find strong support within our department." Finally, general statements in this regard, such as "Students have found that sociology deepens their understanding of

our world and prepares them to contribute to its betterment," are sometimes amplified with reference to specific outcomes: "For example, in a course in feminist perspectives, students have designed and run a camp for young people, teaching media literacy and enhancing self-esteem."

In the case of the few departments operating in institutions with a strong religious mandate, religious values often informed the agenda of social improvement, and were thus emphasized in their promotional messages. For example, "Informed by a Christian perspective, sociology enables us to reflect on social life in a positive redemptive manner." As well, "Even though we know our world belongs to God, there is still so much that we can learn. . . . If you have a passion for justice, compassion for the hurting, or a curiosity about people or relationships, then sociology/ social work might be where God is calling you." While these religious statements were rare, and were only cited in departments from religiously based universities, it is interesting how values of social betterment resonate across different audiences. Values connected to social betterment through the exercise of sociology can be seen in many of the promotional messages, whether they are presented through the lens of a more secular humanist, politically radical, liberal or religious bent, depending on the orientation of the department. However, the reality of how much opportunity students have to bring about real change through their program of study is questionable. As a recruitment strategy, these images may represent an empty promise, to some extent, of what idealistic students may hope to gain in their sociology education as a "social movement."

The Promise of Skills to Be Acquired

. . . [W]hat good is an education if there is no training provided? What is gained from an English degree, for example, if students do not cultivate the rules of good writing, grammar, and punctuation? The essence of these skills entails that they *must be trained*, in that the student patiently incorporates and internalizes nonnegotiable rules from the outside. Certainly, the English major can write original and clever mystery novels, and the engineer can go on to design innovative bridges and car engines, but neither could do so effectively without the proper training to enable the foundation from which these trajectories could spawn. Indeed, it seems that the notion of education as creative self-development cannot be easily detached from training, so their dichotomous opposition seems questionable at best.

Despite these analytical problems, [this raises] a very important point. That is, who benefits most from the skills students acquire in university? Are students being trained to think for themselves among a matrix of competing interests in society, to make ethical and pragmatic decisions according to their own reasoning and weighing of evidence? Or are students simply gaining skill sets that make them more efficient workers for various tasks and roles in the private sector? Working from this basic conceptual split, we identified two different categories representing the types of skills students could expect to receive as a result of an education in sociology. One category was defined as (1) skills that would allow for self-development and critical, independent thinking, while the other houses skills that are suited to (2) particular market niches.

Self-development and critical thinking skills. In the first category, 55 percent of the primarily undergraduate programs place an emphasis on skills oriented to fostering critical, independent thought, and the development of self, while only about 30 percent of doctoral-comprehensive departments do so. Quotations like the following emphasized a general set of skills for personal enrichment that would be suitable across a broad spectrum of life experience: "Such knowledge can enhance our

ability to better achieve personal goals." Other passages were more direct in that students would be able to better think for themselves, and analyze social issues in more critical and systematic ways. For example, "The Department's approach puts strong emphasis on the acquisition of a capacity for independent and critical thought," and "These courses are designed to enable students to think more reflexively about their own life experiences, and to think more critically and analytically about some of the pressing social and global issues of our age." Some argue that such skills can help students think creatively and move beyond the traditional assumptions of the status quo: "Sociology teaches us to think creatively and critically about the world around us," and "Courses enhance students' abilities to examine critically the social conventions and regulations that circumscribe our lives." It is also asserted that such critical thought will lead to the betterment of the self in terms of improved citizenship and well-being: "theoretical and analytical tools . . . contribute in this way to personal enrichment and more effective citizenship."

While it is nice to see these qualities emphasized, it is noteworthy that upper-tier schools are less likely to place these issues front and center in their promotional statements. As upper-tier research institutions hold to a stronger market orientation, abstract goals about self-enrichment and critical thinking are not seen to resonate with students looking for job opportunities when they graduate. The difference shows that upper- and lower-tier schools are devising different niche marketing strategies to attract different types of students. This may indicate that research-based departments are focusing primarily on market-oriented students, while liberal arts and primarily undergraduate schools put more emphasis on students who are less driven by career interests. One should be cautious in drawing these conclusions, however, as our data may hide important differences among primarily undergraduate programs, which would depend in part on the social class of their clientele. For example, undergraduate programs that specialize in providing a quality liberal arts education, such as Acadia and Mount Allison, probably attract more upper-middle class students, who are privileged enough to pursue knowledge for knowledge's sake. In contrast, campuses like Lakehead and Laurentian, who draw a larger percentage of working class students, probably feel more pressure to extol the career virtues of their programs as a result.[2]

Market-based skills. Some departments emphasized the extent to which students would gain skills more tailored to specific career interests, making them attractive to potential employers. Such market skills are emphasized more by doctoral-comprehensive programs (26 percent), while only half as many primarily undergraduate programs do so (13 percent). Examples of such pitches are as follows: "students develop research skills that are applicable to a variety of employment opportunities," and "some of the students apply their social sciences knowledge and analytical skills directly into research, teaching, policy development, human resources and correctional services." Here schools would emphasize specific "tool kits" enabling the students to handle various careers: "research methods and data analytic techniques . . . expand their 'tool kits' by learning how these are used in cutting-edge research . . . these skills allow students to follow many of the career paths in sociology." Such tools are seen as an excellent commodity for entering the labor market: "A sound knowledge of sociology is a significant asset in many careers."

There are a number of reasons why upper-tier programs are more likely to promise specific market-based skill sets. It could be that more career-oriented students aim for the research-intensive campuses, and hence, this is simply what they want to hear. It may also be that larger departments at powerhouse institutions are more enmeshed in business and governmental partnerships in their day-to-day work, rely on more grants, and focus more intensely on quantitative research as this brings more prestige and money into the university. Thus, perhaps research practices and institutional goals become naturally translated into the classroom. Certainly, skills that fit well on a resume probably put students and parents at ease. But if such skills become the main modus operandi of "quality" sociology programs, there is a danger that the market logic of the system is too often uncritically supported. Is the gradual encroachment of the system eroding the original promises of a sociology education? How much should we desire the addition of specific market-based tools in the curriculum, and how much should we fear them for stripping away the potential for critical and independent thought?

The Promise of the Learning Experience

A related measure is the type of learning experience promised to students. We reveal three major categories here, all pitching the benefit of the learning experience in different ways: (1) an elite program, with high quality, cutting-edge researchers setting the curriculum and delivering the material; (2) an accessible program that would not be too challenging and may even be fun; and (3) an enriching program that offers intellectual stimulation and interesting, challenging material. We consider these categories in turn.

Elite program. Departments claiming "elite" programs consistently emphasized the quality of their faculty, usually in terms of research excellence. Quotes, such as "our faculty possess a wealth of expertise acquired through study and research in a variety of countries and are internationally recognized in their areas," and "our faculty members maintain strong research records and stay at the cutting edge of their fields of expertise," were common. Leading programs at medical-doctoral universities boast even more expertise among their faculty. For example, "The department has two Canada Research Chairs, the current Harney Chair of Ethnic and Pluralism Studies, and the endowed S.D. Clark Memorial Chair." As well as emphasizing the best researchers, schools would also push their institutional prominence in various ways. For example, "The Department of Sociology hosts the *Canadian Review of Sociology*, the flagship journal of the Canadian Sociological Association."

Leading programs would also boast about their historical legacy: "The McGill Sociology Department was instrumental in establishing empirical sociology in Canada." These points imply that the programs offered are stronger than their competitors as they draw on the expertise of the best scholars: "Based on the data available, and through our self-study, we place ourselves highly in the realm of North American departments. Faculty in each of our core areas are renowned academic leaders in their respective fields." In sum, these schools try to win over students based on their historical legacy, institutional prominence, and cutting-edge research emphasis. As one would expect, departments from doctoral-comprehensive universities engage in this tactic almost three times as often as departments in primarily undergraduate universities (35 versus 13 percent). Students entering the marketplace are led to believe they will be able to cash in on the cultural capital that prominent research centers offer (Bourdieu [1984] 1979, 2001). In practice, students are unlikely to learn the newest cutting-edge research findings, but follow textbooks or well established readings that are available anywhere. Further, the majority of students do not participate in faculty research programs either. In fact, students enrolled at prestigious institutions are less likely to be taught by true experts as faculty on research leave are replaced with sessional lecturers and graduate students. Instead, a symbolic affiliation is gained, as well as a general trust in the philosophy that the best

researchers in the field are also the most qualified teachers, when they are available.

Even then, there is ongoing debate over this supposed positive relationship between teaching and research. While some argue that research enhances the quality of teaching, others maintain that research and teaching are generally in conflict with each other. The latter group contends that professors' narcissistic preoccupation with their research works against classroom excellence and is of little benefit to students (see, e.g., Gouldner 1970; Nelsen 1991; Newson and Buchbinder 1988; Pocklington and Tupper 2002; Sperber 2000:81–91; Sykes 1988; Terenzini and Pascarella 1991). Not much has changed in the university since the 1940s and the end of World War II regarding the academic schizophrenia resulting from this almost competitive relationship between teaching and research. Indeed, what Caplow and McGee (1965:69) wrote about *The Academic Marketplace* over 45 years ago still holds true today: "For most members of the profession, the real strain in the academic role arises from the fact that they are, in essence, paid to do one job (teaching), whereas the worth of their services is evaluated on the basis of how well they do another (research)." This debate reached somewhat of a crescendo in 1991 with the release of Stuart Smith's (1991) report inquiring into the health of Canadian university education. Many observers were both surprised and angered when Smith criticized the research emphasis of the universities and proposed that they pay greater attention to teaching. This challenged the self-serving myth of mutual enrichment that favored the predilections and interests of the professoriate. As Tom Pocklington and Allan Tupper (2002:111–12) note, "The administrative policies of Canadian universities pound spikes into the coffin of mutual enrichment."

A related issue is the culture of learning that tends to arise at more elite universities, as a result of the heightened career emphasis, as well as the presumed expertise of research-oriented professors. Drawing on his long tenure at an elite American university, William Deresiewicz (2008) laments that the so-called "best and the brightest," are too often nurtured toward an "entitled mediocrity" in order for the "chance to get rich." True intellectual curiosity takes a back seat to the instrumental concern of satisfying course requirements and playing the game required to achieve better grades. Deresiewicz (2008:6) writes that "the few students who are passionate about ideas find themselves feeling isolated and confused. I was talking with one of them last year about his interest in the German Romantic idea of *bildung*, the up-building of the soul. But, he said—he was a senior at the time—it's hard to build your soul when everyone around you is trying to sell theirs." As our most powerhouse institutions push research over teaching, compensating for this with the promise of elite credentials, are the engaging aspects of the learning experience being lost?

Accessible learning. When schools could not boast about the rigor and superiority of the program in terms of cutting-edge research, they would often try to attract students by making the program seem accessible. It should be noted, however, that doctoral-comprehensive programs also adopted the "ease of learning" tack to an equal level as primarily undergraduate programs (30 versus 29 percent). Undoubtedly, part of the draw of a sociology degree is the "bird program" reputation, in that students, many who work long hours to pay for their education, are looking for something less taxing, more easily manageable, and entertaining. This can be seen as gaining benefits by being able to minimize their planned "investments" (time, work effort) in relation to what they gain from the degree.

Much like private schools (Davies and Quirke 2005) and tutoring businesses (Aurini 2004) at the high school level, many departments are increasingly promising small class sizes and the use of individualized, flexible learning styles tailored to student needs.

Promises of accessible material, patient and easy to understand teachers, and small class sizes were common: "The small size of our programme and the dedication of our faculty, allow us to provide personal attention to students and extensive access to faculty. Having relatively few requirements, we allow students substantial flexibility in meeting individual intellectual pursuits." Other examples include: "The Department prides itself on having good student-teacher contact," and "professors employ diverse pedagogies to facilitate student learning." Some promise students "small class sizes, flexible programs, lifelong friendships, caring and experienced professors," ensuring "a context of flexible and personalized instruction." Rather than stressing independence and responsibility, the emphasis is consistently on spoon-feeding strategies, individualized coaching, and personalized instruction. Students can look forward to professors who are not only experts in their field, but who are also kind, caring, considerate, and open to accommodating student needs.

Some departments emphasize that the learning experience will not only be relatively painless and easy, but also entertaining and fun. Nelsen (2007) argues that this phenomenon is linked to students' immersion in the technologically mediated culture of entertainment generally, such that universities increasingly feel obliged to offer "edutainment" in an effort to compete with other media-driven institutions. This increasing slide to "fun and games in higher education" fits not only with a decreased attention span and competing sources of quick and instantaneous information now readily available, but also with the fact that students are more pressed for time with part-time jobs to meet rising tuition costs. As a result, students need to be entertained as well as educated with films, video clips, and various sights and sounds that go beyond the dry delivery of material. Programs would promise "fear, fun, advertising, youth, action film, the entertainment industry, consumerism, and many more." Another department describes the content as "cutting edge social issues such as sweat shops, hate crimes, gang violence, professional wrestling." One department enticingly asks "What can we learn from watching and analyzing films like Trainspotting?" In short, not only will the degree be easy and accessible, but entertaining as well.

Pitches for accessibility may seem very different from the rhetoric of elite programs, but both reveal the same instrumental market logic, which structures and increasingly commodifies higher education. In the final analysis, cutting-edge programs promise the *rewards* of acquiring certifications and cultural and symbolic capital that translates into enhanced market opportunities. In contrast, examples of pitches for ease of learning and more "edutainment" show us that universities are following this market logic by trumpeting the minimal *investments* required by the student in terms of time and effort, thus providing the same profit sum in terms of investment versus reward. As Côté and Allahar (2007) have argued, university is increasingly becoming a business where we must serve our clients in return for their money, and customer satisfaction is put at a premium never before seen in the context of higher education. Thus, administrators and professors must lessen their expectations of students, but are assured a steady influx of clients to meet their budgetary demands.

Engagement and intellectual stimulation. What is sadly missing from both primarily undergraduate as well as doctoral-comprehensive departments is the promise of engagement and intellectual stimulation. Only 13 percent of doctoral-comprehensive schools and 16 percent of primarily undergraduate institutions offer this pitch. Many would argue that an emphasis on authentic intellectual exchanges is the core of a solid education (Puddephatt, Kelly, and Adorjan 2006), yet this is the least common

theme presented in the statements analyzed. Departments who did draw on this theme would offer the following types of statements: "our commitment to providing a stimulating and dynamic environment for learning," a "program that is interesting and informative," or "courses aimed at broadening the student's perspective and enriching the educational experience." Other examples include "We invite you to join with us on this exciting journey of understanding and engagement," and "Our shared goal is to make studies in Sociology exciting, provocative, relevant, intellectually rigorous, and memorable." We believe it is unfortunate that this message is in the minority. Programs with instant career benefits, entertaining and accessible modes of delivery, and cutting-edge curriculum sell better than the promise of thought-provoking material and rigorous, critical thinking. One wonders about the extent to which these sales pitches have their correlates in actual pedagogical practice. . . .

CRITICAL THINKING QUESTIONS

1. Although you may not be a declared sociology major, what attracted you to taking a course in sociology in the first place? Are you planning to take more courses in the discipline? If you are not planning to major in sociology, what are some of the reasons?

2. Some of the questions asked in the reading about sociology are also applicable to university as a whole. Why are you in university? Is it to gain skills, because of intellectual curiosity, or because it will serve as a passport to a higher paying job?

3. What kinds of skills do you learn in university in general and in sociology in particular? Do you think it is noble or foolish to acquire a degree in a discipline just for interest's sake, particularly if it does not provide the necessary skills for the job market?

NOTES

1. One reviewer stated that longitudinal data would help to show how these messages have changed over the last 20 years. This would seem even more relevant due to the aforementioned trends in rising enrollments in sociology since Fabianic was writing. Unfortunately, this type of longitudinal data are not readily available without making use of Web archives, which is beyond the scope of this project. We invite others to explore these trends.

2. This is further complicated by the fact that Lakehead's most recent marketing campaign for students had the slogan "I think for myself." This clearly taps in to the rhetoric of critical thinking and works to downplay career-oriented themes. Hence, the issues here are complex, and institutions may attempt different strategies in efforts to recruit wide segments of the population both locally and from afar. One might argue Lakehead's recent campaign shift is an attempt to win over more middle-class Toronto area students, either to the Thunder Bay campus, or to the newly built satellite campus in Orillia, located in a much closer proximity to Toronto.

REFERENCES

Association of Universities and Colleges of Canada. 2008. *Canadian universities: Our universities*. Available: **http://www.aucc.ca/can_uni/our universities/index e.html**. Accessed December 5, 2008.

Aurini, J. 2004. Educational entrepreneurialism in the private tutoring industry: Balancing profitability with the humanistic face of schooling. *The Canadian Review of Sociology and Anthropology*, 41: 475–91.

Bourdieu, P. [1984] 1979. *Distinction: A social critique of the judgement of taste*. Cambridge, MA: Harvard University Press.

Bourdieu, P. 2001. *The science of science and reflexivity*. Chicago, IL: University of Chicago Press.

Caplow, T., and R. J. McGee. 1965. *The academic marketplace*. Garden City, NY: Doubleday.

Charmaz, K. 2006. *Constructing grounded theory: A practical guide through qualitative analysis*. Thousand Oaks, CA: Sage.

Côté, J. E., and A. L. Allahar. 2007. *Ivory tower blues: A university system in crisis*. Toronto, ON: University of Toronto Press.

Davies, S., and L. Quirke. 2005. Providing for the priceless student: Ideologies of choice in an emerging educational market. *American Journal of Education*, 111: 523–47.

Deresiewicz, W. 2008. The disadvantages of an elite education: Our best universities have forgotten that the reason they exist is to make minds, not careers. *The American Scholar*, Summer, 2008.

Gouldner, A. W. 1970. *The coming crisis of western sociology*. New York: Basic Books.

Mills, C. W. 1961. *The sociological imagination*. New York: Oxford.

Nelsen, R. W. 1991. *Miseducating: Death of the sensible*. Kingston, ON: Cedarcreek Publications.

Nelsen, R. W. 2002. *Schooling as entertainment: Corporate education meets popular culture*. Kingston, ON: Cedarcreek Publications.

Nelsen, R. W. 2006. The community college con: Education that works? In *The professionalization of work*, eds. M. Jacobs and S. Bosanac, 336–57. Whitby, ON: de Sitter Publications.

Nelsen, R. W. 2007. *Fun and games and higher education: The lonely crowd revisited*. Toronto, ON: Between the Lines Press.

Newson, J., and H. Buchbinder. 1988. *The university means business: Universities, corporations and academic work*. Toronto, ON: Garamond Press.

Pocklington, T., and A. Tupper. 2002. *No place to learn: Why universities aren't working*. Vancouver: UBC Press.

Puddephatt, A., B. Kelly, and M. Adorjan. 2006. Unveiling the cloak of competence: Cultivating authenticity in graduate sociology. *The American Sociologist*, 37: 84–98.

Schafer, M. 2005. Who you gonna call? Not the corporate university." *Canadian Dimension*, 39: 26–29.

Smith, S. 1991. *Report: Commission of inquiry on Canadian university education*. Ottawa, ON: Association of Universities and Colleges of Canada.

Sperber, M. 2000. *Beer and circus: How big time sports is crippling undergraduate education*. New York: Henry and Holt Company.

Strauss, A., and J. Corbin. 1998. *Basics of qualitative research: Techniques and procedures for developing grounded theory*. 2nd ed. Thousand Oaks, CA: Sage.

Sykes, C. J. 1988. *ProfScam: Professors and the demise of higher education*. New York: St. Martin's Press.

Terenzini, P. T., and E. T. Pascarella. 1991. *How college affects students: Findings and insights from twenty years of research*. San Francisco, CA: Jossey-Bass.

3

Body Ritual Among
the Nacirema

HORACE MINER

*Most people take their life for granted; when they think about society at all, it is usually
viewed as both natural and good. To help us step back from our society, anthropologist
Horace Miner describes the Nacirema, a peculiar people living in North America (whose
lives should strike you as familiar). Miner's intellectual sleight-of-hand illustrates how
the sociological perspective involves detachment, so that everyday life becomes something new and unusual.*

The anthropologist has become so familiar
with the diversity of ways in which different
peoples behave in similar situations that he is
not apt to be surprised by even the most exotic
customs. In fact, if all of the logically possible combinations of behavior have not been
found somewhere in the world, he is apt to
suspect that they must be present in some yet
undescribed tribe. This point has, in fact, been
expressed with respect to clan organization by
Murdock (1949:71). In this light, the magical
beliefs and practices of the Nacirema present
such unusual aspects that it seems desirable to
describe them as an example of the extremes to
which human behavior can go.

Professor Linton first brought the ritual of
the Nacirema to the attention of anthropologists

twenty years ago (1936:326), but the culture of
this people is still very poorly understood. They
are a North American group living in the territory between the Canadian Cree, the Yaqui
and Tarahumare of Mexico, and the Carib and
Arawak of the Antilles. Little is known of their
origin, although tradition states that they came
from the east. According to Nacirema mythology, their nation was originated by a culture
hero, Notgnihsaw, who is otherwise known for
two great feats of strength—the throwing of a
piece of wampum across the river Pa-To-Mac
and the chopping down of a cherry tree in
which the Spirit of Truth resided.

Nacirema culture is characterized by a
highly developed market economy which has
evolved in a rich natural habitat. While much
of the people's time is devoted to economic
pursuits, a large part of the fruits of these
labors and a considerable portion of the day
are spent in ritual activity. The focus of this

Source: "Body Ritual among the Nacirema" by Horace
Miner. Reprinted courtesy of the American Anthropological Association from *American Anthropologist*, vol. 58,
no. 3, June, 1956.

activity is the human body, the appearance and health of which loom as a dominant concern in the ethos of the people. While such concern is certainly not unusual, its ceremonial aspects and associated philosophy are unique.

The fundamental belief underlying the whole system appears to be that the human body is ugly and that its natural tendency is to debility and disease. Incarcerated in such a body, man's only hope is to avert these characteristics through the use of the powerful influences of ritual and ceremony. Every household has one or more shrines devoted to this purpose. The more powerful individuals in this society have several shrines in their houses, and, in fact, the opulence of a house is often referred to in terms of the number of such ritual centers it possesses. Most houses are of wattle and daub construction, but the shrine rooms of the more wealthy are walled with stone. Poorer families imitate the rich by applying pottery plaques to their shrine walls.

While each family has at least one such shrine, the rituals associated with it are not family ceremonies but are private and secret. The rites are normally only discussed with children, and then only during the period when they are being initiated into these mysteries. I was able, however, to establish sufficient rapport with the natives to examine these shrines and to have the rituals described to me.

The focal point of the shrine is a box or chest which is built into the wall. In this chest are kept the many charms and magical potions without which no native believes he could live. These preparations are secured from a variety of specialized practitioners. The most powerful of these are the medicine men, whose assistance must be rewarded with substantial gifts. However, the medicine men do not provide the curative potions for their clients, but decide what the ingredients should be and then write them down in an ancient and secret language. This writing is understood only by the medicine men and by the herbalists who, for another gift, provide the required charm.

The charm is not disposed of after it has served its purpose, but is placed in the charm-box of the household shrine. As these magical materials are specific for certain ills, and the real or imagined maladies of the people are many, the charm-box is usually full to overflowing. The magical packets are so numerous that people forget what their purposes were and fear to use them again. While the natives are very vague on this point, we can only assume that the idea in retaining all the old magical materials is that their presence in the charm-box, before which the body rituals are conducted, will in some way protect the worshipper.

Beneath the charm-box is a small font. Each day every member of the family, in succession, enters the shrine room, bows his head before the charm-box, mingles different sorts of holy water in the font, and proceeds with a brief rite of ablution. The holy waters are secured from the Water Temple of the community, where the priests conduct elaborate ceremonies to make the liquid ritually pure.

In the hierarchy of magical practitioners, and below the medicine men in prestige, are specialists whose designation is best translated "holy-mouth-men." The Nacirema have an almost pathological horror of and fascination with the mouth, the condition of which is believed to have a supernatural influence on all social relationships. Were it not for the rituals of the mouth, they believe that their teeth would fall out, their gums bleed, their jaws shrink, their friends desert them, and their lovers reject them. They also believe that a strong relationship exists between oral and moral characteristics. For example, there is a ritual ablution of the mouth for children which is supposed to improve their moral fiber.

The daily body ritual performed by everyone includes a mouth-rite. Despite the fact that these people are so punctilious about care of the mouth, this rite involves a practice which strikes the uninitiated stranger as revolting. It was reported to me that the ritual consists of inserting a small bundle of hog hairs into the mouth, along with certain magical powders, and then moving the bundle in a highly formalized series of gestures.

In addition to the private mouth-rite, the people seek out a holy-mouth-man once or twice a year. These practitioners have an impressive set of paraphernalia, consisting of a variety of augers, awls, probes, and prods. The use of these objects in the exorcism of the evils of the mouth involves almost unbelievable ritual torture of the client. The holy-mouth-man opens the client's mouth and, using the above-mentioned tools, enlarges any holes which decay may have created in the teeth. Magical materials are put into these holes. If there are no naturally occurring holes in the teeth, large sections of one or more teeth are gouged out so that the supernatural substance can be applied. In the client's view, the purpose of these ministrations is to arrest decay and to draw friends. The extremely sacred and traditional character of the rite is evident in the fact that the natives return to the holy-mouth-man year after year, despite the fact that their teeth continue to decay.

It is to be hoped that, when a thorough study of the Nacirema is made, there will be careful inquiry into the personality structure of these people. One has but to watch the gleam in the eye of a holy-mouth-man, as he jabs an awl into an exposed nerve, to suspect that a certain amount of sadism is involved. If this can be established, a very interesting pattern emerges, for most of the population shows definite masochistic tendencies. It was to these that Professor Linton referred in discussing a distinctive part of the daily body ritual which is performed only by men. This part of the rite involves scraping and lacerating the surface of the face with a sharp instrument. Special women's rites are performed only four times during each lunar month, but what they lack in frequency is made up in barbarity. As part of this ceremony, women bake their heads in small ovens for about an hour.

The theoretically interesting point is that what seems to be a preponderantly masochistic people have developed sadistic specialists.

The medicine men have an imposing temple, or *latipso*, in every community of any size. The more elaborate ceremonies required to treat very sick patients can only be performed at this temple. These ceremonies involve not only the thaumaturge but a permanent group of vestal maidens who move sedately about the temple chambers in distinctive costume and headdress.

The *latipso* ceremonies are so harsh that it is phenomenal that a fair proportion of the really sick natives who enter the temple ever recover. Small children whose indoctrination is still incomplete have been known to resist attempts to take them to the temple because "that is where you go to die." Despite this fact, sick adults are not only willing but eager to undergo the protracted ritual purification, if they can afford to do so. No matter how ill the supplicant or how grave the emergency, the guardians of many temples will not admit a client if he cannot give a rich gift to the custodian. Even after one has gained admission and survived the ceremonies, the guardians will not permit the neophyte to leave until he makes still another gift.

The supplicant entering the temple is first stripped of all his or her clothes. In everyday life the Nacirema avoids exposure of his body and its natural functions. Bathing and excretory acts are performed only in the secrecy of the household shrine, where they are ritualized as part of the body-rites. Psychological shock results from the fact that body secrecy is suddenly lost upon entry into the *latipso*. A man, whose own wife has never seen him in an excretory act, suddenly finds himself naked and assisted by a vestal maiden while he performs his natural functions into a sacred vessel. This sort of ceremonial treatment is necessitated by the fact that the excreta are used by a diviner to ascertain the course and nature of the client's sickness. Female clients, on the other hand, find their naked bodies are subjected to the scrutiny, manipulation, and prodding of the medicine men.

Few supplicants in the temple are well enough to do anything but lie on their hard beds. The daily ceremonies, like the rites of the holy-mouth-men, involve discomfort and torture. With ritual precision, the vestals awaken their miserable charges each dawn and roll them about on their beds of pain while performing ablutions, in the formal movements of which the maidens are highly trained. At other times they insert magic wands in the supplicant's mouth or force him to eat substances which are supposed to be healing. From time to time the medicine men come to their clients and jab magically treated needles into their flesh. The fact that these temple ceremonies may not cure, and may even kill, the neophyte, in no way decreases the people's faith in the medicine men.

There remains one other kind of practitioner, known as a "listener." This witch-doctor has the power to exorcise the devils that lodge in the heads of people who have been bewitched. The Nacirema believe that parents bewitch their own children. Mothers are particularly suspected of putting a curse on children while teaching them the secret body rituals. The counter-magic of the witch-doctor is unusual in its lack of ritual. The patient simply tells the "listener" all his troubles and fears, beginning with the earliest difficulties he can remember. The memory displayed by the Nacirema in these exorcism sessions is truly remarkable. It is not uncommon for the patient to bemoan the rejection he felt upon being weaned as a babe, and a few individuals even see their troubles going back to the traumatic effects of their own birth.

In conclusion, mention must be made of certain practices which have their base in native esthetics but which depend upon the pervasive aversion to the natural body and its functions. There are ritual fasts to make fat people thin and ceremonial feasts to make thin people fat. Still other rites are used to make women's breasts larger if they are small, and smaller if they are large. General dissatisfaction with breast shape is symbolized in the fact that the ideal form is virtually outside the range of human variation. A few women afflicted with almost inhuman hypermammary development are so idolized that they make a handsome living by simply going from village to village and permitting the natives to stare at them for a fee.

Reference has already been made to the fact that excretory functions are ritualized, routinized, and relegated to secrecy. Natural reproductive functions are similarly distorted. Intercourse is taboo as a topic and scheduled as an act. Efforts are made to avoid pregnancy by the use of magical materials or by limiting intercourse to certain phases of the moon. Conception is actually very infrequent. When pregnant, women dress so as to hide their condition. Parturition takes place in secret, without friends or relatives to assist, and the majority of women do not nurse their infants.

Our review of the ritual life of the Nacirema has certainly shown them to be a magic-ridden people. It is hard to understand how they have managed to exist so long under the burdens which they have imposed upon themselves. But even such exotic customs as these take on real meaning when they are viewed with the insight provided by Malinowski when he wrote (1948:70):

Looking from far and above, from our high places of safety in the developed civilization, it is easy to see all the crudity and irrelevance of magic. But without its power and guidance early man could not have mastered his practical difficulties as he has done, nor could man have advanced to the higher stages of civilization.

CRITICAL THINKING QUESTIONS

1. Did you understand that Miner is describing the American—"Nacirema" spelled backwards? Why do we not recognize this right away?

2. Using Miner's approach, describe a base-ball game, an auction, shoppers in a super-market, or a university classroom.
3. What do we gain from being able to "step back" from our way of life as Miner has done here?

REFERENCES

Linton, R. 1936. *The study of man*. New York: Appleton-Century.
Malinowski, B. 1948. *Magic, science and religion*. Glencoe, IL: Free Press.
Murdock, G. P. 1949. *Social structure*. New York: Macmillan.

4

The Case for Value-Free Sociology

MAX WEBER

The following is part of a lecture given in 1918 at Germany's Munich University by Max Weber, one of sociology's pioneers. Weber lived in politically turbulent times, in which the government and other organizations were demanding that university faculty teach the "right" ideas. Weber responded to these pressures by encouraging everyone to be politically involved as citizens, and yet he maintained that teachers and scholars should prize dispassionate analysis rather than political advocacy. This selection stimulates critical thinking about the mix of fact and value that is found in all sociological research.

Let us consider the disciplines close to me: sociology, history, economics, political science, and those types of cultural philosophy that make it their task to interpret the sciences. It is said, and I agree, that politics is out of place in the lecture-room. It does not belong there on the part of the students. . . . Neither does [it] belong in the lecture-room on the part of the [instructors], and when the [instructor] is scientifically concerned with politics, it belongs there least of all.

To take a practical stand is one thing, and to analyze political structures and party positions is another. When speaking in a political meeting about democracy, one does not hide one's personal standpoint; indeed, to come out

clearly and take a stand is one's damned duty. The words one uses in such a meeting are not means of scientific analysis but means of canvassing votes and winning over others. They are not plowshares to loosen the soil of contemplative thought; they are swords against the enemies: Such words are weapons. It would be an outrage, however, to use words in this fashion in a lecture or in the lecture-room. If, for instance, "democracy" is under discussion, one considers its various forms, analyzes them in the way they function, determines what results for the conditions of life the one form has as compared with the other. Then one confronts the forms of democracy with nondemocratic forms of political order and endeavors to come to a position where the student may find the point from which, in terms of his ultimate ideals, he can take a stand. But the true teacher will beware of imposing from the platform any political position upon the

Source: Excerpts from *Max Weber: Essays in Sociology* by *Max Weber,* edited by H. H. Gerth and C. Wright Mills, translated by H. H. Gerth and C. Wright Mills, copyright © 1946, 1958 by H. H. Gerth and C. Wright Mills. Used by permission of Oxford University Press.

student, whether it is expressed or suggested. "To let the facts speak for themselves" is the most unfair way of putting over a political position to the student.

Why should we abstain from doing this? I state in advance that some highly esteemed colleagues are of the opinion that it is not possible to carry through this self-restraint and that, even if it were possible, it would be a whim to avoid declaring oneself. Now one cannot demonstrate scientifically what the duty of an academic teacher is. One can only demand of the teacher that he have the intellectual integrity to see that it is one thing to state facts, to determine mathematical or logical relations or the internal structure of cultural values, while it is another thing to answer questions of the value of culture and its individual contents and the question of how one should act in the cultural community and in political associations. These are quite heterogeneous problems. If he asks further why he should not deal with both types of problems in the lecture-room, the answer is: because the prophet and the demagogue do not belong on the academic platform.

To the prophet and the demagogue, it is said: "Go your ways out into the streets and speak openly to the world," that is, speak where criticism is possible. In the lecture-room we stand opposite our audience, and it has to remain silent. I deem it irresponsible to exploit the circumstance that for the sake of their career the students have to attend a teacher's course while there is nobody present to oppose him with criticism. The task of the teacher is to serve the students with his knowledge and scientific experience and not to imprint upon them his personal political views. It is certainly possible that the individual teacher will not

entirely succeed in eliminating his personal sympathies. He is then exposed to the sharpest criticism in the forum of his own conscience. And this deficiency does not prove anything; other errors are also possible, for instance, erroneous statements of fact, and yet they prove nothing against the duty of searching for the truth. I also reject this in the very interest of science. I am ready to prove from the works of our historians that whenever the man of science introduces his personal value judgment, a full understanding of the facts ceases. . . .

The primary task of a useful teacher is to teach his students to recognize "inconvenient" facts—I mean facts that are inconvenient for their party opinions. And for every party opinion there are facts that are extremely inconvenient, for my own opinion no less than for others. I believe the teacher accomplishes more than a mere intellectual task if he compels his audience to accustom itself to the existence of such facts. I would be so immodest as even to apply the expression "moral achievement," though perhaps this may sound too grandiose for something that should go without saying.

CRITICAL THINKING QUESTIONS

1. Why does Weber seek to set the campus apart from society as an "ivory tower"?

2. How is the classroom a distinctive setting in terms of political neutrality? If instructors cannot be entirely free from value positions, why should they strive to point out "inconvenient facts" to their students?

3. Do you see arguments for instructors presenting passionate advocacy of issues that are of great political and moral significance?

5

Defining Features of Canadian Sociology

BRUCE RAVELLI

In this brief review, Bruce Ravelli looks at some of the defining features of Canadian sociology. This article should inspire you to think about Canadian society and whether you believe it is reflected in Canadian sociology.

Canadian sociology often mirrors the nature of Canada itself: a diverse landscape where Canadians struggle to find their unique voice within a chorus dominated by Americans. In fact, some analysts suggest that Canadian sociology is a product of its experiences with, and at times its resistance to, the larger and more dominant American sociological tradition (see Brym & Saint-Pierre, 1997; Hiller, 2001; Hiller & Di Luzio, 2001). The dominance of the American sociological tradition in Canada is largely due to its longer history[1] and its sheer size.[2] However, at least four elements influence the presence of a distinctly Canadian sociology:

1. Canada's physical geography, defined by its vast and often challenging physical environment, and its regionalism, evidenced in the important role Quebec plays in Canadian sociology's intellectual development

2. Canadian sociology's focus on the political economy

3. The Canadianization movement of the 1960s and 1970s in response to the number of American faculty in our postsecondary institutions

4. The radical nature of Canadian sociology

CANADA'S GEOGRAPHY AND REGIONALISM

Canada, the world's second-largest country—in terms of total area, not population (Countries of the World, 2002)—is blessed with rich natural resources and a beautiful and diverse landscape. As we will see, these environmental factors have influenced Canadian sociology.

Source: This article was specifically written by the author for an earlier edition of this reader.

According to Hiller (2001), Canadian sociology is not simply a culmination of the varieties of sociology practised in Canada; it is instead the product of Canadian sociologists' efforts to understand the Canadian experience. For Hiller (2001), one of Canadian sociology's defining pursuits has been the attempt to understand a changing national society. Everett Hughes asserted in 1959 that Canadian sociology should be grounded in its own societal context: as society changes, so too should its sociology (cited in Hiller, 2001). Sociology "should reflect both the unique aspects of the society's character as well as the evolution of that society" (Hiller, 2001: 262).

External and internal forces help to shape and define a Canadian sociology. The particular nature of the relationship between Canada's physical landscape and Canadian sociology is seen clearly in Brym and Saint-Pierre (1997). They suggest that one defining characteristic of Canadian sociology is its survivalism (1997: 543) and propose that a core theme of Canadian sociology is the development and maintenance of a community in the face of hostile elements (e.g., geographically, socially) and outside forces (i.e., political and intellectual pressures from the United States and American sociologists). One inside force defining Canadian sociology is the role that regionalism plays in our country's development (e.g., west versus east) and, in particular, Quebec's influence. Quebec has a unique linguistic and cultural influence on Canadian society generally and on Canadian sociology specifically.

The teaching of Canadian francophone sociology began in 1943, when the Faculty of Social Sciences was established at Laval University in Quebec City. Although francophone sociology is comparatively young, it experienced explosive growth from the 1960s to the 1980s, as demonstrated by rising student enrolment and the wealth of research produced by francophone sociologists (Brym & Saint-Pierre, 1997: 544). During the 1960s, a social movement in Quebec called the Quiet Revolution saw the influence of the Catholic Church diminish, replaced by an expanded provincial bureaucracy and, ultimately, a resurgence in nationalistic sentiments (seen in the rising popularity of the separatist movement and the growing influence of the Parti Québécois and its then-leader, René Lévesque).

The Quiet Revolution not only inspired changes in Quebec society and politics, but it also influenced sociologists to focus on issues of social class and social policy (see Brym & Saint-Pierre, 1997; Hiller, 2001). In fact, some Quebec sociologists have played leadership roles in the transformation of francophone society as senior advisors and civil servants for the provincial government (Brym & Saint-Pierre, 1997: 544). This is consistent with Southcott's (1999: 459) position that francophone sociologists are more likely to see themselves as "agents of change" than are their anglophone colleagues. Again, we see that the society in which sociologists work affects their approach to the discipline. One of those approaches involves an interest in the political economy.

CANADIAN FOCUS ON THE POLITICAL ECONOMY

Wallace Clement (2001), a leading figure in Canadian sociology, believes that one of the defining elements of Canadian sociology is its interest in the political economy. The political economy encompasses politics, government, and governing, as well as the social and cultural constitution of markets, institutions, and actors (Clement, 2001: 406). For Clement, this intellectual pursuit is characterized by the attempt to uncover tensions and contradictions within society and use them as the bases for social change.

Arguably, the first Canadian sociologist to investigate Canada's political economy was Harold A. Innis in *The Fur Trade in Canada*

(1970/1930) and *The Cod Fisheries* (1954/1940). In these works, Innis develops what has been termed the *staples thesis*, which contends that Canada's development was based on the exploitation of raw materials sent back to European countries to satisfy their industrial thirsts. Innis suggests that each staple (e.g., commercial: cod, fur, timber; industrial: pulp and paper, minerals) had its own characteristics that imposed a particular logic on its individual development (Clement, 2001: 407). As Canada grew and these economic developments continued, these raw materials were sent abroad, refined into more valuable commodities (e.g., furniture, automobiles), and returned to Canada at vastly inflated prices. Innis suggests that since Canada's economic position was subordinate to Britain and to the United States, Canadians were seen as "hewers of wood, drawers of water"—people who performed menial tasks. Certainly, the historical development of Canada's natural resources suggests that Canadian society has been, at least in part, defined by the realization that Canada is not one of the world's major economic or social forces. This underdog mentality was evident in the attempt by Canadian universities in the 1960s and 1970s to Canadianize our postsecondary education system.

THE CANADIANIZATION MOVEMENT

The development of Canadian anglophone sociology was influenced by American sociology as practised at the University of Chicago (see Brym & Saint-Pierre, 1997; Eichler, 2001; Hiller, 2001; Hiller & Di Luzio, 2001; Langlois, 2000; McKay, 1998).

Founded in 1892 by Albion Small, the department of sociology at the University of Chicago defined the American sociological tradition for much of the early twentieth century. The Chicago School of sociology was dominated by the symbolic-interactionist approach, focusing on social reform and collective social responsibility. The Chicago School's influence was most profound on early francophone sociology in Quebec, particularly at Canada's founding department of sociology, McGill. In fact, many influential sociologists in Canada trained at the University of Chicago (such as C. A. Dawson, Everett Hughes, Harold Innis, A. C. McCrimmon, and Roderick D. McKenzie). The Chicago School was instrumental in defining Canadian sociology, but in the 1950s and 1960s, a movement to increase the number of Canadian faculty teaching at Canadian universities began.

During the late 1960s, Connors and Curtis (1970, cited in Hiller & Di Luzio, 2001: 494) found that more than 60 percent of sociologists in Canada had received their highest degree from a foreign institution. Even in 1971, Hedley and Warburton (1973: 305, cited in Hiller & Di Luzio, 2001: 494) found that in large Canadian sociology departments (those with more than twenty faculty members), more than 50 percent of instructors were American, 20 percent were from other countries, and 30 percent were Canadian. These findings were important as they emphasized the need to hire and train more Canadian sociologists if we ever hoped to investigate and understand Canadian society.

The discipline's Canadianization movement was also prompted by the explosion in the number of university enrolments in Canada beginning in the 1950s. In 1962–63, full-time university enrolment in Canada was 132 681, while only 10 years later (1972–73) it had more than doubled to 284 897. Ten years later (1982–83) the number had reached 640 000 (Hiller & Di Luzio, 2001: 491), and at the end of 1999, the number of full-time Canadian university enrolments hovered around 580 000 (Statistics Canada, 1999). Clearly, the need for Canadian-trained sociologists to teach students about Canadian society was a pressing one. This sentiment was clearly expressed when the Association of Universities and Colleges of Canada appointed a Commission on Canadian Studies in 1972, which resulted in The Symons Report (1975).

The report called on the Canadian academic community to increase its efforts to contribute to the knowledge of their own society. The reaction to this report came in an increase in the number of Canadian society courses taught by sociologists across the country, as well as in an increased focus on publishing sociological materials for Canadian sociology students. The assertion that these measures have worked has some support in the number of part- and full-time students who are undergraduate majors in sociology: the figure rose from 13 638 in 1982–83 to 21 028 in 1996–97 (Hiller & Di Luzio, 2001: 493). These students are making a sociological analysis of their own society, and they are also learning about the comparatively radical nature of Canadian sociology.

THE RADICAL NATURE OF CANADIAN SOCIOLOGY

Brym and Saint-Pierre (1997) suggest that one of the defining features of English-Canadian sociology is its radical nature, seen in its focus on the political economy and feminist ideas and perspectives. The important distinction these authors add, however, is how little of this radicalism is seen by the public (1997: 546). Certainly, Quebec sociologists are more focused on the policy ramifications of their endeavours, but Brym and Saint-Pierre recognize that many leading English-Canadian sociologists (such as Margrit Eichler, Graham Lowe, and Susan McDaniel) are mindful of the impact their ideas have on the larger society (1997: 546). Their investigations into the political economy were instrumental in showing that Canadian sociology was not afraid to uncover the hidden power structures that influence and guide society. Canadian feminist

sociologists continue this tradition by looking at how gender acts as a locus of oppression and domination.

Margrit Eichler (2001) suggests that the simultaneous emergence of the Canadianization movement and the feminist movement led to a politics of knowledge that proved helpful to both groups. By expanding university departments by adding Canadian academics during the 1960s and 1970s, the feminist movement found a new voice on university campuses. In Eichler's paper *Women Pioneers in Canadian Sociology: The Effects of a Politics of Gender and a Politics of Knowledge* (2001), she attempts to reverse the politics of erasure that she argues effectively allowed the historical contributions of female sociologists in Canada to be written out of the literature. Eichler undertakes the project by conducting interviews with ten of the leading female sociologists born before 1930. Through the interviews, Eichler utilizes a life-history approach, allowing the women to tell their own stories about being female sociologists during a period of rapid growth within the university system in general, and sociology departments in particular, as well as in a period when feminist issues first entered the sociological discourse.

One important finding from Eichler's investigation into these women's lives is the fact that they never had problems finding jobs in academe (2001: 393). The expanding university system, as well as the emerging recognition of feminist issues, allowed these women to begin full-time careers with little effort. Although they all faced sexism in some form during their careers, they were able to initiate significant institutional change by their mere presence on campus (e.g., pay equity measures, sexual harassment policies). Their ability to be a critical social presence within the academic community was an important factor in advancing feminist issues on university campuses and in the larger society as the feminist movement gained momentum in Canada.

That impetus led to the establishment of the Royal Commission on the Status of Women in 1967 to "inquire into and report upon the status of women in Canada, and to recommend what steps might be taken by the Federal Government to ensure for women equal opportunities with men in all aspects of Canadian society" (Cross, 2000). The final report was released in 1970 with 167 recommendations and "became the blueprint for mainstream feminist activism" (Womenspace, 2002). The feminist movement inspired women to reflect differently on their social surroundings and reinforced the need to question social convention. The influence on early female sociology pioneers was equally important, as it encouraged them to critique their own intellectual foundations generally and sociology specifically. As Dorothy Smith notes about this time, "Because we were free to take up issues for women, we didn't feel committed to reproducing the discipline, . . . it had the effect . . . of really liberating the discipline in general in Canada, so that you now have an orientation where people feel absolutely comfortable in raising current issues, in addressing what's going on in Canada" (cited in Eichler, 2001: 394). The Royal Commission report opened the debate on women's positions in Canadian society and resulted in the formation of the women's caucus at the Canadian Sociology and Anthropology Association, which still exists today. The feminist movement, and sociology's role within it, is just one example of Canadian sociology's critical foundation and how Canada continues to influence the discipline today.

CONCLUSION

Canadian sociology is defined by its geography, focus on the political economy, the Canadianization movement, and its radical approach to social issues. This brief review should give you some appreciation for the flavour of Canadian sociology and how it represents a unique approach to the discipline and to our understanding of what it means to be Canadian.

CRITICAL THINKING QUESTIONS

1. Do you believe that social forces influence how academics in a given country see the world? Support your answer.

2. Provide examples of how Canadian winters influence the way Canadians think about themselves. Can similar examples be found for how Canadian summers influence our national identity?

3. In your opinion, was the Canadianization movement at universities and colleges necessary? Why or why not?

NOTES

1. The University of Chicago established the first American department of sociology in 1892 and McGill University established the first Canadian one in 1924.

2. The American postsecondary system serves more than 14 800 000 students and the Canadian system around 827 000 (NCES, 2002; Statistics Canada, 1999). In 1999 more than 2400 departments of sociology existed in the United States (ASA, 2002). Canada had around 45 university departments of sociology—including joint sociology/anthropology departments—(McMaster, 2002) and approximately 150 colleges, the majority of which offered at least introductory sociology (ACCC, 2002).

REFERENCES

ACCC (Association of Canadian Community Colleges). 2002. Membership list. [Online]. Available: **http://www.accc.ca/english/colleges/membership_list.cfm**. Accessed October 27, 2002.

ASA (American Sociological Association). 2002. Departmental listings for 1999. [Online]. Available: **http://www.asanet.org/pubs/dod.html**. Accessed October 27, 2002.

Brym, R., and C. Saint-Pierre. 1997. Canadian sociology. *Contemporary Sociology*, 26(5): 543–46.

Clement, W. 2001. Canadian political economy's legacy for sociology. *Canadian Journal of Sociology*, 26(3): 405–20.

Connor, D. M., and E. Curtis. 1970. *Sociology and anthropology in Canada: Some characteristics of the disciplines and their current university programs.* Montreal: Canadian Sociology and Anthropology Association.

Countries of the World. 2002. Country statistics at a glance. [Online]. Available: **http://www.infoplease.com/ipa/A0762380.html.** Accessed July 17, 2002.

Cross, P. 2000. *Report of the Royal Commission on the Status of Women: Where are we after thirty years?* [Online]. Available: **http://www.owjn.org/issues/equality/thirty.htm.** Accessed January 31, 2003.

Eichler, M. 2001. Women pioneers in Canadian sociology: The effects of a politics of gender and a politics of knowledge. *Canadian Journal of Sociology,* 26(3): 375–403.

Hedley, R. A., and R. T. Warburton. 1973. The role of national courses in the teaching and development of sociology: The Canadian case. *Sociological Review,* 21(2): 299–319.

Hiller, H. H. 2001. Legacy for a new millennium: Canadian sociology in the twentieth century as seen through its publications. *Canadian Journal of Sociology,* 26(3): 257–63.

Hiller, H. H., and L. Di Luzio. 2001. Text and context: Another "chapter" in the evolution of sociology in Canada. *Canadian Journal of Sociology,* 26(3): 487–512.

Innis, H. A. 1954. *The cod fisheries: The history of an international economy.* University of Toronto Press (original work published 1940).

Innis, H. A. 1970. *The fur trade in Canada.* Toronto: University of Toronto Press (original work published 1930).

Langlois, S. 2000. A productive decade in the tradition of Canadian sociology. *Canadian Journal of Sociology,* 25(3): 391–97.

McKay, I. 1998. Changing the subject(s) of the "History of Canadian sociology": The case of Colin McKay and Spencerian Marxism, 1890–1940. *Canadian Journal of Sociology,* 23(4): 389–426.

McMaster University. 2002. Sociology institutions—departments. [Online]. Available: **http://www.mcmaster.ca/socscidocs/w3virtsoclib/cansoc.htm.** Retrieved October 27, 2002.

NCES (National Center for Education Statistics). 2002. Digest of education statistics, 2001—Chapter 3: Postsecondary education. [Online]. Available: **http://nces.ed.gov/pubs2002/digest2001/ch3.asp#1.** Accessed January 31, 2003.

Southcott, C. 1999. The study of regional inequality in Quebec and English Canada: A comparative analysis of perspectives. *Canadian Journal of Sociology,* 24(4): 457–84.

Statistics Canada. 1999. University enrolment, full-time and part-time, by sex. [Online]. Available: **http://www.statcan.ca/english/Pgdb/educ03a.htm.** Accessed October 27, 2002.

Womenspace. 2002. *Since the Royal Commission on the Status of Women.* [Online]. Available: **http://herstory.womenspace.ca/RCSW.html.** Retrieved October 23.

6

Arab Women in the Field

SORAYA ALTORKI

Social scientists often rely on ethnography—the study of people using observation or interviews—to provide detailed descriptions of groups, organizations, and communities. Such fieldwork, like other data collection methods, has both strengths and limitations. As Soraya Altorki shows, a major advantage of studying one's own culture includes a familiarity with the people and the environment. The researcher also encounters a number of problems. One of Altorki's challenges, for example, involved resocializing herself into her culture, having been abroad for a number of years. She also had to overcome the informants' reluctance to address sensitive questions about their religious practices and family life to an "outsider."

AT HOME IN THE FIELD

Having been socialized many years in Egypt and identifying with its people, I had regarded it, on one level, to be my home. On another level, however, I had been brought up in a Saudi Arabian family committed in great measure to that country's cultural heritage and the observance of its cultural norms, even while selectively observing certain Egyptian values and practices. Throughout my college days, I had been reminded that I could not do what my Egyptian girlfriends could do, because "our" traditions were different and for "us" such behavior was unacceptable.

Besides, it was not only the constraining elements of Saudi Arabian culture that molded

Source: "At Home in the Field," by Soraya Altorki, in *Arab Women in the Field: Studying Your Own Society,* eds. Soraya Altorki and Camillia Fawzi El-Solh, pp. 51–59. New York: Syracuse University Press, 1998. Reprinted by permission.

my growing-up experiences in Egypt, but also the rich rewards that I reaped from kinship support and shared cultural knowledge. These provided for me the security of a closure that was not attainable in Egypt. Thus, Saudi Arabia was home for me on a more fundamental level.

Arriving in Jiddah [Saudi Arabia], my native city, I knew I wanted to study urban life. Although the entire northern portion of the Arabian Peninsula was virtually unknown to social scientists, early travelers and even scholars avoided its study in favor of the nomad and the camel. Barring Hürgrouje and Burton, almost nothing was known about urban life. In retrospect, I believe that my choice to focus on urban society was partly a reaction to the stereotypical view of Saudi Arabia as a society of nomads and oil wells.

There were also social constraints to my choice. I knew that, as an unmarried woman, I could neither travel alone in the country nor wander around with the nomads. Living alone, anywhere in the country, was out of the question. Thus, for many considerations, an urban-based study seemed most appropriate, and the city of Jiddah the most convenient.

The realities of being an unmarried woman in many ways dictated my field of research, although it did not determine my choice of research topic within that field (Altorki, 1986). This essentially meant that I could work with women and that I had limited access to men. Within these bounds, my choice was absolutely free. . . .

INSIDER/OUTSIDER

Being literally at home in Jiddah, I was spared having to worry about the problems of settling in that most anthropologists face when entering the field. Furthermore, I needed no research permit (or if I did, I never bothered to find out) and no letters of guarantee. Neither was I required to make commitments to local authorities and research institutes concerning the conduct of my work and the use and distribution of my data.

The people I studied saw me as one of themselves. Some of them had ties of kinship and friendship to my family. Others knew my family members by name. This state of affairs provided me with significant advantages. Others, working in their own society, have observed similar benefits in knowing the culture and consequently being able to select their research agenda in consonance with what is most expedient for the research task and what is most feasible within the limits of what will be allowed by the subjects under investigation (see Stephenson and Greer 1981:126).

However, some facets of my life concerned my informants. Why, for example, was I not a married woman with children, like all my peers? And why was I still living abroad rather than residing in Jiddah, awaiting marriage?

My unmarried status at the age of twenty-two made me somewhat of an anomaly. More distressing to the older women among whom I worked was the conclusion that I was more interested in following my studies than in settling down to married life. Although the role of an educated woman had come to be accepted by the community at large and the elite in particular, the problem was in the priorities this role took over what was perceived to be the more important aspect of gender role, namely the status that marriage and motherhood bring. According to both men and women, it is these dimensions of womanhood that are primary. In fact, given the segregation of Saudi Arabian women from men, and their isolation from public life, marriage and motherhood become a woman's avenues to maturity, security, and greater prestige. Being a member of the society, I anticipated this and was well prepared to deal with its consequences.

Although women come of age with marriage, and prestige for them is attained by motherhood, my status within the community had to rest on other things: It relied greatly on my education. Lacking husband and child, I predicated my adulthood on education and depended on the community's acceptance of it as a legitimate goal for women to attain. Men and women alike respected this, although never failing to remind me of the fundamentals of my role as a woman. As one older woman put it to me: "Education is good, but women are weak. No matter how much money they have, no matter their education, they cannot manage without men. May Allah save your father and your brother. But you have to start your own family." That statement accurately reflects the dependence of women on men, a dependence that also correlates with their segregation in Saudi Arabian society. But my role as a Saudi Arabian woman, educated abroad, permitted me more flexibility and autonomy. For one thing, my interaction with men who were not my relatives was tolerated.

My long absence abroad was an additional factor leading to more mobility. While abroad, I had been immersed in a different way of life, and hence women and men alike did not expect me to conform totally to the cultural norms governing the relationship of men and women in Saudi Arabian society. My absence had a complex effect on my reentry into my own community. On the one hand, it allowed more maneuverability in my role as an unmarried woman, and, on the other hand, it made conformity especially expedient in strengthening my ties to my informants.

Repeatedly, men and women expressed their surprise and approval when my behavior showed conformity to Saudi Arabian culture. They were, for example, delighted that my many years in Egypt had not changed my accent to Egyptian. Whenever I showed observance of norms that young people my age had begun to modify, members of the older generation were astonished and particularly delighted. Those of the younger generation, however, saw such conformity as awkward and continued to remind me that times had changed: "Nobody is observing such things these days."

For example, norms of deference to older siblings necessitate that they be addressed in specific terms. To an older brother and kinsmen his age the term is *sidi*, which means "my master." My use of these terms of address was welcomed by all, barring girls of my age who by then were seeking to substitute as equivalent for the term *sidi* those of *akhuya* (my brother) and the sobriquet *abu flan* (father of). In doing this, I took my cues from young men who had obtained their college education abroad, sometimes through graduate school, and who continued to use traditional terms of reference in addressing older female siblings and other kinswomen in their age group.

It was in the same spirit that I observed some norms of modesty, particularly those related to veiling. Such practices were changing at the time of my fieldwork, so that the families I studied showed the whole spectrum of veiling practices, from those who had considerably modified its use to leave the face bare, to those who still observed the traditional practice of covering the face as well. While visiting the homes of the latter, I made sure to conform and to cover my face carefully. This gesture of respect did not go unnoticed: Women and men alike commented that my many years abroad had not made me behave like a "foreigner."

The years abroad had been spent as a student, and now I had come back as a researcher with the intention of recording a way of life that had not previously been studied. Everyone understood that role. Female education was not a novelty. Girls were sent to *faqihas* (informal traditional schools) as far back as older informants could remember; and formal girls' schools were opened by the government in 1960. By the time I went to the field, the first women's university had already opened in Jiddah. College education was thoroughly acceptable for women; indeed, it had become greatly valued.

Thus, I had no problem in defining part of my role to the subjects of my research. I wanted to study social life, family organization, rituals, beliefs, and customs, and to document how these have changed for the younger people in the study. In another way, my role was more ascribed. My return to Jiddah meant taking my place in a family and getting involved in the various ramifications of family life. It also meant belonging to a class with the task of conforming to the behavior of that class. I was aware that I could in fact not conform to that behavior, but I had little choice with regard to involvement in family life.

The ascribed aspects of my role, i.e., gender, age, and kinship, were more fundamental in people's perception of me, which may be unavoidable in doing research among one's own people. My education was important in allowing me to explore areas of social life (e.g., more access to the world of men) that other women could not undertake. Despite my research objective, known and accepted to all the families, I remained primarily a Saudi Arabian woman. As such, I was known to some as the daughter or a sister of a friend, while to others as a member of a lineage they knew from other mutual friends. These considerations were always present in my interaction with others. While criteria centering on the individual are not without relevance in structuring relations, the world of these elite families was in the first instance structured by consanguineous and marital ties, and in the second place by friendship and business networks.

Within this world an individual—whether man or woman—is deeply embedded in the 'aila (family). One's status is, to a considerable degree, ascribed by the status of the 'aila. Individual achievement is an avenue to mobility, but clearly it is the achievement of men and not of women that is associated with family prestige. Recent changes in the wider society have introduced more emphasis on individuality and an increase of distance from the 'aila. This is evidenced in neolocal residence patterns, more individual involvement in marriage choice, relative reduction of parental authority, independent career choices for men, and less observance of traditional obligations to kinsmen (Altorki, 1986).

On the whole, I experienced no problems in establishing rapport—that quality in the relationship between the ethnographer and the host community that the introductions to ethnographic monographs rarely fail to mention, but which probably involves the most enigmatic aspect of our methodological trademark: participant observation. I spoke the language, and the trademark itself had no special meaning for me, although, as I will explain, it had very special implications in my case.

In short, I found practical advantages in my particular field situation: Unencumbered by bureaucratic impediments, comfortably set up in my family's home, fluent in the vernacular,

and personally known in some of the households I was to study, I could begin my research under very auspicious circumstances—or so it seemed until I realized the implications of being an indigenous anthropologist. I discovered that almost every one of the advantages had its negative side.

In a very real sense, my fieldwork experience was a process of resocialization into my own society. Although I was raised in a Saudi Arabian family, my long years of residence abroad had established considerable distance between me and my society. The advantages were that much of the culture was not so familiar that it could easily escape my notice. This problem in the collection of data has been observed by other ethnographers working under similar conditions (cf. Spradley and McCurdy, 1972; Ablon, 1977; Stephenson and Greer, 1981), but it is one that can be overcome by rigorous training. The researcher can counteract familiarity by close observation, meticulous recording of ethnographic scenes, and detailed probing to uncover the "taken-for-granted" world he or she may share with members of the community being studied.

Living at home meant that I had to assume the role expected of a family member in my position within the household group. The ordinary field situation reversed itself in my case. I became what may best be described as an observant participant. My primary duty was to participate. To observe became an incidental privilege.

My status did not afford me immunity from observing all the taboos and attending to all the obligations my culture prescribed for me—an immunity usually granted to foreign anthropologists. I had to accept severe restrictions on my movements and on my interaction with other people. For example, I had no freedom to move in public on my own, and challenging any norms of conduct would have jeopardized my relationships with the families I had decided to study. Had I not conformed,

I would have risked ostracism and termination of my research. Persistently, if slowly, I achieved a precarious balance of roles that allowed me mobility and freedom to do my research as well as to be accepted and taken seriously. I became a conscious witness to my own resocialization as an Arab woman in my society and thus learned and comprehended many aspects of this role in the best possible manner.

This, perhaps, is one of the hidden advantages of being an insider. For example, veiling norms can be observed and described by an outsider, and one can also learn about the meaning of veiling by soliciting relevant information from informants. Yet the participant charged with the task of abiding by the norms experiences the constraints, to be sure, but also the rewards of these norms on a more basic level. In that sense, my resocialization generated data on an experiential level different from that to which an outsider could bear witness. This point has also been observed as a merit of indigenous research elsewhere. Aguilar, for example, summarizing the pros and cons of this kind of research, mentions that its advocates insist "that the covert culture of the insider has the heuristic value of lending psychological reality (or cultural reality) to ethnographic analyses" (1981:16).

My status affected my research in another way. Restricted possibilities for movement outside the house and pervasive segregation of men and women in public confined the research predominantly to the world of women. These realities affected the choice of topic for investigation. I could not study market or political relations, for example. Neither could I investigate any other subject in which men, rather than women, are the dominant actors. Family organization seemed the most accessible for a female researcher, and elites became my focus. Within that, my emphasis was on how ideology and practice affect and are influenced by one another. But, as noted elsewhere, elites

are the least accessible to inquiry, especially through the technique of prolonged participant observation. The families I elected to study formed closed groups, and although the observation of and participation in their daily lives was possible for me as a member of the group, even I could gain their confidence only through patient approaches along the lines of friendship.

Although generous hospitality is highly valued behavior, there remain degrees of formality that the families must always maintain vis-à-vis the whole community. Only with considerable caution can a nonmember see their lives as they live them, as opposed to how they want the rest of the community to perceive them. For example, it takes a long time, coupled with intensive interaction, before people allow a friend to move within their home free of the facade of formality exhibited to outsiders. Indeed, it took between six and eight months before I could develop the friendships that made close observation of their daily lives possible to the degree that my presence was more or less ignored. Being an insider has even more serious consequences for research. Information may be withheld when it relates to behavior that must be concealed from public knowledge. If one is outside the system, one's awareness of goings-on may not be problematical. But as a participant, the researcher constitutes a threat of exposure and judgment. Lewis (1973:588) explains this situation very well:

There is a growing fear that the information collected by an outsider, someone not constrained by group values and interests, will expose the group to outside manipulation and control. . . . The insider, on the other hand, is accountable; s/he must remain in the community and take responsibility for her/his actions. Thus, s/he is forced through self-interest to exercise discretion.

This was one of the hardest areas to overcome in doing research among one's own people. For example, family solidarity and cohesion are greatly valued. Verbally, men and women endorse the ideal of love and support between siblings; respect and obedience in filial relations; and honoring family duties of financial support to the needy and maintenance of elderly parents. In practice, the older generations approximated many of these ideals (Altorki, 1986).

But family conflict does occur, and younger generation members have begun to modify family obligations in general. Differences over inheritance constitute the most serious threat to family solidarity—a threat that mounts as the stakes become higher and people's wealth increases. The ideal remains that such differences must be kept out of the public eye and should be reconciled between family members without recourse to the courts. So important is this family ideal that information about conflict, especially that considered to be serious, was at first not revealed to me. I learned about such conflicts indirectly from domestic servants working in these homes who, by coincidence, happened to be related to women working in my family's household. On other occasions, I obtained relevant information from women with whom I had established such strong ties of friendship that we had come to be considered "sisters." This family idiom symbolized our enclosure in the same kinship group and, by implication, showed our interest in protecting that group and shielding it from public criticism.

On one point, my learning about family conflicts was fortuitous. Is it conceivable that I would have returned from the field with the belief that the ideal of family solidarity was the reality? By being an insider, and from my own kinship network, I "experienced" the fact that reality was different and that disagreement can escalate to conflicts between family members. The problem, however, was in collecting data about conflict from the other families to uncover patterns in its expression and management. What, for example, were the patterns for the expression of intrafamily conflict? How

was it managed, and what are the patterns for its resolution?

In this respect, my status as an insider prevented people from divulging such information for fear of having it exposed to the wider community. Obviously, disseminating information about intrafamilial conflict to the community also implies that the disseminator, i.e., the indigenous anthropologist, has judged it negatively and is now taking an active role in censoring the behavior it bespeaks. While the question of exposure to the public can be bridged by trust and confidence in the researcher, the threat of judgment is harder to overcome. Being a participating family member implies, of course, subscribing to the cultural norms and values of the group and to the sanctions that follow a breach of valued behavior.

These considerations are different for a foreign anthropologist. As an outsider investigating family organization and interfamilial conflict, she or he must gain the confidence of the people and be trusted not to expose family differences to the community. But outsider status does not imply shared cultural knowledge, and thus protects the outsider from applying the same moral judgments. The nonindigenous researcher is outside the system, and for this very reason people may not conceal family differences to the same degree as they would from a member of their own group. In collecting relevant data, the indigenous researcher is twice bound and must be able to overcome barriers to confidence and to potential value judgment.

Other social scientists have made similar observations. Aguilar, for example, highlights the constraints indigenous status may place on access to data (1981:21), although, as he points out, other anthropologists claim the opposite (1981:18). However, the Saudi Arabian case indicates that while confidence can be established, a morally neutral judgment is harder to demonstrate. An effective strategy is to be drawn into the same closure that allows sharing of such delicate information. In my case, the idiom of kinship and the ties of close friendships provided such a closure.

My general familiarity with these families had another irksome drawback. My informants presumed that I knew my own culture, and for a long time they either misinterpreted my questions as implying an unbecoming skepticism or failed to appreciate that I truly did not know what I had asked them to explain. This was especially true for knowledge of religious beliefs and rituals, which for me was a difficult area to explore. Such knowledge is essential to an adult Muslim, and any queries about it reveal a lapse in religious duties. Fed up with my questions, an older woman put it to me this way: "Are you not ashamed that you do not know how to pray at your age? What then did they teach you abroad?"

This revealed to me the cultural givens of the community and the cultural repertoire indispensable to membership in it. The best research strategy to circumvent this role was to openly admit my ignorance and to blame it all on my long absence abroad. Women and men patiently explained matters to me in a desire to resocialize me as a Muslim Arab woman. In fact, it was especially pleasing to the older women, often illiterate, to instruct me despite my higher formal education.

These considerations have been well described by Stephenson and Greer. They note that while familiarity with the culture under study can be a bonus, prior knowledge of the people studied provides no guaranteed advantage. The expectations people may have of the investigator could make it more difficult for her or him to break out of fixed patterns and thus serve to restrict the work at hand (1981:129). The role that the community attributes to the researcher may inhibit other relationships and bias the researcher's thoughts. Moreover, the role ascribed by kinship to the indigenous anthropologist may forcefully draw that person into factionalism within the community and thereby limit the work that can be accomplished. Sometimes, such problems can be circumvented by conscious strategy. As Stephenson and Greer observe, "the researcher can mitigate the effects of already established roles by emphasizing some over others" (1981:127).

CRITICAL THINKING QUESTIONS

1. How did Altorki's sex and background influence her decisions about where and how to conduct her research on Arab society?

2. Field researchers must often balance the advantages and disadvantages of playing "insider" and "outsider" roles. How did being an insider both benefit and limit Altorki's research? What barriers did she have to overcome?

3. What strengths and weaknesses did Altorki encounter as an outsider? Is it possible for researchers who are outsiders to offer information and valid insights about the societies they study? Explain your answer.

REFERENCES

Ablon, J. 1977. Field methods in working with middle class Americans: New issues of values, personality and reciprocity. *Human Organization*, 36(1): 69–72.

Aguilar, J. 1981. Insider research: An ethnography of a debate. In *Anthropologists at home in North America: Methods and issues in the study of one's own society*, ed. D. A. Messerschmidt. Cambridge: Cambridge University Press.

Altorki, S. 1986. *Women in Saudi Arabia: Ideology and behavior among the elite.* New York: Columbia University Press.

Lewis, D. 1973. Anthropology and colonialism. *Current Anthropology*, 14(12): 581–602.

Spradley, J. P., and D. W. McCurdy. 1972. *The cultural experience.* Chicago: Science Research Association.

Stephenson, J. B., and L. S. Greer. 1981. Ethnographers in their own cultures: Two Appalachian cases. *Human Organization*, 40(2): 123–30.

7

North America's Two Distinct Societies

MICHAEL ADAMS (WITH AMY LANGSTAFF AND DAVID JAMIESON)

A sizable proportion of Canada's population, particularly among the left, is concerned that economic and political integration with the United States will inevitably result in cultural homogenization. In the minds of many, Canadians are becoming more like their American counterparts. This excerpt dispels some of those fears and discusses some of the characteristics that make Canadians distinct from their neighbours to the south.

Canada and the United States have reached the point where we can no longer think of each other as foreign countries.

—Harry S. Truman, U.S. president, address, joint sitting of the Canadian Senate and House of Commons, 11 June 1947

He understands I want to make sure our relations with our most important neighbour to the north of us, the Canadians, is strong. . . .

—George W. Bush, reacting to a statement of support for his presidential bid from "Canadian Prime Minister Jean Poutine"; Poutine's thumbs-up was relayed to President Bush at a 2000 campaign stop by Canadian comic and *This Hour Has 22 Minutes* "reporter" Rick Mercer

Canada is the largest country in the world that doesn't exist.

—Richard Rodriguez, American social commentator of Mexican-Indian descent, commenting on the notion that minority groups overtake majority groups, in an interview by Neil Bissoondath on TVO's *Markings*, 3 July 1995

In the days and weeks following 11 September, Canadians' feelings of sympathy for and solidarity with the United States were expressed again and again. Canadian firefighters and medical professionals travelled to New York City to offer assistance to those affected by the terrorist attacks. Families in Newfoundland opened their homes to fearful and distraught Americans whose planes had been diverted into Canada after news of the disaster had spread through airline communication systems. On 14 September, 100,000 Canadians gathered on Parliament Hill to express their grief over the tragedies that had befallen their neighbours.

The reaction was more immediate and heartfelt than in any other nation. It brought to mind a child in a schoolyard tearfully rushing to the aid of an older sibling in serious distress, affection and fellow feeling blotting out all the usual resentment over quotidian bullying or petty squabbles. Certainly, after things had settled down somewhat, some of the usual fault lines between the two countries began to reappear: Canadians began to wonder about what the U.S. response to the attacks would be, and some eventually began to fret openly (if gingerly) about how Canadians would be drawn into the conflict. But for a short time, the differences between Canada and the United States seemed to dissolve.

As the horror receded and daily life slowly resumed, the differences that had seemed so trivial as to be almost non-existent on that Tuesday morning began to reassert themselves little by little. As 2001 wound shakily down and 2002 began, many Canadians once again found themselves beginning to roll their eyes at phrases like "axis of evil" and shake their heads at George W. Bush's repeated references to the women of Afghanistan as "women of cover." Without losing any of our sympathy for the lives lost or irrevocably altered on 11 September, Canadians began to regain some of their sense of distance and difference from the United States and its worldview.

This slow, tentative process was accelerated very suddenly on 17 April 2002, when news of the deaths of four Canadian soldiers in Afghanistan reached North America (or at least, the news *seemed* to reach North America, but for all the attention it received south of the border it might as well have been lost in transit). The four soldiers were killed (and eight others injured) by "friendly fire"; a U.S. fighter pilot dropped a bomb on the Canadians (whom he mistook for enemy soldiers) as they were carrying out a training exercise on the ground.

"Accidents happen in wars," all voices seemed to concede sadly. "Nobody wanted this to happen." But as President Bush made his first, second, third, fourth, and fifth public appearances the next day without ever mentioning the incident—and even ignoring a question shouted by a Canadian reporter as Bush scuttled away from one press conference—sadness turned to anger. Was it really too much to expect that the United States might have been saddened at having killed and wounded a group of young Canadians who were doing their best to help America fight its war? Was it too much to expect that the American president would at least *pretend* to be dismayed, expressing at least some modest words of empathy and regret? Or that the *New York Times* might have spared a little space somewhere ahead of page fourteen on the day following the incident?

Now Canadians were beginning to recall the old simmering resentments of life in Uncle Sam's backyard. Though the feeling of fraternity that had permeated the country in the period immediately following September 11 had been entirely genuine, this familiar feeling of ill use was no less so. Canadians seemed to recall, in April of 2002, that although it may sometimes seem that Canada and the U.S. are "on the same page," that's usually because we're reading over their shoulder.

Because the cultural differences between Canada and the United States tend to exist beneath the consciousness of our daily lives, it is sometimes possible to imagine that those differences do not exist. After all, on any given day, most Canadians, like most Americans, can be spotted in their natural habitats driving cars, consuming too much energy and water, spending a little less time with their nuclear families than they would like, working a little more than is healthy, watching television, and buying some things they could probably survive without. But differences—both subtle and marked—do exist, and do endure. Some are external (gun control, bilingualism, health care), but many exist only inside the minds of Canadians and Americans—in how they see the world, how they engage with it, and how they hope to shape it.

In this chapter, I will offer a closer look at Canadians' and Americans' responses to individual survey questions—responses that attest, one by one, to a broad trend of cultural *divergence*.

But before the big picture, I'd like to share some raw numbers. We begin our portrait of these two neighbours with a comparison of their religious convictions. Canadians are by now quite familiar with evangelists Jerry Falwell, Pat Robertson, Jimmy Swaggart, Jim and Tammy Faye Bakker (who are slowly getting back to the business), and even William Jennings Bryan, who defended creationism in the famous Scopes Monkey trial in the 1920s. We know that Christian fundamentalism has far deeper and more enduring roots in the United States, particularly in the Bible Belt, than here in Canada. What we sometimes fail to remember is that not so long ago, Canadians were more conventionally religious than Americans. In the mid-1950s, 60 percent of Canadians told pollsters they went to church each Sunday; the proportion in the U.S. at that time was only 50 percent. Today, only a fifth of Canadians claim weekly church attendance (22 percent, according to Ekos), whereas the proportion in the U.S. is 42 percent. A 2002 Pew Research Center poll found religion to be important to 59 percent of Americans— the highest proportion in all the developed nations surveyed—and to only 30 percent of Canadians, a rate similar to that found in Great Britain and Italy. Nearly four in ten Canadians do not consider themselves to be members of a religious faith. In the U.S. the proportion of atheists, agnostics, or secular humanists is only 25 percent. In less than a generation, Canadians have evolved from being much more religious than Americans to being considerably less so.

Canadians have not only rejected in large numbers the authority of religious institutions, but have brought this questioning of traditional authority closer to home. Our research shows Canadians to be far less likely

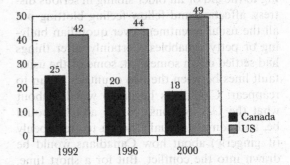

Figure 7.1   Father of Family Must Be Master in His Own House: Canada and the United States: Agree 1992, 1996, & 2000

than Americans to agree with the statement, "The father of the family must be master in his own home." In 1992 we found that 26 percent of Canadians believed Father must be master (down from 42 percent in 1983). In 1992, 42 percent of Americans told us Dad should be on top. Since then the gap has widened: down to 20 percent in Canada and up to 44 percent in the U.S. in 1996, and then down even further (to 18 percent) in Canada in 2000 and up further still (to 49 percent) in the U.S. in that year. The widening gap between the two countries now stands at an astonishing thirty-one points, with Canadians becoming ever less deferential to patriarchal authority and Americans becoming more and more willing to Wait Till Their Father Comes Home to find out if it's okay to watch *The Simpsons*.

Paralleling this differing orientation to patriarchal authority are the two populations' attitudes toward the relative status of the sexes. In a word, Americans are more predisposed to male chauvinism than Canadians, and here again the gap is widening. In 1992, 26 percent of Canadians told us that men are naturally superior to women, while 30 percent of Americans felt the same way. Four years later in 1996, the proportion of Canadians believing in the innate superiority of men declined to 23 percent while the U.S. proportion rose to

32 percent. By 2000, the proportion in Canada stood at 24 percent while that in the U.S. shot up to 38 percent. It only stands to reason, many Americans seem to be telling us, that if God-fearing men are the superior beings on this planet, then they should certainly be the bosses in their own homes.

Canadians' more egalitarian views regarding the status of women and the structure of the family, plus a more skeptical view of traditional institutional authority, also seem to lead them to a more relaxed view of what constitutes a family. Over the past decade, Canadians have consistently felt that two people living together, what we used to call living common-law, in fact constitutes a family. In 2000, 71 percent of Canadians felt a couple that shared a home were a family; up from 66 percent in 1992. Only 54 percent of Americans shared this view, albeit up from 49 percent in 1992. It is almost impossible to imagine a governor of any U.S. state daring to brazenly "live in sin" with his or her "life partner" as can Ontario Premier Ernie Eves. When in 1942 the Conservatives added the adjective "Progressive" to their party name, I doubt they had common-law cohabitation in mind.

What emerges so far is a portrait of two nations evolving in unexpected directions: the once shy and deferential Canadians, who used to wait to be told by their betters what to do and how to think, have become more skeptical of traditional authority and more confident about their own personal decisions and informal arrangements. Americans, by contrast, seeking a little of the "peace and order" that Canadians hoped "good government" would provide, seem inclined to latch on to traditional institutional practices, beliefs, and norms as anchors in a national environment that is more intensely competitive, chaotic, and even violent.

Attitudes toward violence are, in fact, among the features that most markedly differentiate Canadians from Americans. In the year 2000, 50 percent of Canadians told us they felt violence to be all around them, a high figure to be sure,

but nowhere near the 76 percent of Americans who felt the same way. Americans' responses to our questions about violence suggest that they may even be becoming inured to the violence they perceive to be ubiquitous. In 1992, 9 percent of Canadians and 10 percent of Americans told us that violence is a normal part of life, nothing to be concerned about. In 1996, the figure in Canada was still 9 percent, but had grown to 18 percent in the U.S. In 2000, 12 percent of Canadians felt that violence in everyday life was normal, but in the same year 24 percent of Americans felt the same way. For one American in four, representing 70 million people, violence is perceived as a normal part of one's daily routine. The other three-quarters of the population, presumably, are doing all they can to avoid those 70 million, particularly if alone on the street after dark.

We found further evidence that violence is becoming more, not less, normative in America when we asked Americans to agree or disagree that when one is extremely tense or frustrated, a little violence can offer relief, and that "it's no big deal." In 1992, 14 percent of Americans agreed with this sentiment, as did 14 percent of Canadians we polled. In 1996, the proportion was 10 percent in Canada but zoomed to 27 percent in the U.S. By 2000, the proportion in Canada was back up to 14 percent, but had surged further to 31 percent in America, nearly one-third of the population. Again, you might not want to confront one of these folks when they're feeling a bit on edge, particularly when you remember that many of them (including the U.S. Attorney General) believe their Constitution guarantees them the right to bear firearms.

America is and always has been a very competitive society, nurtured by the myth of the American Dream, which suggests that anyone with a little vision and a lot of hard work can achieve material success. Sociologist Seymour Martin Lipset points out that in all categories, crime rates in America are about three times higher than they are in other industrialized countries. Lipset suggests as an explanation for this phenomenon the following: the American Dream, and the concomitant imperative to achieve material success, are so strong in America that many people pursue the goals of wealth and status in reckless, sometimes even criminal, ways. The end is of such monumental importance that the means become almost irrelevant.

Our polling found some interesting results in this area. In 1992, we asked Canadians and Americans whether they would be prepared to take "great risks" in order to get what they want. That year, nearly equal proportions of Canadians (25 percent) and Americans (26 percent) reported that they would indeed be prepared to take great risks to get what they wanted. The same in 1996. But by 2000 still only a quarter of Canadians were prepared to take great risks while the proportion in the U.S. increased to 38 percent—a full eleven points higher than in Canada.

Americans are prepared to put a lot more on the line than Canadians to achieve their version of the American Dream, including personal risks to life and limb. They are also, as it turns out, more willing than Canadians to risk the lives and limbs of others to achieve the same ends. In 1992, 10 percent of Canadians and only 9 percent of Americans told us that it is acceptable to use violence to get what you want. In 1996, 11 percent of Canadians felt this way, but the proportion of Americans rose to 17 percent. By 2000, 13 percent of Canadians felt the use of violence, presumably on or off the ice, was an acceptable way of achieving one's objectives, while the proportion in the U.S. was 23 percent, nearly one in four and almost double the figure in Canada.

Lipset's hypothesis about the possible relationship between crime and the deep-rooted imperative of the American Dream illuminates an interesting contradiction: frustrated by their inability to achieve the Dream by socially acceptable means, those who obtain the trappings of success unlawfully exercise excessive individualism precisely *in order* to conform.

The idea that America's ostensible commitment to individualism may mask a deep impulse toward conformity is borne out in our polling data. We find that Americans are in fact more prone to conformity than their neighbours to the north, who reside in a land that not only tolerates but actually celebrates linguistic, ethnic, and regional group identities. We track three items that shed light on this intriguing question: do people mind changing their habits, do they relate to people who show originality in dress and behaviour, and do they relate to people who repress rather than show their emotions. Our findings are surprising. In 1992, 51 percent of Canadians and 56 percent of Americans reported that they did not like changing their habits. In 1996, 48 percent of Canadians reported being stuck in their ways—a decline of three points—and 58 percent of Americans said the same thing, an increase of two points. By 2000, we had a widening and quite significant gap: only 42 percent of Canadians said they don't like changing their habits while 54 percent of Americans reported the same, now a gap of twelve points showing Canadians to be less conservative and more flexible than Americans in their day-to-day routines.

How about conformity of dress and behaviour: wearing the right costume or uniform for the occasion, not saying or doing anything politically incorrect? Who are the conformists? Who are the rebels? In 1992, 1996, and 2000 a consistent two-thirds of Canadians (68, 68, and 67 percent) told us that they relate to nonconformists. Conversely, in each year, the proportion of Americans who do so dropped: from 64 percent in 1992 to 61 percent in 1996 to 52 percent in 2000. Overall, the gap between the U.S. and Canada stands at 15 percent. That George W. Bush, after his election, instantly reinstated a strict suit-and-tie dress code at the White House illustrates this penchant for order and decorum, in stark contrast to the Clinton-era "wonk casual" image. Meanwhile, Canada's male politicians go out of their way to dress informally, almost invariably replacing their blue suits with open-collared sports shirts when on the campaign trail. One of the truly remarkable silent social revolutions in Canada has been the rapid death of the dress code. Dress-down Friday became dress-down every day in the Canadian workplace in a matter of months. In New York many upscale restaurants still strictly enforce a jacket-and-tie dress code; in Toronto only the stuffiest of private clubs have a store of apparel for the uncouth who show up improperly attired.

And finally, what about emotional informality and openness? Who are more open: the famously friendly "y'all come back real soon" Americans or the reputedly reserved, understated (even cold?) Canadians? In 1992, 32 percent of Canadians told us that they relate best to people who do not show their emotions. In 1996 we found a similar proportion (28 percent), and in 2000 30 percent—essentially no change over the decade. In 1992, the proportion of Americans who preferred the stiff-upper-lip type was 27 percent—five points lower than in Canada, as expected. But in 1996 that proportion rose to 35 percent, and then in 2000 shot up even further to 44 percent—an astounding fourteen-point gap. It's hard to get your head around the idea of a touchy-feely Canadian in contrast to the emotionally restrained, uptight American. But think back—way back—to the strong, silent heroes of American westerns who let their guns do the talking and held their liquor as if it were Ovaltine. The late 90s have seen a tremendous backlash in the U.S. against the early trend toward "feminization." Today that forgotten cowboy, the one who doesn't have much time for fancy language or womanish diplomacy but sure knows what to do with an axis of evil when he sees one, is back in style.

Soon after 9/11, President George Bush and then New York Mayor Rudolph Giuliani urged Americans to demonstrate their patriotism in defiance of the forces of evil who "wish to destroy our way of life." The president and the mayor urged their fellow Americans to go out shopping. This the people did, thus saving the U.S. (and Canada) from recession. These leaders knew they were addressing receptive audiences: hordes of people who not only felt a genuine desire to do something, anything, to respond to those deeply traumatic events in a helpful way, but who had also been weaned on the idea that material possessions are among the most important expressions of one's status, interests, personality, and citizenship in the greatest country on earth. In 1992, 38 percent of Americans told us it was important that people admire the things they own. Similar proportions in 1996 (37 percent) and 2000 (36 percent) said the same thing. In Canada, meanwhile, ostentatious consumption has been in gentle decline: from 34 percent in 1992, to 32 percent in 1996, and down to 29 percent in 2000. Many Canadians are still conspicuous consumers, but they lag behind their American cousins and seem to be drifting away from consuming "things" toward enjoying "experience." Americans brag about the new car they just bought; Canadians are more likely to boast about the trips they have taken.

CRITICAL THINKING QUESTIONS

1. Do you think that people from Canada and the United States are generally the same, or are there significant differences? What are those differences? How would you go about measuring those differences? And finally, what do you think lies at the root of those differences?

2. Studying the differences between Canadians and Americans has been a topic of social research for decades. What kind of evidence does Adams have to offer that our two cultures are not becoming more similar? Give specific examples. What research method does he apply?

3. One fear that persists among Canadians is that as the North American economy becomes more integrated, culture will follow. What is meant by *culture* in this instance? Can you give some examples of cultural products? Do you think there is a connection between the economy and culture?

8

India's Sacred Cow

MARVIN HARRIS

Anthropologist Marvin Harris uses the approach of cultural ecology to investigate how exotic and seemingly inexplicable cultural patterns may turn out to be everyday strategies for human survival in a particular natural environment. In this article, he offers his own favourite example: Why do people in India—many of whom are hungry—refuse to eat beef from the "sacred cows" that are found almost everywhere?

Whenever I get into discussions about the influence of practical and mundane factors on lifestyles, someone is sure to say, "But what about all those cows the hungry peasants in India refuse to eat?" The picture of a ragged farmer starving to death alongside a big fat cow conveys a reassuring sense of mystery to Western observers. In countless learned and popular allusions, it confirms our deepest conviction about how people with inscrutable Oriental minds ought to act. It is comforting to know—somewhat like "there will always be an England"—that in India spiritual values are more precious than life itself. And at the same time it makes us feel sad. How can we ever hope to understand people so different from ourselves? Westerners find the idea that there might be a practical explanation for Hindu

love of the cow more upsetting than Hindus do. The sacred cow—how else can I say it?—is one of our favorite sacred cows.

Hindus venerate cows because cows are the symbol of everything that is alive. As Mary is to Christians the mother of God, the cow to Hindus is the mother of life. So there is no greater sacrilege for a Hindu than killing a cow. Even the taking of human life lacks the symbolic meaning, the unutterable defilement, that is evoked by cow slaughter.

According to many experts, cow worship is the number one cause of India's hunger and poverty. Some Western-trained agronomists say that the taboo against cow slaughter is keeping 100 million "useless" animals alive. They claim that cow worship lowers the efficiency of agriculture because the useless animals contribute neither milk nor meat while competing for croplands and food-stuff with useful animals and hungry human beings. . . .

It does seem that there are enormous numbers of surplus, useless, and uneconomic animals, and that this situation is a direct result of irrational Hindu doctrines. Tourists on their way through Delhi, Calcutta, Madras, Bombay, and other Indian cities are astonished at the liberties enjoyed by stray cattle. The animals wander through the streets, browse off the stalls in the market place, break into private gardens, defecate all over the sidewalks, and snarl traffic by pausing to chew their cuds in the middle of busy intersections. In the countryside, the cattle congregate on the shoulders of every highway and spend much of their time taking leisurely walks down the railroad tracks.

To Western observers familiar with modern industrial techniques of agriculture and stock raising, cow love seems senseless, even suicidal. The efficiency expert yearns to get his hands on all those useless animals and ship them off to a proper fate. And yet one finds certain inconsistencies in the condemnation of cow love. When I began to wonder if there might be a practical explanation for the sacred cow, I came across an intriguing government report. It said that India had too many cows but too few oxen. With so many cows around, how could there be a shortage of oxen? Oxen and male water buffalo are the principal source of traction for plowing India's fields. For each farm of ten acres or less, one pair of oxen or water buffalo is considered adequate. A little arithmetic shows that as far as plowing is concerned, there is indeed a shortage rather than a surplus of animals. India has 60 million farms, but only 80 million traction animals. If each farm had its quota of two oxen or two water buffalo, there ought to be 120 million traction animals—that is, 40 million more than are actually available.

The shortage may not be quite so bad, since some farmers rent or borrow oxen from their neighbors. But the sharing of plow animals often proves impractical. Plowing must be coordinated with the monsoon rains, and by the time one farm has been plowed, the optimum

moment for plowing another may already have passed. Also, after plowing is over, a farmer still needs his own pair of oxen to pull his oxcart, the mainstay of the bulk transport throughout rural India. Quite possibly private ownership of farms, livestock, plows, and oxcarts lowers the efficiency of Indian agriculture, but this, I soon realized, was not caused by cow love.

The shortage of draft animals is a terrible threat that hangs over most of India's peasant families. When an ox falls sick a poor farmer is in danger of losing his farm. If he has no replacement for it, he will have to borrow money at usurious rates. Millions of rural households have in fact lost all or part of their holdings and have gone into sharecropping or day labor as a result of such debts. Each year hundreds of thousands of destitute farmers end up migrating to the cities, which already teem with unemployed and homeless persons.

The Indian farmer who can't replace his sick or deceased ox is in much the same situation as an American farmer who can neither replace nor repair his broken tractor. But there is an important difference: Tractors are made by factories, but oxen are made by cows. A farmer who owns a cow owns a factory for making oxen. With or without cow love, this is a good reason for him not to be too anxious to sell his cow to the slaughterhouse. One also begins to see why Indian farmers might be willing to tolerate cows that give only 500 pounds of milk per year. If the main economic function of the zebu cow is to breed male traction animals, then there's no point in comparing her with specialized American dairy animals, whose main function is to produce milk. Still, the milk produced by zebu cows plays an important role in meeting the nutritional needs of many poor families. Even small amounts of milk products can improve the health of people who are forced to subsist on the edge of starvation.

Agriculture is part of a vast system of human and natural relationships. To judge isolated portions of this "ecosystem" in terms that are relevant to the conduct of American agribusiness leads to some very strange impressions. Cattle figure in the Indian ecosystem in ways that are easily overlooked or demeaned by observers from industrialized, high-energy societies. In the United States, chemicals have almost completely replaced animal manure as the principal source of farm fertilizer. American farmers stopped using manure when they began to plow with tractors rather than mules or horses. Since tractors excrete poisons rather than fertilizers, a commitment to large-scale machine farming is almost of necessity a commitment to the use of chemical fertilizers. And around the world today there has in fact grown up a vast integrated petrochemical-tractor-truck industrial complex that produces farm machinery, motorized transport, oil and gasoline, and chemical fertilizers and pesticides upon which new high-yield production techniques depend.

For better or worse, most of India's farmers cannot participate in this complex, not because they worship their cows, but because they can't afford to buy tractors. Like other underdeveloped nations, India can't build factories that are competitive with the facilities of the industrialized nations nor pay for large quantities of imported industrial products. To convert from animals and manure to tractors and petrochemicals would require the investment of incredible amounts of capital. Moreover, the inevitable effect of substituting costly machines for cheap animals is to reduce the number of people who can earn their living from agriculture and to force a corresponding increase in the size of the average farm. We know that the development of large-scale agribusiness in the United States has meant the virtual destruction of the small family farm. Less than 5 percent of U.S. families now live on farms, as compared with 60 percent about a hundred years ago. If agribusiness were to

develop along similar lines in India, jobs and housing would soon have to be found for a quarter of a billion displaced peasants.

Since the suffering caused by unemployment and homelessness in India's cities is already intolerable, an additional massive build-up of the urban population can only lead to unprecedented upheavals and catastrophes.

With this alternative in view, it becomes easier to understand low-energy, small-scale, animal-based systems. As I have already pointed out, cows and oxen provide low-energy substitutes for tractors and tractor factories. They also should be credited with carrying out the functions of a petrochemical industry. India's cattle annually excrete about 700 million tons of recoverable manure. Approximately half of this total is used as fertilizer, while most of the remainder is burned to provide heat for cooking. The annual quantity of heat liberated by this dung, the Indian housewife's main cooking fuel, is the thermal equivalent of 27 million tons of kerosene, 35 million tons of coal, or 68 million tons of wood. Since India has only small reserves of oil and coal and is already the victim of extensive deforestation, none of these fuels can be considered practical substitutes for cow dung. The thought of dung in the kitchen may not appeal to the average American, but Indian women regard it as a superior cooking fuel because it is finely adjusted to their domestic routines. Most Indian dishes are prepared with clarified butter known as ghee, for which cow dung is the preferred source of heat since it burns with a clean, slow, long-lasting flame that doesn't scorch the food. This enables the Indian housewife to start cooking her meals and to leave them unattended for several hours while she takes care of the children, helps out in the fields, or performs other chores. American housewives achieve a similar effect through a complex set of electronic controls that come as expensive options on late-model stoves.

Cow dung has at least one other major function. Mixed with water and made into a paste, it is used as a household flooring material. Smeared over a dirt floor and left to harden into a smooth surface, it keeps the dust down and can be swept clean with a broom.

Because cattle droppings have so many useful properties, every bit of dung is carefully collected. Village small fry are given the task of following the family cow around and of bringing home its daily petrochemical output. In the cities, sweeper castes enjoy a monopoly on the dung deposited by strays and earn their living by selling it to housewives. . . .

During droughts and famines, farmers are severely tempted to kill or sell their livestock. Those who succumb to this temptation seal their doom, even if they survive the drought, for when the rains come, they will be unable to plow their fields. I want to be even more emphatic: Massive slaughter of cattle under the duress of famine constitutes a much greater threat to aggregate welfare than any likely miscalculation by particular farmers concerning the usefulness of their animals during normal times. It seems probable that the sense of unutterable profanity elicited by cow slaughter has its roots in the excruciating contradiction between immediate needs and long-term conditions of survival. Cow love with its sacred symbols and holy doctrines protects the farmer against calculations that are "rational" only in the short term. To Western experts it looks as if "the Indian farmer would rather starve to death than eat his cow." . . . They don't realize that the farmer would rather eat his cow than starve, but that he will starve if he does eat it. . . .

Do I mean to say that cow love has no effect whatsoever on . . . the agricultural system? No. What I am saying is that cow love is an active element in a complex, finely articulated material and cultural order. Cow love mobilizes the latent capacity of human beings to persevere in a low-energy ecosystem in which there is little room for waste or indolence. Cow love contributes to the adaptive resilience of the human population by preserving temporarily dry or barren but still useful animals; by discouraging the growth of an energy-expensive beef industry; by protecting cattle that fatten in the public domain or at landlord's expense; and by preserving the recovery potential of the cattle population during droughts and famines. . . .

Wastefulness is more a characteristic of modern agribusiness than of traditional peasant economies. . . .

Automobiles and airplanes are faster than oxcarts, but they do not use energy more efficiently. In fact, more calories go up in useless heat and smoke during a single day of traffic jams in the United States than is wasted by all the cows of India during an entire year. The comparison is even less favorable when we consider the fact that the stalled vehicles are burning up irreplaceable reserves of petroleum that it took the earth tens of millions of years to accumulate. If you want to see a real sacred cow, go out and look at the family car.

CRITICAL THINKING QUESTIONS

1. What evidence does Harris offer to support his argument that defining the cow as sacred is a necessary strategy for human survival in India?
2. If survival strategies make sense when we take a close look at them, why do they become so "encased" in elaborate cultural explanations?
3. Does India's recognition of the sacred cow help or hurt that nation's natural environment?
4. Following Harris's logic, can you think of reasons that people in some parts of the world (the Middle East, for instance) do not eat pork?

Society
CLASSIC
CONTEMPORARY
CROSS-CULTURAL

9

Manifesto of the Communist Party

KARL MARX AND FRIEDRICH ENGELS

Karl Marx, collaborating with Friedrich Engels, produced the "Manifesto" in 1848. This document is a well-known statement about the origin of social conflict in the process of material production. The ideas of Marx and Engels have been instrumental in shaping the political lives of more than one-fifth of the world's population, and, of course, they have also been instrumental in the development of the social–conflict paradigm in sociology.

BOURGEOIS AND PROLETARIANS[1]

The history of all hitherto existing society[2] is the history of class struggles.

Freeman and slave, patrician and plebeian, lord and serf, guild-master[3] and journeyman, in a word, oppressor and oppressed, stood in constant opposition to one another, carried on an uninterrupted, now hidden, now open fight, a fight that each time ended, either in a revolutionary reconstitution of society at large, or in the common ruin of the contending classes.

In the earlier epochs of history, we find almost everywhere a complicated arrangement of society into various orders, a manifold gradation of social rank. In ancient Rome we have patricians, knights, plebeians, slaves; in the Middle Ages, feudal lords, vassals, guild-masters, journeymen, apprentices, serfs; in almost all of these classes, again, subordinate gradations.

The modern bourgeois society that has sprouted from the ruins of feudal society has not done away with class antagonisms. It has but established new classes, new conditions of oppression, new forms of struggle in place of the old ones.

Our epoch, the epoch of the bourgeoisie, possesses, however, this distinctive feature; it has simplified the class antagonisms. Society as a whole is more and more splitting up into two great hostile camps, into two great classes directly facing each other: Bourgeoisie and Proletariat.

From the serfs of the Middle Ages sprang the chartered burghers of the earliest towns. From these burgesses the first elements of the bourgeoisie were developed.

The discovery of America, the rounding of the Cape, opened up fresh ground for the

Source: From *Manifesto of the Communist Party*, Part I, by Karl Marx and Friedrich Engels.

rising bourgeoisie. The East Indian and Chinese markets, the [colonization] of America, trade with the colonies, the increase in the means of exchange and in commodities generally, gave to commerce, to navigation, to industry, an impulse never before known, and thereby, to the revolutionary element in the tottering feudal society, a rapid development.

The feudal system of industry, under which industrial production was monopolized by close guilds, now no longer sufficed for the growing wants of the new markets. The manufacturing system took its place. The guild-masters were pushed on one side by the manufacturing middle class; division of labor between the different corporate guilds vanished in the face of division of labor in each single workshop.

Meantime the markets kept ever growing, the demand, ever rising. Even manufacture no longer sufficed. Thereupon, steam and machinery revolutionized industrial production. The place of manufacture was taken by the giant, Modern Industry, the place of the industrial middle class, by industrial millionaires, the leaders of whole industrial armies, the modern bourgeois.

Modern industry has established the world-market, for which the discovery of America paved the way. This market has given an immense development to commerce, to navigation, to communication by land. This development has, in its turn, reacted on the extension of industry; and in proportion as industry, commerce, navigation, railways extended, in the same proportion the bourgeoisie developed, increased its capital, and pushed into the background every class handed down from the Middle Ages.

We see, therefore, how the modern bourgeoisie is itself the product of a long course of development, of a series of revolutions in the modes of production and of exchange.

Each step in the development of the bourgeoisie was accompanied by a corresponding political advance of that class. An oppressed class under the sway of the feudal nobility, an armed and self-governing association in the mediæval commune, [4] here independent urban republic (as in Italy and Germany), there taxable "third estate" of the monarchy (as in France), afterwards, in the period of manufacture proper, serving either the semi-feudal or the absolute monarchy as a counterpoise against the nobility, and, in fact, cornerstone of the great monarchies in general, the bourgeoisie has at last, since the establishment of modern industry and of the world-market, conquered for itself, in the modern representative State, exclusive political sway. The executive of the modern State is but a committee for managing the common affairs of the whole bourgeoisie.

The bourgeoisie, historically, has played a most revolutionary part.

The bourgeoisie, wherever it has got the upper hand, has put an end to all feudal, patriarchal, idyllic relations. It has pitilessly torn asunder the motley feudal ties that bound man to his "natural superiors," and has left remaining no other nexus between man and man than naked self-interest, than callous "cash payment." It has drowned the most heavenly ecstasies of religious fervour, of chivalrous enthusiasm, of philistine sentimentalism, in the icy water of egotistical calculation. It has resolved personal worth into exchange value, and in place of the numberless indefeasible chartered freedoms, has set up that single, unconscionable freedom—Free Trade. In one word, for exploitation, veiled by religious and political illusions, it has substituted naked, shameless, direct, brutal exploitation.

The bourgeoisie has stripped of its halo every occupation hitherto honoured and looked up to with reverent awe. It has converted the physician, the lawyer, the priest, the poet, the man of science, into its paid [wage-laborers].

The bourgeoisie has torn away from the family its sentimental veil, and has reduced the family relation to a mere money relation.

The bourgeoisie has disclosed how it came to pass that the brutal display of vigour in the Middle Ages, which reactionists so much admire, found its fitting complement in the most slothful indolence. It has been the first to show what man's activity can bring about. It has accomplished wonders far surpassing Egyptian pyramids, Roman aqueducts, and Gothic cathedrals; it has conducted expeditions that put in the shade all former Exoduses of nations and crusades.

The bourgeoisie cannot exist without constantly revolutionizing the instruments of production, and thereby the relations of production, and with them the whole relations of society. Conservation of the old modes of production in unaltered form, was, on the contrary, the first condition of existence for all earlier industrial classes. Constant revolutionizing of production, uninterrupted disturbance of all social conditions, everlasting uncertainty and agitation distinguish the bourgeois epoch from all earlier ones. All fixed, fast-frozen relations, with their train of ancient and venerable prejudices and opinions, are swept away, all new-formed ones become antiquated before they can ossify. All that is solid melts into air, all that is holy is profaned, and man is at last compelled to face with sober senses, his real conditions of life, and his relations with his kind.

The need of a constantly expanding market for its products chases the bourgeoisie over the whole surface of the globe. It must nestle everywhere, settle everywhere, establish [connections] everywhere.

The bourgeoisie has through its exploitation of the world-market given a cosmopolitan character to production and consumption in every country. To the great chagrin of reactionists, it has drawn from under the feet of industry the national ground on which it stood. All old-established national industries have been destroyed or are daily being destroyed. They are dislodged by new industries, whose introduction becomes a life and death question for all civilised nations, by industries that no longer work up indigenous raw material, but raw material drawn from the remotest zones; industries whose products are consumed, not only at home, but in every quarter of the globe. In place of the old wants, satisfied by the productions of the country, we find new wants, requiring for their satisfaction the products of distant lands and climes. In place of the old local and national seclusion and self-sufficiency, we have intercourse in every direction, universal interdependence of nations. And as in material, so also in intellectual production. The intellectual creations of individual nations become common property. National one-sidedness and narrow-mindedness become more and more impossible, and from the numerous national and local literatures there arises a world-literature.

The bourgeoisie, by the rapid improvement of all instruments of production, by the immensely facilitated means of communication, draws all, even the most barbarian, nations into civilization. The cheap prices of its commodities are the heavy artillery with which it batters down all Chinese walls, with which it forces the barbarians' intensely obstinate hatred of foreigners to capitulate. It compels all nations, on pain of extinction, to adopt the bourgeois mode of production; it compels them to introduce what it calls civilization into their midst, i.e., to become bourgeois themselves. In a word, it creates a world after its own image.

The bourgeoisie has subjected the country to the rule of the towns. It has created enormous cities, has greatly increased the urban population as compared with the rural, and has thus rescued a considerable part of the population from the idiocy of rural life. Just as it has made the country dependent on the towns, so it has made barbarian and semi-barbarian countries dependent on the civilised ones, nations of peasants on nations of bourgeois, the East on the West.

The bourgeoisie keeps more and more doing away with the scattered state of the population, of the means of production, and of property. It has agglomerated population, centralized means of production, and has concentrated property in a few hands. The necessary consequence of this was political centralization. Independent, or but loosely connected provinces, with separate interests, laws, governments and systems of taxation, became lumped together in one nation, with one government, one code of laws, one national class-interest, one frontier and one customs-tariff.

The bourgeoisie, during its rule of scarce one hundred years, has created more massive and more colossal productive forces than have all preceding generations together. Subjection of Nature's forces to man, machinery, application of chemistry to industry and agriculture, steam-navigation, railways, electric telegraphs, clearing of whole continents for cultivation, canalization of rivers, whole populations conjured out of the ground—what earlier century had even a presentiment that such productive forces slumbered in the lap of social labor?

We see then: The means of production and of exchange on whose foundation the bourgeoisie built itself up, were generated in feudal society. At a certain stage in the development of these means of production and of exchange, the conditions under which feudal society produced and exchanged, the feudal organization of agriculture and manufacturing industry, in one word, the feudal relations of property became no longer compatible with the already developed productive forces; they became so many fetters. They had to burst asunder; they were burst asunder.

Into their places stepped free competition, accompanied by a social and political constitution adapted to it, and by the economical and political sway of the bourgeois class.

A similar movement is going on before our own eyes. Modern bourgeois society with its relations of production, of exchange and of property, a society that has conjured up such gigantic means of production and of exchange, is like the sorcerer, who is no longer able to control the powers of the nether world whom he has called up by his spells. For many a decade past the history of industry and commerce is but the history of the revolt of modern productive forces against modern conditions of production, against the property relations that are the conditions for the existence of the bourgeoisie and of its rule. It is enough to mention the commercial crises that by their periodical return put on its trial, each time more threateningly, the existence of the entire bourgeois society. In these crises a great part not only of the existing products, but also of the previously created productive forces, are periodically destroyed. In these crises there breaks out an epidemic that, in all earlier epochs, would have seemed an absurdity—the epidemic of overproduction. Society suddenly finds itself put back into a state of momentary barbarism; it appears as if a famine, a universal war of devastation had cut off the supply of every means of subsistence; industry and commerce seem to be destroyed; and why? Because there is too much civilization, too much means of subsistence, too much industry, too much commerce. The productive forces at the disposal of society no longer tend to further the development of the conditions of bourgeois property; on the contrary, they have become too powerful for these conditions, by which they are fettered, and so [as] soon as they overcome these fetters, they bring disorder into the whole of bourgeois society, endanger the existence of bourgeois property. The conditions of bourgeois society are too narrow to comprise the wealth created by them. And how does the bourgeoisie get over these crises? On the one hand by enforced destruction of a mass of productive forces; on the other, by the conquest of new markets, and by the more thorough exploitation of the old ones. That is to say, by paving the way for more extensive and more destructive crises, and by diminishing the means whereby crises are prevented.

The weapons with which the bourgeoisie felled feudalism to the ground are now turned against the bourgeoisie itself.

But not only has the bourgeoisie forged the weapons that bring death to itself; it has also called into existence the men who are to wield those weapons—the modern working class— the proletarians.

In proportion as the bourgeoisie, i.e., capital, is developed, in the same proportion is the proletariat, the modern working class, developed, a class of laborers, who live only so long as they find work, and who find work only so long as their labor increases capital. These laborers, who must sell themselves piecemeal, are a commodity, like every other article of commerce, and are consequently exposed to all the vicissitudes of competition, to all the fluctuations of the market.

Owing to the extensive use of machinery and to division of labor, the work of the proletarians has lost all individual character, and, consequently, all charm for the workman. He becomes an appendage of the machine, and it is only the most simple, most monotonous and most easily acquired knack that is required of him. Hence, the cost of production of a workman is restricted, almost entirely, to the means of subsistence that he requires for his maintenance, and for the propagation of his race. But the price of a commodity, and also of labor, is equal to its cost of production. In proportion, therefore, as the repulsiveness of the work increases, the wage decreases. Nay more, in proportion as the use of machinery and division of labor increases, in the same proportion the burden of toil also increases, whether by prolongation of the working hours, by increase of the work enacted in a given time, or by increased speed of the machinery, etc.

Modern industry has converted the little workshop of the patriarchal master into the great factory of the industrial capitalist. Masses of laborers, crowded into the factory, are organized like soldiers. As privates of the industrial army they are placed under the command of a perfect hierarchy of officers and sergeants. Not only are they the slaves of the bourgeois class, and of the bourgeois State, they are daily and hourly enslaved by the machine, by the over-looker, and, above all, by the individual bourgeois manufacturer himself. The more openly this despotism proclaims gain to be its end and aim, the more petty, the more hateful and the more embittering it is.

The less the skill and exertion or strength implied in manual labor, in other words, the more modern industry becomes developed, the more is the labor of men superseded by that of women. Differences of age and sex have no longer any distinctive social validity for the working class. All are instruments of labor, more or less expensive to use, according to their age and sex.

No sooner is the exploitation of the laborer by the manufacturer, so far, at an end, that he receives his wages in cash, than he is set upon by the other portions of the bourgeoisie, the landlord, the shopkeeper, the pawnbroker, etc.

The lower strata of the middle class—the small tradespeople, shopkeepers, and retired tradesmen generally, the handicraftsmen and peasants—all these sink gradually into the proletariat, partly because their diminutive capital does not suffice for the scale on which Modern Industry is carried on, and is swamped in the competition with the large capitalists, partly because their specialised skill is rendered worthless by new methods of production. Thus the proletariat is recruited from all classes of the population.

The proletariat goes through various stages of development. With its birth begins its struggle with the bourgeoisie. At first the contest is carried on by individual laborers, then by the workpeople of a factory, then by the operatives of one trade, in one locality, against the individual bourgeois who directly exploits them. They direct their attacks not against the bourgeois conditions of production, but against the instruments of production themselves; they destroy imported wares that compete with their labor, they smash to pieces machinery, they set factories ablaze, they seek to restore by force the vanished status of the workman of the Middle Ages.

At this stage the laborers still form an incoherent mass scattered over the whole country, and broken up by their mutual competition. If anywhere they unite to form more compact bodies, this is not yet the consequence of their own active union, but of the union of the bourgeoisie, which class, in order to attain its own political ends, is compelled to set the whole proletariat in motion, and is moreover yet, for a time, able to do so. At this stage, therefore, the proletarians do not fight their enemies, but the enemies of their enemies, the remnants of absolute monarchy, the landowners, the non-industrial bourgeois, the petty bourgeoisie. Thus the whole historical movement is concentrated in the hands of the bourgeoisie; every victory so obtained is a victory for the bourgeoisie.

But with the development of industry the proletariat not only increases in number, it becomes concentrated in greater masses, its strength grows, and it feels that strength more. The various interests and conditions of life within the ranks of the proletariat are more and more equalized, in proportion as machinery obliterates all distinctions of labor, and nearly everywhere reduces wages to the same low level. The growing competition among the bourgeois, and the resulting commercial crises, make the wages of the workers ever more fluctuating. The unceasing improvement of machinery, ever more rapidly developing, makes their livelihood more and more precarious; the collisions between individual workmen and individual bourgeois take more and more the character of collisions between two classes. Thereupon the workers begin to form combinations (Trades' Unions) against the bourgeois; they club together in order to keep up the rate of wages; they found permanent associations in order to make provision beforehand for these occasional revolts. Here and there the contest breaks out into riots.

Now and then the workers are victorious, but only for a time. The real fruit of their battles lies, not in the immediate result, but in the ever expanding union of the workers. This union is helped on by the improved means of communication that are created by modern industry, and that place the workers of different localities in contact with one another. It was just this contact that was needed to centralize the numerous local struggles, all of the same character, into one national struggle between classes. But every class struggle is a political struggle. And that union, to attain which the burghers of the Middle Ages, with their miserable highways, required centuries, the modern proletarians, thanks to railways, achieve in a few years.

This organization of the proletarians into a class, and consequently into a political party, is continually being upset again by the competition between the workers themselves. But it ever rises up again, stronger, firmer, mightier. It compels legislative recognition of particular interests of the workers, by taking advantage of the divisions among the bourgeoisie itself. Thus the ten-hours'-bill in England was carried.

Altogether collisions between the classes of the old society further, in many ways, the course of development of the proletariat. The bourgeoisie finds itself involved in a constant battle. At first with the aristocracy; later on, with those portions of the bourgeoisie itself, whose interests have become antagonistic to the progress of industry; at all times, with the bourgeoisie of foreign countries. In all these battles it sees itself compelled to appeal to the proletariat, to ask for its help, and thus, to drag it into the political arena. The bourgeoisie itself, therefore, supplies the proletariat with its own elements of political and general education, in other words, it furnishes the proletariat with weapons for fighting the bourgeoisie.

Further, as we have already seen, entire sections of the ruling classes are, by the advance of industry, precipitated into the proletariat, or are at least threatened in their conditions of existence. These also supply the proletariat with fresh elements of enlightenment and progress.

Finally, in times when the class-struggle nears the decisive hour, the process of dissolution going on within the ruling class, in fact within the whole range of old society, assumes such a violent, glaring character, that a small section of the ruling class cuts itself adrift, and joins the revolutionary class, the class that holds the future in its hands. Just as, therefore, at an earlier period, a section of the nobility went over to the bourgeoisie, so now a portion of the bourgeoisie goes over to the proletariat, and in particular, a portion of the bourgeois ideologists, who have raised themselves to the level of comprehending theoretically the historical movements as a whole.

Of all the classes that stand face to face with the bourgeoisie today, the proletariat alone is a really revolutionary class. The other classes decay and finally disappear in the face of modern industry; the proletariat is its special and essential product.

The lower-middle class, the small manufacturer, the shopkeeper, the artisan, the peasant, all these fight against the bourgeoisie, to save from extinction their existence as fractions of the middle class. They are therefore not revolutionary, but conservative. Nay more, they are reactionary, for they try to roll back the wheel of history. If by chance they are revolutionary, they are so, only in view of their impending transfer into the proletariat, they thus defend not their present, but their future interests, they desert their own standpoint to place themselves at that of the proletariat.

The "dangerous class," the social scum, that passively rotting mass thrown off by the lowest layers of old society, may, here and there, be swept into the movement by a proletarian

revolution; its conditions of life, however, prepare it far more for the part of a bribed tool of reactionary intrigue.

In the conditions of the proletariat, those of old society at large are already virtually swamped. The proletarian is without property; his relation to his wife and children has no longer anything in common with the bourgeois family-relations; modern industrial labor, modern subjection to capital, the same in England as in France, in America as in Germany, has stripped him of every trace of national character. Law, morality, religion, are to him so many bourgeois prejudices, behind which lurk in ambush just as many bourgeois interests.

All the preceding classes that got the upper hand sought to fortify their already acquired status by subjecting at large to their conditions of appropriation. The proletarians cannot become masters of the productive forces of society, except by abolishing their own previous mode of appropriation, and thereby also every other previous mode of appropriation. They have nothing of their own to secure and to fortify; their mission is to destroy all previous securities for, and insurances of, individual property.

All previous historical movements were movements of minorities, or in the interest of minorities. The proletarian movement is the self-conscious, independent movement of the immense majority, in the interest of the immense majority. The proletariat, the lowest stratum of our present society, cannot stir, cannot raise itself up, without the whole superincumbent strata of official society being sprung into the air.

Though not in substance, yet in form, the struggle of the proletariat with the bourgeoisie is at first a national struggle. The proletariat of each country must, of course, first of all settle matters with its own bourgeoisie.

In depicting the most general phases of the development of the proletariat, we traced the more or less veiled civil war, raging within existing society, up to the point where that war breaks out into open revolution, and where the violent overthrow of the bourgeoisie, lays the foundation for the sway of the proletariat.

Hitherto, every form of society has been based, as we have already seen, on the antagonism of oppressing and oppressed classes. But in order to oppress a class, certain conditions must be assured to it under which it can, at least, continue its slavish existence. The serf, in the period of serfdom, raised himself to membership in the commune, just as the petty bourgeois, under the yoke of feudal absolutism, managed to develop into a bourgeois. The modern laborer, on the contrary, instead of rising with the progress of industry, sinks deeper and deeper below the conditions of existence of his own class. He becomes a pauper, and pauperism develops more rapidly than population and wealth. And here it becomes evident, that the bourgeoisie is unfit any longer to be the ruling class in society, and to impose its conditions of existence upon society as an overriding law. It is unfit to rule, because it is incompetent to assure an existence to its slave within his slavery, because it cannot help letting him sink into such a state, that it has to feed him, instead of being fed by him. Society can no longer live under this bourgeoisie, in other words, its existence is no longer compatible with society.

The essential condition for the existence, and for the sway of the bourgeois class, is the formation and augmentation of capital; the condition for capital is wage-labor. Wage-labor rests exclusively on competition between the laborers. The advance of industry, whose involuntary promoter is the bourgeoisie, replaces the isolation of the laborers, due to competition, by their involuntary combination, due to association. The development of modern industry, therefore, cuts from under its feet the very foundation on which the bourgeoisie produces and appropriates products. What the bourgeoisie therefore produces, above all, are

its own grave-diggers. Its fall and the victory of the proletariat are equally inevitable.

CRITICAL THINKING QUESTIONS

1. What are the distinguishing factors of "class conflict"? How does this differ from other kinds of conflict, as between individuals or nations?

2. Why do Marx and Engels argue that understanding society in the present requires investigating the society of the past?

3. On what grounds did Marx and Engels *praise* industrial capitalism? On what grounds did they *condemn* the system?

NOTES

1. By *bourgeoisie* is meant the class of modern capitalists, owners of the means of social production and employers of wage-labor; by *proletariat*, the class of modern wage-laborers who, having no means of production of their own, are reduced to selling their labor-power in order to live.

2. That is, all written history. In 1847, the prehistory of society, the social organization existing previous to recorded history, was all but unknown. Since then, Haxthausen discovered common ownership of land in Russia. Maurer proved it to be the social foundation from which all Teutonic races started in history, and by and by village communities were found to be, or to have been, the primitive form of society everywhere from India to Ireland. The inner organization of this primitive Communistic society was laid bare, in its typical form, by Morgan's crowning discovery of the true nature of the gens and its relation to the tribe. With the dissolution of these primæval communities society begins to be differentiated into separate and finally antagonistic classes. I have attempted to retrace this process of dissolution in "Der Ursprung der Familie, des Privateigenthums und des Staats," 2d ed. Stuttgart 1886.

3. Guild-master, that is, a full member of a guild, a master within, not a head of, a guild.

4. "Commune" was the name taken, in France, by the nascent towns even before they had conquered from their feudal lords and masters, local self-government and political rights as "the Third Estate." Generally speaking, for the economical development of the bourgeoisie, England is here taken as the typical country, [and] for its political development, France.

CLASSIC

CONTEMPORARY

CROSS-CULTURAL

10

Unmarried with Children

KATHRYN EDIN AND MARIA KEFALAS

Since the late 1980s, one of the major changes in U.S. society has been a dramatic increase in unmarried mothers, especially at lower socioeconomic levels. Have these women given up on marriage, as most male, white, and middle-class observers have concluded? According to Kathryn Edin and Maria Kefalas, many of the single women who have children believe in marriage. They are still waiting for the right partner to fulfill their dreams of having a middle-class home with a devoted husband and father.

Jen Burke, a white tenth-grade dropout who is seventeen years old, lives with her stepmother, her sister, and her sixteen-month-old son in a cramped but tidy row home in Philadelphia's beleaguered Kensington neighborhood. She is broke, on welfare, and struggling to complete her GED. Wouldn't she and her son have been better off if she had finished high school, found a job, and married her son's father first?

In 1950, when Jen's grandmother came of age, only one in twenty American children was born to an unmarried mother. Today, that rate is one in three—and they are usually born to those least likely to be able to support a child on their own. In our book, *Promises I Can Keep: Why Poor Women Put Motherhood Before Marriage,*[1] we discuss the lives of 162

Source: "Unmarried with Children" by Kathryn Edin and Maria Kefalas, taken from *Contexts Journal Volume 4*, Number 2, May 2005, pp. 16–22. Used with Permission of the publisher, American Sociology Association.

white, African American, and Puerto Rican low-income single mothers living in eight destitute neighborhoods across Philadelphia and its poorest industrial suburb, Camden. We spent five years chatting over kitchen tables and on front stoops, giving mothers like Jen the opportunity to speak to the question so many affluent Americans ask about them: Why do they have children while still young and unmarried when they will face such an uphill struggle to support them?

ROMANCE AT LIGHTNING SPEED

Jen started having sex with her twenty-year-old boyfriend Rick just before her fifteenth birthday. A month and a half later, she was pregnant. "I didn't want to get pregnant," she claims. "*He* wanted me to get pregnant." "As soon as he met me, he wanted to have a kid with me," she explains. Though Jen's college-bound suburban peers would be appalled by such a declaration, on the streets of Jen's neighborhood, it is something of a badge of honor. "All those other girls he was with, he didn't want to have a baby with any of them," Jen boasts. "I asked him, 'Why did you choose me to have a kid when you could have a kid with any one of them?' He was like, 'I want to have a kid with you.'" Looking back, Jen says she now believes that the reason "he wanted me to have a kid that early is so that I didn't leave him."

In inner-city neighborhoods like Kensington, where child-bearing within marriage has become rare, romantic relationships like Jen and Rick's proceed at lightning speed. A young man's avowal, "I want to have a baby by you," is often part of the courtship ritual from the beginning. This is more than idle talk, as their first child is typically conceived within a year from the time a couple begins "kicking it." Yet while poor couples' pillow talk often revolves around dreams of shared children, the news of a pregnancy—the first indelible sign of the huge changes to come—puts these still-new relationships into overdrive. Suddenly, the would-be mother begins to scrutinize her mate as never before, wondering whether he can "get himself together"—find a job, settle down, and become a family man—in time.

Jen began pestering Rick to get a real job instead of picking up day-labor jobs at nearby construction sites. She also wanted him to stop hanging out with his ne'er-do-well friends, who had been getting him into serious trouble for more than a decade. Most of all, she wanted Rick to shed what she calls his "kiddie mentality"—his habit of spending money on alcohol and drugs rather than recognizing his growing financial obligations at home.

Rick did not try to deny paternity, as many would-be fathers do. Nor did he abandon or mistreat Jen, at least intentionally. But Rick, who had been in and out of juvenile detention since he was eight years old for everything from stealing cars to selling drugs, proved unable to stay away from his unsavory friends. At the beginning of her seventh month of pregnancy, an escapade that began as a drunken lark landed Rick in jail on a carjacking charge. Jen moved back home with her stepmother, applied for welfare, and spent the last two-and-a-half months of her pregnancy without Rick.

Rick sent penitent letters from jail. "I thought he changed by the letters he wrote me. I thought he changed a lot," she says. "He used to tell me that he loved me when he was in jail. . . . It was always gonna be me and him and the baby when he got out." Thus, when Rick's alleged victim failed to appear to testify and he was released just days before Colin's birth, the couple's reunion was a happy one. Often, the magic moment of childbirth calms the troubled waters of such relationships. New parents typically make amends and resolve to stay together for the sake of their child. When surveyed just after a child's birth, eight in ten unmarried parents say they are still together, and most plan to stay together and raise the child.

Promoting marriage among the poor has become the new war on poverty, Bush style. And it is true that the correlation between marital status and child poverty is strong. But poor single mothers already believe in marriage. Jen insists that she will walk down the aisle one day, though she admits it might not be with Rick. And demographers still project that more than seven in ten women who had a child outside of marriage will eventually wed someone. First, though, Jen wants to get a good job, finish school, and get her son out of Kensington.

Most poor, unmarried mothers and fathers readily admit that bearing children while poor and unmarried is not the ideal way to do things. Jen believes the best time to become a mother is "after you're out of school and you got a job, at least, when you're like twenty-one. . . . When you're ready to have kids, you should have everything ready, have your house, have a job, so when that baby comes, the baby can have its own room." Yet given their already limited economic prospects, the poor have little motivation to time their births as precisely as their middle-class counterparts do. The dreams of young people like Jen and Rick center on children at a time of life when their more affluent peers plan for college and careers. Poor girls coming of age in the inner city value children highly, anticipate them eagerly, and believe strongly that they are up to the job of mothering—even in difficult circumstances.

Jen, for example, tells us, "People outside the neighborhood, they're like, 'You're fifteen! You're pregnant?' I'm like, it's not none of their business. I'm gonna be able to take care of my kid. They have nothing to worry about." Jen says she has concluded that "some people . . . are better at having kids at a younger age. . . . I think it's better for some people to have kids younger."

WHEN I BECAME A MOM

When we asked mothers like Jen what their lives would be like if they had not had children, we expected them to express regret over foregone opportunities for school and careers. Instead, most believe their children "saved" them. They describe their lives as spinning out of control before becoming pregnant—struggles with parents and peers, "wild," risky behavior, depression, and school failure. Jen speaks to this poignantly. "I was just real bad. I hung with a real bad crowd. I was doing pills. I was really depressed. . . . I was drinking. That was before I was pregnant." "I think," she reflects, "if I never had a baby or anything, . . . I would still be doing the things I was doing. I would probably still be doing drugs. I'd probably still be drinking." Jen admits that when she first became pregnant, she was angry that she "couldn't be out no more. Couldn't be out with my friends. Couldn't do nothing." Now, though, she says, "I'm glad I have a son . . . because I would still be doing all that stuff." Children offer poor youth like Jen a compelling sense of purpose. Jen paints a before-and-after picture of her life that was common

among the mothers we interviewed. "Before, I didn't have nobody to take care of. I didn't have nothing left to go home for. . . . Now I have my son to take care of. I have him to go home for. . . . I don't have to go buy weed or drugs with my money. I could buy my son stuff with my money! . . . I have something to look up to now." Children also are a crucial source of relational intimacy, a self-made community of care. After a nasty fight with Rick, Jen recalls, "I was crying. My son came in the room. He was hugging me. He's sixteen months and he was hugging me with his little arms. He was really cute and happy, so I got happy. That's one of the good things. When you're sad, the baby's always gonna be there for you no matter what." Lately she has been thinking a lot about what her life was like back then, before the baby. "I thought about the stuff before I became a mom, what my life was like back then. I used to see pictures of me, and I would hide in every picture. This baby did so much for me. My son did a lot for me. He helped me a lot. I'm thankful that I had my baby."

Around the time of the birth, most unmarried parents claim they plan to get married eventually. Rick did not propose marriage when Jen's first child was born, but when she conceived a second time, at seventeen, Rick informed his dad, "It's time for me to get married. It's time for me to straighten up. This is the one I wanna be with. I had a baby with her, I'm gonna have another baby with her." Yet despite their intentions, few of these couples actually marry. Indeed, most break up well before their child enters preschool.

I'D LIKE TO GET MARRIED, BUT . . .

The sharp decline in marriage in impoverished urban areas has led some to charge that the poor have abandoned the marriage norm. Yet we found few who had given up on the idea of marriage. But like their elite counterparts, disadvantaged women set a high financial bar for marriage. For the poor, marriage has become an elusive goal—one they feel ought to be reserved for those who can support a "white picket fence" lifestyle: a mortgage on a modest row home, a car and some furniture, some savings in the bank, and enough money left over to pay for a "decent" wedding. Jen's views on marriage provide a perfect case in point. "If I was gonna get married, I would want to be married like my Aunt Nancy and my Uncle Pat. They live in the mountains. She has a job. My Uncle Pat is a state trooper; he has lots of money. They live in the [Poconos]. It's real nice out there. Her kids go to Catholic school. . . . That's the kind of life I would want to have. If I get married, I would have a life like [theirs]." She adds, "And I would wanna have a big wedding, a real nice wedding."

Unlike the women of their mothers' and grandmothers' generations, young women like Jen are not merely content to rely on a man's earnings. Instead, they insist on being economically "set" in their own right before taking marriage vows. This is partly because they want a partnership of equals, and they believe money buys say-so in a relationship. Jen explains, "I'm not gonna just get into marrying him and not have my own house! Not have a job! I still wanna do a lot of things before I get married. He [already] tells me I can't do nothing. I can't go out. What's gonna happen when I marry him? He's gonna say he owns me!"

Economic independence is also insurance against a marriage gone bad. Jen explains, "I want to have everything ready, in case something goes wrong. . . . If we got a divorce, that would be my house. I bought that house, he can't kick me out or he can't take my kids from me." "That's what I want in case that ever happens. I know a lot of people that happened to. I don't want it to happen to me." These statements reveal that despite her desire to marry, Rick's role in the family's future is provisional at best. "We get along, but we fight a lot. If he's there, he's there, but if he's not, that's why I want a job . . . a job with computers . . . so I could afford my kids, could afford the house. . . . I don't want to be living off him. I want my kids to be living off me."

Why is Jen, who describes Rick as "the love of my life," so insistent on planning an exit strategy before she is willing to take the vows she firmly believes ought to last "forever"? If love is so sure, why does mistrust seem so palpable and strong? In relationships among poor couples like Jen and Rick, mistrust is often spawned by chronic violence and infidelity, drug and alcohol abuse, criminal activity, and the threat of imprisonment. In these tarnished corners of urban America, the stigma of a failed marriage is far worse than an out-of-wedlock birth. New mothers like Jen feel they must test the relationship over three, four, even five years' time. This is the only way, they believe, to ensure that their marriages will last.

Trust has been an enormous issue in Jen's relationship with Rick. "My son was born December 23rd, and [Rick] started cheating on me again . . . in March. He started cheating on me with some girl—Amanda. . . . Then it was another girl, another girl, another girl after. I didn't wanna believe it. My friends would come up to me and be like, 'Oh yeah, your boyfriend's cheating on you with this person.' I wouldn't believe it. . . . I would see him with them. He used to have hickies. He used to make up some excuse that he was drunk—that was always his excuse for everything." Things finally came to a head when Rick got another girl pregnant. "For a while, I forgave him for everything. Now, I don't forgive him for nothing." Now we begin to understand the source of Jen's hesitancy. "He wants me to marry him, [but] I'm not really sure. . . . If I can't trust him, I can't marry him, 'cause we would get a divorce. If you're gonna get married, you're supposed to be faithful!" she insists. To Jen and her peers, the worst thing that could happen is "to get married just to get divorced."

Given the economic challenges and often perilously low quality of the romantic relationships among unmarried parents, poor women may be right to be cautious about marriage. Five years after we first spoke with her, we met with Jen again. We learned that Jen's second pregnancy ended in a miscarriage. We also learned that Rick was out of the picture—apparently for good. "You know that bar [down the street?] It happened in that bar. . . . They were in the bar, and this guy was like badmouthing [Rick's friend] Mikey, talking stuff to him or whatever. So Rick had to go get involved in it and start with this guy. . . . Then he goes outside and fights the guy [and] the guy dies of head trauma. They were all on drugs, they were all drinking, and things just got out of control, and that's what happened. He got fourteen to thirty years."

THESE ARE CARDS I DEALT MYSELF

Jen stuck with Rick for the first two and a half years of his prison sentence, but when another girl's name replaced her own on the visitors' list, Jen decided she was finished with him once and for all. Readers might be asking what Jen ever saw in a man like Rick. But Jen and Rick operate in a partner market where the better-off men go to the better-off women. The only way for someone like Jen to forge a satisfying relationship with a man is to find a diamond in the rough or improve her own economic position so that she can realistically compete for more upwardly mobile partners, which is what Jen is trying to do now. "There's this kid, Donny, he works at my job. He works on C shift. He's a supervisor! He's funny, three years older, and he's not a geek or anything, but he's not a real preppy good boy either. But he's not [a player like Rick] and them. He has a job, you know, so that's good. He doesn't do drugs or anything. And he asked my dad if he could take me out!"

These days, there is a new air of determination, even pride, about Jen. The aimless high school dropout pulls ten-hour shifts entering data at a warehouse distribution center Monday through Thursday. She has held the job for three years, and her aptitude and hard work have earned her a series of raises. Her current salary is higher than anyone in her household commands—$10.25 per hour, and she now gets two weeks of paid vacation, four personal days,

sixty hours of sick time, and medical benefits. She has saved up the necessary $400 in tuition for a high school completion program that offers evening and weekend classes. Now all that stands between her and a diploma is a passing grade in mathematics, her least favorite subject. "My plan is to start college in January. [This month] I take my math test . . . so I can get my diploma," she confides.

Jen clearly sees how her life has improved since Rick's dramatic exit from the scene. "That's when I really started [to get better] because I didn't have to worry about what *he* was doing, didn't have to worry about him cheating on me, all this stuff. [It was] then I realized that I had to do what I had to do to take care of my son. . . . When he was there, I think that my whole life revolved around him, you know, so I always messed up somehow because I was so busy worrying about what *he* was doing. Like I would leave the [GED] programs I was in just to go home and see what he was doing. My mind was never concentrating." Now, she says, "a lot of people in my family look up to me now, because all my sisters dropped out from school, you know, nobody went back to school. I went back to school, you know? . . . I went back to school, and I plan to go to college, and a lot of people look up to me for that, you know? So that makes me happy . . . because five years ago nobody looked up to me. I was just like everybody else."

Yet the journey has not been easy. "Being a young mom, being fifteen, it's hard, hard, hard, you know." She says, "I have no life. . . . I work from 6:30 in the morning until 5:00 at night. I leave here at 5:30 in the morning. I don't get home until about 6:00 at night." Yet she measures her worth as a mother by the fact that she has managed to provide for her son largely on her own. "I don't depend on nobody. I might live with my dad and them, but I don't depend on them, you know." She continues, "There [used to] be days when I'd be so stressed out, like, 'I can't do this!' And I would just cry and cry and cry. . . . Then I look at Colin, and he'll be sleeping, and I'll just look at him and think

I don't have no [reason to feel sorry for myself]. The cards I have I've dealt myself so I have to deal with it now. I'm older. I can't change anything. He's my responsibility—he's nobody else's but mine—so I have to deal with that."

Becoming a mother transformed Jen's point of view on just about everything. She says, "I thought hanging on the corner drinking, getting high—I thought that was a good life, and I thought I could live that way for eternity, like sitting out with my friends. But it's not as fun once you have your own kid. . . . I think it changes [you]. I think, 'Would I want Colin to do that? Would I want my son to be like that . . . ?' It was fun to me but it's not fun anymore. Half the people I hung with are either . . . Some have died from drug overdoses, some are in jail, and some people are just out there living the same life that they always lived, and they don't look really good. They look really bad." In the end, Jen believes, Colin's birth has brought far more good into her life than bad. "I know I could have waited [to have a child], but in a way I think Colin's the best thing that could have happened to me. . . . So I think I had my son for a purpose because I think Colin changed my life. He *saved* my life, really. My whole life revolves around Colin!"

PROMISES I CAN KEEP

There are unique themes in Jen's story—most fathers are only one or two, not five years older than the mothers of their children, and few fathers have as many glaring problems as Rick—but we heard most of these themes repeatedly in the stories of the 161 other poor, single mothers we came to know. Notably, poor women do not reject marriage; they revere it. Indeed, it is the conviction that marriage is forever that makes them think that divorce is worse than having a baby outside of marriage. Their children, far from being liabilities, provide crucial social-psychological resources—a strong sense of purpose and a profound source of intimacy. Jen and the other mothers we came to know are coming of age in an America that is profoundly unequal—where the gap between rich and poor continues to grow. This economic reality has convinced them that they have little to lose and, perhaps, something to gain by a seemingly "ill-timed" birth.

The lesson one draws from stories like Jen's is quite simple: Until poor young women have more access to jobs that lead to financial independence—until there is reason to hope for the rewarding life pathways that their privileged peers pursue—the poor will continue to have children far sooner than most Americans think they should, while still deferring marriage. Marital standards have risen for all Americans, and the poor want the same things that everyone now wants out of marriage. The poor want to marry too, but they insist on marrying well. This, in their view, is the only way to avoid an almost certain divorce. Like Jen, they are simply not willing to make promises they are not sure they can keep.

CRITICAL THINKING QUESTIONS

1. Why does romance among many low-income women not result in marriage? How do these women differ from most middle-class women who have an out-of-wedlock baby?

2. Why is marriage for many low-income women an "elusive goal"? Consider, especially, the economic factors that these mothers describe as well as their expectations for a family provider in the future.

3. Do you agree or not with the women in this study that it's better to raise children as a single parent rather than marry a man who's not "marriage material"? Do you know any middle-class women (including yourself, your mother, relatives, or friends) who have made the same decisions?

NOTE

1. Kathryn Edin and Maria Kefalas. *Promises I Can Keep: Why Poor Women Put Motherhood Before Marriage* (University of California Press, 2005).

11

The Amish: A Small Society

JOHN A. HOSTETLER

Some 100,000 Old Order Amish live in the rolling farmland of Pennsylvania, Ohio, Indiana, and southern Ontario. These descendants of 16th-century Germans, who fled persecution for their religious beliefs, constitute a distinctive "small society" that keeps the larger world at arm's length. This description of the Amish suggests the extent of cultural diversity within North America and raises questions about why some people would reject the "advantages" that many others take for granted.

Small communities, with their distinctive character—where life is stable and intensely human—are disappearing. Some have vanished from the face of the earth, others are dying slowly, but all have undergone changes as they have come into contact with an expanding machine civilization. The merging of diverse peoples into a common mass has produced tension among members of the minorities and the majority alike.

The Old Order Amish, who arrived on American shores in colonial times, have survived in the modern world in distinctive, viable, small communities. They have resisted the homogenization process more successfully than others. In planting and harvest time one can see their bearded men working the fields

with horses and their women hanging out the laundry in neat rows to dry. Many American people have seen Amish families, with the men wearing broad-brimmed black hats and the women in bonnets and long dresses, in railway depots or bus terminals. Although the Amish have lived with industrialized America for over two and a half centuries, they have moderated its influence on their personal lives, their families, communities, and their values.

The Amish are often perceived by other Americans to be relics of the past who live an austere, inflexible life dedicated to inconvenient and archaic customs. They are seen as renouncing both modern conveniences and the American dream of success and progress. But most people have no quarrel with the Amish for doing things the old-fashioned way. Their conscientious objection was tolerated in wartime, for after all, they are meticulous farmers who practice the virtues of work and thrift.

Source: From *Amish Society*, 3rd ed., by John A. Hostetler (Baltimore: The Johns Hopkins University Press, 1980), pp. 3–12. Reprinted with permission.

. . . The Amish are a church, a community, a spiritual union, a conservative branch of Christianity, a religion, a community whose members practice simple and austere living, a familistic entrepreneuring system, and an adaptive human community. . . .

The Amish are in some ways a little commonwealth, for their members claim to be ruled by the law of love and redemption. The bonds that unite them are many. Their beliefs, however, do not permit them solely to occupy and defend a particular territory. They are highly sensitive in caring for their own. They will move to other lands when circumstances force them to do so.

Commonwealth implies a place, a province, which means any part of a national domain that geographically and socially is sufficiently unified to have a true consciousness of its unity. Its inhabitants feel comfortable with their own ideas and customs, and the "place" possesses a sense of distinction from other parts of the country. Members of a commonwealth are not foot-loose. They have a sense of productivity and accountability in a province where "the general welfare" is accepted as a day-to-day reality. Commonwealth has come to have an archaic meaning in today's world, because when groups and institutions become too large, the sense of commonwealth or the common good is lost. Thus it is little wonder that the most recent dictionaries of the American English language render the meaning of commonwealth as "obsolescent." In reality, the Amish are in part a commonwealth. There is, however, no provision for outcasts.

It may be argued that the Amish have retained elements of wholesome provincialism, a saving power to which the world in the future will need more and more to appeal. Provincialism need not turn to ancient narrowness and ignorance, confines from which many have sought to escape. A sense of province or commonwealth, with its cherished love of people and self-conscious dignity, is a necessary basis for relating to the wider world community. Respect for locality, place, custom, and local idealism can go a long way toward checking the monstrous growth of consolidation in the nation and thus help to save human freedom and individual dignity.

. . . Anthropologists, who have compared societies all over the world, have tended to call semi-isolated peoples "folk societies," "primitives," or merely "simple societies." These societies constitute an altogether different type in contrast to the industrialized, or so-called civilized, societies.

The "folk society," as conceptualized by Robert Redfield,[1] is a small, isolated, traditional, simple, homogeneous society in which oral communication and conventionalized ways are important factors in integrating the whole life. In such an ideal-type society, shared practical knowledge is more important than science, custom is valued more than critical knowledge, and associations are personal and emotional rather than abstract and categoric.

Folk societies are uncomfortable with the idea of change. Young people do what the old people did when they were young. Members communicate intimately with one another, not only by word of mouth but also through custom and symbols that reflect a strong sense of belonging to one another. A folk society is *Gemeinschaft*-like; there is a strong sense of "we-ness." Leadership is personal rather than institutionalized. There are no gross economic inequalities. Mutual aid is characteristic of the society's members. The goals of life are never stated as matters of doctrine, but neither are they questioned. They are implied by the acts that constitute living in a small society. Custom tends to become sacred. Behavior is strongly patterned, and acts as well as cultural objects are given symbolic meaning that is often pervasively religious. Religion is diffuse and all-pervasive. In the typical folk society, planting and harvesting are as sacred in their own ways as singing and praying.

The folk model lends itself well to understanding the tradition-directed character of Amish society. The heavy weight of tradition can scarcely be explained in any other way. The Amish, for example, have retained many of the customs and small-scale technologies that were common in rural society in the nineteenth century. Through a process of syncretism, Amish religious values have been fused with an earlier period of simple country living when everyone farmed with horses and on a scale where family members could work together. The Amish exist as a folk or "little" community in a rural subculture within the modern state. . . . The outsider who drives through an Amish settlement cannot help but recognize them by their clothing, farm homes, furnishings, fields, and other material traits of culture. Although they speak perfect English with outsiders, they speak a dialect of German among themselves.

Amish life is distinctive in that religion and custom blend into a way of life. The two are inseparable. The core values of the community are religious beliefs. Not only do the members worship a deity they understand through the revelation of Jesus Christ and the Bible, but their patterned behavior [also] has a religious dimension. A distinctive way of life permeates daily life, agriculture, and the application of energy to economic ends. Their beliefs determine their conceptions of the self, the universe, and man's place in it. The Amish world view recognizes a certain spiritual worth and dignity in the universe in its natural form. Religious considerations determine hours of work and the daily, weekly, seasonal, and yearly rituals associated with life experience. Occupation, the means and destinations of travel, and choice of friends and mate are determined by religious considerations. Religious and work attitudes are not far distant from each other. The universe includes the divine, and Amish society itself is considered divine insofar as the Amish recognize themselves as "a chosen people of God." The Amish do not seek to master nature or to work against the elements, but try to work with them. The affinity between Amish society and nature in the form of land, terrain, and vegetation is expressed in various degrees of intensity.

Religion is highly patterned, so one may properly speak of the Amish as a tradition-directed group. Though allusions to the Bible play an important role in determining their outlook on the world, and on life after death, these beliefs have been fused with several centuries of struggling to survive in [a] community. Out of intense religious experience, societal conflict, and intimate agrarian experience, a mentality has developed that prefers the old rather than the new. While the principle seems to apply especially to religion, it has also become a charter for social behavior. "The old is the best, and the new is of the devil" has become a prevalent mode of thought. By living in closed communities where custom and a strong sense of togetherness prevail, the Amish have formed an integrated way of life and a folklike culture. Continuity of conformity and custom is assured and the needs of the individual from birth to death are met within an integrated and shared system of meanings. Oral tradition, custom, and conventionality play an important part in maintaining the group as a functioning whole. To the participant, religion and custom are inseparable. Commitment and culture are combined to produce a stable human existence.

. . . A century ago, hardly anyone knew the Amish existed. A half-century ago they were viewed as an obscure sect living by ridiculous customs, as stubborn people who resisted education and exploited the labor of their children. Today the Amish are the unwilling objects of a thriving tourist industry on the eastern seaboard. They are revered as hard-working, thrifty people with enormous agrarian stamina, and by some, as islands of sanity in a culture gripped by commercialism and technology run wild.

CRITICAL THINKING QUESTIONS

1. In what ways does this description of the Amish way of life make you think about your own way of life differently?

2. Why would the Amish reject technological advances that most members of our society hold to be invaluable?

3. What might the majority of the North American population learn from the Amish?

NOTE

1. Robert Redfield, "The Folk Society," *American Journal of Sociology*, 52 (Jan. 1947), 293–308. See also his book *The Little Community* (Chicago: University of Chicago Press, 1955).

Socialization

CLASSIC

CONTEMPORARY

CROSS-CULTURAL

12

The Self

GEORGE HERBERT MEAD

The self is not the body but arises in social experience. Explaining this insight is perhaps the greatest contribution of George Herbert Mead. Mead argues that the basic shape of our personalities is derived from the social groupings in which we live. Note, too, that even the qualities that distinguish each of us from others emerge only within a social community.

In our statement of the development of intelligence we have already suggested that the language process is essential for the development of the self. The self has a character which is different from that of the physiological organism proper. The self is something which has a development; it is not initially there, at birth, but arises in the process of social experience and activity, that is, develops in the given individual as a result of his relations to that process as a whole and to other individuals within that process.

We can distinguish very definitely between the self and the body. The body can be there and can operate in a very intelligent fashion without there being a self involved in the experience.

Source: From *Mind, Self and Society: From the Standpoint of a Social Behaviorist* by George Herbert Mead (Chicago: University of Chicago Press, 1934), pp. 135–42, 144, 149–56, 158, 162–64. Copyright © 1934 by the University of Chicago Press. Reprinted with permission of the University of Chicago Press.

The self has the characteristic that it is an object to itself, and that characteristic distinguishes it from other objects and from the body. It is perfectly true that the eye can see the foot, but it does not see the body as a whole. We cannot see our backs; we can feel certain portions of them, if we are agile, but we cannot get an experience of our whole body. There are, of course, experiences which are somewhat vague and difficult of location, but the bodily experiences are for us organized about a self. The foot and hand belong to the self. We can see our feet, especially if we look at them from the wrong end of an opera glass, as strange things which we have difficulty in recognizing as our own. The parts of the body are quite distinguishable from the self. We can lose parts of the body without any serious invasion of the self. The mere ability to experience different parts of the body is not different from the experience of a table. The table presents a different feel from what the hand does when one hand feels another, but it is an experience of something with which we come definitely into contact. The body does not experience itself as a whole, in the sense in which the self in some way enters into the experience of the self.

It is the characteristic of the self as an object to itself that I want to bring out. This characteristic is represented in the word "self," which is a reflexive, and indicates that which can be both subject and object. This type of object is essentially different from other objects, and in the past it has been distinguished as conscious, a term which indicates an experience with, an experience of, one's self. It was assumed that consciousness in some way carried this capacity of being an object to itself. In giving a behavioristic statement of consciousness we have to look for some sort of experience in which the physical organism can become an object to itself.[1]

When one is running to get away from someone who is chasing him, he is entirely occupied in this action, and his experience may be swallowed up in the objects about him, so that he has, at the time being, no consciousness of self at all. We must be, of course, very completely occupied to have that take place, but we can, I think, recognize that sort of a possible experience in which the self does not enter. We can, perhaps, get some light on that situation through those experiences in which in very intense action there appear in the experience of the individual, back of this intense action, memories and anticipations. Tolstoi as an officer in the war gives an account of having pictures of his past experience in the midst of his most intense action. There are also the pictures that flash into a person's mind when he is drowning. In such instances there is a contrast between an experience that is absolutely wound up in outside activity in which the self as an object does not enter, and an activity of memory and imagination in which the self is the principal object. The self is then entirely distinguishable from an organism that

is surrounded by things and acts with reference to things, including parts of its own body. These latter may be objects like other objects, but they are just objects out there in the field, and they do not involve a self that is an object to the organism. This is, I think, frequently overlooked. It is that fact which makes our anthropomorphic reconstructions of animal life so fallacious. How can an individual get outside himself (experientially) in such a way as to become an object to himself? This is the essential psychological problem of selfhood or of self-consciousness; and its solution is to be found by referring to the process of social conduct or activity in which the given person or individual is implicated. The apparatus of reason would not be complete unless it swept itself into its own analysis of the field of experience; or unless the individual brought himself into the same experiential field as that of the other individual selves in relation to whom he acts in any given social situation. Reason cannot become impersonal unless it takes an objective, noneffective attitude toward itself; otherwise we have just consciousness, not self-consciousness. And it is necessary to rational conduct that the individual should thus take an objective, impersonal attitude toward himself, that he should become an object to himself. For the individual organism is obviously an essential and important fact or constituent element of the empirical situation in which it acts; and without taking objective account of itself as such, it cannot act intelligently, or rationally.

The individual experiences himself as such, not directly, but only indirectly, from the particular standpoints of other individual members of the same social group, or from the generalized standpoint of the social group as a whole to which he belongs. For he enters his own experience as a self or individual, not directly or immediately, not by becoming a subject to himself, but only insofar as he first becomes an object to himself just as other individuals are objects to him or in his experience; and he becomes an object to himself only by taking the attitudes of other individuals toward himself within a social environment or context of experience and behavior in which both he and they are involved.

The importance of what we term "communication" lies in the fact that it provides a form of behavior in which the organism or the individual may become an object to himself. It is that sort of communication which we have been discussing—not communication in the sense of the cluck of the hen to the chickens, or the bark of a wolf to the pack, or the lowing of a cow, but communication in the sense of significant symbols, communication which is directed not only to others but also to the individual himself. So far as that type of communication is a part of behavior it at least introduces a self. Of course, one may hear without listening; one may see things that he does not realize; do things that he is not really aware of. But it is where one does respond to that which he addresses to another and where that response of his own becomes a part of his conduct, where he not only hears himself but responds to himself, talks and replies to himself as truly as the other person replies to him, that we have behavior in which the individuals become objects to themselves . . . .

The self, as that which can be an object to itself, is essentially a social structure, and it arises in social experience. After a self has arisen, it in a certain sense provides for itself its social experiences, and so we can conceive of an absolutely solitary self. But it is impossible to conceive of a self arising outside of social experience. When it has arisen we can think of a person in solitary confinement for the rest of his life, but who still has himself as a companion, and is able to think and to converse with himself as he had communicated with others. That process to which I have just referred, of responding to one's self as another responds to it, taking part in one's own conversation with others, being aware of what one is saying and using that awareness of what

one is saying to determine what one is going to say thereafter—that is a process with which we are all familiar. We are continually following up our own address to other persons by an understanding of what we are saying, and using that understanding in the direction of our continued speech. We are finding out what we are going to say, what we are going to do, by saying and doing, and in the process we are continually controlling the process itself. In the conversation of gestures what we say calls out a certain response in another and that in turn changes our own action, so that we shift from what we started to do because of the reply the other makes. The conversation of gestures is the beginning of communication. The individual comes to carry on a conversation of gestures with himself. He says something, and that calls out a certain reply in himself which makes him change what he was going to say. One starts to say something, we will presume an unpleasant something, but when he starts to say it he realizes it is cruel. The effect on himself of what he is saying checks him; there is here a conversation of gestures between the individual and himself. We mean by significant speech that the action is one that affects the individual himself, and that the effect upon the individual himself is part of the intelligent carrying-out of the conversation with others. Now we, so to speak, amputate that social phase and dispense with it for the time being, so that one is talking to one's self as one would talk to another person.[2]

This process of abstraction cannot be carried on indefinitely. One inevitably seeks an audience, has to pour himself out to somebody. In reflective intelligence one thinks to act, and to act solely so that this action remains a part of a social process. Thinking becomes preparatory to social action. The very process of thinking is, of course, simply an inner conversation that goes on, but it is a conversation of gestures which in its completion implies the expression of that which one thinks to an audience. One separates the significance of what he is saying to others from the actual speech and gets it ready before saying it. He thinks it out, and perhaps writes it in the form of a book; but it is still a part of social intercourse in which one is addressing other persons and at the same time addressing one's self, and in which one controls the address to other persons by the response made to one's own gesture. That the person should be responding to himself is necessary to the self, and it is this sort of social conduct which provides behavior within which that self appears. I know of no other form of behavior than the linguistic in which the individual is an object to himself, and, so far as I can see, the individual is not a self in the reflexive sense unless he is an object to himself. It is this fact that gives a critical importance to communication, since this is a type of behavior in which the individual does so respond to himself.

We realize in everyday conduct and experience that an individual does not mean a great deal of what he is doing and saying. We frequently say that such an individual is not himself. We come away from an interview with a realization that we have left out important things, that there are parts of the self that did not get into what was said. What determines the amount of the self that gets into communication is the social experience itself. Of course, a good deal of the self does not need to get expression. We carry on a whole series of different relationships to different people. We are one thing to one man and another thing to another. There are parts of the self which exist only for the self in relationship to itself. We divide ourselves up in all sorts of different selves with reference to our acquaintances. We discuss politics with one and religion with another. There are all sorts of different selves answering to all sorts of different social reactions. It is the social process itself that is responsible for the appearance of the self; it is not there as a self apart from this type of experience.

A multiple personality is in a certain sense normal, as I have just pointed out . . .

The unity and structure of the complete self reflects the unity and structure of the social process as a whole; and each of the elementary selves of which it is composed reflects the unity and structure of one of the various aspects of that process in which the individual is implicated. In other words, the various elementary selves which constitute, or are organized into, a complete self are the various aspects of the structure of that complete self answering to the various aspects of the structure of the social process as a whole; the structure of the complete self is thus a reflection of the complete social process. The organization and unification of a social group is identical with the organization and unification of any one of the selves arising within the social process in which that group is engaged, or which it is carrying on.[3]

. . . Another set of background factors in the genesis of the self is represented in the activities of play and the game. . . . We find in children . . . imaginary companions which a good many children produce in their own experience. They organize in this way the responses which they call out in other persons and call out also in themselves. Of course, this playing with an imaginary companion is only a peculiarly interesting phase of ordinary play. Play in this sense, especially the stage which precedes the organized games, is a play at something. A child plays at being a mother, at being a teacher, at being a policeman; that is, it is taking different roles, as we say. We have something that suggests this in what we call the play of animals: A cat will play with her kittens, and dogs play with each other. Two dogs playing with each other will attack and defend, in a process which if carried through would amount to an actual fight. There is a combination of responses which checks the depth of the bite. But we do not have in such a situation the dogs taking a definite role in the sense that a child deliberately takes the role of another. This tendency on the part of children is what we are working with in the kindergarten where the roles which the children assume are made the basis for training. When a child does assume a role he has in himself the stimuli which call out that particular response or group of responses. He may, of course, run away when he is chased, as the dog does, or he may turn around and strike back just as the dog does in his play. But that is not the same as playing at something. Children get together to "play Indian." This means that the child has a certain set of stimuli that call out in itself the responses that they would call out in others, and which answer to an Indian. In the play period the child utilizes his own responses to these stimuli which he makes use of in building a self. The response which he has a tendency to make to these stimuli organizes them. He plays that he is, for instance, offering himself something, and he buys it; he gives a letter to himself and takes it away; he addresses himself as a parent, as a teacher; he arrests himself as a policeman. He has a set of stimuli which call out in himself the sort of responses they call out in others. He takes this group of responses and organizes them into a certain whole. Such is the simplest form of being another to one's self. It involves a temporal situation. The child says something in one character and responds in another character, and then his responding in another character is a stimulus to himself in the first character, and so the conversation goes on. A certain organized structure arises in him and in his other which replies to it, and these carry on the conversation of gestures between themselves.

If we contrast play with the situation in an organized game, we note the essential difference that the child who plays in a game must be ready to take the attitude of everyone else involved in that game, and that these different roles must have a definite relationship to each other. Taking a very simple game such as hide-and-seek, everyone with the exception of the one who is hiding is a person who is hunting. A child does not require more than the person who is hunted and the one who is hunting. If a child is playing in the first sense he just goes on playing, but there is no basic organization gained. In that early stage he passes from one to another just as a whim takes him. But in a game where a number of individuals are involved, then the child taking one role must be ready to take the role of everyone else. If he gets in a ball game he must have the responses of each position involved in his own position. He must know what everyone else is going to do in order to carry out his own play. He has to take all of these roles. They do not all have to be present in consciousness at the same time, but at some moments he has to have three or four individuals present in his own attitude, such as the one who is going to throw the ball, the one who is going to catch it, and so on. These responses must be, in some degree, present in his own make-up. In the game, then, there is a set of responses of such others so organized that the attitude of one calls out the appropriate attitudes of the other.

This organization is put in the form of the rules of the game. Children take a great interest in rules. They make rules on the spot in order to help themselves out of difficulties. Part of the enjoyment of the game is to get these rules. Now, the rules are the set of responses which a particular attitude calls out. You can demand a certain response in others if you take a certain attitude. These responses are all in yourself as well. There you get an organized set of such responses as that to which I have referred, which is something more elaborate than the roles found in play. Here there is just a set of responses that follow on each other indefinitely. At such a stage we speak of a child as not yet having a fully developed self. The child responds in a fairly intelligent fashion to the immediate stimuli that come to him, but they are not organized. He does not organize his life as we would like to have him do, namely, as a whole. There is just a set of responses of the type of play. The child reacts to a certain stimulus, and the reaction is in himself that is called out in others, but he is not a whole self. In his game he has to have an organization of these roles; otherwise he cannot play the game. The game represents the passage in the life of the child from taking the role of others in play to the organized part that is essential to self-consciousness in the full sense of the term.

. . . The fundamental difference between the game and play is that in the former the child must have the attitude of all the others involved in that game. The attitudes of the other players which the participant assumes organize into a sort of unit, and it is that organization which controls the response of the individual. The illustration used was of a person playing baseball. Each one of his own acts is determined by his assumption of the action of the others who are playing the game. What he does is controlled by his being everyone else on that team, at least insofar as those attitudes affect his own particular response. We get then an "other" which is an organization of the attitudes of those involved in the same process.

The organized community or social group which gives to the individual his unity of self may be called "the generalized other." The attitude of the generalized other is the attitude of the whole community.[4] Thus, for example, in the case of such a social group as a ball team, the team is the generalized other insofar as it enters—as an organized process or social activity—into the experience of any one of the individual members of it.

If the given human individual is to develop a self in the fullest sense, it is not sufficient for him merely to take the attitudes of other human individuals toward himself and toward one another within the human social process, and to bring that social process as a whole into his individual experience merely in these terms: He must also, in the same way that he takes the attitudes of other individuals toward himself and toward one another, take their attitudes toward

the various phases or aspects of the common social activity or set of social undertakings in which, as members of an organized society or social group, they are all engaged; and he must then, by generalizing these individual attitudes of that organized society or social group itself, as a whole, act toward different social projects which at any given time it is carrying out, or toward the various larger phases of the general social process which constitutes its life and of which these projects are specific manifestations. This getting of the broad activities of any given social whole or organized society as such within the experiential field of any one of the individuals involved or included in that whole is, in other words, the essential basis and prerequisite of the fullest development of that individual's self: Only insofar as he takes the attitudes of the organized social group to which he belongs toward the organized, cooperative social activity or set of such activities in which that group as such is engaged, does he develop a complete self or possess the sort of complete self he has developed. And on the other hand, the complex cooperative processes and activities and institutional functionings of organized human society are also possible only insofar as every individual involved in them or belonging to that society can take the general attitudes of all other such individuals with reference to these processes and activities and institutional functionings, and to the organized social whole of experiential relations and interactions thereby constituted—and can direct his own behavior accordingly.

It is in the form of the generalized other that the social process influences the behavior of the individuals involved in it and carrying it on, i.e., that the community exercises control over the conduct of its individual members; for it is in this form that the social process or community enters as a determining factor into the individual's thinking. In abstract thought the individual takes the attitude of the generalized other[5] toward himself, without reference to its expression in any particular other individuals;

and in concrete thought he takes that attitude insofar as it is expressed in the attitudes toward his behavior of those other individuals with whom he is involved in the given social situation or act. But only by taking the attitude of the generalized other toward himself, in one or another of these ways, can he think at all; for only thus can thinking—or the internalized conversation of gestures which constitutes thinking—occur. And only through the taking by individuals of the attitude or attitudes of the generalized other toward themselves is the existence of a universe of discourse, as that system of common or social meanings which thinking presupposes at its context, rendered possible.

. . . I have pointed out, then, that there are two general stages in the full development of the self. At the first of these stages, the individual's self is considered simply by an organization of the particular attitudes of other individuals toward himself and toward one another in the specific social acts in which he participates with them. But at the second stage in the full development of the individual's self that self is constituted not only by an organization of these particular individual attitudes, but also by an organization of the social attitudes of the generalized other or the social group as a whole to which he belongs. . . . So the self reaches its full development by organizing these individual attitudes of others into the organized social or group attitudes, and by thus becoming an individual reflection of the general systematic pattern of social or group behavior in which it and the others are all involved—a pattern which enters as a whole into the individual's experience in terms of these organized group attitudes which, through the mechanism of his central nervous system, he takes toward himself, just as he takes the individual attitudes of others.

. . . A person is a personality because he belongs to a community, because he takes over the institutions of that community into his own conduct. He takes its language as a medium by which he gets his personality, and then through a process of taking the different roles that all the others furnish he comes to get the attitude of the members of the community. Such, in a certain sense, is the structure of a man's personality. There are certain common responses which each individual has toward certain common things, and insofar as those common responses are awakened in the individual when he is affecting other persons he arouses his own self. The structure, then, on which the self is built is this response which is common to all, for one has to be a member of a community to be a self. Such responses are abstract attitudes, but they constitute just what we term a man's character. They give him what we term his principles, the acknowledged attitudes of all members of the community toward what are the values of that community. He is putting himself in the place of the generalized other, which represents the organized responses of all the members of the group. It is that which guides conduct controlled by principles, and a person who has such an organized group of responses is a man who we say has character, in the moral sense.

. . . I have so far emphasized what I have called the structures upon which the self is constructed, the framework of the self, as it were. Of course we are not only what is common to all: Each one of the selves is different from everyone else; but there has to be such a common structure as I have sketched in order that we may be members of a community at all. We cannot be ourselves unless we are also members in whom there is a community of attitudes which control the attitudes of all. We cannot have rights unless we have common attitudes. That which we have acquired as self-conscious persons makes us such members of society and gives us selves. Selves can only exist in definite relationships to other selves. No hard-and-fast line can be drawn between our own selves and the selves of others, since our own selves exist and enter as such into our experience only insofar as the selves of others exist and enter as such into our experience also. The individual possesses a self only in relation to the selves of the other members of his social group; and the structure of his self expresses or reflects the general behavior pattern of this social group to which he belongs, just as does the structure of the self of every other individual belonging to this social group.

CRITICAL THINKING QUESTIONS

1. How does Mead distinguish between body and the self? What makes this a radically *social* view of the self?
2. How is the self both a subject and an object to itself? How is the ability to assume "the role of the other" vital to our humanity?
3. The idea that socialization produces conformity is easy to understand, but explain Mead's argument that individual distinctiveness is also a result of social experience.

NOTES

1. Man's behavior is such in his social group that he is able to become an object to himself, a fact which constitutes him a more advanced product of evolutionary development than are the lower animals. Fundamentally it is this social fact—and not his alleged possession of a soul or mind with which he, as an individual, has been mysteriously and supernaturally endowed, and with which the lower animals have not been endowed—that differentiates him from them.

2. It is generally recognized that the specifically social expressions of intelligence, or the exercise of what is often called "social intelligence," depend upon the given individual's ability to take the roles of, or "put himself in the place of," the other individuals implicated with him in given social situations; and upon his consequent sensitivity to their attitudes toward himself and toward one another. These specifically social expressions of intelligence, of course, acquire unique significance in terms of our view that the whole nature of intelligence is social to the very core—that this putting of one's self in the places of others, this taking by one's self of their roles or attitudes, is not merely one of the various aspects or expressions of intelligence or intelligent behavior, but is the very essence of its character. Spearman's "X factor" in intelligence—the unknown factor which, according to him, intelligence contains—is simply (if our social theory of intelligence is correct) this ability of the intelligent individual to take the attitude of the other, or the attitudes of others, thus realizing the significations or grasping the meanings of the symbols or gestures in terms of which thinking proceeds; and thus being able to carry on with himself the internal conversation with these symbols or gestures which thinking involves.

3. The unity of the mind is not identical with the unity of the self. The unity of the self is constituted by the unity of the entire relational pattern of social behavior and experience in which the individual is implicated, and which is reflected in the structure of the self; but many of the aspects or features of this entire pattern do not enter into consciousness, so that the unity of the mind is in a sense an abstraction from the more inclusive unity of the self.

4. It is possible for inanimate objects, no less than for other human organisms, to form parts of the generalized and organized—the completely socialized—other for any given human individual, insofar as he responds to such objects socially or in a social fashion (by means of the mechanism of thought, the internalized conversation of gestures). Any thing—any object or set of objects, whether animate or inanimate, human or animal, or merely physical—toward which he acts, or to which he responds, socially, is an element in what for him is the generalized other; by taking the attitudes of which toward himself he becomes conscious of himself as an object or individual, and thus develops a self or personality. Thus, for example, the cult, in its primitive form, is merely the social embodiment of the relation between the given social group or community and its physical environment—an organized social means, adopted by the individual members of that group or community, of entering into social relations with that environment, or (in a sense) of carrying on conversations with it; and in this way that environment becomes part of the total generalized other for each of the individual members of the given social group or community.

5. We have said that the internal conversation of the individual with himself in terms of words or significant gestures—the conversation which constitutes the process or activity of thinking—is carried on by the individual from the standpoint of the "generalized other." And the more abstract that conversation is, the more abstract thinking happens to be, the further removed is the generalized other from any connection with particular individuals. It is especially in abstract thinking, that is to say, that the conversation involved is carried on by the individual with the generalized other, rather than with any particular individuals. Thus it is, for example, that abstract concepts are concepts stated in terms of the attitudes of the entire social group or community; they are stated on the basis of the individual's consciousness of the attitudes of the generalized other toward them, as a result of his taking these attitudes of the generalized other and then responding to them. And thus it is also that abstract propositions are stated in a form which anyone—any other intelligent individual—will accept.

Socialization	
CLASSIC	
CONTEMPORARY	
CROSS-CULTURAL	

13

"It's Like They Have Two Parents": Consequences of Inconsistent Socialization of Inuit Children

ANNE S. DOUGLAS

When cultures meet, conflict often arises. In this reading, Anne Douglas documents tensions between the existing Inuit culture—which is based on kinship, family, and an emphasis on group rights—and the imposing Western culture, which uses formal education to socialize its members to norms of individuality.

INTRODUCTION

"It's like they have two [sets of] parents." This was how Kowtak Joseph, a respected grandmother in the High Arctic community of Arctic Bay (Nunavut), described students at the local school. . . . I had come to Arctic Bay to learn how much control this community had over its school and, as a corollary, how Inuit were accommodating the demands of school on their lives. Kowtak Joseph summed up this challenge. While acknowledging the students' predicament, her words also addressed the confusion of her fellow parents.

Most Arctic Bay parents accepted school: they wanted their children to learn "new survival skills." But school was also introducing new behavioural

Source: From *Études/Inuit/Studies, Volume 33*, Number 1–2, 2009, pp. 35–54. Used with permission of the author and the publisher.

standards. What was acceptable there was inconsistent with the responsive behaviour that parents typically expected from children and adults. As a result, many questioned what was happening. Parents in Western cultures exert some local control over academic orientation and curriculum through parents' meetings and committees. Most accept the prevailing socialisation at school as being compatible with the way they themselves rear their children. Immigrants likewise accept it because they have chosen to bring up their children in a new cultural setting (Ogbu 1992).

In Arctic Bay, parents could contribute to their children's schooling through a locally elected Community Education Council (CEC) and through community-wide parents' meetings. Initially, school itself was a novelty for many. Arctic Bay was relatively new and extended families were still moving there from their camps in the mid to late 1970s. A large number of parents had thus never attended school; quite a few had some elementary schooling, and a handful some years of high school. While some of the parents' questions at school meetings addressed academic content, their main preoccupation was the school's influence on their children's behaviour. Their challenge lay in proving the legitimacy of their concerns to the school authorities. However, what mattered to the former was sometimes irrelevant to the latter. The school authorities, for their part, were often frustrated by the parents' seeming inability to grasp the implicit rationale for schooling. The "two parents" could not easily negotiate common ground because they had differing expectations for methods and goals. The differences came down to conflicting requirements for personal responsibility.

This article illustrates how school has incrementally intruded on customary socialisation by Inuit families. . . .

PERSONHOOD AND SOCIOCULTURAL IMPLICATIONS

Personhood is the socially oriented part of the self (Fortes 1973 in Dorais and Searles 2001: 17). Its expression is interdependent with society and explains "a wide range of behaviour, emotions and events" (La Fontaine 1985: 126). Universally, adults socialise children to conform to worldviews that give meaning to beings, objects, and events (Geertz 1973; Rosaldo 1984; Tambiah 1990). Each society endows the objects and events in its surrounding environment with cultural ideas, thereby turning them into symbols that evoke action, thought, and feeling. In general, outsiders lack the insight to identify another culture's symbols (*ibid.*).

There are two contrasting understandings of an individual's relationship to society. People who value social bonds and responsibilities over individuality adopt a sociocentric orientation; people with the opposite view, an egocentric one (Shweder and Bourne 1984; Tambiah 1990;

Wagner 1981). The two perspectives also have contrasting styles of reasoning, as seen in the practice of knowledge and modes of emotional experience. For instance, sociocentricity fosters self-effacement while egocentricity promotes competitiveness and affective neutrality (Lave and Wenger 1991; Leacock 1985; Rogoff 1990; Rosaldo 1984; Stairs 1992; Tambiah 1990). These orientations should be regarded as ideal types. In all societies, personhood reflects a balance between social integration and individuation (La Fontaine 1985; Wagner 1981). . . .

PERSONHOOD IN MAINSTREAM CANADIAN SOCIETY

Because mainstream Canada is a Westernised society, it subscribes to the modern view that individual phenomena (e.g., humans) are abstracted from their context. The domain of work is equated with the scientifically observable world and people participate in it as autonomous units with individual rights. Their economic security and social worth lie in the value attributed to their work (La Fontaine 1985; Marcuse 1966; Tambiah 1990; Taylor 1989). The working world is a series of institutions ranging from vast government bureaucracies to small businesses. These institutions reflect the goals of economic growth and individual competition; on them depend social order and organisation, and they enable people to connect to society through roles that are mediated by impersonal regulations. When and where one works is the main constraint of this world (Marcuse 1966; Tambiah 1990).

The family, though likewise an institution, is viewed as separate from and less significant than the domain of work. In this private sphere people are liberated from work's restraints; they can express their social independence through personal and private choices. As the institution of intended socialisation and integration, school is the bridge between family and society.

Here children learn the standardised personhood that applies in all non-family settings.

PERSONHOOD IN INUIT SOCIETY

Personhood in Inuit society has many facets, being rich and complex. First, Inuit society exemplifies socio-centric organisation. Unlike mainstream Canada, it has but one institution—kinship. While social order is maintained through kinship rules, Inuit themselves embody these rules, which serve the goal of group survival.

Inuit Social Organisation

Inuit kin in north Baffin Island include blood relatives, affinal relatives (those through marriage), adoptees, and name-sakes (people named after a usually deceased relative). . . . The kind of relationship is defined by the kin term that each member of the pair uses for the other, and it embodies specific rules of conduct that include respect, obedience, and cooperation. Kin terms also convey the appropriate emotional attachment between two kin, ranging from close affection to complete avoidance—the customary response to opposite-sex in-laws, among others. These multiple relationships are potential roles, lying in abeyance until the appropriate setting activates them. A group is defined by the sum of all possible kin interactions.

Before several families now living in Arctic Bay moved into the settlement, they had lived in extended family camps in and around Admiralty Inlet, exemplifying a "family-oriented society" (Burch 1975: 294). Indeed, as one High Arctic resident put it, "Each family *was* its own community" (Nasook 1990: 50). A family group needed a minimum of two couples, perhaps parents and a married child, or two siblings (Burch 1975;

Damas 1963). But the total number of people could fluctuate; the group adapted readily if other kin joined up or if some members left for other destinations.

Inuit Socialisation

Children were initiated into the obligations of kinship from infancy. Inuit told me how, as small children, they had been taught to recite the terms for their kin. . . . Kinship knowledge was the basis for recognition that the group comes first. To impress this covenant on children, and because compliance entailed demanding responsibilities, their socialisation was "intensely personal" (Diamond 1974: 172 in Leacock 1985: 83). Biological parents were usually the most constant teachers, but other kin group members took part (Briggs 1970, 1998; Washburne 1940). As adults usually outnumbered children in those days, one child had many teachers. Children grew up surrounded by expectations to be respectful, obedient, cooperative, and restrained. . . .

From my Western perspective, the socialisation methods seemed innovative. Parents used few words but acted effectively. A mother would ignore a child's requests until the child had given up; or would give a direct, stern look to make the child comply. At times a slightly wrinkled nose conveyed "no," or slightly raised eyebrows "yes." But adults generally ignored children who, from my perspective, truly deserved a response (*cf.* Briggs 1998). On the other hand, I also saw Inuit parents ignore children acting disruptively. Similar behaviour would be verbally censured in "southern" families. In fact, the adults appeared oblivious. Nor would they warn against a potential danger, such as a child reaching for a knife or a hot teapot. If harm occurred, someone attended to it; otherwise the outcome, unless destructive, was ignored.

In time I recognised that many parents were constantly, yet unobtrusively, alert to their children. Apparent signs of parental indifference were in fact reinforcements of the valued behaviours of self-discipline, self-sufficiency, and non-interference (Kingston 2008; Minor 1992). Parents consciously fostered these behaviours by consistently modelling them, and, though unobserved or unrecognised by me, were quite likely employing other tactics. As children are inclined to conform, and, as in the case of these Inuit children, their own wishes were consistently thwarted, they would inevitably begin to pay attention to their parents and fall in line with their example. . . .

Briggs (1970, 1982, 1987, 1991, 1998) showed how parents urged, if not forced, children to internalise necessary emotions by drawing them into various rituals, or games, that arouse complex and conflicting feelings. These rituals provoked a sense of danger that ultimately made children conform to socially approved values and behaviour. Thus, a child might be encouraged to protect and nurture a small animal or younger child, then abruptly be told to harm or destroy it—the confused child felt torn. The desired goal here was to recognize that non-violence is sanctioned although violence is also sometimes unavoidable. After being consistently and repeatedly drawn into similar rituals, children would become increasingly cooperative, yet also self-sufficient. . . .

All in all, these socialisation practices generate attitudes of mutual respect and trust. Inuit show these attitudes by not interfering with one another (Kingston 2008; Minor 1992; Ridington 1988). When inclined to comment on another's actions, they do so indirectly (Kingston 2008; Minor 1992; Morrow 1990). Moreover this atmosphere of trust allows Inuit to tolerate a high degree of uncooperative or disruptive behaviour in another group member—up to the point where it threatens group survival (Kingston 2008; Minor 1992; Rasing 1994).

The Embodiment of Personhood

Inuit socialisation is holistic. Its methods impress a variety of attributes simultaneously, instilling kin interdependence yet also fostering the complementary principle of individual self-sufficiency or autonomy. Here is the rationale: by developing and fulfilling a capacity to be both skilful and knowledgeable, one becomes more responsible towards and for others. Thus, in the Inuit context, personal self-sufficiency should not be confused with social independence. . . .

Being technologically and environmentally knowledgeable is key to self-sufficient personhood. Inuit children traditionally learned requisite skills by observing and imitating experienced kin, just as an apprentice learns skills and concepts in authentic contexts (Bodenhorn 1988; Lave and Wenger 1991; Wertsch 1991). Knowledge is autonomously created yet communally shared. In the manner of its production and circulation, knowledge is a metaphor for kinship, that is, each person's knowledge is available for all to use, but one only uses what is expedient at a given time (Roepstroff 1998). This knowledge tradition depends on people being able to trust each other's "informed intelligence" (Ridington 1998: 107).

TWO SOCIALISATION SYSTEMS MEET

School came to Arctic Bay in 1959. The first teacher, Miss Hinds, noted that her nine students were attentive, hardworking, and "among the most intelligent of any Eskimos I had taught up to this time" (in Macpherson 1991: 125). Most of them could already read and write; family members had taught them Inuktitut syllabics (Hinds 1968). The next teacher felt the same way. The students proved eager to learn and "progressed very rapidly" (Dalby 1962: 15). The girls in particular appeared mature beyond their years and reflected "the self-reliance and perseverance of an individualistic nature" (*ibid.*: 16).

The first official school was built in 1962. By 1967 it had two rooms, two teachers, and 30 students. By 1993 it was in its fourth building with 200 students. Meanwhile, the community had grown from five families to 550 residents (247 or 44% under 14 years of age). The Canadian government's policy of compulsory education prompted relocation from family camps to the settlement. Once there, families began to adapt their individual groups to this larger community through marriage and naming. They also allocated board memberships on the new "southern" institutions equally among themselves. The community became one large extended family (*cf.* Nasook 1990). At the same time, the original families continued their customary obligations: immediate kin sought to keep their homes near each other, visited each other frequently, and shared a daily meal. While kinship is no longer necessary for contemporary Inuit social organisation, it continues to influence social activity, particularly hunting (Wenzel 1995). Knowing who are kin helps explain why one woman would spend the night helping another sew—the two are first cousins. Or why the community's best hunter would accompany a town-based young man on his first hunt—the former is the latter's uncle. Name relationships may be the community's most enduring kinship practice. . . .

Nonetheless it would be inaccurate and unjust to view this Inuit community as a collective whole. A continuum already existed with respect to school experience. As the population grew, several other continua evolved regarding child rearing. While some parents continued to practise their customary socialisation, others were more explicitly controlling with their children. Still others were a mixture of both. Then some were neither traditional nor controlling in the "southern" manner. They may have thought that their children would pick up appropriate behaviour or that other people would watch over them. Such parents were not consciously negligent. They may have been raised by a group of kin who were no longer available to assist them, and were unaware of specific parenting responsibilities, particularly in a nuclear family. In spite of these different outlooks, community life had a distinctive spirit. Community activities, together with family life, mattered more than school for most adults. As Sipporah Oyukuluk (pers. comm. 1993) emphasised, "There's life, and then there's school." . . .

. . . When students shift to English and individual subjects, they start learning how to compartmentalise abstract knowledge out of context. They find this novel learning style challenging for several reasons (Bodenhorn 1988; Lave and Wenger 1991; Wertsch 1991). First, they are accustomed to appropriating new information in context and over time, thereby accommodating the knowledge in greater depth. Hence, a teacher-in-training found her summer course so interesting that she planned to take it again although she had met the curriculum requirement (Lucy Taqtu, pers. comm. 1994). Second, school knowledge is standardised and impersonal: one teacher provides the same knowledge simultaneously to a group of students who are assessed individually. The teacher is also directive, the method being teacher-centred. Third, because they are used to focused thinking, some students have trouble skipping discontinuously from one idea to another. The teachers move ahead too quickly for them; some students think they talk too much. Students fall behind if unable to keep up with the teacher's pace. Some repeat a grade or two, and others drop out. . . .

The parents could not ignore school; it separated them from their children. But school needed their support and expected them to respond as southern parents would. These Inuit parents encompassed broad ranges of age and school experience. Some were barely in their 20s and others in their mid to late 60s. The latter were largely parents who had adopted children two generations younger. While some parents had never gone to school, those who had gone possessed qualitatively different experiences; the older schooled parents had undergone more rigorous schooling than had the younger ones. In the 1960s and 1970s academic standards had been higher and discipline stricter. Because of their widely differing backgrounds, parents expressed a variety of responses to school. Some were concerned about matters that were irrelevant to others. The intensity of concern also varied. There were, so to speak, circles of concern that might or might not overlap if not coincide with each other. In its early days, school had been an adjunct to the community. Now it was pervasive. Parents looked for aspects of school to which they could relate, while some were reluctant to go to school because they were ill at ease. Classroom assistant Sarah Alooloo (pers. comm. 1993) believed some parents "feel tense because they don't know what they are supposed to do; they feel left behind. They don't know how to 'help' in the classroom." One parent said she and others went to school infrequently because "We don't know each other's languages; the only communication we have is smiling" (Tina Pauloosie, pers. comm. 1992).

Lack of Discipline

Whatever their degree of involvement in school, parents were frustrated by the dearth of discipline. They noticed this dearth when visiting the school. Others noticed it through their children's attitudes and their discussions with other parents. Nute Arnaujumajuq (pers. comm. 1991), a parent and the community's mayor, blamed both the lax academic standards and the inadequate discipline on Baffin School Board policy. Having spent some years at a residential school in Churchill, Arnaujumajuq claimed school board policy reflected the political mood of Inuit Tapirisat in the early 1970s. Many of that

generation had suffered in school at the hands of Qallunaat [non-Inuit]. While learning new skills, they had endured consistent lack of self-worth and cultural deprivation. Today, they wished to protect younger generations from their experience. But, according to Arnaujumajuq, they failed to realise the negative effects of relaxed discipline. They thus failed to develop an appropriate code of discipline whereby students could work and learn. Their educational philosophy is described in Board policy:

[. . .] the school must be committed to serving the rights of the child within the cultural framework of the community.

2. School complements the family as a place where the child learns to become an individual and a responsible person. It is an extension of the family which is the primary focus of the child and the first centre of learning. It goes without saying, therefore, that there must be close ties between the school and the family. [. . .]

4. The school is a place where young people develop an identity. Where young adults arrive at a realistic sense of what they are, what they want, what they need, and what their responsibilities are to the community. [. . .] (BDBE 1988: Policy 1.4)

These policy goals raise complex challenges. They attempt to reconcile two distinct social institutions: the Inuit family and school. This vision is also contradictory. It endorses the primacy of the Inuit family as "the first centre of learning" yet portrays school not only as an "extension of the family" but also as the "place where young people develop an identity." While the policy reduces cultural deprivation, it has negative side effects. The Qallunaaq principal complied with the policy by promoting school as a friendly, non-threatening place and by supporting the Inuit professional teachers. However, the principal was both overprotective and overly informal with these teachers, and maintained a jocular, light-hearted relationship. This approach was to their disadvantage because it kept some of them from growing into full maturity as adult Inuit models and as disciplined teachers.

The principal's attitude was also detrimental to the Qallunaat teachers. They were left to fend for themselves. The principal may not have condoned delinquent student behaviour, but nonetheless gave little open support to staff members when they tried to control it. Qallunaat teachers told me they had done their best to defuse unruly situations. They had sound classroom practices that depended on the students being present and attentive. Yet they felt frustrated by their difficulty in exerting control in a generally lax atmosphere. When Qallunaat teachers chastised students or imposed discipline, some students failed to comply and later told their parents. Some parents, concerned that their children were being badly treated, confronted the teachers. Teacher Susan Riach (pers. comm. 1993) recalled how one angry mother came to school and said, "I'm going to call the RCMP!" While transgressing the non-interference norm of her own Inuit culture, this parent had no trouble exercising her rights in the mainstream social setting of school.

Even when students attended regularly, the lax atmosphere undermined their efforts to learn. Angus Murray (pers. comm. 1993) recognised the intelligence of many students, and was frustrated by those who said the work was "too hard." He believed students had so long been able to avoid effort that this avoidance was now ingrained. He pointed to one student who, although spending most of his time at his family camp, always caught up quickly and usually surpassed his classmates. This student obviously had maintained the customary attentive, disciplined approach to learning. The students in the junior grades had fewer disciplinary problems, many being still conditioned to obey. Moreover their teachers were from the community and familiar (if not related) to them. While the Inuit teachers had learned to control the class and hold the students' attention, they tended to ignore the less compliant ones, unless they were extremely disruptive. At some point a teacher would sit a disruptive child beside herself, but generally without admonishment. While these teachers might tolerate disruptive behaviour more than would their Qallunaat counterparts, they might also be waiting for their students to show signs of developing *isuma* ["a major criterion of maturity" (Briggs 1991: 267; 1998: 233) required for picking up "desirable behaviour" and acquiring knowledge (Briggs 1987: 10)]. In contrast, Qallunaat teachers labelled some noncompliant students as "slow learners." . . . .

Attendance

Lack of discipline led to concerns about poor attendance, which was not unique to Arctic Bay (Briggs 1997). Historically, attendance had been poor; the school did all it could to improve the situation. Each month the names of the "perfect attenders" were announced on the community radio. These students also received awards at a monthly ceremony in the school gym. The school needed the parents' help. Some of them made a concerted effort to get their children to school; others were more or less encouraging. Still others, however, felt that the children should be responsible for going to school on their own. The school employed a School Community Counsellor whose primary responsibility was to visit families with truant children. This was a priority of the NWT Department of Education. The counsellor was not entirely comfortable with her job. During visits to parents in their homes "they turn their faces" from her. Parents resented this intrusion, especially coming from a member of their own community. Some might also have wished to respect their children's choice to attend or not. . . . .

Cultural Inclusion Classes

Some parents welcomed the authentic representation of their culture in the required "Cultural Inclusion" classes taught by community members. The classes are intended to develop "knowledge and skills in aspects of Inuit culture" (BDBE 1988: Policy 1.5). They were essential for one mother who had no time to teach her children at home. Some interested parents expressed concern that the students did not finish their work, and moreover the articles they made were "too easy," e.g., mittens for the girls or fish nets for the boys. Rebecca Williams (pers. comm. 1991) explained that children always had to finish their tasks in traditional Inuit culture; other parents echoed those sentiments. Moses Oyukuluk (pers. comm. 1993) would prefer to see the boys get out and "make big things, like houses." Olayuk Kigutikajuk (CEC meeting 1992), an accomplished sewer, requested that the CEC allow the girls to use real skins instead of duffle. The classes challenged both the instructors and the students (Douglas 1994). Some students took the classes seriously, but the majority appeared disinterested and some wandered off. They were insufficiently attuned to their own culture, had lost interest in it, or were confused by the use of another teaching method. Moreover, the Qallunaaq principal did not consider the classes to have academic value and appeared frustrated by the instructors' seeming inability to teach, although they were all experienced practitioners. While parents discussed Culture Inclusion classes with ease, some had trouble assessing their children's academic work. Paunarjuk Enoogoo (pers. comm. 1991) confided, "We didn't use to learn things by talking." As one parent queried at a 1992 CEC meeting, "How can I tell if a piece of paper with writing on it is finished?"

Participation of Parents

Many parents wanted to do what school expected of them but knew neither precisely what it was nor how to do it. In 1990, one concerned parent even asked the CEC for a course in contemporary parenting. Some parents thus sensed they were not attending to something that they should be doing, and recognised they might not live up to school's expectations. While many parents were unable to transcend the language barrier, a few hesitated to contravene the implicit non-interference code of Inuit culture by participating in school like a southern parent.

The school staff tried hard to encourage parental support of the students. Most teachers sent home envelopes of students' work every two weeks, and all teachers filled out report cards three times during the school year. Concurrent with the report periods, teachers held scheduled interviews with parents to discuss their children's progress and report cards. A special effort was made to accommodate parents by offering them tea, coffee, and cookies in the staff lounge. Many parents appeared to be content with the procedure, some looked uncomfortable, and others chose not to come. Parents who hesitated to come explained they did not understand what was expected of them or thought the teacher would discuss discipline problems. One parent said some of them resented being told their children had academic problems; they left the school thinking, "I don't like my child to embarrass me like that." This parent obviously found the process intrusive as it reflected badly on her, as a parent, and on her child, as a student. There was further potential for embarrassment when the Qallunaaq teacher required an interpreter for the interview; none of these teachers spoke Inuktitut, and few of the Inuit parents with English-language skills had the fluency to discuss academic concerns. According to another parent, the presence of a third person, the interpreter, made an already awkward situation more so; it was mortifying for her to have another Inuk as a witness. In addition, an experienced Inuk teacher, Morty Alooloo (pers. comm. 1992), considered the Qallunaat teachers' style of communication to be intimidating. She said that Inuit are sensitive to body language and that the teachers' predisposition to look directly into parents' eyes made them uncomfortable. She added that many Inuit are frightened by the sound of Qallunaat's voices and their forceful (i.e., authoritarian) manner of speaking.

Several Qallunaat teachers confirmed these views. They agreed that most parents were anxious to know whether their children listened, obeyed, and came on time. Many parents were reportedly concerned about whether their children were "good" in school; "good" meaning appropriate behaviour rather than academic success. One parent queried, "Isn't that what Qallunaat want, that the students are good in school?" Susan Riach (pers. comm. 1993) further explained parental discomfort with interviews. As she began to tell one parent that her child needed to improve a particular aspect of schoolwork, the interpreter interrupted to say, "I can't tell her that!" The interpreter was resisting normative school practices not only by refusing to take part in an intrusive procedure, but also by defending a fellow Inuk from it.

Many parents had tried to support school but were distressed by its indifference towards students after they dropped out, and some even thought that school was implicated in the problem. As one parent said, students drop out due to lack of interest. According to another, students lack interest because the classes are too large. During a 1993 CEC meeting, Leah Okadluk stated that students drop out because they have no one to talk to when they have a problem. One parent suggested that 16-year-olds drop out because at that age they do not like to be told what to do. Most parents could not understand that school operates under the same regulations as those of other institutions in mainstream society: once students 16 and older stop attending, school has no further responsibility. From the perspective of their own holistic orientation, parents expected school to continue to be responsible since it had taken over their children's socialisation. For those parents, school

seemed to tell students they could do whatever they wanted once they turned 16. Charlie Inuaraq worried that at that age school had not yet prepared them to do anything. Despite their anxieties and concerns, parents recognised they were partly responsible for their children's education. Many had moved into the community for that reason. In the words of Nute Arnaujumajuq (pers. comm. 1991), "Inuit are making changes, but very slowly. It will take a long time to get school where it should be."

DISCUSSION AND CONCLUSION

When Inuit children become students, they are released from a familiar set of social requirements and submitted to another and uniquely different one. The new requirements are manifested through impersonal external regulations, new interpersonal relations, and constraints of time and place (Briggs 2001). The students are thus imprinted with the standardised expectations of personhood in mainstream society. But without the emotional messages that once nudged them toward correct behaviour, these young Inuit find the school atmosphere bland and devitalised.

Inuit parents confront a dilemma. It is difficult for them to know what their children are experiencing in school. They would like to find a way of monitoring the new influences on their children, but they are confused as to what their responsibilities should be. Both school and parents want children to be properly educated, yet a subtle power struggle exists as to whose rules should prevail. Each is frustrated by the other's seeming lack of discipline. From the school's perspective, many parents will not make their children obey its regulations and are not amenable to discussing their children's work with the teachers. For their part, parents are disheartened that their children fail to exhibit some form of disciplined behaviour. This is the least they would expect from school, yet school does not teach it in a form they can identify. . . .

School board policy exacerbates, if not distorts, an already confusing situation. The original policy makers wanted to free the school from harsh and unjustified discipline. Unwittingly, however, they undermined both the essence of their own social practice and the school's capacity for acceptable discipline. . . . Moreover, the original policy makers had been so culturally deprived that they felt compelled to safeguard their culture by making it explicit. Thus they created an ethnic identity by insisting that school affirm Inuit culture through the language of instruction and through course content. Members of a cultural group assert their uniqueness in this way when they encounter another one that inhibits or threatens the expression of their culture. . . .

However, an ethnic identity is not a culture; it is a means whereby a cultural group can draw out its distinctions interculturally and politically. Authentic cultural practice is intra-cultural; it lies in relationships. . . .

Because people embody culture, school is inevitably a site of socio-cultural change. In fact, when Inuit relate to school in any capacity, they are inescapably drawn into the process of change. School puts Inuit personhood to a hard test. As interpersonal relationships become increasingly threatened, Inuit sense their own fragility. Each Inuk expresses personhood as a matter of individual history and choice. While kin cooperation is no longer an urgent social priority, many Inuit still count on it for both practical and emotional reasons. Moreover most Inuit still value their kin relationships and the accompanying socio-centric worldview; a sufficient social base exists to ensure their continuation. Contemporary Inuit parents are now challenged to maintain and model the behaviour and attitudes they prize while accommodating new survival skills. In this, they will be assisted by a disciplined, focused approach to the task at hand that has always been a hallmark of Inuit culture.

CRITICAL THINKING QUESTIONS

1. What was the goal of schooling when it was initially introduced to Arctic Bay? What did Inuit parents expect from the school?

2. What do you think of the Inuit parents' methods of socialization? How do their techniques compare with how you were socialized?

3. The Inuit community often has priorities that differ from those of the formal education system. This has resulted in conflict. Can you think of any policies or approaches that might better incorporate the needs of the Inuit community in creating and reaching shared goals?

REFERENCES

BDBE (Baffin Divisional Board of Education). 1988. *Policy manual.* Iqaluit: Baffin Divisional Board of Education.

Bodenhorn, Barbara. 1988. *Documenting Inupiat family relationships in changing times.* Report prepared for the North Slope Borough Commission on Inupiat History, Language and Culture and Alaska Humanities Forum.

Briggs, Jean L. 1970. *Never in anger: Portrait of an Eskimo family.* Cambridge: Harvard University Press.

———.1982. Living dangerously: The contradictory foundations of value in Canadian Inuit society. In *Politics and history in band societies,* eds. E. Leacock and R. Lee. Cambridge: Cambridge University Press, 109–139.

———.1987. In search of emotional meaning. *Ethos,* 15(1): 8–15.

———.1991. Expecting the unexpected: Canadian Inuit training for an experimental lifestyle. *Ethos,* 19(3): 259–287.

———.1997. From trait to emblem and back: Living and representing culture in everyday Inuit life. *Arctic Anthropology,* 34(1): 227–235.

———.1998. *Inuit morality play.* New Haven and London: Yale University Press.

Burch, Ernest S. 1975. *Eskimo kinsmen: changing family relationships in Northwest Alaska.* St. Paul, MN: West Publishing.

Dalby, Ronald. 1962. Twentieth-century school (Part 2). *North*, 9(4): 12–18.

Damas, David. 1963. *Igulligmiut kinship and local groupings: A structural approach*. Ottawa: National Museum of Canada, Bulletin, 64.

Dorais, Louis-Jacques and Edmund (Ned) Searles. 2001. Inuit identities. *Études/Inuit/Studies*, 25(1–2): 283–319.

Douglas, Anne S. 1994. Recontextualizing formal schooling within an Inuit community. *Canadian Journal of Education*, 19(2): 154–164.

Geertz, Clifford. 1973. *The interpretation of cultures*. New York: Basic Books.

Hinds, Margery. 1968. *High arctic venture*. Toronto: Ryerson Press.

Kingston, Deanna P. 2008. The persistence of conflict avoidance among King Island Inupiat. *Études/Inuit/Studies*, 32(2): 151–167.

La Fontaine, Jean S. 1985. Person and individual: Some anthropological reflections. In *The category of the person: Anthropology, philosophy, history*, eds. M. Carrithers, S. Collins, and S. Lukes. Cambridge: Cambridge University Press: 123–140.

Lave, Jean, and E. Wenger. 1991. *Situated learning: Legitimate peripheral participation*. Cambridge: Cambridge University Press.

Leacock, Eleanor. 1985. Individuals and society in anthropological theory. *Dialectical Anthropology*, 10(1–2): 69–91.

Macpherson, Norman J. 1991. *Dreams and visions: Education in the Northwest Territories from early days to 1984*. Yellowknife: Department of Education, Government of the Northwest Territories.

Marcuse, Herbert. 1966. *One-dimensional man: Studies in the ideology of advanced industrial societies*. Boston: Beacon Press.

Minor, Kit. 1992. *Issumatuq: Learning from the traditional healing wisdom of the Canadian Inuit*. Halifax: Fernwood Publishing.

Nasook, Noah. 1990. Interview. *Inuktitut*, 17: 39–55.

Ogbu, John U. 1992. Understanding cultural diversity and learning. *Educational Researcher*, 21(8): 5–14.

Rasing, Wilfred C. E. 1994. *Too many people: Order and nonconformity in Iglulingmiut social process*. Nijmegen: Katholieke Universiteit, Faculteit der Rechtsgeleerdheid.

Ridington, Robin. 1988. Knowledge, power, and the individual in subarctic hunting societies. *American Anthropologist*, 90: 98–110.

Rogoff, Barbara. 1990. *Apprenticeship in thinking: Cognitive development in social context*. New York: Oxford University Press.

Rosaldo, Michelle Z. 1984. Toward an anthropology of self and feeling. In *Culture theory: Essays on mind, self, and emotion*, eds. A. Shweder and R. A. Levine. Cambridge: Cambridge University Press, 137–157.

Shweder, Richard A., and Edmund J. Bourne. 1984. Does the concept of the person vary cross-culturally? In *Culture theory: Essays on mind, self, and emotion*, eds. R. A. Shweder and R. A. Levine. Cambridge: Cambridge University Press: 159–191.

Stairs, Arlene. 1992. Self-image, world-image: Speculations on identity from experiences with Inuit. *Ethos*, 20(1): 116–126.

Tambiah, Stanley J. 1990. *Magic, science, religion, and the scope of rationality*. Cambridge: Cambridge University Press.

Taylor, Charles. 1989. *Sources of the self: The making of the modern identity*. Cambridge: Harvard University Press.

Wagner, Roy. 1991. *The invention of culture*. Chicago: University of Chicago Press.

Washburne, Heluiz (with Anauta Blackmore). 1940. *Land of the good shadows: The life story of Anauta, an Eskimo woman*. New York: John Day.

Wertsch, James V. 1991. A sociocultural approach to socially shared cognition. In *Perspectives on socially shared cognition*, eds. L. B. Resnick, J. M. Levine, and S. D. Teasely. Philadelphia: University of Pittsburgh, Learning Research and Development Center, 85–100.

14

Parents' Socialization of Children in Global Perspective

D. TERRI HEATH

One of the most important functions of the family worldwide is the socialization of children. Although parents might receive help from others (such as relatives, neighbours, and professional caregivers), most communities expect parents themselves to raise their children to be productive and responsible adults. Across vastly different cultural environments, D. Terri Heath shows the universal importance of closeness with parents in affecting the academic achievement, psychological well-being, substance use and juvenile delinquency, and general behaviour of children worldwide.

THE BENEFITS OF CLOSE PARENT–YOUTH RELATIONSHIPS IN ADOLESCENCE

This article . . . [describes] how a positive relationship between parents and children later enhances the life satisfaction and psychological well-being of older youths and protects them from juvenile delinquency and substance abuse. As the cross-cultural examples illustrate, youth who perceive a close relationship with their parents exhibit more positive outcomes in each of these four areas. Life satisfaction and psychological well-being are described first, followed by illustrative cross-cultural examples. Next is a description of the impact of close parent-child relationships and their protective value on the

substance abuse and juvenile delinquency of adolescents. Relevant, illustrative cross-cultural examples conclude this section.

Life satisfaction is a subjective measure of an individual's perception of his/her quality of life. Rather than objective measures of income, education, accumulation of wealth, and home ownership, life satisfaction is the level of individual satisfaction each person perceives in his/her own life: that which is privately known and privately evaluated. A multitude of factors influence life satisfaction, and because it is a personal evaluation, these factors differ for individuals. A study of life satisfaction among Hong Kong adolescents illustrates the profound effects peers and parents can exert on an adolescent's life satisfaction.

Psychological well-being is a measure of multiple submissions: self-esteem, locus of control, anxiety, loneliness, and sociability. Persons who exhibit high self-esteem, an internal locus

Source: From *Families in Multicultural Perspective*, eds. Bron B. Ingoldsby and Suzanna Smith, pp. 161–86. Copyright © 1995 Guilford Press, NY. Reprinted with permission.

of control, low anxiety and loneliness, and high sociability are considered to have strong psychological well-being. Just as with life satisfaction, many factors can influence psychological well-being, but this section focuses specifically on the association between strong relationships with parents and positive outcomes for youth and young adults.

Hong Kong

Adolescence is a transitional period in the life cycle. Associations with family and peers are changing, and adolescents often feel increased pressure to succeed in social relationships outside their families. Their level of attachment, identification, and frequency of consultation with parents relative to that with peers influences the life satisfaction of adolescents in general and, specifically, their satisfaction with school, family, and others. Hong Kong, on the south coast of China, is heavily influenced by current political and economic changes in China. Chinese culture, with its emphasis on family and community over individual independence, continues to play a significant role in the culture of Hong Kong. Because the orientation of adolescents toward their peers and parents has important implications for their satisfaction with life, Hong Kong offers a unique look at this relationship in a rapidly developing society. In a study of 1,906 students, ages thirteen to sixteen, adolescents who were more oriented toward their parents, as well as those who were more oriented toward their peers, were equally satisfied with school, their acceptance by others, the government, and the media. However, those adolescents who are most oriented toward their parents were additionally satisfied with life in general, their families, and the environment (Man, 1991). Man (1991) concludes that "in a predominantly Chinese society like Hong Kong, the family remains a highly important determinant of the adolescents' life satisfaction" (p. 363).

Iran

Parents continue to influence the lives of their children as young adults through parental interactions, guidance, and shared history. When young adults are dissatisfied with their parents, their adult psychological well-being appears to be negatively influenced. When Iranian students, ages seventeen to thirty-nine, studying at universities in Iran and the United States, were asked about their childhood dissatisfactions with their parents, an interesting pattern emerged. Those adults who perceived the most childhood dissatisfaction with parents were most likely to experience current loneliness, anxiety, external locus of control, misanthropy, neurosis, and psychosis when compared to adults who scored low on the dissatisfaction scale. They were also more likely to experience lower self-esteem and lower sociability, as well as decreased satisfaction with peer relationships, than were adults who had perceptions of childhood satisfaction with parents (Hojat, Borenstein, & Shapurian, 1990). There were no differences between the Iranian students studying at U.S. universities and those studying at Iranian institutions. The authors conclude that when a child's needs for closeness, attachment, and intimacy are not fulfilled to the child's satisfaction in early childhood, the result can be adult dissatisfactions with peer relationships and decreased psychological well-being in adulthood.

Puerto Rico

Can a child's need for closeness and intimacy be adequately fulfilled when the parents of the child are either alcohol dependent or mentally ill? By comparing three groups of children—those with an alcoholic parent, with a mentally ill parent, and with other parents without obvious diagnoses—researchers in Puerto Rico believe that children and adolescents, ages four to sixteen, with alcoholic or mentally ill parents are more likely than other children to be exposed to adverse family environments, such as stressful life events, marital discord, and family dysfunction. In addition, the children in these families were more maladjusted than were children in families without a diagnosed parent, according to reports by psychiatrists, parents, and the children themselves (Rubio-Stipec et al., 1991). (However, the teachers of these three groups of children were unable to detect differences in child behavior, probably because 43 percent of them rated their familiarity with the child as "not good.") It appears from this research that children of alcoholic or mentally ill parents suffer negative consequences during childhood, and these consequences are readily apparent to psychiatrists, their parents, and even the children themselves.

In many cultures, adolescence is a period of rapid psychological growth and a shift in orientation from parents to peers. Adolescents move through this period from childhood at the beginning to adulthood at the end. Most choose educational and career paths during this period. Many choose marriage partners. They move from residing with their parents to residing with peers, with spouses, or by themselves. Because this is a time of such change, some adolescents cope with the transitions by engaging in problematic behaviors (e.g., drug and alcohol abuse and juvenile delinquency). This section presents some of the factors that contribute to problematic behaviors for youth in Canada and three subcultures in the United States: Native American, white, and Hispanic.

Canada

Social control theorists contend that adolescent alcohol consumption is influenced by the degree to which youth are influenced by peers more than parents. A study of alcohol consumption by Canadian eleventh and twelfth graders demonstrates this relationship (Mitic, 1990). Students were divided into three groups:

(1) those who drank only with their parents, (2) those who drank only with their peers, and (3) those who drank both with and without their parents. The consumption rates of this last group were further divided into the amount of drinking with and without parents. As might be expected, students who drank only with parents consumed the least amount of alcohol. Those who drank with both parents and peers consumed the most alcohol and drank more heavily when they were with peers. It appears that what parents model for their children regarding alcohol consumption has only a small influence in the youths' consumption behaviors when the parents are not present.

Hispanics and Whites in the United States

Researchers found that Hispanic and white youth (ages nine to seventeen) in the United States are also significantly influenced in their drug and alcohol consumption by their relationships with friends and parents. For white and Hispanic adolescents who used either licit substances (e.g., cigarettes and alcohol), marijuana, or other illicit substances (e.g., cocaine, heroin, and prescription drugs used for recreational purposes), the single most important influence was the percentage of friends who used marijuana. Those youths who had higher percentages of friends who used marijuana were more likely to use each category of drug (licit, marijuana, and other illicit) than were youths who had fewer friends who used marijuana; this is equally true for both Hispanic and white youth. Although both users and abstainers were more affiliated with their parents than their peers, users were more strongly influenced by their peers; more likely to believe that their friends, rather than their parents, understand them best; and more likely to respect the ideas of their friends in different situations. The only cultural difference was that, in general, Hispanic youths respected their parents' views more than did white youths, regardless of whether they used or abstained from drugs and alcohol (Coombs, Paulson, & Richardson, 1991). Coombs et al. conclude that "youths having viable relationships with parents are less involved with drugs and drug-oriented peers" (p. 87).

Ojibway Native Americans

Delinquent behavior represents a dysfunctional response to stressors and strains in adolescence. On Native American reservations in the United States, an orientation toward parents and tribal elders appears to protect some youth from these negative behaviors. High percentages of Native American Ojibway adolescents, ages twelve to eighteen, reported inappropriate or illegal activities, such as using alcohol (85 percent), stealing something (70 percent), skipping school (64 percent), smoking marijuana (53 percent), and intentional damage to property (45 percent). However, those who spent more time with their family in chores, recreation, family discussions, and meals were less involved in negative behaviors. As expected, those youth who spent more time in activities away from their families—such as listening alone to the radio, and partying with drugs and alcohol—were at greatest risk for delinquent behaviors and court adjudications (Zitzow, 1990). Ojibway youths who spent more time in activities with parents and tribal elders were less likely to engage in delinquent behaviors resulting in court adjudications.

Summary

This last section focuses on how close parent-youth relationships are associated with the life satisfaction, psychological well-being, lack of substance use, and absence of delinquent behavior in adolescents. Without exception,

adolescents in all six studies benefit from increased involvement with healthy parents. Parental involvement enhanced life satisfaction among adolescents in Hong Kong and contributed to psychological well-being among Iranian college students and Puerto Rican youths. The presence of parents was associated with less alcohol consumption among Canadian adolescents, a strong bond with parents was associated with less drug consumption by Hispanic and white youth in the United States, and spending time with parents and tribal elders was associated with less involvement in delinquent behaviors for Native American adolescents in the United States.

CONCLUSION

In reviewing the literature on cross-cultural research on parent-child relations for this chapter, a clear trend became increasingly apparent. When parents are more involved and/or have greater expectations of their children's behavior, children demonstrate better outcomes. As is apparent from the illustrative examples, greater parental involvement is an active involvement, not a passive one. It is acquired not simply by the amount of time parents and children spend together but rather by how the time is spent. An involved parent is not one who spends the majority of the day near his/her child but rarely interacting with the child. It is, instead, the parent who uses opportunities to share activities such as teaching the child a local trade, reading together, or fostering a close, supportive relationship through companionship. This active, involved parent appears much more likely to rear a successful child. Illustrative cross-cultural examples presented here of high-quality interaction between parents and children, such as . . . establishing firm limits and offering support in China, and engaging adolescents in activities with parents and tribal elders in the United States, has been associated with better child outcomes. These patterns emerged even when examining parent-son versus parent-daughter relations, relationships among family members in developing versus developed countries, or parent-child relationships in families that resided in Western cultures versus Eastern ones.

CRITICAL THINKING QUESTIONS

1. According to Heath, are there greater differences or similarities across cultures in the relationship between parent–child closeness and adolescent behaviour?

2. What are some of the factors that contribute to the problematic behaviour of adolescents both cross-culturally and within Canada?

3. What does Heath mean by "parental involvement"? What other variables might also have an impact on parent–child relationships that are not discussed in this selection?

REFERENCES

Coombs, R. H., M. J. Paulson, and M. A. Richardson. 1991. Peer versus parental influence in substance use among Hispanic and Anglo children and adolescents. *Journal of Youth and Adolescence*, 20(1): 73–88.

Hojat, M., B. D. Borenstein, and R. Shapurian. 1990. Perception of childhood dissatisfaction with parents and selected personality traits in adulthood. *Journal of General Psychology*, 117(3): 241–53.

Man, P. 1991. The influence of peers and parents on youth life satisfaction in Hong Kong. *Social Indicators Research*, 24(4): 347–65.

Mitic, W. 1990. Parental versus peer influence on adolescents' alcohol consumption. *Psychological Reports*, 67: 1273–74.

Rubio-Stipec, M., H. Bird, G. Canino, and M. Alegria. 1991. Children of alcoholic parents in the community. *Journal of Studies on Alcohol*, 52(1): 78–88.

Zitzow, D. 1990. Ojibway adolescent time spent with parents/ elders as related to delinquency and court adjudication experiences. *American Indian and Alaska Native Mental Health Research*, 4(1): 53–63.

Social Interaction in Everyday Life

CLASSIC

CONTEMPORARY

CROSS-CULTURAL

15

The Presentation of Self

ERVING GOFFMAN

Face-to-face interaction is a complex process by which people both convey and receive information about each other. In this selection, Erving Goffman presents basic observations about how everyone tries to influence how others perceive them. In addition, he suggests ways in which people can evaluate how honestly others present themselves.

When an individual enters the presence of others, they commonly seek to acquire information about him or to bring into play information about him already possessed. They will be interested in his general socioeconomic status, his conception of self, his attitude toward them, his competence, his trustworthiness, etc. Although some of this information seems to be sought almost as an end in itself, there are usually quite practical reasons for acquiring it. Information about the individual helps to define the situation, enabling others to know in advance what he will expect of them and what they may expect of him. Informed in these ways, the others will know how best to act in order to call forth a desired response from him.

Source: From *The Presentation of Self in Everyday Life* by Erving Goffman, copyright © 1959 by Erving Goffman, Bantam Doubleday Dell Publishing Group, Inc. Reprinted with permission.

For those present, many sources of information become accessible and many carriers (or "sign-vehicles") become available for conveying this information. If unacquainted with the individual, observers can glean clues from his conduct and appearance which allow them to apply their previous experience with individuals roughly similar to the one before them or, more important, to apply untested stereotypes to him. They can also assume from past experience that only individuals of a particular kind are likely to be found in a given social setting. They can rely on what the individual says about himself or on documentary evidence he provides as to who and what he is. If they know, or know of, the individual by virtue of experience prior to the interaction, they can rely on assumptions as to the persistence and generality of psychological traits as a means of predicting his present and future behavior.

However, during the period in which the individual is in the immediate presence of the others, few events may occur which directly provide the others with the conclusive information they will need if they are to direct wisely their own activity. Many crucial facts lie beyond the time and place of interaction or lie concealed within it. For example, the "true" or "real" attitudes, beliefs, and emotions of the individual can be ascertained only indirectly, through his avowals or through what appears to be involuntary expressive behavior. Similarly, if the individual offers the others a product or service, they will often find that during the interaction there will be no time and place immediately available for eating the pudding that the proof can be found in. They will be forced to accept some events as conventional or natural signs of something not directly available to the senses. In Ichheiser's terms,[1] the individual will have to act so that he intentionally or unintentionally *expresses* himself, and the others will in turn have to be *impressed* in some way by him.

The expressiveness of the individual (and therefore his capacity to give impressions) appears to involve two radically different kinds of sign activity: the expression that he *gives,* and the expression that he *gives off*. The first involves verbal symbols or their substitutes which he uses admittedly and solely to convey the information that he and the others are known to attach to these symbols. This is communication in the traditional and narrow sense. The second involves a wide range of action that others can treat as symptomatic of the actor, the expectation being that the action was performed for reasons other than the information conveyed in this way. As we shall have to see, this distinction has an only initial validity. The individual does of course intentionally convey misinformation by means of both of these types of communication, the first involving deceit, the second feigning.

. . . Let us now turn from the others to the point of view of the individual who presents himself before them. He may wish them to think highly of him, or to think that he thinks highly of them, or to perceive how in fact he feels toward them, or to obtain no clear-cut impression; he may wish to ensure sufficient harmony so that the interaction can be sustained, or to defraud, get rid of, confuse, mislead, antagonize, or insult them. Regardless of the particular objective which the individual has in mind and of his motive for having this objective, it will be in his interests to control the conduct of the others, especially their responsive treatment of him. This control is achieved largely by influencing the definition of the situation which the others come to formulate, and he can influence this definition by expressing himself in such a way as to give them the kind of impression that will lead them to act voluntarily in accordance with his own plan. Thus, when an individual appears in the presence of others, there will usually be some reason for him to mobilize his activity so that it will convey an impression to others which it is in his interests to convey. Since a girl's dormitory mates will glean evidence of her popularity from the calls she receives on the phone, we can suspect that some girls will arrange for calls to be made, and Willard Waller's finding can be anticipated:

It has been reported by many observers that a girl who is called to the telephone in the dormitories will often allow herself to be called several times, in order to give all the other girls ample opportunity to hear her paged.[2]

Of the two kinds of communication—expressions given and expressions given off—this report will be primarily concerned with the latter, with the more theatrical and contextual kind, the nonverbal, presumably unintentional kind, whether this communication be purposely engineered or not. As an example of what we must try to examine, I would like to cite at length a novelistic incident in which Preedy, a vacationing Englishman, makes his first appearance on the beach of his summer hotel in Spain:

But in any case he took care to avoid catching anyone's eye. First of all, he had to make it clear to those potential companions of his holiday that they were of no concern to him whatsoever. He stared through them, round them, over them—eyes lost in space. The beach might have been empty. If by chance a ball was thrown his way, he looked surprised; then let a smile of amusement lighten his face (Kindly Preedy), looked round dazed to see that there were people on the beach, tossed it back with a smile to himself and not a smile at the people, and then resumed carelessly his nonchalant survey of space.

But it was time to institute a little parade, the parade of the Ideal Preedy. By devious handlings he gave any who wanted to look a chance to see the title of his book—a Spanish translation of Homer, classic thus, but not daring, cosmopolitan too—and then gathered together his beach-wrap and bag into a neat sand-resistant pile (Methodical and Sensible Preedy), rose slowly to stretch at ease his huge frame (Big-Cat Preedy), and tossed aside his sandals (Carefree Preedy, after all).

The marriage of Preedy and the sea! There were alternative rituals. The first involved the stroll that turns into a run and a dive straight into the water, thereafter smoothing into a strong splashless crawl towards the horizon. But of course not really to the horizon. Quite suddenly he would turn on to his back and thrash great white splashes with his legs, somehow thus showing that he could have swum further had he wanted to, and then would stand up a quarter out of water for all to see who it was.

The alternative course was simpler, it avoided the cold-water shock and it avoided the risk of appearing too high-spirited. The point was to appear to be so used to the sea, the Mediterranean, and this particular beach, that one might as well be in the sea as out of it. It involved a slow stroll down and into the edge of the water—not even noticing his toes were wet, land and water all the same to *him!*—with his eyes up at the sky gravely surveying portents, invisible to others, of the weather (Local Fisherman Preedy).[3]

The novelist means us to see that Preedy is improperly concerned with the extensive impressions he feels his sheer bodily action is giving off to those around him. We can malign Preedy further by assuming that he has acted merely in order to give a particular impression, that this is a false impression, and that the others present receive either no impression at all, or, worse still, the impression that Preedy is affectedly trying to cause them to receive this particular impression. But the important point for us here is that the kind of impression Preedy thinks he is making is in fact the kind of impression that others correctly and incorrectly glean from someone in their midst. . . . .

There is one aspect of the others' response that bears special comment here. Knowing that the individual is likely to present himself in a light that is favorable to him, the others may divide what they witness into two parts; a part that is relatively easy for the individual to manipulate at will, being chiefly his verbal assertions, and a part in regard to which he seems to have little concern or control, being chiefly derived from the expressions he gives off. The others may then use what are considered to be the ungovernable aspects of his expressive behavior as a check upon the validity of what is conveyed by the governable aspects. In this a fundamental asymmetry is demonstrated in the communication process, the individual presumably being aware of only one stream of his communication, the witnesses of this stream and one other. For example, in Shetland Isle one crofter's wife, in serving native dishes to a visitor from the mainland of Britain, would listen with a polite smile to his polite claims of liking what he was eating; at the same time she would take note of the rapidity with which the visitor lifted his fork or spoon to his mouth, the eagerness with which he passed food into his mouth, and the gusto expressed in chewing the food, using these signs as a check on the stated feelings of the eater. The same woman, in order to discover what one acquaintance (A) "actually" thought of another acquaintance (B), would wait until B was in the presence of A but engaged in conversation with still another person (C). She would then covertly examine the facial expressions of

A as he regarded B in conversation with C. Not being in conversation with B, and not being directly observed by him, A would sometimes relax usual constraints and tactful deceptions, and freely express what he was "actually" feeling about B. This Shetlander, in short, would observe the unobserved observer.

Now given the fact that others are likely to check up on the more controllable aspects of behavior by means of the less controllable, one can expect that sometimes the individual will try to exploit this very possibility, guiding the impression he makes through behavior felt to be reliably informing.[4] For example, in gaining admission to a tight social circle, the participant observer may not only wear an accepting look while listening to an informant, but may also be careful to wear the same look when observing the informant talking to others; observers of the observer will then not as easily discover where he actually stands. A specific illustration may be cited from Shetland Isle. When a neighbor dropped in to have a cup of tea, he would ordinarily wear at least a hint of an expectant warm smile as he passed through the door into the cottage. Since lack of physical obstructions outside the cottage and lack of light within it usually made it possible to observe the visitor unobserved as he approached the house, islanders sometimes took pleasure in watching the visitor drop whatever expression he was manifesting and replace it with a sociable one just before reaching the door. However, some visitors, in appreciating that this examination was occurring, would blindly adopt a social face a long distance from the house, thus ensuring the projection of a constant image.

This kind of control upon the part of the individual reinstates the symmetry of the communication process, and sets the stage for a kind of information game—a potentially infinite cycle of concealment, discovery, false revelation, and rediscovery. It should be added that since the others are likely to be relatively unsuspicious of the presumably unguided aspects of the individual's conduct, he can gain much by controlling it. The others of course may sense that the individual is manipulating the presumably spontaneous aspects of his behavior, and seek in this very act of manipulation some shading of conduct that the individual has not managed to control. This again provides a check upon the individual's behavior, this time his presumably uncalculated behavior, thus re-establishing the asymmetry of the communication process. Here I would like only to add the suggestion that the arts of piercing an individual's effort at calculated unintentionality seem better developed than our capacity to manipulate our own behavior, so that regardless of how many steps have occurred in the information game, the witness is likely to have the advantage over the actor, and the initial asymmetry of the communication process is likely to be retained. . . .

In everyday life, of course, there is a clear understanding that first impressions are important. Thus, the work adjustment of those in service occupations will often hinge upon a capacity to seize and hold the initiative in the service relation, a capacity that will require subtle aggressiveness on the part of the server when he is of lower socioeconomic status than his client. W. F. Whyte suggests the waitress as an example:

The first point that stands out is that the waitress who bears up under pressure does not simply respond to her customers. She acts with some skill to control their behavior. The first question to ask when we look at the customer relationship is, "Does the waitress get the jump on the customer, or does the customer get the jump on the waitress?" The skilled waitress realizes the crucial nature of this question. . . .

The skilled waitress tackles the customer with confidence and without hesitation. For example, she may find that a new customer has seated himself before she could clear off the dirty dishes and change the cloth. He is now leaning on the table studying the menu. She greets him, says, "May I change the cover, please?" and, without waiting for an answer, takes his menu away from him so that he moves back from the table, and she goes about her work. The relationship is handled politely but firmly, and there is never any question as to who is in charge.[5]

When the interaction that is initiated by "first impressions" is itself merely the initial interaction in an extended series of interactions involving the same participants, we speak of "getting off on the right foot" and feel that it is crucial that we do so. Thus, one learns that some teachers take the following view:

You can't ever let them get the upper hand on you or you're through. So I start out tough. The first day I get a new class in, I let them know who's boss. . . . You've got to start off tough, then you can ease up as you go along. If you start out easy-going, when you try to get tough, they'll just look at you and laugh.[6]

. . . In stressing the fact that the initial definition of the situation projected by an individual tends to provide a plan for the cooperative activity that follows—in stressing this action point of view—we must not overlook the crucial fact that any projected definition of the situation also has a distinctive moral character. It is this moral character of projections that will chiefly concern us in this report. Society is organized on the principle that any individual who possesses certain social characteristics has a moral right to expect that others will value and treat him in an appropriate way. Connected with this principle is a second, namely that an individual who implicitly or explicitly signifies that he has certain social characteristics ought in fact to be what he claims he is. In consequence, when an individual projects a definition of the situation and thereby makes an implicit or explicit claim to be a person of a particular kind, he automatically exerts a moral demand upon the others, obliging them to value and treat him in the manner that persons of his kind have a right to expect. He also implicitly foregoes all claims to be things he does not appear to be[7] and hence foregoes the treatment that would be appropriate for such individuals. The others find, then, that the individual has informed them as to what is and as to what they *ought* to see as the "is."

One cannot judge the importance of definitional disruptions by the frequency with which they occur, for apparently they would occur more frequently were not constant precautions taken. We find that preventive practices are constantly employed to avoid these embarrassments and that corrective practices are constantly employed to compensate for discrediting occurrences that have not been successfully avoided. When the individual employs these strategies and tactics to protect his own projections, we may refer to them as "defensive practices"; when a participant employs them to save the definition of the situation projected by another, we speak of "protective practices" or "tact." Together, defensive and protective practices comprise the techniques employed to safeguard the impression fostered by an individual during his presence before others. It should be added that while we may be ready to see that no fostered impression would survive if defensive practices were not employed, we are less ready perhaps to see that few impressions could survive if those who received the impression did not exert tact in their reception of it.

In addition to the fact that precautions are taken to prevent disruption of projected definitions, we may also note that an intense interest in these disruptions comes to play a significant role in the social life of the group. Practical jokes and social games are played in which embarrassments which are to be taken unseriously are purposely engineered.[8] Fantasies are created in which devastating exposures occur. Anecdotes from the past—real, embroidered, or fictitious—are told and retold, detailing disruptions which occurred, almost occurred, or occurred and were admirably resolved. There seems to be no grouping which does not have a ready supply of these games, reveries, and cautionary tales, to be used as a source of humor, a catharsis for anxieties, and a sanction for inducing individuals to be modest in their claims and reasonable in their projected expectations. The individual may tell of himself through dreams of getting into impossible positions. Families tell of the time a guest got his dates mixed and arrived when neither the house nor anyone in it was ready for him. Journalists tell of times when an all-too-meaningful misprint occurred, and the paper's assumption of objectivity or decorum was humorously discredited. Public servants tell of times a client ridiculously misunderstood form instructions, giving answers which implied an unanticipated and bizarre definition of the situation.[9] Seamen, whose home away from home is rigorously he-man, tell stories of coming back home and inadvertently asking mother to "pass the fucking butter."[10] Diplomats tell of the time a near-sighted queen asked a republican ambassador about the health of his king.[11]

To summarize, then, I assume that when an individual appears before others he will have many motives for trying to control the impression they receive of the situation.

CRITICAL THINKING QUESTIONS

1. How does the "presentation of self" contribute to a definition of a situation in the minds of participants? How does this definition change over time?

2. Apply Goffman's approach to the classroom. What are the typical elements of the instructor's presentation of self? A student's presentation of self?

3. Can we evaluate the validity of people's presentations? How?

NOTES

1. Gustav Ichheiser, "Misunderstandings in Human Relations," supplement to *The American Journal of Sociology* 55 (Sept., 1949), 6–7.

2. Willard Waller, "The Rating and Dating Complex," *American Sociological Review* 2 (1937), 730.

3. William Sansom, *A Contest of Ladies* (London: Hogarth, 1956), pp. 230–32.

4. The widely read and rather sound writings of Stephen Potter are concerned in part with signs that can be engineered to give a shrewd observer the apparently incidental cues he needs to discover concealed virtues the gamesman does not in fact possess.

5. W. F. Whyte, "When Workers and Customers Meet," chap. 7, *Industry and Society*, ed. W. F. Whyte (New York: McGraw-Hill, 1946), pp. 132–33.

6. Teacher interview quoted by Howard S. Becker, "Social Class Variations in the Teacher-Pupil Relationship," *Journal of Educational Sociology* 25, p. 459.

7. This role of the witness in limiting what it is the individual can be has been stressed by Existentialists, who see it as a basic threat to individual freedom. See Jean-Paul Sartre, *Being and Nothingness*, trans. Hazel E. Barnes (New York: Philosophical Library, 1956), pp. 365ff.

8. Goffman, op. cit., pp. 319–27.

9. Peter Blau, "Dynamics of Bureaucracy" (Ph.D. dissertation, Department of Sociology, Columbia University, forthcoming, University of Chicago Press), pp. 127–29.

10. Walter M. Beattie, Jr., "The Merchant Seaman" (unpublished M.A. Report, Department of Sociology, University of Chicago, 1950), p. 35.

11. Sir Frederick Ponsonby, *Recollections of Three Reigns* (New York: Dutton, 1952), p. 46.

16

The Music Ringtone as an Identity Management Device

CHRISTOPHER J. SCHNEIDER

In this article, adapted to include Canadian statistics, Christopher Schneider draws on his research into ringtones to illustrate how this new technology is used to establish one's identity.

INTRODUCTION

The creation of the mobile, or cellular (cell) phone (these terms will be used interchangeably) has extended telephone use, which was once largely considered a private affair, into the public sphere and, subsequently, everyday life. The novel ideas portrayed in Goffman's (1959) influential *The Presentation of Self in Everyday Life*, concerning imagery of the theater and social interaction, are useful when considering the use of cell phone ringtones as props to convey a particular and, one might add, favorable identity to an audience. Goffman's central thesis contends that as social actors take into account their situational contexts; they select particular props to create a certain

Source: From *Studies in Symbolic Interaction*, Volume 33, pp. 35–45. Copyright © 2009 Emerald Group Publishing Limited, used with permission of the publisher.

definition of self (depending on the situation, audience, time, place, and manner).

Notably missing from Goffman's body of work is an extended discussion of youth identity formation, especially from within the context of a total institution where one need not necessarily be confined permanently. This assumed identity becomes restricted in a place that captures the interest and time of its members; however, it may also serve as a physical barrier to social intercourse with the outside world (Goffman, 1961, 1963). For example, daily activities in the secondary education system, including learning, exercise, and eating, are conducted in the same place, in the company of other pupils required to do the same. These activities are tightly scheduled in prearranged time slots leading into other activities, and are controlled by a single fixed authority, all in an effort to fulfill the stated aims of the institution (Goffman, 1961). In these ways, the secondary education system represents a total institution.

The importance of amending Goffman's ideas here on the presentation of self, in light of new technological developments, is relevant to our greater understanding of identity management. This chapter updates and builds on Goffman's work in the following ways: it (1) explores youth identity formation in the confines of the secondary education system, and (2) considers recent developments in communication and information technologies that contribute to this process, particularly the cell phone ringtone and its ability to provide super or hyper auditory "tie-signs" relating to one's identity (Goffman, 1961, 1971).

According to Goffman (1971), tie-signs consist of fragmented pieces of public information conveyed by acting participants in the social realm. Through select social action, these pieces of information connect otherwise *anonymous relationships* between social participants, transforming the social encounter into the beginning of an *anchored relationship* where circumstances arise for the establishment of a particular social identity (Goffman, 1971). Establishing social identity at this early stage in a relationship is important, as "the beginning of an anchored relationship can depend on the memory each has of having seen the other before in a context that implies for each a relevant social identity for the other" (Goffman, 1971, p. 191). The manner and degree to which a ringtone, as an auditory tie-sign, is interpreted is therefore consequential to the establishment of social identity.

PREVIOUS RESEARCH

Although there has been a proliferation of mobile technology in everyday life, empirical research on the social implications of mobile phone use has not kept pace with this development. To be sure, studies have been done, but they have not focused enough attention on the importance of mobile

phone use on the practices that enable people to manage their identities in the presence of others. The specific concern here rests with the information people reveal about their identities during mobile phone usage and its potential impact on social interaction. However, the extant literature focuses on the national and global effects of mobile phone technology, addressing the intended (staying in touch) and unintended (*always* staying in touch) consequences of this technology on everyday social life (Agar, 2005; Ito, Okabe, & Matsuda, 2005; Katz and Aakhus, 2002). Other consequences of mobile technology on everyday social life that have been examined, include both unwanted surveillance and the increased sense of security gained from being able to communicate with others where conventional phone lines are unavailable (Harper & Hamill, 2005; Levinson, 2004; Ling, 2004; Lyon, 2006; Reid & Reid, 2005; Rheingold, 2002; Schuchardt, 2003; Strate, 2003).

DATA AND METHODS

This project occurred over the span of several months during the fall of 2006 while I was employed as a secondary education substitute teacher. Access to this setting, one that is highly protected from outsiders, allowed me to become more intimately familiar with select aspects of youth culture. The informal data gathered over the course of these dozens of observations, although not overtly reflected in the overall write-up of this project, informed its basic structure, direction, and outline.

This project is unique in that it did not begin as a formal ethnography per se but, rather, later in some less distinct ways, developed into one. No formal structured interviews were conducted during this period due to the extreme (ages 13–18) sensitivity of the observed population. In an effort to avoid any ethical dilemmas, jottings of the day's observations, activities, and conversations were taken down immediately on my return home, when I was both off school grounds and out of the immediate vicinity of anyone associated with the school.

Extensive observations were conducted on school grounds between August 2006 and December 2006, immediately before, during (in the hallways and cafeteria), and after school and, most importantly, within the confines of the classroom. These descriptions of secondary education social life revealed that identity development and maintenance, especially among these youth, relies heavily (perhaps more than in other populations because of their limited freedoms) on props, most specifically, the cell phone.

Despite formal policy against cell phone use, students would forthrightly ask if they could use their cell phones for text messaging and games after they completed their tasks (some teachers, myself included, allowed this behavior, whereas others did not). When this question was asked (as it most always was), I used my status as both teacher and trained observer to cautiously, mindful of the population, question students about their cell phones (discovering that most possessed them), their use of these devices and, in particular, their selection and use of their ringtones.

DEMOGRAPHICS OF RINGTONES

According to the Office of Consumer Affairs of Industry Canada (2006), mobile phones have become "ubiquitous in today's society and are now an important part of most of Canadians' telecommunications activities." There were 16.8 million wireless subscribers in Canada in 2006 (Statistics Canada, 2006) with this number increasing to 25.1 million by the end of June 2011 (Canadian Wireless Telecommunications Association, 2011). As of January 1, 2011, Canada's population was estimated at 34,278,400 (Statistics Canada, 2011). It is almost certain that the number of wireless phone subscribers will continue to increase.

The ringtones of early 1980's mobile phones usually consisted of a few pre-programmed monophonic (single melodic line) sounds. These

tones had no significance or practical use other than as a perceived indicator of social status (i.e., having a cell phone) and to alert the listener to an incoming call. In the past few years, however, the popularity of ringtones has exploded with the introduction of "realtones," sometimes referred to as realtunes, truetones, or mastertones. These particular ringtones are 30-second excerpts of popular music recordings, such as those featured on the radio or on the top music charts (e.g., Billboard Canadian Hot 100). These tones can be easily downloaded or programmed into mobile phones compatible with this technology, which includes most, if not all, contemporary cell phones.

The Billboard Hot Ringtones chart debuted at the end of 2004. In 2008, in response to the increased popularity of ringtones in Canada, ringtone award certification (by sales) was officially introduced by the Canadian Recording Industry Association (CRIA). Much like Billboard's charts for album sales and radio airplay, the Billboard Hot Ringtones chart reflects the top polyphonic (multiple melodic line) ringtone sales for each week. It is based on aggregated data collected from all of the major cell phone carriers and distributors that is claimed to represent more than 90% of the market. The Hot Ringtones chart, according to Billboard, reflects "the most comprehensive market sample of ringtones worldwide and the single most comprehensive starting sample of any chart produced by Billboard to date" (Billboard Bows Ringtones Chart, 2004). The chart is endorsed both by The Cellular Telecommunications and Internet Association (CITA) (formed as a nonprofit organization in 1984) and the Mobile Entertainment Forum, a global trade association representing participants in the mobile entertainment industry.

The ringtone broadcasts information individually selected (in this instance, music), which, I contend, helps define who a person is. Apart from pre-programmed default ringtones (tones that come standard in all modern mobile phones), downloadable ringtones are purposefully selected more often than default tones (these are individually selected as well). In these instances the user must seek to acquire them (i.e., possess enough technological proficiency to download them) and pay an additional fee. These fees vary, depending on the tone; for instance, monophonic tones tend to be less expensive, whereas realtones are more expensive. The simple fact that a user might pay between $1.99 and $3.99 for a 30-second snippet of a particular song (which, in all likelihood, the user may already possess), when the entire version can in some circumstances be purchased legally for as little as 88 cents, is certainly suggestive of the extent to which the ringtone factors into the concept of managing one's identity.

THE RINGTONE AS AN IDENTITY MANAGEMENT DEVICE

The secondary education system operates as a *total institution,* established for the purpose of pursuing work-like tasks (Goffman, 1961). The most basic features of any total institution concern the restriction or control of information, communication, and physical movement. Goffman (1961) contends that it is "characteristic of inmates that they come to the institution with a 'presenting culture'" (p. 12). Culture is necessary for the creation of a social reality (Berger & Luckmann, 1967). Popular culture provides both shared meaning and rules of social action, thus creating the conditions necessary for human beings to symbolically communicate meaning with one another. Popular culture can be loosely described as a fluid set of characteristics, beliefs, and practices collectively accepted and understood as the basis of normalcy. Music, for example, is a significant part of popular culture, informing daily life, including shared perceptions of deviance (Schneider, 2011).

Research literature supports the assertion that age is the single greatest factor in determining one's allegiance to music (see Denisoff, 1975; Grossberg, 1992, 1997; Rose, 1994a), and is especially the case when considering rap and hip-hop music (Keyes, 2004; Rose, 1994b). According to a survey conducted by Media Awareness Network (2005), as cited by the Office of Consumer Affairs of Industry Canada, "Canadian youth are *significant* wireless users" (*emphasis added*). The survey data denotes that, "6% of Grade 4 children said they owned a cellular phone; by Grade 11, the proportion reached 46%" (Media Awareness Network, 2005). A report published in *The Globe and Mail* (Canada's national newspaper of record) indicates that youth groups "ranked customizable ringtones as one of the three most desirable things to look for in a wireless phone" (Everett-Green, 2002). In the United States, according to the NPD Group, a market research firm, in 2006, youth consumers were more likely to download music ringtones. According to data collected in a monthly survey in July 2006, 26% of those that downloaded ringtones were between the ages of 13 and 17, whereas 22% were between the ages of 18 and 24, with females downloading slightly more ringtones than males (NPD Group, 2006).

Ringtone selection among the observed population coincides in many ways with the research literature concerning youth music selection and hip-hop. Some popular ringtones, for instance, included songs by hip-hop artists Akon ("Smack That"—a top selling ringtone in Canada certified 8X platinum in April 2008; 1X platinum certification is awarded by the CRIA for sales of 40,000) and Fergie ("Big Girls Don't Cry"). Students I observed were especially reluctant to discuss their selection of "Smack That" as a ringtone, because the lyrics referred to the performance of sexual acts.

Maybe go to my place and just kick it, like Taebo, and possibly bend you over, look back and watch me smack that, all on the floor, smack that give me some more, smack that until you get sore, smack that oooh (Akon, 2007)

The mere mention of this ringtone, for instance, would often induce giggle-like behavior in the classroom. The assumption was, of course, that I was unaware of the lyrical content. However, students sometimes indicated that they selected these and other suggestive ringtones (e.g., "Crazy Bitch" by the rock and roll group Buckcherry), not only because they liked the songs, but also, and importantly, because of the record producers' apparent ability to "get away with" broadcasting inappropriate content (sexual or otherwise) right under the noses of unknowledgeable adults by wrapping in the cloak of popular culture.

Culturally, politically, and socially, at least in Canada, those under a certain age (i.e., 18) are legally and collectively categorized as "youths" or "minors," often with little (if any) regard and, in some instances, no tolerance for individualism or individualist-like behavior. As an example, consider the secondary education system where conformity to some rules (many of which are arbitrary) is not only expected, but also rigidly enforced. Acts or displays of individualism, many of which are perfectly normal and legal (say, wearing a baseball cap), that fall outside the established rules are punished and sometimes severely so (with suspension or expulsion). Youth spend a majority of their daily lives and, indeed, waking moments, in the confines of the education system; thus, the narrow social space that exists outside this system for youth to freely create and manage identities during social interaction takes on added importance.

The construction of social identity occurs within a vast framework of communication, in which many actors who are sometimes unfamiliar with one another participate. These anonymous relationships, according to Goffman (1971), become meaningful only when participants act in response to fragments of information about one another that are made publicly available. Thus, the relations between these persons become mediated by "tie-signs" (p. 194) which point to or reveal "who they are." Ringtones perform the function of a special kind of tie-sign in everyday life.

The ringtone as an auditory tie-sign then simultaneously expresses both *intentional* and *unintentional* acts of impression management (as do many props); however, music is symbolically laden perhaps more than other physical objects and, therefore, it can be assumed that meanings derived from a ringtone can be multiple or fragmented, depending on song selection, audience members, and the time, place, and manner in which the ringtone is broadcasted (Goffman, 1959, 1971). "A tie-sign is in fact dependent on the context for its meaning" (Goffman, 1971, p. 197), and these contexts can vary considerably.

Consider, for instance, the popular ringtone "Bad Boys" (originally released as a full-length single in 1993), recorded by reggae group Inner Circle. The ringtone peaked on Billboard's Hot Ringtones Chart at number 30 and has remained on the chart for over 110 weeks. The song was made popular by the television program *COPS* (currently in its 24th season) and also by the films *Bad Boys* and *Bad Boys 2,* starring Will Smith and Martin Lawrence. The lyrics are sung over a smooth-flowing reggae composition:

Bad boys, bad boys, whatchagoin' do? Bad boys, bad boys, whatchagoin' do? Whatchagoin' do when Sherrif John Brown come for you? Tell me, whatchagoin' do? (Inner Circle, 1993)

The lyrics, as stated, are not too difficult to decipher. However, to those familiar enough with either *COPS* or the *Bad Boys* films, the ringtone could be thought to convey contradictory signals to an audience that could readily interpret the tune as either a testament to the enforcement of the law and rendering of justice, thus validating the *hosts' crimefighter image* (Cavender, 1998) or, considering the content of the show (e.g., lawlessness, disorderly conduct, belligerence, intoxication, and violence), as mocking the law-enforcement community. The ringtone could also offer panopticonic surveillance suggestions to those familiar with the television program: break the law and we (i.e., the police) will find you (see Foucault, 1995; Marx, 1995). Someone unfamiliar with the above television program and films could interpret the tune in various other ways (e.g., reggae has a reputation as party or anthem music and is widely associated with marijuana use).

Mobile phone technology has created new standards of etiquette and consumption practices, prompting users to sometimes exert control over the unintended revelation of individual ringtone selection. In these circumstances, such as the school classroom, students would most always set their cell phones to "silent" or "vibrate" to avoid reprimand or confiscation. In other front-stage regions, users are freely able to manage multiple ringtones on one mobile phone (a process I call *tone-shifting*), a similar activity to the various ways in which human actors modify their style of dress for different social settings.

In ordinary social situations, however, performance blunders, such as failure to control the revelation of ringtone selection, can and do occur (I refer to this as an *identity blitzkrieg*). In these events, the temporary loss of the ability to control these fragmented pieces of information about oneself creates the threat that an audience could interpret that information as contradicting their previously formed positive impression of the actor (Goffman, 1971), which could seriously *disrupt the ongoing social interaction*. If actors become incapable of reliably controlling the information revealed about themselves, then it makes impression management, and, in turn, social interaction highly problematical for all concerned (Goffman, 1959).

When interpreted unfavorably, the ringtone could invite or generate unfavorable reaction from an audience, jeopardizing their initial favorable definition of the person, even though recovery of a positive identity may be later possible. Ringtone technology is unique, then, in its capacity to change swiftly the impression (either positively or negatively) that an actor is making on an audience. Thus, it can undermine our attempts to create or maintain a favorable impression on others.

CONCLUSION

This chapter spotlights the importance of the need for more empirical research assessing the relationships between technology, identity, and social interaction. Though the ringtone is meaningful, it is not the only element in establishing a social identity, nor is social identity the only element in shaping social interaction. Nevertheless, ringtone preferences are potent tie-signs of people's identities and, thereby, can dramatically affect social interaction; thus, Goffman's ideas on the presentation of self need to be amended in light of ways that new technological developments create new challenges for our managing the impression that we make on other people during social interaction. The next steps in this research program should include exploring the effects of ringtones on the impression management practices among different populations in other institutional settings and, more importantly, the general impact on identity of music that people buy and listen to and the public places where they go to listen to it. This is part of future writing on the subject.

CRITICAL THINKING QUESTIONS

1. The article states that "age is the single greatest factor in determining one's allegiance to music." Can you think of some examples of this? How, for example, does the amount of music you listen to differ from that of your parents? What about the type of music?

2. Relatedly, how does social class influence someone's choice of music? What kind of music do you expect your professor to listen to? The prime minister? A mechanic?

3. What does the author mean when he writes that a ringing telephone can seriously undermine ongoing social interactions? In terms of impression management, what does this mean? How do you manage your telephone and have you ever witnessed an embarrassing situation with respect to cellphones? Have you been engaged in such an incident yourself?

REFERENCES

Agar, J. 2005. *Constant touch: A global history of the mobile phone.* Cambridge, UK: Totem Books.

Akon. 2007. "Smack That." Ringtone. Verizon Wireless/ Umvd/Import.

"Billboard bows ringtones chart." 2004, October 26. Available: **http://www.billboard.com/news/billboard-bows-ringtones-chart-1000684908**. Accessed January 5, 2007.

Berger, P., and T. Luckmann. 1967. *The social construction of reality.* New York: Penguin Press.

Cavender, G. 1998. "The Shadow of shadows": Television reality crime programming. In *Entertaining crime,* eds. M. Fishman and G. Cavender. New York: Aldine De Gruyter.

Canadian Wireless Telecommunications Association. 2011. Facts & figures: Wireless phone subscribers in Canada. Available: **http://cwta.ca/facts-figures**. Accessed January 8, 2012.

Denisoff, R. S. 1975. *Solid gold: The popular record industry.* New Brunswick, NJ: Transaction Books.

Everett-Green, R. 2002, December 21. Ringing up musical dollars; excuse me, is your cell playing The Real Slim Shady? *Globe and Mail,* Weekend Review, p. R3.

Foucault, M. 1995. *Discipline & punish: The birth of the prison* (Original work published 1977). New York: Random House.

Goffman, E. 1959. *The presentation of self in everyday life.* New York: Doubleday Press.

Goffman, E. 1961. *Asylums.* New York: Anchor Books.

Goffman, E. 1963. *Stigma.* New York: Simon & Schuster, Inc.

Goffman, E. 1971. *Relations in public.* New York: Harper & Row.

Grossberg, L. 1992. *We gotta get out of this place.* New York: Routledge.

Grossberg, L. 1997. *Dancing in spite of myself.* Durham, NC: Duke University Press.

Harper, R., and Hamill, L. 2005. Kids will be kids: The role of mobiles in teenage life. In *Mobile world: Past, present and future,* eds. L. Hamill and A. Larson. Guilford, UK: Springer Publishing.

Inner Circle. 1993. Bad boys. Ringtone. Verizon Wireless/ Big Beat/Wea. 2007.

Ito, M., D. Okabe, and M. Matsuda. (Eds). 2005. *Personal, portable, pedestrian: Mobile phones in Japanese life.* Cambridge, MA: MIT Press.

Katz, E. J., and M. Aakhus. (Eds). 2002. *Perpetual contact: Mobile communication, private talk, public performance.* Cambridge, UK: Cambridge University Press.

Keyes, C. 2004. *Rap music and street consciousness.* Champaign Urbana, IL: University of Illinois Press.

Levinson, P. 2004. *Cellphone: The story of the world's most mobile medium and how it has transformed everything!* New York: Palgrave Macmillan.

Ling, Rich. 2004. *The mobile connection: The cell phone's impact on society.* San Francisco, CA: Morgan Kaufmann Publishers.

Lyon, D. 2006. *Theorizing surveillance: The panopticon and beyond.* Devon, UK: Willan.

Marx, G. T. 1995. Electric eye in the sky: Some reflections on the new surveillance and popular culture. In *Cultural criminology,* eds. J. Ferrell and C. R. Sanders. Boston: Northeastern University Press.

Media Awareness Network. 2005. Young Canadians in a wired world, phase II – student survey (November).

NPD Group, Inc. 2006, September 20. Rap/Hip-hop ringtones rule the market. Available: **http://wireless.npd.com/news091106.html**. Accessed January 4, 2007.

Office of Consumer Affairs of Industry Canada. 2006. The expansion of cell phone service. Available: **http://www.ic.gc.ca/eic/site/oca-bc.nsf/eng/ca02267.html#n2**. Accessed January 2012.

Reid, D. J., and Reid, F. J. M. 2005. Kids will be kids: The role of mobiles in teenage life. In *Mobile world: Past, present and future,* eds. L. Hamill and A. Larson. Guilford, UK: Springer Publishing.

Rheingold, H. 2002. *Smart mobs: The next social revolution.* Cambridge, MA: Perseus Books.

Rose, T. 1994a. *Microphone fiends: Youth music and youth culture.* New York: Routledge.

Rose, T. 1994b. *Black noise: Rap music and black culture in contemporary America.* Middletown, CT: Wesleyan University Press.

Schuchardt, R. M. 2003. How to quit smoking using only your cell phone. *Explorations in Media Ecology, 2*(1), 25–34.

Schneider, C. J. 2011. Popular culture, rap music, "bitch" and the development of the censorship frame. *American Behavioral Scientist* 55: 36–56.

Statistics Canada. 2006. Telecommunications statistics, first quarter 2006. *The Daily,* catalogue number 11-001-XIE (September 13, 2006).

Statistics Canada. 2011. Canada's population estimates. Available: **http://www.statcan.gc.ca/daily-quotidien/110324/dq110324b-eng.htm**. Accessed January 8, 2012.

Strate, L. 2003. The cell phone as environment. *Explorations in Media Ecology, 2*(1): 19–24.

Groups and Organizations

CLASSIC

CONTEMPORARY

CROSS-CULTURAL

17

Primary Groups

CHARLES HORTON COOLEY

Charles Horton Cooley argues that human nature is a social nature and is clearly expressed in group life. Cooley describes primary groups as "spheres of intimate association and cooperation" that are vital to the process of socialization.

By primary groups I mean those characterized by intimate face-to-face association and cooperation. They are primary in several senses, but chiefly in that they are fundamental in forming the social nature and ideals of the individual. The result of intimate association, psychologically, is a certain fusion of individualities in a common whole, so that one's very self, for many purposes at least, is the common life and purpose of the group. Perhaps the simplest way of describing this wholeness is by saying that it is a "we"; it involves the sort of sympathy and mutual identification for which "we" is the natural expression. One lives in the feeling of the whole and finds the chief aims of his will in that feeling.

It is not to be supposed that the unity of the primary group is one of mere harmony and love. It is always a differentiated and usually a competitive unity, admitting of self-assertion and various appropriative passions; but these passions are socialized by sympathy, and come, or tend to come, under the discipline of a common spirit. The individual will be ambitious, but the chief object of his ambition will be some desired place in the thought of the others, and he will feel allegiance to common standards of service and fair play. So the boy will dispute with his fellows a place on the team, but above such disputes will place the common glory of his class and school.

The most important spheres of this intimate association and cooperation—though by no means the only ones—are the family, the play-group of children, and the neighborhood or community group of elders. These are practically universal, belonging to all times and all

Source: From *Social Organization: A Study of the Larger Mind* by Charles Horton Cooley (New York: Schocken Books, a subsidiary of Pantheon Books, 1962; orig. 1909), pp. 23–31. Reprinted with permission.

stages of development; and are accordingly a chief basis of what is universal in human nature and human ideals. The best comparative studies of the family, such as those of Westermarck[1] or Howard,[2] show it to us as not only a universal institution, but as more alike the world over than the exaggeration of exceptional customs by an earlier school had led us to suppose. Nor can anyone doubt the general prevalence of play-groups among children or of informal assemblies of various kinds among their elders. Such association is clearly the nursery of human nature in the world about us, and there is no apparent reason to suppose that the case has anywhere or at any time been essentially different.

As regards play, I might, were it not a matter of common observation, multiply illustrations of the universality and spontaneity of the group discussion and cooperation to which it gives rise. The general fact is that children, especially boys after about their twelfth year, live in fellowships in which their sympathy, ambition, and honor are engaged even more often than they are in the family. Most of us can recall examples of the endurance by boys of injustice and even cruelty, rather than appeal from their fellows to parents or teachers—as, for instance, in the hazing so prevalent at schools, and so difficult, for this very reason, to suppress. And how elaborate the discussion, how cogent the public opinion, how hot the ambitions in these fellowships.

Nor is this facility of juvenile association, as is sometimes supposed, a trait peculiar to English and American boys; since experience among our immigrant population seems to show that the offspring of the more restrictive civilizations of the continent of Europe form self-governing play-groups with almost equal readiness. Thus Miss Jane Addams, after pointing out that the "gang" is almost universal, speaks of the interminable discussion which every detail of the gang's activity receives, remarking that "in these social folkmotes, so to speak, the young citizen learns to act upon his own determination."[3]

Of the neighborhood group it may be said, in general, that from the time men formed permanent settlements upon the land, down, at least, to the rise of modern industrial cities, it has played a main part of the primary, heart-to-heart life of the people. Among our Teutonic forefathers the village community was apparently the chief sphere of sympathy and mutual aid for the commons all through the "Dark" and Middle Ages, and for many purposes it remains so in rural districts at the present day. In some countries we still find it with all its ancient vitality, notably in Russia, where the *mir,* or self-governing village group, is the main theatre of life, along with the family, for perhaps fifty million peasants.

In our own life the intimacy of the neighborhood has been broken up by the growth of an intricate mesh of wider contacts which leaves us strangers to people who live in the same house. And even in the country the same principle is at work, though less obviously, diminishing our economic and spiritual community with our neighbors. How far this change is a healthy development, and how far a disease, is perhaps still uncertain.

Besides these almost universal kinds of primary association, there are many others whose form depends upon the particular state of civilization; the only essential thing, as I have said, being a certain intimacy and fusion of personalities. In our own society, being little bound by place, people easily form clubs, fraternal societies and the like, based on congeniality, which may give rise to real intimacy. Many such relations are formed at school and college, and among men and women brought together in the first instance by their occupations—as workmen in the same trade, or the like. Where there is a little common interest and activity, kindness grows like weeds by the roadside.

But the fact that the family and neighborhood groups are ascendant in the open and plastic time of childhood makes them even now incomparably more influential than all the rest.

Primary groups are primary in the sense that they give the individual his earliest and completest experience of social unity, and also in the sense that they do not change in the same degree as more elaborate relations, but form a comparatively permanent source out of which the latter are ever springing. Of course they are not independent of the larger society, but to some extent reflect its spirit; as the German family and the German school bear somewhat distinctly the print of German militarism. But this, after all, is like the tide setting back into creeks, and does not commonly go very far. Among the German, and still more among the Russian, peasantry are found habits of free cooperation and discussion almost uninfluenced by the character of the state; and it is a familiar and well-supported view that the village commune, self-governing as regards local affairs and habituated to discussion, is a very widespread institution in settled communities, and the continuator of a similar autonomy previously existing in the clan. "It is man who makes monarchies and establishes republics, but the commune seems to come directly from the hand of God."[4]

In our own cities the crowded tenements and the general economic and social confusion have sorely wounded the family and the neighborhood, but it is remarkable, in view of these conditions, what vitality they show; and there is nothing upon which the conscience of the time is more determined than upon restoring them to health.

These groups, then, are springs of life, not only for the individual but for social institutions. They are only in part moulded by special traditions, and, in larger degree, express a universal nature. The religion or government of other civilizations may seem alien to us, but the children or the family group wear the common life, and with them we can always make ourselves at home.

By human nature, I suppose, we may understand those sentiments and impulses that are human in being superior to those of lower animals, and also in the sense that they belong to mankind at large, and not to any particular race or time. It means, particularly, sympathy and the innumerable sentiments into which sympathy enters, such as love, resentment, ambition, vanity, hero-worship, and the feeling of social right and wrong.

Human nature in this sense is justly regarded as a comparatively permanent element in society. Always and everywhere men seek honor and dread ridicule, defer to public opinion, cherish their goods and their children, and admire courage, generosity, and success. It is always safe to assume that people are and have been human.

To return to primary groups: The view here maintained is that human nature is not something existing separately in the individual, but a *group-nature* or *primary phase of society*, a relatively simple and general condition of the social mind. It is something more, on the one hand, than the mere instinct that is born in us—though that enters into it—and something else, on the other, than the more elaborate development of ideas and sentiments that makes up institutions. It is the nature which is developed and expressed in those simple, face-to-face groups that are somewhat alike in all societies; groups of the family, the playground, and the neighborhood. In the essential similarity of these is to be found the basis, in experience, for similar ideas and sentiments in the human mind. In these, everywhere, human nature comes into existence. Man does not have it at birth; he cannot acquire it except through fellowship, and it decays in isolation.

If this view does not recommend itself to common sense I do not know that elaboration will be of much avail. It simply means the application at this point of the idea that society and individuals are inseparable phases of a common whole, so that wherever we find an individual fact we may look for a social fact to go with it.

If there is a universal nature in persons there must be something universal in association to correspond to it.

What else can human nature be than a trait of primary groups? Surely not an attribute of the separate individual—supposing there were any such thing—since its typical characteristics, such as affection, ambition, vanity, and resentment, are inconceivable apart from society. If it belongs, then, to man in association, what kind or degree of association is required to develop it? Evidently nothing elaborate, because elaborate phases of society are transient and diverse, while human nature is comparatively stable and universal. In short the family and neighborhood life is essential to its genesis and nothing more is.

Here as everywhere in the study of society we must learn to see mankind in psychical wholes, rather than in artificial separation. We must see and feel the communal life of family and local groups as immediate facts, not as combinations of something else. And perhaps we shall do this best by recalling our own experience and extending it through sympathetic observation. What, in our life, is the family and the fellowship; what do we know of the we-feeling? Thought of this kind may help us to get a concrete perception of that primary group-nature of which everything social is the outgrowth.

CRITICAL THINKING QUESTIONS

1. Are primary groups necessarily devoid of conflict? How does Cooley address this issue?

2. Why does Cooley employ the term "primary" in his analysis? What are the characteristics of the implied opposite of primary groups: "secondary groups"?

3. What is Cooley's view of human nature? Why does he think that society cannot be reduced to the behaviour of many distinct individuals?

NOTES

1. *The History of Human Marriage.*
2. *A History of Matrimonial Institutions.*
3. *Newer Ideals of Peace*, p. 177.
4. De Tocqueville, *Democracy in America*, vol. 1, chap 5.

18

The Characteristics of Bureaucracy

MAX WEBER

According to Max Weber, human societies have historically been oriented by tradition of one kind or another. Modernity, in contrast, is marked by a different form of human consciousness: a rational world view. For Weber, there is no clearer expression of modern rationality than bureaucracy. In this selection, Weber identifies the characteristics of this organizational form.

Modern officialdom functions in the following specific manner:

I. There is the principle of fixed and official jurisdictional areas, which are generally ordered by rules, that is, by laws or administrative regulations. (1) The regular activities required for the purposes of the bureaucratically governed structure are distributed in a fixed way as official duties. (2) The authority to give the commands required for the discharge of these duties is distributed in a stable way and is strictly delimited by rules concerning the coercive means, physical, sacerdotal, or otherwise, which may be placed at the disposal of officials. (3) Methodical provision is made for the regular and

Source: From *Max Weber: Essays in Sociology*, by Max Weber, edited by H. H. Gerth and C. Wright Mills, translated by H. H. Gerth and C. Wright Mills. Copyright © 1946, 1958 by H. H. Gerth and C. Wright Mills. Used by permission of Oxford University Press.

continuous fulfillment of these duties and for the execution of the corresponding rights; only persons who have the generally regulated qualifications to serve are employed.

In public and lawful government these three elements constitute "bureaucratic authority." In private economic domination, they constitute bureaucratic "management." Bureaucracy, thus understood, is fully developed in political and ecclesiastical communities only in the modern state, and, in the private economy, only in the most advanced institutions of capitalism. Permanent and public office authority, with fixed jurisdiction, is not the historical rule but rather the exception. This is so even in large political structures such as those of the ancient Orient, the Germanic, and Mongolian empires of conquest, or of many feudal structures of state. In all these cases, the ruler executes the most important measures through personal trustees, table-companions, or court-servants. Their commissions and authority are not precisely delimited and are temporarily called into being for each case.

II. The principles of office hierarchy and of levels of graded authority mean a firmly ordered system of super- and subordination in which there is a supervision of the lower offices by the higher ones. Such a system offers the governed the possibility of appealing the decision of a lower office to its higher authority, in a definitely regulated manner. With the full development of the bureaucratic type, the office hierarchy is monocratically organized. The principle of hierarchical office authority is found in all bureaucratic structures: in state and ecclesiastical structures as well as in large party organizations and private enterprises. It does not matter for the character of bureaucracy whether its authority is called "private" or "public."

When the principle of jurisdictional "competency" is fully carried through, hierarchical subordination—at least in public office—does not mean that the "higher" authority is simply authorized to take over the business of the "lower." Indeed, the opposite is the rule. Once established and having fulfilled its task, an office tends to continue in existence and be held by another incumbent.

III. The management of the modern office is based upon written documents ("the files"), which are preserved in their original or draft form. There is, therefore, a staff of subaltern officials and scribes of all sorts. The body of officials actively engaged in a "public" office, along with the respective apparatus of material implements and the files, make up a "bureau." In private enterprise, "the bureau" is often called "the office."

In principle, the modern organization of the civil service separates the bureau from the private domicile of the official,

and, in general, bureaucracy segregates official activity as something distinct from the sphere of private life. Public monies and equipment are divorced from the private property of the official. . . . In principle, the executive office is separated from the household, business from private correspondence, and business assets from private fortunes. The more consistently the modern type of business management has been carried through, the more are these separations the case. The beginnings of this process are to be found as early as the Middle Ages.

It is the peculiarity of the modern entrepreneur that he conducts himself as the "first official" of his enterprise, in the very same way in which the ruler of a specifically modern bureaucratic state spoke of himself as "the first servant" of the state. The idea that the bureau activities of the state are intrinsically different in character from the management of private economic offices is a continental European notion and, by the way of contrast, is totally foreign to the American way.

IV. Office management, at least all specialized office management—and such management is distinctly modern—usually presupposes a thorough and expert training. This increasingly holds for the modern executive and employee of private enterprises, in the same manner as it holds for the state official.

V. When the office is fully developed, official activity demands the full working capacity of the official, irrespective of the fact that his obligatory time in the bureau may be firmly delimited. In the normal case, this is only the product of a long development, in the public as well as in the private office. Formerly, in all cases, the normal state of affairs was reversed: Official business was discharged as a secondary activity.

VI. The management of the office follows general rules, which are more or less stable, more or less exhaustive, and which can be learned. Knowledge of these rules represents a special technical learning which the officials possess. It involves jurisprudence, or administrative or business management.

VII. The reduction of modern office management to rules is deeply embedded in its very nature. The theory of modern public administration, for instance, assumes that the authority to order certain matters by decree—which has been legally granted to public authorities—does not entitle the bureau to regulate the matter by commands given for each case, but only to regulate the matter abstractly. This stands in extreme contrast to the regulation of all relationships through individual privileges and bestowals of favor, which is absolutely dominant in patrimonialism, at least insofar as such relationships are not fixed by sacred tradition.

All this results in the following for the internal and external position of the official.

I. Office holding is a "vocation." This is shown, first, in the requirement of a firmly prescribed course of training, which demands the entire capacity for work for a long period of time, and in the generally prescribed and special examinations which are prerequisites of employment. Furthermore, the position of the official is in the nature of a duty. This determines the internal structure of his relations, in the following manner: Legally and actually, office holding is not considered a source to be exploited for rents or emoluments, as was normally the case during the Middle Ages and frequently up to the threshold of recent times. . . . Entrances into an office, including one in the private economy, is considered an acceptance of a specific obligation of faithful management in return for a secure existence. It is decisive for the specific nature of modern loyalty to an office that, in the pure type, it does not establish a relationship to a *person*, like the

vassal's or disciple's faith in feudal or in patrimonial relations and authority. Modern loyalty is devoted to impersonal and functional purposes. . . .

II. The personal position of the official is patterned in the following way:

(1) Whether he is in a private office or a public bureau, the modern official always strives and usually enjoys a distinct *social esteem* as compared with the governed. His social position is guaranteed by the prescriptive rules of rank order and, for the political official, by special definitions of the criminal code against "insults of officials" and "contempt" of state and church authorities.

The actual social position of the official is normally highest where, as in old civilized countries, the following conditions prevail: a strong demand for administration by trained experts; a strong and stable social differentiation, where the official predominantly derives from socially and economically privileged strata because of the social distribution of power; or where the costliness of the required training and status conventions are binding upon him. The possession of educational certificates—to be discussed elsewhere—are usually linked with qualification for office. Naturally, such certificates or patents enhance the "status element" in the social position of the official. . . .

Usually the social esteem of the officials as such is especially low where the demand for expert administration and the dominance of status conventions are weak. This is especially the case in the United States; it is often the case in new settlements by virtue of their wide fields for profit-taking and the great instability of their social stratification.

(2) The pure type of bureaucratic official is *appointed* by a superior authority. An official elected by the governed is not a purely bureaucratic figure. Of course, the formal existence of an election does not

by itself mean that no appointment hides behind the election—in the state, especially, appointment by party chiefs. Whether or not this is the case does not depend upon legal statutes but upon the way in which the party mechanism functions. Once firmly organized, the parties can turn a formally free election into the mere acclamation of a candidate designated by the party chief. As a rule, however, a formally free election is turned into a fight, conducted according to definite rules, for votes in favor of one of two designated candidates. . . .

(3) Normally, the position of the official is held for life, at least in public bureaucracies; and this is increasingly the case for all similar structures. As a factual rule, *tenure for life* is presupposed, even where the giving of notice or periodic reappointment occurs. In contrast to the worker in a private enterprise, the official normally holds tenure. Legal or actual life-tenure, however, is not recognized as the official's right to the possession of office, as was the case with many structures of authority in the past. Where legal guarantees against arbitrary dismissal or transfer are developed, they merely serve to guarantee a strictly objective discharge of specific office duties free from all personal considerations. . . .

(4) The official receives the regular *pecuniary* compensation of a normally fixed *salary* and the old age security provided by a pension. The salary is not measured like a wage in terms of work done, but according to "status," that is, according to the kind of function (the "rank") and, in addition, possibly, according to the length of service. The relatively great security of the official's income, as well as the rewards of social esteem, make the office a sought-after position. . . .

(5) The official is set for a "*career*" within the hierarchical order of the public service. He moves from the lower, less important, and lower paid to the higher positions. The average official naturally desires a mechanical fixing of the conditions of promotion: if not of the offices, at least of the salary levels. He wants these conditions fixed in terms of "seniority," or possibly according to grades achieved in a developed system of expert examinations.

CRITICAL THINKING QUESTIONS

1. In what respects is bureaucracy impersonal? What are some of the advantages and disadvantages of this impersonality?

2. Through most of human history, kinship has been the foundation of social organization. Why is kinship missing from Weber's analysis of bureaucracy? On what other basis are people selected for bureaucratic positions?

3. Why does bureaucracy take a hierarchical form? Do you think formal organization must be hierarchical?

19

McJobs: McDonaldization and the Workplace

GEORGE RITZER

About two decades ago, George Ritzer coined the term "McDonaldization" to refer to a set of organizational principles—including efficiency, uniformity, predictability, and control—that play an important part in today's society. Here, he describes the way McDonald's and similar organizations control not just their workers, but also their customers.

In recent years the spread of McDonaldized systems has led to the creation of an enormous number of jobs. Unfortunately, the majority of them can be thought of as McDonaldized jobs, or "McJobs." While we usually associate these types of positions with fast-food restaurants, and in fact there are many such jobs in that setting (over 2.5 million people worked in that industry in the United States in 1992 [Van Giezen, 1994]), McJobs have spread throughout much of the economy with the growing impact of McDonaldization on work settings which had previously experienced relatively little rationalization.

It is worth outlining some of the basic realities of employment in the fast-food industry in the United States since those jobs serve as a model for employment in other McDonaldized

settings (Van Giezen, 1994). The large number of people employed in fast-food restaurants accounts for over 40 percent of the approximately six million people employed in restaurants of all types. Fast-food restaurants rely heavily on teenage employees—almost 70 percent of their employees are twenty years of age or younger. For many, the fast-food restaurant is likely to be their first employer. It is estimated that the first job for one of every fifteen workers was at McDonald's; one of every eight Americans has worked at McDonald's at some time in his or her life. The vast majority of employees are part-time workers: The average work week in the fast-food industry is 29.5 hours. There is a high turnover rate: Only slightly more than half the employees remain on the job for a year or more. Minorities are overrepresented in these jobs—almost two-thirds of employees are women and nearly a quarter are non-white. These are low-paid occupations, with many earning the minimum wage, or slightly more. As a result, these jobs are greatly affected by changes in the minimum wage: An upward revision has an important effect on the income of these workers. However, there is a real danger that many workers would lose their positions as a result of such increases, especially in economically marginal fast-food restaurants.[1]

Although the McDonaldization of society is manifest at all levels and in all realms of the social world, the work world has played a particularly pivotal role in this. On the one hand, it is the main source of many of the precursors of McDonaldization, including bureaucracies, scientific management, assembly lines, and so on. More contemporaneously, the kinds of jobs, work procedures, and organizing principles that have made McDonald's so successful have affected the way in which many businesses now organize much of their work. In fact, it could well be argued that the primary root of the McDonaldization of the larger society is the work world. On the other hand, the McDonaldization of the larger society has, in turn, served to further rationalize the work world. We thus have a self-reinforcing and enriching process that is speeding the growth and spread of McDonaldization.

The process of McDonaldization is leading to the creation of more and more McJobs.[2] The service sector, especially at its lower end, is producing an enormous number of jobs, most of them requiring little or no skill. There is no better example of this than the mountain of jobs being produced by the fast-food industry. However, new occupational creation is not the only source of McJobs: Many extant low-level jobs are being McDonaldized. More strikingly, large numbers of middle-level jobs are also being deskilled and transformed into McJobs.

McJobs are characterized by the five dimensions of McDonaldization. The jobs tend to involve a series of simple tasks in which the emphasis is on performing each as efficiently as possible. Second, the time associated with many of the tasks is carefully calculated and the emphasis on the quantity of time a task should take tends to diminish the quality of the work from the point of view of the worker. That is, tasks are so simplified and streamlined that they provide little or no meaning to the worker. Third, the work is predictable: employees do and say essentially the same things hour after hour, day after day. Fourth, many non-human technologies are employed to control workers and reduce them to robotlike actions. Some technologies are in place, and others are in development, that will lead to the eventual replacement of many of these "human robots" with computerized robots. Finally, the rationalized McJobs lead to a variety of irrationalities, especially the dehumanization of work. The result is the extraordinarily high turnover rate described above and difficulty in maintaining an adequate supply of replacements.[3]

The claim is usually made by spokespeople for McDonaldized systems that they are offering a large number of entry-level positions that help give employees basic skills they will need in order to move up the occupational ladder within such systems (and many of them do). This is likely to be true in the instances in which the middle-level jobs to which they move—for example, shift leader, assistant manager, or manager of a fast-food restaurant—are also routinized and scripted. In fact, it turns out that this even holds for the positions held by the routinized and scripted instructors at [McDonald's training program at] Hamburger University who teach the managers, who teach the employees, and so on. However, the skills acquired in McJobs are not likely to prepare one for, help one to acquire, or help one to function well in, the far more desirable postindustrial occupations which are highly complex and require high levels of skill and education. Experience in routinized actions and scripted interactions do not help much when occupations require thought and creativity. . . .

At the cultural level, large numbers of people in the United States, and increasingly throughout much of the rest of the world, have come to value McDonaldization in general, as well as its fundamental characteristics. McDonaldization, as well as its various principles, has become part of our value system. That value system has, in turn, been translated into a series of principles that have been exported to, adopted by, and adapted to, a wide range of social settings. . . .

. . . . For example, the behavior of customers at fast-food restaurants is being affected in much the same way as the behavior of those who work in those restaurants.

The constraints on the behavior of employees and customers in McDonaldized systems are of both a structural and a cultural nature. Employees and customers find themselves in a variety of McDonaldized structures that demand that they behave in accord with the dictates of those structures. For example, the drive-through window associated with the fast-food restaurant (as well as other settings such as banks) structures both what customers in their cars and employees in their booths can and cannot do. They can efficiently exchange money for food, but their positions (in a car and a booth) and the press of other cars in the queue make any kind of personal interaction virtually impossible. Of course, many other kinds of behavior are either made possible, or prohibited, by such structures. In Giddens's (1984) terms, such structures are both enabling and constraining.

At a cultural level, both employees and customers are socialized into, and have internalized, the norms and values of working and living in a McDonaldized society. Employees are trained by managers or owners who are likely, themselves, to have been trained at an institution like McDonald's Hamburger University (Schaaf, 1994). Such institutions are as much concerned with inculcating norms and values as they are with the teaching of basic skills. For their part, customers are not required to attend Hamburger University, but

they are "trained" by the employees themselves, by television advertisements, and by their own children who are often diligent students, teachers, and enforcers of the McDonald's way. This "training," like that of those employees who attend Hamburger University, is oriented not only to teaching the "skills" required to be a customer at a fast-food restaurant (e.g., how to queue up in order to order food), but also the norms and values of such settings as they apply to customers (e.g., customers are expected to dispose of their own debris; they are not expected to linger after eating). As a result of such formal and informal training, both employees and customers can be relied on to do what they are supposed to, and what is expected of them, with little or no personal supervision. . . .

. . . . McJobs are not simply the deskilled jobs of our industrial past in new settings; they are jobs that have a variety of new and distinctive characteristics. . . . . Industrial and McDonaldized jobs both tend to be highly routinized in terms of what people do on the job. However, one of the things that is distinctive about McDonaldized jobs, especially since so many of them involve work that requires interaction and communication, especially with consumers, is that what people say on the job is also highly routinized. To put this another way, McDonaldized jobs are tightly scripted: They are characterized by *both* routinized actions (for example, the way McDonald's hamburgers are to be put down on the grill and flipped [Love, 1986: 141–2]) and scripted interactions (examples include "May I help you?"; "Would you like a dessert to go with your meal?"; "Have a nice day!"). Scripts are crucial because, as Leidner (1993) points out, many of the workers in McDonaldized systems are interactive service workers. This means that they not only produce goods and provide services, but they often do so in interaction with customers.

The scripting of interaction leads to new depths in the deskilling of workers. Not only have employee actions been deskilled; employees' ability to speak and interact with customers is now being limited and controlled. There are not only scripts to handle general situations, but also a range of subscripts to deal with a variety of contingencies. Verbal and interactive skills are being taken away from employees and built into the scripts in much the same way that manual skills were taken and built into various technologies. At one time distrusted in their ability to *do* the right thing, workers now find themselves no longer trusted to *say* the right thing. Once able to create distinctive interactive styles, and to adjust them to different circumstances, employees are now asked to follow scripts as mindlessly as possible. . . .

One very important, but rarely noted, aspect of the labor process in the fast-food restaurant and other McDonaldized systems is the extent to which customers are being led, perhaps even almost required, to perform a number of tasks without pay that were formerly performed by paid employees. For example, in the modern gasoline station the driver now does various things for free (pumps gas, cleans windows, checks oil, even pays through a computerized credit card system built into the pump) that were formerly done by paid attendants. In these and many other settings, McDonaldization has brought the customer *into* the labor process: The customer is the laborer! This has several advantages for employers, such as lower (even nonexistent) labor costs, the need for fewer employees, and less trouble with personnel problems: Customers are far less likely to complain about a few seconds or minutes of tedious work than employees who devote a full work day to such tasks. Because of its advantages, as well as because customers are growing accustomed to and accepting of it, I think customers are likely to become even more involved in the labor process.

This is the most revolutionary development, at least as far as the labor process is concerned, associated with McDonaldization. As a result of this dramatic change, the analysis of the labor process must be extended to what customers do in McDonaldized systems. The distinction between customer and employee is eroding, or in postmodern terms "imploding," and one can envision more and more work settings in which customers are asked to do an increasing amount of "work." More dramatically, it is also likely that we will see more work settings in which there are no employees at all! In such settings customers, in interaction with nonhuman technologies, will do *all* of the human labor. A widespread example is the ATM in which customers (and the technology) do all of the work formerly done by bank tellers. More strikingly, we are beginning to see automated loan machines which dispense loans as high as $10,000 (Singletary, 1996). Again, customers and technologies do the work and, in the process, many loan-officer positions are eliminated. Similarly, the new automated gasoline pumps allow (or force) customers to do all of the required tasks; in some cases and at certain times (late at night) no employees at all are present.

In a sense, a key to the success of McDonaldized systems is that they have been able to supplement the exploitation of employees with the exploitation of customers. Lest we forget, Marx "put at the heart of his sociology—as no other sociology does—the theme of exploitation" (Worsley, 1982: 115). In Marxian theory, the capitalists are seen as simply paying workers less than the value produced by the workers, and as keeping the rest for themselves. This dynamic continues in contemporary society, but capitalists have learned that they can ratchet up the level of exploitation not only by exploiting workers more, but also by exploiting a whole new group of people—consumers. In Marxian terms, customers create value in the tasks they perform for McDonaldized systems. And they are not simply paid less than the value they produce, they are paid *nothing at all*. In this way, customers are exploited to an even greater degree than workers. . . .

While no class within society is immune to McDonaldization, the lower classes are the most affected. They are the ones who are most likely to go to McDonaldized schools, live in inexpensive, mass-produced tract houses, and work in McDonaldized jobs. Those in the upper classes have much more of a chance of sending their children to non-McDonaldized schools, living in custom-built homes, and working in occupations in which they impose McDonaldization on others while avoiding it to a large degree themselves.

Also related to the social class issue is the fact that the McDonaldization of a significant portion of the labor force does not mean that all, or even most, of the labor force is undergoing this process. In fact, the McDonaldization of some of the labor force is occurring at the same time that another large segment is moving in a postindustrial, that is, more highly skilled, direction (Hage & Powers, 1992). Being created in this sector of society are relatively high-status, well-paid occupations requiring high levels of education and training. In the main, these are far from McJobs and lack most, or all, of the dimensions discussed at the beginning of this [reading]. The growth of such postindustrial occupations parallels the concern in the labor process literature with flexible specialization occurring side by side with the deskilling of many other jobs. This points to a bifurcation in the class system. In spite of appearances, there is no contradiction here; McDonaldization and postindustrialization tend to occur in different sectors of the labor market. However, the spread of McJobs leads us to be dubious of the idea that we have moved into a new postindustrial era and have left behind the kind of deskilled jobs we associate with industrial society.

CRITICAL THINKING QUESTIONS

1. Describe ways in which McDonaldization is evident in a number of familiar settings (not just the workplace, but perhaps shopping malls and even the college or university campus). What elements of McDonaldization can you find?

2. In what ways does a McDonaldized setting control not just workers but customers as well? Why do organizations want to control customers?

3. Why does McDonaldization seem to appeal to many people? Do you think this process is good for society as a whole or harmful? Why?

NOTES

This chapter combines a paper, "McJobs," published in Rich Feller and Garry Walz (eds.), *Career Transitions in Turbulent Times* (Greensboro, N.C.: ERIC/CASS Publications, 1996) and the Invited Plenary Address, International Labour Process Conference, Blackpool, England, April, 1995.

1. Although a study by Katz and Krueger (1992) indicates an employment increase accompanying a rise in the minimum wage.

2. As we will see below, other kinds of high-status, high-paying postindustrial occupations are also growing.

3. There are, of course, many other factors involved in turnover.

REFERENCES

Giddens, Anthony. 1984. *The constitution of society: Outline of the theory of structuration.* Berkeley, CA: University of California Press.

Hage, Jerald, and Charles H. Powers. 1992. *Post-industrial lives: Roles and relationships in the 21st century.* Newbury Park, CA: Sage.

Leidner, Robin. 1993. *Fast food, fast talk: Service work and the routinization of everyday life.* Berkeley, CA: University of California Press.

Love, John. 1986. *McDonald's: Behind the arches.* Toronto: Bantam Books.

Schaaf, Dick. 1994. Inside Hamburger University. *Training,* December: 18–24.

Singletary, Michelle. 1996. Borrowing by the touch. *Washington Post,* 30 March: C1, C2.

Van Giezen, Robert W. 1994. Occupational wages in the fast-food restaurant industry. *Monthly Labor Review,* August: 24–30.

Worsley, Peter. 1982. *Marx and Marxism.* Chichester, UK: Ellis Horwood.

"Even if I Don't Know What I'm Doing, I Can Make It Look Like I Do": Becoming a Doctor in Canada

BRENDA L. BEAGAN

Sociologists use the term "social structure" to refer to the relatively stable patterns of social interaction and organized relationships that persist over time. Brenda Beagan's article shows how medical students who are trained at Canadian universities are socialized to fit into existing social structures rather than to change them. Notice how medical students incorporate their new professional identity as they move through their studies.

When students enter medical school they are lay people with some science background. When they leave four years later they have become physicians; they have acquired specialized knowledge and taken on a new identity of medical professional. What happens in those four years? What processes of socialization go into the making of a doctor? . . . .

This study draws on survey and interview data from students and faculty at one Canadian medical school to examine the processes of professional identity formation and how they are experienced by diverse undergraduate medical students in the late 1990s. As the results will show, the processes are remarkably unchanged from the processes documented forty years ago. . . .

Source: Brenda L. Beagan. 2001. "Even If I Don't Know What I'm Doing I Can Make It Look Like I Know What I'm Doing": Becoming a doctor in the 1990s. *The Canadian Review of Sociology and Anthropology* 38(3): 275–92.

FIRST EXPERIENCES BECOME COMMONPLACE

When identifying how they came to think of themselves as medical students, participants described a process whereby what feels artificial and unnatural initially comes to feel natural simply through repetition. For many students, a series of "first times" were transformative moments.

Denise:[1] I think there are sort of seminal experiences. The first cut in anatomy, the first time you see a patient die, first time you see a treatment that was really aggressive and didn't work. . . . First few procedures that I conducted myself, first time I realized that I really did have somebody's life in my hands. . . . It seems like a whole lot of first times. The first time you take a history, the first time you actually hear the murmur. There are a lot of "Ah-ha!" sort of experiences.

Part of the novelty is the experience of being entitled—even required—to violate conventional social norms, touching patients' bodies, inquiring about bodily functions, probing emotional states: "You have to master a sense that you're invading somebody, and to feel like it's all right to do that, to invade their personal space. . . ."

CONSTRUCTING A PROFESSIONAL APPEARANCE

Students are quite explicitly socialized to adopt a professional appearance: "When people started to relax the dress code a letter was sent to everybody's mailbox, commenting that we were not to show up in jeans, and a tie is appropriate for men." Most students, however, do not require such reminders; they have internalized the requisite standards.

Dressing neatly and appropriately is important to convey respect to patients, other medical staff, and the profession. It probably also helps in patients taking students seriously. (survey comment)

Asked whether or not they ever worry about their appearance or dress at the hospital, 41 percent of the survey respondents said they do not, while 59 percent said they do.

There were no statistically significant differences by gender, class background or "minority" status, yet gendered patterns emerged when students detailed their concerns in an open-ended question. Most of the men satisfied their concerns about professional appearance with a shave and a collared shirt, perhaps adding a tie: "I do make sure that I am dressed appropriately when I see patients i.e. well-groomed, collared shirt (but no tie)." Women, on the other hand, struggled with the complex messages conveyed by their clothing, trying to look well-dressed yet not convey sexual messages. For women, "dressed up" normally means feminine while a professional image is intended to convey competence. Striking a balance at the intersection can be difficult: "Is it professional enough? Competent looking? . . . I do not want

to appear 'sexy' on the job." As one student noted, while both men and women sometimes violate standards of professional dress, men's violations tend to involve being too informal; women's may involve dressing too provocatively, thereby sexualizing a doctor–patient encounter.

CHANGES IN LANGUAGE, THINKING AND COMMUNICATION SKILLS

Acquiring a huge vocabulary of new words and old words with new meanings—what one student called "medical-ese"—is one of the central tasks facing medical students, and one of the major bases for examining them (Sinclair, 1997). Students were well aware of adopting the formal language of medicine.

Dawna: All of a sudden all I can think of is this lingo that people won't understand. My brother told me the other day, "Sometimes I just don't understand what you are talking about anymore." I don't realize it! I'll use technical terms that I didn't think that other people wouldn't know.

The language of medicine is the basis for constructing a new social reality. Even as it allows communication, language constructs "zones of meaning that are linguistically circumscribed" (Berger & Luckmann, 1966: 39). Medical language encapsulates and constructs a worldview wherein reducing a person to body parts, tissues, organs and systems becomes normal, natural, "the only reasonable way to think" (Good & Good, 1993: 98–9). Students described this as learning to pare away "extraneous" information about a patient's life to focus on what is clinically relevant.

Becky: I see how it happens. . . . The first day of medicine we're just people. We relate by asking everything about a person, just like you'd have a conversation with anybody. And then that sort of changes and you become focused on the disease . . . because right now there's just too much. It's overwhelming. I'm hoping that as I learn more and become more comfortable with what I know and I can apply it without having to consciously go through every step in my mind, that I'll be able to focus on the *person* again.

In part through the language of medicine students learn a scientific gaze that reduces patients to bodies, allowing them to concentrate on what is medically important—disease, procedures, and techniques (Haas & Shaffir, 1987).

Not surprisingly, students may simultaneously lose the communication abilities they had upon entering medical school.

Dr. W.: Their ability to talk to people becomes corrupted by the educational process. They learn the language of medicine but they give up some of the knowledge that they brought in. . . . The knowledge of how to listen to somebody, how to be humble, how to hear somebody else's words. . . . It gets overtaken by the agenda of medical interviewing.

Another faculty member noted that students' communication skills improved significantly during their first term of first year, but "by the end of fourth year they were worse than they had been before medical school."

LEARNING THE HIERARCHY

Key to becoming a medical student is learning to negotiate the complex hierarchy within medicine, with students positioned at the bottom. A few faculty saw this hierarchy as a fine and important tradition facilitating students' learning.

Dr. U.: You're always taught by the person above you. Third-year medical students taught by the fourth-year student. . . . Fourth-year student depends on the resident to go over his stuff. Resident depends on maybe the senior or the chief resident or the staff person. So they all get this hierarchy which is wonderful for learning because the attendings can't deal with everybody.

Students, and most faculty, were far less accepting of this traditional hierarchy—particularly of students' place in it.

Both faculty and students pointed out the compliance the hierarchical structure inculcates in students, discouraging them from questioning those above them.

Dr. G.: If they don't appear compliant and so on they will get evaluated poorly. And if you get evaluated poorly then you might not get a good residency position. There's that sort of thing over their shoulders all of the time . . . the fear.

For students being a "good medical student" means not challenging clinicians.

Valerie: If I ever saw something blatantly sexist or racist or wrong I hope that I would say something. But you get so caught up in basically clamming up, shutting up, and just taking it. . . . Is it going to ruin my career, am I going to end up known as the fink, am I going to not get the [residency] spot that I want because I told?

Though virtually every student described seeing things on the wards that they disagreed with, as long as there was no direct harm to a patient they stayed silent and simply filed away the incident in their collection of "things not to do when I am a doctor."

Other researchers have noted that medical students develop an approach geared to getting along with faculty, pleasing them whatever their demands (Becker et al., 1961: 281; Bloom, 1973: 20; Sinclair, 1997: 29). Some students, however, had internalized the norm of not criticizing clinicians, adopting an unspoken "code of silence" not just to appease faculty, but as part of being a good physician. In particular, one should never critique a colleague in front of patients.

Mark: As students we all critique the professors and our attendings. . . . But I don't think we'd ever do that in front of a patient. It's never been told to us not to. But most of us wouldn't do that. Even if a patient describes something their doctor has prescribed to them or a treatment they've recommended which you know is totally wrong, maybe even harmful, I think most of us, unless it was really harmful, would tend to ignore it and just accept, "This is the doctor and his patient. What happens between them is okay."

These students had developed a sense of alliance with other members of the profession rather than with lay people and patients—a key to professional socialization. Several faculty referred to good medical students as "good team players" (cf. Sinclair, 1997), invoking a notion of belonging.

Dr. M.: That sense of belonging, I think, is a sense of belonging to the profession. . . . You're part of the process of health care. . . . I mean, you haven't a lot of the responsibility, but at least you're connected with the team.

For some students, too, the desire to present a united front for patients was expressed as being a good team player: "You have to go along with some things . . . in front of the patient. For teams it wouldn't be good to have the ranks arguing amongst themselves about the best approach for patient care." To remain good team players, many students, residents and physicians learn to say nothing even when they see colleagues and superiors violating the ethics and standards of the profession; such violations are disregarded as matters of personal style (Light, 1988).

RELATIONSHIP TO PATIENTS

As students are learning their place in the hierarchy within medicine, they are simultaneously learning an appropriate relationship to patients. Within the medical hierarchy students feel powerless at the bottom. Yet in relation to patients even students hold a certain amount of power. In the interviews there were widely diverging views on the degree of professional authority physicians and student-physicians should display.

Some faculty drew a very clear connection between professionalism and the "emotional distancing" Fox documented in medicine in 1957, describing students developing a "hard shell" as a "way of dealing with feelings" to prevent over-identifying with patients. Emotional involvement and over-identification are seen as dangerous; students must strike a balance between empathy and objectivity, learning to overcome or master their emotions (Conrad, 1988; Haas & Shaffir, 1987): "I only become of use if I can create some distance so that I can function."

Dr. E.: Within the professional job that you have to do, one can be very nice to patients but there's a distancing that says you're not their friend, you're their doctor.

In contrast, several faculty members rejected the "emotional distancing" approach to medicine in favour of one based in egalitarian connection.

Dr. V.: I reject that way of dealing with it. . . . When I'm seeing a patient I have to try to get into understanding what's bothering them. And in fact it's a harder job, I mean I need to understand well enough so I can help them to understand. 'Cause the process of healing is self-understanding.

These faculty members talked about recognizing and levelling power or sharing power. They saw professional distancing as the loss of humanitarianism, the adoption of a position of superiority, aloofness, emphasizing that clinicians need to know their patients as something more than a diagnosis. Women were slightly over-represented among those expressing the egalitarian perspective, but several male clinicians also advocated this position.

PLAYING A ROLE GRADUALLY BECOMES REAL

Along with emotional distancing, Fox (1957) identified "training for uncertainty" as key to medical socialization, including the uncertainty arising from not knowing everything, and not knowing enough. Alongside gathering the knowledge and experience that gradually reduces feelings of uncertainty, students also grow to simply tolerate high levels of uncertainty. At the same time they face routine expectations of certainty—from patients who expect them "to know it all" and faculty who often expect them to know far more than they do and who evaluate the students' competence (Haas & Shaffir, 1987). Students quickly learn it is risky to display lack of certainty; impression management becomes a central feature of clinical learning (Conrad, 1988). Haas and Shaffir (1987: 110) conclude that the process of professionalization involves above all the successful adoption of a cloak of competence such that audiences are convinced of the legitimacy of claims to competence.

Robert Coombs argues that medical professional socialization is partly a matter of playing the role of doctor, complete with the props of white coat, stethoscope, name tag, and clipboard (1978: 222). The symbols mark medical students off as distinct from lay people and other hospital staff, differentiating between We and They. Students spoke of "taking on a role" that initially made them feel like "total frauds," "impostors."

Erin: It was really role-playing. You were doing all these examinations on these patients which were not going to go into their charts, were not going to ever be read by anybody who was treating the people so it really was just practice. Just play-acting.

They affirmed the importance of the props to successful accomplishment of their role play—even as it enhanced the feeling of artifice: "During third year when we got to put the little white coat on and carry some instruments around the hospital, have a name tag . . . it definitely felt like role-playing."

Despite feeling fraudulent, the role play allows students to meet a crucial objective: demonstrating to faculty, clinical instructors, nurses and patients that they know something. They quickly learn to at least look competent.

Nancy: Even if I don't know what I'm doing I can make it *look* like I know what I'm doing. . . . It was my acting in high school. . . . I get the trust of the patient. . . .

RESPONSES FROM OTHERS

The more students are treated by others as if they really were doctors the more they feel like doctors (cf. Coombs, 1978). In particular, the response from other hospital personnel and patients can help confirm the student's emerging medical professional identity.

Rina: The more the staff treats you as someone who actually belongs there, that definitely adds to your feeling like you do belong there. . . . It's like, "Wow! This nurse is paging me and wants to know *my* opinion on why this patient has no urine output?!"

For many students, patients were the single most important source of confirmation for their emerging identity as physicians. With doctors and nurses, students feel they can easily be caught out for what they don't know; with patients they feel fairly certain they can pull off a convincing performance, and they often realize they do know more than the average person.

One response from others that has tremendous impact is simply being called doctor by others (Konner, 1987; Shapiro, 1987). Survey results show 68 percent ($n = 48$) of students had been called doctor at least occasionally by people other than family or friends. All but two fully recalled the first time they were called doctor and how they felt about it. Not being called doctor—especially when your peers are—can be equally significant. In previous accounts, being white and being male have greatly improved a medical student's chances of being taken for a doctor (Dickstein, 1993; Gamble, 1990; Kirk, 1994; Lenhart, 1993). In this study, although social class background, minority status and first language made no difference, significantly more men than women were *regularly* called doctor and significantly more women had *never* been called doctor.[2]

These data suggest a lingering societal assumption that the doctor is a man. According to the interviews, women medical students and physicians are still often mistaken for nurses.

Two of the male students suggested the dominant assumption that a doctor is a man facilitates their establishing rapport with patients and may ease their relationships with those above them in the medical hierarchy: "I've often felt because I fit like a stereotypical white male, that patients might see me as a bit more trustworthy. A bit more what they'd like to see. Who they want to see." Goffman notes that the part of a social performance intended to impress others, which he calls the "front," and which includes clothing, gender, appearance and manner, is predetermined: "When an actor takes on an established social role, usually he finds that a particular front has already been established for it" (1959: 27). In this case it appears that the role doctor, or medical student, still carries an attached assumption of maleness. . . .

CONCLUSION

What is perhaps most remarkable about these findings is how little has changed since the publication of *Boys in White* (Becker et al., 1961) and *Student Physician* (Merton et al., 1957), despite the passage of forty years and the influx of a very different student population. The basic processes of socializing new members into the profession of medicine remain remarkably similar, as students encounter new social norms, a new language, new thought processes, and a new world view that will eventually enable them to become full-fledged members of "the team" taking the expected role in the medical hierarchy.

Yet, with the differences in the 1990s student population, there are also some important differences in experiences. The role of medical student continues to carry with it certain expectations of its occupant. At a time when medical students were almost exclusively white, heterosexually identified, upper- or middle-class men, the identity may have "fit" more easily than it does for students who are women, who are from minority racial groups, who identify as gay or lesbian or working-class. If role-playing

competence and being reflected back to yourself as "doctor" are as central to medical socialization as Haas and Shaffir (1987) suggest, what does it mean that women students are less likely than their male peers to be called doctor? This research has indicated the presence of a lingering societal assumption that Doctor = Man. Women students struggle to construct a professional appearance that male students find a straightforward accomplishment. Women search for ways to be in a relationship with their patients that are unmarked by gender. Despite the fact that they make up half of all medical students in Canada, women's experiences of medical school remain different. In this research, almost half (six of fourteen) of the women students interviewed indicated that they do not identify themselves as medical students in casual social settings outside school lest they be seen as putting on airs; none of the male students indicated this. It remains for future research to determine whether gender differences in the "fit" of the physician role make a difference to medical practice. . . .

CRITICAL THINKING QUESTIONS

1. One new experience for medical students is learning *medical-ese*. Have you faced a similar process during your college or university education? Explain.

2. Why do you think that the traditional hierarchy in medical schools (i.e., faculty at the top, students at the bottom) is seen by many as a good thing?

3. Which groups of students were most likely to resist professional socialization? Why would this be the case?

NOTES

1. All names are pseudonyms.
2. Never been called doctor, 14 percent of women, 0 percent of men; occasionally or regularly, 57 percent of women, 78 percent of men (Cramer's V = 0.32).

REFERENCES

Becker, H. S., B. Geer, A. L. Strauss, and F. C. Hughes. 1961. *Boys in white: Student culture in medical school.* Chicago: University of Chicago Press.

Berger, P. L., and T. Luckmann. 1966. The social construction of reality: A treatise in the sociology of knowledge. New York: Doubleday and Co.

Bloom, S. W. 1973. *Power and dissent in the medical school.* New York: The Free Press.

———. 1988. Structure and ideology in medical education: An analysis of resistance to change. *Journal of Health and Social Behavior*, 29: 294–306.

Conrad, E. 1988. Learning to doctor: Reflections on recent accounts of the medical school years. *Journal of Health and Social Behavior*, 29: 323–32.

Coombs, R. H. 1978. *Mastering medicine.* New York: Free Press.

Dickstein, L. J. 1993. Gender bias in medical education: Twenty vignettes and recommended responses. *Journal of the American Medical Women's Association*, 48(5): 152–62.

Fox, R. C. 1957. Training for uncertainty. In *The student-physician: Introduction studies in the sociology of medical education*, eds. R. K. Merton, G. G. Reader, and E. L. Kendall, 207–44. Cambridge, MA: Harvard University Press.

Gamble, V. N. 1990. On becoming a physician: A dream not deferred. In *The black women's health book: Speaking for ourselves*, ed. E. C. White, 52–64. Seattle, WA: Seal Press.

Goffman, E. 1959. *The presentation of self in everyday life.* New York: Doubleday.

Good, B. J., and M. J. DelVecchio Good. 1993. "Learning medicine." The constructing of medical knowledge at Harvard medical school. In *Knowledge, power, and practice: The anthropology of medicine and everyday life*, eds. S. Lindbaum, and M. Lock, 81–107. Berkeley: University of California Press.

Haas, J., and W. Shaffir. 1987. *Becoming doctors: The adoption of a cloak of competence.* Greenwich, CT: JAI Press.

Kirk, J. 1994. A feminist analysis of women in medical schools. In *Health, illness, and health care in Canada*, 2nd ed., eds. B. S. Bolaria, and H. D. Dickenson, 158–82. Toronto: Harcourt Brace.

Konner, M. 1987. *Becoming a doctor: A journey of initiation in medical school.* New York: Viking.

Lenhart, S. 1993. Gender discrimination: A health and career development problem for women physicians. *Journal of the American Medical Women's Association*, 48(5): 155–59.

Light, D. W. 1988. Toward a new sociology of medical education. *Journal of Health and Social Behavior*, 29: 307–22.

Merton, R. K., G. G. Reader, and P. L. Kendall. 1957. *The student physician: Introductory studies in the sociology of medical education.* Cambridge, MA: Harvard University Press.

Shapiro, M. 1987. *Getting doctored: Critical reflections on becoming a physician.* Toronto: Between the Lines.

Sinclair, S. 1997. *Making doctors: An institutional apprenticeship.* New York: Berg.

Deviance

CLASSIC

CONTEMPORARY

CROSS-CULTURAL

21

The Functions of Crime

EMILE DURKHEIM

Common sense leads us to view crime, and all kinds of deviance, as pathological—that is, as harmful to social life. Despite the obvious social costs of crime, however, Durkheim argues that crime is normal because it is part of all societies. Furthermore, he claims that crime makes important contributions to the operation of a social system.

Crime is present not only in the majority of societies of one particular species but in all societies of all types. There is no society that is not confronted with the problem of criminality. Its form changes; the acts thus characterized are not the same everywhere; but, everywhere and always, there have been men who have behaved in such a way as to draw upon themselves penal repression. . . . There is, then, no phenomenon that presents more indisputably all the symptoms of normality, since it appears closely connected with the conditions of all collective life. To make of crime a form of social morbidity would be to admit that morbidity

is not something accidental, but, on the contrary, that in certain cases it grows out of the fundamental constitution of the living organism; it would result in wiping out all distinction between the physiological and the pathological. No doubt it is possible that crime itself will have abnormal forms, as, for example, when its rate is unusually high. This excess is, indeed, undoubtedly morbid in nature. What is normal, simply, is the existence of criminality. . . .

Here we are, then, in the presence of a conclusion in appearance quite paradoxical. Let us make no mistake. To classify crime among the phenomena of normal sociology is not to say merely that it is an inevitable, although regrettable, phenomenon, due to the incorrigible wickedness of men; it is to affirm that it is a factor in public health, an integral part of all healthy societies. This result is, at first glance, surprising enough to have puzzled even ourselves for a long time. Once this first surprise

Source: Reprinted with permission of The Free Press, a Division of Simon & Schuster Adult Publishing Group, from *The Rules of Sociological Method* by Emile Durkheim, translated by Sarah A. Solovay and John H. Mueller. Edited by George E. G. Catlin. Copyright © 1938 by George E. G. Catlin; copyright renewed 1966 by Sarah A. Solovay, John H. Mueller, and George E. G. Catlin.

has been overcome, however, it is not difficult to find reasons explaining this normality and at the same time confirming it.

In the first place crime is normal because a society exempt from it is utterly impossible. Crime . . . consists of an act that offends certain very strong collective sentiments. In a society in which criminal acts are no longer committed, the sentiments they offend would have to be found without exception in all individual consciousnesses, and they must be found to exist with the same degree as sentiments contrary to them. Assuming that this condition could actually be realized, crime would not thereby disappear; it would only change its form, for the very cause which would thus dry up the sources of criminality would immediately open up new ones.

Indeed, for the collective sentiments which are protected by the penal law of a people at a specified moment of its history to take possession of the public conscience or for them to acquire a stronger hold where they have an insufficient grip, they must acquire an intensity greater than that which they had hitherto had. The community as a whole must experience them more vividly, for it can acquire from no other source the greater force necessary to control these individuals who formerly were the most refractory. For murderers to disappear, the horror of bloodshed must become greater in those social strata from which murderers are recruited; but, first it must become greater throughout the entire society. Moreover, the very absence of crime would directly contribute to produce this horror; because any sentiment seems much more respectable when it is always and uniformly respected.

One easily overlooks the consideration that these strong states of the common consciousness cannot be thus reinforced without reinforcing at the same time the more feeble states, whose violation previously gave birth to mere infraction of convention—since the weaker ones are only the prolongation, the attenuated form, of

the stronger. Thus robbery and simple bad taste injure the same single altruistic sentiment, the respect for that which is another's. However, this same sentiment is less grievously offended by bad taste than by robbery; and since, in addition, the average consciousness has not sufficient intensity to react keenly to the bad taste, it is treated with greater tolerance. That is why the person guilty of bad taste is merely blamed, whereas the thief is punished. But, if this sentiment grows stronger, to the point of silencing in all consciousnesses the inclination which disposes man to steal, he will become more sensitive to the offenses which, until then, touched him but lightly. He will react against them, then, with more energy; they will be the object of greater opprobrium, which will transform certain of them from the simple moral faults that they were and give them the quality of crimes. For example, improper contracts, or contracts improperly executed, which only incur public blame or civil damages, will become offenses in law.

Imagine a society of saints, a perfect cloister of exemplary individuals. Crimes, properly so called, will there be unknown; but faults which appear venial to the layman will create there the same scandal that the ordinary offense does in ordinary consciousnesses. If, then, this society has the power to judge and punish, it will define these acts as criminal and will treat them as such. For the same reason, the perfect and upright man judges his smallest failings with a severity that the majority reserve for acts more truly in the nature of an offense. Formerly, acts of violence against persons were more frequent than they are today, because respect for individual dignity was less strong. As this has increased, these crimes have become more rare; and also, many acts violating this sentiment have been introduced into the penal law which were not included there in primitive times.. . .[1]

Crime is, then, necessary; it is bound up with the fundamental conditions of all social life, and by that very fact it is useful, because these conditions of which it is a part are themselves indispensable to the normal evolution of morality and law.

Indeed, it is no longer possible today to dispute the fact that law and morality vary from one social type to the next, nor that they change within the same type if the conditions of life are modified. But, in order that these transformations may be possible, the collective sentiments at the basis of morality must not be hostile to change, and consequently must have but moderate energy. If they were too strong, they would no longer be plastic. Every pattern is an obstacle to new patterns, to the extent that the first pattern is inflexible. The better a structure is articulated, the more it offers a healthy resistance to all modification; and this is equally true of functional, as of anatomical, organization. If there were no crimes, this condition could not have been fulfilled; for such a hypothesis presupposes that collective sentiments have arrived at a degree of intensity unexampled in history. Nothing is good indefinitely and to an unlimited extent. The authority which the moral conscience enjoys must not be excessive; otherwise no one would dare criticize it, and it would too easily congeal into an immutable form. To make progress, individual originality must be able to express itself. In order that the originality of the idealist whose dreams transcend his century may find expression, it is necessary that the originality of the criminal, who is below the level of his time, shall also be possible. One does not occur without the other.

Nor is this all. Aside from this indirect utility, it happens that crime itself plays a useful role in this evolution. Crime implies not only that the way remains open to necessary changes but that in certain cases it directly prepares these changes. Where crime exists, collective sentiments are sufficiently flexible to take on a new form, and crime sometimes helps to determine the form they will take. How many times, indeed, it is only an anticipation of future morality—a step toward what will be! According to Athenian law, Socrates was a criminal, and his condemnation was no more than just. However, his crime, namely, the independence of his thought, rendered a service not only to humanity but to his country. . . .

From this point of view the fundamental facts of criminality present themselves to us in an entirely new light. Contrary to current ideas, the criminal no longer seems a totally unsociable being, a sort of parasitic element, a strange and unassimilable body, introduced into the midst of society. On the contrary, he plays a definite role in social life.

CRITICAL THINKING QUESTIONS

1. On what grounds does Durkheim argue that crime should be considered a "normal" element of society?
2. Why is a society devoid of crime an impossibility?
3. What are the functional consequences of crime and deviance?

NOTES

1. Calumny, insults, slander, fraud, etc.

22

Hunting Humans

ELLIOTT LEYTON

Deviance

CLASSIC

CONTEMPORARY

CROSS-CULTURAL

Most research on serial murderers searches for shortcomings in the individual perpetrator, most often some kind of physical deficiency such as a brain injury. Sociologists, however, tend to argue that the rise of serial murderers can be explained by culture and economic circumstances.

THE HISTORICAL METAMORPHOSES

"We are encountering more and more . . . [of those who] have turned the life instinct on its head: Meaning for them can only come from acts of destruction."

—Roger Kramer and Ira Weiner [1]

Multiple murderers are not "insane" and they are very much products of their time. Far from being a randomly occurring freakish event, the arrival of the multiple murderer is dictated by specific stresses and alterations in the human community. Moreover, far from being deluded, he is in many senses an embodiment of the central themes in his civilization as well as a reflection of that civilization's critical tensions. He is thus a creature and a

creation of his age. As such, we would expect him to change his character over time, and all the evidence suggests that that is precisely what he does. The pre-industrial multiple killer was an aristocrat who preyed on his peasants; the industrial era produced a new kind of killer, most commonly a new bourgeois who preyed upon prostitutes, homeless boys, and housemaids; and in the mature industrial era, he is most often a faded bourgeois who stalks middle class victims as well as vulnerables. Thus for each historical epoch, both the social origins of the killers and the social characteristics of their victims are highly predictable: They are thus very much men of their time. . . .

THE MODERN ERA

This is the American Dream. . . . In America, anything is possible if you work for it."

—Vice-Presidential candidate, 1984

Culture

No quality of American culture is more jarring than the *culture of violence*. Its continued assertion (sometimes subliminal, sometimes blatant) of the nobility of violence is propagated with excitement and craft in all popular cultural forms, including films, television, print, and the Internet. This cultural predilection must have been immeasurably enhanced by the daily television coverage of the Vietnam War, which for the first time brought real bloodletting into every American living room and rendered death sacred no more. Subtly encouraged thus to act out their fantasies, our killers would find that their murderous acts would both validate and relieve their grievances. Whether in the media or at the level of the street, the glowing mythology often surrounding violence creates a situation in which the most trivial provocation can result in a savage explosion. Moreover, such vulnerables are primed for their purple displays by a *culture of fear* in which people are "taught" to be fearful of one another, ever poised for the onset of sexual and physical assault.

In *Seductions of Crime*, Katz's marvellous study of the "moral and sensual attractions in doing evil" in modern American culture, Katz shows how homicide is commonly conceived and expressed as "righteous slaughter" (which is to say that it is both ethically correct and emotionally conditioned); and how remorse and regret are largely removed from the equation. Here then we can find an armed street culture in which "dissing" one another—showing disrespect in matters as insignificant as maintaining eye contact for too long, or bumping into another, or "stealing" a lover or a parking place—can be perceived and felt as legitimate provocation for a homicide, or even a mass murder.

Across the nation, as many as one half of American homicides are provoked by such "trivial altercation." Moreover, the culture permits the "impassioned killers" to see themselves as somehow fundamentally moral, "defending both the morality of the social system and a personal claim of moral worth," even "upholding the respected social statuses of husband, mother, wife, father, property owner, virile male, deserving poor/self-improving welfare mother, and responsible debtor." It is precisely here—in condoning an atmosphere tolerant of physical confrontation—that American civilization unwittingly encourages those at the bottom to cross the line to homicidal assault. It is precisely here, at the level of "deep culture," that the dominant ethos desensitizes its population to murder.

Why should trivial altercations provoke so many killings? Gottfredson and Hirschi conclude that the under-socialized members of *any* civilization "will tend to be impulsive, insensitive, physical, risk-taking, short-sighted, and nonverbal" and are therefore most likely to risk criminal acts. In such under-controlled persons, outbursts of violence can be sparked by mere "momentary irritation," because "people with low self-control tend to have minimal tolerance for frustration and little ability to respond to conflict through verbal rather than physical means." Thus the noisome "irritation caused by a crying child [or a noisy neighbor] is often the stimulus for physical abuse," and the disrespect from "a taunting stranger in a bar is often the stimulus for aggravated assault." Those who exercise such limited control are more commonly found among the working classes, and those who have the least to lose are always more prone to violent display. But in a culture that validates and conditions these beliefs and behaviours, the responses are found with greater frequency and throughout the social order.

This, then, is the cultural milieu which has for two centuries glorified violence as an appropriate and manly response to frustration. *The History of Violence in America* documented the public response to a bank robbery in which a young girl was shot in the leg: The Kansas City *Times* reiterated the dominant cultural theme by describing the robbery as "so diabolically daring and so utterly in contempt of fear that we are bound to admire it and revere its perpetrators." A few days later, the same newspaper underlined this when it commented that

It was as though three bandits had come to us from storied Odenwald, with the halo of medieval chivalry upon their garments and shown us how the things were done that the poets sing of. Nowhere else in the United States or in the civilized world, probably, could this thing have been done.[2]

Social Structure

If the culture thus underwrites an explosive response to low levels of frustration, and if it has evolved over the centuries to separate its peoples from one another through fear, then changes in the social structure that add to the levels of frustration escalate still further the risk of multiple murder.

In the immediate aftermath of the Second World War, the industrial economies moved into an era of unprecedented expansion and prosperity. With the growth of the industrial sector came a parallel development of all government and social service agencies—running the gamut from education to medicine to welfare. This remarkable growth in both the corporate and social sectors created two postwar decades in which individuals with even the most marginal of qualifications and abilities could enter occupations which offered a real measure of dignity and recompense. These were quiet years for homicide in general and multiple murder in particular as the population scrambled to better itself. The increase in the rate of production of these most modern of killers began again in the mid-1960s and has continued ever since: This directly paralleled, and may well have owed its initial impetus to, the *closure* that was taking place in the American economy. From the mid-1960s onwards, the myriad of middle-class positions that had been created since the Second World War began to be filled, or reduced in number and "downsized." Inexorably, more and more socially ambitious but untalented (or unconnected) young men and women must have

found it difficult to achieve their goals of "successful" careers and crisp identities. A proportion of these people—we can never know precisely how many—began to fantasize about revenge. A tiny but increasing percentage of them began to react to the frustration of their blocked social mobility by transforming their fantasies into a vengeful reality.

Thus the *character* of both killers and victims underwent a further transformation. The social origins of the killers continued to fall: Gone were the aristocrats of the fifteenth century, and the doctors and teachers of the nineteenth century. Now the killers were drawn from the ranks of the working and lower-middle classes; for the most part they were security guards, computer operators, postal clerks, and construction workers. Conversely, the social origins of the victims pursued an opposite path: Where they had been peasants in the fifteenth century; housemaids, homeless boys, and prostitutes in the nineteenth century, now they were as likely to be drawn from the middle-class neighbourhoods: university students, aspiring models, and shoppers in middle-class malls. Both killer and victim had altered their form because the nature of the homicidal protest had changed radically. It was no longer the threatened aristocrat testing the limits of his power; no longer the morbidly insecure new bourgeois tasting the limits of his hard-won power. Now it was an excluded individual wreaking vengeance on the symbol and source of his excommunication.

Was this increase a consequence only of the predatory nature of capitalism? The evidence does not warrant such a conclusion. The structures of humiliation and deprivation coalesce around *any* hierarchical industrial system, whether it be capitalist or communist; and neither system appears to hold any monopoly on alienation and exclusion, dehumanization and depersonalization. We would thus have expected the communist bloc states also to produce multiple murderers—but in varying numbers, according to the degree with which their respective cultures glorify and venerate violence. Unfortunately, we cannot confirm these speculations since communist bloc states restricted the flow of information to their citizens; but the Soviet-era "Vampire of Silesia" . . . is an interesting illustration of what we might expect, as was the well-known case of the prolific killer Andrei Chikatilo. Valery Chalidze's review of Soviet crime made it clear that multiple murder was common enough in the former USSR. In the early 1960s, Chalidze wrote, one man "became well known to the Moscow public" for murdering children in their own apartments: Curiously, the official explanation given for his behaviour was precisely the same as any Western psychiatrist or court might offer—"his crimes appeared to be the acts of a maniac, and the general belief was that his motives were sexual." Since the collapse of the Soviet Union, indigenous homicide and multiple murder rates appear to have escalated radically, but a full understanding of this awaits further analysis.[3]

The simple fact of human social life is that in order for individuals to behave "normally," they must grow up feeling that they have some place in the social order—which is to say a coherent and socially constructed identity. Unfortunately, individuals who bear these social characteristics often come to feel excluded from the social order—a separation I have often heard in "reform schools," where juveniles refer to civilians as "humans"— and such exclusion can exact a fearful price. But many people who bear these social characteristics grow into a mature and balanced adulthood. Why should some fail to do so? Several other factors are necessary in the biography before a multiple murderer can be produced. He must also be inculcated with an ambition—or a "dream"— which either circumstances rob from him (as when DeSalvo's wife Irmgard refused him admission to the lower-middle class), or which he cannot feel at ease in living (as when Bundy spurned his long-sought socialite fiancée). He is never Durkheim's contented man, who:

vaguely realizes the extreme limit set to his ambitions and aspires to nothing beyond. . . . He feels that it is not well to ask more. Thus, an end and goal are set to the passions. . . . This relative limitation

and the moderation it involves, make men contented with their lot while stimulating them moderately to improve it; and this average contentment causes the feeling of calm, active happiness, the pleasure in existing and living which characterizes health for societies as well as for individuals.

It is in this light that we must interpret and understand the fierce social ambition of so many of our multiple murderers—and the feeling of being a robot that torments so many of them as they pursue their goals.[4]

Finally, for the production of multiple murderers to reach the unprecedented levels that it has in the America of the early twenty-first century, we require the existence of cultural forms that can mediate between killer and victim in a special sense—ridding the potential victims of any humanity, and the potential killer of any responsibility. Both sociologists Christopher Lasch and Barbara Ehrenreich have argued most persuasively that we have developed these forms with little refinement. Lasch devoted a volume to delineating the nature of this "culture of competitive individualism" which carries "the logic of individualism to the extreme of a war of all against all, the pursuit of happiness to the dead end of a narcissistic preoccupation with the self." Ehrenreich dwelt upon the sources of this ideology which so encouraged the severing of responsibility between people. She saw its roots in the developing post-war male culture of "escape—literal escape from the bondage of breadwinning." Here, men were urged to take part in the superficial excitement of "the nightmare anomie of the pop psychologists' vision: a world where other people are objects of consumption, or the chance encounters of a 'self' propelled by impulse alone."[5]

Thus the freedom for which mankind had struggled over the centuries proved to be a two-edged sword. The freedom from the suffocation of family and community, the freedom from systems of religious thought, the freedom to explore one's self, all entailed heavy penalties to society—not the least of which was the rate of multiple murder. Whether the industrial system was socialist or capitalist, its members were forced to look upon themselves and others as marketable commodities. It can hardly be surprising then that some fevered souls, feeling like automatons, might choose to coalesce their fuzzy identity in a series of fearful acts. Their ambitions crushed, some would lash out in protest at objects (most often sexual) which they had been taught to see as essentially insignificant. Now the question asked by the killer Bundy seems less inappropriate: "What's one less person on the face of the earth, anyway?"

Each of our case studies reveals that at a certain point in his life, the future killer experiences a kind of *internal* social crisis, when he realizes that he cannot be what he wishes to be—cannot live his version of the American dream. When these killers reach that existential divide, the seed is planted for a vengeance spree. Sometimes their motives are entirely conscious (as with the D.C. Snipers, Essex, Bundy, and Panzram); while with others (like Berkowitz and DeSalvo), they are only dimly understood. In either case, it is unrealizable ambition that motivates them, as they launch a kind of sub-political and personal assault on society, aiming always at the class or group they feel oppresses or excludes them. Some require minimal justification for their acts, obtaining temporary relief from their rage through the killings and then "forgetting" or compartmentalizing their memories, as when DeSalvo remarked: "I was there, it was done, and yet if you talked to me an hour later, or half hour later, it didn't mean nothing." Still others construct elaborate intellectual (Panzram) or spiritual (Berkowitz's demons) rationalizations to explain and justify their killings. Only a few (such as Joseph Kallinger, and California's Herbert Mullins, who murdered to "stop earthquakes") detach themselves so much from conventional reality that they construct their own universes, thereby entering that state the psychiatrists call madness.

Yet what they are *all* orchestrating is a kind of social levelling, in which they rewrite the universe to incorporate themselves: No one expressed this more clearly than Starkweather

when he said that "dead people are all on the same level." They are all engaged in the same process, claiming their "manhood" by punishing the innocent; in doing so they recreate the dehumanized industrial system in a form that gives themselves a central position. One hundred eyes for an eye: It is by no means the first time in human history that retaliating men have grossly exceeded the degree of the original insult. Neither do they form their missions in a private vacuum, bereft of all advice, for the larger culture encodes in them a respect for violent display—an especially central theme in the media messages beamed at the working class—and the ready availability of stimulating materials in books and magazines, films, videotapes, and the Internet, teaches them to link their lust with violence. If we were charged with the responsibility for designing a society in which all structural and cultural mechanisms leaned toward the creation of the killers of strangers, we could do no better than to present the purchaser with the shape of modern America.

The Negotiation of Murderous Identity

The twilight of the human race on this planet may well have been the thirty or forty thousand years our ancestors dwelt in relatively egalitarian (one assumes) hunting and gathering societies. In such non-stratified societies, there was little specialization of labour, little production of surplus, and few opportunities for aggressive and ambitious individuals to overcome the reluctance of their fellows to submit to any expropriation of the social commodities for which human beings compete—power, prestige, and wealth. However, something like 10,000 years ago all our ancestors began to make the shift from hunting and gathering to agriculture and pastoralism—new forms of economy that captured a larger amount of energy for each hour of work. When eight could thus do the work to feed ten, the stage was set for the production of a surplus and the expropriation of that surplus by an emerging class of elites. And so the form and structure of society was entirely rewritten: Now rank and hierarchy, not mutual obligation, began to emerge as *the* organizing principles of human society. That development provided the framework for the growth over the millennia of social classes: clusters of individuals with mutual interests who stood in opposition to individuals of other social classes. Over time, new classes emerged and struggled for ascendancy, as did the bourgeoisie in the nineteenth century. Thus some groups are more threatened than others in different periods of history. It is precisely at the point in time when a single class is most threatened (when its rights are challenged by another class, its legitimacy questioned by a discontented proletariat, or its newfound status imprecisely defined) that we can expect to find some members of that class beginning to fantasize about killing members of another class.

Thus the multiple murderer does not appear at random through history. He appears at special points in social evolution, during periods of particular tension. Durkheim's thoughts on destruction (although he was concerned with self-destruction) are central here. Despite the glories of humanity, it remains a fragile species. Its equilibrium is in such a delicate state of balance that any crisis (financial, industrial, or social) in the larger system disorients the individuals in that system. It matters not whether they are crises of prosperity or of poverty: It merely matters that individuals' expectations are profoundly shaken.

Every disturbance of equilibrium, even though it achieves greater comfort and a heightening of general vitality, is an impulse to voluntary death. Whenever serious readjustments take place in the social order, whether or not due to a sudden growth or to an unexpected catastrophe, men are more inclined to self-destruction.

In the archaic, pre-industrial period, it was the old and "noble" landed aristocracy which was most threatened by the rebellious peasantry and the rising mercantile classes. It makes a certain terrible sense that it was among this threatened class that fantasies of disordered

self-indulgent sexuality might turn to the torture and murder of the lower orders. During the industrial revolution of the late eighteenth and nineteenth centuries, while the aristocracy retired to its estates to lick its wounds and the rising bourgeoisie revelled in its ascendancy, it was the new marginal middle classes—men like Wagner and Dr. Cream—who, insecure in their unaccustomed roles, would grow obsessed with a sense of possible exposure and failure. During that period, it would primarily be doctors, government clerks, and school teachers who might discipline those of the lower orders—who perhaps whispered about past errors or who flaunted their indifference.[6]

In the early twentieth century, a new homicidal theme emerged. Proletarian revolt became a minor expression, in which those (like Panzram) who glimpsed their utter exclusion, who felt their torture at the hands of the bourgeois institutions constructed for their "rehabilitation," wreaked a similar havoc. These proletarians would continue into the modern era, as with the D.C. Snipers, but they would be a minor theme: Their class would find alternative forms of protest, either in direct political action, or in smothering their claims in drugs and alcohol, or just as commonly in theft. Murder for its own sake had relatively little appeal to a class with such immediate problems.

The major homicidal form of the modern era is the man who straddles the border between the upper-working class and the lower-middle class. Often, as with Robert Hansen in Alaska or cousins Kenneth Bianchi and Angelo Buono in Los Angeles (The "Hillside Stranglers"), they continue a metaphor from the earlier era and discipline unruly prostitutes and runaways. Commonly, too, they punish those above them in the system—preying on unambiguously middle-class figures such as university women. In any case, they are all justifying their behaviour and drawing their ideas from a *dehumanizing mass culture* that glorifies and legitimizes violence as an appropriate—even "manly"—response to the disappointments that are a normal part of life. In such a cultural milieu, self-control remains untaught, even stigmatized as submission and cowardice.

All class-based industrial nation-states, regardless of their professed ideologies, transform their members into either winners or losers. By the mid-1960s, however, the increasing closure of middle-class positions meant there would be many more losers, many more who were alienated and despairing. Moreover, as these positions were closing, other social forces within society continued their transformation of neighbours into strangers: The constriction of the extended family, the expansion of the anonymous city and suburb, the geographic mobility of individual familial units, and the disintegration of marriage and parenthood all made it progressively easier for the potential killer to overcome his scruples. The murder and mutilation of such enemy-strangers is but the abuse of a commodity. Thus we find the source of our new multiple murderer primarily among the ambitious who failed—or who believed they would fail—and who seek another form of success in the universal celebrity and attention they will receive through their extravagant homicides. In the performance of this task they are aided immensely by the extraordinary tolerance the social system offers their activities, providing only paltry resources for the monitoring and apprehension of potential killers.

Whether they kill all at once in a bloody hour or day, or whether they kill over an extended period, whether their motives appear to be economic, "sexual," or "psychotic," the objects of our study are all much of a kind. They all decide independently to construct a program of killing many strangers. On the surface of things they appear to be doing it for the thrill of sexual excitement or the intoxication of conquest; but the truth is they do it to relieve a burning grudge engendered by their failed ambition. Some are so finished with life that they wish to die when they have discharged their brief task: They come to be called "mass murderers," and they leave it up to a bewildered public to decipher their message. Others

wish to live and tell their stories and bask in their fame: They usually come to be called "serial murderers."

"The tragedy and irony is that what has produced this abomination is the achievement of the freedom for which mankind has struggled for centuries—freedom to explore one's self without reference to rigid systems of thought. That freedom exacts a terrible price, for it releases humans too much from their social contract. Under such conditions, those whose ambitions are denied (and there are more of these each year since the 1960s when closure first occurred), in a culture which so glamorizes and rewards violence, find a solution to all their problems in that purple explosion. As many more come to feel excluded in this time of industrial and social crisis, we can expect many more to follow the path of the University of Chicago undergraduate William Heirens, who searched for something—he knew not what—in the dissected entrails of a kidnapped child, and wrote in lipstick upon the walls of another victim's apartment: 'FOR HEAVEN'S SAKE CATCH ME BEFORE I KILL MORE I CANNOT CONTROL MYSELF.'"[7] . . .

Reducing Violence

Every civilization occasionally produces individuals with a personality many psychologists and psychiatrists gloss as "psychopathic." By this they refer to those who have little or no feeling for others, low levels of impulse control, no remorse or guilt for what they might do, and whose primary pleasure lies in the sadistic abuse and manipulation or even obliteration of others. If modern societies are remarkably similar to one another, they nevertheless vary enormously in the proportion of their psychopathic population that goes on to commit rape, torture, and murder. Indeed, we suspect that in most societies the majority of "psychopaths" go on to live relatively normal lives, perhaps rising in politics, university administration, government, or the corporate world. In others they are more likely to act upon their illegal sexual fantasies. Why this difference?

America is one of the world's great civilizations. Its contributions to art, literature, theatre, film, music, medicine, and science and technology are unparalleled, as are its veneration of personal freedom, its industrial capacity, and its military prowess. But its crime problem is also without parallel: Americans are five to ten times more likely to be murdered than western Europeans, and three to four times more likely than Canadians—all this despite the nation's harsh treatment of its criminals. How can they escape from this trap?

America's pattern of bullyboy politics and pugnacious personalities was established long before Teddy Roosevelt instructed his minions to "carry a big stick," a reiteration of a much older American cultural principle which seems to revere aggressivity. "In America," wrote Clancy Sigal, "murderers are more valued, certainly more admired, than their victims." No wonder Lewis Lapham thundered that by the 1980s, America's film heroes "had become paramilitary figures . . . paranoid and enraged—angry at anybody and everybody to whom they could assign the fault for the world's evil."[8]

Sadly, there is nothing unique in the world about a man (and occasionally a woman) who goes on a killing rampage. But these atrocities happen far more often in modern America than anywhere else. Where did they learn the script they are acting out? A civilization pays a tragic price if it encodes in its citizens any of the following notions:

. . . That violence has an intoxicating beauty and nobility

. . . That a man must personally avenge his dishonour

. . . That it is acceptable to demean or abuse any vulnerable class, gender, or ethnic group

. . . That wealth, power, and prestige are everything that matters

. . . That winning is glorious and losing is shameful

. . . That the suffering of others is their fault, not ours.

Some scholars have argued that the cause of all this lies buried in the institutionalized oppression at the bottom of the hierarchy, released as child abuse by the disordered family toiling at the bottom of society and avenged later in life as a (often sexualized) killing spree; but perhaps a more significant element in the formation of murderous personalities is *cultural,* the set of ideas implanted in the maturing child about the righteousness of slaughter, the cultural codes that "teach" young persons—especially males—that violence is appropriate in a variety of social situations beyond self-defence. Moreover, a nation that does not bend its energies to ameliorating the deprivation and alienation of those on the bottom pays a heavy price in murder. It is no coincidence that the nations of western Europe—England, France, the Netherlands, Germany, Austria, and the Scandinavian nations—with their generous welfare and educational systems are the ones that (along with Japan) produce the lowest homicide rates in the world. America would do well to remove its ideological blinkers and examine its friends more closely.

The Integration of Theory

How much further can we expect to advance in our understanding of the wellsprings of human aggression? Alas, not much further so long as we maintain the present fratricidal structure of modern science—in which the disciplines compete with one another, like the cheapest politicians, for funding and dominance. This is an intellectual disaster, choking the hope of all scientific advance and dooming the field to stagnation.

In his magisterial work *Europe and the People without History* Eric Wolf remarked that the primary intellectual achievement of the twentieth century was also its greatest weakness. Science had divided human behaviour and experience into manageable "bits" such as history, biology, economy, psychology, society, and so on; but then, lost in these arbitrary distinctions, made no comparable attempt to reassemble what had been so artificially dismembered. Indeed, we are only at the beginning of our understanding of human behaviour (healthy or otherwise), and a true and deepened comprehension of pathological aggression is unlikely to emerge until the insights from each discipline are integrated in a meaningful and balanced way.

The basic dilemmas remain unchanged: The social sciences have charted the cultural and structural pressures that ultimately create pathological behaviour; yet they are unable to explain why the majority of people exposed to these social pressures do not kill. The psychological sciences have dissected a portion of the psychological and biological vulnerability to aggressive behaviour in any individual; yet they are unable to explain why there are such massive differences between societies (and genders and social classes) in their levels of violence. Everywhere in the world, physical violence is overwhelmingly a male domain; yet radical feminist analysis is rarely able to transcend mere sexism in its analysis of the cause of differences between men and women.

One of the most intriguing possibilities is the proper integration of the levels of understanding offered by these various academic disciplines. Thus the social and economic forces that create so many violent and "dysfunctional" families could be analyzed, together with the psychological mechanisms that severely abused children develop to cope with their obliteration. In turn, these socioeconomic and psychological factors would, in cases of individuals with biological/chemical deficits that mitigate against impulse control, create individuals "programmed" to revel in the display of vengeful savagery. Such a balanced and integrated enterprise awaits its polymathic leader.

CRITICAL THINKING QUESTIONS

1. Do you think that a cultural explanation of serial murder is valid? Why or why not? What advantage does a cultural explanation have over medical or psychological ones?

2. Do you think violence in mass media desensitizes us? Serial killers are often celebrated in popular culture (e.g., movies, books). In your opinion, does this have an effect on how we think about this crime?

3. What does Leyton mean by the phrase "culture of violence"? Provide some examples of how violence is celebrated in our society.

NOTES

1. Kramer and Weiner 1983:73.
2. Frantz, in Graham and Gurr (eds) 1969.
3. Chalidze 1977: 107.
4. Durkheim 1961: 918.
5. Lasch 1979: 21; and Ehrenreich 1983: 51, 182.
6. Durkheim 1961: 918.
7. Heirens, in Freeman 1955.
8. Clancy Sigal, *Guardian Weekly*, Sept. 1993; Lewis Lapham, *Harper's*, Apr. 1994.

REFERENCES

Chalidze, Valery. 1977. *Criminal Russia: Essays on crime in the Soviet Union.* New York: Random House.

Durkheim, Emile. 1961. Anomic suicide. In *Theories of society: Foundations of modern sociological theory,* eds. Talcott Parsons, Edward Shils, Kasper Naegele, and Jesse R. Pitts. New York: Free Press.

Ehrenreich, Barbara. 1983. *The hearts of men: American dreams and the flight from commitment.* New York: Anchor.

Freeman, Lucy. 1955. *"Before I kill more ..."* New York: Crown.

Graham, H.D., and T.R. Gurr (eds.). 1969. *The history of violence in America: historical and comparative perspectives.* New York: Praeger.

Kramer, Roger and Ira Weiner. 1983. Psychiatry on the borderline. *Psychology Today* 17: 70–73.

Lasch, Christopher. 1979. *The culture of narcissism: American life in an age of diminishing expectations.* New York: Warner.

23

Canadian Cannabis: Marijuana as an Irritant/Problem in Canada–U.S. Relations

PAUL GECELOVSKY

What is considered deviant changes in terms of time and place. Alcohol and marijuana are both good examples in that countries around the world have different attitudes toward the two substances (e.g., alcohol is illegal in some Muslim countries). Canada has a more open attitude toward marijuana, and Gecelovsky provides some detail of how important this crop is to the British Columbian economy. But the Americans are not happy about this type of entrepreneurial activity.

In a recent survey of the Canada–U.S. relationship, Munroe Eagles noted that the "popular impression" for many Americans was that Canadians were "out of step with their more conservative neighbor to the south" (Eagles 2006, 821). John Herd Thompson made a similar claim in his review of the bilateral relationship over the 1994–2003 period, writing that Canadians are perceived by some Americans as being "left wing wimps" (Thompson 2003, 17). One area in which Canada may be regarded as out of step with the United States, and Canadians as left wing wimps, is the issue of marijuana. There are real and noticeable differences between Canada and the U.S. in the way each side deals with the issue of marijuana. The following pages examine the marijuana issue in terms of the growing volume of the drug being

smuggled into the United States from Canada, the increased potency of the strains of marijuana grown in Canada, and the differences in judicial deterrents adopted to penalize possession and cultivation. This is followed by a look at a couple of possibilities that have the potential to transform the marijuana irritant into the marijuana problem in Canada–U.S. relations.

The amount of marijuana being produced in Canada and then illegally exported to the United States is of increasing concern to all levels of American law enforcement. While British Columbia (B.C.), Ontario, and Quebec are all of concern to U.S. officials, British Columbia presents the largest source of Canadian marijuana for the U.S. market, so the discussion will focus primarily upon that province. The marijuana cultivation industry in B.C. is thriving, as demonstrated by the fact that the province accounted for almost 40 percent of all growing operations found by law enforcement officials

Source: American Review of Canadian Studies, Summer 2008; 38(2): CBCA Reference p. 207.

in Canada in 2003, the last year for which full data are available (CCJS 2004). During that year, the province also had the highest rate of cultivation "incidents" in Canada, at 79 per 100,000 people. What this means is that 79 marijuana cultivation operations were found for every 100,000 people in the province. This is nearly triple the national rate of 27 per 100,000 people, and 33 times higher than second-place New Brunswick, at 46. More marijuana cultivation facilities were uncovered by Canadian law enforcement officials in B.C. (3274) than in all of the other provinces combined (2564), except Quebec (2939), in 2003 (CCJS 2004). In their study of the B.C. marijuana growing industry over the 1997–2003 period, Darryl Plecas, Aili Malm, and Bryan Kinney identified over 25,000 cultivation operations uncovered by police officers in the province (Plecas, Malm, and Kinney 2005). In terms of the monetary value of marijuana, it is estimated that the annual wholesale value of the provincial industry is approximately C$6 billion, or what is equivalent to about 5 percent of the annual provincial gross domestic product. To provide some perspective, the B.C. marijuana industry is relatively equal in dollar value to the province's public sector, and bigger than the legal exports of sawmill products (C$4.6 billion) and oil and gas (C$2.5 billion). In terms of employment, it is estimated that the provincial marijuana industry employs roughly 150,000 people (Mulgrew 2006, 109).

The size of the B.C. marijuana industry is of concern to U.S. law officials, because upwards of 90 percent of the crop is exported to the American market (Hamilton et al. 2004, 36). More disconcerting to American law enforcement is that there has been a "sharp rise" in the smuggling of marijuana into the United States from Canada and that this has resulted in a near tripling in both the *number* of seizures and the *volume* of marijuana seized over the 2001–2004 period, the last period for which data are available (U.S. Department of Justice 2006). The 2006 International Narcotics

Control Strategy Report (INCSR) prepared by the U.S. Department of State indicated that marijuana cultivation is a "thriving industry in Canada" and that "large scale cross-border trafficking" is "a serious concern" of the American government (U.S. Department of State 2006).

It is not just the volume of marijuana being smuggled from Canada to the United States that is of concern to Americans; it is also the potency of the marijuana. Of particular interest is the marijuana cultivated in British Columbia: the so-called B.C. Bud. The U.S. Drug Enforcement Agency assessed B.C. Bud for its tetrahydrocannabinol (THC) content—the psychoactive drug in marijuana—and found that its THC content was 25 percent. In comparison, the average THC content is 7 percent for marijuana consumed in the United States today and only 2 percent for marijuana smoked in the 1970s (Hamilton et al. 2004, 36). The result of this is that, as Ian Mulgrew has noted, British Columbia "is a marijuana Mecca" and B.C. Bud is "a globally recognized brand name" that stands "in a pantheon of pot beside such legends as Acapulco Gold or California Sinsemilla" and "is sought by cannabis cognoscenti and commands the highest price" (Mulgrew 2006, 21). The INCSR, in 2006, listed Canada as "a principal drug concern" due to the "continuing large-scale production of high-potency, indoor grown marijuana for export to the United States" (U.S. Department of State 2006). Moreover John Walters, Director of the White House Office of National Drug Control Policy (the U.S. drug czar), critically remarked that "Canada is exporting to [the United States] the crack of marijuana" (Hamilton et al. 2004, 36).

While the increasing volume of marijuana being smuggled into the United States from Canada and the high potency of the drug are of importance to Americans, the source of gravest concern is what is perceived by Americans to be lax Canadian laws regarding marijuana possession and cultivation. The reasoning goes that if Canada adopted more stern measures and penalties concerning marijuana, the flow to the United States would be abated somewhat. The first area in which Canada is seen as being out of step with the United States is in penalties for marijuana possession. This was demonstrated in the 2003–2006 period, wherein the Chrétien and Martin governments in Canada proposed, wrote, and introduced legislation to decriminalize possession of marijuana of 15 grams or less. The American response to this was immediate and forceful. The U.S. drug czar, John Walters, pledged to "respond to the threat" that this posed to the United States (Klein 2003, 12). One of the means proposed to deal with the threat was the "re-criminalizing" of marijuana possession at the American border. Christopher Sands has noted that some members of Congress and the media in the United States "advanced the notion that such possession could be 're-criminalized' by U.S. border officials if it appeared on the criminal record of a Canadian requesting entry into the United States, even as a misdemeanor" (Sands 2006, 130). The American concerns over decriminalization of marijuana were allayed with the election, in January 2006, of the Conservative government led by Stephen Harper. The Harper government had campaigned on a promise to end the decriminalization initiative of the Martin government and, therefore, did not reintroduce the marijuana legislation after it died in committee at the end of the 38th Parliament.

While the decriminalization issue has been resolved for the duration of the present Conservative government, the laxity of Canadian laws pertaining to the production of marijuana is still troubling to many Americans. Of the 25,000 growing operations identified by B.C. law enforcement between 1997 and 2003 mentioned previously, less than 17,000 were investigated and less than one-half of those were prosecuted (Plecas, Malm, and Kinney 2005). Plecas, Malm, and Kinney found that charges were entered in less than one-half of all raids conducted on marijuana operations in British Columbia over the last seven years.

Moreover, they noted that only about one in ten of those convicted were sentenced to a jail term, with the average sentence being five months (Plecas, Malm, and Kinney 2005, 50). The authors compared the sentences handed out in B.C. with what would have happened had these cases come to trial in Washington State, just south of the border. Under sentencing guidelines found in Washington State, one-half of the convictions would have resulted in mandatory jail sentences of at least five years and over two-thirds of those convicted would have served some time in prison (Plecas, Malm, and Kinney 2005, 56). In comparison, the sentences received in Canada appear lenient. Mulgrew has noted that marijuana cultivators in Canada view judicial punishments not as a deterrent but rather as "an operating cost" (Mulgrew 2006, 5). Marijuana cultivation "has been a relatively minimum-risk activity due to low sentences meted out by Canadian courts," as noted in the 2006 INCSR. The report further "encourage[d] Canada to take steps to improve its ability to expedite investigations and prosecutions" and to "strengthen judicial deterrents" (U.S. Department of State 2006).

The result of all this is that Canada is regarded as being soft on marijuana use and cultivation. Evidence of this is provided by Canada being consistently mentioned in the annual Presidential Determination on Major Drug Transit or Major Illicit Drug Producing Countries. While Canada has thus far escaped being placed on the Majors List (i.e., those states listed as major drug transit or producing countries), it is the only state not on the list to have been mentioned in the reports over the last five years. For 2007, Canada and North Korea are the only two states not on the list but noted in the Presidential Determination (U.S. Office of the President 2006).

The Canadian and American governments cooperate on a wide range of policy issues, and the bilateral relationship is mostly without major controversy or difficulty. The differences in the Canadian and American approaches to marijuana are regarded primarily as an irritant in the relationship, but one of a number of policy areas on which Canada and the United States differ. There are, however, two ways in which the marijuana irritant could become the marijuana *problem* in the bilateral relationship. The first would be if the marijuana irritant were to become more directly linked with homeland security in the United States. Marijuana is still largely regarded as a law enforcement issue, not a national security problem. It is perceived more as a state-level concern than a national policy issue. This may change, however. For instance, if it is determined that groups in Canada on the U.S. list of foreign terrorist organizations maintained by the State Department are using marijuana to generate revenue for their operations, including purchasing weaponry and planning attacks in the U.S., this could result in the marijuana issue being redefined as part of the war on terror and, therefore, a homeland security problem. A second, and related, manner in which the marijuana irritant could become more problematic for Canada is if the Bush administration, or the U.S. Congress, began to link more closely the export to the U.S. of marijuana from Canada with cocaine and other drugs from Mexico in the current American war on drugs. Thus far, Canadian officials have been relatively successful in persuading American government officials of the differences in the scale and nature of the drug threats emanating from Canada and from Mexico. The result of this has been to differentiate the northern border with Canada from the southern border with Mexico (Sokolsky and Legassé 2006).

If either of the two scenarios outlined above were to occur, and the marijuana irritant were to become the marijuana problem, this would have significant implications for Canada. Two main lines of potential American response may be outlined briefly. The first would entail a further intensification and militarization of the Canada–U.S. border, or movement toward what Peter Andreas has referred to as a "Mexicanization of the Canadian border" (Andreas 2005). This, in turn, would cause a significant reduction in and delay of human and commercial cross-border

traffic, thereby negatively impacting the bilateral commercial relationship for both countries. A second manner in which the United States might respond should marijuana become a problem in the Canada–U.S. relationship is to increase pressure on Canada to more closely align Canadian marijuana policy with that of the United States.

CRITICAL THINKING QUESTIONS

1. What is your attitude toward marijuana? Should smoking it be considered a criminal activity? Do you think smoking marijuana constitutes deviant behaviour? Why or why not?

2. Why do you think alcohol is legal in both Canada and the United States and marijuana is not? Do you think the two substances are that much different?

3. What do you think would happen if marijuana was made legal in Canada? Would the United States object? Why do Americans take such a hard line on marijuana and drugs in general?

REFERENCES

Andreas, Peter. 2005. The Mexicanization of the US–Canada border: Asymmetric interdependence in a changing security context. *International Journal*, 60: 449–62.

Canadian Centre for Justice Statistics. 2004. Canadian crime statistics 2003. Available: **http://statscan.ca/english/freepub/85-205XIE/0000385-205-XIE.pdf**. Accessed April 17, 2007.

Eagles, Munroe. 2006. Canadian-American relations in a turbulent era. *PS: Political Science and Politics*, 39: 821–24.

Hamilton, Anita, Ben Bergman, Laura Blue, Chris Daniels, Deborah Jones, and Elaine Shannon. 2004. This Bud's for the U.S. *Time*, 164: 36–7.

Klein, Naomi. 2003. Canada: Hippie nation? *The Nation* (July 21/28): 12.

Mulgrew, Ian. 2006. *Bud Inc.: Inside Canada's marijuana industry.* Toronto: Vintage.

Pleces, Darryl, Aili Malm, and Bryan Kinney. 2005. Marihuana growing operations in British Columbia revisited, 1997–2003. Available: **http://www.ucfv.ca/pages/Special/Marihuana_Grow_Ops_in_BC_Study.pdf**. Accessed April 17, 2007.

Sexuality
CLASSIC
CONTEMPORARY
CROSS-CULTURAL

24

Understanding Sexual Orientation

ALFRED C. KINSEY, WARDELL B. POMEROY, AND CLYDE E. MARTIN

In 1948, Alfred Kinsey and his colleagues published the first modern study of sexuality in the United States—and raised plenty of eyebrows. For the first time, people began talking openly about sex, questioning many common stereotypes. Here Kinsey reports his finding that sexual orientation is not a matter of clear-cut differences between heterosexuals and homosexuals, but is better described as a continuum by which most people combine elements of both.

THE HETEROSEXUAL–HOMOSEXUAL BALANCE

Concerning patterns of sexual behavior, a great deal of the thinking done by scientists and laymen alike stems from the assumption that there are persons who are "heterosexual" and persons who are "homosexual," that these two types represent antitheses in the sexual world, and that there is only an insignificant class of "bisexuals" who occupy an intermediate position between the other groups. It is implied that every individual is innately—inherently—either heterosexual or homosexual. It is further implied that from the time of birth one is fated to be one thing or the other, and that there is

Source: From *Sexual Behavior in the Human Male* by Alfred C. Kinsey, Wardell B. Pomeroy, and Clyde E. Martin. (Philadelphia: W. B. Saunders Company, 1948), pp. 636–39. Reprinted by permission of The Kinsey Institute.

little chance for one to change his pattern in the course of a lifetime.

It is quite generally believed that one's preference for a sexual partner of one or the other sex is correlated with various physical and mental qualities, and with the total personality which makes a homosexual male or female physically, psychically, and perhaps spiritually distinct from a heterosexual individual. It is generally thought that these qualities make a homosexual person obvious and recognizable to anyone who has a sufficient understanding of such matters. Even psychiatrists discuss "the homosexual personality" and many of them believe that preferences for sexual partners of a particular sex are merely secondary manifestations of something that lies much deeper in the totality of that intangible which they call the personality.

It is commonly believed, for instance, that homosexual males are rarely robust physically, are uncoordinated or delicate in their movements, or perhaps graceful enough but not strong and vigorous in their physical expression. Fine skins, high-pitched voices, obvious hand movements, a feminine carriage of the hips, and peculiarities of walking gaits are supposed accompaniments of a preference for a male as a sexual partner. It is commonly believed that the homosexual male is artistically sensitive, emotionally unbalanced, temperamental to the point of being unpredictable, difficult to get along with, and undependable in meeting specific obligations. In physical characters there have been attempts to show that the homosexual male has a considerable crop of hair and less often becomes bald, has teeth which are more like those of the female, a broader pelvis, larger genitalia, and a tendency toward being fat, and that he lacks a linea alba. The homosexual male is supposed to be less interested in athletics, more often interested in music and the arts, more often engaged in such occupations as bookkeeping, dress design, window display, hairdressing, acting, radio work, nursing, religious service, and social work. The converse to all of these is supposed to represent the typical heterosexual male. Many a clinician attaches considerable weight to these things in diagnosing the basic heterosexuality or homosexuality of his patients. The characterizations are so distinct that they seem to leave little room for doubt that homosexual and heterosexual represent two very distinct types of males. . . .

It should be pointed out that scientific judgments on this point have been based on little more than the same sorts of impressions which the general public has had concerning homosexual persons. But before any sufficient study can be made of such possible correlations between patterns of sexual behavior and other qualities in the individual, it is necessary to understand the incidences and frequencies of the homosexual in the population as a whole, and the relation of the homosexual activity to the rest of the sexual pattern in each individual's history.

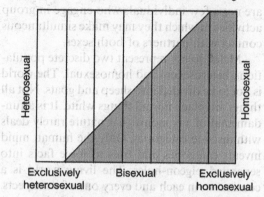

Figure 24.1 Heterosexual–homosexual rating scale.

The histories which have been available in the present study make it apparent that the heterosexuality or homosexuality of many individuals is not an all-or-none proposition. It is true that there are persons in the population whose histories are exclusively heterosexual, both in regard to their overt experience and in regard to their psychic reactions. And there are individuals in the population whose histories are exclusively homosexual, both in experience and in psychic reactions. But the record also shows that there is a considerable portion of the population whose members have combined, within their individual histories, both homosexual and heterosexual experience and/or psychic responses. There are some whose heterosexual experiences predominate, there are some whose homosexual experiences predominate, there are some who have had quite equal amounts of both types of experience (see Figure 24.1).

Some of the males who are involved in one type of relation at one period in their lives may have only the other type of relation at some later period. There may be considerable fluctuation of patterns from time to time. Some males may be involved in both heterosexual and homosexual activities within the same period of time. For instance, there are some who engage in both heterosexual and homosexual activities in the same year, or in the same month or week, or even in the same day. There are not a few individuals who engage in group activities in which they may make simultaneous contact with partners of both sexes.

Males do not represent two discrete populations, heterosexual and homosexual. The world is not to be divided into sheep and goats. Not all things are black nor all things white. It is a fundamental of taxonomy that nature rarely deals with discrete categories. Only the human mind invents categories and tries to force facts into separated pigeon-holes. The living world is a continuum in each and every one of its aspects. The sooner we learn this concerning human sexual behavior the sooner we shall reach a sound understanding of the realities of sex.

CRITICAL THINKING QUESTIONS

1. Why do you think people have long thought of heterosexuality and homosexuality as opposite and mutually exclusive (that is, only in terms of "exclusively heterosexual" or "exclusively homosexual," as in Figure 24.1)?

2. Kinsey suggests that anyone's sexual orientation may well change over time. Do you agree? Why or why not?

3. Why do people tend to label someone with any degree of homosexual experience as a "homosexual"? (After all, we don't do the same in the case of any heterosexual experience.)

25

"I'll Scratch Your Back if You'll Scratch Mine": The Role of Reciprocity, Power and Autonomy in the Strip Club

JACQUELINE LEWIS

This study is an example of how qualitative methods, in this case face-to-face personal interviews, are employed to gather sociological data. This research depicts how work in strip clubs is organized along gender and occupational lines (bartender, server, etc). It also compares stripping to other service jobs and illustrates how sex work is not all that different from other kinds of work in that it is stratified and governed by both competition and cooperation.

The Canadian economy has increasingly become more service-based (Little, 1999), resulting in changing labour relations (Sallaz, 2002). In an effort to reduce labour costs, the service industry relies on the "tipping system." Although this emphasis results in a loss of worker commitment to the business (Sallaz, 2002), it motivates the worker to work hard to please customers and push the products that result in the accrual of earnings/tips and business revenue. In addition to reducing labour costs, one of the main benefits of the tipping system for the business owner is "that it keeps the . . . staff firmly at the front line in the battle to turn a profit" (Citron, 1989: 9). Workers in the service sector, however, "must be granted a much wider degree of autonomy to customize their service offerings" (Sallaz, 2002: 406). This organizational feature provides

workers with further incentive and freedom "to pursue their own interests at the expense of the company" (Paules, 1991: 55).

Although strip clubs are part of the service industry, they differ in terms of the way staff members earn their money. In most strip clubs in Southern Ontario, the majority of workers do not receive a salary from the club and some actually pay a fee to work there. As a result, they tend to operate as private entrepreneurs. These structural elements of the strip club create a work environment that inspires little in the way of worker commitment. Instead, workers focus on themselves, providing client services and engaging in co-operative activities that increase earnings and/or provide some sort of resource (e.g., support, security, friendship). The workplace structure also encourages the use of resistance strategies as a way to deal with the lack of security tied to jobs in the industry (Paules, 1991).

Source: The Canadian Journal of Sociology and Anthropology, August 2006: 43(3), 297–298, 300–305, 309–310.

Various staff members play an integral role in the daily operations of the strip club: dancers, waitresses, shooter girls, bartenders, disc jockeys (DJs), doorpersons/bouncers and hostesses. Although strip clubs, like other sectors of the service industry, are highly gendered and sexualized establishments (Paules, 1991), there is a complex interplay of power dynamics among workers as each strives to enhance her/his autonomy, security and income. The result is a variety of mutually interdependent relationships between the various staff members.

The focus of this article is the social organization of the strip club. It examines the interplay of power relations in the club and how workers in this environment are able to enhance autonomy and use the resources at their disposal to decrease the inherent uncertainties of their job. Interconnections between and co-operative activities engaged in by workers as a means to deal with exploitive labour practices, as well as to create a socially and/or economically supportive work environment, are also explored.

METHODOLOGY

The findings reported in this paper are based on a study that explored the work and careers of exotic dancers. There were two primary means of data collection: participant observation and interviewing. Field observations were conducted at ten strip clubs in four cities in southern Ontario.

In-depth interviews were conducted with thirty female exotic dancers and eight strip club staff members (disc jockeys, waitresses, shooter girls, bartenders, hostesses and doormen). The positions held by all except one of the staff members were gender-specific (i.e., women were waitresses, shooter girls and hostesses, while men were bartenders, doormen and disc jockeys). The exception was a woman who was working as a bartender at the time of her interview.

Although a semi-structured interview guide was used for each interview, interviews were conducted in an informal manner in order to allow participants to freely express themselves and [permit] the exploration of new lines of questioning that arose during the interview. When new questions appeared relevant to future interviews, they were incorporated into the interview guide. Interview questions were designed to explore: entry into the strip club work environment; work history and future plans; the nature of the work and work environment, including relationships with customers and co-workers; strategies used to maintain personal power and manage the work situation; and significant other and reference group relationships.

THE SOCIAL ORGANIZATION OF THE STRIP CLUB

Strip clubs are highly gendered establishments where jobs tend to be gender-stratified and women outnumber men. In them, women predominantly do "the grunt work" or stereotypical "women's work." They fill the roles of dancer, waitress and shooter girl, all of which require extended time on the floor of the strip club, interacting directly with customers (men) and servicing customers' needs. In contrast, men fill the roles of manager, bartender, doorman/bouncer and disc jockey (see Price, 2000), which require smaller degrees of direct customer service.

Gender and managerial power, however, are not the only forms of power relevant to the social organization of the strip club. Economic power also plays a role. It is determined by opportunities to earn money and, ultimately, by money earned. Dancers' economic power in the strip clubs is tied to their direct or indirect involvement with the way the club and most of its workers earn money. In the strip club, dancing serves as "the pivot around which much of the social and economic life . . . revolves" (Prus and Irini, 1980: 4). In the interviews we conducted, it was obvious that many of the staff recognized the economic power of dancers and the importance of their relationships with dancers to their own incomes.

You've got to treat these girls with respect because without them you wouldn't have a job. That's why these customers are coming here, to see naked women, not to drink, because you can drink anywhere. (Doorman)

In the following section, the relationships between dancers, disc jockeys, waitresses and doormen are used to explore the complex interplay between the various forms of power found in the strip club, including the modes of resistance and adaptation available to strip club workers as a result of the clubs' social organization. The focus is on the individual and collective adaptations employed by strip club workers to deal with their work environment.

DISC JOCKEYS AND DANCERS

The power associated with the job of disc jockey is tied to it being a male-dominated position that carries some managerial power in a gendered industry. Disc jockeys are responsible for "keeping an eye on the girls [the dancers]," part of which involves determining whose turn it is to do a stage show and how long shows will last. Although all dancers are supposed to appear on stage in a specified order and dance for three songs, disc jockeys have the power to make alterations if they so desire. They also are able to choose who will do special performances, such as "shower shows."

For a $75 club fee bachelors can get a shower show. . . . They bring the bachelor right onstage . . . and we [the disc jockeys] get one of the girls to join the bachelor in the shower. . . . The DJ chooses the dancer. Usually we go from the top of the list down, but if there is a girl I'm mad at then she's going to do showers all night. They can't refuse. (Disc jockey)

The disc jockey's power is also directly related to the nature of the service they provide dancers during stage shows. There are two elements involved: stage show maintenance and security assistance. When dancers are on stage, disc jockeys can put on light shows and "talk up the girls" to "try to get guys interested in the show." Such promotional activities increase the potential for tipping during and table dance requests at the end of a stage show.

The DJ can get the crowd going for you and get them to pay attention. And you get more tips if the crowd's happy and they're excited. (Dancer)

In addition, disc jockeys assist dancers with their stage shows by paying attention to "how the show is going" and attending to their needs.

Sometimes you are up there and it isn't going well. . . . You look at the DJ and make little signals. . . . The DJs are pretty cool about that, they'll shorten your songs. (Dancer)

Due to their close proximity to the stage, disc jockeys are also the dancers' closest source of security and protection during stage performances. Disc jockeys usually watch dancers during their shows to make sure that men do not touch them when they are offering tips.[1] If the disc jockey observes any type of aggressive or inappropriate movement on a man's part he lets the customer know he is in violation of club rules and directs him how to behave.

When the girls are onstage I keep an eye on the guys tipping them. They are supposed to lie still and are not allowed to touch them [the dancers]. If they start to move I remind them "Don't touch." I do this to stop them, but also to alert the dancer that something is up. (Disc jockey)

Dancers know how important it is to be able to rely on the disc jockey during their performances, whether it is because they want the audience "pumped up," want relief from "a bad set" or are in a vulnerable position while accepting tips. Having a good working relationship with a disc jockey is one way to ensure that he stays alert. Both dancers and disc jockeys report feeling that tipping helps maintain good work relations and serves as an incentive or reward for disc jockeys to provide quality services to dancers.

Most of the dancers tip. A lot will give me two or three bucks . . . and some of them don't. And the ones that usually don't we don't do nothing for. (Disc jockey)

If you don't tip them [disc jockeys] and you're not nice to them, they don't do as much for you on stage. Whether it's your light shows, or just saying stuff about you, or promoting tips. (Dancer)

In addition, both dancers and disc jockeys acknowledge that due to their role in the club, disc jockeys "have the power" to impact the quality of dancers' work lives. As one disc jockey noted:

If we [disc jockeys and dancers] don't have a good relationship we basically won't be doing anything for them . . . we won't play their music . . . or we screw something up on purpose, which we do a lot. If they're not nice to us then basically we're not gonna be nice to them . . . and they'll find it a little rougher.

Knowledge of this provides dancers with a further incentive to "kiss up" to disc jockeys and "tip them extra" in order to "stay in their good books." During interviews dancers talked about how the disc jockey is someone who has the ability to "make their job easier or tougher," someone who "can either be your best friend or your worst enemy" and therefore "someone you want on your side."

Although the disc jockey appears to have a lot of power vis-à-vis the dancers, it is mostly in the form of managerial power. Their economic power is restricted by their limited opportunities to earn money. They are typically not paid a wage by clubs and instead rely on income generated by a club-mandated "DJ fee" that all dancers are required to pay the club daily if they want to work. In the clubs we studied, the amount that disc jockeys received from the DJ fee ranged from five to ten dollars per dancer. Their only other real income-generating opportunities involve "encouraging" dancers to tip them for their services. In either case, the disc jockeys' earnings come primarily from dancers.

Since it is the dancers who provide the services that customers come to the club for, and are typically the major recipients of customer money, they are in an advantageous economic position. Their economic power helps balance out some of the power differential between them and the disc jockeys. Dancers use their economic power when they tip the disc jockey beyond the club-mandated fee and disc jockeys use their power to help dancers "drum up tips." Tips between workers are used to maintain good working relations and ensure service provision. When dancers use tips to "bribe" disc jockeys so they can violate club policies (e.g., leave their shift early; not go on stage during a particular shift), it provides dancers with a mechanism to ensure autonomy in the work place.

I mean you kiss up to the DJ so that you can get out of going on stage, or you bribe them. "Here's twenty bucks, I don't want to go on stage"-type thing. (Dancer)

CONCLUSION

The structural elements of the strip club create a work environment that motivates workers to engage in income-generating activities. Work structures that use the tipping system encourage workers to "push" business products that increase business revenues, but they do so at a cost. The workers in such an environment are less likely to feel a sense of loyalty, commitment, or lasting ties to their workplace than workers who receive a liveable wage or salary from an employer (see Paules, 1991; Sallaz, 2002).

The informal economic system that was found to develop among strip club staff works as a feedback loop, feeding back into and reinforcing itself. Staff members learn that it is easier to do one's job with a supporting cast (Prus and Sharpe, 1977). Those who work co-operatively are rewarded both socially (in terms of social support, future opportunities to earn money and to violate club polices unnoticed) and economically (in terms of financial gain). In addition, it is likely that, in working together, the staff may experience a greater sense of autonomy, personal empowerment and enhanced economic security in an ever more exploitive work environment.

CRITICAL THINKING QUESTIONS

1. How are the tasks in a strip club divided according to gender? And along what lines is a strip club stratified? Who has economic power and why?

2. How does the reciprocal relationship between disc jockeys and strippers play out? How are disc jockeys paid and how does this influence their relationship with strippers?

3. Many service workers directly interact with the public. In terms of behaviour and expectations, what makes service-sector jobs different from industrial ones? What are the similarities between stripping and other service jobs? Are there pronounced differences in terms of organization between a restaurant

and a strip club? Do you think that putting them both in the category of service work amounts to a fair comparison?

NOTES

1. In southern Ontario, when men offer tips to dancers performing on stage, they lie on the stage and put their "tip" between their teeth or lips. The dancer then kneels on the stage and slowly crawls over top of the customer (without touching him), until her face is above his genital area and her genital area is above his face. As she slowly crawls back she removes the money with her teeth, lips, hand, or breasts.

REFERENCES

Citron, Z. 1989. "Waiting for nodough: The case against tipping." *The New Republic* (January 2): 9–10.

Little, D. 1999. "Employment and remuneration in the service industries since 1984." Ottawa: Statistics Canada. Available at: **http://www.statcan.ca/bsolc/english/bsolc?catno'63F0002X1999024**.

Paules, G. F. 1991. *Dishing it out: Power and resistance among waitresses in a New Jersey restaurant.* Philadelphia: Temple University Press.

Prus, R. C. and S. Irini. 1980. *Hookers, rounders, and desk clerks: The social organization of the hotel community.* Toronto: Gage Publishing Limited.

Prus, R. C. and C. R. D. Sharpe. 1977. *Road hustler: The career contingencies of professional card and dice hustlers.* Toronto: Lexington Books.

Sallaz, J. J. 2002. "House rules: Autonomy and interests among service workers in the contemporary casino service industry." *Work and Occupation*, 29(4): 394–427.

26

Homosexual Behavior in Cross-Cultural Perspective

J. M. CARRIER[*]

Although sexuality is a biological process, the meaning of sexuality is culturally variable. Carrier shows that attitudes toward homosexuality are far from uniform around the world. Some societies are quite accommodating about sexual practices that other societies punish harshly.

The available cross-cultural data clearly show that the ways in which individuals organize their sexual behavior vary considerably between societies (Westermarck, 1908; Ford & Beach, 1951; Broude & Greene, 1976). Although biological and psychological factors help explain variations of sexual behavior between individuals within a given society, intercultural variations in patterns of human sexual behavior are mainly related to social and cultural differences occurring between societies around the world. The purpose of this chapter is to consider what kinds of variations in homosexual behavior occur between societies, and to determine which

sociocultural factors appear to account for the variance of the behavior cross-culturally.[1]

THE CROSS-CULTURAL DATA

Data available on homosexual behavior in most of the world's societies, past or present, are meager. Much is known about the dominant middle-class white populations of the United States, England, and northern European countries where most scientific research on human sexual behavior has been done, but very little is known about homosexual behavior in the rest of the world. The lack of knowledge stems from the irrational fear and prejudice surrounding the study of human sexual behavior and from the difficulties associated with the collection of information on a topic that is so personal and highly regulated in most societies.

Most of the cross-cultural information on sexual behavior has been gathered by Western

*The author is particularly indebted to Evelyn Hooker for her invaluable and criticism; and to the Gender Identity Research Group at UCLA for an early critique of the ideas presented in this paper.

anthropologists. The quality of the information collected and published, however, varies considerably. Based on a survey of the literature, Marshall and Suggs (1971) report that: "Sexual behavior is occasionally touched upon in anthropological publications but is seldom the topic of either articles or monographs by anthropologists." Broude and Greene (1976), after coding the sexual attitudes and practices in 186 societies using the Human Relations Area Files, note:[2]

. . . information of any sort on sexual habits and beliefs is hard to come by . . . when data do exist concerning sexual attitudes and practices, they are often sketchy and vague; what is more, such information is usually suspect in terms of its reliability, either because of distortions on the part of the subjects or because of biases introduced by the ethnographer. . . .

Cross-cultural data on homosexual behavior is further complicated by the prejudice of many observers who consider the behavior unnatural, dysfunctional, or associated with mental illness, and by the fact that in many of the societies studied the behavior is stigmatized and thus not usually carried out openly. Under these circumstances, the behavior is not easily talked about. At the turn of the twentieth century such adjectives as disgusting, vile, and detestable were still being used to describe homosexual behavior; and even in the mid-1930s some anthropologists continued to view the behavior as unnatural. In discussing sodomy with some of his New Guinea informants, Williams (1936), for example, asked them if they "had ever been subjected to an unnatural practice." With the acceptance of the view in the mid-1930s that homosexual behavior should be classified as a mental illness (or at best dysfunctional), many anthropologists replaced "unnatural" with the medical model. This model still finds adherents among researchers at present, especially those in the branch of anthropology referred to as psychological anthropology.

Because of the prejudice with which many researchers and observers approached the subject, statements about the reported absence of homosexual behavior, or the limited extent of the behavior where reported, should be viewed with some skepticism. Mead (1961) suggests that statements of this kind "can only be accepted with the greatest caution and with very careful analysis of the personality and training of the investigator." She further notes that "denials of a practice cannot be regarded as meaningful if that practice is verbally recognized among a given people, even though a strong taboo exists against it."

This chapter will mainly utilize the published research findings of empirical studies which have considered homosexual behavior in some detail. It will examine homosexual behavior in preliterate, peasant, and complex modern societies in all the major geographical regions of the world.[3] Where necessary, these findings will be supplemented with information found in accounts given by travelers, missionaries, and novelists.

SOCIOCULTURAL FACTORS

A number of sociocultural factors help explain variations of homosexual behavior between societies. Two of the most important are cultural attitudes and proscriptions related to cross-gender behavior, and availability of sexual partners.[4] The latter is in turn related to such variables as segregation of sexes prior to marriage, expectations with respect to virginity, age at marriage, and available economic resources and/or distribution of income.

Cross-Gender and Homosexual Behavior

Different expectations for male persons as opposed to female persons are culturally elaborated from birth onward in every known society. Although behavioral boundaries between the sexes may vary culturally, male persons are clearly differentiated from female persons; and progeny is assured by normative societal rules which correlate male and female gender roles with sexual behavior, marriage, and the family. There is a general expectation in every society that a majority of adult men and women will cohabit and produce the next generation. Social pressure is thus applied in the direction of marriage. The general rule is that one should not remain single.

The cross-cultural data on human sexual behavior suggest that a significant relationship exists between much of the homosexual behavior reported cross culturally and the continuing need of societies to deal with cross-gender behavior. Feminine male behavior, and the set of anxieties associated with its occurrence in the male part of the population, appears to have brought about more elaborate cultural responses temporally and spatially than has masculine female behavior. There are no doubt many reasons why this is so, but it appears to be related in general to the higher status accorded men than women in most societies; and, in particular, to the defense role that men have historically played in protecting women and children from outsiders.

Societies in which homosexual behavior can be linked to cultural responses to cross-gender behavior may be categorized according to the type of response made. Three major cultural types have been identified: those societies which make a basic accommodation to cross-gender behavior, those societies which outlaw the behavior as scandalous and/or criminal, and those societies which neither make an accommodation to such behavior nor outlaw it but instead have a cultural formulation which tries to ensure that cross-gender behavior does not occur.

Accommodating Societies

Societies making an accommodation to cross-gender behavior in one form or another have been reported in many different parts of the world. Munroe et al. (1969), for example, put together a list of societies having what they call "institutionalized male transvestism . . . the permanent adoption by males of aspects of female dress and/or behavior in accordance with customary expectations within a given society." Their list includes Indian societies in North and South America, island societies in Polynesia and Southeast Asia, and preliterate and peasant societies in mainland Asia and Africa. Although reported for both sexes, male cross-gender behavior appears in the literature more often than female.

A folk belief exists in some of these societies that in every generation a certain number of individuals will play the gender role of the opposite sex, usually beginning at or prior to puberty and often identified at a very early age. The Mohave Indians of the American Southwest, for example, used to hold the following belief—typical of many Indian societies in North America—about cross-gender behavior of both sexes:

Ever since the world began at the magic mountain . . . it was said that there would be transvestites. In the beginning, if they were to become transvestites, the process started during their intrauterine life. When they grew up they were given toys according to their sex. They did not like these toys however. (Devereux, 1937)

In southern Mexico one group of Zapotec Indians believes that "effeminate males" are born, not made: "Typical comments include, But what can we do; he was born that way; he is like God made him. A related belief also exists that . . . it is a thing of the blood" (Royce, 1973). In Tahiti, the belief exists that there is at least one cross-gender behaving male, called a *māhū* in all villages: "When one dies then another substitutes . . . God arranges it like this. It isn't allowed (that there should be) two *māhū* in one place" (Levy, 1973).

Cross-gender behavior is accepted in other societies because it is believed that some supernatural event makes people that way prior to birth, or that the behavior is acquired through some mystical force or dream after birth. In India, for example, the following belief exists about the *Hijadās*, cross-gender behaving males thought to be impotent at birth who later have their genitals removed:

When we ask a *Hijadā* or an ordinary man in Gujarat "Why does a man become a *Hijadā*?" the usual reply is "One does not become a *Hijadā* by one's own will; it is only by the command of the *mātā* that one becomes a *Hijadā*." The same idea is found in a myth about the origin of the *Hijadās*. It is said that one receives the *mātā's* command either in dreams or when one sits in meditation before her image. (Shah, 1961)

Among the Chukchee of northeastern Asia, a role reversal was accepted because of an unusual dream or vision:

Transformation takes place by the command of the *ka'let* (spirits) usually at the critical age of early youth when shamanistic inspiration first manifests itself. (Bogores, 1904)

Among the Lango in Africa:

A number of Lango men dress as women, simulate menstruation, and become one of the wives of other males. They are believed to be impotent and to have been afflicted by some supernatural agency. (Ford & Beach, 1951)

Although not necessarily accepted gladly, the various folk beliefs make the behavior acceptable, and a certain number of cross-gender behaving individuals are to be expected in every generation. Expectations about the extent to which the opposite gender role is to be played, however, appear to have changed over time with acculturation. Affected individuals in the past often were required to make a public ritualized change of gender and cross-dress and behave in accordance with their new identity. Among the Mohave, for example, there was an initiation ceremony and it was important for the initiate "to duplicate the behavior pattern of his adopted sex and make 'normal' individuals of his anatomic sex feel toward him as though he truly belonged to his adopted sex" (Devereux, 1937). The *māhū* in Tahiti were described in the latter part of the eighteenth century as follows:

These men are in some respects like the Eunichs [*sic*] in India but are not castrated. They never cohabit with women but live as they do. They pick their beard out and dress as women, dance and sing with them and are as effeminate in their voice. (Morrison, 1935)

Affected individuals in most societies at present are allowed a choice as to the extent they want to play the role; e.g., how far they want to identify with the opposite sex, whether they want to cross-dress or not, etc. Levy (1973) notes, for example, that in Tahiti: "Being a *māhū* does not now usually entail actually dressing as a woman." The North American Indian societies who used to have initiation ceremonies discontinued them long ago; and, although expectations about cross-gender behaving individuals persist, only remnants of the original belief system are remembered currently. They continue, however, to be tolerant and "there apparently is no body of role behavior aimed at humiliating boys who are feminine or men who prefer men sexually" (Stoller, 1976).

The link between cross-gender behavior and homosexual behavior is the belief that there should be concordance between gender role and sexual object choice. When a male behaves like a female, he should be expected therefore to want a male sexual partner and to play the female sex role—that is, to play the insertee role in anal intercourse or fellatio. The same concordance should be expected when a female behaves like a male. As a result of beliefs about concordance, it is important to note that a society may not conceptualize the sexual behavior or its participants as "homosexual."

There is some evidence in support of this linking of gender role and homosexual behavior in societies making an accommodation and providing a social role for cross-gender behaving individuals. Kroeber (1940), for example, concluded from his investigations that: "In most of primitive northern Asia and North America, men of homosexual trends adopted women's dress, work, and status, and were accepted as nonphysiological but institutionalized women." Devereux's Mohave informants said that the males who changed their gender role to female had male husbands and that both anal intercourse and fellatio were practiced, with the participants playing the appropriate gender sex role. The informants noted the same concordance for females who behaved like males.

Unfortunately, the anthropological data do not always make clear whether cultural expectations in a given society were for concordance between gender role and erotic object; or, in terms of actual behavior, how many cross-gender behaving individuals chose same sex, opposite sex, or both sexes as erotic objects. In the paper I just quoted, Kroeber also concluded: "How far invert erotic practices accompanied the status is not always clear from the data, and it probably varied. At any rate, the North American attitude toward the berdache stresses not his erotic life but his social status; born a male, he became accepted as a woman socially."

Many anthropologists and other observers confounded their findings by assuming an equivalence between "transvestite" and "homosexual."[5] Thus, when an informant described cross-gender behavior, they may have concluded without foundation that a same-sex erotic object choice was part of the behavior being described, and that they were eliciting information on "homosexuals." Angelino and Shedd (1955) provide supporting evidence. They reviewed the literature on an often used anthropological concept, berdache, and concluded that the "term has been used in an exceedingly ambiguous way, being used as a synonym for homosexualism, hermaphroditism, transvestism, and effeminism." They also note that the meaning of berdache changed over time, going from kept boy/male prostitute, to individuals who played a passive role in sodomy, to males who played a passive sex role and cross-dressed.

In spite of the confusion between "transvestite" and "homosexual," the available data suggest that in many of the societies providing a social role for cross-gender behavior, the selection of sexual partners was based on the adopted gender role; and, though they might be subjected to ridicule, neither partner in the sexual relationship was penalized for the role played.

The *māhū* role in Tahiti provides a contemporary look at how one Polynesian society continues to provide a social role for cross-gender behavior. According to Levy (1973),

villagers in his area of study do not agree on the sexual behavior of the *māhū*—some "believe that *māhū* do not generally engage in homosexual intercourse." Information from both *māhū* and non-*māhū* informants, however, leads to the conclusion that probably a majority of the *māhū* prefer adolescent males with whom they perform "ote moa" (literally, "penis sucking"). The following are some aspects of the role and the community response to it:

It is said to be exclusive. Its essential defining characteristic is "doing woman's work," that is, a role reversal which is publicly demonstrated—either through clothes or through other public aspects of women's role playing. Most villagers approve of, and are pleased by, the role reversal. But homosexual behavior is a covert part of the role, and it is disapproved by many villagers. Men who have sexual relations with the *māhū* . . . do not consider themselves abnormal. Villagers who know of such activities may disapprove, but they do not label the partners as unmanly. The *māhū* is considered as a substitute woman for the partner. A new word, raerae, which reportedly originated in Papeete, is used by some to designate nontraditional types of homosexual behavior. (Levy, 1973)

It should also be noted that in Levy's village of study *māhū* were the only adult men reported to be engaging in homosexual intercourse.

Another contemporary example of a social role for cross-gender behavior is the *Hijadā* role provided cross-gender behaving males in northwestern India. Given slightly different names by different observers (*Hijarās, Hinjrās,* and *Hijirās*), these males appear to be playing the same role. There is general agreement on the fact that they cross-dress, beg alms, and collect dues at special ceremonies where they dance and sing as women. There is a considerable difference of opinion, however, as to whether they engage in homosexual intercourse or in any sexual activity for that matter. From the available data, it appears that they live mostly in towns in communes, with each commune having a definite jurisdiction of villages and towns "where its members can beg alms and collect dues" (Shah, 1961). They are also reported to live separately by themselves.

From the findings of Carstairs (1956) and Shah (1961), one can at least conclude that the *Hijadās* living alone are sexually active:

Carstairs is wrong in considering all the Hijadās as homosexual, but there seems to be some truth in his information about the homosexuality of the Deoli Hijadā (Note: Deoli is the village of Carstairs' study.) Faridi and Mehta also note that some Hijadās practice "sodomy." This, however, is not institutionalized homosexuality. (Shah, 1961)

The finding by Opler (1960) that "they cannot carry on sexual activities and do not marry" may apply to the majority of *Hijadās* living in communes. The question of what kind of sexual behavior the *Hijadās* practice, if any, cannot be answered definitively with the data available. That they are still a viable group in India is confirmed by a recent Associated Press release:

About 2000 eunuchs dressed in brightly colored saris and other female garb were converging on this northern town from all over India this weekend for a private convention of song, dance and prayer.

Local reaction to the gathering was mixed. "They're perverts," commented a local peanut vendor. "We should have nothing to do with them. They should be run out of town."

A New Delhi social worker . . . said they sometimes supplement their income as paid lovers of homosexuals. (Excerpts from AP, February 6, 1979)

Disapproving Societies

Societies in which cross-gender behavior produces strong emotional negative reactions in large segments of the population tend to have the following commonalities: (1) negative reactions produced by the behavior are essentially limited to the male part of the population and relate mainly to effeminate males; (2) cross-gender behavior is controlled by laws which prohibit cross-dressing, and by laws and public opinion which consider other attributes associated with the behavior as scandalous; (3) gender roles are sharply dichotomized; and (4) a general belief exists that anyone demonstrating cross-gender behavior is homosexual.

A number of complex modern and peasant societies in the Middle East, North Africa, southern Europe, and Central and South America have the commonalities listed. The author's research in Mexico (Carrier, 1976 and 1977) illustrates how homosexual behavior in these societies appears to be linked to social responses to cross-gender behavior. The comments that follow are limited to male homosexual behavior. Female homosexuality is known to exist in these societies, but too little is known about the behavior to be included in the discussion.

Mexican Homosexual Behavior. The Mexican mestizo culture places a high value on manliness. One of the salient features of the society is thus a sharp delimitation between the roles played by males and females. Role expectations in general are for the male to be dominant and independent and for the female to be submissive and dependent. The continued sharp boundary between male and female roles in Mexico appears to be due in part to a culturally defined hypermasculine ideal model of manliness, referred to under the label *machismo*. The ideal female role is generally believed to be the reciprocal of the macho (male) role.[6]

As a consequence of the high status given manliness, Mexican males from birth onward are expected to behave in as manly a way as possible. Peñalosa (1968) sums it up as follows: "Any signs of feminization are severely repressed in the boy." McGinn (1966) concludes: "The young Mexican boy may be severely scolded for engaging in feminine activities, such as playing with dolls or jacks. Parents verbally and physically punish feminine traits in their male children." The importance of manly behavior continues throughout the life span of Mexican males.

One result of the sharp dichotomization of male and female gender roles is the widely held belief that effeminate males basically prefer to play the female role rather than the male. The link between male effeminacy and homosexuality is the additional belief that as a result of this role preference effeminate males are sexually interested only in masculine males with whom they play the passive sex role. Although the motivations of males participating in homosexual encounters are without question diverse and complex, the fact remains that in Mexico cultural pressure is brought to bear on effeminate males to play the passive insertee role in sexual intercourse, and a kind of de facto cultural approval is given (that is, no particular stigma is attached to) masculine males who want to play the active insertor role in homosexual intercourse.

The beliefs linking effeminate males with homosexuality are culturally transmitted by a vocabulary which provides the appropriate labels, by homosexually oriented jokes and word games (*albures*), and by the mass media. The links are established at a very early age. From early childhood on, Mexican males are made aware of the labels used to denote male homosexuals and the connection is always clearly made that these homosexual males are guilty of unmanly effeminate behavior.

The author's data also support the notion that prior to puberty effeminate males in Mexico are targeted as sexual objects for adolescent and adult males, and are expected to play the passive insertee sex role in anal intercourse. Following the onset of puberty, they continue to be sexual targets for other males because of their effeminacy. The consensus of my effeminate respondents in Mexico is that regardless of whether they are at school, in a movie theater, on the downtown streets, in a park, or in their own neighborhood, they are sought out and expected to play the anal passive sex role by more masculine males. As one fourteen-year-old respondent put it, in response to the question of where he had looked for sexual contacts during the year prior to the interview: "I didn't have to search for them . . . they looked for me."

The other side of the coin is represented by masculine male participants in homosexual encounters. Given the fact that effeminate males in Mexico are assumed homosexual and thus considered available as sexual outlets, how do the cultural factors contribute to the willingness of masculine males to play the active insertor sex role? The available data suggest that, insofar as the social variables are concerned, their willingness to participate in homosexual encounters is due to the relatively high level of sexual awareness that exists among males in the society, to the lack of stigmatization of the insertor sex role, and to the restraints that may be placed on alternative sexual outlets by available income and/or by marital status. The only cultural proscriptions are that "masculine" males should not play the passive sex role and should not be exclusively involved with homosexual intercourse.

The passive sex role is by inference— through the cultural equivalence of effeminacy with homosexuality—prescribed for "effeminate" males. It becomes a self-fulfilling prophecy of the society that effeminate males (a majority?) are eventually, if not from the beginning, pushed toward exclusively homosexual behavior. Some do engage in heterosexual intercourse, and some marry and set up households; but these probably are a minority of the identifiably effeminate males among the mestizos of the Mexican population.

Brazilian Homosexual Behavior. Both Young (1973) and Fry (1974) note the relationship between cross-gender behavior and homosexuality in Brazil:

Brazilians are still pretty hung-up about sexual roles. Many Brazilians believe in the *bicha/bofe* (femme/ butch) dichotomy and try to live by it. In Brazil, the average person doesn't even recognize the existence of the masculine homosexual. For example, among working-class men, it is considered all right to fuck a *bicha,* an accomplishment of sorts, just like fucking a woman. (Young, 1973)

In the simplest of terms, a male is a man until he is assumed or proved to have "given" in which case he becomes a *bicha.* With very few exceptions, males who "eat" *bichas* are not classified as anything other than "real men." Under this classificatory scheme they differ in no way from males who restrict themselves to "eating" females. (Note: the male who gives is an insertee, the one who eats is an insertor.) (Fry, 1974)

Southern European Homosexual Behavior. Contemporary patterns of male homosexual behavior in Greece appear similar to those observed by the author in Mexico. An American anthropologist who collected data on homosexual behavior in Greece while working there on an archaeological project (Bialor, 1975) found, for example, that preferences for playing one sex role or the other (anal insertor or anal insertee) appear to be highly developed among Greek males. Little or no stigma is attached to the masculine male who plays the active insertor role. The social setting in modern Greece also appears to be strikingly similar to that in modern Mexico. Karlen (1971) describes it as follows:

The father spends his spare time with other men in cafes; society is a male club, and there all true companionship lies. Women live separate, sequestered lives. Girls' virginity is carefully protected, and the majority of homicides are committed over the "honor" of daughters and sisters. In some Greek villages a woman does not leave her home unaccompanied by a relative between puberty and old age. Women walk the street, even in Athens, with their eyes down; a woman who looks up when a man speaks to her is, quite simply, a whore. The young male goes to prostitutes and may carry on homosexual connections; it is not unusual for him to marry at thirty having had no sexual experience save with prostitutes and male friends. (p. 16)

In an evaluation of the strategy of Turkish boys' verbal dueling rhymes, Dundes, Leach, and Ozkok (1972) make the following observations about homosexual behavior in Turkey:

It is extremely important to note that the insult refers to passive homosexuality, not to homosexuality in general. In this context there is nothing insulting about being the active homosexual. In a homosexual relationship, the active phallic aggressor gains status; the passive victim of such aggression loses status. It is important to play the active role in a homosexual relationship; it is shameful and demeaning to be forced to take the passive role.

Moroccan Homosexual Behavior. The author does not know of any formal studies of homosexual behavior in Morocco. The available information suggests, however, that contemporary patterns of homosexual behavior in Morocco are similar to those in Mexico; that is, as long as Moroccan males play the active, insertor sex role in the relationship, there is never any question of their being considered homosexual. Based on his field work in Morocco shortly after the turn of the century, Westermarck (1908) believed that "a very large proportion of the men" in some parts of the country were involved in homosexual activity. He also noted that "in Morocco active pederasty is regarded with almost complete indifference, whilst the passive sodomite, if a grown-up individual, is spoken of with scorn. Dr. Polak says the same of the Persians." Contemporary patterns of homosexual behavior in the Islamic Arab countries of North Africa are probably similar to those in Morocco. . . .

DISCUSSION

Heterosexual intercourse, marriage, and the creation of a family are culturally established as primary objectives for adults living in all of the societies discussed above. Ford and Beach (1951) concluded from their cross-cultural survey that "all known cultures are strongly biased in favor of copulation between males and females as contrasted with alternative avenues of sexual expression." They further note that this viewpoint is biologically adaptive in that it favors perpetuation of the species and social group, and that societies favoring other nonreproductive forms of sexual expression for adults would not be likely to survive for many generations.

Homosexual intercourse appears to be the most important alternative form of sexual expression utilized by people living around the world. All cultures have established rules and regulations that govern the selection of a sexual partner or partners. With respect to homosexual behavior, however, there appear to be greater variations of the rules and regulations. And male homosexual behavior generally appears to be more regulated by cultures than female homosexual behavior. This difference may be the result of females being less likely than males to engage in homosexual activity; but it may also just be the result of a lack of data on female as compared with male homosexual behavior cross-culturally.

Exclusive homosexuality, however, because of the cultural dictums concerning marriage and the family, appears to be generally excluded as a sexual option even in those societies where homosexual behavior is generally approved. For example, the two societies where all male individuals are free to participate in homosexual activity if they choose, Siwan and East Bay, do not sanction exclusive homosexuality.[7] Although nearly all male members of these two societies are reported to engage in extensive homosexual activities, they are not permitted to do so exclusively over their adult life span. Davenport (1965) reports that "East Bay is a society which permits men to be either heterosexual or bisexual in their behavior, but denies the possibility of the exclusively homosexual man." He notes that "they have no concept and therefore no word for the exclusive homosexual." There are not much data available on the Siwans, but it has been reported that whether single or married, Siwan males "are expected to have both homosexual and heterosexual affairs" (Ford & Beach, 1951).

In East Bay there are two categories of homosexual relationships. One category appears similar to that found in a number of Melanesian societies; an older man plays the active (insertor) sex role in anal intercourse with younger boys "from seven to perhaps eleven years of age." Davenport notes:

The man always plays the active role, and it is considered obligatory for him to give the boy presents in return for accommodating him. A man would not engage his own son in such a relationship, but fathers do not object when friends use their young sons in this way, provided the adult is kind and generous. (p. 200)

The other category is between young single men of the same age group who play both sex roles in anal intercourse. The young men, however, "are not regarded as homosexual lovers. They are simply friends or relatives, who, understanding each other's needs and desires, accommodate one another thus fulfilling some of the obligations of kinship and friendship." This category may be related to several social factors which limit heterosexual contacts of young single men. First, the population is highly masculine with a male/female ratio of 120:100 in the fifteen- to twenty-five-year-old age group. Second, females have historically been brought in as wives for those who could afford the bride price. Third, sexual relations between unmarried individuals and adultery are forbidden. Both relationships are classed as larcenies and "only murder carries a more severe punishment." At first marriage a bride is expected to be a virgin. Chastity is highly valued in that it indicates adultery is less likely to occur after marriage. And fourth, there is "an extensive system for separating the sexes by what amounts to a general social avoidance between men and women in all but a few situations." From early adolescence on, unmarried men and boys sleep and eat in the men's house; and married men spend much of their time there during the day. Davenport notes that both masturbation and anal copulation are socially approved and regarded as substitutes for heterosexual intercourse by members of the society. Female homosexual activity is not reported in East Bay.

Among Siwan males the accepted homosexual relationship is "between a man and a boy but not between adult men or between two young boys" (Bullough, 1976). They are reported to practice anal intercourse with the adult man always playing the active (insertor) sex role. In this society, boys are more valued than girls. Allah (1917) reports that

. . . bringing up of a boy costs very little whereas the girl needs ornaments, clothing, and stains. Moreover the boy is a very fruitful source of profit for the father, not for the work he does, but because he is hired by his father to another man to be used as a catamite. Sometimes two men exchange their sons. If they are asked about this, they are not ashamed to mention it.

Homosexual activity is not reported for Siwan females.

The way in which cross-gender behavior is linked to homosexual behavior, and the meaning ascribed to the "homosexual" behavior by participants and significant others, differ between the three categories of societies identified in this study. What is considered homosexuality in one culture may be considered appropriate behavior within prescribed gender roles in another, a homosexual act only on the part of one participant in another, or a ritual act involving growth and masculinity in still another. Care must therefore be taken when judging sexual behavior cross-culturally with such culture-bound labels as "homosexual" and "homosexuality."

From a cultural point of view, deviations from sexual mores in a given society appear most likely to occur as a result of the lack of appropriate sexual partners and/or a result of conditioning in approved sexual behavior which is limited by age or ritual (for example, where homosexual intercourse is only appropriate for a certain age group and/or ritual time period and inappropriate thereafter). Homosexual activity initiated by sociocultural variables may, over time through interaction with personality variables, produce an outcome not in accordance with the sexual mores of the society.

The findings presented in this chapter illustrate the profound influence of culture on the structuring of individual patterns of sexual behavior. Whether from biological or psychological causation, cross-gender behaving individuals in many societies must cope with a cultural formulation which equates their behavior with homosexual activity and thus makes it a self-fulfilling prophecy that they become homosexually involved. There are also individuals in many societies who might prefer to be exclusively homosexual but are prevented from doing so by cultural edicts. From whatever causes that homosexual impulses originate, whether they be biological or psychological, culture provides an additional dimension that cannot be ignored.

CRITICAL THINKING QUESTIONS

1. What type of society tends to be accepting of homosexuality? What kind of society is disapproving of this sexual orientation? Why?
2. What insights can be drawn from this article that help to explain violence and discrimination directed toward gay people in Canadian society?
3. Are data about sexuality easily available to researchers? Why not?

NOTES

1. Homosexual behavior or activity will be used here to describe sexual behavior between individuals of the same sex; it may have nothing to do with sexual object choice or sexual orientation of the individual involved. Additionally, the terms "sex role" and "gender role" will be used to describe different behavioral phenomena. As Hooker (1965) points out, they "are often used interchangeably, and with resulting confusion." Following her suggestion the term "sex role," when homosexual practices are described, will refer to typical sexual performance only. "The gender connotations (M-F) of these performances need not then be implicitly assumed." The term "gender role" will refer to the expected attitudes and behavior that distinguish males from females.

2. The Human Relations Area Files (HRAF) contain information on the habits, practices, customs, and behavior of populations in hundreds of societies around the world. These files utilize accounts given not only by anthropologists but also by travelers, writers, missionaries, and explorers. Most cross-cultural surveys of sexual behavior, like those of Ford and Beach and Broude and Greene, have been based on HRAF information. A major criticism of the HRAF information on sexual behavior relates to the difficulty of assessing the reliability of the data collected in different time periods by different people with varying amounts of scientific training as observers.

3. "Preliterate" refers to essentially tribal societies that do not have a written language; "peasant" refers to essentially agrarian literate societies; and "complex modern" refers to highly industrialized societies.

4. In one of the first scholarly surveys of homosexual behavior done by an anthropologist, Westermarck (1908) concluded that: "A very important cause of homosexual practices is absence of the other sex."

5. The confounding of transvestism with homosexuality still occurs. For example, Minturn, Grosse, and Haider (1969) coded male homosexuality with transvestism in a recent study of the patterning of sexual beliefs and behavior, "because it is often difficult to

distinguish between the two practices, and because they are assumed to be manifestations of the same psychological processes and to have similar causes."

6. The roles described represent the normative cultural ideals of the mestizoized national culture. Mestizos are Mexican nationals of mixed Indian and Spanish ancestry. They make up a large majority of the population, and their culture is the dominant one.

7. Both societies are small, each totaling less than 1,000 inhabitants. The Siwans live in an oasis in the Libyan desert. The people of East Bay (a pseudonym) live in a number of small coastal villages in an island in Melanesia.

REFERENCES

Allah, M. 1917. Siwan customs. *Harvard African Studies*, 1: 7.

Angelino, A., and C. Shedd. 1955. A note on berdache. *American Anthropologist*, 57: 121–25.

Associated Press. 1979. Eunuchs gather for convention in India. *Panipat*, February 6, 1979.

Bialor, P. 1975. Personal communication.

Bogores, W. 1904. The Chukchee. *Memoirs of American Museum of Natural History*, 2: 449–51.

Broude, G., and S. Greene. 1976. Cross-cultural codes on twenty sexual attitudes and practices. *Ethnology*, 15(4): 410–11.

Bullough, V. 1976. *Sexual variance in society and history*, 22–49. New York: John Wiley.

Carrier, J. 1976. Cultural factors affecting urban Mexican male homosexual behavior. *Archives of Sexual Behavior*, 5(2): 103–24.

———. 1977. Sex-role preference as an explanatory variable in homosexual behavior. *Archives of Sexual Behavior*, 6(1): 53–65.

Carstairs, G. 1956. Hinjra and Jiryan: Two derivatives of Hindu attitudes to sexuality. *British Journal of Medical Psychology*, 2: 129–32.

Davenport, W. 1965. Sexual patterns and their regulation in a society of the southwest Pacific. In *Sex and behavior*, 164–207. New York: John Wiley.

Devereux, G. 1937. Institutionalized homosexuality of the Mohave Indians. In *The problem of homosexuality in modern society*, 183–226. New York: E. P. Dutton.

Dundes, A., J. Leach, and B. Ozkok. 1972. The strategy of Turkish boys' verbal dueling. In *Directions in sociolinguistics: The ethnography of communication*. New York: Holt.

Ford, C. S., and F. A. Beach. 1951. *Patterns of sexual behavior*. New York: Harper & Row.

Fry, P. 1974. Male homosexuality and Afro-Brazilian possession cults. Unpublished paper presented to Symposium on Homosexuality in Crosscultural Perspective, 73rd Annual Meeting of the American Anthropological Association, Mexico City.

Hooker, E. 1965. An empirical study of some relations between sexual patterns and gender identity in male homosexuals. In *Sex research: New developments*, 24–25. New York: Holt.

Karlen, A. 1971. *Sexuality and homosexuality: A new view*. New York: W. W. Norton.

Kroeber, A. 1940. Psychosis or social sanction. *Character and Personality*, 8: 204–15. Reprinted in *The nature of culture*, 313. Chicago: University of Chicago Press, 1952.

Levy, R. 1973. *Tahitians*. Chicago: University of Chicago Press.

Marshall, D., and R. Suggs. 1971. *Human sexual behavior*, 220–21. New York: Basic Books.

McGinn, N. 1966. Marriage and family in middle-class Mexico. *Journal of Marriage and Family Counseling*, 28: 305–13.

Mead, M. 1961. Cultural determinants of sexual behavior. In *Sex and internal secretions*, 1433–79. Baltimore: Williams & Wilkins.

Minturn, L., M. Grosse, and S. Haider. 1969. Cultural patterning of sexual beliefs and behavior. *Ethnology*, 8(3): 3.

Morrison, J. 1935. *The journal of James Morrison*. London: Golden Cockeral Press.

Munroe, R., J. Whiting, and D. Hally. 1969. Institutionalized male transvestism and sex distinctions. *American Anthropologist*, 71: 87–91.

Opler, M. 1960. The Hijarā (hermaphrodites) of India and Indian national character: A rejoinder. *American Anthropologist*, 62(3): 505–11.

Peñalosa, F. 1968. Mexican family roles. *Journal of Marriage and Family Counseling*, 30: 680–89.

Royce, A. 1973. Personal communication.

Shah, A. 1961. A note on the Hijadās of Gujarat. *American Anthropologist*, 63(6): 1325–30.

Stoller, R. 1976. Two feminized male American Indians. *Archives of Sexual Behavior*, 5(6): 536.

Westermarck, E. 1908. On homosexual love. In *The origin and development of the moral ideas*. London: Macmillan.

Williams, F. 1936. *Papuans of the trans-fly*. London: Oxford University Press.

Young, A. 1973. Gay gringo in Brazil. In *The gay liberation book*, eds. L. Richmond and G. Noguera, 60–7. San Francisco: Ramparts Press.

27

The Vertical Mosaic: An Analysis of Social Class and Power in Canada

JOHN PORTER

In this chapter from the highly regarded book The Vertical Mosaic, *Porter highlights the importance of studying Canadian social class structures. Porter traces the Canadian belief that there are no clearly defined classes in Canada back to the frontier environment and the settlement of Canada.*

THE CANADIAN MIDDLE CLASS IMAGE

One of the most persistent images that Canadians have of their society is that it has no classes. This image becomes translated into the assertion that Canadians are all relatively equal in their possessions, in the amount of money they earn, and in the opportunities which they and their children have to get on in the world. An important element in this image of classlessness is that, with the absence of formal aristocracy and aristocratic institutions, Canada is a society in which equalitarian values have asserted themselves over authoritarian values. Canada, it is thought, shares not only a continent with the United States, but also a democratic ideology which rejects the historical class and power structures of Europe.

Source: From *The Vertical Mosaic* by John Porter. Toronto: University of Toronto Press, 1965, pp. 3–6. Reprinted with the permission of the publisher.

Social images are one thing and social realities another. Yet the two are not completely separate. Social images are not entirely fictional characters with only a coincidental likeness to a real society, living or dead. Often the images can be traced to an earlier historical period of the society, its golden age perhaps, which, thanks to the historians, is held up, long after it has been transformed into something else, as a model way of life. As well as their historical sources, images can be traced to their contemporary creators, particularly in the world of the mass media and popular culture. When a society's writers, journalists, editors, and other image-creators are a relatively small and closely linked group, and have more or less the same social background, the images they produce can, because they are consistent, appear to be much more true to life than if their group were larger, less cohesive, and more heterogeneous in composition.

157

The historical source of the image of a classless Canada is the equality among pioneers in the frontier environment of the last century. In the early part of the [twentieth] century there was a similar equality of status among those who were settlers in the west, although, as we shall see, these settlers were by no means treated equally. A rural, agricultural, primary producing society is a much less differentiated society than one which has highly concentrated industries in large cities. Equality in the rural society may be much more apparent than real, but the rural environment has been for Canada an important source of the image of equality. Later we shall examine more closely how the historical image has become out of date with the transformation of Canadian society from the rural to the urban type.

Although the historical image of rural equality lingers, it has gradually given way in the urban industrial setting to an image of a middle level classlessness in which there is a general uniformity of possessions. For families these possessions include a separate dwelling with an array of electrical equipment, a car, and perhaps a summer cottage. Family members, together or as individuals, engage in a certain amount of ritualistic behaviour in churches and service clubs. Modern advertising has done much to standardize the image of middle class consumption levels and middle class behaviour. Consumers' magazines are devoted to the task of constructing the ideal way of life through articles on child-rearing, homemaking, sexual behaviour, health, sports, and hobbies. Often, too, corporations which do not produce family commodities directly will have large advertisements to demonstrate how general social well-being at this middle level is an outcome of their own operations.

That there is neither very rich nor very poor in Canada is an important part of the image. There are no barriers to opportunity. Education is free. Therefore, making use of it is largely a question of personal ambition. Even university education is available to all, except that it may require for some a little more summer work and thrift. There is a view widely held by many university graduates that they, and most other graduates, have worked their way through college. Consequently it is felt anyone else can do the same.

In some superficial respects the image of middle class uniformity may appear plausible. The main values of the society are concerned with the consumption of commodities, and in the so-called affluence that has followed World War II there seem to have been commodities for everybody, except, perhaps, a small group of the permanently poor at the bottom. Credit facilities are available for large numbers of low-income families, enabling them, too, to be consumers of commodities over and above the basic necessities of life. The vast array of credit facilities, some of them extraordinarily ingenious, have inequalities built into them, in that the cost of borrowing money varies with the amount already possessed. There are vast differences in the quality of goods bought by the middle income levels and the lower income levels. One commodity, for instance, which low-income families can rarely purchase is privacy, particularly the privacy of a house to themselves. It is perhaps the value of privacy and the capacity to afford it which has become the dividing line between the real and the apparent middle class.

If low-income families achieve high consumption levels it is usually through having more than one income earner in the household. Often this is the wife and mother, but it may be an older child who has left school, and who is expected to contribute to the family budget. Alternatively, high consumption levels may be achieved at a cost in leisure. Many low-income family heads have two jobs, a possibility which has arisen with the shorter working day and the five-day week. This "moonlighting," as it is called in labour circles, tends to offset the progress which has been made in raising the level of wages and reducing the hours of work. There is no way of knowing how extensive "moonlighting" is, except that we know that trade unions denounce it as a practice which tends to take away the gains which have been obtained for workers. For large segments of the population, therefore, a high level of consumption is obtained by means which are alien to a true middle class standard. [When] . . . we . . . examine closely the distribution of income, we . . . see what a small proportion of Canadian families were able to live a middle class style of life in the middle 1950s, the high tide of post-war affluence.

At the high end of the social class spectrum, also in contrast to the middle level image, are the families of great wealth and influence. They are not perhaps as ostentatious as the very wealthy of other societies, and Canada has no "celebrity world" with which these families must compete for prestige in the way Mills has suggested is important for the very rich in American society.[1]

Almost every large Canadian city has its wealthy and prominent families of several generations. They have their own social life, their children go to private schools, they have their clubs and associations, and they take on the charitable and philanthropic roles which have so long been the "duty" of those of high status. Although this upper class is always being joined by the new rich, it still contributes, as we shall see later, far more than its proportionate share to the elite of big business.

The concentration of wealth in the upper classes is indicated by the fact that in Canada in 1955 the top one per cent of income recipients received about 40 per cent of all income from dividends.

Images which conflict with the one of middle class equality rarely find expression, partly because the literate middle class is both the producer and the consumer of the image. Even at times in what purports to be serious social analysis, middle class intellectuals project the image of their own class onto the social classes above and below them. There is scarcely any critical analysis of Canadian social life upon which a conflicting image could be based. The idea of class differences has scarcely entered into the stream of Canadian academic writing

despite the fact that class differences stand in the way of implementing one of the most important values of western society, that is equality.[2] The fact, which we shall see later, that Canada draws its intellectuals either from abroad or from its own middle class, means that there is almost no one producing a view of the world which reflects the experience of the poor or the underprivileged. It was as though they did not exist. It is the nature of these class differences and their consequences for Canadian society that [we] . . . seek to explore.

Closely related to differences in class levels are differences in the exercising of power and decision-making in the society: Often it is thought that once a society becomes an electoral democracy based on universal suffrage, power becomes diffused throughout the general population so that everyone participates somehow in the selection of social goals. There is, however, a whole range of institutional resistances to the transfer of power to a democratic political system.[3] . . .

CRITICAL THINKING QUESTIONS

1. Is Porter's assertion that Canadians believe they exist within a classless society still valid today? Why or why not?

2. Porter's work was published in 1965. Do any of his observations continue to be revealing in a contemporary analysis of Canadian society?

3. According to Porter, does democracy ensure the equal allocation of power and influence within society? Why or why not?

NOTES

1. C. W. Mills, *The Power Elite* (New York, 1956), chap. 4.

2. Nor does class appear as a theme in Canadian literature. See R. L. McDougall, "The Dodo and the Cruising Auk," *Canadian Literature*, no. 18 (Autumn 1963).

3. For a comparative study of social mobility see S. M. Lipset and R. Bendix, *Social Mobility in Industrial Society* (Berkeley, 1959).

28

Discomforting Comfort Foods:
Stirring the Pot on Kraft Dinner
and Social Inequality in Canada

MELANIE ROCK, LYNN MCINTYRE,
AND KRISTA RONDEAU

This reading looks at food from the perspective of social class and tracks how people in poverty treat Kraft Dinner differently from those who are well to do.

INTRODUCTION

Kraft Dinner was perhaps the first food product sold in a kit with a long shelf life, and with rapid home-based assembly in mind. While Kraft Dinner is currently sold in a variety of flavors and formats, the ever-popular original version is sold in a cardboard box containing 225 g of dried macaroni made with enriched wheat flour and an envelope of powdered cheddar cheese. Kraft launched this product in Canada and the United States in 1937, when Depression-era hardships created a niche for an inexpensive meatless entrée; this niche market subsequently expanded with rationing during WWII (Jacobson and Salamie 2002). Today, Kraft Dinner is the top-selling grocery product in Canada (Allossery 2000). Canadians annually purchase

Source: From *Agriculture and Human Values, Volume 26,* Issue 3, September 2009, pp. 167–176. Copyright © Springer Science and Business Media. Used with permission of the publisher.

about 90 million boxes of Kraft Dinner, and consumption is spread remarkably evenly across the country, and in terms of age group, gender, occupational status, household income and level of education. Approximately 30% of all respondents in a random sample of Canadians reported consuming Kraft Dinner in the previous 30 days (Print Measurement Bureau 2003). These figures do not take into account the consumption of imitator products marketed under private store labels. Similar to the way that the brand name Kleenex is synonymous with facial tissues, both Anglophones and Francophones in Canada often extend the term "Kraft Dinner" to boxed macaroni and cheese. Boxes of store-brand as well as brand-name Kraft Dinner are often sold for less than $1CAD each. By way of comparison, the sale price for a brand-name tube of toothpaste or a pound of tomatoes, when in season, is about $1.60CAD.

Kraft Dinner is part of Canadian popular culture and reflects socioeconomic status or class differences. For instance, the Toronto-based pop rock group Barenaked Ladies scored an enduring hit with their song, "If I had a $1,000,000" (Bateman 2007) which includes the refrain, "If I had a million dollars, we wouldn't have to eat Kraft Dinner, but we would, we'd just eat more." While Kraft Dinner consumption is quite evenly spread across the socioeconomic spectrum, as hinted in the lyrics for "If I had a $1,000,000," obligatory consumption of Kraft Dinner is associated with poverty. Furthermore, an association of Kraft Dinner consumption with financial distress exists in parallel with an association of Kraft Dinner consumption with feeling soothed and reassured. Reflecting the increased usage of the term "comfort food" in the English language, several dictionaries now include comfort food as an entry. Dictionary definitions include: (1) a food that comforts or affords solace; hence, any food (frequently with a high sugar or carbohydrate content) that is associated with childhood or with home cooking (*Oxford English Dictionary* 2007); and (2) a food prepared in a traditional style having a usually nostalgic or sentimental appeal (Merriam-Webster 2007). "In essence," according to *The Encyclopedia of Food and Culture,* "comfort food provides individuals with a sense of security during troubling times by evoking emotions associated with safer and happier times" (Locher 2002, p. 443). In the United States (Locher et al. 2005), Kraft Macaroni and Cheese ranks as a common comfort food, as does Kraft Dinner in Canada.

The common practice of individuals donating Kraft Dinner and its imitators for charitable food distribution builds on associating Kraft Dinner with both poverty and with comfort. Furthermore, many food banks and some food corporations actively promote donations of Kraft Dinner and its imitators. A plastic bag issued by the Calgary Inter-Faith Food Bank Society, for example, lists "non-perishable food suggestions;" among them "macaroni and cheese." Notices routinely appear in community newspapers across the country, urging people to donate food and suggesting Kraft Dinner by name, thus: "Some

of the items needed include cereal, peanut butter, canned fruit, tuna, canned vegetables, pork and beans, pasta, rice and Kraft Dinner" (Tayti 2000). "Each of our stores features pre-packaged food bundles containing the most needed food items according to the local food banks," notes a public relations statement issued by a large supermarket chain (Safeway Canada 2007), and these bundles uniformly contain a box of private-label macaroni and cheese in the style of Kraft Dinner. In addition, adorning the bins set out by this supermarket chain to collect food bank donations is a poster of a school-aged boy shown smiling and eating a bowl of what looks to be Kraft Dinner.

Food Insecurity in Canada

Food insecurity is an important social problem in Canada, with significant implications for public health (Tarasuk and Vozoris 2003; Ricciuto and Tarasuk 2007). In higher-income societies such as Canada, food insecurity has been defined as "the inability to obtain sufficient, nutritious, personally acceptable food through normal food channels or the uncertainty that one will be able to do so" (Davis and Tarasuk 1994, p. 51). By extension, food-secure people have the ability to obtain nutritious, personally acceptable food through normal food channels, and do not fear losing this ability. In 2004, 9.2% of all Canadian households were food-insecure, and the prevalence of severe food insecurity in female lone-parent households was five times greater than in couple-led households (Health Canada 2007). Furthermore, the data collected in this 2004 survey clearly showed a relationship between income and food insecurity. Households in which the main source of income was "social assistance" (59.7%) or "worker's compensation/employment insurance" (29.0%) were more likely to report food insecurity than households with other main sources of income.

Despite the gravity of the problem, the dominant response to food insecurity in Canada remains extra-governmental charitable programs, commonly termed "food banks," which focus on the collection and distribution of donated food. These locally based programs emerged as an ad hoc response to the recession of the early 1980s, but have since evolved into a loosely connected network and are now deeply entrenched in Canadian society. Food bank use has increased by over 99% since 1989 and at least 649 food banks operated across Canada, in all provinces and territories, as of March 2006 (Canadian Association of Food Banks 2006, p. 4). Persistent food insecurity undoubtedly contributes to the perpetuation of food banks, but it has also been shown that food banks fulfill important functions for corporate donors. For example, these donations spare corporations from paying landfill tipping fees and other costs entailed in disposing of products that, for many reasons (including manufacturing errors, damaged packaging, stocked past expiry date, wilted, or unpopular) cannot be sold at a profit (Tarasuk and Eakin 2005). Donations also assist corporations in projecting a positive image of corporate citizenship (DeLind 1994), especially to the food-secure majority. While corporate donations likely comprise most of the food distributed through Canadian food banks, donations from individuals account for about 25% of all charitable food distribution in major metropolitan areas (Tarasuk and Eakin 2005, p. 178), and likely more than that in smaller centers (Tarasuk and Eakin 2005, p. 180). The perspectives of food-secure people about food insecurity have yet to be thoroughly examined. This paper contrasts the perceptions of Canadians who are food-secure with the perceptions of Canadians who are food-insecure through the different meanings that they ascribe to Kraft Dinner.

MATERIALS AND METHODS

This paper relies on transcripts of face-to-face interviews with people living in food-secure and food-insecure households, transcripts of focus groups involving people living in food-insecure households, and newspaper articles. The interviews with food-secure individuals that we draw on in this paper were conducted in French with 18 francophone residents of Montreal. A purposive sample (Bernard 2006, pp. 189–191) was identified via the first author's social network. Approximately half of the interviewees worked in social services as counselors or community developers, or both. Social service providers were of particular interest because their work routinely brings them into contact with people living in poverty; hence, they are well-positioned to compare food-secure with food-insecure contexts. The semi-structured interview guide included a question asking respondents to comment on why Kraft Dinner is so often offered as a charitable food donation. The intent here was to collect information on social patterns of thinking and acting (Spradley 1979). Rigorous transcription (Poland 1995) was possible for eleven interviews. All of these interviewees were white, middle-class people who grew up in Quebec and who speak French as their first language. The youngest person interviewed was in her early 30s at the time of the interview, while the oldest were in their late 60s. Three were men and eight were women. This gender bias reflects the composition of the social service workforce. For the present paper, transcript segments in which these participants reflected on Kraft Dinner's status as a common food donation were analyzed.

The second source of data for this paper was a study that sought to stabilize and increase milk consumption in low-income households (McIntyre et al. 2007a). Individual and group interviews were conducted for this policy-oriented study with 54 low-income lone mothers, all of whom were raising two or more children less than 14 years of age in the province of Nova Scotia. In follow-up focus group interviews involving a mix of the original respondents and new participants, 34 women were invited to comment on promising policy strategies that had emerged from the first round. This exclusively female sample was composed of predominantly white women aged approximately 20 to 40 years, reflecting the fact that most had young children. All transcripts (five individual interviews and nine group interviews) included discussion of food banks, and three out of nine focus group transcripts included the term "Kraft Dinner" or the common acronym "KD." For the present paper, transcript segments in which participants discussed Kraft Dinner or food banks were re-analyzed.

The third source of primary data for our paper was a study designed to document the occurrence and extent of food insecurity among low-income mothers and their children in the Atlantic Canada region (McIntyre et al. 2002, 2003a, b). As part of this mixed-method study, in-depth interviews took place with 24 low-income lone mothers who had also provided quantitative dietary intake data. The women ranged in age from 21 to 41 years; 20 (83%) were of white Canadian background, three (13%) were of African Canadian background, and one woman (4%) was of aboriginal descent. All 24 of these interview transcripts included at least one of the following terms: "food bank," "food banks," "Kraft Dinner," and "KD." These transcript segments were re-analyzed as part of the new dataset.

The fourth source of primary data came from newspaper articles archived either in the *InfoGlobe* database or in the *Canadian Newstand* database. *InfoGlobe* contains the full-text archive of *The Globe and Mail*, a Toronto-based newspaper that targets an elite readership and that is distributed across Canada. *Canadian Newstand* archives Canada's other nationally distributed newspaper, the *National Post*, and over 200 other daily or weekly newspapers that serve cities and smaller communities. Of the more than 1,500 articles published between 1990 and 2003 that were retrieved from the databases *Canadian Newstand* and *InfoGlobe* because they mentioned Kraft Dinner, 155 articles mentioned food banks. These 155 articles were added to our dataset. . . .

Our analysis focused on comparing the statements made by food-secure people with those made by people experiencing food insecurity. More specifically, we focused on contrasting the views expressed by food-secure lone mothers residing in Atlantic Canada. Because the newspapers in our sample targeted a middle-class readership, most of the newspaper data reflected food-secure perspectives. On occasion, however, the newspaper articles described or quoted people experiencing food insecurity. Including the newspaper articles in our analysis helped us to validate, in a separate sample consisting of documents not originally produced for research purposes, the differences between food-secure and food-insecure perspectives that we observed in the transcript data. This approach to validation is often called triangulation (Webb et al. 1981 [1966]; Bryman 2001, p. 275).

RESULTS

We were able to use our various data sources to discern food-secure and food-insecure perspectives on Kraft Dinner. The results of our study are organized according to thematic content. We first outline food-secure perspectives on Kraft Dinner, and then turn to food-insecure perspectives.

Food-secure Perspectives on Kraft Dinner

Palatable, Especially for Children. One reason why food-secure people frequently offer Kraft Dinner as a charitable food donation is because they regard the item as palatable. By palatable, we mean agreeable to the mind as well as satisfying to taste. Familiarity is an important element of this perceived palatability, for Kraft Dinner is presumed to be familiar to the eventual recipients of charitable food donations. As one social service provider put it, "I have the impression it's [given] because it is seen as a simple product that is well-known" . . . (Interview #YUL-0323). A different social service provider concurred that people tended to have the impression that members of the working class enjoy Kraft Dinner, and thought this impression helped to account for why it was so often donated . . . (Interview #YUL-0314). Along these lines, a lawyer suggested that Kraft

Dinner is so often given "probably because it's known and appreciated" among the eventual recipients . . . (Interview #YUL-0130).

Across Canada, Kraft Dinner is strongly associated with childhood and youth. For instance, one newspaper article referred to "[t]hat definitive college student and kid staple, Kraft Dinner" (KD 1998, When only KD will do). This association of Kraft Dinner with children and youth was also found among Quebec Francophones. For example, one social service provider said, "I think that it is well-liked by children and younger people. It has the style of taste that they like. You know that a child is going to eat it up, but if you serve him something else, he won't necessarily eat it" . . . (Interview #YUL-0125).

Implicit in these responses to the question about Kraft Dinner's status as a common food donation is the understanding that many food-insecure households include children. Another implicit understanding is that because it is enjoyed by many food-secure children and adults, it ought to be acceptable to members of a food-insecure household. A union official put it this way: "You might serve it to your own kids, to your own family, or even to yourself. In the end, you make it yourself" . . . (Interview #YUL-0126).

The fact that Kraft Dinner is sold as a boxed do-it-yourself kit, as opposed to pre-cooked and in a can, also seems to confer the perception of palatability. For instance, the union official continued from the quotation above by saying, "It's not reheated. That's the big difference; you have to reheat what's in a can you know." An archivist said, "It's frankly less disgusting than a can of . . . of stewed meatballs in a can, you know. At least it's not canned food" . . . (Interview #YUL-0201).

Often several boxes of Kraft Dinner are donated at once, which may allow an individual donor to feel and look generous without spending very much money. One social service worker remarked on the common Christmas-time practice of bulk Kraft Dinner donations in office environments:

You think in terms of charity instead of sharing, so you want to make a finite amount of your money go as far as possible. And so if you budget ten dollars, then you arrive with ten boxes of Kraft Dinner. That seems like you're giving more and are more generous, or you have the impression that you are feeding more people, than if you arrive with, I don't know, a chicken in a—a de-boned chicken or a box of chocolates. . . . (Interview #YUL-0316)

Kraft Dinner is a palatable donation—in the sense of being pleasing to a food-secure mind—partly because it is so cheap.

A Complete Meal That Is Easy to Prepare. Besides palatability, many food-secure people regard Kraft Dinner as suitable for donation because of preparation ease. "It's easy to prepare and we assume, I suppose that people assume everyone knows how to prepare it," said a lawyer in an interview . . . (Interview #YUL-0130). "It's easy for adults to make quickly," noted one social service provider. "It's not too complicated" . . . (Interview #YUL-0125).

The standard or classic instructions read as follows:

- STIR pasta into six cups (1.5 L) boiling water.
- BOIL rapidly, stirring occasionally, 7–8 min or to desired tenderness. Drain.
- ADD 3 Tbsp. (45 mL) butter or margarine, 1/4 cup (50 ml) milk and the Cheese Sauce Mix. Stir until pasta is evenly coated.

What Kraft calls the Sensible Solution instructions differ somewhat. They call for 1 Tbsp of non-hydrogenated margarine and 1/2 cup of skim milk. Not only are the package instructions easy to follow, meal preparation is thought to be simplified because nothing additional need be prepared or added when serving Kraft Dinner. A social service provider speculated:

Personally, I have the impression that when people give it [Kraft Dinner] to food banks it's because they say to themselves, "When you eat pasta, you feel less hungry." And so I have the impression that if you say, "Well, there's a bit of cheese," that makes for a bit of protein. And perhaps people are going to feel that they have eaten something better than just pasta alone. . . . (Interview #YUL-0301)

An archivist also supported this impression: "Simply put, there's the idea of a complete meal, in the sense of protein, pasta. Instead of giving a package of white spaghetti, you give a kit that is a meal" . . . (Interview #YUL-0201). "It's complete," said another respondent, a lawyer. "You don't have to add anything else, not even seasonings, not even salt" . . . (Interview #YUL-0130).

And yet, the package instructions indeed call for additional supplies and ingredients: water and a pot in which to boil the pasta, fuel and a stove, butter or margarine, and fresh milk. Access to these items is taken for granted when food-secure people think about Kraft Dinner as a do-it-yourself kit for a making a basic yet complete meal. Along these lines, a college professor said, "You have water! Butter, margarine, you have these too!" . . . (Interview #YUL-0129). Access to butter or margarine and to fresh milk is also assumed when food-secure people talk about Kraft Dinner as something that always tastes the same.

This notion of taste consistency is also part of what makes it palatable, perhaps especially from a child's point of view—but as a result, for parents too, and for prospective donors who imagine food-insecure households with children as the eventual recipients. As a union official put it, "Kraft Dinner is always, always the same. So by serving it, you're a good parent too. It works for you too. You're a good parent, you have prepared it, and you have prepared something that is consistent" . . . (Interview #YUL-0125).

Convenient and Safe to Store. Along with palatability and presumed simplicity of preparation, the ease with which Kraft Dinner can be stored helps account for its status as a well-regarded staple food bank donation. The interviews conducted with food-secure Montrealers suggested that Kraft Dinner is routinely found in food-secure households partly because it is so easily stored for consumption at a much later date: it is non-perishable, compact, cheap and often sold in bulk. And the fact that it is so often stored in food-secure households helps account for why it so often donated. As one social service provider put it:

Since it's not expensive, people will rarely buy just one box. They will buy three or four. So you might buy a case. When you have a case at your house, and people come by for food donations, you have a lot. So why not give even half? . . . (Interview #YUL-0323)

In summary, food-secure Canadians perceive Kraft Dinner as a complete meal that is palatable for a variety of ages but especially for children, easy to prepare, easy to store, and easy to donate. The reasoning that leads food-secure Canadians to purchase Kraft Dinner themselves appears to be embedded in singling out Kraft Dinner for charitable donation from what they have stored in their cupboards. But the fact that Kraft Dinner is cheap looms large in rendering Kraft Dinner as especially appropriate for donation. Kraft Dinner is considered "good enough" for consumption in many food-secure households, yet not "too good" for poor people to afford on their own, and so food-secure donors presume familiarity among the eventual recipients. Furthermore, Kraft Dinner is cheap enough that food-secure people can easily afford to donate several boxes. For food-secure people, then, Kraft Dinner can provide comfort through physical or vicarious consumption; vicarious consumption may be achieved by offering it to a child or by offering it as a charitable donation.

Food-insecure Perspectives on Kraft Dinner Consumption

Hunger-killer of Last Resort. Kraft Dinner is part of how many food-insecure households experience financial distress. Kraft Dinner may be obtained from a food bank, but the product is also frequently purchased because of its low cost. When an interviewer asked a lone mother to list the foods on hand when times are tough or money is tight, the answer was "Kraft Dinner, of course". . . (Interview #HM-203). Often, Kraft Dinner is consumed near the end of the month, when most other food has run out, and there is either no money left for food, or only enough to purchase Kraft Dinner. Reported one lone mother, "I get real low, low, low like there's only one box of Kraft Dinner in the house, I know that one box of Kraft Dinner is going to be there like the day before my check comes" (Interview #HM-201). Another lone mother said:

Usually the last week is the worst, then I find I get depressed, I get upset. I get where I just . . . I don't even want to eat because I don't know, you know. I don't know if me eating that's like if I put on soup or something, I don't know if that, you know, maybe the next day it will be Kraft Dinner or something and one of the kids won't want it and we don't have a whole lot that I can offer. But when you have no vegetables, no nothing, all you have is Kraft Dinner and, um, like stuff like that, Kraft Dinner, Mr. Noodles, stuff like that, I mean . . . I don't want my kids to go on that for a week. (Interview #HM-209)

Some food-insecure mothers indicated, however, that they purchased Kraft Dinner because it is their children's favorite food. But these women distinguish genuine Kraft Dinner from imitator products. For example, one mother said,

It has to be real. Well I don't blame them [her children]. Did you ever taste, taste that other stuff? The cat won't even eat it, I'll put it to you that way. Because there has been a couple of times that I made it and they wouldn't eat it so I see if the cat will eat it, the cat won't even eat it." (Interview #HM-137)

Such remarks suggest that consistency over time, which is part of the food-secure perception of Kraft Dinner as a palatable donation, cannot be fully achieved with cheaper imitations consumed under duress.

An Incomplete Meal. In direct contrast with the food-secure perception of Kraft Dinner as a meal-in-a-box, the additional commodities required to prepare Kraft Dinner according to the package instructions are rationed or lacking altogether in food-insecure households. Fuel consumption is closely monitored—access to electricity and natural gas can be removed if bills are not paid; butter or

margarine may also be unavailable. Milk is required to make Kraft Dinner according to the package instructions; and to be palatable, the milk should not be powdered but fresh. Yet in many food-insecure households, the most precious commodity of all is fresh milk. As soon as food-insecure households run out of money for the month, they cannot purchase fresh milk. A lone mother explained:

I used to buy myself milk all the time, and now I try to have one litre of milk in just for the Kraft Dinner spaghetti, forget me and my milk, you know what I'm saying. I shouldn't be doing that because I'm getting on in years and I should be making sure I have that calcium but you do. You have to pick and choose. (Interview #HM-205)

Similarly, a newspaper article reported on what, for food-secure readers, would be exotic circumstances: a "42-year-old single mother of three who makes the rounds of alleys at night scrounging for returnable bottles so she can buy milk for her kids . . . The children eat a lot of watered-down Kraft dinners 'but they don't complain as long as it fills them up,' she said" (KD-2003, Help for the needy). Consumers in the province of British Columbia may add a cash donation to their bill at supermarket check-outs, which "means that fresh local items such as fruit, milk and eggs can be donated to food banks" (KD-1997, Food banks), but such voucher programs remain uncommon enough to be considered newsworthy. In any case, the supply of fresh milk in food banks remains driven by charitable impulse, not by nutritional need. Thus, the Kraft Dinner consumed in food-insecure households across Canada toward the end of each month is often watered-down, prepared with powdered milk or prepared without any milk whatsoever, adding symbolically and physically to discomfort.

Monotony. One consequence of a restricted food budget is a monotonous diet, which in the Canadian context is often materially and symbolically tied to Kraft Dinner. The association of obligatory Kraft Dinner consumption with low income was conveyed in many newspaper articles in our dataset, including the following example: "The

Ryders don't use the local food bank. When asked how they feed a family of five on their limited income, Travis responded, 'We eat a lot of Kraft Dinner.'" (KD-1999, A home of their own). One lone mother, speaking of her daughter, said, "On other days, when we have no money, she has to eat Kraft Dinner or French fries . . . She gets tired of the same meals. She don't even want to eat. She says, 'Mommy, I ain't eating Kraft Dinner again today. We ate it all last week'" (Interview #HM-138). And it is not only the children in food-insecure households who are eating Kraft Dinner. As another lone mother put it, "The things that I eat mostly, are stuff like Kraft Dinner, or a sandwich, that is if there is any bread left after [my son] and [my daughter] go through the bag, and Pepsi. That's my meals" (Interview #HM-074).

Some people regard Kraft Dinner as the Rubicon of food insecurity: "I'm an inventive cook. I detest Kraft Dinner and hotdog suppers. I just refuse" (KD-1991, Going without, Recession). Others maintain that Kraft Dinner should be transformed:

You know and I might not always have a good meal to throw together but I mean even with a Kraft Dinner I can do wonders with a box of Kraft Dinner. I can. I put my peas and carrots in there and some soya sauce, oh yeah, and we do that right up. (Interview #HM-138)

Note that Kraft Dinner can only be made over in this way if some vegetables and a condiment can be procured. Note also that the sense that Kraft Dinner should be avoided or reworked departs from the food-secure perception that, as sold, Kraft Dinner is palatable and complete.

Discomfort, overall, permeates Kraft Dinner in food-insecure households. Because Kraft Dinner is often used to manage cash crunches, Kraft Dinner purchases may involve discomfort because these purchases are made in situations of serious financial constraint or in anticipation of impending financial crisis. In food-insecure households, Kraft Dinner is truly synonymous with lack of money to purchase other foods, contributes to dietary monotony, and compounds anxiety about maintaining a supply of fresh milk. We noted that the food-insecure respondents did not distinguish between Kraft Dinner packages that were purchased or received from a charitable program. It seems as if it is the Kraft Dinner itself, and not its source, that evokes discomforting feelings. While our dataset did not include discussion of consuming donated Kraft Dinner compared with purchased Kraft Dinner, there was extensive discussion of the nutritional inadequacy of food bank fare and of the stigma associated with resorting to a food bank.

DISCUSSION

We have shown that Kraft Dinner means different things to food-insecure compared with food-secure Canadians. Whereas food-secure Canadians tend to associate Kraft Dinner with comfort, food-insecure Canadians tend to associate Kraft Dinner with discomfort.

Although an estimated 73% of the population believes that hunger is a significant problem in Canada (Canadian Association of Food Banks 2006, p.9), our analysis suggests considerable ignorance among food-secure Canadians about the particulars of the food insecurity experience. For example, food-secure Canadians do not generally associate food insecurity with fresh milk scarcity. Dairy products are carefully apportioned to different members of food-insecure households, with the youngest children given first priority (McIntyre et al. 2002, 2003a, b); meanwhile, fresh milk is both scarce and its availability of tremendous symbolic significance (McIntyre et al. 2007b). In light of research showing fluctuations in nutrition over the course of a month in parallel with cash flows in food-insecure households (McIntyre et al. 2007; Tarasuk et al. 2007), and also of research suggesting that food shopping for loved ones may amount to an everyday sacrificial ritual (Miller 1998), a genuine Kraft Dinner prepared with the requisite amount of fresh milk might be construed in some food-insecure households as an elusive goal.

The ill-informed food-secure perspective influences food donations, illustrated in part by the prevalence of Kraft Dinner as a commonly donated food item. Rather than providing comfort to food-insecure Canadians, donated Kraft Dinner contributes to discomfort among food-insecure recipients. Ignorance among food-secure people of what it is like to be poor amidst plenty may partly account for the perpetuation of local food charity as the dominant response in Canada to food insecurity (see also Rock 2006).

One limitation of this study is that our data on food-insecure perceptions came from interviews and focus groups with women who head up households on their own. Yet men also experience food insecurity in Canada, and their perceptions of Kraft Dinner could differ from women's. Our data on food-secure perceptions, moreover, come from newspapers and from a small sample of interviews during which people were asked to comment on the common practice of donating Kraft Dinner for charitable redistribution. Thus, an important limitation of this paper is that actual individual donation practices were not studied. Not all of the interviewees had donated to food banks, nor did the study aim to establish that all had donated Kraft Dinner or a similar product in the past. Nevertheless, all interviewees readily agreed that Kraft Dinner and its imitators are commonly donated, and the newspaper data supported this contention.

As noted by Tarasuk and Eakin (2005, pp. 184–185), most previous research on food insecurity in Canada has regarded the proliferation and subsequent entrenchment of food banks across Canada as a function of demand, that is, as a direct result of food insecurity. Their work has shown that the way in which food banks operate actually masks the severity and extent of food insecurity (Tarasuk and Eakin 2003), while also conveniently providing food manufacturers, wholesalers, and retailers with a low-cost way of disposing of unwanted products (Tarasuk and Eakin 2005). "The entwining of food bank work with the needs of the food industry must also serve to obscure the inadequacies and inappropriateness of food banks as a response to the problems of food insecurity and contribute to the entrenchment of this secondary food system," they observe (Tarasuk and

Eakin 2005, p. 184). In an earlier paper examining an annual food drive in Michigan, USA, DeLind (1994) also critiqued the entwining of charitable food assistance with corporate agendas. We share the view that need alone cannot account for the popularity of food banks and other forms of charitable food assistance, and we suggest that, in addition to corporate interests, the perceptions held by food-secure people merit scrutiny. Food-secure individuals not only donate, they vote. And not only do they vote in elections of government officials, they vote with their feet when shopping. The use of food insecurity by food corporations in public relations, and the perpetual lack of publicly funded initiatives to redress food insecurity, cannot be fully explained without considering public perceptions.

To recognize the discomfort that results from obligatory consumption of Kraft Dinner requires food-secure people to view the world as it is actually seen and experienced by food-insecure people. By obligatory consumption of Kraft Dinner, we mean any product in the style of Kraft Dinner purchased under financial duress, as well as any such product obtained from a food bank or other charitable program. First, obligatory consumption of Kraft Dinner prepared without all requisite ingredients, fresh milk in particular, is not palatable. Second, obligatory consumption of Kraft Dinner or any other food received through recourse to a charitable program is a stigmatizing experience because charitable redistribution does not constitute a normal food channel. If understood as "the inability to obtain sufficient, nutritious, personally acceptable food through normal food channels or the uncertainty that one will be able to do so" (Davis and Tarasuk 1994, p. 51), food banks cannot resolve food insecurity. Third, over time, repetitive consumption of Kraft Dinner and its imitators contributes to a monotonous and nutritionally unbalanced diet. While Kraft Dinner does provide some key nutrients, it provides little dietary fiber and may contribute to excess sodium, especially if consumed routinely in large portions.

Previous studies have underscored the importance of specific foods in making social class distinctions (Bourdieu 1984 [1979]; Mintz 1985; Roseberry 1997; Penfold 2002), yet questions regarding social inequality deserve further attention in contemporary research on food cultures (Mintz and Du Bois 2002; Phillips 2006). By contrasting how food-secure and food-insecure people perceive Kraft Dinner, the palpable salience of social class came to the fore in our analysis. Stark differences in how food-secure and food-insecure Canadians experience the world are thrown into relief when a box of Kraft Dinner travels from a food-secure household to a food-insecure household via a food bank. Rather than a comforting satiety, one finds discomforting penury. The "biographies" or "social lives" (Appadurai 1986; Kopytoff 1986) of donated Kraft Dinner boxes are structured by social knowledge, i.e., that Kraft Dinner is palatable, easy to store, and easy to prepare in food-secure households, so it must retain these properties in food-insecure households—social knowledge which is also a form of ignorance. In the contemporary Canadian context, confidence of mainstream society regarding Kraft Dinner's stability is part of "ignorance-qua-knowledge" (cf. Gershon and Raj 2000) that helps to constitutes "food-secure" and "food-insecure" as interrelated social positions. The social dynamics that produce health and wealth, in other words, also produce sickness and poverty; so much so that central or dominant perspectives exert structuring effects on lives led at the peripheries (Nguyen and Peschard 2004; Moore 2006). Living in the shadow of abundance (Storper 2000), meanwhile, is part of the discomfort synonymous with food insecurity. Ultimately, Kraft Dinner "tastes" entirely different, depending upon whether a given box ends up being consumed in a food-secure or in a food-insecure household. . . .

CRITICAL THINKING QUESTIONS

1. How do people who are food-insecure perceive Kraft dinner differently from those who have enough food?

2. How might the diet of a middle- or upper-class person differ from that of a person in poverty? Relatedly, in terms of social class, how do restaurants differ?

3. As the reading illustrates, social class matters when it comes to food. What about drinks? And can preference for particular foods and drinks also be gendered?

REFERENCES

Allossery, P. 2000. Kraft hits its mark in a cheesy moment. And why Kraft's new ad campaign brings it back to form. *National Post* C.04.

Appadurai, A. 1986. Introduction: commodities and the politics of value. In *The social life of things: commodities in cultural perspective*, ed. A. Appadurai, 3–63. Cambridge, UK: Cambridge University Press.

Bateman, J. 2007. Barenaked Ladies. Encyclopedia of music in Canada 2007. Available: **http://thecanadianencyclopedia.com/index.cfm?PgNm=TCE&Params=U1SEC843622.** Accessed February 22, 2007.

Bernard, H. R. 2006. *Research methods in anthropology: Qualitative and quantitative approaches*. Lanham, MD: AltaMira Press.

Borkan, J. 1999. Immersion/crystallization. In *Doing qualitative research*, eds. B. Crabtree and W. L. Miller, 179–194. London: Sage.

Bourdieu, P. 1984 [1979]. *Distinction: a social critique of the judgment of taste*. Cambridge, MA: Harvard University Press.

Bryman, A. 2001. *Social research methods*. Oxford. UK: Oxford University Press.

Canadian Association of Food Banks. 2007. HungerCount 2006. Canadian Association of Food Banks 2006. Available: **http://www.cafb-acba.ca/documents/2006_HungerCount_EN_designed.pdf.** Accessed February 21, 2007.

Davis, B., and V. Tarasuk. 1994. Hunger in Canada. *Agriculture and Human Values*, 11(4): 50–57.

DeLind, L. B. 1994. Celebrating hunger in Michigan: a critique of an emergency food program and an alternative for the future. *Agriculture and Human Values*, 11(4): 58–68.

Gershon, I., and D. S. Raj. 2000. The symbolic capital of ignorance. *Social Analysis*, 44(2): 3–14.

Glaser, B. G., and A. L. Strauss. 1967. *The discovery of grounded theory: strategies for qualitative research*. Chicago: Aldine.

Health Canada. 2007. Income-related household food security in Canada. Canadian Community Health Survey, Cycle 2.2, Nutrition (2004) 2007. Available: **http://www.hc-sc.gc.ca/fn-an/surveill/nutrition/commun/income_food_sec-sec_alim_e.html.** Accessed August 24, 2007.

Jacobson, R. R., and D. E. Salamie. 2002. Kraft Foods. In *International directory of company histories*, vol. 45, ed. J. P. Pederson, 235–244. Detroit, Michigan: St. James Press.

Kopytoff, I. 1986. The cultural biography of things: commoditization as process. In *The social life of things: commodities in cultural perspective*, ed. A. Appadurai, 64–91. Cambridge, UK: Cambridge University Press.

Locher, J. L. 2002. Comfort food. In *Encyclopedia of food and culture*, ed. S. H. Katz, 442–443. New York: Charles Scribner's Sons.

Locher, J. L., W. C. Yoels, D. Maurer, and J. Van Ells. 2005. Comfort foods: an exploratory journey into the social and emotional significance of food. *Food and Foodways*, 13: 273–297.

McIntyre, L., N. T. Glanville, S. Officer, B. Anderson, K. D. Raine, and J. B. Dayle. 2002. Food insecurity of low-income lone mothers and their children in Atlantic Canada. *Canadian Journal of Public Health*, 93(6): 411–415.

McIntyre, L., N. T. Glanville, K. D. Raine, J. B. Dayle, B. Anderson, and N. Battaglia. 2003a. Do low-income lone mothers compromise their nutrition to feed their children? *Canadian Medical Association Journal*, 168(6): 686–691.

McIntyre, L., S. Officer, and L. M. Robinson. 2003b. Feeling poor: the felt experience of low-income lone mothers. *Affilia: Journal of Women and Social Work*, 18(3): 316–331.

McIntyre, L., V. Tarasuk, and T. Jinguang Li. 2007a. Improving the nutritional status of food-insecure women: first, let them eat what they like. *Public Health Nutrition*, 10(11): 1288–1298.

McIntyre, L., P. Williams, and N. T. Glanville. 2007b. Milk as metaphor: low income lone mothers' characterization of their challenges in acquiring milk for their families. *Ecology of Food and Nutrition*, 46: 263–279.

Merriam-Webster. 2007. Comfort food 2007. Available: http://www.m-w.com. Accessed August 24, 2007.

Miles, M.B., and A. M. Huberman. 1994. *Qualitative data analysis*. Thousand Oaks, CA: Sage.

Miller, D. 1998. *A theory of shopping*. Ithaca, NY: Cornell University Press.

Mintz, S. 1985. *Sweetness and power: the place of sugar in modern history*. New York: Viking Press.

Mintz, S., and C. Du Bois. 2002. The anthropology of food and eating. *Annual Review of Anthropology* 31: 99–119.

Moore, S. 2006. Peripherality, income inequality, and life expectancy: revisiting the income inequality hypothesis. *International Journal of Epidemiology*, 35(3): 623–632.

Nguyen, V.-K., and K. Peschard. 2004. Anthropology, inequality, and disease: a review. *Annual Review of Anthropology*, 32: 447–474.

Oxford English Dictionary. 2007. Comfort food 2007. Available: http://dictionary.oed.com. Accessed August 24, 2007.

Penfold, S. 2002. "Eddie Shack was no Tim Horton": Donuts and the folklore of mass culture in Canada. In *Food nations: selling taste in consumer societies*, eds. W. Belasco and P. Scranton, 48–66. London, New York: Routledge.

Phillips, L. 2006. Food and globalization. *Annual Review of Anthropology*, 35: 37–57.

Poland, B. D. 1995. Transcription quality as an aspect of rigor in qualitative research. *Qualitative Inquiry*, 1(3): 290–310.

Print Measurement Bureau. 2003. PMB 2003 category reports: groceries 2003. Available: www.pmb.ca. Accessed February 24, 2004.

QSR International. 2006. NVivo 7, Version 7.0.247.0 [computer software]. Doncaster, Victoria, Australia: QSR International Pty. Ltd.

Ricciuto, L. E., and V. S. Tarasuk. 2007. An examination of income-related disparities in the nutritional quality of food selections among Canadian households from 1986–2001. *Social Science and Medicine*, 64(1): 186–198.

Rock, M. 2006. "We don't want to manage poverty": community groups politicize food insecurity and charitable food donations. *Promotion and Education: International Journal for Health Promotion and Education*, 13(1): 36–41.

Roseberry, W. 1997. The rise of yuppie coffees and the reimagination of class in the United States. *American Anthropologist*, 98(4): 762–775.

Safeway Canada. 2007. Safeway community caring. National sponsorships and programs. Food bank 2007. Available: http://shop.safeway.com/corporate/safeway/community_can/food_bank.asp. Accessed February 21, 2007.

Spradley, J. 1979. *The ethnographic interview*. New York: Holt, Rinehart and Winston.

Storper, M. 2000. Lived effects of the contemporary economy: globalization, inequality, and consumer society. *Public Culture*, 12(2): 375–410.

Tarasuk, V., and J. M. Eakin. 2003. Charitable food assistance as symbolic gesture: an ethnographic study of food banks in Ontario. *Social Science and Medicine*, 56(7): 1505–1515.

———. 2005. Food assistance through "surplus" food: insights from an ethnographic study of food bank work. *Agriculture and Human Values*, 22(2): 177–186.

Tarasuk, V., and N. Vozoris. 2003. Household food insufficiency is associated with poorer health. *Journal of Nutrition*, 133(1): 120–126.

Tarasuk, V., L. McIntyre, and J. Li. 2007. Low-income women's dietary intakes are sensitive to the depletion of household resources in one month. *Journal of Nutrition*, 137(8): 1980–1987.

Tayti, M. 2000. Invitations out for Welland food drive. *Tribune* B.3.

Webb, E., D. T. Campbell, R. D. Schwartz, and L. Sechrest. 1981 [1966]. *Unobtrusive research: Nonreactive research in the social sciences*. Chicago: Rand McNally.

29

Introduction to *The Canadian Fact Book on Poverty*

DAVID P. ROSS, KATHERINE J. SCOTT, AND PETER J. SMITH

This classic statement summarizes what it means to be poor in Canada and introduces students to politically contentious issues such as the definition and measurement of poverty. This book is published by the Canadian Council on Social Development, an organization that conducts research on poverty and economic inequality in Canada. The CCSD maintains a website that features some of the most recent poverty statistics available.

When most Canadians think of poverty, the image is of sickly children on the edge of starvation. In highly industrialized societies, however, this scene is not typical. What prevails instead is deprivation and need. In Canada, people suffer deeply not because the necessities of life barely exist for the population at large—the state of affairs in many Third World countries—but because an unequal distribution of income blocks access to Canada's abundance. Poverty in this country is a matter not of starving but rather of begging for food at food banks and shelters, and of being shunted from one substandard shelter arrangement to another. For an increasing number of people, it even means living on the street and panhandling. This dreary picture is the result of an unequal distribution of riches rather than a lack of riches.

Source: David P. Ross, Katherine J. Scott, and Peter J. Smith. 2000. In *The Canadian Fact Book on Poverty,* pp. 1–7. Ottawa: The Canadian Council on Social Development.

Poverty of the type typically found in industrial countries is a serious matter, and pockets of Third World poverty do exist in Canada, in some of our inner cities and on the reserves of Aboriginal peoples. There is no shortage of statistics documenting a link between poverty in Canada and various debilitating behaviours and conditions. For the sake of the many sceptics, let it be stressed that the authors do not claim that lack of income itself causes these human conditions—one cannot demonstrate causation with statistics—but only that these conditions are strongly associated with low income. The question of causation is left to the reader's own judgement.

The statistics are especially striking for children—a segment of the population that is unequipped to overcome poverty by any efforts of its own. Income levels and the well-being of Canadian children are undeniably linked, as a pioneering study by the Canadian Council on

Social Development (CCSD) has documented. Some of these links are:

- Poor children (family income less than $20,000) are 1.3 times more likely to be growing up in substandard housing as are children from middle-income families (family income $45,000), and 2.4 times as likely as are children from high-income families (income above $80,000).

- Poor children are 1.9 times more likely to be living in neighbourhoods with lots of problems, such as fighting, drug dealing and vandalism, than are children in middle-income families, and 2.4 times more likely than are children in high-income families.

- Poor children are 1.4 times more likely to engage in aggressive behaviour than are children in middle-income families or higher-income families.

- Poor children are 1.5 and 1.7 times as likely to be hyperactive than are children from middle- and high-income families, respectively.

- Poor children are more likely to exhibit delinquent behaviours compared to middle- and high-income families: 1.8 and 2.6 times respectively.

- Serious health problems that affect a child's functioning such as vision, hearing, speech, mobility and cognition are 1.7 and 2.6 times more likely to be found in poor children than in children from middle- and high-income families, respectively.

- Four- and five-year-old children from poor families are 2.2 and 4.5 times more likely to exhibit delayed development on vocabulary tests than are the children from middle- and high-income families. In fact, over one-third (36 percent) of poor children are judged to have delayed language development.

- Children from poor families are 1.8 times as likely to be registered in special education classes than are children from middle- and high-income families. Children enrolled in special education classes are at higher risk

for falling behind in school and dropping out before high school completion.

- Poor children are 1.3 times less likely to participate in organized sports than are children from middle-income families and 2.8 times less likely than are children from high-income families. Almost three-quarters (72 percent) of poor children do not participate compared to only one-quarter of children from high-income families.

- Older teens aged 16 to 19 years are normally expected to be either in school or in a job. However, poor children are 2.5 and 4.4 times more likely to be engaged in neither activity (in a sense, they are "idle") compared to teens from middle- and higher-income families.

This partial catalogue of misfortune makes clear that children who grow up in low-income families stand out in a variety of ways from their better-off peers. They are less healthy, have less access to skill-building activities, have more destructive habits and behaviours, live more stressful lives, and are subject to more humiliation. In short, they have less stable and less secure existences, and as a result are less likely to be secure as adults.

In a day and age when education, emotional maturity, leadership, and social and communication skills are prized as essential for prospering in an increasingly knowledge-based society, it is not promising that so many Canadian children are starting off with such disadvantage. The days of just making sure that children had enough to eat and a roof over their heads in order to produce strong arms and backs is long gone. The skills and attributes valued today require more than a start in life at a minimum subsistence level. In fact, the CCSD study (from which the above findings are taken) shows that after studying 27 living conditions and outcomes, the likelihood of a poor outcome dramatically diminishes up to a family income level of $30,000 in 80 percent of the cases. Further, in 50 percent of the cases, risk rapidly diminishes up to the $40,000 family income level. If a high level of child well-being is an important objective of a society, these are the income levels that need to be discussed in terms of setting a floor on income inequality in Canada.

The cataloguing of misfortune is not restricted to children. Adults with low incomes also suffer debilitating conditions according to a Statistics Canada study:

- Adults in low-income households (less than $30,000 income) are 4.6 times more likely to report being in poor or only fair health compared to high-income adults (over $60,000), and 2.2 times more likely than middle-income adults ($30,000 to $60,000). In fact, one-fifth of poor adults report being in poor or only fair health.

- Serious health problems that affect an adult's functioning such as vision, hearing, speech, mobility and cognition are 1.3 and 2.0 times more likely to be found in poor adults than in middle- and high-income adults respectively. Two-fifths of low-income adults have these health problems.

- Suffering from chronic health conditions such as asthma, high blood pressure, stomach ulcers and the effects of stroke is more prevalent in low-income adults. Whereas 55 percent of low-income adults had two or more of these conditions, this was true for only 32 percent of middle-income adults and 13 percent of those with high incomes.

- The mental state of adults who responded to the Statistics Canada survey has been summed up in a mental health distress index. The results show that low-income adults are 2.4 times more likely to have a high distress score than are high-income adults, and 1.8 times more likely than are middle-income adults.

- Low-income adults are 1.3 times more likely to express low self-esteem compared to high-income adults. Esteem relates to whether a person feels they have a number of good qualities, are worth as much as others, have a positive attitude towards self, and whether they believe they are failures or not.

These results for adults cannot confirm that the debilitating conditions in each case are caused by low income. In some cases, it may be that the conditions are the cause of low incomes. However, this brief portrait does confirm that low income is associated with a disproportionate number of special problems. Thus, to integrate these people into society requires a special effort. To facilitate a permanent escape from poverty, such an effort must include special services to assist people in overcoming or adapting to some of the problems as well as income transfers to address their current poverty.

While noting the links between income and many child and adult outcomes, it would be gratifying to report that the inequality between rich and poor is narrowing and as a consequence, some of the riskier outcomes are being ameliorated. Unfortunately, the opposite is true—inequality is widening. For example, between 1973 and 1997, the share of total earnings in Canada going to the bottom 20 percent of families with children fell steeply from a paltry 5.3 percent to 2.6 percent, which represents several billion dollars in total. In contrast, the share of earnings going to the top 20 percent increased from an already generous 38.4 percent to 42.8 percent. This is income redistribution in reverse. Fortunately, after government transfers and income taxes, the picture improves: the bottom 20 percent received 7.7 percent of all income in 1973, but even this small amount had deteriorated to 7.0 percent in 1997, while the top 20 percent increased their share from 35.5 percent to 37.2 percent. So, over time, both labour market earnings and government assistance have let down the poor.

A DAY IN A LIFE OF POVERTY

Aside from the negative links between low income and child well-being, what does it mean in real-life terms to be raised in poverty in a well-off industrialized country such as Canada? Although some individuals raised in poor families turn out to be happy and successful adults, such exceptions do not disprove the rule. Most poor Canadian individuals or families suffer the effects of continual deprivation: a relentless feeling of being boxed in; a feeling that life is dictated by the requirements simply of surviving each day. In this way of life there is no choice, there is no flexibility, and if something unexpected happens—such as sickness, accident, family death, fire or theft, rent increase—there is no buffer to deal with the emergency. Life is just today, because tomorrow offers no hope.

Perhaps the easiest way to comprehend what a day in a life of poverty is like is to describe a family's left-over income after it pays for basic shelter, food and clothing. How much money does a typical poor family consisting of two adults and two children, and living in a large urban area, have at its disposal? In 1997, while the traditional Statistics Canada low income cut-off line for such a family was set at $28,100, the average two-parent family with two children was in fact below this line by an amount equal to $10,050, leaving it with $18,050 annually on which to live.

Compare this to the family's basic expenditures on shelter, food and clothing. Using the Canadian Mortgage and Housing Corporation (CMHC) survey of shelter costs across the country, the median rent for a three-bedroom apartment amounted to $8,495 per year (weekly equivalent of $40.84 per person). To adhere to Agriculture Canada's Nutritious Food Basket as a guide to basic food costs, the family required $6,885 (weekly equivalent of $33.10 per person). Using the Montreal Diet Dispensary guidelines for basic living, estimated clothing costs totalled $2,208 (weekly equivalent of $10.61 per person). This amounts to $17,588 per year for the typical poor four-member family. Deducting this from its gross income of $18,050 leaves a surplus of only $462 for the year, or $2.22 per person per week.

This $2.22 per week must be used to meet all other needs such as personal care, household needs, furniture, telephone, transportation, school supplies, health care and so on. There is no money for entertainment, recreation, reading material, insurance, and charitable or religious donations.

It is easy to understand why poor families:

- cut into their budget for essentials;
- rent substandard housing;
- move often in attempts to save rent;
- purchase poor-quality food that lacks freshness or variety;
- supplement their food budget with trips to food banks;
- own a minimum selection of mainly used clothing.

DEFINING AND MEASURING POVERTY

There are two basic approaches to defining and measuring poverty in Canada. When taken to their respective extremes, they establish the possible income bounds of poverty. Numerous intermediate measures fall between these extremes.

- *Absolute measure:* The first approach is based on the belief that one can determine an *absolute* measure of poverty by examining an essential basket of goods and services deemed necessary for physical survival. The cost of this basket represents an objective dollar measure of poverty. The strictest application of this approach results in a standard of living sufficient only to keep the human body together. This purely physical approach stipulates a budget whose components are food provided by a charitable group or food bank, shelter provided by a community hostel, secondhand clothing, and access to basic remedial health care. The poverty line implied by such a budget would be very low; an annual income in the order of $2,000 per person would probably cover it.

The consequence of the absolute approach, if rigorously applied, is an utter absence of choice and flexibility in how one lives. The shape of one's life is determined rigidly by the requirements of a fixed and rock-bottom physical existence.

• ***Relative approach:*** At the other definitional extreme is the *relative* approach, which is based on the belief that any definition of poverty must take into account social and psychological as well as physical well-being. The relative approach is based on social inclusion and equity, that is, on some notion of the extent to which society should tolerate inequality in the distribution of income. It argues that someone who has so little that he or she stands out in relation to the surrounding community will feel marginalized. Marginalized people, whether children or adults, affect the social cohesion of a community because they no longer feel part of what they see as an indifferent or hostile society.

In the rich countries of the industrialized world, the income level associated with a relative definition of poverty will be many times the level required to assure physical survival. In fact, an argument frequently voiced against relative definitions of poverty is that a typical poor family in Canada would be wealthy if the family lived in the Third World. But poor Canadians do not live in the Third World; they live in communities that have First World living costs and in which wealth surrounds them daily. Hence the justification for a relative measure.

Not surprisingly, there is no consensus on the question of which basic approach should be adopted. Most approaches compromise between the two, that is, they attempt to define a basket of goods and services that assures a minimum standard of living which is acceptable in social as well as purely physical terms. The difference in these approaches is their judgement of what constitutes a minimum that respects the need to function with dignity in society. The difference between the lower guidelines based on absolute or physical definitions of poverty, and the higher ones based on relative or social definitions, is considerable.

To a great extent, the enduring debate about the proper definition of poverty is academic. Although poverty standards have been loosely used as a guide to the level of payments under the federal government's elderly benefit programs, and to determine eligibility for school lunch programs and the like, they have not been used to set the level of the income safety net. The income of poor households falls well below the recommended incomes of the most widely accepted definitions of poverty. For example, the income of the average Canadian poor family in 1997 was $8,559 below the widely recognized low-income line established by Statistics Canada (and $8,942 below in the case of a lone-parent mother). It is accurate to conclude, therefore, that basic assistance to Canada's poor population is guided mainly by the absolute approach to the definition of poverty. The growth and persistence of food banks and the homeless underscore this conclusion.

CRITICAL THINKING QUESTIONS

1. What is the difference between a relative and absolute poverty line? Do you think poverty should be measured on a relative or absolute basis?

2. Why do you think there is so much debate about where the poverty line should be drawn? Where do you think it should be placed? The Statistics Canada low-income cut-off for a family of four living in a large urban area is $39,399 (before taxes). Is this too generous or too stingy? Prepare an approximate budget (rent, food, clothing, transportation, etc.).

3. What is the government's role in combating poverty? Do you think market forces are capable of dealing with poverty on their own? Can you think of countries where there are no welfare state programs? What is the likely result of not having any welfare programs?

30

Free Trade and the Third World

PETER URMETZER

The debate about the relationship between the First and Third World is a seemingly unending one. Are First World countries wealthy because they exploit poor countries or because they are more productive? This reading examines the role of international institutions, including the World Bank, World Trade Organization, and the International Monetary Fund, and how they govern economic interaction between rich and poor countries.

True individual freedom cannot exist without economic security and independence. People who are hungry and out of a job are the stuff of which dictatorships are made.

—Franklin D. Roosevelt

FREE TRADE AND THE THIRD WORLD

Based on the lottery that is life, or at least so the story goes, some countries are naturally better endowed with resources than others. Some, like Canada, find themselves with vast tracts of timber, whereas others, like Brazil, may have perfect conditions for growing coffee. One country's workforce may be skilled at manufacturing automobiles, another's at

Source: Peter Urmetzer. 2003. In *From Free Trade to Forced Trade: Canada in the Global Economy,* pp. 165–169, 170–178, 179–183. Toronto: Penguin Canada.

producing shirts, and if all engage in trade, according to the theory, all will be better off. This makes one wonder, why do poor countries, at least for the most part, continue to be poor? Not only that, why, as we shall soon see, is this gap widening? The answer may, ironically, have less to do with free trade than with too much interference by the West. By trying their best to ensure that the market system rules supreme in the Third World, the World Bank and the International Monetary Fund (IMF), and to some degree the World Trade Organization (WTO), might well have made things worse.

The World Bank and the IMF

The two institutions just mentioned, the World Bank and the IMF, are frequently mentioned in the same breath as the WTO, and for good reason: They share a common history. The World

Bank and the IMF, and to a lesser degree the WTO, are all part of a monetary framework designed by Britain and the United States around the end of the Second World War.

The World Bank and the IMF are often referred to as the Bretton Woods Twins, and are considered sister institutions in that they fulfill similar roles. Both are located in Washington, DC, which should give some indication of who dominates these institutions. Another clue that hints at the cozy relationship between the US administration and these organizations is that some commentators have come to include the World Bank and the IMF when they refer to Washington (or the Washington Consensus). The World Bank and the IMF are a direct result of the Bretton Woods negotiations, which took place in New Hampshire in 1944. Given the geopolitical climate at the end of the Second World War, it should come as no surprise that only two countries mattered in these negotiations: Great Britain (represented by John Maynard Keynes) and the United States (represented by Harry Dexter White). After nearly six decades, these institutions are now well integrated into the American world order. With a few exceptions, such as Cuba and North Korea, this vision has been adopted around the world. By default, the free market system has replaced much of the socialist system in what used to be referred to as the Second World, the erstwhile Soviet Union.

The World Bank and the IMF epitomize the relationship between the First and the Third Worlds, a system in which political power directly corresponds to economic strength. Being the world's wealthiest nation in such a system, the United States reigns. This hierarchy is explicit within the World Bank and the IMF, as voting strength is directly related to the size of a country's economy. On this basis, the United States effectively has veto power over any decisions these institutions make. Although the IMF has provided assistance to countries in the First World, all World Bank loans (with the exception of a small number in its early days) and the majority of IMF interventions have been in the Third World. And as is often the case in these situations, these monies come with strings attached. It is not altogether surprising that these strings can be traced to Anglo-Saxon ideas about the free market: no social programs, no deficit, low inflation, privatization, and no subsidies, with few allowances for labour or environmental standards. Not only are these policies an integral part of these institutions' ideologies, but they are explicitly practised in what are called the Structural Adjustment Programs (SAP).

World Bank

There is no such institution as the World Bank. It is merely a term of convenience used to describe two related institutions: the IBRD (International Bank for Reconstruction and Development) and the IDA (International Development Association). Both institutions, as well as the IMF and the WTO, are also part of the UN. The World Bank's headquarters is located, as already mentioned, in Washington, DC, with offices in New York, Paris, Geneva, London, and Tokyo.[1]

The majority of loans by the World Bank are from the IBRD. In 1999, for example, of the US $29 billion lent out by the World Bank, $22 billion, or around three-quarters of the total, originated with the IBRD. The other 25 percent of loans were associated with the IDA. Together these institutions have lent an amount fast approaching half a trillion dollars since their inception, a tidy sum, but one that still greatly underestimates the power of the World Bank. When the World Bank first lends money to a Third World country, the loan serves as a signal to private investors that the country is a safe haven for investment. In 1998, of the long-term debt owed by the Third World (in contrast with the short-term debt that is the bailiwick of the

IMF), only 16 percent was owed to the World Bank. The other 84 percent was owed to private banks (57 percent) and other governments (27 percent). These figures do not include investments such as foreign direct investment, or FDI (the establishment of branch plants, buying of real estate, etc.). This private/public mix tends to favour public debt as risk increases. For example, 72 percent of South American debt is held in private hands, compared with only 24 percent in equatorial Africa.

There is considerable evidence that the bank was instrumental in the proliferation of Third World debt. In no way was this due to malice, but rather to two unfortunate and unanticipated developments. One, as part of its mandate, the World Bank attempted to help countries industrialize, which included sponsoring megaprojects such as dams, bridges, and other infrastructure. In order to finance these projects, Third World countries were encouraged to borrow. At first this did not present much of a problem, as in the 1960s and 1970s interest rates were low. But this would soon change. Central banks around the world—including the Federal Reserve in the United States, the Bundesbank in West Germany, and the Bank of Canada in Canada—declared war on inflation in the mid-1970s. Their primary policy instrument in this war was high interest rates. This meant that both debts and interest payments everywhere, including those of the Third World, skyrocketed. Put simply, when the Third World was first seduced into going on a borrowing spree money was cheap; when it was time to pay, it was dear.

The second reason for the Third World debt crisis is less well recognized. The West reasoned that if countries wanted to get on the right track towards modernization, they needed to trade more. More trade required that poor countries produce things that could be sold in foreign markets. As it was, these countries were primarily engaged in subsistence agriculture, and Western consumers were not all that interested in buying more rice or corn. Change, for

the most part, meant the exploitation of natural resources and a shift from food to cash crops (crops like coffee, which could be sold on the international market rather than consumed locally). An increased reliance on cash crops and natural resources, encouraged by the World Bank throughout the Third World, soon resulted in world markets being flooded with commodities like coffee, cocoa, rubber, and copper. And as any student of economics knows, when there are too many products on the market, prices drop. Things even got worse. In the push to modernize, Third World countries were also encouraged to export so they could acquire foreign exchange (US dollars, German marks) needed to buy products like machinery and oil, essential ingredients for industrialization. But this little plan soon backfired. Growing cash crops instead of food for local consumption led to increased reliance on food imports, which became relatively more expensive as commodity prices fell and local currencies lost value.

In short, the increase in interest rates coincided with falling commodity prices. Through no fault of its own, the Third World was suddenly faced with higher expenditures (in terms of increased debt maintenance) and lower income (due to falling commodity prices). Rather than going towards the purchase of products to modernize Third World economies as originally intended, foreign exchange went to pay foreign debts. It is important to keep in mind that these developments were not the result of the natural workings of the market but were initially orchestrated by the First World. In direct contradiction of free market doctrines, these programs were forced onto poor countries, illustrating once again that laissez-faire is planned. And badly planned at that.

Consequently, Third World debt soared, resulting in the 1980s debt crisis. At least from the perspective of the Third World, this crisis has yet to be resolved. Rather than take the blame and eliminate Third World debt, or at least substantially alleviate it, the World Bank used this opportunity to provide the Third World with another dose of First World medicine. When a country is in danger of defaulting on its debt, the World Bank and the IMF step in with emergency measures. The logic behind these programs is that the only remedy that will work is strict adherence to free market principles. These programs, commonly referred to as austerity programs, are officially known as Structural Adjustment Programs (SAP). These include privatization and downsizing of government; the promotion of exports and liberalization of imports; reduction or even elimination of subsidies to agriculture, food, health care, and education; and programs to curb inflation (including higher interest rates and reduction in wages).

Not surprisingly, these programs have failed to meet their objectives. Third World debt has continued to increase and its economies have faltered. The IMF and the World Bank have come under increasing scrutiny for their policies, both from the inside (including Joseph Stiglitz, the 2001 Nobel Prize winner in economics and former chief economist of the World Bank, who shared the prize with George Akerlof and Michael Spence) and the outside (the most prominent of their many critics being Paul David Hewson; a.k.a. the short guy with the funny glasses; a.k.a. Bono, the lead singer of the pop group U2).

The IMF (International Monetary Fund)

Like the World Bank, the IMF is part of the UN and a direct result of the Bretton Woods negotiations. The IMF, in particular, has been criticized for being overly secretive, and has historically been much less open to criticism than the World Bank. The IMF's major concern is international monetary co-operation and stability. When an emergency situation arises, such as balance of payment problems,

currency instability, or inability to meet financial obligations, the IMF steps in and provides emergency loans. As of 2001, the IMF had approximately US $65 billion of loans outstanding. As with World Bank loans, monies are tied to SAPs, which gives the IMF considerable sway over how a country's economy is managed. In comparison with the World Bank, details of what the IMF does are less clear. This can partly be blamed on the already mentioned lack of transparency. The World Bank also has the advantage of sharing similarities with regular banks, in that it lends money, which is easy to understand. Besides having no domestic counterpart, the responsibilities of the IMF are a little more technical. Furthermore, the IMF's mandate has changed considerably since its inception.

The primary role of the IMF following the Second World War was to supervise exchange rates. This was known as the Bretton Woods exchange system, whereby each country's currency was pegged to the American dollar, which, in turn, was pegged to the price of gold at US $35 per ounce. Some Canadians may remember that the price of foreign currencies, including that of the American dollar, fluctuated little between the war and the mid-1970s. For a variety of reasons, former US president Richard Nixon abandoned that system in 1971, and currencies were allowed to float. Suddenly, the price of currencies around the world became much more volatile (and as Canadians know too well, seemed only to drop). With the closing of the gold window, as it is sometimes referred to, one of the major responsibilities of the IMF had evaporated. But other commitments soon presented themselves. With the rapid rise in oil prices throughout the 1970s (which hurt importing countries) and the increase in interest rates (which hurt indebted countries), the IMF began to concentrate on short-term loans to countries that encountered balance of payment difficulties. Its role was further expanded when a series of Third World countries, starting with Mexico in 1982, came perilously close to defaulting on their debts.

The IMF also played a prominent role in the 1998 Asian crisis, but this debacle differed significantly from the 1980s debt crisis. The latter was largely caused by the increase in interest rates and affected mostly governments and big private banks. In contrast, in the Asian crisis the majority of investments were speculative in nature and involved private investors. Much of the foreign financing that had gone into Indonesia, South Korea, and Thailand went into risky ventures such as real estate speculation, and critics have pointed out that IMF loans did more for American, Japanese, and European investors than for the governments directly affected by the crisis. While the IMF guaranteed the investments of Westerners, austerity measures imposed on Indonesia, including the prohibition of subsidies for rice and cooking fuel, almost certainly contributed to the social unrest that the country underwent in 1999. According to the rules of the market, investors who greedily bankrolled foreign undertakings they knew little about should have suffered their own losses. But as it turned out, this was just another example of how institutions like the IMF are unable to stand by and do nothing when the judgment of the market fails to meet their expectations.

The Theory Behind Development

Essentially, the World Bank, the IMF, and the WTO are attempting to universalize the doctrines of laissez-faire, an ideology that originated in Great Britain in the eighteenth and nineteenth centuries. From there, mirroring colonization, it travelled to North America, Australia, and New Zealand, where the ideology still dominates. These ideas were also exported to other British colonies, including India and South Africa, and leaped the English Channel to the Continent, but there laissez-faire found a less welcoming environment and was tempered by the moderating influences of the host countries. In the twentieth century, dissemination of the free market ideology has continued unabated. It has now become the mission of institutions like the WTO and the World Bank to disseminate and enforce these ideas in the Third World.

Another important ideology that underlies institutions like the World Bank, the WTO, and the IMF is the old saw, promulgated by early social theorists, that societies must go through an evolution of stages on their way to industrial status. It is worthwhile noting that this thesis, usually referred to as modernization theory, has, in a variety of incarnations, been around for centuries, and yet its more optimistic prophecies have never come to fruition. This theory became fashionable in eighteenth- and nineteenth-century Europe, and attempted to explain the transition from an agricultural to an urban society. This change was accompanied by much tumult, and social theorists shared a desire to make sense of it all. Whereas some, like Adam Smith, saw order, others, like Karl Marx, saw chaos. Based on their observations, these theorists sought to establish principles from which they could generalize; that is, to apply their theories to all times and places. Not surprisingly, these theorists all observed a society that was slowly evolving from agrarian to industrial status. This evolutionary element provided an integral component for many theories, including those of French theorist Emile Durkheim, the Englishman Herbert Spencer, and the German Ferdinand Tonnies. All contrasted a decaying feudal, traditional, or agricultural order with a burgeoning industrial, urban, or modern one. Marx's theory stood apart only in that it had more stages—primitive communism, slavery, feudalism, capitalism, socialism, and communism—but the underlying evolutionary impetus was the same. Many academics have judged these theories as perspicacious for their time, but are reluctant to vouch for their universal application. This hesitancy is understandable for, given the benefit of hindsight, we know that not all societies have gone through these same stages of evolution. As a matter of fact, to this day there are still more people on this planet toiling away in agrarian than industrial societies.

The fact that theories of evolution have been discredited by more than two hundred years of history has not discouraged twentieth-century pundits from continuing with this train of thought. Today these theories comfortably fit under the rubric of modernization theory. Its proponents point to countries like Taiwan and South Korea as evidence of what is in store for the rest of the world. Beyond that, they forecast the eventual industrialization, and eventually post-industrialization, of all countries. In essence, these theories are no different than those espoused by theorists in the eighteenth century. The only difference is that today this thesis has left the theoretical realm and found practical applications through institutions like the World Bank and the WTO.

Suffering under the delusion that the West's economic success is rooted in laissez-faire, organizations like the WTO and the World Bank have put their faith in the market to solve the problem of global inequality. These institutions, as well as free traders in general, allege that open markets will eventually increase the wealth of all those who choose to participate in the global economy. Advocates of free trade have used this line of reasoning in a roundabout way to attack anti–free traders, accusing them of being anti-poor. They argue that by denying poor countries the opportunity to trade, anti-globalists also deny them a chance to become wealthy. But this road to wealth, we are forewarned, is a long one, and we cannot expect results to happen overnight.

In 1950, the GDP per capita of industrialized countries (excluding Japan) was approximately double that of Third World countries. By 1998, this gap had widened considerably, as the industrial countries' GDP per capita had increased to approximately five times that of the Third World. Whereas that of Asia and Latin America increased marginally (approximately doubling), GDP per capita failed to increase in Africa and dropped to 1950s levels after the fall of communism in the erstwhile Soviet countries.

And the further one goes back, the more apparent becomes the growing disparity in wealth between the First and Third Worlds. Angus Maddison, an economic historian with the OECD (Organisation for Economic Cooperation and Development), has examined the incomes of six regions over a 172-year period (Western Europe, North America, and Australia make up one region; Eastern Europe, Southern Europe, Latin America, Asia, and Africa are the other five).[2] In 1820, the ratio of economic output between the richest and poorest of these regions was 3:1. From that date on, the world economy grew at a monumental rate, although this growth affected each region differently. This should not be unexpected, given colonization as well as huge gaps in technology. Trade throughout that period also increased, particularly in the post-war era. At any rate, between 1820 and 1992 the ratio between the richest and poorest regions had grown from the original 3:1 to 16:1. When countries are considered instead of regions, this disparity becomes even more dramatic, growing from 3:1 in 1820 to 72:1 in 1992. At no time throughout this period did this process of polarization let up, let alone reverse. This even applies to the very prosperous post-war era, a period throughout which trade increased dramatically. The World Bank, despite claims that globalization is supposed to provide opportunities for less-developed countries, has published similar data. In terms of wealth, then, the world was a much more egalitarian place in the 1820s than in the 1990s, casting a shadow of doubt on theories that project a better future for the Third World on the basis of free trade or industrialization. Such promises have failed to materialize in the past 180 years and there is no reason to believe that they will bear fruit any time soon.

These theories, as advocated by the World Bank, and the WTO, have failed to produce the predicted results because they ignore the inter-relationships between countries, particularly that of the First and Third Worlds. Sociologists are keenly aware of how power imbalances affect relationships, whether between individuals or groups. From that perspective, it becomes clear that not all countries are equal. Suriname cannot boast the same influence on the world stage as the United States, for example. The reason, as Andre Gunder Frank has pointed out, is a history of colonialism. While that era has largely come to an end, First World countries continue to exert considerable power over the Third World in other, primarily economic, ways.

One reason that this disparity of wealth endures is precisely because of organizations like the World Bank and the WTO. Third World debt in 1998 was US $2.4 trillion (that's twelve zeros and approximately three and a half times Canada's yearly GDP). That same year, in order to service that debt, Third World countries paid US $296 billion in interest payments. This is more money than travelled the other direction in terms of aid. In other words, the industrialized world continues to be a net benefactor in this relationship. In the process, Third World economies are slowly being enslaved on account of their debts. For example, in Zambia 30 percent of government spending goes to paying off foreign debt, with only 10 percent going to social services, including health and education.

Ironically, despite their allegiance to free markets, these institutions are unable to keep their hands off them. First, they feel the inevitable evolutionary process towards modernization has to be nudged along, which does not necessarily have to be a bad thing. The transference of technology, knowledge, or capital investment can be of utmost value to poor countries. But even if modernization theory were correct in its fundamental premise that societies evolve, it does not necessarily follow that this process can be hurried along. There is good reason to believe that too quick a transition can ruin, rather than benefit, an economy. Witness, for example, the devastation that followed the sudden collapse of the Soviet economy a little over a decade ago. The transition from socialism to free market meant the economy went into free fall. When change is too rapid, or imposed from the outside as is often the case in the Third World, the effect may not always be that favourable. Second, the World Bank has always worked on the assumption that what is good for the First World must be equally good for the Third. But taken out of their Western context, free trade, privatization, and strict monetary policies have caused more ill to Third World economies than good. Not that free trade, privatization, and strict monetary policies have been all that successful in the First World either, but such policies make even less sense in economies that are still primarily agricultural.

And last, but not least, the evidence showing that First World countries are wealthy because of their strict adherence to free market principles is far from conclusive. First, the benefits of free trade, as we have discussed, are dubious to begin with. Second, First World countries all have generous education and health programs, which they sometimes deny to Third World countries. (Even in the United States, often considered a welfare-state laggard, 45 percent of health care is publicly funded, which amounted to US $522 billion in 1998. Publicly funded education cost another US $498 billion in the 1998–1999 school year, which adds up to over $1 trillion in government expenditures on a yearly basis for these two programs alone.) Industrialized countries also have huge civil services that provide many well-paying jobs. Third, there is consideration neither of differences in culture, nor of the power relationship, between the First and Third Worlds. When intervention is neutral (that is, money comes with no strings attached), it may not be altogether bad. But as we have seen, in its eagerness to pull the Third World out of poverty, First World policies have only succeeded in making the Third World go into more debt.

This is not to say that debt should be avoided at all costs. In order for economies to grow, they require capital, and borrowing funds can play an invaluable role in this process. The expansion of the British Empire was expedited by the availability of easy money, and many governments today borrow money to invest in their future. But there is a crucial difference between First and Third World debt, in that the former is usually owed internally and the latter externally. The biggest shortcoming associated with foreign debt is the control that the lender is able to exert over the indebted. It is precisely for this reason that many religions have proscribed debt. The Bible counsels that "the borrower is a servant to the lender." In that sense, large debts have enslaved Third World countries, making it difficult for them to become independent. Programs that have attempted to alleviate debts through rescheduling, such as the notorious SAP, have only succeeded in imposing more Western control over the Third World.

CRITICAL THINKING QUESTIONS

1. Why do you think some countries are rich and others are poor? It is often believed that people in Third World countries are less motivated than people in industrialized countries. Do you agree? Do you think the root cause for global economic inequality is structural (e.g., a history of colonialism) or behavioural (e.g., poor economic management)?

2. Why are the World Bank and the International Monetary Fund often referred to as sister institutions? Do you think the poorest countries should repay their debts, or (as Bono from U2 has championed) should their debts be forgiven?

3. Many cultures in the past have made it illegal to charge interest on loans. Is debt necessarily a bad thing? What is the power relationship between those who lend money and those who owe? Discuss the advantages and disadvantages of borrowing money for various institutions, including governments and corporations. What about the role of debt in your own life (e.g., purchasing a car or paying for an education)?

NOTES

1. The factual information about the World Bank is from its website, as well as from Susan George and Fabrizio Sabelli. *Faith and Credit: The World Bank's Secular Empire*. Toronto: Penguin Books, 1994.

2. Angus Maddison. 1995. *Monitoring the World Economy, 1820–1992*. Paris: OECD.

Gender

CLASSIC

CONTEMPORARY

CROSS-CULTURAL

31

Sex and Temperament in Three Primitive Societies

MARGARET MEAD

The work of anthropologist Margaret Mead laid the foundation for much of our contemporary sociological research and debate on gender. Are "masculine" and "feminine" traits innate or learned? Do men and women differ because of nature (heredity) or nurture (socialization)? Based on her studies of three "primitive peoples" in New Guinea, Margaret Mead argues that cultural conditioning is more important than biology in shaping women's and men's behaviour.

We have now considered in detail the approved personalities of each sex among three primitive peoples. We found the Arapesh—both men and women—displaying a personality that, out of our historically limited preoccupations, we would call maternal in its parental aspects, and feminine in its sexual aspects. We found men, as well as women, trained to be cooperative, unaggressive, responsive to the needs and demands of others. We found no idea that sex was a powerful driving force either for men or for women. In marked contrast to these attitudes, we found among the Mundugumor that both men and women developed as ruthless, aggressive, positively sexed individuals, with the maternal cherishing aspects of personality at a minimum. Both men and women approximated

to a personality type that we in our culture would find only in an undisciplined and very violent male. Neither the Arapesh nor the Mundugumor profit by a contrast between the sexes; the Arapesh ideal is the mild, responsive man married to the mild, responsive woman; the Mundugumor ideal is the violent aggressive man married to the violent aggressive woman. In the third tribe, the Tchambuli, we found a genuine reversal of the sex attitudes of our own culture, with the woman the dominant, impersonal, managing partner, the man the less responsible and the emotionally dependent person. These three situations suggest, then, a very definite conclusion. If those temperamental attitudes which we have traditionally regarded as feminine—such as passivity, responsiveness, and a willingness to cherish children—can so easily be set up as the masculine pattern in one tribe, and in another be outlawed for the majority of women as well as for the majority of men, we no longer have any basis for regarding such aspects of behaviour as sex-linked. And this conclusion becomes even stronger when we consider the actual reversal in Tchambuli of the position of dominance of the two sexes, in spite of the existence of formal patrilineal institutions.

The material suggests that we may say that many, if not all, of the personality traits which we have called masculine or feminine are as lightly linked to sex as are the clothing, the manners, and the form of head-dress that a society at a given period assigns to either sex. When we consider the behaviour of the typical Arapesh man or woman as contrasted with the behaviour of the typical Mundugumor man or woman, the evidence is overwhelmingly in favour of the strength of social conditioning. In no other way can we account for the almost complete uniformity with which Arapesh children develop into contented, passive, secure persons, while Mundugumor children develop as characteristically into violent, aggressive, insecure persons. Only to the impact of the whole of the integrated culture upon the growing child can we lay the formation of the contrasting types. There is no other explanation of race, or diet, or selection that can be adduced to explain them. We are forced to conclude that human nature is almost unbelievably malleable, responding accurately and contrastingly to contrasting cultural conditions. The differences between individuals who are members of different cultures, like the differences between individuals within a culture, are almost entirely to be laid to differences in conditioning, especially during early childhood, and the form of this conditioning is culturally determined. Standardized personality differences between the sexes are of this order, cultural creations to which each generation, male and female, is trained to conform. There remains, however, the problem of the origin of these socially standardized differences.

While the basic importance of social conditioning is still imperfectly recognized—not only in lay thought, but even by the scientist specifically concerned with such matters—to go beyond it and consider the possible influence of variations in hereditary equipment is a hazardous matter. The following pages will read very differently to one who has made a part of his thinking a recognition of the whole amazing mechanism of cultural conditioning—who has really accepted the fact that the same infant could be developed into a full participant in any one of these three cultures—than they will read to one who still believes that the minutiae of cultural behaviour are carried in the individual germ-plasm. If it is said, therefore, that when we have grasped the full significance of the malleability of the human organism and the preponderant importance of cultural conditioning, there are still further problems to solve, it must be remembered that these problems come after such a comprehension of the force of conditioning; they cannot precede it. The forces that make children born among the Arapesh grow up into typical Arapesh personalities are entirely social, and any discussion of the variations which do occur must be looked at against this social background.

With this warning firmly in mind, we can ask a further question. Granting the malleability of human nature, whence arise the differences between the standardized personalities that different cultures decree for all of their members, or which one culture decrees for the members of one sex as contrasted with the members of the opposite sex? If such differences are culturally created, as this material would most strongly suggest that they are, if the newborn child can be shaped with equal ease into an unaggressive Arapesh or an aggressive Mundugumor, why do these striking contrasts occur at all? If the clues to the different personalities decreed for men and women in Tchambuli do not lie in the physical constitution of the two sexes—an assumption that we must reject both for the Tchambuli and for our own society—where can we find the clues upon which the Tchambuli, the Arapesh, the

Mundugumor, have built? Cultures are man-made, they are built of human materials; they are diverse but comparable structures within which human beings can attain full human stature. Upon what have they built their diversities?

We recognize that a homogeneous culture committed in all of its gravest institutions and slightest usages to a cooperative, unaggressive course can bend every child to that emphasis, some to a perfect accord with it, the majority to an easy acceptance, while only a few deviants fail to receive the cultural imprint. To consider such traits as aggressiveness or passivity to be sex-linked is not possible in the light of the facts. Have such traits, then, as aggressiveness or passivity, pride or humility, objectivity or a preoccupation with personal relationships, an easy response to the needs of the young and the weak or a hostility to the young and the weak, a tendency to initiate sex-relations or merely to respond to the dictates of a situation or another person's advances—have these traits any basis in temperament at all? Are they potentialities of all human temperaments that can be developed by different kinds of social conditioning and which will not appear if the necessary conditioning is absent?

When we ask this question we shift our emphasis. If we ask why an Arapesh man or an Arapesh woman shows the kind of personality that we have considered in the first section of this book, the answer is: Because of the Arapesh culture, because of the intricate, elaborate, and unfailing fashion in which a culture is able to shape each new-born child to the cultural image. And if we ask the same question about a Mundugumor man or woman, or about a Tchambuli man as compared with a Tchambuli woman, the answer is of the same kind. They display the personalities that are peculiar to the cultures in which they were born and educated. Our attention has been on the differences between Arapesh men and women as a group and Mundugumor men and women as a group. It is as if we had represented the Arapesh

personality by a soft yellow, the Mundugumor by a deep red, while the Tchambuli female personality was deep orange, and that of the Tchambuli male, pale green. But if we now ask whence came the original direction in each culture, so that one now shows yellow, another red, the third orange and green by sex, then we must peer more closely. And leaning closer to the picture, it is as if behind the bright consistent yellow of the Arapesh, and the deep equally consistent red of the Mundugumor, behind the orange and green that are Tchambuli, we found in each case the delicate, just discernible outlines of the whole spectrum, differently overlaid in each case by the monotone which covers it. This spectrum is the range of individual differences which lie back of the so much more conspicuous cultural emphases, and it is to this that we must turn to find the explanation of cultural inspiration, of the source from which each culture has drawn.

There appears to be about the same range of basic temperamental variation among the Arapesh and among the Mundugumor, although the violent man is a misfit in the first society and a leader in the second. If human nature were completely homogeneous raw material, lacking specific drives and characterized by no important constitutional differences between individuals, then individuals who display personality traits so antithetical to the social pressure should not reappear in societies of such differing emphases. If the variations between individuals were to be set down to accidents in the genetic process, the same accidents should not be repeated with similar frequency in strikingly different cultures, with strongly contrasting methods of education.

But because this same relative distribution of individual differences does appear in culture after culture, in spite of the divergence between the cultures, it seems pertinent to offer a hypothesis to explain upon what basis the personalities of men and women have been differently standardized so often in the history of the human race. This hypothesis is an extension of that advanced by Ruth Benedict in her *Patterns of Culture*: Let us assume that there are definite temperamental differences between human beings which if not entirely hereditary at least are established on a hereditary base very soon after birth. (Further than this we cannot at present narrow the matter.) These differences finally embodied in the character structure of adults, then, are the clues from which culture works, selecting one temperament, or a combination of related and congruent types, as desirable, and embodying this choice in every thread of the social fabric—in the care of the young child, the games the children play, the songs the people sing, the structure of political organization, the religious observance, the art and the philosophy.

Some primitive societies have had the time and the robustness to revamp all of their institutions to fit one extreme type, and to develop educational techniques which will ensure that the majority of each generation will show a personality congruent with this extreme emphasis. Other societies have pursued a less definitive course, selecting their models not from the most extreme, most highly differentiated individuals, but from the less marked types. In such societies the approved personality is less pronounced, and the culture often contains the types of inconsistencies that many human beings display also; one institution may be adjusted to the uses of pride, another to a casual humility that is congruent neither with pride nor with inverted pride. Such societies, which have taken the more usual and less sharply defined types as models, often show also a less definitely patterned social structure. The culture of such societies may be likened to a house the decoration of which has been informed by no definite and precise taste, no exclusive emphasis upon dignity or comfort or pretentiousness or beauty, but in which a little of each effect has been included.

Alternatively, a culture may take its clues not from one temperament, but from several temperaments. But instead of mixing together into an inconsistent hotchpotch the choices and emphases of different temperaments, or blending them together into a smooth but not particularly distinguished whole, it may isolate each type by making it the basis for the approved social personality for an age-group, a sex-group, a caste-group, or an occupational group. In this way society becomes not a monotone with a few discrepant patches of an intrusive colour, but a mosaic, with different groups displaying different personality traits. Such specializations as these may be based upon any facet of human endowment—different intellectual abilities, different artistic abilities, different emotional traits. So the Samoans decree that all young people must show the personality trait of unaggressiveness and punish with opprobrium the aggressive child who displays traits regarded as appropriate only in titled middle-aged men. In societies based upon elaborate ideas of rank, members of the aristocracy will be permitted, even compelled, to display a pride, a sensitivity to insult, that would be deprecated as inappropriate in members of the plebeian class. So also in professional groups or in religious sects some temperamental traits are selected and institutionalized, and taught to each new member who enters the profession or sect. Thus the physician learns the bedside manner, which is the natural behaviour of some temperaments and the standard behaviour of the general practitioner in the medical profession; the Quaker learns at least the outward behaviour and the rudiments of meditation, the capacity for which is not necessarily an innate characteristic of many of the members of the Society of Friends.

So it is with the social personalities of the two sexes. The traits that occur in some members of each sex are specially assigned to one sex, and disallowed in the other. The history of the social definition of sex-differences is filled with such arbitrary arrangements in the intellectual and artistic field, but because of the assumed congruence between physiological sex and emotional endowment we have been less able to recognize that a similar arbitrary selection is being made among emotional traits also. We have assumed that because it is convenient for a mother to wish to care for her child, this is a trait with which women have been more generously endowed by a carefully teleological process of evolution. We have assumed that because men have hunted, an activity requiring enterprise, bravery, and initiative, they have been endowed with these useful attitudes as part of their sex-temperament.

Societies have made these assumptions both overtly and implicitly. If a society insists that warfare is the major occupation for the male sex, it is therefore insisting that all male children display bravery and pugnacity. Even if the insistence upon the differential bravery of men and women is not made articulate, the difference in occupation makes this point implicitly. When, however, a society goes further and defines men as brave and women as timorous, when men are forbidden to show fear and women are indulged in the most flagrant display of fear, a more explicit element enters in. Bravery, hatred of any weakness, of flinching before pain or danger—this attitude which is so strong a component of some human temperaments has been selected as the key to masculine behaviour. The easy unashamed display of fear or suffering that is congenial to a different temperament has been made the key to feminine behaviour.

Originally two variations of human temperament, a hatred of fear or willingness to display fear, they have been socially translated into inalienable aspects of the personalities of the two sexes. And to that defined sex-personality every child will be educated, if a boy, to suppress fear, if a girl, to show it. If there has been no social selection in regard to this trait, the proud temperament that is repelled by any betrayal of feeling will display itself, regardless of sex, by

keeping a stiff upper lip. Without an express prohibition of such behaviour the expressive unashamed man or woman will weep, or comment upon fear or suffering. Such attitudes, strongly marked in certain temperaments, may by social selection be standardized for everyone, or outlawed for everyone, or ignored by society, or made the exclusive and approved behaviour of one sex only.

Neither the Arapesh nor the Mundugumor have made any attitude specific for one sex. All of the energies of the culture have gone towards the creation of a single human type, regardless of class, age, or sex. There is no division into age-classes for which different motives or different moral attitudes are regarded as suitable. There is no class of seers or mediums who stand apart drawing inspiration from psychological sources not available to the majority of the people. The Mundugumor have, it is true, made one arbitrary selection, in that they recognize artistic ability only among individuals born with the cord about their necks, and firmly deny the happy exercise of artistic ability to those less unusually born. The Arapesh boy with a tinea infection has been socially selected to be a disgruntled, antisocial individual, and the society forces upon sunny cooperative children cursed with this affliction a final approximation to the behaviour appropriate to a pariah. With these two exceptions no emotional role is forced upon an individual because of birth or accident. As there is no idea of rank which declares that some are of high estate and some of low, so there is no idea of sex-difference which declares that one sex must feel differently from the other. One possible imaginative social construct, the attribution of different personalities to different members of the community classified into sex-, age-, or caste-groups, is lacking.

When we turn however to the Tchambuli, we find a situation that while bizarre in one respect, seems nevertheless more intelligible in another. The Tchambuli have at least made the point of sex-difference; they have used the obvious fact of sex as an organizing point for the formation of social personality, even though they seem to us to have reversed the normal picture. While there is reason to believe that not every Tchambuli woman is born with a dominating, organizing, administrative temperament, actively sexed and willing to initiate sex-relations, possessive, definite, robust, practical and impersonal in outlook, still most Tchambuli girls grow up to display these traits. And while there is definite evidence to show that all Tchambuli men are not, by native endowment, the delicate responsive actors of a play staged for the women's benefit, still most Tchambuli boys manifest this coquettish play-acting personality most of the time. Because the Tchambuli formulation of sex-attitudes contradicts our usual premises, we can see clearly that Tchambuli culture has arbitrarily permitted certain human traits to women, and allotted others, equally arbitrarily, to men.

CRITICAL THINKING QUESTIONS

1. How do female and male personality traits differ among the Arapesh, the Mundugumor, and the Tchambuli?

2. How does Mead explain these differences? What does she mean, for example, when she states that "human nature is unbelievably malleable to cultural conditions"?

3. Most people in North America still describe men as aggressive, strong, confident, and ambitious while characterizing women as emotional, talkative, romantic, and nurturing. Does this mean that biology is more important than environment in shaping our personality and behaviour?

32

Sk8er Girls: Skateboarders, Girlhood and Feminism in Motion

SHAUNA POMERANTZ, DAWN H. CURRIE, AND DEIDRE M. KELLY

Gender plays an important role in all social situations, even in subcultures that generally reject the values and norms of mainstream society. This reading discusses the importance of gender at a Vancouver skate park in order to illustrate the obstacles that young women face when participating in what is generally a male-dominated sport.

Most skaters are young teenage boys who think they are kings and the world sits below them. Trying to tell them that women should be able to skate without being harassed may be an impossible task, but it must be done.

—Jigsaw Youth

Skate parks are generally awash in a grey, graffiti-ridden concrete that is the necessary landscape for practicing tricks. Vancouver has several good places for skateboarding, but most are burdened with a reputation for drugs and vandalism. The largest indoor park in the city was recently shut down for its high level of drug trafficking and defacement of property. Underground skaters who detest anything remotely mainstream avoid the parks,

Source: Reprinted from *Women's Studies International Forum*, Vol. 27, Shauna Pomerantz, Dawn H. Currie and Deidre M. Kelly, "Sk8er Girls: Skateboarders, Girlhood and Feminism in Motion," pp. 550–552, 2004, with permission from Elsevier.

confining their practice to the streets, the parking lots of local establishments, and the (now monitored by security) area surrounding the art gallery downtown. For those skaters who do not mind mainstream skateboarding, the parks are the best place to practice, learn tricks, and participate in skate culture. But no matter which skate park or street location you choose to frequent, one thing is abundantly clear—there are very few girl skateboarders.

As Sandy, a self-proclaimed skateboarding "coach" for her friends, announced in no uncertain terms, "Like, a lot of girls don't skateboard!"[1] Skateboarding is not a common activity for girls and finding a girl on a skateboard is rare. Despite the recent media frenzy around teen pop singer Avril Lavigne, who has been dubbed a "skate punk" for her style and loose connections to skateboarding, girls are often relegated to the sidelines while the boys "do their thing." Further evidence can be found by visiting skate parks, where girls hang off the railing as watchers, fans, and girlfriends. Evidence of this can also be found on numerous Internet skater zines dedicated to girls.[2] One girl skater writes, "Every time I venture out to skate, either alone or with friends, I am in some way harassed, threatened, or opposition to my skating is voiced in some manner." And there is this testimonial of frustration by Morgan:

Once upon a time, I was a lonely girl skater in a big city. I went to the indoor park a few times a week, but there were never any other girls there and the guys seemed to want little to do with the girl in the corner teaching herself kickturns. As much as I loved skating, it was necessary to give myself a serious pep talk to get motivated to go back to the park each day.

These accounts of life at the skate park indicate the gendered nature of skater culture, where girls have to work much harder and overcome many more obstacles than boys to gain legitimate skater status. The subordination and delegitimation of girls to boys is a common theme in youth sub/cultures. Paul Willis (1981) represents girls in working class "lad" culture as sexual objects for the more powerful boys. In Dick Hebdige's (1979) analysis of punk culture, girls are represented as accoutrement and secondary figures. McRobbie and Garber (1997 [1976]) first pointed out that youth cultural studies theorists saw girls as backdrop characters in male dominated subcultures, whose lives revolved around finding a boyfriend, looking attractive, and being promiscuous. But in their own analysis of girls in male subcultures, they concluded that traditional sex roles were also dominant in biker culture, mod culture, and hippy culture. Girls were given very little status and almost no legitimation. In skater culture, girls are assigned a similar kind of derogatory positioning. Yet despite the sexism of the skate park and of skateboarding in general, there are still some girls who choose to take up the label of "skater."

The members of the Park Gang were 14 and 15 years old at the time of the study. They all lived in an area of Vancouver known for its family orientation, professional demographic, and urban chic. Four were Canadian-born Chinese girls, two were White, one was a Canadian-born Latina, and one was half First Nations, half White. This racial mix is representative of the city of Vancouver itself, which is ethnically and racially highly diverse. With the exception of one girl, who attended a Catholic school, the girls all attended a large urban high school known for its Asian population and academic achievement. Skateboarding was a passion for four of the girls; two of the girls called themselves "coaches" in the sense that they skated but preferred to "just help"; and two of the girls were skaters by association, meaning that they were involved in skate culture, music, and style—like all of the Park Gang—but without the desire to actually skate. They all hung out at a skate park that would be considered amateurish compared to the larger and more daunting parks downtown. This particular park was connected to a community centre in an affluent neighbourhood. It was relatively clean and safe.

Given their occupation of a subject position that held the possibility for a feminist politics, we found it interesting that some of the Park Gang espoused a postfeminist ethos. Sara, for example, did not see the relevance of feminism today because she had never encountered a situation where "I wanted to, like, do something because, like, it wasn't how I wanted it to be." And Emily did not think being a girl carried any stigma whatsoever: "I think it's pretty much even with guys now." To some of the Park Gang, feminism had become a form of reverse discrimination. Emily noted that feminists were not trying to make things equal, but rather "boost" the women above the men: "Like, it's constantly, like, a fight, instead of just being equal. They [feminists] just want to be better than men." Pete also expressed the idea that feminism was a form of discrimination. "I think sometimes feminism is brought a bit too far," she said. "Um, like, there is, 'Yeah, I want to be equal to the men, get paid the same wage for doing the same job.' And then there is, 'I'm going to go out and be a fire fighter just for the sake of having women in the force.'" Although some of the Park Gang expressed postfeminist sentiments, their desire to "do" skateboarding told a different story.

Members of the Park Gang were relatively new skaters when we met them. They came to the sport through older brothers or boys at school. Grover noted that she got started because a friend did not want to learn alone:

There are not too many girl skateboarders so it is kind of better—she felt more comfortable if there was, like, you know, another person that, you know, could be with her. And so she asked if I wanted to try it, so I said sure, and, um, her brothers started teaching us and I found it was something that, it was a lot of fun, so I just stayed with it, so I'm still learning.

When more of the Park Gang decided to try skateboarding, they ventured into the skate park with their boards for the first time, hoping to gain acceptance and practice. But the park proved to be a location of struggle that was dominated by skater boys, who put the girls under surveillance. The skater boys were always asking members of the Park Gang to show them what they could do and Zoey spoke of the constant questioning of the girls' abilities. They often asked her, "Why don't you skate *more*?" She admitted that, "Sometimes we don't want to skate around them 'cause, like, they do really good stuff and we're just kind of learning."

The Park Gang quickly realized that being the only girl skaters at the park singled them out for some harassment. To the skater boys who dominated the park and acted as its gate-keepers, the park was their space—a space that left very little room for girls, unless they were occupying the traditionally feminine subject positions of watcher, fan, or girlfriend. Gracie theorized that girls skate less than boys due to this kind of territorial attitude: "Some [girls] are kind of, like, scared, because, um, of what

people might think of them." When asked what she meant, Gracie noted that the lack of girls who skated at the park might make the boys question girls' right to belong. Onyx added that the skater boys viewed the Park Gang as "invading their space." Grover felt that the Park Gang threatened the skater boys "just because, you know, girls are doing their sport." She went on to explain the attitudes of some of the boys at the park.

Sometimes, they'll be kind of, like, rude, like, I don't know if it's on purpose, but they just, you know, have this kind of attitude. . . . I guess they think they're so good and one of them or two of them— I'm not sure if all of them are, like, sponsored by skateboarding companies—so they always feel, like, you know, they're kind of superior and so, you know, we're only a year younger, so it's kind of, like, we're obviously not as good as them, but they kind of forget that they had to start somewhere too, so, and it would be harder for us because we're girls.

The territory of the park became a contested space. The boys saw it as theirs. The girls wanted access. Grover, Gracie, and Onyx understood that the boys were threatened by their presence, but wished the boys could appreciate how hard it was for girls to get started. They wanted the boys to see them as equals who deserved the same kind of camaraderie that they gave each other. But instead, the boys saw them as interlopers with little legitimate claim to the space. Some of the boys accused some of the Park Gang of being "posers." Often, girls who try to gain skater status are seen as posers. A poser wears the right clothes, such as wide sneakers with fat laces, brand-name pants and hoodies, and, of course, carries a skateboard. But posers do not really skate. Although boys can be posers too, girls who attempt access to the label "skater" are singled out for this derogatory title. It is assumed that girls hang around the skate park as a way to meet skater boys, to flirt.

When this accusation was levelled at some of the Park Gang, they immediately took action to prove the skater boys wrong. Zoey recounted the story.

There's this one time where a couple of the guys thought we were just—they said it out loud that we're just there for the guys and we're like, "No!" And they're like, "But you're here all the time, like almost every day, skateboarding, and so are we." So we did this whole thing where we didn't come there for quite a while just to show them; and then we came back and they stopped bugging us about it.

The girls involved in the park boycott practiced at an elementary school for two weeks and went to the park only when they knew the boys would not be around. When asked what they had gained by boycotting the park, Zoey responded, "That we're not there just for the guys and we're not there to watch them and be around them." Suddenly, the girls received more respect and experienced less harassment from the skater boys. Zoey noted a distinct change in their attitude. "I guess to some level, they treated us like an equal to them, kind of." Instead of placing the girls under surveillance, the skater boys watched the Park Gang in order to see "how they were doing." They suddenly became curious about the girls' progress. When asked if they thought they had successfully changed the opinions of the skater boys, Zoey enthusiastically replied, "Well yes!"

The girls involved in the boycott retreated to a safe space where they were not being monitored. When they re-emerged, they were ready to fully occupy the subject position of "skater." In so doing, the girls challenged who a "skater" could be by challenging the skater boys' power over who had legitimate claim to the park. This discursive struggle for naming and authorization necessitated an understanding of the discourse of the park. The boys were interfering in the girls' desire to occupy the subject position of "skater." By blocking the subject position of "skater," the boys retained some control over the girls' sense of who they were. Recognizing how unfair this was, the girls responded by gaining control over their own subjectivity. They retreated to a space where they were free to think of themselves as "skaters." When they returned to the park, they were armed with both a sense of confidence about their skating abilities and a sense of entitlement to the "skater" label. They took authorizing power away from the boys and legitimated themselves.

Before the boycott, the skater girls were thought of in a very specific way: as posers, flirts, or interlopers. But through the boycott, the girls believed they altered how the boys thought of them and, more significantly, how they thought of themselves. In their efforts to change the meaning of "skater," the Park Gang acknowledged how they had been subordinated at the park and successfully resignified the commonly accepted process of belonging. They carved out a space for girls where none used to exist. In this way, the Park Gang legitimated the subject position of "skater" for girls at the park and expanded the possibilities for subjectivity within girlhood. As Pete pointed out, "Lots of girls have actually started [skating] because my group started and then they kind of feel in power. I think they kind of feel empowered that they can start now, that it's okay for girls to skate."

CRITICAL THINKING QUESTIONS

1. Do you agree with one of the interview subjects when she says that women are "pretty much even with guys now"? Do you think this is true in general? Do you think this is true in the skate park?

2. What other sports are divided along gender lines? Can you name a sport in which men and women compete side by side? Why do you think the gender divide persists? Do you think women should be able to play on the same teams as men, in the National Hockey League, for example?

3. The authors observe that the skate park was a contested space. What do they mean by this? Can you think of other spaces, past and present, that are contested? Do

you think the behaviour of the boys is sexist?

NOTES

1. All names are pseudonyms chosen by the girls in the study.
2. Examples of online skater girl zines include: frontsidebetty.com, withitgirl.com, sk8girl.com, girlskateboarding.com, girlsskatebetter.com, and gurlzonboards.com.

REFERENCES

Hebdige, Dick. 1979. *Subculture: The meaning of style*. London: Methuen.

McRobbie, Angela, and Jenny Garber. 1997 [1976]. Girls and subcultures. In *The subcultures reader*, eds. Ken Gelder and Sarah Thornton, 112–120. London: Routledge.

Willis, Paul E. 1981. In *Learning to labor: How working class kids get working class jobs*, ed. Morningside, 51–70. New York: Columbia University Press.

33

Domestic Violence: A Cross-Cultural View

ELAINE LEEDER

Gender

CLASSIC

CONTEMPORARY

CROSS-CULTURAL

Domestic violence is a global problem and occurs in both industrialized and developing countries. Elaine Leeder discusses why women and children, especially girls, experience physical abuse in nations as diverse as India, Japan, Vietnam, and Africa. This dark side of family life reflects structural inequality and cultural attitudes about gender.

FAMILY VIOLENCE IN INDIA

The Indian government and feminist organizations are concerned about wife battering, child abuse and neglect, and infanticide, which occur quite regularly there. [Earlier] I mentioned bride burnings in India, called "dowry deaths," which occur as a result of rising demands for the dowry given from the bride's side to the groom's family. I also briefly mentioned female infanticide. Those are extreme forms of gender violence. However, in this [reading] we focus on the regular and daily patterns of domestic violence that take place in India.

Many forms of domestic violence in India occur as a result of rising industrialization and modernization. Families have rising economic

Source: The Family in Global Perspective: A Gendered Journey by Elaine Leeder. Thousand Oaks, CA: Sage, 2004, pp. 244–48, 251–54.

expectations, and the problems are acted out at home. Wife battering is a fairly common occurrence (Rao, 1997). Mild forms of wife beating are commonplace, and many men and women admit freely in interviews that it is justified if the woman does not "behave herself." Interestingly, though, in one study only 22 percent of the women admitted on surveys to having been beaten; it is unacceptable to admit abuse, yet it seems to be such a common practice that it is not considered worthy of mention. Only women for whom abuse is a serious or chronic problem are willing to admit it. Otherwise it is such an everyday affair that it is not considered a problem.

In rural India, women believe that alcohol and inadequate dowries provoke the abuse. Some drunken husbands beat their wives without provocation, and women who are beaten complain that the problem is exacerbated by the drunken fits of their husbands. Alcohol is widely available, as it is in the United States, and many of the men say that their drinking is due to a feeling of hopelessness caused by poverty. Their lack of options for breaking out of poverty leads them to drink to "forget their troubles."

Also, as dowry demands have escalated in the past 20 years, many parents have been unable to keep up with the inflation. Some girls are kept hostage by their in-laws in an attempt to extract larger amounts of money from the girls' parents. When those demands are not met, the young bride is beaten, often living in terror of what might become of her. Her power is also diminished in the home after she has been beaten. Sometimes "family resources are transferred away from the wife and her children to other members of the household . . . and the husband and wife are unable to construct a strong marital bond."

It appears that if women have male children they are less likely to be beaten. Having fulfilled societal expectations seems to provide a deterrent to abuse. A rural woman is more likely to be beaten if she has been sterilized. Sterilization is a major form of birth control in rural India; after bearing enough children, a woman often chooses it as contraception. It appears that a man feels freer to beat a woman who has been sterilized, perhaps out of fear of her infidelity.

In rural India, abuse is tolerated under certain circumstances, which include dowry problems, a wife's infidelity, her neglect of household duties, or her disobedience to her husband's dictates. Abuse is also tolerated if a husband beats his wife when he is drunk but is otherwise a good husband. But if a man batters his wife beyond levels considered tolerable for the village, or if he beats her for reasons not considered legitimate by the village, then a village elder or a local monk will intervene to stop the violence.

Finally, we should mention that living outside of marriage is not an option for an Indian woman. There are no alternatives to marriage for Indian women at this time. Although many women work outside of the home, the types of jobs available are limited, pay is quite low, and marriage is considered the norm.

Clearly, wife battering is a prevalent and "normal" family dynamic in India. It is part of the social fabric, so much so that it is not even commented on unless it is extreme. So too is child abuse.

Child abuse has occurred since time immemorial and exists across cultures. Usually it is the poorer classes who get the attention of public health and welfare services. But middle-class practices are more reflective of whether or not abuse is common in a society. In India middle-class families have experienced a greater amount of stress as the country modernizes and industrializes. India is becoming more urban, and this points to a rise in child abuse among Indian families (Segal, 1995). There is intense competition and effort at upward mobility. This also puts stress on the family. In addition, there is a well-established pattern of corporal punishment in raising children. Children are socialized to obey their parents, and there is strict discipline, even though infants are highly indulged. The family is highly hierarchical, and now that families are moving away from the joint family, there is less support for raising children and sharing household tasks. All these factors create an environment that's ripe for an increase in child abuse rates.

The use of corporal punishment is so well entrenched in Indian society that even the middle and upper classes admit to using it. In one study of 319 highly educated, college-graduate parents in three cities in India, a full 56.9 percent reported having used "acceptable" forms of violence, while 41.9 percent engaged in "abusive" violence, and 2.9 percent admitted using "extreme" violence on their children. Unfortunately we have no specific studies of middle- and upper-class parents in the United States with which to compare this data. Suffice it to say that in the United States we have comparably high rates of child abuse, too (Gelles & Straus, 1986). Remember that in the United States *at least* a million children are abused a year.

Female infanticide and child neglect are also major child abuse issues in India, particularly in rural villages. Barbara Miller (1987) has spent years studying abuse in rural north India and has found significant discrimination against girl children there. There is a strong preference for sons. Boys are needed as economic assets, for farming, and for the money they send home if they move away. They are more likely to stay with their families after marriage and maintain their parents in old age. Girls move away when they marry and cannot contribute to the family upkeep. Sons bring dowries and perform rituals among the Hindus when the father dies; therefore boys are important to the maintenance of family life, while girls are seen as a drain economically. This strong preference for sons has led to disappointment when a girl is born, withholding of medical care for girls, and preferential feeding of boy children.

Infanticide is the killing of a child under one year old, and is the most extreme form of child abuse. *Neonaticide* is the killing of an infant up to 24 hours old, and *feticide* is the abortion of a baby in utero, particularly when it is done as sex selection. After a child is 12 months old, the killing is considered a homicide. In north India, the killing of female infants is quite an old phenomenon. The British discovered it as early as 1789 and outlawed it by 1870. In some parts of India during that time, the sex ratio was 118 men to 100 women. Nowadays, systematic, indirect female infanticide still exists. Girls are not actively killed; they are just neglected so badly that they die from lack of care. The numbers seem to cross class and caste, with even wealthier families preferring sons. This is also true for well-educated families.

In India there is also sex-selective abortion. Although there is a lack of definitive data, anecdotal evidence indicates that it is quite widespread. One study found that in one hospital, of the 700 amniocenteses done, 250 were male and 450 were female. A full 430 of the 450 females were aborted, while all the male fetuses were brought to full term.

Now that I have presented this data, I urge a suspension of any ethnocentric value judgments.

It is true that these figures are disturbing and certainly are contrary to Western-based humanistic values. Let's try to keep a view that is culturally relative, to understand why people would engage in such behavior. Understanding why it is done, and being aware of one's own bias, might lead us to think of what can be done about it. There are groups working in India and through the United Nations who have declared this problem a public health issue and are trying to prevent or reduce the incidence of these practices.

WIFE BATTERING IN JAPAN

Now let's focus our lens on another part of Asia, this time Japan. In previous chapters we talked about the way the Japanese family is organized, and how unlike it is to families in the United States, even though both countries are highly industrialized. In Japan the incidence of wife battering is quite high. In one study (Yoshihama & Sorenson, 1994), a survey was done of 796 married women, in which more than three-fourths reported at least one type of violence perpetrated by a male intimate partner. This ranged from a slap to an assault with a deadly weapon, from verbal ridicule to restriction of social activities, and from incompliance with contraception to forced, violent sex. About two-thirds of the most serious physically violent incidents resulted in injury.

Unlike the United States, Japan has no specific laws against wife battering as a crime, and there is no governmental funding for services that address the problem. Often, if women get help, it is through services intended for other purposes, like homes established under child welfare laws. Fully one-third of the women who use other services, like shelters that protect prostitutes, were actually battered women seeking protection from their abusers. A husband's violence is one of the primary reasons women list when they are seeking divorce, and contrary to the myths of the quiet, passive Japanese man, violence is an integral part of family life in Japanese society.

Often, when a woman seeks to end a violent marriage, the violence does not end. This is true in the United States as well as Japan. Violence often escalates during the process of separation and divorce. It is as if the man does not want to let go of his property, holding tighter and becoming more abusive as he fears the loss. Male violence in Japan seems to cross all socioeconomic strata and can lead to serious consequences. Women report broken bones, lacerations requiring stitches, ruptured eardrums, and other injuries requiring medical care.

Domestic violence in Japan is still an unrecognized problem. There is not even a word for it in Japanese; language has been adapted from the English to refer to it. An increasing level of media attention is being focused on the problem at the time of the publication of this book, but the level is far below that with which we are familiar in the West. This is a problem that bears watching closely, to see how well Japan deals with a problem that many countries are starting to grapple with. . . .

DOMESTIC VIOLENCE IN VIETNAM

. . . The Socialist Republic of Vietnam is rich in culture, deep in religion, and ancient yet modern. It is beautiful, with pristine beaches, huge rivers, and rice paddies galore. Eighty percent of the population lives in the rural areas, and it has a 94 percent literacy rate. We in the United States think that Vietnam is a place of war, and it was, in fact, for most of the past century. In 1945 Vietnam became independent of France, fought for its freedom, and then fought against the Americans, who established their presence there after the French pulled out.

The war has had a significant impact on family life in Vietnam. With the revolution in 1945 came the first attempts to change the inferior position of women there. Laws were passed to equalize the rights, positions, and interests of women. Unfortunately, today the vestiges of Confucian ideology still

linger. Men act as kings in their homes even while the women in the workforce make more money than their husbands (Quy, 1996). Women are employed in the labor market in great numbers, but still do the "second shift" that's common in the United States. After work at the factory, Vietnamese women spend five to six hours a night on housework at home. This has been called the "invisible violence" of Vietnam, because while there may not be physical violence between men and women, intimidation and fear drive the relationships. This inequity occurs for both urban educated and rural poor women. Many women feel that their situation is predestined, in accordance with Confucian ideology.

Then there is the "visible violence" that recently has led to a large number of divorces in Vietnam. One report indicates that as many as 87.5 percent of the divorces in 1992 were a result of violence or violence-related causes. There are numerous injuries and deaths related to violence in the home, although exact numbers are not available. What is known is that 17.5 percent of the deaths in Vietnam in 1992 were caused by family violence.

One of the reasons given for this problem is low socioeconomic status. Poor men, in particular, feel that it is permissible to take out their frustration and anger on their wives and children. Another reason given is the "feudal attitude": the old Confucian ideas of "thinking highly of men and slightly of women" seem to inform beliefs about hitting one's wife. Sometimes men take lovers, or even concubines, who come to live in the home with the wife, against the wife's will.

Other reasons for violence are drinking, gambling, adultery, and jealousy. Although there are no numbers available on this, the researcher conducted interviews with battered wives who attributed the abusive behavior to a few of these factors. Another reason given was what we would call the "intra-individual theory": that there is "mad blood" in the perpetrator. In Vietnam this means that there are people who always feel anxious and angry and tend to shift the blame onto others, especially their next of kin.

In Vietnamese law, men and women are considered equal. Violence toward wives and children is specifically prohibited and is considered a violation of human rights, and the government has established a series of local and state programs for intervention. There are also laws against the preference for male children, although as we will see, these have certainly not had much of an impact. Interestingly, however, the incidence of rape in Vietnam seems to be low, specifically as compared with the United States (Goodstein, 1996). The Vietnamese Women's Union plays a role at the local level, watching out for the rights of women (Johnson, 1996).

As in many parts of the world, preference for a son remains strong in Vietnam, especially in light of the family planning policy there, which recommends only two children per family (Haughton & Haughton, 1995). Payments must be made to the government should a family have more than two children, although the sanctions are not as strict as they are in neighboring China. Following the Confucian model, in Vietnam there is still the belief that a son will care for you in old age and that a son is an investment, while a daughter will leave. Even though women in Vietnam are well educated (remember, the literacy rate is 94 percent) and well integrated into the workforce, the Vietnamese still prefer male children.

Another problem related to violence in Vietnam is the trafficking in women (Barry, 1996). Vietnam's traditional values, like fate and filial piety, shape the culture and make it ripe for exploitation by the "sex work" industry. Other countries in the region, like Japan, Thailand, and Australia, have well-established sex industries that have begun moving into Vietnam as the country moves toward economic development. Vietnam has a history of sexual exploitation of women, most notably during the Vietnam War, when more than 500,000 women served as prostitutes to the U.S. troops. Many were rape victims or war widows needing to earn a living. Now many women are being forced into prostitution as part of the growing sex trade industry. Because prostitution provides immediate cash incentives for the women when other work is not available, it is becoming an increasingly viable option as the country moves toward a more westernized model of economics.

Vietnam, although a socialist country with some new elements of capitalism, seems to have similar domestic violence problems as other parts of the world: violence against wives, son sex-preference, and a growing sex trade. It appears that not many places in the world are free of domestic violence.

DOMESTIC VIOLENCE IN AFRICA

. . . In Uganda, violence against one's wife is accepted as legitimate; when it is mentioned, most men just shrug and say, "It's our culture" (Doro, 1999). If a woman attacks her husband, the violence is considered criminal. The U.S. Department of State Uganda Report on Human Rights Practices for 1998 says that violence against women, including rape, is quite common. There are no specific laws against wife battering, although a law passed in 1997 provides protection for families, including wives and children. But it is hard to implement the law since law enforcement officials view the problem the way the public does, as not a problem.

Families in Uganda endure violence in silence, and violence is worse in the countryside than it is in the city. According to the Human Rights Report, the pattern is similar in other African countries, too. Women have few rights, neighbors don't want to get involved, and the women lie about their injuries if asked about them at medical facilities.

Several women's organizations in coalition are actively pursuing reform and holding public workshops to lobby for a revision of the Domestic Relations Act. Most of the trouble in getting anything done is related to lack of funding. Many of the countries in Africa do not have adequate funds to handle the many social problems they have, like AIDS, and they have put domestic violence issues on the back burner, because they think, after all, "It is our culture."

Other studies done in Africa are also not comprehensive. One study of domestic violence in Nigeria found that polygamy lends itself more to wife battering than do monogamous marriages (Efoghe, 1990). In this study, more polygamous marriages were violent than were monogamous marriages. Another study, of child sexual abuse in Zimbabwe, found that sexual abuse of children is not as prevalent there as it is internationally, with only about 10 percent of the population being victims of this kind of abuse (Khan, 1995). The authors of the study wonder whether this discrepancy reflects underreporting, or if sexual abuse of children is really not a big problem in Zimbabwe.

Finally, let's remember that Africa and parts of Southwest Asia perform ritual circumcision of girls. In Somalia, Kenya, the Sudan, Tanzania, Ethiopia, Egypt, Uganda, Chad, Mali, Senegal, Cameroon, Zaire, and Nigeria, to name just a few, girls are cut and scraped to make their bodies more attractive and marriageable. This practice has been framed as a human rights abuse, as well as a form of child abuse that is being taken up as a problem by the United Nations and the World Health Organization.

CRITICAL THINKING QUESTIONS

1. How is domestic violence similar in India, Japan, Vietnam, and Africa? How does it differ? Also, Leeder notes that rising industrialization and modernization increase the likelihood of family violence. Why, then, is wife battering also common in industrialized countries such as Japan and the United States?

2. Why do most of the women in these countries never complain about domestic violence? What individual, legal, historical, and cultural factors help explain their silence?

3. Leeder urges the reader to suspend "any ethnocentric value judgments" about family violence. What does she mean? And, if we do so, does this mean that the global community shouldn't interfere with a country's violent practices against women and children?

REFERENCES

Barry, K. 1996. Industrialization and economic development: The costs to women. In *Vietnam women in transition*, ed. K. Barry. New York: St. Martin's Press.

Doro, M. 1999. August 4. Available: End Violence@edc-cit.org.

Efoghe, G. B. 1990. Nature and type of marriage as predictors of aggressiveness among married men in Ekpoma, Bendel State of Nigeria. *International Journal of Sociology of the Family*, 20 (Spring): 67–78.

Gelles, R., and M. Straus. 1986. Societal change and change in family violence from 1975–1985 as revealed in two national surveys. *Journal of Marriage and the Family*, 48 (3): 465–80.

Goodstein, L. 1996. Sexual assessment in the U.S. and Vietnam: Some thoughts and questions. In *Vietnam women in transition*, ed. K. Barry, 275–86. New York: St. Martin's Press.

Haughton, J., and D. Haughton. 1995. Son preference in Vietnam. *Studies in Family Planning*, 26, 6 (Nov/Dec): 325–38.

Johnson, M. 1996. Violence against women in the family: The U.S. and Vietnam. In *Vietnam women in transition*, ed. K. Barry. New York: St. Martin's Press.

Khan, N. 1995. Patterns of child sexual abuse in Zimbabwe: An overview. *Zimbabwe Journal of Educational Research*, 7, 2 (July): 181–208.

Miller, B. 1987. Female infanticide and child neglect in rural North India. In *Child survival*, ed. N. Scheper-Hughes, 95–112. Dordrecht: D. Reidel Publishing Co.

Quy, L. 1996. Domestic violence in Vietnam. In *Vietnam women in transition*, ed. K. Barry, 263–74. New York: St. Martin's Press.

Rao, V. 1997. Wife beating in rural south India: A qualitative and econometric analysis. *Social Science and Medicine*, 44 (8): 1169–80.

Segal, U. 1995. Child abuse by the middle class: A study of professionals in India. *Child Abuse and Neglect*, 19 (2): 217–31.

Yoshihama, M., and S. Sorenson. 1994. Physical, sexual and emotional abuse by male intimates: Experiences of women in Japan. *Violence and Victims*, 9 (1): 63–77.

34

The Souls of Black Folk

W. E. B. DU BOIS

W. E. B. Du Bois, a pioneering U.S. sociologist and the first African American to receive a doctorate from Harvard University, describes how a colour-conscious society casts black people as strangers in their own homes. One result, Du Bois explains, is that African Americans develop a "double-consciousness," seeing themselves as Americans but always gazing back at themselves through the eyes of the white majority, as people set below and apart by colour.

Between me and the other world there is ever an unasked question: unasked by some through feelings of delicacy; by others through the difficulty of rightly framing it. All, nevertheless, flutter round it. They approach me in a half-hesitant sort of way, eye me curiously or compassionately, and then, instead of saying directly, How does it feel to be a problem? they say, I know an excellent colored man in my town; or, I fought at Mechanicsville; or, Do not these Southern outrages make your blood boil? At these I smile, or am interested, or reduce the boiling to a simmer, as the occasion may require. To the real question, How does it feel to be a problem? I answer seldom a word.

And yet, being a problem is a strange experience—peculiar even for one who has never been anything else, save perhaps in babyhood

Source: From *The Souls of Black Folk* by W. E. B. Du Bois (New York: Penguin, 1982; orig. 1903), pp. 43–53.

and in Europe. It is in the early days of rollicking boyhood that the revelation first bursts upon one, all in a day, as it were. I remember well when the shadow swept across me. I was a little thing, away up in the hills of New England, where the dark Housatonic winds between Hoosac and Taghkanic to the sea. In a wee wooden school-house, something put it into the boys' and girls' heads to buy gorgeous visiting-cards—ten cents a package—and exchange. The exchange was merry, till one girl, a tall newcomer, refused my card—refused it peremptorily, with a glance. Then it dawned upon me with a certain suddenness that I was different from the others; or like, mayhap, in heart and life and longing, but shut out from their world by a vast veil. I had thereafter no desire to tear down that veil, to creep through; I held all beyond it in common contempt, and lived above it in a region of blue sky and great wandering shadows. That sky was bluest when I could beat my mates at examination-time, or beat them at a foot-race, or even beat their stringy heads. Alas, with the years all this fine contempt began to fade; for the words I longed for, and all their dazzling opportunities, were theirs, not mine. But they should not keep these prizes, I said; some, all, I would wrest from them. Just how I would do it I could never decide: by reading law, by healing the sick, by telling the wonderful tales that swam in my head—some way. With other black boys the strife was not so fiercely sunny: Their youth shrunk into tasteless sycophancy, or into silent hatred of the pale world about them and mocking distrust of everything white; or wasted itself in a bitter cry, Why did God make me an outcast and a stranger in mine own house? The shades of the prison-house closed round about us all: walls strait and stubborn to the whitest, but relentlessly narrow, tall, and unscalable to sons of night who must plod darkly on in resignation, or beat unavailing palms against the stone, or steadily, half hopelessly, watch the streak of blue above.

After the Egyptian and Indian, the Greek and Roman, the Teuton and Mongolian, the Negro is a sort of seventh son, born with a veil, and gifted with second-sight in this American world—a world which yields him no true self-consciousness, but only lets him see himself through the revelation of the other world. It is a peculiar sensation, this double-consciousness, this sense of always looking at one's self through the eyes of others, of measuring one's soul by the tape of a world that looks on in amused contempt and pity. One ever feels his twoness—an American, a Negro; two souls, two thoughts, two unreconciled strivings; two warring ideals in one dark body, whose dogged strength alone keeps it from being torn asunder.

The history of the American Negro is the history of this strife, this longing to attain self-conscious manhood, to merge his double self into a better and truer self. In this merging he wishes neither of the older selves to be lost. He would not Africanize America, for America has too much to teach the world and Africa. He would not bleach his Negro soul in a flood of white Americanism, for he knows that Negro blood has a message for the world. He simply wishes to make it possible for a man to be both a Negro and an American, without being cursed and spit upon by his fellows, without having the doors of Opportunity closed roughly in his face.

This, then, is the end of his striving: to be a coworker in the kingdom of culture, to escape both death and isolation, to husband and use his best powers and his latent genius. These powers of body and mind have in the past been strangely wasted, dispersed, or forgotten. The shadow of a mighty Negro past flits through the tale of Ethiopia the Shadowy and of Egypt the Sphinx. Through history, the powers of single black men flash here and there like falling stars, and die sometimes before the world has rightly gauged their brightness. Here in America, in the few days since Emancipation, the black man's turning hither and thither in hesitant and doubtful striving has often made his very strength to lose effectiveness, to seem like absence of power, like weakness. And yet it is not weakness—it is the contradiction of double aims. The double-aimed struggle of the black artisan on the one hand to escape white contempt for a nation of mere hewers of wood and drawers of water, and on the other hand to plough and nail and dig for a poverty-stricken horde—could only result in making him a poor craftsman, for he had but half a heart in either cause. By the poverty and ignorance of his people, the Negro minister or doctor was tempted toward quackery and demagogy; and by the criticism of the other world, toward ideals that made him ashamed of his lowly tasks. The would-be black savant was confronted by the paradox that the knowledge his people needed was a twice-told tale to his white neighbors, while the knowledge which would teach the white world was Greek to his own flesh and blood. The innate love of harmony and beauty that set the ruder souls of his people a-dancing and a-singing raised but confusion and doubt in the soul of the black artist; for the beauty revealed to him was the soul-beauty of a race which his larger audience despised, and he could not articulate the message of another people. This waste of double aims, this seeking to satisfy two unreconciled ideals, has wrought sad havoc with the courage and faith and deeds of ten thousand thousand people, has sent them often wooing false gods and invoking false means of salvation, and at times has even seemed about to make them ashamed of themselves.

Away back in the days of bondage they thought to see in one divine event the end of all doubt and disappointment; few men ever worshipped Freedom with half such unquestioning faith as did the American Negro for two centuries. To him, so far as he thought and dreamed, slavery was indeed the sum of all villainies, the cause of all sorrow, the root of all prejudice; Emancipation was the key to a promised land of sweeter beauty than ever stretched before the eyes of wearied Israelites. In song and exhortation swelled one refrain—Liberty; in his tears and curses the God he implored had Freedom in his right hand. At last it came, suddenly, fearfully, like a dream. With one wild carnival of blood and passion came the message in his own plaintive cadences:

> Shout, O children!
> Shout, you're free!
> For God has bought your liberty!

Years have passed away since then—ten, twenty, forty; forty years of national life, forty years of renewal and development, and yet the swarthy spectre sits in its accustomed seat at the Nation's feast. In vain do we cry to this our vastest social problem:

> Take any shape but that, and my firm nerves
> Shall never tremble!

The Nation has not yet found peace from its sins; the freedman has not yet found in freedom his promised land. Whatever of good may have come in these years of change, the shadow of a deep disappointment rests upon the Negro people—a disappointment all the more bitter because the unattained ideal was unbounded save by the simple ignorance of a lowly people.

The first decade was merely a prolongation of the vain search for freedom, the boon that seemed ever barely to elude their grasp, like a tantalizing will-o'-the-wisp, maddening and misleading the headless host. The holocaust of war, the terrors of the Ku Klux Klan, the lies of carpet-baggers, the disorganization of industry, and the contradictory advice of friends and foes, left the bewildered serf with no new watchword beyond the old cry for freedom. As the time flew, however, he began to grasp a new idea. The ideal of liberty demanded for its attainment powerful means, and these the Fifteenth Amendment gave him. The ballot, which before he had looked upon as a visible sign of freedom, he now regarded as the chief means of gaining and perfecting the liberty with which war had partially endowed him. And why not? Had not votes made war and emancipated millions? Had not votes enfranchised the freedmen? Was anything impossible to a power that had done all this? A million black men started with renewed zeal to vote themselves into the kingdom. So the decade flew away, the revolution of 1876 came, and left the half-free serf weary, wondering, but still inspired. Slowly but steadily, in the following years, a new vision began gradually to replace the dream of political power—a powerful movement, the rise of another ideal to guide the unguided, another pillar of fire by night after a clouded day. It was the ideal of "book-learning"; the curiosity, born of compulsory ignorance, to know and test the power of the cabalistic letters of the white man, the longing to know. Here at last seemed to have been discovered the mountain path to Canaan; longer than the highway of Emancipation and law, steep and rugged, but straight, leading to heights high enough to overlook life.

Up the new path the advance guard toiled, slowly, heavily, doggedly; only those who have watched and guided the faltering feet, the misty minds, the dull understandings, of the dark pupils of these schools know how faithfully, how piteously, this people strove to learn. It was weary work. The cold statistician wrote down the inches of progress here and there, noted also where here and there a foot had slipped or someone had fallen. To the tired climbers, the horizon was ever dark, the mists were often cold, the Canaan was always dim and far away. If, however, the vistas disclosed as yet no goal, no resting-place, little but flattery and criticism, the journey at least gave leisure for reflection and self-examination; it changed the child of Emancipation to the youth with dawning self-consciousness, self-realization, self-respect. In those sombre forests of his striving his own soul rose before him, and he saw himself, darkly, as through a veil; and yet he saw in himself some faint revelation of his power, of his mission. He began to have a dim feeling that, to attain his place in the world, he must be himself, and not another. For the first time he sought to analyze the burden he bore upon his back, that dead-weight of social degradation partially masked behind a half-named Negro problem. He felt his poverty; without a cent, without a home, without land, tools, or savings, he had entered into competition with rich, landed, skilled neighbors. To be a man is hard; but to be a poor race in a land of dollars is the very bottom of hardships. He felt the weight of his ignorance, not simply of letters, but of life, of business, of the human-ities; the accumulated sloth and shirking and awkwardness of decades and centuries shackled his hands and feet. Nor was his burden all poverty and ignorance. The red stain of bastardy, which two centuries of systematic legal defilement of Negro women had stamped upon his race, meant not only the loss of ancient African chastity, but also the hereditary weight of a mass of corruption from white adulterers, threatening almost the obliteration of the Negro home.

A people thus handicapped ought not to be asked to race with the world, but rather allowed to give all its time and thought to its own social problems. But alas! while soci-ologists gleefully count his bastards and his prostitutes, the very soul of the toiling, sweat-ing black man is darkened by the shadow of a vast despair. Men call the shadow prejudice, and learnedly explain it as the natural defence of culture against barbarism, learning against ignorance, purity against crime, the "higher" against the "lower" races. To which the Negro cries Amen! and swears that to so much of this strange prejudice as is founded on just hom-age to civilization, culture, righteousness, and progress, he humbly bows and meekly does obeisance. But before that nameless prejudice that leaps beyond all this he stands helpless, dismayed, and well-nigh speechless; before that personal disrespect and mockery, the ridi-cule and systematic humiliation, the distortion of fact and wanton license of fancy, the cynical ignoring of the better and the boisterous wel-coming of the worse, the all-pervading desire to inculcate disdain for everything black, from Toussaint to the devil—before this there rises a sickening despair that would disarm and discourage any nation save that black host to whom "discouragement" is an unwritten word.

But the facing of so vast a prejudice could not but bring the inevitable self-questioning, self-disparagement, and lowering of ideals which ever accompany repression and breed in an atmosphere of contempt and hate. Whis-perings and portents came borne upon the four winds: Lo! we are diseased and dying, cried the dark hosts; we cannot write, our voting is vain; what need of education, since we must always cook and serve? And the Nation echoed and enforced this self-criticism saying: Be content to be servants, and nothing more; what need of higher culture for half-men? Away with the black man's ballot, by force or fraud—and behold the suicide of a race! Nevertheless, out of the evil came something of good—the more careful adjustment of education to real life, the clearer perception of the Negroes' social responsibilities, and the sobering realization of the meaning of progress.

So dawned the time of *Sturm und Drang*: Storm and stress today rocks our little boat on the mad waters of the world-sea; there is within and without the sound of conflict, the burning of body and rending of soul; inspiration strives with doubt, and faith with vain questionings. The bright ideals of the past— physical freedom, political power, the training of brains and the training of hands—all these in turn have waxed and waned, until even the last grows dim and overcast. Are they all wrong, all false? No, not that, but each alone was over-simple and incomplete—the dreams of a credulous race-childhood, or the fond imaginings of the other world which does not know and does not want to know our power. To be really true, all these ideals must be melted and welded into one. The training of the schools we need today more than ever—the training of deft hands, quick eyes and ears, and above all the broader, deeper, higher culture of gifted minds and pure hearts. The power of the ballot we need in sheer self-defence—else what shall save us from a second slavery? Freedom, too, the long-sought, we still seek, the freedom of life and limb, the freedom to work and think, the freedom to love and aspire. Work, culture, liberty—all these we need, not singly but together, not successively but together, each growing and aiding each, and all striving toward that vaster ideal that swims before the Negro people, the ideal of human brotherhood, gained through the unifying ideal of Race; the ideal of fostering and developing the traits and talents of the Negro, not in opposition to or contempt for other races, but rather in large conformity to the greater ideals of the American Republic, in order that some

day on American soil two world-races may give each to each those characteristics both so sadly lack. We the darker ones come even now not altogether empty-handed: There are today no truer exponents of the pure human spirit of the Declaration of Independence than the American Negroes; there is no true American music but the wild sweet melodies of the Negro slave, the American fairy tales and folklore are Indian and African; and, all in all, we black men seem the sole oasis of simple faith and reverence in a dusty desert of dollars and smartness. Will America be poorer if she replace her brutal dyspeptic blundering with light-hearted but determined Negro humility? or her coarse and cruel wit with loving jovial good-humor? or her vulgar music with the soul of the Sorrow Songs?

Merely a concrete test of the underlying principles of the great republic is the Negro Problem, and the spiritual striving of the freedmen's sons is in the travail of souls whose burden is almost beyond the measure of their strength, but who bear it in the name of an historic race, in the name of this the land of their fathers' fathers, and in the name of human opportunity.

CRITICAL THINKING QUESTIONS

1. What does Du Bois mean by the "double-consciousness" of African Americans?
2. Du Bois writes that people of colour aspire to realizing a "better and truer self." What do you think he imagines such a self to be?
3. What are some of the reasons, according to Du Bois, that Emancipation (from slavery in 1863) brought disappointment to former slaves, at least in the short run?
4. Does this essay seem optimistic or pessimistic about the future of race relations? Why?

35

Why Is Our Educational System Still Guilty of Whiteness?

PATRINA DUHANEY

In this essay Patrina Duhaney recounts her experiences as a black student in an educational system that is primarily populated by, and biased toward, white students and faculty.

Generations of Black students have learned the importance of academic success. . . . . Taylor and Krahn (2005) found that approximately 75 per cent of visible minority [high school] students, compared to 51 per cent of Canadian-born students who were not from visible minorities, were more likely to have higher university aspirations. One main reason why higher education has remained so relevant in Black communities is that Black people have always had to fight for their right to participate in education and to maintain their identity once in the school system (Freeman, 2003). Black people have also recognized the liberating power and privilege attached to education. . . . .

Despite their educational aspirations, however, not all Black individuals have equal

Source: Taken from *Canadian Social Work Review, Vol. 1,* Number 1 (2010). Permission granted by author, Patrina Duhaney.

access to education. In fact, Black students are globally under-represented at all levels of education (Freeman, 2003). Among students surveyed in 2007, only 19 per cent identified themselves as members of a visible minority group and only 3 per cent identified themselves as Aboriginal (CAUT, 2009). A number of complex social, demographic, economic, and political factors combine to create barriers to higher education (Looker & Lowe, 2001). Black students who have gained access to universities have done so with great difficulty. Teranishi (2007) explains that the challenges encountered by racialized students have to do with the uneven distribution of opportunities awarded to them. Students have had to prove that they are "just as good" academically as White students. . . . As a little girl, I was always told that I should aspire to get a good education because once I had it no one could take it away from me. Throughout my years in middle school and high school, I also learned that a good education meant doing well; unless I did well, I would not make it to the next level. A student's academic success is often measured by how well she or he is able to master course content and is evaluated on a set of criteria deemed to be objective (Marchak, 1996). The reward is often a letter or number grade and advancement to a higher academic level (Kelly, 2008). As a Black student, one of the ways that I have been able to demonstrate my competency is by aspiring to get a certain grade, specifically an A. . . .

I was prompted to write this piece as a result of the numerous discussions . . . with fellow students and professors that have taken place while I was completing my graduate studies. I felt at times that I was implicated in some of the discussions about marks, as I had carried the label of being "overly concerned," "obsessed," or "neurotic" about marks. In a sense, the institution and its inhabitants had perceived me as a "mad" woman. After all, I must have experienced some form of psychosis that caused me to place such a high value on achieving high grades. At other times, I have felt the need to explain my strong desire to attain an A average in my studies. It has been frustrating and infuriating to have to justify and revalidate my personal values and the desire to achieve a certain educational attainment. . . . I have felt "othered" and racialized more than ever during my years in university. . . .

RACIALIZATION AND WHITENESS

. . . [T]he Human Rights Commission (2010) defines racialization as the process whereby society constructs race as real, different, and unequal in ways that matter to economic, political, and social life. The above terms provide a starting point for understanding the process of racialization; however, Collins (cited in Murji & Solomos, 2005) and Galabuzi (2006) offer

a more comprehensive definition that speaks to the lived experiences of racialized people. According to Collins, racialization is more than simply an issue of representation, but is tied to social practices through which racialized people are excluded from political, economic, and social spheres. Through these processes, Galabuzi notes, the dominant group enjoys a certain amount of privilege while oppressing and further marginalizing racialized groups. . . . Specifically, it is through Whiteness that White people have been understood as being without race and have enjoyed a certain level of power and privilege. Furthermore, as Ladson-Billings (1998) states, although there is no fixedness to these categories, in a racialized society where Whiteness is positioned as normative, everyone is ranked and categorized in relation to the dominant group. . . . Whiteness is historically, socially, culturally, and politically produced. This social stratification is advantageous to the process of Whiteness because it allows for the subjugation of racialized groups. Whiteness is significant in situating my experiences in the school system because White people tend to represent the dominant group within and outside academic institutions. . . .

UNIVERSITY LIFE

Racist hierarchical structures are present in economic, political, and social domains. These structures allocate certain privileges to the dominant group in society while subsequently working to exclude racialized people in all areas, including education (DeCuir & Dixson, 2004). . . . According to DeCuir and Dixson, racism is especially problematic for African-American students attending predominantly White schools. . . . Students attending Canadian schools have also communicated similar concerns. For example, Codjoe (2001) found that Black students' primary concerns include hostile school environments, negative racial stereotyping, differential treatment by race, lack of representation of Black perspectives, and low expectations on the part of teachers. Furthermore, colleges and universities demographically depict White cultures and White climates, fostering a one-way assimilation process in which Black students are forced to adapt to White views, norms, and practices (Feagan, Vera & Imani, 1996). Depending on how well they adapt to the structures and standards of the dominant culture, students are able to achieve a sense of belonging (Harvey, 1984), but this sense of belonging is problematic because it is superficial. In conforming, one often loses one's own identity, which is a great price to pay.

The encounters that Black students experience imply that they are inferior to Whites. As Harvey (1984) states, "the schooling process, the social mechanism that is ostensibly designed to inspire and uplift, and obviously contribute positively to the mental health of its recipients, has not met the needs of Black students, either on the cognitive of the affective levels" (p. 449). Black students are often put in situations that require them either to conform or to resist the deleterious effects of Whiteness.

Through the process of Whiteness, Black students often face challenges in the education system that mirror the daily challenges they encountered as members of a White society. Fegin, Vera and Imani (1996) cite discrimination as one such challenge. They found that acts of discrimination within the educational system were not considered unusual disruptions of students' everyday lives, but rather as recurring and integral experiences of being Black in a White-dominated society. Black students have encountered major barriers in their pursuit of an education, both socially and within the educational system (Fegin, Vera & Imani, 1996). Many Black students face trans-generational pressures that greatly affect not only their conceptions of themselves but also how their communities view them. Much

of this pressure comes from the tradition and history of Black people in the educational system. Black people's struggle to have access to education can be traced to the days of slavery, when they were prevented from learning to read or write (Chambers, 2009). After emancipation, Black people were forced to attend segregated schools, which were substandard to schools for Whites. Junne (2003) argues that discrimination forced many Black people to create their own schools and assume responsibility for educating their own children. Eventually, desegregated schools were introduced, but Black students rarely shared the same level of access and resources (Chambers, 2009). For example, Cummins (1997) notes that Black students were seldom placed in advanced streams but rather predominantly in basic, vocationally oriented programs. In essence, this substandard education has undermined both the educational and occupational potential of Black students (Smith & Lalonde, 2003). For many generations, Black students have had to maintain a certain level of academic performance to continue to justify their presence in White institutions. One reason is that achievement has been thought of in racial terms (Pollock, 2001), based on the idea that various racial groups had different outcomes in terms of achievement. . . .

As a Black student, I have been guided by the familial emphasis on education as I moved through the educational system. During middle school and high school, I always made the honour role. During my adolescent years I felt the great demand to make it to university. After all, I would be the first child in my family to attend university. I realized very early that I could not go very far with an undergraduate degree. In fact, I had two undergraduate degrees, but they were not enough to secure a "good" career. In the final year of my second degree, my faculty advisor told me that I was considered a good student because of the marks that were reflected on my transcript; for some reason that comment resonated with me. Marks had gotten me through middle school, then to high school, then into a prestigious university. Marks, among other things, also ensured that I was able to make it to graduate school. Once there, I realized I had to maintain a certain mark to ensure that I remained in the program. Furthermore, because I wanted to get into a doctorate program, I would also need good marks to be competitive as well as to receive funding. While a few faculty members liked to say, "Marks don't matter," I would reply, "Marks matter!" A quick perusal of schools offering a PhD in social work reveals that students are required to have at least a B+ average; however, having this minimum will not necessarily ensure a spot in the program. Other schools asked for an A– average. One may ask, "Why are you so hung up about marks?" My response is that I have had to be concerned with marks. Marks prove my ability and credibility. Through marks I have been able to prove to universities that I am a good student, which directly translates into me being a good person. In addition, marks have allowed me to escape the labels that have been given to other Black students: labels such as unintelligent, unmotivated, and underachieving. The constant need to justify my presence in White universities through marks has come at a great cost.

I have been accused of being "Whitewashed" and of "acting White" simply because I have done well in school and because I have acquired a certain level of education. "Acting White" was a term used by scholars to characterize racialized students who did well academically and were shunned by their peers as a result (Cook & Ludwig, 1997; Schultz, 2008). The phrase "acting White" is very contentious and has been used to refer to a number of social practices and attitudes. Its meanings have been open to many interpretations; however, these meanings have affected how Black students have come to identify themselves. It has affected how I continue to define and re-define myself. In some contexts, I am told I act "too White,"

while in other contexts I have not been "White enough" to enjoy certain power and privileges awarded to White people.

The Canadian educational system, for the most part, is based on a White Eurocentric curriculum that has deprived Black students of their ancestral histories and cultural heritage. Within this colonial curriculum, White people have claimed authority of experience, knowledge, and text (Dei, 1996). They have had the power to establish the curriculum, evaluate performance, and assess capacities (Marchak, 1996). They have also acted as gatekeepers, controlling who gains access or is denied access to universities. To evaluate the efforts of students, universities use a meritocratic system based on a grade scale. The manner in which students' abilities are assessed and evaluated by universities is considered necessary to test students' acquisition of knowledge. Grades have worked as a mechanism of access for many Black students, including myself. Although my positionality in society as a marginalized woman does not award me with the same amount of privilege as my White classmates, I am aware that I am privileged because of the degrees I have attained at three Canadian universities. It is through this meritocratic system that I have been able to legitimize my academic abilities and justify my rightful place within these institutions. I have used the educational system as a "vehicle for challenging the prevailing, stigmatized representations of Blackness" (Gosine, 2002, p. 87). However, similar to the students in a study conducted by James (1997), I too question the basis of the merit system universities use to evaluate a student's abilities. Grading practices vary from one professor to another and from one university to another (Kelly, 2008), but a student's knowledge and understanding of course content cannot simply be represented by a letter or numerical grade (Randall & Engelhard, 2010). Universities are now taking into consideration factors such as attendance, participation, and group work to reward students' abilities. However, because the assigning of marks remains very subjective, Black students still fall short when it comes to getting higher grades. Thus, as Dei (2008) states, the educational system needs "to explore a wide range of teaching, instructional, and learning models, as well as strategies and practices for educational administration, that will bring profound change" (p. 348), not only in schools but in the lives of Black students.

. . . While I do not believe I have assimilated to the confines of Whiteness, I have conformed in some instances and resisted in others. For example, I have had to adapt to White norms and practices as a survival mechanism although, in doing so, I feel that I have lost parts of my identity. As Giles and Hughes (2009) state, "the more people of colour morph into what the White [Canadian] hegemony demands of us, the more we lose elements of our sense of authentic self. . . . They tell us to get a 'quality' education, but when we do, we are considered uppity, accused of having unearned success, and our credentials and abilities are constantly called into question" (p. 693). Our educational system is still guilty of Whiteness despite the work that has been done to eradicate racism and discrimination. . . .

CRITICAL THINKING QUESTIONS

1. Why is there such a disparity between the proportion of visible-minority high school students with higher-education aspirations and the proportion actually enrolled in universities? What kinds of barriers might account for this gap?

2. What is racialization? Do you agree that it's a current process in today's society? Consider your own race, social status, and cultural history.

3. Do you agree with Duhaney's assertion that the Canadian education system is still guilty

of "whiteness"? Have you ever compared yourself academically to someone else based on racial stereotypes? How can you change your mindset to break that cycle?

REFERENCES

Canadian Association of University Teachers (CAUT). 2009. *CAUT almanac of post-secondary education in Canada 2009–2010*. Available: **http://www.caut.ca/uploads/2009_CAUT_Almanac.PDF**. Accessed April 13, 2010.

Chambers, T. V. 2009. The "receivement gap": School tracking policies and the fallacy of the "achievement gap." *Journal of Negro Education*, 78(4): 417–431.

Codjoe, H. 2001. Fighting a "public enemy" of Black academic achievement: The persistence of racism and the schooling experiences of Black students in Canada. *Race Ethnicity and Education*, 4(4): 343–375.

Cook, P., and J. Ludwig. 1997. Weighing the "burden of 'acting White'": Are there race differences in attitudes toward education? *Journal of Policy Analysis and Management*, 16(2): 256–278.

Cummins, J. 1997. Minority status and schooling in Canada. *Anthropology & Education Quarterly*, 28(3): 411–430.

DeCuir, J., and A. Dixson. 2004. "So when it comes out, they aren't that surprised that it is there": Using CRT as a tool of analysis of race and racism in education. *Educational Researcher*, 33: 26–31.

Dei, G. 1996. *Anti-racism education: Theory and practice*. Halifax, NS: Fernwood Publishers.

Dei, G. J. 2008. Schooling as community: Race, schooling, and the education of African youth. *Journal of Black Studies*, 38(3): 346–366.

Feagin, J., H. Vera, and K. Imani. 1996. *The agony of education: Black students at a white university*. New York: Routledge.

Freeman, K. 2003. Black populations globally: The challenges and promises in their educational experiences. *Comparative Education Review*, 47(1): 1–2.

Fryer, R. 2006. "Acting White": The social price paid by the best and brightest minority students. *Education Next*, 6(1).

Galabuzi, G. E. 2006. *Canada's economic apartheid: The social exclusion of racialized groups in the new century*. Toronto: Canadian Scholars' Press.

Giles, M., and R. Hughes. 2009. CRiT walking race, place, and space in the academy. *International Journal of Qualitative Studies in Education*, 22(6): 687–696.

Gosine, K. 2002. Essentialism versus complexity: Conceptions of racial identity construction in educational scholarship. *Canadian Journal of Education*, 27(1): 81–100.

Harvey, W. 1984. The educational system and Black mental health. *Journal of Negro Education*, 53(4): 444–454.

Human Rights Commission. 2010. *Racial discrimination, race and racism*. Available: **http://www.ohrc.on.ca/en/resources/factsheets/race**. Accessed April 21, 2010.

James, C. E. 1997. Contradictory tensions in the experiences of African Canadians in a Faculty of Education with an access program. *Canadian Journal of Education*, 22(2): 158–174.

Junne, G. H. 2003. *The history of blacks in Canada: A selectively annotated bibliography*. Westport, CN: Greenwood Press.

Kelly, S. 2008. What types of students' effort are rewarded with high marks? *Sociology of Education*, 81(1): 32–52.

Ladson-Billings, G. 1998. Just what is critical race theory and what's it doing in a nice field like education? *Qualitative Studies in Education*, 11(1): 7–24. Available: **http://diversitypedagogy.com/Diversity%20ideologies (implications%20for%20schooling)/Ladson-Billings. Just%20what%20is%20critical%20theory.pdf**. Accessed April 26, 2010.

Looker, E., and G. Lowe. 2001. *Post-secondary access and student financial aid in Canada: Current knowledge and research gaps*. Available: **http://www.nan.on.ca/upload/documents/edu-post-sec-report-on-access.pdf**. Accessed April 15, 2010.

Marchak, P. M. 1996. *Racism, sexism, and the university: The political science affair at the University of British Columbia*. Montreal & Kingston: McGill-Queen's University Press.

Murji, K., and J. Solomos. 2005. *Racialization: Studies in theory and practice*. New York: Oxford University Press.

Pollock, M. 2001. How the question we ask most about race in education is the very question we most suppress. *Educational Researcher*, 30(9): 2–12.

Randall, J., and G. Engelhard. 2010. Examining the grading practices of teachers. *Teaching and Teacher Education*, 26(7): 1372–1380.

Schultz, S. 2008, November 9. Revenge of the black nerd. *New York Daily News*. Available: **http://nymag.com/news/intelligencer/52025**. Accessed April 20, 2010.

Smith, A., and R. N. Lalonde. 2003. "Racelessness" in a Canadian context? Exploring the link between Black students' identity, achievement, and mental health. *Journal of Black Psychology*, 29(2): 142–164.

Taylor, A., and H. Krahn. 2005. *Aiming high: Educational aspirations of visible minority youth*. Available: **http://www.statcan.gc.ca/pub/11–00x/2005003/article/8966-eng.pdf**. Accessed April 12, 2010.

Teranishi, R. 2007. Race, ethnicity, and higher education policy: The use of critical quantitative research. *New Directions for Institutional Research*, 13: 37–49.

36

Canada's Aging Population

NEENA CHAPPELL, LYNN MCDONALD, AND MICHAEL STONES

Population aging is an interesting sociological phenomenon because it illustrates the power of demographic trends over the individual. As you read this selection, think about how our aging population might affect you in terms of job opportunities, taxes, and having children.

We now look at how the Canadian population has aged over the last 150 years, and how it is expected to age in the coming decades. Projections about the future age structure depend on assumptions about future levels of fertility, mortality, and migration. In particular, if our fertility rates were to undergo another boom, our future age structure would be younger than projected. Figure 36.1 presents data on the percentage of the population aged 65 and over from 1881 to 1993, with projections to 2036. It can be observed that our population has been aging continuously over the entire period; in other words, population aging is not new. However, certain time periods have experienced more rapid aging than others. Clearly, the decades to come will experience a large increase in the proportion of the population aged 65 and over. This

Source: Excerpted from *Aging in Contemporary Canada, 2ce* by Neena Chappell, Lynn MacDonald, Michael Stones, pp. 29–37. Copyright © 2003, 2008 Pearson Education Canada Inc.

increase is a direct result of the aging of the baby boomers—the large cohort of persons born between 1946 and 1962—who will begin entering traditionally defined old age (i.e., age 65) in 2011. Between then and 2027, when the youngest baby boomers turn age 65, the ranks of the older population will grow substantially. The effect of the baby boom on the percentage of the population aged 65 and over will gradually dissipate; by 2050, most of the youngest boomers will be dead.

It is also important to note that the elderly population is itself aging, that is, among those aged 65 and over, there is an increasing number and percentage of persons who are aged 80 and over. In 2000, there were approximately 910 000 Canadians aged 80 and over, making up 3 percent of the total population. In 1981, the comparable percentage was 2.4 percent, and in 1961 it was 1.4 percent. In fact, the population aged 80 and over is proportionately the fastest growing age segment in Canada.

Figure 36.1   Proportion of People Aged 65 Years and Over in the Total Population, Canada, 1881–2036

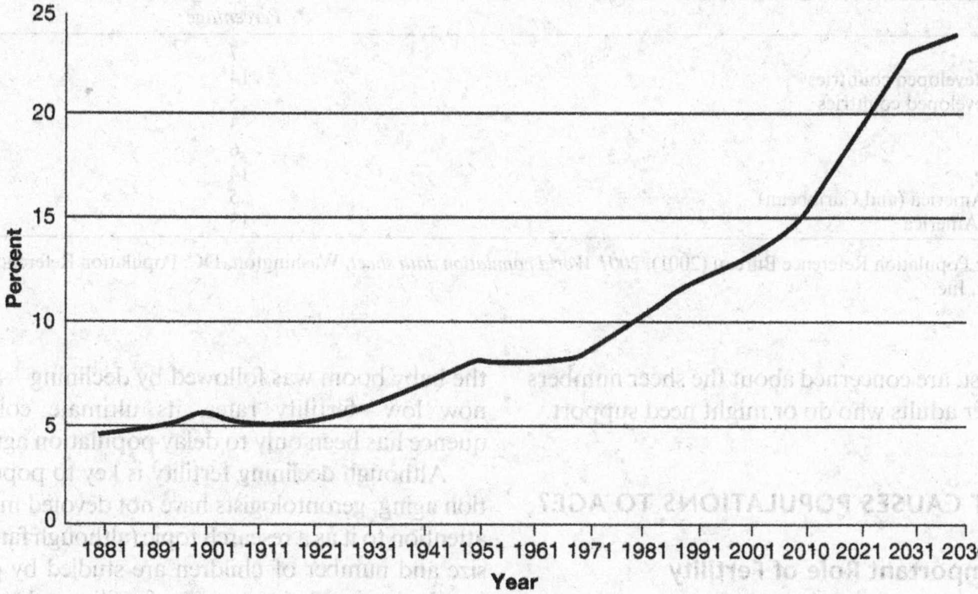

Source: Statistics Canada, *Population ageing and the elderly*, Catalogue No. 91-533 (April 7, 1993): 13.

CANADIAN POPULATION AGING IN COMPARATIVE PERSPECTIVE

Approximately 7 percent of the world's population is aged 65 and over, with a sharp division between more developed and less developed nations (see Table 36.1). The youngest populations occur in Africa; the oldest populations are in Europe. With 13 percent of our population aged 65 and over, the Canadian population is, comparatively speaking, quite old. However, many European nations are substantially older than Canada. For example, Sweden, Belgium, Italy, and Greece all have 17 percent of their populations aged 65 and over; and the figure is 16 percent in France, Germany, Spain, and the United Kingdom (Population Reference Bureau, 2001). In contrast, the percentage aged 65 and over is as low as 2 percent in Niger and Uganda in Africa and Bhutan in South Central Asia.

So far, we have been considering relative proportions only; absolute numbers are also

important to take into account. The number of older persons in the continent with the greatest proportion of old people, Europe (including Russia), totals approximately 102 million; in Asia, the 6 percent figure translates into approximately 221 million elderly persons. India alone, with only 4 percent of its population aged 65 and over, contains about 44.1 million elders—almost 10 million more people than the total population of Canada (Population Reference Bureau, 2001). Thus, the developed and developing worlds face different age structure issues. In the North, we are dealing with a relatively high proportion of elderly, compared with other age groups; in the South (or the Third World), the issue is one of a large and growing *number* of elderly people, although they do not constitute a large fraction of the overall population. To the degree that elderly people require special resources (and only some do), the North faces a relatively smaller proportion of working-age people to support them. Southern countries, in

TABLE 36.1   Percentage of Population Aged 65 and Over, by Region: Circa 2001

Region	Percentage
World	7
More developed countries	14
Less developed countries	5
Africa	3
Asia	6
Europe	14
Latin America (and Caribbean)	5
North America	13

Source: Population Reference Bureau (2001). *2001 World population data sheet.* Washington, DC: Population Reference Bureau, Inc.

contrast, are concerned about the sheer numbers of older adults who do or might need support.

WHAT CAUSES POPULATIONS TO AGE?

The Important Role of Fertility

Why is it that developed countries such as Canada have an age structure that is so much older than that in developing countries? The answer may surprise you: the main factor accounting for population aging is declining fertility, as established by noted U.S. demographer Ansley Coale (1956) 50 years ago. As fertility declines, the number and proportion of children in a population decline, and the proportion of older people correspondingly increases. In youthful Africa, the total fertility rate (the average number of children born to a woman by the end of her childbearing years) is 5.3; in old Europe, the comparable figure is 1.4 (and the Canadian total fertility rate is 1.5) (Population Reference Bureau, 2001).

The reason that Canada (and the United States) has a younger population than most European countries is because we had a large and long baby boom after World War II, as noted above. The immediate effect of this boom was to increase the proportion of children and then young adults in our population, that is, to "young" our population. However, because the baby boom was followed by declining—and now low—fertility rates, its ultimate consequence has been only to delay population aging.

Although declining fertility is key to population aging, gerontologists have not devoted much attention to it as a research topic (although family size and number of children are studied by gerontologists in relation to aging families and social support . . .). Fertility levels and trends have been, and remain, the purview of demographers, who have identified a number of factors that acted as important causes of fertility decline in the West: urbanization and the declining value and increased costs of children in cities; the decline of the family wage and the consequent increase in women's labour force participation; increasing levels of education, particularly for women; the women's movement; and increasingly available and effective means to control reproduction (e.g., Balakrishnan, Lapierre-Adamcyk and Krotki, 1993; Ford and Nault 1996; Matthews, 1999). Apart from academic specialization, one reason why gerontologists have not studied fertility is that fertility has become less predictive of population aging as mortality rates have been lowered. After a population reaches a life expectancy at birth of 70 years, almost all young people survive past their risky first year; thus, any further declines in mortality are concentrated at older ages. These declines translate into relatively more growth in the older age groups, and therefore population aging.

Population Pyramids

It is common to graphically represent age structures by what are termed **population pyramids**; these illustrate the proportion of males and females in each age group (usually five-year age groups up to the older ages, where there is aggregation due to small numbers) in a population. There are three ideal types of pyramids: (1) expansive pyramids, which have a broad base (and look most like pyramids), reflecting a high proportion of children in the population, the result of high past and present fertility levels; (2) constrictive pyramids, in which the base is somewhat narrower than the middle, and which occur when fertility has been rapidly declining; and (3) stationary pyramids, which have a narrow base and approximately equal percentages of people in each age group, tapering off at older ages, and which are the result of a lengthy period of low fertility. Figure 36.2 presents Canadian population pyramids for selected years from 1881 to 2036. We can see that in 1881, the Canadian age structure was expansive, reflecting high fertility which had not yet begun to decline; decreases in fertility are evident in the 1921 pyramid, as the base of the pyramid is narrowing; continuing constriction is interrupted by the baby boom, the beginnings of which can be observed in the 1951 pyramid; in 1991, the pyramid has taken on the classic characteristics of the constrictive type as a result of the significant decline in fertility that commenced in the mid-1960s; and the future pyramids in 2011 and 2036 increasingly take on the stationary shape.

Mortality Decline

While declines in fertility are the major cause of population aging, decreases in mortality (deaths) are important as well. This is more intuitive. Because we associate population aging with more older people, we automatically equate population aging with higher life expectancy (the flip side of lower mortality).

Life expectancy refers to the number of years that a person in a given country/population can expect to live. Conceptually, life expectancy is virtually identical to *longevity*; the difference between them lies in measurement issues. Life expectancy is calculated in a very strict way, using what is termed life table analysis (see Box 36.1); longevity is not associated with any particular statistical technique. Both life expectancy and longevity are distinct from **lifespan,** which, in demography, refers to the number of years that humans could live under ideal conditions. In other disciplines the concept of lifespan is sometimes used differently. In psychology, for example, it refers to developmental changes over the course of a human life.

Table 36.2 shows trends in life expectancy at birth and at age 65 for the period from 1921 (when Canada began a national system of death registration) to 2001. We can see that life expectancy increased steadily over the course of the 20th century. The major gains in life expectancy at birth were made in the earlier part of the period. For example, from 1921 to 1961, life expectancy at birth increased almost 10 years for males and nearly 14 years for females. Over this same period, life expectancy at age 65 increased a mere 0.6 years for men and 2.5 years for women. However, after 1961, life expectancy at age 65 increased more sharply. These trends indicate that young Canadians were the first to benefit from mortality reductions; it was only later that longevity in later life increased appreciably. This is the typical experience of developed countries.

It is not known whether life expectancy will continue to increase as we move through the 21st century, and indeed this is a subject of a fair amount of debate. Part of the debate concerns the length of the human lifespan. Some . . . argue that Western populations are approaching a biologically fixed maximum or finite lifespan—probably in the range of 85 to 100 years. Others suggest that the human lifespan can be extended by many more years, due to advances in molecular medicine . . .

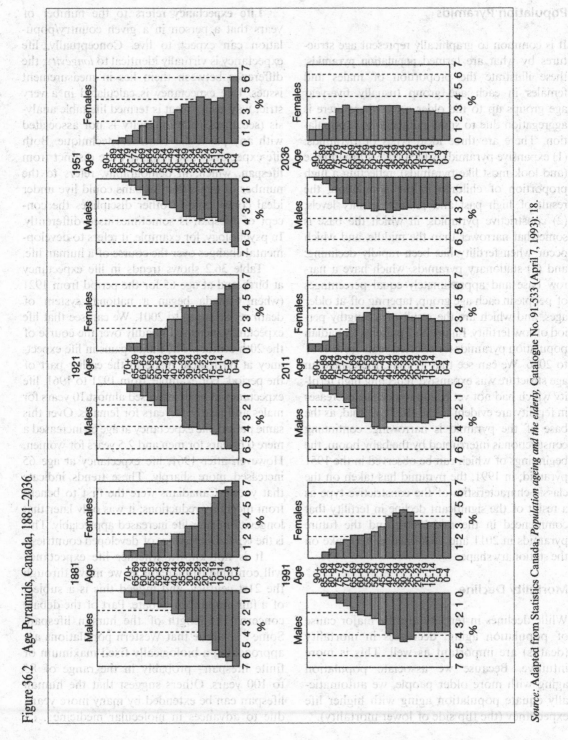

Figure 36.2 Age Pyramids, Canada, 1881–2036.

Source: Adapted from Statistics Canada, *Population ageing and the elderly,* Catalogue No. 91-533 (April 7, 1993): 18.

Box 36.1   Measuring Life Expectancy

Life expectancy is a summary measure of mortality in a population. Statistics on life expectancy are derived from a mathematical model known as a life table. Life tables create a hypothetical cohort (or group) of 100,000 persons (usually of males and females separately) and subject it to the age-gender-specific mortality rates (the number of deaths per 1,000 or 10,000 or 100,000 persons of a given age and gender) observed in a given population. In doing this, we can trace how, say, the 100,000 hypothetical persons (called a synthetic cohort) would shrink in numbers due to deaths as they age. The average age at which these persons are likely to have died is the life expectancy at birth. Life tables also provide data on life expectancy at other ages; the most commonly used statistic other than life expectancy at birth is life expectancy at age 65 years, that is, the number of remaining years of life that persons aged 65 years can expect to live.

Life expectancy statistics are very useful as summary measures of mortality, and they have an intuitive appeal that other measures of mortality, such as rates, lack. However, it is important to interpret data on life expectancy correctly. If it is reported that life expectancy at birth in a given population is 75 years in 2000, this does not mean that all members of the population can expect to live to the age of 75 years. Rather, it means that babies born in that population in 2000 would have a life expectancy at birth of 75 years, if they live their lives subject to the age-specific mortality rates of the entire population in 2000. This is not likely; as they age, age-specific mortality rates will almost certainly change in some ways. Also, older people in that population will have lived their lives up to the year 2000 under a different set of age-specific mortality rates. Thus, it is important to be aware of the hypothetical nature of life expectancy statistics.

or dietary improvements . . . , for example. A third, intermediate position is that there is no rigid limit to the human lifespan and unforeseen biomedical technological breakthroughs could gradually increase our lifespan.

A considerable amount of research, based on the foundational assumption of a finite human lifespan, has focused on the concept of **dependency-free life expectancy** (also called *dependence-free life expectancy, healthy life expectancy, active life expectancy, disability-free life expectancy,* and *functional life expectancy*).

These varying terms refer to the number of years that people in a given population can expect to live in (reasonably) good health, with no or only minor disabling health conditions. Much of the research on dependency-free life expectancy tests, in varying ways, the validity of the **compression of morbidity** hypothesis, originally formulated by Fries (1983). This hypothesis states that, at least among Western populations, more and more people are able to postpone the age of onset of chronic disability; hence, the period of time between onset of

TABLE 36.2   Life Expectancy at Birth and at Age 65 Years, Males and Females: Canada, 1921–2001

| | Males | | Females | |
	At Birth	At Age 65	At Birth	At Age 65
1921	58.8	13.0	60.6	13.6
1931	60.0	13.0	62.1	13.7
1941	63.0	12.8	64.6	13.4
1951	66.4	13.3	70.9	15.0
1961	68.4	13.6	74.3	16.1
1971	69.4	13.8	76.5	17.6
1981	71.9	14.6	79.1	18.9
1991	74.3	15.6	80.8	19.8
2001	77.0	17.0	82.1	20.5

Source: E.G. Moore & M.W. Rosenberg, with D. McGuinness (1997). *Growing old in Canada: Demographic and geographic perspectives.* Toronto, ON: Statistics Canada and ITP Nelson (p. 12); A. Bélanger, Y. Carrière, & S. Gilbert (2000). *Report on the demographic situation in Canada, 2000.* (Catalogue No. 91-209-XPE). Ottawa, ON: Statistics Canada, Table A9; Population Reference Bureau. (2005). *2005 World population data sheet.* Washington, DC: Population Reference Bureau, Inc.

becoming seriously ill or disabled and dying is shortening or compressing. The general idea is that we are moving to a situation in which we will all live hale and hearty lives until a very old age and then die quickly.

One of the challenges for an aging society is that the biomedical model dominant in the Canadian health-care system is largely geared toward acute illness and often does not provide the most appropriate care for the chronic conditions seniors suffer. Even though recent research suggests that the onset of chronic conditions is later than it used to be, seniors still have many years living with these types of problems.

Research on dependency-free life expectancy in Canada reveals an important gender difference (Martel & Bélanger, 2000). While, at age 65, women can expect to live about four years longer than men, their expectation of dependency-free years of life is not quite a year more than that of men. In other words, older women will spend proportionately more of the remaining years of their lives (32.4 percent) in poor health than will men (21.1 percent). . . . .

The Role of Migration

It is commonly thought that one way to cope with population aging is to try to avoid it by "younging" the population through increased immigration. The reasoning is that because migrants tend to be young, their numbers will counteract population aging. However, migration plays a relatively small role in population aging, especially at the national level. Canada's Chief Statistician, Ivan Fellegi (1988), has estimated that Canada would have to allow in more than 600 000 immigrants per year in order for immigration to have a measurable impact on our age structure. The Canadian government sets its annual immigration targets in the neighbourhood of 200 000 to 225 000 (and has failed to meet these targets in recent years). An approximate tripling of the number

of immigrants who enter Canada annually has not occurred and does not seem likely despite current plans from Ottawa at the present time. There are also additional costs for immigrant services, such as teaching English or French as a second language, and public opinion is less than enthusiastic about current levels of immigration, let alone increased levels. Following the terrorist attacks on September 11, 2001, on the World Trade Center in New York and the Pentagon in Washington, D.C., immigration has become even more difficult.

In summary, Canada's aging population is due to the combined effect of declining fertility and declining mortality, with international migration playing a fairly minor role. Historically, fertility has been the major determinant of our age structure. In the absence of another baby boom—which no one is predicting—and in the face of low fertility, mortality will take on increasing importance in determining our age structure.

CRITICAL THINKING QUESTIONS

1. What are some potential social problems associated with an aging population? According to the authors, the North and South face different challenges in terms of aging. Some social scientists argue that there are no problems inherent with an aging population. Do you agree?

2. What are some of the reasons that might explain the dramatic decline in fertility in Canada over recent decades? Can you explain this sociological phenomenon via your own life circumstances? Are you thinking about having a family, and if so, how many children do you think is optimum and why?

3. As the authors state, people are living longer lives in both industrial and developing countries. What are some of the reasons behind this trend? Can you name additional reasons for population aging besides those listed (think technology and social policy)?

REFERENCES

Balakrishnan, T. R., E. Lapierre-Adamcyk, and K. J. Krotki. 1993. *Family and childbearing in Canada: A demographic analysis.* Toronto: University of Toronto Press.

Coale, A. J. 1956. The effects of changes in mortality and fertility on age composition. *Milbank Memorial Fund Quarterly*, 34: 79–114.

Fellegi, I. P. 1988, October. Can we afford an aging society? *Canadian Economic Observer*, 4.1–4.33.

Ford, D., and F. Nault. 1996. Changing fertility patterns, 1974 to 1994. *Health Report*, 8(3), 39–46. (Catalogue No. 83-003). Ottawa: Statistics Canada.

Fries, J. F. 1983. Compression of morbidity. *Milbank Memorial Fund Quarterly*, 61: 397–419.

Martel, L., and A. Belanger. 2000. Dependence-free life expectancy in Canada. *Health Reports*, 58: 26–29. (Catalogue No. 11-008). Ottawa: Statistics Canada.

Matthews, B. J. 1999. The gender system and fertility: An exploration of the hidden links. *Canadian Studies in Population*, 26: 21–38.

Population Reference Bureau. 2001. *2001 World population data sheet.* Washington, DC: Population Reference Bureau, Inc.

Schwartz, W. B. 1998. *Life without disease: The pursuit of medical utopia.* Berkeley, CA: University of California Press.

Walford, R. L. 1983. *Maximum life span.* New York: Norton.

37

Our Aging World

FRANK B. HOBBS AND BONNIE L. DAMON

The average age in societies around the world is rising. Even now, demographers report, the eighty-and-over age group is the fastest-growing portion of the elderly population. Frank B. Hobbs and Bonnie L. Damon describe the growing number of elderly persons worldwide, compare the growth of the elderly population in developed and developing countries, and raise important questions about the future implications of our aging world.

POPULATION AGING IS WORLDWIDE

To set the aging of the United States in context it is useful to look at aging in the rest of the world. Fertility rates and infant and maternal mortality have declined in most nations. Also, mortality from infectious and parasitic diseases has declined. The world's nations generally have improved other aspects of health and education. All of these factors have interacted so that every major region in the world shows an increased proportion of the population that will be sixty-five or older by 2020.

There were 357 million persons aged sixty-five and over in the world in 1994 [see Table 37.1]. They represent 6 percent of the world's population. By the year 2000, there would be about

Source: From *65+ in the United States*. U.S. Bureau of the Census, Current Population Reports, Special Studies, P23–190 (Washington, D.C.: Government Printing Office, 1996), pp. 24–27.

418 million elderly. The annual growth rate for the elderly was 2.8 percent in 1993–94 (compared with an average annual rate for the total world population of 1.6 percent). Such growth is expected to continue far into the twenty-first century.

Numerical growth of the elderly population is worldwide. It is occurring in both developed and developing countries. The average annual growth rate in 1993–94 of persons sixty-five years and over was 3.2 percent in developing countries compared with 2.3 percent in the developed world. In absolute numbers, from 1993 to 1994, the net balance of the world's elderly population (sixty-five years and over) increased by over 1,000 persons every hour. Of this increase, 63 percent occurred in developing countries.

Over half (55 percent) of the world's elderly lived in developing nations in 1994. These developing regions could be home to nearly two-thirds (65 percent) of the world's elderly by the year

TABLE 37.1 World Population by Age and Sex, 1994 and 2000

	Population (millions)			Percentage of Total			
Year and Age	Both Sexes	Male	Female	Both Sexes	Male	Female	Males per 100 Females
1994							
All ages	5,640	2,841	2,798	100.0%	100.0%	100.0%	101.5
Under 15 years	1,790	917	873	31.7	32.3	31.2	105.1
15 to 64 years	3,492	1,771	1,722	61.9	62.3	61.5	102.9
65 years and over	357	153	204	6.3	5.4	7.3	75.2
2000							
All ages	6,161	3,103	3,057	100.0	100.0	100.0	101.5
Under 15 years	1,877	962	915	30.5	31.0	29.9	105.2
15 to 64 years	3,866	1,959	1,907	62.7	63.1	62.4	102.8
65 years and over	418	182	236	6.8	5.9	7.7	77.1

Source: U.S. Bureau of the Census, International Data Base.

2020. Thirty nations had elderly populations of at least 2 million in 1994. . . . Current population projections indicate there will be fifty-five such nations by 2020.

Among countries with more than 1 million population, Sweden has the highest proportion of people aged sixty-five and over, with 18 percent in 1994—about the same as the state of Florida. Sweden also has the highest proportion aged eighty and over with 5 percent. The Caribbean is the oldest of the major developing regions with 7 percent of its population sixty-five or older in 1994.

By 2020, the elderly will constitute from one-fifth to nearly one-fourth of the population of many European countries. For example, Census Bureau projections indicate that 23 percent of Germany's population would be elderly compared with 22 percent for Italy, Finland, Belgium, Croatia, Denmark, and Greece. The elderly population of twelve additional European countries with more than 1 million population will constitute at least one-fifth of the total country population. The United States would be 16 percent.

Japan's population age sixty-five and over is expected to grow dramatically in the coming decades. According to projections, the percentage of Japan's population that is elderly could grow from 14 percent (17.1 million) in 1994 to 17 percent (21.0 million) in 2000 and to 26 percent

(32.2 million) by 2020. . . . This is a rapid rise in a short time. Japan's population eighty years and over also is projected to grow very rapidly, from 3 percent of their total population in 1994 to 7 percent by 2020. Already the Japanese are reducing retirement benefits and making other adjustments to prepare for the economic and social results of a rapidly aging society.

In 1994, the world had an estimated 61 million persons aged eighty or older. That number is expected to increase to 146 million by the year 2020. Persons eighty years and over constituted only 1 percent of the world's total population in 1994 and more than 20 percent of the world's elderly (28 percent in developed countries, 16 percent in developing nations).

DEVELOPED COUNTRIES NOW HAVE MOST OF THE WORLD'S OLDEST POPULATION

Although the developed countries of the world represented only 22 percent of the total world population in 1994, the majority of the world's population aged eighty and over live in developed countries. However, it is projected that by 2020, the majority will live in developing countries. For many nations, the eighty-and-over age group will be the fastest

TABLE 37.2 Projected Population for Countries with More Than One Million Persons Aged 80 Years and Over, 1994 and 2020

	Rank		Population Aged 80 Years and Over (in thousands, based on rank in 1994)	
Country/Area	1994	2020	1994	2020
China, Mainland	1	1	9,010	28,737
United States	2	2	7,760	13,007
India	3	3	4,021	12,639
Japan	4	4	3,597	9,362
Russia	5	5	3,317	7,191
Germany	6	6	3,313	5,889
France	7	8	2,563	3,754
United Kingdom	8	9	2,342	3,400
Italy	9	7	2,221	4,142
Ukraine	10	12	1,421	2,923
Spain	11	13	1,287	2,488
Brazil	*	10	*	3,132
Indonesia	*	11	*	3,034
Mexico	*	14	*	2,296
Poland	*	15	*	1,877
Turkey	*	16	*	1,751
Canada	*	17	*	1,595
Thailand	*	18	*	1,477
Pakistan	*	19	*	1,385
Romania	*	20	*	1,264
South Korea	*	21	*	1,221
Vietnam	*	22	*	1,199
Argentina	*	23	*	1,072
Iran	*	24	*	1,039

Source: U.S. Bureau of the Census, International Data Base.

*Indicates population 80 years and over in 1994 was less than 1 million.

growing portion of the elderly population. In 2000, 26 percent of the elderly in the United States would be eighty or older, which, among countries with a population size of at least 5 million, would rank sixth, behind Sweden, Denmark, Switzerland, Cuba, and the United Kingdom.

In 1994, China had the largest number of persons aged eighty or older followed by the United States [see Table 37.2]. Nine additional countries had over 1 million persons eighty years and over in 1994. By 2020, this list is expected to include thirteen additional countries, ten of which are developing countries. In many developing countries, the population eighty and over in 2020 is likely to at least quadruple from 1994. This highlights the problems governments may have in planning support services for this burgeoning population group.

The rapid growth of the oldest old has various health and economic implications for individuals, families, and governments throughout the world. The oldest old often have severe chronic health problems which demand special attention. The nature and duration of their illnesses are likely to produce a substantial need for prolonged care. Developing nations already have diluted resources. They are the most limited in being able to provide preventive measures and, in future years, supportive services. The United States and other countries face enormous investments and payments to maintain current levels of services for the oldest old.

CRITICAL THINKING QUESTIONS

1. What are some of the reasons for the growth of aging populations worldwide?

2. In the 1990s, the majority of the world's population aged eighty and over lived in developed countries. How is this expected to change by 2020? As the average length of life continues to increase in both developed and developing countries, who, if anyone, is responsible for improving the quality of extended life?

3. Hobbs and Damon observe that "the United States and other countries face enormous investments and payments to maintain current levels of services for the old." What, specifically, are examples of such investments and payments? Who will pay for the necessary services for elderly populations—individuals? families? government? corporations? people in the labour force? others?

38

Alienated Labor

KARL MARX

The human species, argues Karl Marx, is social by nature and expresses that social nature in the act of production. But within the capitalist economic system, Marx claims, the process of production does not affirm human nature but denies it. The result is what he terms "alienated labor."

[We] have shown that the worker sinks to the level of a commodity, and to a most miserable commodity; that the misery of the worker increases with the power and volume of his production; that the necessary result of competition is the accumulation of capital in a few hands, and thus a restoration of monopoly in a more terrible form; and finally that the distinction between capitalist and landlord, and between agricultural laborer and industrial worker, must disappear, and the whole of society divide into the two classes of property *owners* and *property-less workers.* . . .

Thus we have now to grasp the real connexion between this whole system of alienation—private property, acquisitiveness, the separation of labor,

Source: "Alienated Labor," by Karl Marx from *Karl Marx: Early Writings*, trans. and ed. by T. B. Bottomore. Copyright © 1963, McGraw-Hill Companies. Reprinted with permission.

capital and land, exchange and competition, value and the devaluation of man, monopoly and competition—and the system of *money.* . . .

We shall begin from a *contemporary* economic fact. The worker becomes poorer the more wealth he produces and the more his production increases in power and extent. The worker becomes an ever cheaper commodity the more goods he creates. The *devaluation* of the human world increases in direct relation with the *increase in value* of the world of things. Labor does not only create goods; it also produces itself and the worker as a *commodity*, and indeed in the same proportion as it produces goods.

This fact simply implies that the object produced by labor, its product, now stands opposed to it as an *alien being*, as a *power independent* of the producer. The product of labor is labor which has been embodied in an object and turned into a physical thing; this product is an *objectification* of labor. The performance of work is at the same time its objectification. The performance of work appears in the sphere of political economy as a *vitiation*[1] of the worker, objectification as a *loss* and as *servitude to the object*, and appropriation as *alienation*.

So much does the performance of work appear as vitiation that the worker is vitiated to the point of starvation. So much does objectification appear as loss of the object that the worker is deprived of the most essential things not only of life but also of work. Labor itself becomes an object which he can acquire only by the greatest effort and with unpredictable interruptions. So much does the appropriation of the object appear as alienation that the more objects the worker produces the fewer he can possess and the more he falls under the domination of his product, of capital.

All these consequences follow from the fact that the worker is related to the *product of his labor* as to an *alien* object. For it is clear on this presupposition that the more the worker expends himself in work the more powerful becomes the world of objects which he creates in face of himself, the poorer he becomes in his inner life, and the less he belongs to himself. It is just the same as in religion. The more of himself man attributes to God the less he has left in himself. The worker puts his life into the object, and his life then belongs no longer to himself but to the object. The greater his activity, therefore, the less he possesses. What is embodied in the product of his labor is no longer his own. The greater this product is, therefore, the more he is diminished. The *alienation* of the worker in his product means not only that his labor becomes an object, assumes an *external* existence, but that it exists independently, *outside himself*, and alien to him, and that it stands opposed to him as an autonomous power. The life which he has given to the object sets itself against him as an alien and hostile force.

Let us now examine more closely the phenomenon of *objectification*; the worker's production and the *alienation* and *loss* of the object it produces, which is involved in it. The worker can create nothing without *nature*, without the *sensuous external world*. The latter is the material in which his labor is realized, in which it is active, out of which and through which it produces things.

But just as nature affords the *means of existence* of labor, in the sense that labor cannot *live* without objects upon which it can be exercised, so also it provides the *means of existence* in a narrower sense; namely the means of physical existence for the *worker* himself. Thus, the more the worker *appropriates* the external world of sensuous nature by his labor the more he deprives himself of *means of existence*, in two respects: First, that the sensuous external world becomes progressively less an object belonging to his labor or a means of existence of his labor, and secondly, that it becomes progressively less a means of existence in the direct sense, a means for the physical subsistence of the worker.

In both respects, therefore, the worker becomes a slave of the object; first, in that he receives an *object of work*, i.e., receives *work*, and secondly, in that he receives *means of subsistence*. Thus the object enables him to exist, first as a *worker* and secondly, as a *physical subject*. The culmination of this enslavement is that he can only maintain himself as a *physical subject* so far as he is a *worker*, and that it is only as a *physical subject* that he is a worker.

(The alienation of the worker in his object is expressed as follows in the laws of political economy: The more the worker produces the less he has to consume; the more value he creates the more worthless he becomes; the more refined his product the more crude and misshapen the worker; the more civilized the product the more barbarous the worker; the more powerful the work the more feeble the worker; the more the work manifests intelligence the more the worker declines in intelligence and becomes a slave of nature.)

Political economy conceals the alienation in the nature of labor insofar as it does not examine the direct relationship between the worker (work) and production. Labor certainly produces marvels for the rich but it produces privation for the worker. It produces palaces, but hovels for the worker. It produces beauty, but deformity for the worker. It replaces labor by machinery, but it casts some of the workers back into a barbarous kind of work and turns the others into machines. It produces intelligence, but also stupidity and cretinism for the workers.

The direct relationship of labor to its products is the relationship of the worker to the objects of his production. The relationship of property owners to the objects of production and to production itself is merely a *consequence* of this first relationship and confirms it. We shall consider this second aspect later.

Thus, when we ask what is the important relationship of labor, we are concerned with the relationship of the *worker* to production.

So far we have considered the alienation of the worker only from one aspect; namely, *his relationship with the products of his labor*. However, alienation appears not merely in the result but also in the *process of production*, within *productive activity* itself. How could the worker stand in an alien relationship to the product of his activity if he did not alienate himself in the act of production itself? The product is indeed only the *résumé* of activity, of production. Consequently, if the product of labor is alienation, production itself must be active alienation—the alienation of activity and the activity of alienation. The alienation of the object of labor merely summarizes the alienation in the work activity itself.

What constitutes the alienation of labor? First, that the work is *external* to the worker, that it is not part of his nature; and that, consequently, he does not fulfill himself in his work but denies himself, has a feeling of misery rather than well-being, does not develop freely his mental and physical energies but is physically exhausted and mentally debased. The worker, therefore, feels himself at home only during his leisure time, whereas at work he feels homeless. His work is not voluntary but imposed, *forced labor*. It is not the satisfaction of a need, but only a *means* for satisfying other needs. Its alien character is clearly shown by the fact that as soon as there is no physical or other compulsion it is avoided like the plague. External labor, labor in which man alienates himself, is a labor of self-sacrifice, of mortification. Finally, the external character of work for the worker is shown by the fact that it is not his own work but work for someone else, that in work he does not belong to himself but to another person. . . .

We arrive at the result that man (the worker) feels himself to be freely active only in his animal functions—eating, drinking, and procreating, or at most also in his dwelling and in personal adornment—while in his human functions he is reduced to an animal. The animal becomes human and the human becomes animal.

Eating, drinking, and procreating are of course also genuine human functions. But abstractly considered, apart from the environment of human activities, and turned into final and sole ends, they are animal functions.

We have now considered the act of alienation of practical human activity, labor, from two aspects: (1) the relationship of the worker to the *product of labor* as an alien object which dominates him. This relationship is at the same time the relationship to the sensuous external world, to natural objects, as an alien and hostile world; (2) the relationship of labor to the *act of production* within *labor*. This is the relationship of the worker to his own activity as something alien and not belonging to him, activity as suffering (passivity), strength as powerlessness, creation as emasculation, the *personal* physical and mental energy of the worker, his personal life (for what is life but activity?), as an activity which is directed against himself, independent of him and not belonging to him. This is *self-alienation* as against the [afore]mentioned alienation of the *thing*.

We have now to infer a third characteristic of *alienated labor* from the two we have considered.

Man is a species-being not only in the sense that he makes the community (his own as well as those of other things) his object both practically and theoretically, but also (and this is simply another expression for the same thing) in the sense that he treats himself as the present, living species, as a *universal* and consequently free being.

Species-life, for man as for animals, has its physical basis in the fact that man (like animals) lives from inorganic nature, and since man is more universal than an animal so the range of inorganic nature from which he lives is more universal. Plants, animals, minerals, air, light, etc. constitute, from the theoretical aspect, a part of human consciousness as objects of natural science and art; they are man's spiritual inorganic nature, his intellectual means of life, which he must first prepare for enjoyment and perpetuation. So also, from the practical aspect, they form a part of human life and activity. In practice man lives only from these natural products, whether in the form of food, heating, clothing, housing, etc. The universality of man appears in practice in the universality which makes the whole of nature into his inorganic body: (1) as a direct means of life; and equally (2) as the material object and instrument of his life activity. Nature is the inorganic body of man; that is to say nature, excluding the human body itself. To say that man *lives* from nature means that nature is his *body* with which he must remain in a continuous interchange in order not to die. The statement that the physical and mental life of man, and nature, are interdependent means simply that nature is interdependent with itself, for man is a part of nature.

Since alienated labor (1) alienates nature from man; and (2) alienates man from himself, from his own active function, his life activity; so it alienates him from the species. It makes *species-life* into a means of individual life. In the first place it alienates species-life and individual life, and secondly, it turns the latter, as an abstraction, into the purpose of the former, also in its abstract and alienated form.

For labor, *life activity, productive life*, now appear to man only as *means* for the satisfaction of a need, the need to maintain his physical existence. Productive life is, however, species-life. It is life creating life. In the type of life activity resides the whole character of a species, its species-character; and free, conscious activity is the species-character of human beings. Life itself appears only as a *means of life*.

The animal is one with its life activity. It does not distinguish the activity from itself. It is *its activity*. But man makes his life activity itself an object of his will and consciousness. He has a conscious life activity. It is not a determination with which he is completely identified. Conscious life activity distinguishes man from the life activity of animals. Only for this reason is he a species-being. Or rather, he is only a self-conscious being, i.e., his own life is an object for him, because he is a species-being. Only for this reason is his activity free activity. Alienated labor reverses the relationship, in that man because he is a self-conscious being makes his life activity, his *being*, only a means for his *existence*.

CRITICAL THINKING QUESTIONS

1. Does Marx argue that work is inevitably alienating? Why does work within a capitalist economy produce alienation?

2. In what different respects does labour within capitalism alienate the worker?

3. Based on this analysis, under what conditions do you think Marx would argue that labour is not alienating?

NOTE

1. Debasement.

39

Experiences of Social Class: Learning from Occupational Therapy Students

BRENDA L. BEAGAN

This reading brings to light some of the problems that people from working-class backgrounds experience when they enter middle-class jobs (in this case, occupational therapy). It discusses poverty and, above all, the impact of social class. This study also uses a somewhat novel method of data collection. Professor Beagan asked students to write about their experiences, which she then systematically analyzed and documented. Permission to be included in the research was given by the students involved in the study.

This paper analyses the personal accounts of occupational therapy students on the ways their own occupational lives have been affected by growing up in working-class or impoverished families and communities. The student accounts provide a unique blending of profession-specific understanding of occupation and experiential understanding of social class.

The working class includes about a third of the Canadian population, men and women usually working at manual (blue-collar), clerical (pink-collar) or retail jobs (MacIonis, Clarke, & Gerber, 1997). They generally have a high school education, but not post-secondary. The lower class, about 20 percent of Canadians, live in poverty; some rely on social assistance for their only source of income, some work

Source: Brenda L. Beagan. 2007. "Experiences of Social Class: Learning from Occupational Therapy Students." *Canadian Journal of Occupational Therapy*, 74(2): 126–128, 129, 130–131.

at low-prestige, minimum-wage jobs. They may or may not have a high school education (MacIonis, Clarke, & Gerber, 1997). With universal access to basic health care, the impact of poverty on health is not as dramatic as in the United States. Nevertheless, lower-income Canadians die earlier and suffer more illnesses than Canadians with higher incomes, regardless of age, sex, race and geographic location (Health Canada, 2004; Raphael et al., 2005).

METHODS

This paper is based on student assignments submitted for an undergraduate occupational therapy course in which the impact of social factors on occupational engagement and opportunities were explored. The class occurred in the second term of the first year of the program. In one exercise, students were asked to write an occupational autobiography in which they analysed the ways their own membership in particular social groups had shaped their occupational lives. In these essays, several students explored the ways growing up in working-class or impoverished families affected their occupations in profound and ongoing ways.

With written permission from these students, this paper drew on parts of their essays as qualitative data.

RESULTS

The Participants

The 17 students (3 male and 14 female) whose essays were used as data all self-identified as coming from working-class, lower-class or impoverished family backgrounds, for at least part of their lives. Three were raised by single mothers; three students had parents with chronic illnesses or disabilities; four had at least one parent struggling with alcoholism. Five students experienced significant periods of time when social assistance or employment insurance was the main source of family income. In general, however, these students grew up in families that were considered among the working poor, where one or both parents were employed yet wages were insufficient to bring the family above the poverty line. Their parents worked in a range of positions including: childcare, homecare, manual labour, farming, fishing, factory work, manual trades, clerical work and retail.

Experiences of poverty differed among the students. None of the students described ever being homeless, but several remembered shortages of food when they were young: "I can remember a very empty fridge at times." All of the students described times when money was limited and they had to do without. Treats and luxuries were rare: "My mother couldn't even spare me a quarter when I asked her for money to buy penny candies at the store." Students described restricted or non-existent leisure opportunities, having no telephone, wearing hand-me-down clothing, using food banks, and living in sub-standard housing: "Our apartment was clean but always cold." The broad themes that emerged from their essays included shame and stigma, "passing" as middle class, leisure and responsibilities, experiences of family and schooling, and positive qualities.

The Shame and Sigma of Poverty

Students identified marginalization and stigma as central to their experience of living in poverty. They argued that people who are not middle-class are "regularly discriminated against because these individuals are seen as lazy or intellectually inferior." Stigma attaches a powerful, negative social label that diminishes a person's self concept. Many students wrote about housing or neighbourhoods that were stigmatized, causing them tremendous shame and embarrassment.

I never invited friends over to my house. . . . I did not want my friends to see how shabby and ugly my home was. I thought they would see that I was poor and not like me anymore.

Some students noted that the shame accompanying social stigma is not easily overcome. One student is still too embarrassed to bring his girlfriend to the house where he grew up. Another was not particularly ashamed of her home while she was growing up, but since entering occupational therapy school has made friends with people "from higher social classes":

People talk about coming and visiting in the summer time to my home town but I am embarrassed about the condition of my parents' house and that people will think my family is dirty or lazy based on what they see.

Students also described particular shame and stigma concerning clothing and physical appearance. Especially in junior high and high school they were teased, judged and ridiculed when they wore clothes identifiable as inexpensive or not brand-name.

I got picked on, stigmatized, labelled and left out due to the fact that we had little money and I wore second hand clothing. The worst was going to school in what was a new article of clothing for me, unaware that the same article was one a classmate of mine gave to the second hand store last week.

One student described a direct impact on her daily occupations. She could never afford to have the right sneakers to avoid ridicule, so she stopped participating in gym class: "I would bring 'dress' shoes and pretend I'd forgotten my sneakers."

The relentless mockery and derision had profound effects on some students' sense of self-worth. Several described learning to hate themselves, and learning to loathe going to school: "I was constantly made fun of and picked on because I did not have the latest style clothes, or the coolest sneakers. . . . I felt like dirt." Not surprisingly, messages so hurtful can have lasting effects. A few students described a pervasive belief that they were not good enough. As one said, "I believe that it is a mistake that I was accepted into the [occupational therapy] program. I feel that I am not smart enough or good enough."

Occupied with "Passing"

In response to shame and stigma, almost all of the students at some point engaged in activities that could be defined as attempts to "pass" as middle class. "Passing" occurs when members of social groups, who face discrimination, attempt to be identified as members of a higher-status social group. Students tried to pass as middle class to avoid or lessen the stigma attached to a lower-class status: "I put all my energy into having middle-class friends and 'appearing' to be of middle-class descent. . . . I always felt that I was an impostor." One student described herself as extremely self-conscious: "I lived in fear

that others would come to the realization that I was poor."

Students employed multiple strategies in their efforts to pass. Some found involvement in particular leisure occupations, such as teams or sports, that allowed them to fit in or pass, at least in that venue. For example, one student had a mentor who sponsored her involvement in figure skating. Many friends then assumed she belonged to the middle class because of her engagement in skating: "When I was at the arena I felt as though I could hide who I really was and pretend to be who I wished I was." More commonly, however, students described how they invested considerable energy in lying and hiding, and in devising strategies to avoid risky situations that might blow their cover and prevent them from passing as middle class.

One night after a party when a group of friends was driving me home, they saw the trailer court and began making redneck jokes. I then directed them to a house that was not mine and was dropped off there so I would not hear them make more jokes about where I lived.

One student had a simple strategy for hiding her lack of money from university friends: "When we went out to eat, I had water or tea and told them I had already eaten."

If an occupation can be understood as an activity invested with meaning, cultural significance, and power (Christiansen & Townsend, 2004), these students accurately point out that passing as middle class can become an occupation in and of itself. They invest time, energy, thought, care, skill, and effort into producing an appearance of middle-class membership.

It is an occupation to produce one's class identity, or in my case to mask or cover up my class identity. In my youth I spent a lot of my time pretending that I was in a higher social class than I actually belonged to.

Finally, it is clear that the desire to pass, and the habits and strategies developed in the service of that goal, are not easily abandoned upon entry to university or to occupational therapy school. A few students described the direct impact on their self-care occupations with implications for time use.

My dress and self-care began to consume a large part of my daily routine. As I wrote this paper I came to realize why I cannot leave the house in old clothes and I have to shower every day, wear make up and feel good about the outfit I choose for the day. I worry about who will see me and what they will think, and this is a result of being paranoid as a child about how people felt about how I looked and whether they could tell I was poor.

Another student noted that she has to wash her hair daily, "even when it is not dirty."

Not only clothing, cleanliness and appearance are loaded with potential for revealing a student's true class status, but also manners and etiquette. One student described a particularly powerful way her childhood poverty, and her desire to pass as middle class, continue to affect her daily in the self-care occupation of eating.

In elementary school I would pretend that I had forgotten my lunch because I did not want to eat in front of people. I was sure my eating habits and etiquette were less than those of my friends. I was so hungry that I had difficulties retaining information and therefore learning. Even in university, I go to the library in another building to eat lunch because I am not comfortable eating in front of others.

This student, who already feels marginalized, further isolates herself every day by eating on her own where no one she knows will see her, lest they detect lower-class manners.

Experiences of Family

Family was often experienced as another site of shame or stigma, especially when students were younger. One student avoided having her friends interact with her family lest they figure out her mother's single-parent status. Another skipped her prom and graduation and noted, "I did not want my classmates to see my parents and make fun of them and judge me." Others simply did the best they could to hide their parents from view, and saw their jobs, their possessions, and their actions as embarrassing. Families had the potential to reveal the true class status of someone successfully passing as middle class. For example, one student passed through involvement in figure skating until her peers met her mother.

My social class started to become evident when my mother began to attend my practices. I was so embarrassed of her and ashamed to admit that she was my mother. She did not dress like the other mothers; she was a little unkempt and very outspoken. . . . She was supposed to be well-kept, well-spoken, nice to look at and polite, like all the other kids' mothers. I was not right, nor was my family, for the sport I was in.

Shame concerning family seemed particularly deep-rooted and powerful in dating relationships. Several students were still unwilling to let romantic partners meet their families.

A few students also wrote about having what they perceived to be unusual adult responsibilities or concerns. Some wrote about pervasive awareness of family financial pressures and parental sacrifices to provide for the family: "A child's occupations should never be about money." Others felt they had to somehow take care of their parents.

I would go to bed crying, wishing there was some way I could help my parents out, feeling guilty because I had eaten too much that day and deprived another family member of having a full stomach.

Last, these students' experiences of family were complicated by the fact that university—especially entering a professional school—represented upward class mobility for them. Several students wrote about feeling pressure from family members proud of their admission to a health professional program. These pressures were often complicated by conflicting messages and emotions. While students were expected to "do better" than their parents had, the parents were often proud of their working-class heritage, and did not want their successful, upwardly mobile offspring to forget where they came from, or start thinking that they were better than anyone else. A few students struggled with how to act around friends and family "from home," not wanting to be seen as putting on airs.

Personal Qualities from Class Background

All of the students emphasized that growing up in poverty or in a working-class family was not an entirely negative experience. They identified ways in which important learning, positive characteristics or qualities, and specific values derived from their social class status. Several students spoke of their own determination, drive, strength, independence, compassion and work ethic as class-related.

I can stretch a dollar further than anybody I know; I can find a deal where nobody else can; I have learned to balance my time between work, play and school without a second to waste; but most of all, I have learned that I am a much more resilient person than I would have ever imagined.

Some developed work skills, leadership skills and time management strategies from years of job experience. Several students wrote about a fierce sense of pride that can be both an asset and a drawback. Some felt that they were quick to spot pity—which they resented—and slow to accept help, assistance, or gifts. Some described a compelling need for respect: "I desire to be respected and treated as though I am worth more than how much money I have."

Lastly, many of the students detailed values, particularly relating to family, friends and possessions, which they attributed to their class backgrounds. They wrote about how their shame concerning family turned to admiration as they grew older, as they learned to recognize the strength, resourcefulness, skills and dependability their parents had displayed. A

few students suggested that being raised with few material possessions allowed them to focus more on interpersonal relationships.

I learned to appreciate everything I have, especially the small things. . . . I have learned that what makes life happy and worth living are the people who surround you every day, not the material things that surround you or that you can buy.

Again, such values can be assets and drawbacks in occupational therapy school. If family and friends are priorities, why remove yourself from loved ones in the name of future success?

I often struggle with being away from friends and family to better myself. That is not how I was raised. . . . I was raised to believe in the quality of time not the quantity of goods. . . . Life was good for me as a kid, why don't I just go home and work the day to day and forget about putting myself in debt for the sake of school?

DISCUSSION

The student essays suggest that distinctive, class-based experiences shape people's ways of being in the world. The pervasive stigma and shame that accompany poverty caused them to restrict their own social occupations and avoid situations where friends would encounter their homes, their family members, or other aspects of their lives that might reveal class status. For some, mockery and ridicule of their clothing and appearance resulted in a lasting sense of low self-worth. For most, the clearest legacy of stigma was engagement in the occupation of passing. Numerous small strategies helped to conceal their own class backgrounds and accentuate attributes of the middle class. In the interest of passing, self-care occupations may become imbued with whole new levels of meaning.

Our experiences of the world lead to internalized predispositions to act in patterned ways that may become habits, or social roles with attached "scripts" and expectations (Kielhofner,

2002). At the same time, our sense of personal capacity and self-efficacy develop through experiencing the impact we are able to have on the world around us, in order to meet our goals or needs. Constant reminders that our efforts have little impact can result in a sense of power-lessness and reduced sense of capacity: "When shame or fear of failure governs a person's sense of capacity, there is disincentive to take risks, to learn new skills" (Kielhofner, p. 48).

Beyond the individual, whole social groups (e.g., social classes, cultural groups, racialized groups) can internalize a diminished sense of capacity and efficacy (Bourdieu, 1977). This might be expressed in the notion, 'That's not for the likes of us,' or 'Our people don't do that,' concerning, for example, higher educa-tion (Bellamy, 1994). Thus invisible processes of exclusion are implemented; members of marginalized groups, in effect, exclude them-selves by perceiving occupations as beyond their reach, or not legitimately belonging to them.

This idea was profoundly expressed in student descriptions of education. One young man "felt like an outsider trespassing on someone else's land." Olson argues that educational institutions show "a systematic preference for middle-class values, language, and views of the world" (1995, p. 201). The culture of education is middle class; students are evaluated not only on their academic merits, but also on their ability to display expected behaviours. Working-class students arrive without the right values, norms, skills, and commonplace understandings to move easily through the system. Feeling out of place, some disengage through poor attendance, poor performance, or more direct rebellion. One student detailed a deep sense of not belonging at the occupational therapy school leading to behaviours she interpreted as self-sabotage—an externalization of the belief, 'That's not for the likes of us.'

In part, students from low-income back-grounds feel marginalized in higher education because they do not have the right social cap-ital: social networks and relationships that include the right kinds of people with the right kinds of connections and knowledge (Bourdieu, 1986). As one student wrote, her middle-class friends seemed to have "some sort of invisible knowledge" concerning options for university that she "didn't know how to get." That know-ledge, which came from growing up around "the sophisticated conversations of lawyers and doctors," is middle-class social capital.

The students may also lack middle-class cul-tural capital: knowing how to operate smoothly in the midst of middle-class norms (Bourdieu, 1986). These norms are the intangibles that make someone a competent member of a par-ticular culture. The absence of middle-class occupations leaves some students with perceived gaps in cultural knowledge—they have not been to the right places, watched the right television shows, or experienced the right activities.

CRITICAL THINKING QUESTIONS

1. Have you ever been in a situation where you have felt uncomfortable because of your social or class background? Discuss the situation and how and why you felt dif-ferent from the other people (clothing, speech, etc.).

2. What does the author mean by "passing"? Beagan writes about the norms and expect-ations of the middle class. Can you name some of these and describe how they might differ from those of the working class?

3. Beagan observes that Canadians with working-class backgrounds have a shorter life expectancy and are generally less healthy than their middle-class counter-parts. How do you explain these differences?

REFERENCES

Bellamy, L. A. 1994. Capital, habitus, field, and practice: An introduction to the work of Pierre Bourdieu. In *Sociology of education in Canada: Critical perspectives on theory, research and practice*, eds. L. Erwin and L. MacLennan, 120–36. Toronto: Copp Clark Longman.

Bourdieu, P. 1972/1977. *Outline of a theory of practice* (trans. R. Nice). Cambridge, MA: Cambridge University Press.

Bourdieu, P. 1973/1986. The forms of capital. In *Handbook of theory and research for the sociology of education*, ed. J. C. Richardson (trans. R. Nice), 241–58. New York: Greenwood Press.

Christiansen, C. G., and E. A. Townsend. 2004. *Introduction to occupation: The art and science of living.* Upper Saddle River, NJ: Prentice Hall.

Ginsberg, E. ed. 1996. *Passing and the fictions of identity.* Durham, NC: Duke University Press.

Health Canada. 2004. *Population health.* Available: **http://www.hcsc.gc.ca/hppb/phdd/determinants**. Accessed July 13, 2004.

Kielhofner, G. 2002. *Model of human occupation: Theory and application*, 3rd ed. Baltimore, MD: Lippincott Williams & Wilkins.

MacIonis, J. J., J. N. Clarke, and L. M. Gerber. 1997. *Sociology: The Canadian edition*, 2nd ed. Scarborough, ON: Prentice-Hall Canada.

Olson, P. 1995. Poverty and education in Canada. In *Social change and education in Canada*, eds. R. Ghosh and D. Ray, 196–208. Toronto: Harcourt Brace.

Raphael, D., J. Macdonald, R. Colman, R. Labonte, K. Hayward, and R. Torgerson. 2005. Researching income and income distribution as determinants of health in Canada: Gaps between theoretical knowledge, research practice, and policy implementation. *Health Policy*, 72, 217–32.

40

The Economy and Society

JIM STANFORD

Jim Stanford, a researcher with the Canadian Auto Workers union (one of the country's largest unions), questions the legitimacy of mainstream economics and suggests some alternatives.

WHAT IS THE ECONOMY?

The economy is simultaneously mystifying and straightforward. Everyone has experience with the economy. Everyone participates in it. Everyone knows something about it—long before the pinstripe-wearing economist appears on TV to tell you about it. . . .

At its simplest, the "economy" simply means all the work that human beings perform, in order to produce the things we need and use in our lives. (By work, we mean all productive human activity, not just employment; we'll discuss that distinction later.) We need to organize and perform our work (economists call that PRODUCTION). And then we need to divide up the fruits of our work (economists call that DISTRIBUTION).

What kind of work are we talking about? Any kind of work is part of the economy, as long as it's aimed at producing something we need or want. Factory workers, office workers. Executives, farmers. Teachers, nurses. Homemakers, homebuilders. All of these people perform productive work, and all of that work is part of the economy.

What do we produce when we work? Production involves both goods and services. GOODS are tangible items that we can see and touch: food and clothes, houses and buildings, electronics and automobiles, machines and toys. SERVICES are tasks that one or several people perform for others: cutting hair and preparing restaurant meals, classroom instruction and brain surgery, transportation and auditing.

Where do we perform this work? Productive work occurs almost everywhere: in private companies, in government departments and

Source: Used with permission of the author Jim Stanford and the publisher, Fernwood Publishing Co. Ltd.

public agencies, and in the home. In cities, in towns, on farms, and in forests.

Why do we work? We must survive, and hence we require the basic material needs of life: food, clothing, shelter, education, medical care. Beyond that, we want to get the most out of our lives, and hence we aim for more than subsistence. We want a greater quantity, and a greater variety, of goods and services: for entertainment, for travel, for cultural and personal enrichment, for comfort. We may also work because we enjoy it. Perversely for economists (most of whom view work solely as a "disutility"), most people are happier when they have work to do—thanks to the social interaction, financial well-being, and self-esteem that good work provides.

How do we distribute, and eventually use, the economic pie we have baked together? In many different ways. Some things are produced directly for our own use (like food grown in a garden, and then cooked in a household kitchen). Most things we must buy with money. We are entitled to consume certain products— like walking down a paved street, listening to the radio, or going to school—without directly paying anything. Importantly, some of what we produce must be re-invested, in order to spark even more economic activity in the future.

So when you think about the "economy," just think about work. What work do we do? What do we produce? And what do we do with what we've produced?

THE ECONOMY AND SOCIETY

The economy is a fundamentally *social* activity. Nobody does it all by themselves (unless you are a hermit). We rely on each other, and we interact with each other, in the course of our work.

It is common to equate the economy with private or individual wealth, profit, and self-interest, and hence it may seem strange to describe it as something "social." Indeed, free-market economists adopt the starting premise that human

beings are inherently selfish (even though this assumption has been proven false by biologists and anthropologists alike).

In fact, the capitalist economy is not individualistic at all. It is social, and in many ways it is cooperative. The richest billionaire in the world couldn't have earned a dollar without the supporting roles played by his or her workers, suppliers, and customers. Indeed, our economic lives are increasingly intertwined with each other, as we each play our own little roles in a much bigger picture. That's why most of us live in cities (where the specialized, collective nature of the economy is especially visible). And that's how we can interact economically with people in other countries, thousands of miles away.

The economy is about work: organizing it, doing it, and dividing up its products. And at work, one way or another, we interact with other people.

The link between the economy and society goes two ways. The economy is a fundamentally social arena. But society as a whole depends strongly on the state of the economy. Politics, culture, religion, and international affairs are all deeply influenced by the progress of our economy. Governments are re-elected or turfed from office depending on the state of the economy. Family life is organized around the demands of work (both inside and outside the home). Being able to comfortably support oneself and one's family is a central determinant of happiness.

So the economy is an important, perhaps even dominant, force in human development. That doesn't mean that we should make "sacrifices" for the sake of the economy—since the whole point of the economy is to meet our material needs, not the other way around. And it certainly doesn't mean that we should grant undue attention or influence to economists. But it does mean that we will understand a great deal about our history, our current social reality, and our future evolution as a species, when we understand more about economics.

WHAT IS ECONOMICS?

Economics is a social science, not a physical science. (Unfortunately, many economists are confused on this point! They foolishly try to describe human economic activity with as much mechanical precision as physicists describe the behaviour of atoms.) Economics is the study of human economic behaviour: the production and distribution of the goods and services we need and want.

This broad field encompasses several sub-disciplines: economic history; money and finance; household economics; labour studies and labour relations; business economics and management; international economics; environmental economics; and others. A broad (and rather artificial) division is often made between MICROECONOMICS (the study of the economic behaviour of individual consumers, workers, and companies) and MACROECONOMICS (the study of how the economy functions at the aggregate level).

This all seems relatively straightforward. Unfortunately, the dominant stream in modern economics (NEOCLASSICAL ECONOMICS) . . . makes it more complicated than it needs to be. Instead of addressing broad questions of production and distribution, neoclassical economics focuses narrowly on *markets* and *exchange*. The purpose of economics, in this mindset, was defined by one of its leading practitioners (Lord Lionel Robbins) back in 1932, in a definition that is still taught in economics courses today:

"Economics is the science which studies human behaviour as a relationship between given ends and scarce means which have alternative uses."

Embedded in this definition is a very peculiar (and rather dismal) interpretation of economic life. Scarcity is a normal condition. Humans are "endowed" with arbitrary amounts of useful resources. By trading through markets, they can extract maximum well-being from that endowment—just like school kids experience greater happiness by trading their duplicate superhero cards with one another in the playground. An "efficient" economy is one which maximizes, through trade, the usefulness of that initial endowment—regardless of how output is distributed, what kinds of things are produced, or how rich or poor people are at the end of the day. (This curious narrow concept of efficiency is called ALLOCATIVE EFFICIENCY.)

. . . [B]y defining the fundamental economic "question" in this particular way, neoclassical economics misses many important economic issues related to production, innovation, development, and fairness.

I prefer to keep things simple. We'll stick with a much broader definition of economics: the study of how humans work, and what we do with the fruits of our labour. Part of this involves studying markets and exchange—but only part. Economics also involves studying many other things: history, technology, tradition, family, power, and conflict.

ECONOMICS AND POLITICS

Economics and politics have always gone hand-in-hand. Indeed, the first economists called their discipline "political economy." The connections between economics and politics reflect, in part, the importance of economic conditions to political conditions. The well-being of the economy can influence the rise and fall of politicians and governments, even entire social systems.

But here, too, the influence goes both ways. Politics also affects the economy—and economics itself. The economy is a realm of competing, often conflicting interests. Determining whose interests prevail, and how conflicts are managed, is a deeply political process. (Neoclassical economists claim that anonymous "market forces" determine all these outcomes, but don't be fooled: what they call the "market" is itself a social institution in which some people's interests are enhanced at the expense of others'.) Different economic actors use their political influence and power to advance their respective economic interests. The extent to which groups of people tolerate economic outcomes (even unfavourable ones) also depends on political factors: such as whether or not they believe those outcomes are "natural" or "inevitable," and whether or not they feel they have any power to bring about change.

Finally, the social science which aims to interpret and explain all this scrabbling, teeming behaviour—economics—has its own political assumptions and biases. . . . [M]ost economic theories over the years have been motivated by political considerations. Modern economics (including this book!) is no different: economics is still a deeply political profession.

MEASURING THE ECONOMY

GROSS DOMESTIC PRODUCT (GDP) is the most common way to measure the economy. But beware: it is a deeply flawed measure. GDP adds up the value of all the different goods and services that are produced *for money* in the economy. GDP is thus one measure of the total value of the work we do—but only the work we do for money.

In the private sector of the economy, GDP is based on the market prices of everything that's bought and sold. In the public and nonprofit sectors, it is based on the cost of everything that's produced. In both cases, statisticians must deduct the costs of the many inputs and supplies purchased in any particular industry, from the total value produced by that industry. (This is so that we don't double-count the work that went into all those inputs.) In this way, GDP is designed to only include the VALUE ADDED by new work at each stage of production.

An obvious drawback of GDP is that it excludes the value of work that is *not* performed for money. This is a highly arbitrary and misleading exclusion. For example, most people perform unpaid chores in their households, and many must care for other family members (especially children and elders). Some of this household work can be "outsourced" to paid cleaners, nannies, and restaurants (the richer you are, the more you can outsource), in which case it is included in GDP. But if you "do it yourself," then it doesn't count! Volunteer work and community participation are other forms of valuable, productive work excluded from GDP.

This phony distinction has big consequences for how we measure the economy. Unfortunately, things that we measure often take on extra importance (with the media, and with policy-makers), purely because they *can* be measured. GDP underestimates the total value of work performed in the economy, and hence misjudges our productivity. It undervalues the unpaid work done within our homes and our communities. Because of sexism at home and in the workplace, most of that unpaid work is done by women; hence, GDP underestimates the economic contribution of women.

It's especially misguided to interpret GDP as a measure of human well-being. We've seen that there are many valuable things that are not included in GDP. On the other hand, many of the goods and services that *are* counted in GDP are utterly useless, annoying, or even destructive to human well-being—like dinner-hour telephone solicitations, many pharmaceuticals, excess consumer packaging, and armaments production. Moreover, just because a society produces more GDP never ensures that most members of society will ever receive a larger slice of that growing pie.

So we must be cautious in our use of GDP statistics, and we must never equate GDP with prosperity or well-being.

Despite these caveats, GDP is still an important and relevant measure. It indicates the value of all production that occurs for money. This is an important, appropriate piece of information for many purposes. (For example, the ability of governments to collect taxes depends directly on the money value of GDP.) We need to

GDP and Human Well-Being

The United Nations Development Program produces an annual ranking of countries according to their "human development." The UN defines human development on the basis of three key indicators: GDP per capita, life expectancy, and educational attainment. We've already seen that GDP is a highly misleading measure, so the UN's approach is far from perfect. It attaches no value to social equity, leisure time, and other important human goals.

Nevertheless, it is interesting to compare the ranking of countries according to human development, with their ranking according to GDP. In general, countries with high human development also have high levels of GDP per capita (partly because GDP is itself one of the three variables considered, and partly because higher GDP allows a society to devote more resources to health and education). This indicates that economic growth is indeed very important to standard of living.

However, the link between GDP and human development is not perfect. Some countries (such as the Nordic countries) rank higher in the UN list than they do on the basis of GDP alone. This indicates they are more efficient at translating GDP into genuine human welfare (usually thanks to extensive public services, financed with high taxes). On the other hand, countries which rank lower on the UN list than in the GDP standings are relatively ineffective at translating GDP into well-being; these countries (like the US and the UK) have relatively low taxes and relatively weak public programs.

Table 40.1 summarizes the key human development statistics for selected countries. High-tax Norway (where government spends over 50 percent of GDP on public programs) ranks first; low-tax America ranks eighth (despite having the second-highest GDP in the world). For each country, the difference between its GDP rank and its human development rank summarizes its success at translating GDP into genuine well-being; this difference is reported in the fourth column (shaded). A positive score in this column indicates that a country makes the most of its GDP; a negative score indicates the opposite. Socialist Cuba—where average health outcomes are superior to those in the US—manages to do more, given its GDP, to improve human welfare than any other country in the world. On the other hand, oil-rich Equatorial Guinea does the worst job of any country at channelling GDP into well-being. South Africa also has a very low human development ranking, despite its relatively advanced economy (by African standards), primarily because of low life expectancy and a very unequal distribution of income.

understand the weaknesses of GDP, and supplement it with other measures. Above all, we must remember that expanding GDP is never an end in itself. At best, properly managed, it can be a means to an end (the goal of improving human well-being). Indeed, there is a positive but imperfect relationship between GDP and human welfare (see box). This suggests that we need to be concerned with how much we produce, but equally with what we use it for.

To be meaningful, GDP figures must take several additional factors into account. If the apparent value of our work grows purely because of INFLATION (which is a general increase in the prices of *all* goods and services), then there hasn't been any real improvement in the economy. Therefore we distinguish between NOMINAL GDP (measured in dollars/pounds) and REAL GDP (which deducts the effect of inflation). There are many other economic variables (such as wages and interest rates) for which this distinction between nominal and real values is also important. ECONOMIC GROWTH is usually measured by the expansion of real GDP.

In addition, a country's GDP could expand simply because its population was growing—but this does not imply that the country is becoming more prosperous. This is important when comparing growth rates across countries. For example, in countries with near-zero population growth (such as Europe and Japan), even a slow growth of real GDP can translate into improved living standards; this is not the case where population is growing more quickly. Therefore, economists often divide GDP by population, to get a measure called GDP PER CAPITA. This, too, can be expressed in both nominal and real terms. Growth in real GDP per capita over time is often used as a rough indicator of prosperity—although we must always remember that GDP excludes many valuable types of work, and says nothing about how production is distributed.

TABLE 40.1   GDP and Human Well-Being

Country	Human Development Index Rank (HDI)	GDP Rank	GDP Rank – HDI Rank*	GDP per Capita (US$)	Life Expectancy (years)	Educational Attainment Index†
Norway	1	4	3	38,454	79.6	.99
Iceland	2	5	3	33,051	80.9	.98
Australia	3	14	11	30,331	80.5	.99
Ireland	4	3	−1	38,827	77.9	.99
Sweden	5	16	11	29,541	80.3	.98
Canada	6	10	4	31,263	80.2	.97
Japan	7	18	11	29.251	82.2	.94
US	8	2	−6	39,676	77.5	.97
UK	18	13	−5	30,821	78.3	.97
China	81	90	9	5,896	71.9	.84
India	126	117	−9	3,139	63.6	.61
Human Development "Over-Achievers":						
Uruguay	43	62	+19	9,421	75.6	.95
Cuba	50	93	+43	5,700	77.6	.93
Armenia	80	112	+32	4,101	71.6	.91
Madagascar	143	169	+26	857	55.6	.66
Human Development "Under-Achievers":						
Hong Kong	22	12	−10	30,822	81.8	.88
Saudi Arabia	76	45	−31	13,825	72.0	.72
Turkey	92	70	−22	7,753	68.9	.81
Equatorial Guinea	120	30	−90	20,510	42.8	.77
South Africa	121	55	−66	11,192	47.0	.80

Source: UN Human Development Report, 2006.

*A positive score indicates better HDI ranking than GDP ranking.

†Index based on literacy rate and combined school enrolment.

WHAT IS A GOOD ECONOMY?

Economics tries to explain how the economy works. But economists are equally (and justifiably) concerned with trying to make it work *better*. This inherently requires the economist (and every citizen) to make value judgements about what kind of economy is more desirable. Most economists, unfortunately, are not honest about those value judgements; they like to pretend that their profession is "scientific" and hence value-free, but this is a charade.

Deciding what economic goals to pursue will reflect the priorities and interests of different individuals, communities, and classes. It is an inherently subjective choice. ....

CRITICAL THINKING QUESTIONS

1. As Stanford states, the economy is central to modern life, often to the detriment of social issues. Name some things that are important to your life that are *non*-economic.

2. Can money buy happiness? It's obvious that some money is necessary in order to eke out a comfortable existence, but is there a point where enough is enough? How would your views on this inform economic distribution in Canada?

3. Stanford notes that the field of economics is not a science because it's *not* value free. What does he mean by that? How can values determine one's perspective toward economic policy? Provide some examples.

Politics,
Government,
and the Military

CLASSIC

CONTEMPORARY

CROSS-CULTURAL

41

The Power Elite

C. WRIGHT MILLS

Conventional wisdom suggests that U.S. society operates as a democracy, guided by the "voice of the people." C. Wright Mills argues that above ordinary people—and even above many politicians—are "the higher circles," those who run the corporations, operate the military establishment, and manipulate the machinery of the state. It is this relatively small handful of people whom Mills calls "the power elite."

The powers of ordinary men are circumscribed by the everyday worlds in which they live, yet even in these rounds of job, family, and neighborhood they often seem driven by forces they can neither understand nor govern. "Great changes" are beyond their control, but affect their conduct and outlook nonetheless. The very framework of modern society confines them to projects not their own, but from every side, such changes now press upon the men and women of the mass society, who accordingly feel that they are without purpose in an epoch in which they are without power.

But not all men are in this sense ordinary. As the means of information and of power are centralized, some men come to occupy positions in American society from which they can look down upon, so to speak, and by their decisions mightily affect, the everyday worlds of ordinary men and women. They are not made by their jobs; they set up and break down jobs for thousands of others; they are not confined by simple family responsibilities; they can escape. They may live in many hotels and houses, but they are bound by no one community. They need not merely "meet the demands of the day and hour"; in some part, they create these demands, and cause others to meet them. Whether or not they profess their power, their technical and political experience of it far transcends that of the underlying population. What Jacob Burckhardt said of "great men," most Americans might well say of their elite: "They are all that we are not."

The power elite is composed of men whose positions enable them to transcend the ordinary environments of ordinary men and women; they are in positions to make decisions having major consequences. Whether they do or do not make such decisions is less important than the fact that

Source: From *The Power Elite*, New Edition, by C. Wright Mills. Copyright © 1956, 2000 by Oxford University Press, Inc.; renewed 1984 by Yaraslava Mills. Reprinted by permission of Oxford University Press, Inc.

they do occupy such pivotal positions: Their failure to act, their failure to make decisions, is itself an act that is often of greater consequence than the decisions they do make. For they are in command of the major hierarchies and organizations of modern society. They rule the big corporations. They run the machinery of the state and claim its prerogatives. They direct the military establishment. They occupy the strategic command posts of the social structure, in which are now centered the effective means of the power and the wealth and the celebrity which they enjoy.

The power elite are not solitary rulers. Advisers and consultants, spokesmen and opinion-makers are often the captains of their higher thought and decision. Immediately below the elite are the professional politicians of the middle levels of power, in the Congress and in the pressure groups, as well as among the new and old upper classes of town and city and region. Mingling with them, in curious ways which we shall explore, are those professional celebrities who live by being continually displayed but are never, so long as they remain celebrities, displayed enough. If such celebrities are not at the head of any dominating hierarchy, they do often have the power to distract the attention of the public or afford sensations to the masses, or, more directly, to gain the ear of those who do occupy positions of direct power. More or less unattached, as critics of morality and technicians of power, as spokesmen of God and creators of mass sensibility, such celebrities and consultants are part of the immediate scene in which the drama of the elite is enacted. But that drama itself is centered in the command posts of the major institutional hierarchies.

The truth about the nature and the power of the elite is not some secret which men of affairs know but will not tell. Such men hold quite various theories about their own roles in the sequence of event and decision. Often they are uncertain about their roles, and even more often they allow their fears and their hopes to affect their assessment of their own power. No matter how great their actual power, they tend to be less acutely

aware of it than of the resistances of others to its use. Moreover, most American men of affairs have learned well the rhetoric of public relations, in some cases even to the point of using it when they are alone, and thus coming to believe it. The personal awareness of the actors is only one of the several sources one must examine in order to understand the higher circles. Yet many who believe that there is no elite, or at any rate none of any consequence, rest their argument upon what men of affairs believe about themselves, or at least assert in public.

There is, however, another view: Those who feel, even if vaguely, that a compact and powerful elite of great importance does now prevail in America often base that feeling upon the historical trend of our time. They have felt, for example, the domination of the military event, and from this they infer that generals and admirals, as well as other men of decision influenced by them, must be enormously powerful. They hear that the Congress has again abdicated to a handful of men decisions clearly related to the issue of war or peace. They know that the bomb was dropped over Japan in the name of the United States of America, although they were at no time consulted about the matter. They feel that they live in a time of big decisions; they know that they are not making any. Accordingly, as they consider the present as history, they infer that at its center, making decisions or failing to make them, there must be an elite of power.

On the one hand, those who share this feeling about big historical events assume that there is an elite and that its power is great. On the other hand, those who listen carefully to the reports of men apparently involved in the great decisions often do not believe that there is an elite whose powers are of decisive consequence.

Both views must be taken into account, but neither is adequate. The way to understand the power of the American elite lies neither solely in recognizing the historic scale of events nor in accepting the personal awareness reported by men of apparent decision. Behind such men and behind the events of history, linking the two, are the major institutions of modern society. These hierarchies of state and corporation and army constitute the means of power; as such they are now of a consequence not before equaled in human history—and at their summits, there are now those command posts of modern society which offer us the sociological key to an understanding of the role of the higher circles in America.

Within American society, major national power now resides in the economic, the political, and the military domains. Other institutions seem off to the side of modern history, and, on occasion, duly subordinated to these. No family is as directly powerful in national affairs as any major corporation; no church is as directly powerful in the external biographies of young men in America today as the military establishment; no college is as powerful in the shaping of momentous events as the National Security Council. Religious, educational, and family institutions are not autonomous centers of national power; on the contrary, these decentralized areas are increasingly shaped by the big three, in which developments of decisive and immediate consequence now occur.

Families and churches and schools adapt to modern life; governments and armies and corporations shape it; and, as they do so, they turn these lesser institutions into means for their ends. Religious institutions provide chaplains to the armed forces where they are used as a means of increasing the effectiveness of its morale to kill. Schools select and train men for their jobs in corporations and their specialized tasks in the armed forces. The extended family has, of course, long been broken up by the industrial revolution, and now the son and the father are removed from the family, by compulsion if need be, whenever the army of the state sends out the call. And the symbols of all these lesser institutions are used to legitimate the power and the decisions of the big three.

The life-fate of the modern individual depends not only upon the family into which he was born or which he enters by marriage, but increasingly upon the corporation in which he spends the most alert hours of his best years; not only upon the school where he is educated as a child and adolescent, but also upon the state which touches him throughout his life; not only upon the church in which on occasion he hears the word of God, but also upon the army in which he is disciplined.

If the centralized state could not rely upon the inculcation of nationalist loyalties in public and private schools, its leaders would promptly seek to modify the decentralized educational system. If the bankruptcy rate among the top 500 corporations were as high as the general divorce rate among the 37 million married couples, there would be economic catastrophe on an international scale. If members of armies gave to them no more of their lives than do believers to the churches to which they belong, there would be a military crisis.

Within each of the big three, the typical institutional unit has become enlarged, has become administrative, and, in the power of its decisions, has become centralized. Behind these developments there is a fabulous technology, for as institutions, they have incorporated this technology and guide it, even as it shapes and paces their developments.

The economy—once a great scatter of small productive units in autonomous balance—has become dominated by two or three hundred giant corporations, administratively and politically interrelated, which together hold the keys to economic decisions.

The political order, once a decentralized set of several dozen states with a weak spinal cord, has become a centralized, executive establishment which has taken up into itself many powers previously scattered, and now enters into each and every cranny of the social structure.

The military order, once a slim establishment in a context of distrust fed by state militia, has become the largest and most expensive feature of government, and, although well-versed in smiling public relations, now has all the grim and clumsy efficiency of a sprawling bureaucratic domain.

In each of these institutional areas, the means of power at the disposal of decision makers have increased enormously; their central executive powers have been enhanced; within each of them modern administrative routines have been elaborated and tightened up.

As each of these domains becomes enlarged and centralized, the consequences of its activities become greater, and its traffic with the others increases. The decisions of a handful of corporations bear upon military and political as well as upon economic developments around the world. The decisions of the military establishment rest upon and grievously affect political life as well as the very level of economic activity. The decisions made within the political domain determine economic activities and military programs. There is no longer, on the one hand, an economy, and, on the other hand, a political order containing a military establishment unimportant to politics and to money-making. There is a political economy linked, in a thousand ways, with military institutions and decisions. On each side of the world-split running through central Europe and around the Asiatic rimlands, there is an ever-increasing interlocking of economic, military, and political structures. If there is government intervention in the corporate economy, so is there corporate intervention in the governmental process. In the structural sense, this triangle of power is the source of the interlocking directorate that is most important for the historical structure of the present.

The fact of the interlocking is clearly revealed at each of the points of crisis of modern capitalist society—slump, war, and boom. In each, men of decision are led to an awareness of the interdependence of the major institutional orders. In the nineteenth century, when the scale of all institutions was smaller, their liberal integration was achieved in the automatic economy, by an autonomous play of market forces, and in the automatic political domain, by the bargain and the vote. It was then assumed that out of the imbalance and friction that followed the limited decisions then possible a new equilibrium would

in due course emerge. That can no longer be assumed, and it is not assumed by the men at the top of each of the three dominant hierarchies.

For given the scope of their consequences, decisions—and indecisions—in any one of these ramify into the others, and hence top decisions tend either to become coordinated or to lead to a commanding indecision. It has not always been like this. When numerous small entrepreneurs made up the economy, for example, many of them could fail and the consequences still remain local; political and military authorities did not intervene. But now, given political expectations and military commitments, can they afford to allow key units of the private corporate economy to break down in slump? Increasingly, they do intervene in economic affairs, and as they do so, the controlling decisions in each order are inspected by agents of the other two, and economic, military, and political structures are interlocked.

At the pinnacle of each of the three enlarged and centralized domains, there have arisen those higher circles which make up the economic, the political, and the military elites. At the top of the economy, among the corporate rich, there are the chief executives; at the top of the political order, the members of the political directorate; at the top of the military establishment, the elite of soldier-statesmen clustered in and around the Joint Chiefs of Staff and the upper echelon. As each of these domains has coincided with the others, as decisions tend to become total in their consequence, the leading men in each of the three domains of power—the warlords, the corporation chieftains, the political directorate—tend to come together, to form the power elite of America.

The higher circles in and around these command posts are often thought of in terms of what their members possess: They have a greater share than other people of the things and experiences that are most highly valued. From this point of view, the elite are simply those who have the most of what there is to have, which is generally held to include money, power, and prestige—as well as all the ways of life to which these lead. But the elite are not simply those who have the most, for they could not "have the most" were it not for their positions in the great institutions. For such institutions are the necessary bases of power, of wealth, and of prestige, and at the same time, the chief means of exercising power, of acquiring and retaining wealth, and of cashing in the higher claims for prestige.

By the powerful we mean, of course, those who are able to realize their will, even if others resist it. No one, accordingly, can be truly powerful unless he has access to the command of major institutions, for it is over these institutional means of power that the truly powerful are, in the first instance, powerful. Higher politicians and key officials of government command such institutional power; so do admirals and generals, and so do the major owners and executives of the larger corporations. Not all power, it is true, is anchored in and exercised by means of such institutions, but only within and through them can power be more or less continuous and important.

Wealth also is acquired and held in and through institutions. The pyramid of wealth cannot be understood merely in terms of the very rich; for the great inheriting families, as we shall see, are now supplemented by the corporate institutions of modern society: Every one of the very rich families has been and is closely connected—always legally and frequently managerially as well—with one of the multimillion-dollar corporations.

The modern corporation is the prime source of wealth, but, in latter-day capitalism, the political apparatus also opens and closes many avenues to wealth. The amount as well as the source of income, the power over consumer's goods as well as over productive capital, are determined by position within the political economy. If our interest in the very rich goes beyond their lavish or their miserly consumption, we must examine their relations to modern forms of corporate property as well as to the state; for such relations now determine the chances of men to secure big property and to receive high income.

Great prestige increasingly follows the major institutional units of the social structure. It is obvious that prestige depends, often quite decisively, upon access to the publicity machines that are now a central and normal feature of all the big institutions of modern America. Moreover, one feature of the hierarchies of corporation, state, and military establishment is that their top positions are increasingly interchangeable. One result of this is the accumulative nature of prestige. Claims for prestige, for example, may be initially based on military roles, then expressed in and augmented by an educational institution run by corporate executives, and cashed in, finally, in the political order, where, for General Eisenhower and those he represents, power and prestige finally meet at the very peak. Like wealth and power, prestige tends to be cumulative: The more of it you have, the more you can get. These values also tend to be translatable into one another: The wealthy find it easier than the poor to gain power; those with status find it easier than those without it to control opportunities for wealth.

If we took the 100 most powerful men in America, the 100 wealthiest, and the 100 most celebrated away from the institutional positions they now occupy, away from their resources of men and women and money, away from the media of mass communication that are now focused upon them—then they would be powerless and poor and uncelebrated. For power is not of a man. Wealth does not center in the person of the wealthy. Celebrity is not inherent in any personality. To be celebrated, to be wealthy, to have power requires access to major institutions, for the institutional positions men occupy determine in large part their chances to have and to hold these valued experiences.

The people of the higher circles may also be conceived as members of a top social stratum, as a set of groups whose members know one another, see one another socially and at business, and so, in making decisions, take one another into account. The elite, according to this conception, feel themselves to be, and are felt by others to be, the inner circle of "the upper social classes." They form a more or less compact social and psychological entity; they have become self-conscious members of a social class. People are either accepted into this class or they are not, and there is a qualitative split, rather than merely a numerical scale, separating them from those who are not elite. They are more or less aware of themselves as a social class and they behave toward one another differently from the way they do toward members of other classes. They accept one another, understand one another, marry one another, tend to work and to think if not together at least alike.

Now, we do not want by our definition to prejudge whether the elite of the command posts are conscious members of such a socially recognized class, or whether considerable proportions of the elite derive from such a clear and distinct class. These are matters to be investigated. Yet in order to be able to recognize what we intend to investigate, we must note something that all biographies and memoirs of the wealthy and the powerful and the eminent make clear: No matter what else they may be, the people of these higher circles are involved in a set of overlapping "crowds" and intricately connected "cliques." There is a kind of mutual attraction among those who "sit on the same terrace"—although this often becomes clear to them, as well as to others, only at the point at which they feel the need to draw the line; only when, in their common defense, they come to understand what they have in common, and so close their ranks against outsiders.

The idea of such ruling stratum implies that most of its members have similar social origins, that throughout their lives they maintain a network of informal connections, and that to some degree there is an interchangeability of position between the various hierarchies of money and power and celebrity. We must, of course, note at once that if such an elite stratum does exist, its social visibility and its form, for very solid historical reasons, are quite different from those of the noble cousinhoods that once ruled various European nations.

That American society has never passed through a feudal epoch is of decisive importance to the nature of the American elite, as well as to American society as a historic whole. For it means that no nobility or aristocracy, established before the capitalist era, has stood in tense opposition to the higher bourgeoisie. It means that this bourgeoisie has monopolized not only wealth but prestige and power as well. It means that no set of noble families has commanded the top positions and monopolized the values that are generally held in high esteem; and certainly that no set has done so explicitly by inherited right. It means that no high church dignitaries or court nobilities, no entrenched landlords with honorific accouterments, no monopolists of high army posts have opposed the enriched bourgeoisie and in the name of birth and prerogative successfully resisted its self-making.

But this does not mean that there are no upper strata in the United States. That they emerged from a "middle class" that had no recognized aristocratic superiors does not mean they remained middle class when enormous increases in wealth made their own superiority possible. Their origins and their newness may have made the upper strata less visible in America than elsewhere. But in America today there are in fact tiers and ranges of wealth and power of which people in the middle and lower ranks know very little and may not even dream. There are families who, in their well-being, are quite insulated from the economic jolts and lurches felt by the merely prosperous and those farther down the scale. There are also men of power who in quite small groups make decisions of enormous consequence for the underlying population. . . .

CRITICAL THINKING QUESTIONS

1. What institutions form the "interlocking triangle" in Mills's analysis? Why does he think these are the most powerful social institutions?

2. Explain how Mills argues that the existence of a power elite is not a consequence of people per se but a result of the institutions of U.S. society.

3. Does the lack of an aristocratic history mean that power is dispersed throughout U.S. society?

... where. But in America today there are in fact
... bers and ranges of wealth and power of which

42

The Political Spectrum:
Do You Know Left from Right?

PETER URMETZER

and they...
another, many... one another, tend to work and to
think, if not together...
Now, we do not want by our definition to prejudge whether the elite of the command posts are
conscious members of such a socially recognized
... of whether consciderable proportions of the
elite...
These are matters to be investigated. Yet in order
to be able to recognize what we intend to investigate, we must note something that all biographies
and memoir of the wealthy and the powerful
and the eminent make clear. No matter what else
they may be, the people of these higher circles are
involved in a set of overlapping "crowds" and
intricately connected "cliques." There is a kind
of mutual attraction among those who "sit on

The political spectrum is often confusing to students because terms can have a multitude of different meanings depending on the context. This article looks at that context as well as the history of the term "liberalism."

Politics is first and foremost about how national (or provincial or municipal) wealth is distributed. Lower taxes, more generous social programs, minimum-wage laws, regulation of business and banks—all revolve around the issue of who gets what and how much. On another level, politics is also about how citizens should conduct themselves and what kind of behaviour is deemed acceptable, and, equally as important, unacceptable. Should we decriminalize marijuana, institute the death penalty, allow people of the same sex to marry? The question we will attempt to answer is whether there is any economic and social coherence to these varying issues.

The most common way of bringing some semblance of order to these disparate ideas is to categorize people and political parties along the left–right spectrum. This spectrum can be perplexing to some degree, yet it forms a

crucial basis for understanding politics at any and all levels: national, global, even the local school board or workplace. We'll examine a number of issues with respect to the social and economic dimensions of the political spectrum. The objective is to clear up some of the inevitable confusion.

Most of us are familiar with the labels used by commentators to categorize people, political parties, and even organizations and media outlets as "right wing" or "conservative," "liberal," or "left wing." These labels are often intimidating to students, since not only is the terminology confusing (What exactly *is* a liberal, anyway?), but the spectrum itself is applicable to different spheres: the political, the economic, and the social. For example, a person may be liberal with regard to social issues and conservative when it comes to matters economic.

It's useful to begin with an overview of the Canadian political landscape, highlighting

Source: This article was written specifically for this edition.

where the major parties are situated. The Conservative Party generally leans toward the right, whereas the New Democratic Party (NDP) veers toward the left, as does the Green Party. The Liberal Party has historically been considered, and identifies itself as, a centrist party; it has adopted policies from both the left and right depending on the national mood as well as political opportunity. Likewise, the Bloc Québécois is somewhat difficult to classify, as it encompasses elements of both left and right. Canada also has an active Communist Party (the extreme left), which is represented in only a few ridings. Finally, a variety of fringe parties come to prominence from time to time; these include the Marijuana Party, although it hasn't been motivated to run the past few elections.

In the United States, the Democrats are situated on the left and the Republicans on the right. However, many political commentators wonder just how left the Democrats are. As the novelist and social critic Gore Vidal (1977) famously observed, "There is only one party in the United States, the Property Party . . . and it has two right wings: Republican and Democrat."

The best way to acquire an understanding of the subject is to examine its historical roots. The left–right continuum originated with the French National Assembly, where the more conservative-thinking members were placed on the right side of the assembly and the more progressive members on the left. At the most fundamental level, this continuum, as Vidal noted, is about property. Communists, on the extreme left, endeavour to make private property illegal, whereas those on the extreme right identify property rights as the most crucial of all societal freedoms. The spectrum can also be seen from the perspective of individualism (right) and collectivism (left), and for this reason affects much of what goes on in the economic arena, particularly how we theorize an individual's relationship to the economy and society in general. Those on the right of the political spectrum believe that individuals are solely responsible for their own misfortune

or success and demand that the state play no role in rectifying this. Thus, when a person is out of work, poor, or both—topics central to sociology—someone on the right would blame the individual rather than acknowledge the social context. British prime minister Margaret Thatcher once proclaimed that "There is no such thing as society," implying that only individuals matter. In the political arena, this means that fiscal conservatives generally refuse to support unemployment insurance or social assistance. Some right-wingers go so far as to say that welfare-state intervention (i.e., taxing the well-off in order to fund programs for the poor) is immoral because it effectively steals resources from those individuals who have legitimately earned them. Someone on the left, meanwhile, is likely to place emphasis on the social context, and would argue that poverty and unemployment are structural and therefore require social policy in order to be kept in check.

The continuum can also be expressed as the amount of faith political parties put in the market; in other words, how much economic responsibility should be ceded to market forces. Market loyalty mostly serves as a shorthand for a stubborn aversion to state intervention. There exists a looming distrust of government among the right, which in turn stimulates an aspiration to privatize all economic activities. In the current Canadian political climate, debates about which services should be privatized extend to such areas as health care, education, and electricity generation and distribution. According to the most ardent of economic liberals, everything but police and military should be governed by the market. The American political philosopher Robert Nozick (2003) referred to this as the minimal or night watchman state. In this scenario, the sole responsibility of the state is to defend the nation from external threats and protect private property from threats within, and no more. All other services are to remain private.

It's easy to understand why capital as a class would favour privatization, as this translates into the potential for additional profits. Labour, on the other hand, which sits on the left wing of the political assembly, is generally more suspicious of markets; it champions public welfare programs because in their absence workers become solely dependent on the market for survival. Social assistance, for example, means that workers have some recourse: rather than begging in the streets, starving, or resorting to crime, individuals can collect at least a subsistence income. While this is a positive for workers, it amounts to a negative for business. Social programs mean that fewer and less-desperate workers are available for employment, and consequently wages must invariably rise, increasing overhead for business. This would seem to be a simple equation wherein labour's gain is capital's loss. Yet sociologists would argue that social programs benefit society as a whole, including business. To demonstrate the economic advantages of the welfare state, one has only to look at the economic distribution in most third world countries, where few welfare-state programs exist and workers are forced to toil in often dismal conditions for subsistence wages. With no money to spend, business has few customers to sell its products to. The end result is that only a small minority enjoys wealth while the vast majority of the population remains poor.

THE SOCIAL DIMENSION

The economic continuum, then, pertains to private property rights, the market, and individualism, which are all related. But the left–right continuum is complicated by matters that have little to do with the economic realm and instead pertain to the social organization of society. For example, those on the right oppose abortion and gun control and support the death penalty and a strong military. The left, in turn, takes the opposite position on each of these issues.

While it's possible to be an economic liberal and a social conservative, more often than not there is congruence between the social and the economic sphere, in that a conservative is so on both counts. Someone who supports small government and lower taxes is also likely to be against same-sex marriage and abortion. In Canada such a person is likely to vote for the Conservatives, in the United States the Republicans. Why this overlap of the economic and social exists is beyond simple explanation. One could easily trace these views to an element of religiosity on the part of the right (particularly its stance against abortion and gay and lesbian unions). Yet historically, many of the founders of the left-leaning NDP came from religious backgrounds. Tommy Douglas, often credited as the founder of Canada's national health care system, was a Baptist minister before he became premier of Saskatchewan. So religion remains an inadequate explanation.

A logical way to proceed might be to gather empirical evidence in order to determine what ties these views together. Yet such a route is unlikely to be fruitful, as all kinds of inconsistencies would quickly arise. Using logic and empirical evidence to explain people's political leanings is destined to end in failure. Viewpoints and attitudes of a social nature are seldom grounded in scientific evidence, but rather are informed by the most basic of sociological concepts: values and beliefs. And when it comes to politics, it's best to think in terms of a constellation of values and beliefs that are passed from one generation to the next through the process of socialization. A person who grows up in a conservative household is likely to adopt the values, attitudes, and beliefs, both social and economic, from within that family, a family that is in turn part of a larger culture. In short, social actors don't choose their values based on logical or scientific merit so much as internalize them through their association with groups.

We may be tempted to mock the idea of values and assert that they have little impact on people's behaviour. It's therefore worth being reminded that one of the most powerful theses in sociology concerns the power of values. Weber's theory of the Protestant ethic traced how a change in religious outlook facilitated the rise of capitalism. According to Weber, the Protestant religion altered people's attitudes toward work and consumption and thereby helped bring about fundamental changes in the economy. Weber observed that while capitalism thrived in regions where Protestantism reigned, its progress appeared to be hindered in areas where other religions (e.g., Catholicism, Hinduism, Confucianism) dominated. In his analysis, the values and beliefs that originated within the Protestant sect of Calvinism ultimately helped transform the way the economy was organized. Capitalism was an unintended consequence of this change in attitudes. Protestants tended to work hard and save their money, which created the necessary capital (investment) for capitalism to flourish. The principles of hard work, individual responsibility, and self-reliance, according to Weber, serve to underpin a flourishing capitalist economy. This belief system has stubbornly survived to this day, even though the religious impetus behind it has weakened and in political terms has all but disappeared.

It needs to be stressed that people adhere to these values not because they match empirical observations but because they're part of their culture. A significant number of wealthy North Americans are blessed with economic advantages that include prosperous, well-connected backgrounds and improved access to education. These advantages are in turn passed on to their offspring. At the same time, some of the hardest-working people are poor. In light of this contradictory evidence, why do people continue to believe in the values of individual initiative and hard work? The reason is that social actors internalize the values of their culture, and values of self-reliance are constantly reinforced by family, teachers, and the mass media. These

values long ago became part of the culture, and they persist despite obvious examples to the contrary. The same applies to social values: for example, life is considered sacred, which leads some people to oppose abortion, yet those same people will often support the death penalty. This is only one illustration of how little sway logic has in explaining belief systems. People believe what they do based on the groups they associate with and the kind of behaviour practised and deemed acceptable within that group. In the end, political beliefs both social and economic are difficult to dislodge precisely because they don't succumb to logic and empirical evidence. And with the appeal to logic often closed off, it becomes exceedingly difficult to change people's values and beliefs.

LIBERALISM

The many uses of the term "liberal" can be especially confusing, and consequently benefit from further elucidation. The words "free" and "liberal" essentially mean the same thing, the former being Germanic in origin, the latter Latin.[1] In ancient Rome, those fortunate enough to elude slavery were literally free (*liber* in Latin). Interestingly, the word "liberal" first came to English via education. In Rome, those who were free could afford to while away their time studying logic, rhetoric, and music, collectively referred to as the "liberal arts." In contrast, those who were enslaved were compelled to engage in the servile arts, such as construction and mechanics. This categorization was introduced to England by way of French in the fourteenth century, with the educational distinction intact. In contemporary times, philosophy, history, and literature are still referred to as "liberal arts," while the term "servile arts" (known today as the "vocational sector" or simply the "trades") has fallen out of favour.

With time, the "liberal" component of "liberal arts" came to have a life of its own. Recall that, according to Marx and Engels, class conflict constitutes the motor of history, and that the class divisions are crucial to an understanding of the social world. The class connotation that separated slave from freeman has endured to some degree. In fourteenth-century England the vast majority of people had no access to formal education, and anyone fortunate enough to acquire a liberal arts education was very likely to be from the landed aristocracy or gentry. Thus, anything "liberal" came to be associated with someone from the upper classes. Today we have more freedom to choose our level of education, and the rigid class division between the liberal and servile arts has become less obvious. Yet cultural divisions between the upper and lower classes linger. Literature, ballet, and classical music still enjoy a higher status than stock car racing, heavy metal, or comics. A certain sense of class privilege is also associated with privately funded liberal arts colleges in the U.S., such as Harvard and Yale, particularly when compared with technical institutions. With ever-rising tuition fees, upwards of fifty thousand dollars per annum, this traditional kind of liberal education isn't easily available to the average working or middle class student.

Just as it did in the fourteenth century, education informs one's world view today. A student of the liberal arts tends to be more open-minded, which constitutes another important meaning of the word. A liberal is generally of the opinion that people should do as they please and participate in whatever activities they choose as long as it causes no demonstrable harm to others. Within that worldview, such private matters should not be governed by the intrusive presence of the state. As Prime Minister Pierre Elliott Trudeau once declared, "The state has no business in the bedrooms of the nation." In that sense, Trudeau was a social liberal.

Liberalism has another important genealogical lineage. In the late seventeenth century, liberalism outgrew its association with education,

status, and open-mindedness and came to encompass an economic dimension. It was at this time that liberalism turned into a political movement. At its forefront was the English philosopher John Locke, who notably included property under the freedoms to be practised and protected. Some of Locke's ideas were incorporated into the American Constitution of 1776, and in this way his views played a foundational role in American political culture. To a select few, the defence of private property amounts to the most important feature of liberalism; in some circles it has effectively overwhelmed the meaning of the word. When the Mont Pelerin Society in Switzerland, the Fraser Institute in Canada, and the Heritage Foundation in the United States advocate freedom, it's not women's rights or educational access they're interested in; it's private property. The same is true for "freedom" parties across the world (in Austria and Italy, for example): it is the protection of private property that defines these parties. This explains why an economic liberal occupies the right of the political spectrum (a lineage of political thought that is often simply referred to as "classic liberalism").

Much confusion arises because a social liberal is quite different from an economic liberal, and the two can occupy different ends of the political spectrum (that is, an economic liberal is right wing whereas a social liberal is left wing). As we just saw, the social liberal harkens back to the time when "liberal" was meant to describe someone with a liberal arts education; in other words, someone from the upper classes who was likely to be open-minded. The property component was added some centuries later. The underlying problem stems from the fact that the label "liberal" is often used indiscriminately, without specifying whether it applies to the economic or social realm. Context is everything here.

In American politics, "liberal" has taken on yet another meaning, one that has only a little to do with the traditional free thinker and even less to do with the economic individualist. In the United States, the term "liberal" has come to stand as a euphemism for someone who has socialist tendencies. In the 1988 presidential election, for example, when George Bush Sr. accused Democratic candidate Michael Dukakis of being a liberal, he didn't mean an economic liberal or a free thinker, but rather someone who supports social programs at the expense of market freedom. Put slightly differently, a liberal is someone who privileges group rights over individual rights and does not oppose government intervention. This sort of liberal usually opposes the unencumbered freedom of the individual in the economic arena and is generally more concerned with outcomes such as equality. In this usage, which is primarily American, a liberal is left of centre both socially and economically.

And if that's not confusing enough, add the prefix "neo" (Latin for *new*) and the word reverts to its focus on the economic. A neoliberal is someone who is insistently pro–free market and anti-government. If that sounds familiar, it's because there is little definitional difference between an economic liberal and a neoliberal. "Neoliberalism" is a term primarily used as a label by those on the left who are critical of free-market enthusiasts like George W. Bush, Margaret Thatcher, and organizations like the World Trade Organization and the World Bank. The term is seldom, if ever, used by people to describe their own political perspective and essentially amounts to a pejorative.

In summary, the term "liberal" is used in the United States to describe someone on the left, often as a term of disparagement, by people who cannot bring themselves to utter the word "socialist." In Canada and elsewhere, a liberal can be someone who is open-minded or uncomfortable with government involvement in the social sphere. And finally, an economic liberal is someone who privileges markets over the state, and individuals above all. In other words, a "liberal" can include someone anywhere along the spectrum—no wonder there's so much confusion.

CONCLUSION

It's important to keep in mind that this is a mere introduction to the topic. As a student of politics and sociology both in and out of university, you'll encounter the political spectrum in a variety of forums, and will no doubt add to your knowledge of this system of classification. One of the things you cannot expect is consistency.

Language is constantly changing, and nowhere is this more apparent than in the world of politics. From that perspective, liberalism isn't the only confusing term you're likely to encounter. One could trace similarly storied histories for most of the terms that reside on the political spectrum: conservatism (and neoconservatism), socialism (including social democracy, communism, and fifty varieties of Marxism), anarchism (both social and individual, as well as anarcho-syndicalism), libertarianism, and the list goes on. Each term comes with its own history and its own multitude of meanings that it has collected over its centuries-long journey. These meanings are in constant flux, and any definition is necessarily incomplete, since meanings are modified when political movements try to accommodate terms to their own agendas. When political ideals are applied and practised in the real world they are forced to change in response to practical considerations and the varied demands of a given movement's members. The underlying problem is that there often exists plenty of disagreement within political parties, interest groups, and organizations about what it means to be a liberal or a social democrat. Conflict can exist between the social and economic factions of a movement, and often any one issue (like immigration or an environmental tax) can cause rifts within a party or organization. The meaning of the word can also mutate based on changes in policy direction. A successful political campaign means that everyone wants to be associated with that party and therefore feels comfortable with that label. On the other hand, a historical event like a war can tarnish a label to the point that it falls out of favour permanently. It might be difficult to imagine now, but at one time both "fascism" and "dictator" had positive connotations.

CRITICAL THINKING QUESTIONS

1. Where on the political spectrum do you fall, left or right? Are your political views different from those of your parents or friends? Is political socialization important, and at what stage (at home, at university, through the mass media)?

2. Would a modern industrial economy even be possible without social programs? Why or why not? Consider how the left and right would differ in their position on each of the following issues. Who would support and who would oppose unemployment insurance, social assistance, affirmative action, increased tuition fees, private health care, and national daycare?

3. The Occupy Movement asserts that there is something profoundly wrong with the distribution of income in the United States and Canada. Do you agree that 99 percent of the population isn't getting their fair share of the pie while the top 1 percent is reaping all the benefits of economic growth? What determines such economic inequality? What policy changes would lead to a more equitable distribution?

NOTE

1. Most of the information on the history of the term "liberal" is from Merriam-Webster Inc. (1991) and *The Oxford English Dictionary*, Second Edition (Simpson and Weiner, 1989).

REFERENCES

Merriam-Webster Inc. 1991. *The Merriam-Webster new book of word histories*. Springfield, Massachusetts: Merriam-Webster Inc.

Nozick, Robert. 2003. *Anarchy, state, and utopia*. Oxford: Blackwell.

Simpson, John, and Edmund Weiner (eds). 1989. *The Oxford English dictionary, second edition*. Oxford: Oxford University Press.

Vidal, Gore. 1977. *Matters of fact and of fiction: Essays 1973–1976*. New York: Random House, p. 268.

Politics,
Government,
and the Military

CLASSIC

CONTEMPORARY

CROSS-CULTURAL

43

Is Biotechnology the Answer? The Evidence from NAFTA

GERARDO OTERO AND GABRIELA PECHLANER

Biotechnology and free trade have combined to transform food production, and by extension, the food we eat. Not only has this affected, in differing ways, the three countries that make up NAFTA; it has also meant changes to eating patterns in those countries.

Since genetically modified food crops were first commercialized in the mid-1990s, they have been touted as a miracle technology that, if only given the chance, will make deserts bloom and put an end to world poverty. The intensity of these claims is not tempered by the fact that most transgenic crops are unintended for direct human consumption.

Grown in large industrial monocultures, transgenic soybeans (which account for two thirds of global biotech food production), corn (one quarter of production), cotton, and canola are sold in volatile global markets as the raw material for cattle feed, agro-fuel, cooking oil, and sweeteners, among other products. Five agrochemical companies—Bayer, Syngenta, BASF, Dow AgroSciences, and the

Monsanto Company—dominate the development and production of these products, while their customers are mostly well-capitalized, medium- to large-size farmers looking to mass-produce cash crops.

Even though such a crop system is ill-suited to feeding people, last year's spike in global food prices nonetheless spurred a return to the hopeful industry rhetoric among policy makers and commentators who strongly endorsed transgenic food as a necessary solution to the crisis.[1] World hunger, in this view, can only be eradicated with larger, cheaper, and more efficient crop yields in poor countries, and transgenic crops are said to hold this promise. As one particularly adamant commentator put it recently: "It would be criminal to disregard the hope that biotechnology offers to the world's most malnourished people."[2]

But to fully answer the question of whether agricultural biotechnology can help solve the food crisis, we must consider its political economy

Source: Taken from *NACLA Report on the Americas,
Volume 042*, issue 2, May/June 2009, pp. 27–31. Reprinted
with permission.

and the differing power relations that rich and poor countries have with it, especially within the context of trade liberalization, privatization, and what we call "neoregulation" (more on this below). The biotechnology revolution of the 1990s was superimposed on the reforms brought about under neoliberal globalism, and in the years since, transgenic crops have inundated both the countryside and supermarkets. They are the flagship technology of agricultural neoliberalism, going hand in glove with free trade agreements.

For this reason, the three countries of North America, economically integrated since 1994 under NAFTA, provide a good opportunity to analyze the differential impact that transgenic products have had in nations with varying levels of capitalist development. The contrasts are predictably stark, given that one of these countries, the United States, is the top global biotech farmer, home to more than half the world's farmland devoted to growing transgenic crops. Three-quarters of publicly traded biotechnology companies are U.S.-based, and U.S. spending on biotechnology research and development, both private and public, is vastly greater than that of any other country.[3] The most prominent U.S.-based producer, the Monsanto Company, sold 88% of transgenic seeds in 2004.[4] Clearly, the U.S. biotechnology sector has a significant stake in disseminating transgenic agriculture while maintaining its dominant position in both research and development and in patenting new organisms.

Canada, in contrast, invests 1.5% of what the United States does in development and has a much smaller land area dedicated to producing transgenic crops. But as the fourth-highest producer by production area (after the United States, Argentina, and Brazil), Canada is a significant player, globally speaking.[5]

Today Mexico devotes 247,000 acres of land to growing transgenic cotton and soy, ranking 13th in the world for transgenic acreage in 2008, according to the International Service for the Acquisition of Agri-Biotech Applications,

a trade group.[6] Compared with the United States' and Canada's adoption of transgenic crops, of course, Mexico's is minuscule, and its control over research and development practically nonexistent. But Mexico has nonetheless been significantly affected by transgenic crops—less through directly adopting them for cultivation but indirectly through trade, as the country has become progressively more dependent on importing basic grains, including soybeans (almost 100% imported) and corn (23%), from the United States. Most of Mexico's imported U.S. transgenic corn is destined to become cattle feed, syrup, and oil.

In sum: The United States dominates agricultural biotechnology, Canada is somewhere between a "taker" and "promoter" of it, and Mexico exerts little influence on the technology's development, grows a small amount, and is primarily affected by transgenics' dissemination through its obligatory U.S. imports under NAFTA. But to get a clear idea of what importing transgenic crops has meant for Mexico in contrast with the United States and Canada, we have to compare the empirical data on food consumption in the three countries before and during the NAFTA years.

Unfortunately, the UN Food and Agriculture Organization's data on North American food consumption do not cover the period leading up to and including the 2008 food crisis, but we can still extrapolate the structural trends from 1985 to 2003, the latest year for which they are available. Comparing the three NAFTA countries' per capita food consumption (see figure 43.1), we note several trends and shifts that set the context for 2008.

First, while the United States clearly consumes more food than both Canada and Mexico, it may be surprising to some that in 1985, years before NAFTA's inauguration, Mexico's per capita food consumption was slightly higher than it was in 2003. Starting exactly in 1994, however, Canada's food consumption surpassed Mexico's and continued growing, approaching U.S. levels by 2003.

Figure 43.1 NAFTA Region Food Consumption (1,000 kcal/capita/day)

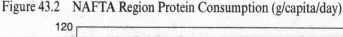

Mexico was left behind in per capita food consumption by its northern partners, even prior to the sharp food price increases beginning in 2007.

If we break down the analysis by food components—protein, vegetables, and fats—we can also see some interesting contrasts, which give us a clear indication of each country's food strength or vulnerability. In per capita protein consumption (see figure 43.2), all three countries experienced slight increases, but Mexico's was 15 to 25 grams per day below that of Canada and the United States at any given time between 1985 and 2003. What increase there is in Mexico's protein intake is likely due to the importation after 1994 of cheaper meat from the United States, where most feed grains are subsidized and produced with transgenic seeds, together with increased purchasing power among middle- and upper-income Mexicans.

The contrasts change when we move on to per capita vegetable consumption (figure 43.3): While the United States consumed more vegetables than Canada and Mexico, and increased its per capita vegetable intake between 1985 and 2003, Canada's consumption, on the rise since before NAFTA, surpassed Mexico's by

Figure 43.2 NAFTA Region Protein Consumption (g/capita/day)

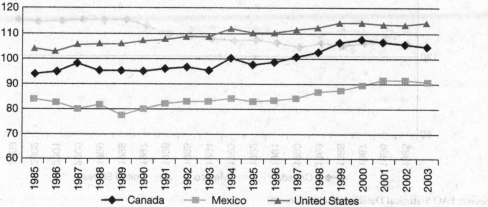

Figure 43.3   NAFTA Region Vegetable Consumption (1,000 kcal/capita/day)

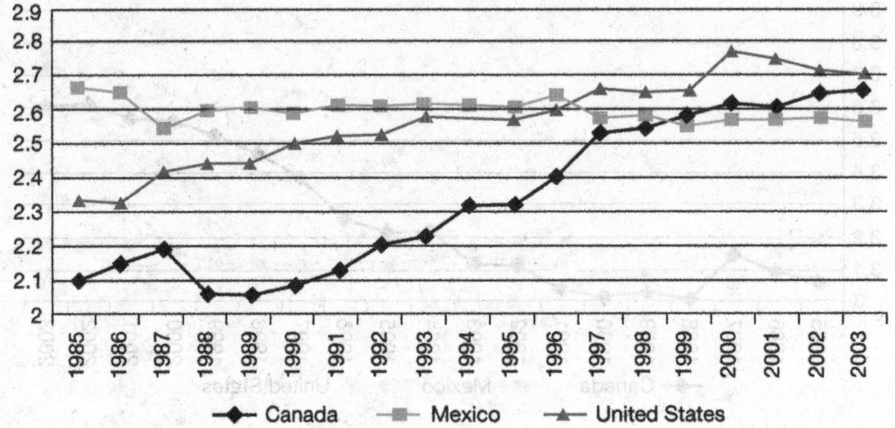

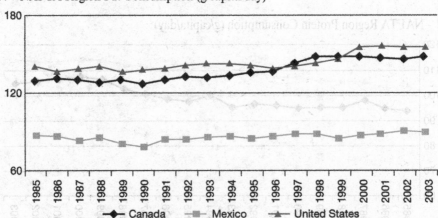

1998. Mexico's vegetable intake, which started the period at a higher level than Canada's, declined slightly. This is ironic, given that during the same period Mexico substantially increased its fruit and vegetable exports to Canada and the United States.[7] Evidently this means that, while capitalized Mexican farmers were able to take good advantage of liberalized trade through NAFTA, average Mexican consumers lost purchasing power and were less able to afford the fruits and vegetables leaving their country for the international market.

Finally, Mexico's per capita fat consumption (figure 43.4), which has always been less than half of Canada's and the United States', remained fairly stable, with a slight decline in the early phase of the neoliberal turn in 1986–90. Canada and the United States, meanwhile, increased their fat consumption.

Mexican economists have corroborated these trends, which clearly indicate an unfavorable evolution of Mexican food consumption relative to those of Canada and the United States. Transgenics arrived in Mexico together

Figure 43.4   NAFTA Region Fat Consumption (g/capita/day)

Source: FAO Statistical Database (faostat.fao.org)

with the massive economic and social disloca-tions of NAFTA: 2 million jobs lost in the countryside; mass migrations of campesinos to cities or to North America; and a mere 1.7% annual national economic growth rate, com-pared with an average 6.1% during the previous four decades.[8] In short, the negative impacts of trade liberalization, which greatly expanded U.S. and Canadian transgenic exports, have been far greater for Mexico than for its two NAFTA partners even prior to the 2008 food price crisis. Once the crisis started, these dispro-portionately negative impacts only deepened.

Increasing transgenic corn and transgenic-fed meat imports to Mexico led, on the one hand, to making more peasants redundant; on the other hand, it allowed for an increase in meat consumption, partly at the expense of vegetable consumption, by those who could afford it. In a country where purchasing power is deeply unequal, mass-produced transgenics fostered a high-protein diet for the few.

The large population of Mexicans with very low purchasing power is extremely vulnerable to price shocks, like so many in the developing world, where the proportion of family budgets spent on food is about four times larger than in developed nations. An average 15% increase in Latin American and Caribbean consumer price indexes in 2006–07 pushed the rate of indigence in the region "by almost three points from 12.7% to 15.9%," according to the UN Economic Commission for Latin America and the Caribbean (CEPAL), meaning almost 16 million Latin Americans became destitute as a result of high prices.[9]

The idea, then, that we can solve the food crisis by simply increasing yields is problematic in a world where most people go hungry not because there isn't plentiful food, but because they cannot afford what food exists. Importing cheaply produced transgenics did nothing to shield Mexicans from the onslaught of high corn prices: When prices increased by 15% in December, consumption dipped by 30%.[10]

Whatever level of transgenic cultivation Mexico undertakes in the future is unlikely to help feed the country. Even if transgenic varieties were proven to be more efficient and environmentally friendly, their adoption in developing countries does not constitute a transfer of technology. Rather, U.S.-based com-panies sell transgenic seeds, often packaged together with herbicides and other agrochem-icals, on a contractual basis to farmers for each season. More direct adoption of transgenic crops in Mexico will likely increase the country's dependence on high-input, capital-intensive agriculture and further threaten peasant pro-duction. It will, in other words, exacerbate the negative social effects already familiar from the Green Revolution—the Rockefeller Founda-tion's effort to "modernize" agriculture, which began in Mexico during the 1940s with the introduction of industrial farming technology.

Furthermore, it is larger, more capitalized farmers who adopt transgenics to produce soy-beans and corn for the lucrative export market, diverting land for domestic food production. Thus the paradox of Argentina: The second-largest transgenic cultivator after the United States, and one of the world's top agricultural exporters, saw growing internal hunger in the early years of the 21st century.[11]

While peasant production isn't highly pro-ductive in economic terms (i.e., in terms of turning a profit), it effectively provides nourish-ment for those who depend on it for sustenance and otherwise have few alternatives in an econ-omy that fails to provide sufficient employment for urban migrants. Replacing peasant agricul-ture with industrial agriculture for export, of which biotech is a crucial component, forces peasants to depend on remittances from rela-tives abroad and therefore increases food insecurity, even if overall production increases.

Study after study has demonstrated the limitations of corporate-driven biotechnol-ogy, including strong doubts about its effective economic performance, its associated rise in pesticide use, its strong bias in favor of large transnational corporations, and its limited benefits to small farmers or the hungry.[12]

Our findings support the view that, while agricultural production and productivity are increasing, the benefits of capitalized farming are not necessarily accruing to small farmers or the hungry.[13] With the introduction of agricultural biotechnology in Latin America, regional and social polarization is quickly expanding beyond what the Green Revolution produced, as fewer and larger farmers dominate agriculture while others are bankrupted. These trends will likely be aggravated by the recent food price inflation. Excluding a bottom-up process of plant breeding and technological innovation that is effectively people- rather than profit-centered, the current form of biotechnology development can hardly help alleviate the food crisis.

In June 2008, the FAO concluded its summit in Rome with a declaration calling on governments to commit $20 billion for "agriculture research," provide food aid, and spark "a new green revolution." However, the FAO declaration takes no official position for or against transgenics. In a hopeful development, and despite the best efforts of Ed Schafer, the USDA secretary, transgenics didn't get much attention at the summit as a possible solution to the food crisis.[14] The FAO's declaration makes proposals that include important measures that could help lead to a sustainable agriculture, and its statement on "biofuels" reflects skepticism on the subject. More importantly, though, the declaration is notable for its focus on small-peasant farmers and the importance of maintaining biodiversity.

The wholesale subscription to the ideology of neoliberal globalism, and its consequent economic and policy paradigm, can carry a very high price for the people in developing countries. Our analysis suggests the wisdom of reinstating policies supporting local agriculture, increasing local food production, and decreasing the reliance on imports, without moving into all-out protectionism.

Supporting small-scale producers has at least two long-term advantages. First, even if they are not nearly as efficient as the more capitalized (and subsidized!) farmers of the North, small-scale producers have been able to feed millions of peasant families.[15] Keeping farmers on the land, as opposed to economically inducing them to migrate, also preserves rural communities as vibrant entities. Many studies have found that migration from rural communities sharply increases work for the women who remain. Second, small-scale production has also been found to be important for preserving plant-biological diversity. The FAO took steps to endorse supporting small-scale production with its 2008 declaration. It is time for states to listen.

CRITICAL THINKING QUESTIONS

1. This article starkly illustrates the link between the global and the local. How have international treaties affected the average Mexican, and for that matter, Canadian and American diets?

2. How has NAFTA affected food consumption in Mexico with respect to economic class? In other words, what has transgenic food meant in terms of being rich or poor?

3. Are you concerned about genetically engineered food? Do you think such foods should be labelled? Who would oppose labelling and why? Are you generally optimistic or pessimistic about technological developments with respect to food?

NOTES

1. Sam Cage, "Food Prices May Ease Hostility to Gene-Altered Crops," *Reuters*, July 9, 2008; Jamie Lee, "GM Crops May Be Answer to Food Crisis: Ecologist," *Reuters*, June 30, 2008; Fiona Harvey and George Parker, "Top UK Scientist Pushes for GM Crops," *Financial Times*, July 8, 2008.

2. Bjorn Lomborg, "Another 'Green Revolution,'" *National Post* (Canada), March 25, 2009.

3. U.S. funding research reached a record 44.825 billion (in Canadian dollars) in 2002. ETC Group, "Oligopoly, Inc. 2005: Concentration in Corporate Power," ETC Group Communique no. 91 (December 2005), available at **etc-group.org/en/materials/publications.html?pub_id=42**, Trefor Munn-Venn and Paul Mitchell, "Biotechnology in Canada: A Technology Platform for Growth," *The Conference Board of Canada Report* (December 2005), p. 4 (available at **www.agwest.sk.ca/biotech/documents/115-D6-Biotechnology%20in%20Canada.pdf)**, with data from National Science Foundation.

4. See statistics compiled in ETC Group, "Global Seed Industry Concentration-2005," ETC Group Communique no. 90 (September/October 2005), available online at **mindfully.org/Farm/2005/Global-Seed-Industry6sep05.htm**.

5. Eight percent of publicly traded biotechnology companies are based in Canada: ETC Group, "Oligopoly Inc. 2005." Canada devoted $695 million (Canadian) to biotechnology research and development in 2002. Munn-Venn and Mitchell, "Biotechnology in Canada."

6. International Service for the Acquisition of Agri-Biotech Applications, available at **isaaa.org/resources/publications/briefs/39/pptslides/default/html**.

7. Gabriela Pechlaner and Gerardo Otero, "The Neoliberal Food Regime: Neoregulation and the New Division of Labor in North America," article under review.

8. Mexican economist José Luis Calva, cited in G.L. Zaragoza, "Balance negative en el agro después de 14 años de TLCAN: acadérnicos," *La Jornada* (Mexico), March 1, 2008.

9. Adjusting for income increases, CEPAL estimates that the figure will actually be 10 million, but this estimate may not have properly taken into account the overproduction glut that helped bring down food prices in 2008. United Nations Economic Commission for Latin America and the Caribbean, "Food Price Hikes May Increase Poverty and Indigence by Over Ten Million People in Latin America and the Caribbean," CEPAL News 28, no. 4 (April 2008): 1.

10. *Notimex*, "Subieron 15% los alimentos básico y *cayó* 30% el consume," January 7, 2009.

11. Miguel Teubal, "Genetically Engineered Soybeans and the Crises of Argentina's Agriculture Model," in Gerardo Otero, ed., *Food for the Few: Neoliberal Globalism and Biotechnology in Latin America* (University of Texan Press, 2008), 189–216.

12. Strong doubts about effective economic performance: Kathy McAfee, "Exporting Crop Biotechnology: The Myth of Molecular Miracles," In Otero, ed., *Food for the Few,* 61–90; pesticide use and bias in favor of large transnational corporations: Friends of the Earth International, *Who Benefits From GM Crops?*, report series available at **foei.org/en/publications**; limited benefits to small farmers or the hungry: Teubal, "Genetically Engineered Soybeans and the Crises of Argentina's Agricultural Model."

13. See also Otero and Pechlaner, "Latin American Agriculture, Food, and Biotechnology: Temperate Dietary Adoption and Unsustainablity," in Otero, ed., *Food for the Few,* 31–60; Pechlaner and Otero, "The Neoliberal Food Regime"; Teubal, "Genetically Engineered Soybeans."

14. Robert Marquand, "Food Crisis Softens Resistance to Genetically Modified (GM) Food," *The Christian Science Monitor,* June 6, 2008.

15. Armando Bartra, "Rebellious Cornfields: Toward Food and Labour Self-Sufficiency," in Gerardo Otero., ed., *Mexico in Transition: Neoliberal Globalism, the State and Civil Society* (Zed Books, 2004), 18–36; David Barkin, "The Reconstruction of a Modern Mexican Peasantry," *The Journal of Peasant Studies* 30, no. 1 (2002): 73–90.

44

Marriage in the Stalled Revolution

ARLIE RUSSELL HOCHSCHILD

In the 1960s, increasingly more women began joining the workforce. This has not necessarily meant that the sharing of housework and child rearing has become more equitable. The result is that most women end up putting in a "second shift" once they return home from their paid employment.

Each marriage bears the footprints of economic and cultural trends which originate far outside marriage. A rise in inflation which erodes the earning power of the male wage, an expanding service sector which opens up jobs for women, new cultural images—like the woman with the flying hair—that make the working mother seem exciting, all these changes do not simply go on *around* marriage. They occur *within* marriage, and transform it. Problems between husbands and wives, problems which seem "individual" and "marital," are often individual experiences of powerful economic and cultural shock waves that are not caused by one person or two. Quarrels that erupt . . . result mainly from a friction between faster-changing women and slower-changing men, rates of change which themselves result from the different rates at which the industrial economy has drawn men and women into itself.

There is a "his" and "hers" to the economic development of the United States. In the latter part of the nineteenth century, it was mainly men who were drawn off the farm into paid, industrial work and who changed their way of life and their identity. At that point in history, men became more different from their fathers than women became from their mothers. Today the economic arrow points at women; it is women who are being drawn into wage work, and women who are undergoing changes in their way of life and identity. Women are departing more from their mothers' and grandmothers' way of life, men are doing so less.*

* This is more true of white and middle-class women than it is of black or poor women, whose mothers often worked outside the home. But the trend I am talking about—an increase from 20 percent of women in paid jobs in 1900 to 55 percent in 1986—has affected a large number of women.

Both the earlier entrance of men into the industrial economy and the later entrance of women have influenced the relations *between* men and women, especially their relations within marriage. The former increase in the number of men in industrial work tended to increase the power of men, and the present growth in the number of women in such work has somewhat increased the power of women. On the whole, the entrance of men into industrial work did not destabilize the family whereas *in the absence of other changes*, the rise in female employment has gone with the rise in divorce. . . . Here I'll focus on the current economic story, that which hangs over the marriages I describe in this book. Beneath the image of the woman with the flying hair, there has been a real change in women without much change in anything else.

The exodus of women into the economy has not been accompanied by a cultural understanding of marriage and work that would make this transition smooth. The workforce has changed. Women have changed. But most workplaces have remained inflexible in the face of the family demands of their workers and at home, most men have yet to really adapt to the changes in women. This strain between the change in women and the absence of change in much else leads me to speak of a "stalled revolution."

A society which did not suffer from this stall would be a society *humanely* adapted to the fact that most women work outside the home. The workplace would allow parents to work part time, to share jobs, to work flexible hours, to take parental leaves to give birth, tend a sick child, or care for a well one. As Delores Hayden has envisioned in *Redesigning the American Dream*, it would include affordable housing closer to places of work, and perhaps community-based meal and laundry services. It would include men whose notion of manhood encouraged them to be active parents and share at home. In contrast, a stalled revolution lacks social arrangements that ease life for working parents, and lacks men who share the second shift.

If women begin to do less at home because they have less time, if men do little more, if the work of raising children and tending a home requires roughly the same effort, then the questions of who does what at home and of what "needs doing" become key. Indeed, they may become a source of deep tension in the marriage, tensions I explore here one by one.

The tensions caused by the stall in this social revolution have led many men and women to avoid becoming part of a two-job couple. Some have married but clung to the tradition of the man as provider, the woman as homemaker. Others have resisted marriage itself. In *The Hearts of Men*, Barbara Ehrenreich describes a "male revolt" against the financial and emotional burden of supporting and raising a family. In *Women and Love*, Shere Hite describes a "female revolt" against unsatisfying and unequal relationships with men. But the couples I focused on are not in traditional marriages and not giving up on marriage. They are struggling to reconcile the demands of two jobs with a happy family life. Given this larger economic story, and given the present stalled revolution, I wanted to know how the two-job family was progressing.

As I drove from my classes at Berkeley to the outreaching suburbs, small towns, and inner cities of the San Francisco Bay to observe and ask questions in the homes of two-job couples, and back to my own two-job marriage, my first question about who does what gave way to a series of deeper questions: What leads some working mothers to do all the work at home themselves—to pursue what I call a supermom strategy—and what leads others to press their husbands to share the responsibility and work of the home? Why do some men genuinely want to share housework and child-care, others fatalistically acquiesce, and still others actively resist?

What do each husband's ideas about manhood lead him to think he "should feel" about what he's doing at home and at work? What does he really feel? Do his real feelings conflict with what he thinks he should feel? How does he resolve the conflict? The same questions apply to wives. What influence does each person's consequent "strategy" for handling his or her feelings and actions with regard to the second shift affect his or her children, job, and marriage? Through this line of questioning, I was led to the complex web of ties between a family's needs, the sometime quest for equality, and happiness in modern marriage, the real topic of this book.

We can describe a couple as rich or poor and that will tell us a great deal about their two-job marriage. We can describe them as Catholic, Protestant, Jewish, black, Chicano, Asian, or white and that will tell us something more. We can describe their marriage as a combination of two personalities, one "obsessive compulsive," say, and the other "narcissistic," and again that will tell us something. But knowledge about social class, ethnicity, and personality takes us only so far in understanding who does and doesn't share the second shift, and whether or not sharing the work at home makes marriages happier.

When I sat down to compare one couple that shared the second shift with another three that didn't, many of the answers that would seem obvious—a man's greater income, his longer hours of work, the fact that his mother was a housewife or his father did little at home, his ideas about men and women—all these factors didn't really explain why some women work the extra month a year and others don't. They didn't explain why some women seemed content to work the extra month, while others were deeply unhappy about it. When I compared a couple who was sharing and happy with another couple who was sharing but miserable, it was clear that purely economic or psychological answers were not enough. Gradually, I felt the need to explore how *deep* within each man and woman gender ideology goes. I felt the need to understand the ways in which some men and women seemed to be egalitarian "on top" but traditional "underneath," or the other way

around. I tried to sensitize myself to the difference between shallow ideologies (ideologies which were contradicted by deeper feelings) and deep ideologies (which were reinforced by such feelings). I explored how each person reconciled ideology with his or her own behavior, that of a partner, and with the other realities of life. I felt the need to explore what I call loosely "gender strategies."

THE TOP AND BOTTOM OF GENDER IDEOLOGY

A gender strategy is a plan of action through which a person tries to solve problems at hand, given the cultural notions of gender at play. To pursue a gender strategy, a man draws on beliefs about manhood and womanhood, beliefs that are forged in early childhood and thus anchored to deep emotions. He makes a connection between how he thinks about his manhood, what he feels about it, and what he does. It works in the same way for a woman.

A woman's gender ideology determines what sphere she *wants* to identify with (home or work) and how much power in the marriage she wants to have (less, more, or the same amount). I found three types of ideology of marital roles: traditional, transitional, and egalitarian. Even though she works, the "pure" traditional wants to identify with her activities at home (as a wife, a mother, a neighborhood mom), wants her husband to base his at work and wants less power than he. The traditional man wants the same. The "pure" egalitarian, as the type emerges here, wants to identify with the same spheres her husband does, and to have an equal amount of power in the marriage. Some want the couple to be jointly oriented to the home, others to their careers, or both of them to jointly hold some balance between the two. Between the traditional and the egalitarian is the transitional, any one of a variety of types of blending of the two. But, in contrast to the traditional, a transitional woman wants to identify with her role at work as well as at home. Unlike the egalitarian, she believes her husband should base his identity more on work than she does. A typical transitional wants to identify *both* with the caring for the home and with helping her husband earn money, but wants her husband to focus on earning a living. A typical transitional man is all for his wife working, but expects her to take the main responsibility at home too. Most men and women I talked with were "transitional." At least, transitional ideas came out when I asked people directly what they believed.

In actuality, I found there were contradictions between what people said they believed about their marital roles and how they seemed to *feel* about those roles. Some men seemed to me egalitarian "on top" but traditional "underneath." Others seemed traditional on top and egalitarian underneath.[1] Often a person attached deep feelings to his or her gender ideology in response to what I call early "cautionary tales" from childhood, as well as in response to his or her present situation. Sometimes these feelings *reinforced* the surface of a person's gender ideology. For example, the fear Nancy Holt was to feel of becoming a submissive mother, a "doormat," as she felt her mother had been, infused emotional steam into her belief that her husband Evan should do half the second shift.

On the other hand, the dissociation Ann Myerson was to feel from her successful career undermined her ostensible commitment both to that career and to sharing the second shift. Ann Myerson's surface ideology was egalitarian; she *wanted* to feel as engaged with her career as her husband was with his. This was her view of the "proper experience" of her career. She thought she *should* love her work. She *should* think it mattered. In fact, as she confessed in a troubled tone, she didn't love her work and didn't think it mattered. She felt a conflict between what she thought she ought to feel (according to her surface ideology)— emotionally involved in her career—and what she did feel—uninvolved with it. Among other things, her gender strategy was a way of trying to resolve that conflict.

The men and women I am about to describe seem to have developed their gender ideology by unconsciously synthesizing certain cultural ideas with feelings about their past. But they also developed their ideology by taking opportunity into account. Sometime in adolescence they matched their personal assets against the opportunities available to men or women of their type; they saw which gender ideology best fit their circumstances, and—often regardless of their upbringing—they identified with a certain version of manhood or womanhood. It "made sense" to them. It felt like "who they were." For example, a woman sizes up her education, intelligence, age, charm, sexual attractiveness, her dependency needs, her aspirations, and she matches these against her perception of how women like her are doing in the job market and the "marriage market." What jobs could she get? What men? What are her chances for an equal marriage, a traditional marriage, a happy marriage, any marriage? Half-consciously, she assesses her chances—chances of an interesting, well-paid job are poor? her courtship pool has very traditional men? She takes these into account. *Then* a certain gender ideology, let's say a traditional one, will "make sense" to her. She will embrace the ideology that suits her perception of her chances. She holds to a certain version of womanhood (the "wilting violet," say). She identifies with its customs (men opening doors), and symbols (lacy dress, long hair, soft handshakes, and lowered eyes). She tries to develop its "ideal personality" (deferential, dependent), not because this is what her parents taught her, not because this corresponds to how she naturally "is," but because these particular customs now *make sense* of her resources and of her overall situation in a stalled revolution. The same principle applies to men. However wholehearted or ambivalent, a person's gender ideology tends to fit their situation.

GENDER STRATEGIES

When a man tries to apply his gender ideology to the situations that face him in real life, unconsciously or not he pursues a gender strategy.[2] He outlines a course of action. He might become a "superdad"—working long hours and keeping his child up late at night to spend time with him or her. Or he might cut back his hours at work. Or he might scale back housework and spend less time with his children. Or he might actively try to share the second shift.

The term "strategy" refers both to his plan of action and to his emotional preparations for pursuing it. For example, he may require himself to suppress his career ambitions to devote himself more to his children, or suppress his responsiveness to his children's appeals in the course of steeling himself for the struggle at work. He might harden himself to his wife's appeals, or he might be the one in the family who "lets" himself see when a child is calling out for help.

In the families I am about to describe, then, I have tried to be sensitive to the fractures in gender ideology, the conflicts between what a person thinks he or she ought to feel and what he or she does feel, and to the emotional work it takes to fit a gender ideal when inner needs or outer conditions make it hard.

As this social revolution proceeds, the problems of the two-job family will not diminish. If anything, as more couples work two jobs these problems will increase. If we can't return to traditional marriage, and if we are not to despair of marriage altogether, it becomes vitally important to understand marriage as a magnet for the strains of the stalled revolution, and to understand gender strategies as the basic dynamic of marriage.

THE ECONOMY OF GRATITUDE

The interplay between a man's gender ideology and a woman's implies a deeper interplay between his gratitude toward her, and hers toward him. For how a person wants to identify himself or herself influences what, in the back and forth of a marriage, will seem like a gift and what will not. If a man doesn't think it fits the kind of "man" he wants to be to have his wife earn more than he, it may become his "gift" to her to "bear it" anyway. But a man may also feel like the husband I interviewed, who said, "When my wife began earning more than me I thought I'd struck gold!" In this case his wife's salary is the gift, not his capacity to accept it "anyway." When couples struggle, it is seldom simply over who does what. Far more often, it is over the giving and receiving of gratitude.

FAMILY MYTHS

As I watched couples in their own homes, I began to realize that couples sometimes develop "family myths"—versions of reality that obscure a core truth in order to manage a family tension.[3] Evan and Nancy Holt managed an irresolvable conflict over the distribution of work at home through the myth that they now "shared it equally." Another couple unable to admit to the conflict came to believe "we aren't competing over who will take responsibility at home; we're just dreadfully busy with our careers." Yet another couple jointly believed that the husband was bound hand and foot to his career "because his work demanded it," while in fact his careerism covered the fact that they were avoiding each other. Not all couples need or have family myths. But when they do arise, I believe they often manage key tensions which are linked, by degrees, to the long hand of the stalled revolution.

After interviewing couples for a while, I got into the practice of offering families who wanted it my interpretations of how they fit into the broader picture I was seeing and what I perceived were their strategies for coping with the second shift. Couples were often relieved to discover they were not alone, and were encouraged to open up a dialogue about the inner and outer origins of their troubles.

Many couples in this book worked long hours at their jobs and their children were very young: in this way their lot was unusually hard. But in one crucial way they had it far easier than most two-job couples in America: most were middle class. Many also worked for a company that embraced progressive policies toward personnel, generous benefits and salaries. If *these* middle-class couples find it hard to juggle work and family life, many other two-job families across the nation—who earn less, work at less flexible, steady, or lucrative jobs, and rely on poorer daycare—are likely to find it much harder still.

Anne Machung and I began interviewing in 1976, and accomplished most of our interviews in the early 1980s. I finished in 1988. About half of my later interviews were follow-up contacts with couples we'd talked to earlier; the other half were new.

How much had changed from 1976 to 1988? In practical terms, little: most women I interviewed in the late 1980s still do the lion's share of work at home, do most of the daily chores and take responsibility for running the home. But something was different, too. More couples *wanted* to share and imagined that they did. Dorothy Sims, a personnel director, summed up this new blend of idea and reality. She eagerly explained to me that she and her husband Dan "shared all the housework," and that they were "equally involved in raising their nine-month-old son Timothy." Her husband, a refrigerator salesman, applauded her career and "was more pleased than threatened by her high salary"; he urged her to develop such competencies as reading ocean maps, and calculating interest rates (which she'd so far "resisted learning") because these days "a woman should." But one evening

at dinner, a telling episode occurred. Dorothy had handed Timothy to her husband while she served us a chicken dinner. Gradually, the baby began to doze on his father's lap. "When do you want me to put Timmy to bed?" Dan asked. A long silence followed during which it occurred to Dorothy—then, I think, to her husband—that this seemingly insignificant question hinted to me that it was *she*, not he, or "they," who usually decided such matters. Dorothy slipped me a glance, put her elbows on the table, and said to her husband in a slow, deliberate voice, "So, what do *we* think?"

When Dorothy and Dan described their "typical days," their picture of sharing grew even less convincing. Dorothy worked the same nine-hour day at the office as her husband. But she came home to fix dinner and to tend Timmy while Dan fit in a squash game three nights a week from six to seven (a good time for his squash partner). Dan read the newspaper more often and slept longer.

Compared to the early interviews, women in the later interviews seemed to speak more often in passing of relationships or marriages that had ended for some other reason but in which it "was also true" that he "didn't lift a finger at home." Or the extra month alone did it. One divorcee who typed part of this manuscript echoed this theme when she explained, "I was a potter and lived with a sculptor for eight years. I cooked, shopped, and cleaned because his art 'took him longer.' He said it was fair because he worked harder. But we both worked at home, and I could see that if anyone worked longer hours I did, because I earned less with my pots than he earned with his sculpture. That was *hard* to live with, and that's really why we ended."

Some women moved on to slightly more equitable arrangements in the early 1980s, doing a bit less of the second shift than the working mothers I talked to in the late 1970s. Comparing two national surveys of working couples, F. T. Juster found the male slice of the second shift rose from 20 percent in 1965 to 30 percent in 1981, and my study may be a local reflection of this slow national trend.[4] But women like Dorothy Sims, who simply add to their extra month a year a new illusion that they aren't doing it, represent a sad alternative to the woman with the flying hair—the woman who doesn't think that's who she is.

CRITICAL THINKING QUESTIONS

1. How does the family you grew up in differ from that of your parents or grandparents' with respect to gender relations? Do you imagine that gender relations might be more equitable if you were to have a family?
2. Name some examples of changes in the economy or culture that affect relations between men and women. How is an industrial economy different from an agrarian or a post-industrial economy in terms of gender roles?
3. Explain what Hochschild means by the term "gender strategy." What might be an example of this strategy?

NOTES

1. In a 1978 national survey, Joan Huber and Glenna Spitze found that 78 percent of husbands think that if husband and wife both work full time, they should share housework equally (*Sex Stratification: Children, Housework and Jobs.* New York: Academic Press, 1983). In fact, the husbands of working wives at most average a third of the work at home.

2. The concept of "gender strategy" is an adaptation of Ann Swidler's notion of "strategies of action." In "Culture in Action—Symbols and Strategies," *American Sociological Review* 51 (1986): 273–86, Swidler focuses on how the individual uses aspects of culture (symbols, rituals, stories) as "tools" for constructing a line of action. Here I focus on aspects of culture that bear on our ideas of manhood and womanhood, and I focus on our emotional preparation for and the emotional consequences of our strategies.

3. For the term *family myth* I am indebted to Antonio J. Ferreira, "Psychosis and Family Myth," *American Journal of Psychotherapy* 21 (1967): 186–225.

4. Juster, F.T. 1986. A note on recent changes in time use. In *Studies in the measurement of time allocation*, eds. F. T. Juster and F. Stafford. Ann Arbor: Institute for Social Research.

45

'Bringing Up' and 'Growing Up': Parents, Children, and Family Life

GILLIAN RANSON

This article reviews the family from a sociological perspective and highlights an ideology that prescribes dissimilar roles for men and women. As you read, think about your own experiences as part of a family and how these are influenced by social norms.

THE IDEOLOGICAL CONTEXT OF PARENTING

The Canadian sociologist Dorothy Smith has argued that an ideological 'code' organizes the activities of individuals in North American families. She calls this code SNAF, for 'Standard North American Family'. Smith describes SNAF as follows:

It is a conception of the family as a legally married couple sharing a household. The adult male is in paid employment; his earnings provide the economic basis of the family household. The adult female may also earn an income, but her primary responsibility is to the care of husband, household and children. (Smith, 1993: 52)

Source: Ranson, Gillian, in *Canadian Families Today: New Perspectives*, David Cheal ed. © Oxford University Press Canada 2007. Reprinted by permission of the publisher.

Smith argues that SNAF describes the way families are *supposed* to run; it's the model by which, in North American society, all families are judged. This code suggests that mothers, though they may have paid employment, are ultimately responsible for the practical care of children. And fathers, though they may also get involved with child care, are helpers rather than family managers; their main family responsibility is to provide adequate financial support.

The strong ideological connection between mothers and nurture, and fathers and breadwinning, is often traced back to the effects of industrialization. As this economic form gradually replaced agricultural economies in Europe and North America from the early nineteenth century onward, so the basis of family financial support shifted to wages earned in industrial workplaces. As workplaces increasingly became separated from the homes and family holdings of an earlier era, and were populated largely by

267

a male workforce, they came to be constructed symbolically as the domain of men, while homes—and the daily care of children—were the symbolic domain of women.

This symbolic allocation of family roles corresponded to middle-class social reformers' fears, at the end of the nineteenth century, about the stability of working-class families in the wake of major social and economic change. In Canada, concern about women in industrial workplaces was based on fears for their health, their safety, and their virtue, which stemmed from deeply held moral beliefs about the sanctity—and the responsibilities—of motherhood. Concerns about child labour were linked to middle-class views of childhood as a period of dependency, separate from the responsibilities—and freedoms—of adult life. Mothers and fathers were believed to have 'biologically prescribed roles within the domestic unit' (Chunn, 2003: 191).

The model of motherhood that has emerged from this history establishes one woman (the biological mother) as primarily responsible for mothering during her children's formative years, with the children constructed reciprocally as needing her constant care and attention (Glenn, 1994; Wearing, 1984). Men as fathers are also reciprocally constructed as breadwinners, discharging their family responsibilities primarily by financial provision. This ideological construction of mothers and fathers was based on the situation of the white, middle-class family; it never reflected the family experiences of working-class or ethnically more diverse families. But as Smith noted, this construction became ideologically dominant, shaping the way people behave in families and how they make sense of what they do.

Fatherhood and Fathering

To consider first the case of fatherhood, current research confirms the 'breadwinner' or 'good provider' model as both durable and pervasive in North America. Men are expected to provide for their families, no matter how else they are involved as fathers (Daly and Palkovitz, 2004; Doucet, 2004; LaRossa, 1997, Wilkie, 1993). But current scholarly work on fatherhood is raising some interesting questions about what it means to be a 'good provider', and whether this role is the best way to represent what contemporary fathers do for and with their children.

As Christiansen and Palkovitz (2001) point out, there are some negative connotations attached to the traditional provider role. Historically, the separation of homes and workplaces as a consequence of industrialization took fathers away from their families. As providers, they were required to be good workers, so their primary commitment was to their jobs. Christiansen and Palkovitz cite studies showing breadwinner fathers labelled as 'distant, strict, harsh, authoritarian and incompetent' (Christiansen and Palkovitz, 2001: 88).

Christiansen and Palkovitz argue that these negative connotations detract from the significant contribution fathers make to their families by their financial provision. Indeed, others (e.g., Walker and McGraw, 2000) have argued that this may be the best thing fathers *can* do for their families. Most labour markets are characterized by significant job segregation by gender. Men tend to have jobs that pay better, so their generally superior earnings may influence their standing as primary breadwinners. Christiansen and Palkovitz point out that, when couples first become parents, many mothers cut back on or quit their paid employment. Since this is also a time when household expenses mount, many men commit more time to work to compensate (see also Fox, 2001; Walzer, 1996). In many working-class families, fathers work two jobs to help families make ends meet. To label such fathers as distant and uninvolved in their families does them a grave injustice (Christiansen and Palkovitz, 2001).

But research also indicates that the identification of fathers with financial support has a moral dimension, closely linked to understandings of appropriate masculinity. Men see breadwinning as something they must do to fulfill their responsibilities not only as fathers but as men. . . .

While the continuing expectation is that fathers will provide, this demand has been tempered by the recognition that, these days, most families have two adult incomes. Since the 1960s, increasing numbers of mothers have entered the workforce. The fact of mothers contributing to their families' financial support has led to questions about fathers sharing the hands-on caregiving long considered to be mothers' responsibility. Several scholars have commented on the changing image of fathers, suggesting that the 'distant breadwinner' is giving way to a new image, the 'new father', described by Pleck (1987) as follows:

This new father differs from older images of involved fatherhood in several key respects: he is present at the birth; he is involved with his children as infants, not just when they are older; he participates in the actual day-to-day work of child care, and not just play; he is involved with his daughters as much as his sons. (Pleck, 1987: 93)

. . . Attention to changing images of good fathering and the emergence (or re-emergence) of the new involved father raises questions about what this involvement actually means in practice. Writing about fathering in the US in the late 1980s, sociologist Ralph LaRossa contended that there was a lag between the *culture* and the *conduct* of fatherhood. Because the image of the new father was so pervasive, people assumed that, as mothers' paid work drew them away from their family responsibilities, fathers must be picking up the slack. But there is some debate about how much more domestic work—including child care—fathers really are picking up (LaRossa, 1988).

The consensus from many research studies is that fathers are certainly doing more than their own fathers did, but not as much as the mothers of their children—even those mothers in full-time paying jobs (Beaujot, 2000; Daly, 2004; Silver, 2000). There are also important

class differences. For example, a common strategy in dual-earning working-class families is to have parents work alternating shifts so that outside child care and its attendant costs are minimized. This positions fathers to share both caregiving and breadwinning with their partners on a much more equal basis. Yet studies show that this non-traditional behaviour is usually accompanied by traditional gender ideologies in which the father is still framed as the breadwinner (Deutsch and Saxon, 1998; Hochschild, 1989). . . .

Motherhood and Mothering

The perceived cultural superiority of biological parenthood has already been noted. But the association of fatherhood with its biological base is not nearly as strong as with motherhood. Where fathering is understood as needing to be learned, mothering is still often recognized as instinctual. One young mother, interviewed in a Canadian study, put it this way:

I think more than anything it's your instinctive mothering or your mothering instincts or whatever, because they're primal and they're first and foremost. It doesn't matter if anything else is going on in the world, you're going to protect and look after your child before anything. . . . I feel very—not possessive, but I think very close. I could be one of those African women that carry their babies around all the time. (Ranson, 2004: 93)

Biology is obviously implicated in the processes of pregnancy, birth, and lactation. But what is implied in the interview excerpt above is a similarly biological basis for *mothering*, the practices of child care and nurture associated with being a mother. From this perspective, the next logical step is to see these practices as somehow universal, a bond that joins all mothers. Motherhood, furthermore, has historically been understood as women's destiny and the core of their identity as women. The symbolic assignment of women to the sphere of home and children in the wake of industrialization, as described earlier, was based on just such common-sense understandings of women's 'nature'.

It was also based on a particular set of social and economic events at a particular point in time and in particular parts of the world, which positioned the biological mother as the sole caregiver and nurturer of children (Ambert, 1994). The current cultural dominance of this ideological construction of mothering masks significant class, race, and ethnic differences in the way mothering is practised. . . .

In North American society, the heyday of stay-at-home mothers managing the households and children of breadwinner fathers was during the post-war economy of the 1950s, when many families could survive on one income and when the demographic phenomenon of the baby boom was beginning. . . . This is the era the US sociological theorist Talcott Parsons was describing when he theorized a woman's family role (based on the primacy of the mother-child bond) as the *expressive* leader, responsible for the emotional nurture of family members, and a man's as the *instrumental* leader, responsible above all for financial support (Parsons, 1955). Other commentators point out that the period of the 1950s was an anomaly, produced by a number of factors—economic growth, suburbanization, a strong collective desire for the life-affirming comfort of marriage and family life after the years of war. In North America, other forces for change were soon to reorganize family life once again.

The most important of these changes, as mentioned in the discussion on fathering, was the movement of women into the paid labour force, particularly in the 1960s and 1970s. In Canada, for example, women's labour force participation rate moved from 29.1 per cent in 1961 to 51.8 per cent in 1981 (Beaujot, 2000: 136). Over the decades, their work histories have become much more similar to men's. Where once childbirth signalled the end of paid employment and a turn to full-time child-rearing, mothers began to take temporary maternity leaves and then return to paid work. In 2002, 62 per cent of mothers whose youngest child was under three were in paid employment; 68 per cent of those whose youngest child was aged three to five also had paying jobs (Statistics Canada, 2003). . . .

These mothers face what US sociologist Sharon Hays (1996) calls 'cultural contradictions'. On the one hand, they must confront the expectations of the workplace—rational, efficiency-oriented, the domain of the 'instrumental' (in other words, male) worker. On the other hand, they must conform to prevailing ideological expectations about mothering and motherhood, which require them to be devoted, selfless nurturers with primary responsibility for their children.

Hays has labelled the dominant contemporary ideology of mothering as 'intensive mothering'. She describes it by drawing on the practices and beliefs of Rachel, one of the mothers she interviewed for her study. Rachel is a married professional woman with a two-year-old daughter, Kristin. According to Hays, Rachel believes that as the mother she must be the central caregiver (even though Kristin is also cared for by her emotionally involved father and by qualified child-care providers). Rachel also believes she must put her child's needs before her own, and must attend to all those needs at all the different stages of Kristin's emotional and intellectual development. This in turn requires her to draw on expert knowledge about child development so she will know what to do. And Rachel also understands that this is an emotionally demanding task, since the foundation of this kind of mothering is love. In sum, says Hays, intensive mothering calls for methods of child-rearing that are 'child-centered, expert-guided, emotionally absorbing, labor-intensive, and financially expensive' (Hays, 1996: 8).

Intensive mothering, like breadwinning for fathers, has a moral dimension as well. It acts as a measuring stick, or a template, for what mothers *should* do. The fact that many mothers are not in a position to engage in mothering that is expert-guided or labour-intensive or financially expensive does not diminish its ideological power. Hays included working-class and poor mothers in her study, and found that they had different standards for what good mothers should provide, as well as different ideas about how to meet children's needs. But, Hays argues, 'all these mothers share a set of fundamental assumptions about the importance of putting their children's needs first and dedicating themselves to providing what is best for their kids, as they understand it' (ibid, 86).

PERSPECTIVES ON THE NEEDS OF CHILDREN

Ideas about appropriate mothering and fathering are intricately connected to and, indeed, follow from ideas about children and their needs. Some of the shifts in thinking, as noted above, have resulted from economic and other social change. But they have also followed from changes in expert opinion about child development and, more fundamentally, the moral nature and value of children. These changes, in turn, are linked to changing understandings of *childhood* as both a developmental stage and a socially constructed space. . . .

Ehrensaft (2001) claims that understandings of childhood throughout history have moved between two poles of a continuum. At one end is the child as miniature adult, at the other the child as 'innocent cherub'. Each historical era develops an image of childhood and children that fits the context in which those children must grow. In earlier historical time periods, but also in other parts of the contemporary world, children's early independence and their economic contributions to their family's support have been, and continue to be, essential to family survival. In the context of contemporary industrialized societies, children are better placed to be 'innocent cherubs' (Erensaft, 2001: 308). . . .

The Canadian Context

In Canada, infant mortality in the late nineteenth and early twentieth centuries was the issue that first mobilized experts to provide advice for mothers. Mothers, as noted above, had clearly been positioned as those most responsible for their children's welfare, and they had already been the focus of social reformers' concerns about family life.

Especially in urban areas, infant mortality rates were a legitimate source of concern. In 1901, for example, the City of Toronto reported that 160 of every 1,000 babies died before their first birthday. In 1907 that rate climbed to 197. In Montreal, about one-third of all infants died (Arnup, 1994: 14–15). . . . But while reformers had been putting pressure on governments to recognize the scale of the problem, Arnup notes that infant mortality began to receive serious government attention when it was viewed in the context of the nation's health. A significant number of potential Canadian recruits for military service during World War I had to be turned away because of ill health. National health concerns were compounded by the effects of the war (Canada sustained some 250,000 casualties, 60,681 of them fatal). Some 50,000 Canadians also died from the post-war Spanish influenza epidemic. This damage, in a population just over eight million, was serious indeed. Arnup cites a 1922 editorial in the *Canadian Medical Association Journal* calling for 'a more careful medical oversight of all children during their early years of growth' (ibid., 19).

Arnup's 1994 book, *Education for Motherhood: Advice for Mothers in Twentieth-Century Canada*, goes on to document the way concerns about infant health were taken up. She notes that while departments of health and divisions of child welfare were established at every level of government, in practice little was done to address the poverty, malnutrition, and poor housing that were the root causes of

The Social Conditions of Motherhood

Motherhood as a biological phenomenon is the basis for powerful cultural understandings about how mothers are supposed to behave as mothers. Mothers' practices are often seen as instinctual, universal, and 'natural'. Mothers are supposed to know what to do with their babies, just as the 'maternal instinct' is supposed to ensure that they will love their babies unconditionally. Because of this love, they are also assumed to be totally invested in their babies' survival.

But scholars point out that far from being 'natural' and 'universal', mothering practices are shaped by the social and economic context in which mothers live (Glenn, 1994; Ambert, 1994). How a very different environment can produce very different mothering practices is vividly shown in the work of anthropologist Nancy Scheper-Hughes, who worked in the 1960s as a medic among desperately poor mothers in an urban slum community in Brazil.

Scheper-Hughes found that in an environment of poverty and high infant mortality, mothers developed differential patterns of nurturing, distinguishing infants likely to thrive, and therefore considered 'keepers', from those they thought of as having been born 'already wanting to die'. Keepers were tended in the careful, committed way associated with Western 'mother love'. Babies in the second category were left for nature to take its course. Scheper-Hughes reports that these babies were often carefully washed, combed, and powdered—but not fed. When they died, they usually did so 'with candles propped up in tiny waxen hands to light their way to the afterlife' (Scheper-Hughes, 1999: 258). They were considered little angels, returning to the place from which they had just come. Scheper-Hughes argues that a high expectancy of infant death is 'a powerful shaper of maternal thinking and practice'. She adds:

> I am *not* arguing that mother love, as we understand it, is deficient or absent in this threatened little human community but rather that its life history, its course, is different, shaped by overwhelming economic and cultural constraints. (Ibid., 257)

much infant ill health. Instead, responsibility was placed squarely on mothers, and an elaborate educational campaign was mounted to train mothers in their proper duties. The campaign was conducted through well-baby clinics, lectures in department stores, radio programs, and columns in women's magazines, as well as in the informational material produced by the professionals in the child health bureaucracy.

Arnup shows how, over the decades of the twentieth century, the advice changed as physicians and other professionals changed their views about what children needed. Concerns about infant mortality in the early decades of the century led to a preoccupation with feeding and a focus on schedules and regimentation. After World War II, concern about rigidly training children to develop good habits gave way to a new maturational-developmental approach to child development. . . .

[Canadian sociologist Glenda Wall (2004)] argues that advice based on 'new brain research' builds on earlier (and now largely discredited) theories of developmental psychology stressing the importance of mother–infant bonding. These theories resonate with the dominant ideology of mothering. So does the advice based on 'new brain research'. In fact, it extends the requirements of intensive mothering already discussed. Wall considers that it also conforms to a trend in child-rearing ideology towards perfecting children, at a time of rapid social and economic change and uncertainty about the future. At the same time, the tendency is to privatize child-rearing responsibilities even as, with the 'new brain research' initiatives, those responsibilities become more burdensome. The focus of programs and policies like Ontario's Early Years Centres is to provide parents with information and leave them to raise perfect children without further support (ibid).

PARENTING IN PRACTICE

Advice to parents, based on expert opinion about what children need, ties in to dominant ideologies of mothering and fathering like those described earlier. These shape not only what people do, but how they make sense of what they do and what they think they ought to do. The 'ought' is important, because in practice many people do not conform to the ideal. Dominant images of mothering and fathering may work in the 'Standard North American Family' described by Smith (1993), but are much more difficult to conform to in non-SNAF families.

For example, in 2001 about 16 per cent of Canadian families were single-parent (predominantly single-mother) families. Conforming to a dominant image of mothering (or fathering) can't be managed easily when the other parent is absent, or even present but not resident in the household. There are different complications when parents separate or divorce, then form new relationships. This often has the effect of introducing new adult relationships—which may or may not be considered 'parental'—into children's lives. If both of the new partners bring children into the relationship, the complications redouble.

Stepfamilies and 'Blended' Families

Statistics Canada defines a stepfamily as one in which at least one of the children in the household is from a previous relationship of one of the parents. In a 'simple' stepfamily, the children of only one of the spouses live in the household. In a 'blended' family, there are children of both partners from one or more previous relationships, or children from the current union and at least one prior one. According to General Social Survey data, Canada had 503,100 stepfamilies in 2001, compared to 430,500 in 1995. This represented almost 12 per cent of all Canadian couples with children in 2001, compared with 10 per cent in 1995 (Statistics Canada, 2002a). About 50 per cent of stepfamilies contained only the children of the female partner. About 10 per cent contained only the male partner's children. The remainder, about 40 per cent, were 'blended'. In most of these cases (81 per cent) they were formed after the birth of a child to the couple. The other 19 per cent included

children from previous relationships of both partners (Statistics Canada, 2002b).

Juby (2003–4) notes that these statistics suggest stepfamilies are still a minority family type. She argues that the stepfamily experience is in fact much more widespread than cross-sectional survey data (like those derived from the General Social Survey) indicate. Such data, she points out, show the prevalence of the stepfamily experience at a given point in time but are unable to show how common it is over the lifetime of the population. Juby adds that another reason survey statistics underestimate the extent of the stepfamily experience is that family statistics are usually based on families as *residential* units. This means, for example, that situations where children live mostly with one parent (in one 'residential unit'), while the other parent has formed a new relationship and had other children in another 'residential unit', are not counted in the stepfamily statistics. Juby cites the conjugal history of Martin and Louise to make her point. They lived together for a couple of years, then married when their son Thomas was conceived. Later they had a second child, Laura. When Laura was four, they separated. Martin later moved in with Marie, and two years later, Martin and Marie had a baby, Jessica. Because Thomas and Laura lived mostly with their mother, their step-parent relationships through their father's family didn't 'count', statistically speaking. Juby feels strongly that they *should* count.

Juby and her colleagues have attempted to overcome the shortcomings of cross-sectional data in their study of stepfamily and blended family networks by using data from the children being followed through the National Longitudinal Study of Children and Youth. Their findings strikingly illustrate the extent to which Canadian children are likely to experience stepfamily relationships in the course of their lives. For example, of the children included in the study whose parents had separated, one-third of the fathers and a quarter of the mothers had remarried or started living with someone other than the child's other parent within three years of separation. Close to half the new relationships formed by separated parents were with people who already had children from a previous relationship. Overall, almost one in five children aged between birth and 13 years in 1996–7 had at least one stepsibling or half-sibling in their family network (Juby et al., 2005).

The study by Juby et al. also noted some other interesting characteristics of stepfamilies. For example, since children most often live with their mothers after separation and divorce, the children in their study sample were much more likely to be living with mothers and stepfathers (84 per cent) than with fathers and stepmothers. For the same reason, the study also found that stepsiblings rarely shared the same residence. In fact, Thomas and Laura, described above, are quite characteristic of the study findings. But for Juby, the fact that they don't share a permanent residence with their father and his new family does not diminish the significance of the stepfamily experience in their lives.

The reality is that these relationships *are* of great importance, at many different levels. Even though Thomas and Laura spend only weekends and holidays with their father and his new family, there are important implications for them all. For Martin, being a part-time Dad to Thomas and Laura involves frequent emotional adjustments as his children come and go. He's also affected financially, since he needs a bigger house with separate bedrooms for Laura and Thomas, and he contributes to the cost of Louise's house through monthly child support payments. Marie has to deal with the challenges of being a part-time stepmother, and Thomas and Laura with having two 'mothers'. Once Jessica comes along, Thomas and Laura also have to cope with the potential threat to their father's affection posed by the new baby, who, unlike them, lives with him all the time. As for Jessica, she must learn to negotiate the complicated universe into which she was born. She will never be the oldest or the only child in the family network . . . she has to shift back and forward between the positions

of younger half-sibling when Thomas and Laura are in the house, and only child when they leave. (Juby, 2003: 5–6)

The complexities of separations and new unions have given rise to the phenomenon of the 'new extended family' (Cherlin and Furstenberg, 1994) whose boundaries are ambiguous and in which family roles are not always clear. Cherlin and Furstenberg note that, in a marriage following divorce, a step-parent does not replace the stepchild's non-resident parent, as was usually the case in earlier generations when remarriages followed the death of a spouse. The lack of norms and guidelines available to step-parents suggest that the step-parent role is 'incompletely institutionalized'. What also seems to be the case, as step-parents discover in practice, is that 'they have been issued only a limited license to parent' (ibid., 367). Step-parents, like the adoptive parents discussed earlier in the research by Miall and March (2003), experience all the difficulties of social parenting, often in situations where biological parents may also be in the picture.

This is challenging for all concerned. Cherlin and Furstenberg cite research suggesting that the adjustment can take years to complete. The situation is particularly tricky for stepmothers, who typically don't live with their stepchildren but must establish a connection to them on visits. A stepmother is also competing with the children's biological mother, with whom they usually have a closer connection. As one stepmother put it, 'When they come back from their mom's on Sunday night, I want to cry. They treat me different[ly]. They want me to know I am not their real mom' (Mason et al., 2002: 514). Stepfathers, on the other hand, may be competing with non-custodial fathers, many of whom see little of their children. In this context stepfathers may be able to fill a vacuum (Cherlin and Furstenberg, 1994).

In spite of the challenges, evidence suggests that step-parents make a significant difference to the families they join. In an extensive study of stepfamily functioning in the US, Mason et al. (2002) found that step-parents served as primary caregivers. They also performed the 'yeoman work' of helping with homework and shuttling the children back and forth, just as biological parents do. The researchers found that, 'on the more delicate issues of giving advice and setting and enforcing rules', step-parents were less often the leaders but still participated actively. They also made a major difference to the economic well-being of their stepchildren (Mason et al., 2002: 518).

Same-Sex Families

Stereotypical expectations about 'mothering' and 'fathering', based on the dominant ideologies described earlier, also do not work well for same-sex couples with children. About 15 per cent of the 15,200 female same-sex couples counted for the first time in the 2001 Canadian census had children living with them, as did about 3 per cent of the 19,000 male same-sex couples. In cases where these children were born to prior heterosexual relationships, biological mothers and fathers may still be present and active in the child's family network. In cases where two women, or two men, each with children, form a new partnership, the step- or blended-family dynamics just described are also characteristic.

Increasingly, however, children are being born or adopted into same-sex families. While adoption is an option for gay men, it is not yet widespread in Canada, and information about gay adoptive fathers is almost non-existent. The situation is different for lesbian mothers. Because of the possibility for women to make use of donor insemination (DI) using either known or unknown donors, increasing numbers of children are being born within lesbian relationships. Known donors, as biological fathers, may have a role in the child's life, but more often as 'kindly uncles' than as fathers (Dunne, 2000). The major challenge in such families is to accommodate two mothers, one of whom gave birth to the child, the other of whom is a 'social' rather than a biological mother. Reimann (1997), in a study of US lesbian families, concluded that the distinction between the biological mother and the non-biological mother affected couples in three main areas: *public* motherhood, which is concerned with how motherhood is defined through the law and social customs; *relational* motherhood, which refers to the definition of motherhood shared by parents and their children in the family; and *personal* motherhood, which links to the idea of motherhood as personal identity (Reimann, 1997: 164–5). Studies suggest that while co-mothers confront challenges in all three domains, lesbian couples work hard, and with some success, to achieve a more egalitarian sharing of parenting and household work than that often found in the households of heterosexual couples. Based on her Canadian study of lesbian families, Nelson (1996) comments:

Lesbian D.I. couples . . . present a substantial challenge to established maternal culture by demanding that they (both partners) not be differentiated on the basis of having given birth or not. By insisting that non-biological mothers are mothers too, these women have the potential to alter the understanding mothers have of motherhood. In this sense, lesbian motherhood through donor insemination can be seen as a revolutionary activity. (Nelson, 1996: 101)

Research information is lacking for gay adoptive fathers. But it is easy to see that the need to accommodate two fathers, while probably not involving a comparison of biological and non-biological fatherhood, would still require negotiation in the public, relational, and personal domains identified by Reimann.

Other Challenges to 'Ideal' Mothering and Fathering

Even among two-parent heterosexual couples raising their own biological children, parenting practices are shaped by factors that make ideal mothering and fathering hard to achieve. Poverty, ill health, unemployment, and the presence of children with special needs all pose challenges for parents. Most parents 'share in the cultural mandate to support their children, attend to their physical well-being, help them stay out of trouble and push them to achieve' (Daly, 2004: 1). But they differ in their interpretation of all these parenting responsibilities and their capacity to fulfill them.

Socio-economic class and the concomitant level of access to material and cultural resources are major influences on parenting. In an ethnographic study of middle-class, working-class, and poor families in the US, Lareau (2002) found that middle-class families (both white and black) engaged in what she called 'concerted cultivation' of their children. In part, this involves the kind of financially expensive, labour-intensive promotion of their children's talents and abilities (through a variety of organized extracurricular activities) covered in Hays's (1996) description of intensive mothering. These parents also stressed language use and the development of reasoning, with talking as the major means of disciplining their children. In contrast, the working-class and poor parents emphasized the 'accomplishment of natural growth'. Lareau commented: 'These parents believe that as long as they provide love, food and safety, their children will grow and thrive' (Lareau, 2002: 748–9). Working-class parents involved their children in fewer organized activities; they used language less in disciplining their children; they were more directive; and they placed more emphasis on physical discipline than did the middle-class parents. Lareau found that the middle-class pattern of 'concerted cultivation' produced an emerging sense of entitlement in children, who were confident about speaking up and asking questions. In contrast, the working-class pattern of the accomplishment of natural growth seemed to produce an attitude, in both parents and children, of outward deference and compliance to authority (ibid, 749).

The need in most families to organize family responsibilities around paid work is stressful for parents. In working-class families, long hours of work, occasionally at more than one job, may be necessary to make ends meet. In middle-class families, especially in times of economic uncertainty and restructuring, the expectations placed on professional jobs often expand as organizations downsize. Long hours may be necessary both to keep up and to stay hired. Employers are only slowly becoming aware of the need for 'work–family balance', and have been equally slow to offer programs that would help (Duxbury and Higgins, 2002).

At the same time, the 'concerted cultivation' in parenting identified by Lareau, the time- and labour-intensive implications of intensive mothering, and the pressures on breadwinner fathers to be more involved in their families put other time pressures on families. In a book appropriately titled *The Time Bind*, US sociologist Arlie Hochschild describes the time pressures many parents face at home as a consequence of long hours at work. Hochschild (1997) argues that there is now a need to strive for workplace-like efficiency at home as well, as parents schedule and multi-task to get everything done. In an earlier (1989) study, Hochschild identified the 'second shift' that mothers put in at home on top of their regular working day. Now, she argues, parents need to do a 'third shift' of emotional work to compensate children for the time-crunched second shift.

Parenting organized around paid work and the worker-like, rational efficiency required of time-stressed parents at home are elements of what Daly (2004) calls the current 'culture of parenting'—the 'background undercurrents that guide what seem right, natural or appropriate' (Daly, 2004: 1). So are the ideologies of mothering and fathering already discussed, along with their implications, as Daly notes, for gender practice. Daley points out that parenting today also takes place in a culture of consumption, in which children's needs and wants exert a powerful influence on how time and money are spent. Finally, Daly notes that parenting takes place in a media culture, in which children are at the centre of a highly politicized debate about the effects of media technology—including, increasingly, computer technology. Daly concludes:

For all parents, this is an environment that requires the ongoing refinement of navigation skills that will take them through uncharted waters. The culture of parenthood is a culture without prescription where knowledge of the traditional rules of the game is less important than a well-stocked tool box that positions them to puzzle through with their children changing gender practices, work expectations, media culture and consumer pressures. Above all, the culture of parenting is one that is shaped by the challenges of an emergent future rather than a settled past. (Daly, 2004: 7)

CHILDREN AND THEIR FAMILIES

. . . The current 'culture of parenting', as described above by Daly, places stress on children as well as parents. The hurried, time-stretched, hyper-organized environment of many middle-class families may produce children whose access to piano lessons and soccer camps and math tutors gives them considerable cultural capital, which will probably parlay into privilege in the competitive adult world they will shortly enter. As part of the practices of intensive mothering described by Hays (1996), this environment also produces children accustomed to having their needs met and feeling entitled to being heard (Lareau, 2002). But if many children's needs are indulged in middle-class households like these, other needs may not be met so well. Daly notes that, contrary to popular belief, parents may not be spending less time with their children. Rather, the time parents and children spend together has become more 'goal-oriented, structured, and saturated with activity' (Daly, 2004: 3). This is vividly illustrated in the comment of one of Hochschild's interviewees, a mother in full-time paid employment:

Quality time is seven-thirty to eight-thirty at night, and then it's time for bed. I'm ready at seven-thirty, but Melinda has other ideas. As soon as quality time comes she wants to have her bath or watch TV; *no way* is she going to play with Mommy. Later, when I'm ready to drop, *then* she's ready for quality time. (Hochschild, 1997: 216)

Children, especially very young ones, have their own ideas about how to spend time. Hochschild points out what all parents know: when left to their own devices, children's pace of life is different. They dawdle, then they run, in what she calls the 'stop and go of childhood itself' (ibid.). Ehrensaft, who described the competing images of children as either 'miniature adults' or 'innocent cherubs', would see the dawdling, playful child as the innocent cherub. But increasingly, children are expected to be 'miniature adults', fitting in with all the time demands and absences from home required by adult work schedules. The paradox is that when they *are* home, they may be indulged and often materially overcompensated by parents who feel guilty about the needs they may not be meeting. Ehrensaft calls such children 'kinderdults' (half children—'Kinder' is the German word for children—and half adults). They live in a world where in one sense childhood has disappeared and in another sense, because of children's prolonged dependence on their parents while completing their education, it goes on longer than it has in the past (Ehrensaft, 2001: 305–6). . . .

CONCLUSION

The challenges and difficulties of raising children will not put people off. The vast majority of young Canadians intend to raise families, no doubt because they are aware of the rich rewards of a relationship, and an endeavour, like no other. As this chapter has shown, however, people do not go about the job of parenting as free agents, able to make up the rules as they go along. In any culture, parenting practices are shaped by powerful ideologies about mothering and fathering. Mothering and fathering are constructed in response to prevailing understandings about the nature and needs of children; these needs change as expert opinion changes. But mothers and fathers also face economic pressures, shaped in part by their understandings of their children's material needs. Working to meet these needs obligates them to employers who see them as workers, not parents. Both mothers and fathers experience 'cultural contradictions' (Hays, 1996).

One way out of the dilemma is to provide parents with more public support. . . . When child-centred policies lead to child-centred programs—like quality daycare, as one example—the lives of many parents will be made easier, and the lives of children will be enriched.

CRITICAL THINKING QUESTIONS

1. What does the "ideological code" prescribe for Canadian families? Do you feel pressure to conform to that norm? How does this norm differ for men and women?

2. Do you think young Canadians feel pressure to have a family? Where does this pressure originate? Is there, in your opinion, a cost to that social pressure on people who don't want to have children? What role do sociological norms play in this?

3. In industrialized countries, families are small in contrast to pre-industrial societies. What are some possible reasons for this (both social and economic)? How has the value of children changed?

REFERENCES

Ambert, Anne-Marie. 1994. An international perspective on parenting: Social change and social constructs. *Journal of Marriage and the Family*, 56: 529–43.

Arnup, Katherine. 1994. *Education for motherhood.* Toronto: University of Toronto Press.

Beaujot, Roderic. 2000. *Earning and caring.* Peterborough, ON: Broadview Press.

Cherlin, Andrew J., and Frank F. Furstenberg. 1994. Stepfamilies in the United States: A reconsideration. *Annual Review of Sociology*, 20: 359–81.

Christiansen, Shawn, and Rob Palkovitz. 2001. Why the "good provider" role still matters: Providing as a form of paternal involvement. *Journal of Family Issues*, 22: 84–106.

Chunn, Dorothy. 2003. Boys will be men, girls will be mothers: The legal regulation of childhood in Toronto and Vancouver. In *Histories of Canadian children and youth*, eds. Nancy Janovicek and Joy Parr. Toronto: Oxford University Press.

Daly, Kerry. 2004. The changing culture of parenting. Ottawa: Vanier Institute of the Family.

—— and Rob Palkovitz. 2004. Guest editorial: Reworking work and family issues for fathers. *Fathering*, 2: 211–13.

Deutsch, F., and S. Saxon. 1998. Traditional ideologies, non-traditional lives. *Sex Roles*, 38: 331–62.

Doucet, Andrea. 2004. "It's almost like I have a job, but I don't get paid": Fathers at home reconfiguring work, care and masculinity. *Fathering*, 2: 277–303.

Dunne, Gillian. 2000. Opting into motherhood: Lesbians blurring the boundaries and transforming the meaning of parenthood and kinship. *Gender & Society*, 14(1): 11–35.

Duxbury, Linda, and Chris Higgins. 2002. *2001 National work-life conflict study: Report one.* Ottawa: Health Canada.

Ehrensaft, Diane. 2001. The kinderdult: The new child born to conflict between work and family. In *Working Families: The Transformation of the American Home*, eds. Rosanna Hertz and Nancy L. Marshall. Berkeley: University of California Press, 304–22.

Fox, Bonnie. 2001. The formative years: How parenthood creates gender. *Canadian Review of Sociology and Anthropology*, 38: 373–90.

Glenn, Evelyn Nakano. 1994. Social constructions of mothering: A thematic overview. In *Mothering: Ideology, experience and agency*, eds. Evelyn Nakano Glenn, Grace Chang, and Linda Rennie Forcie. New York: Routledge.

Hays, Sharon. 1996. *The cultural contradictions of motherhood.* New Haven: Yale University Press.

Hochschild, Arlie. 1989. *The second shift.* New York: Avon.

——. 1997. *The time bind.* New York: Metropolitan Books.

Juby, Heather. 2003. Yours, mine and ours: New boundaries for the modern stepfamily. *Transitions*, 33(4): 3–6.

Lareau, Annette. 2002. Invisible inequality: Social class and childrearing in black families and white families. *American Sociological Review*, 67: 747–76.

LaRossa, Ralph. 1988. Fatherhood and social change. *Family Relations*, 37: 451–8.

Mason, M., S. Harrison-Jay, G. M. Svare, and N. H. Wolfinger. 2002. Stepparents: De facto parents or legal strangers? *Journal of Family Issues*, 23(4): 507–22.

Miall, Charlene, and Karen March. 2003. A comparison of biological and adoptive mothers and fathers: The relevance of biological kinship and gendered constructs of parenthood. *Adoption Quarterly*, 6: 7–39.

Nelson, Fiona. 1996. *Lesbian motherhood: An exploration of Canadian lesbian families*. Toronto: University of Toronto Press.

Parsons, Talcott. 1955. The American family: Its relations to personality and to the social structure. In *Family socialization and interaction process*, eds. Talcott Parsons and Robert F. Bales. Glencoe, Ill.: Free Press.

Pleck, Joseph. 1987. American fathering in historical perspective. In *Changing men: New directions in research on men and masculinity*, ed. Michael Kimmel. Newbury Park, Calif.: Sage.

Ranson, Gillian. 2004. Paid work, family work and the discourse of the full-time mother. In *Mother matters: Motherhood as discourse and practice*, ed. Andrea O'Reilly. Toronto: Association for Research on Mothering.

Reimann, R. 1997. Does biology matter? Lesbian couples' transition to parenthood and their division of labor. *Qualitative Sociology*, 20(2): 153–85.

Scheper-Hughes, Nancy. 1999. (M)Other love: Culture, scarcity and maternal thinking. In *Through the Prism of Difference*, eds. Maxine Baca Zinn, Pierrette Hondagneu-Sotelo, and Michael A. Messner. Boston: Allyn and Bacon.

Silver, Cynthia. 2000. Being there: The time dual-earner couples spend with their children. *Canadian Social Trends*, 57: 26–9.

Smith, Dorothy. 1993. The Standard North American Family: SNAF as an ideological code. *Journal of Family Issues*, 14: 50–65.

Statistics Canada. 2002a. *Profile of Canadian families and households: Diversification continues*. Catalogue no. 96F0030XIE2001003. Ottawa: Ministry of Industry.

——. 2002b. *The Daily*, 11 July. Available: **http://www.statcan.ca/Daily/English/020711/d020711a.htm**.

Walker, Alexis, and Lori McGraw. 2000. Who is responsible for responsible fathering? *Journal of Marriage and the Family*, 62: 563–9.

Wall, Glenda. 2004. Is your child's brain potential maximized? Mothering in an age of new brain research. *Atlantis*, 8: 41–50.

Walzer, Susan. 1996. Thinking about the baby: Gender and divisions of infant care. *Social Problems*, 43: 219–34.

Wearing, Betsy. 1984. *The ideology of motherhood*. Sydney: George Allen and Unwin.

Wilkie, Jane. 1993. Changes in U.S. men's attitudes toward the family provider role, 1972–1989. *Gender & Society*, 7: 261–79.

46

Mate Selection and Marriage Around the World

BRON B. INGOLDSBY

The institution of marriage is very popular throughout the world. Yet, how mates are chosen varies considerably from one culture to another. As Bron B. Ingoldsby shows, free-choice mate selection—which is common in Western countries—is not how couples have been paired with their prospective spouses in most other societies.

MATE SELECTION PROCEDURES

Historically, there have been three general approaches to choosing one's mate: marriage by capture, marriage by arrangement, and free-choice mate selection. I examine each of them in turn.

Marriage by Capture

Although it has probably never been the usual method of obtaining a wife, men have taken women by force in many times and places. This typically occurred in patriarchal societies in which women were often considered property. Often women were seized as part of the spoils

Source: "Mate Selection and Marriage," by Bron B. Ingoldsby in *Families in Multicultural Perspective*, eds. Bron B. Ingoldsby and Suzanna Smith, pp. 143–5. Copyright © 1995 Guilford Press, NY. Reprinted by permission of Guilford Press.

of war, and other times a specific woman was forced into marriage because the man wanted her and could not afford the brideprice or obtain the permission of her parents. The capture and marriage of a woman was legal in England until the reign of Henry VII, who made it a crime to abduct an heiress (Fielding, 1942).

The ancient Hebrews would seize wives under certain circumstances. A dramatic example is recounted in the Old Testament (Judges, chapter 21), where it was arranged for young women to be kidnapped from two different areas to serve as wives so that the tribe of Benjamin would not die out after a war that they had lost.

There was also a formal procedure for dealing with wives captured in warfare (Deuteronomy 21: 10–14):

When thou goest forth to war against thine enemies, and the Lord thy God hath delivered them into thine hands, and thou has taken them captive, And seest among the captives a beautiful woman, and hast a desire unto her, that thou wouldest have her to thy wife; Then thou shalt bring her home to thine house; and she shall shave her head, and pare her nails; And she shall put the raiment of her captivity from off her, and shall remain in thine house, and bewail her father and her mother a full month: and after that thou shalt go in unto her, and be her husband, and she shall be thy wife. And it shall be, if thou have no delight in her, then thou shalt let her go whither she will; but thou shalt not sell her at all for money, thou shalt not make merchandise of her, because thou has humbled her.

At least she was given time to get used to the idea and never sold into slavery! Fielding (1942) cites a number of different cultures, including the Australian aborigines, who frequently resorted to marriage by capture in the recent past. The Yanomamö of Venezuela (an Amazonian tribe) are reported (Peters, 1987) to use capture as one of their mate selection options. One village is often raided by another for the specific purpose of finding wives. If a man captures a young, attractive female, he must be careful as other men from his own village will try to steal her from him.

In the popular musical *Seven Brides for Seven Brothers*, the concept of marriage by capture is acted out, and one of the songs is based on the historical incident of the rape of the Sabine women. There are many cultures that still have remnants of the old practice of marriage by capture in their wedding ceremonies. In each of them, the match is prearranged, but the husband pretends to take his bride by force, and she feigns resistance.

One example is the Roro of New Guinea. On the wedding day, the groom's party surrounds the bride's home and acts out an assault on it. The bride attempts to run away but is caught. Then a sham battle ensues, with the bride's mother leading the way and crying at the loss of her daughter when she is taken off to the groom (Fielding, 1942).

Marriage by Arrangement

It appears that the most common method of mate selection has been by arrangement. Typically, the parents, often with the aid of certain relatives or professional matchmakers, have chosen the spouse for their child. This form of mate choice is more common when extended kin groups are strong and important. Essentially, marriage is seen as of group, rather than individual, importance, and economics is often the driving force rather than love between the principals.

Arranged marriages have been considered especially important for the rulers of kingdoms and other nobility. Care had to be taken to preserve bloodlines, enhance wealth, and resolve political issues. It is believed, for instance, that the majority of King Solomon's 700 wives and 300 concubines were acquired for the purpose of political alliances.

Stephens (1963) identifies four major reasons that determine mate choice in societies in which marriages are arranged. The first is price. The groom's family may need to pay for the bride, with either money or labor. In some cultures, the situation is reversed, with the bride's family paying a dowry to the husband. In other cases, there is a direct exchange, where both families make payments to each other or simply trade women for each other's sons.

The second consideration is *social status*. That is, the reputation of the family from which the spouse for one's child will come is very important. A third determinant is any *continuous marriage arrangement*. This refers to a set pattern for mate selection, which is carried on from generation to generation. For instance, cousin marriages are preferred in many societies.

The final criteria for mate choice are *sororate* and *levirate* arrangements, which refer to second marriages and tend to be based on bride-price obligations. These terms are more fully explained later in the [reading]. Stephens also notes nineteen societies (including, for example, some large ones such as China and Renaissance Europe) that have practiced child betrothals or child marriages. This means that the marriage is arranged before puberty and can even be worked out before the child is born.

In addition to marriage by capture, the Yanomamö also practice variety within arranged marriages. The ideal match is between cross-cousins, and the majority of unions fall into this category. Most betrothals are made before the girl is three years of age. Men initiate these arrangements at about the time they become hunters, which is shortly after they turn fifteen. Another acceptable form of mate selection is sister exchange. Two unrelated single males wish to acquire wives and have sisters who are not promised to anyone, so they simply trade sisters (Peters, 1987).

Some societies have provided an "out" for couples who have strong personal preferences that go against the arrangement of their families. This is to permit elopement. Stephens (1963: 200) gives this account of the Iban of Borneo:

When a young woman is in love with a man who is not acceptable to her parents, there is an old custom called *nunghop bui*, which permits him to carry her off to his own village. She will meet him by arrangement at the waterside, and step into his boat with a paddle in her hand, and both will pull away as fast as they can. If pursued he will stop every now and then to deposit some article of value on the bank, such as a gun, a jar, or a favor for the acceptance of her family, and when he has exhausted his resources he will leave his own sword. When the pursuers observe this they cease to follow, knowing he is cleared out. As soon as he reaches his own village he tidies up the house and spreads the mats, and when his pursuers arrive he gives them food to eat and toddy to drink, and sends them home satisfied. In the meanwhile he is left in possession of his wife.

Following is a detailed look at some of the specific mechanisms of arranged marriages.

Brideprice. Throughout much of human history, marriage has been seen as chiefly an economic transaction. As an old German saying goes, "It is not man that marries maid, but field marries field, vineyard marries vineyard, cattle marry cattle" (Tober, 1984: p. 12). The purpose of a brideprice is to compensate the family of the bride for the loss of her services.

It is extremely common and is indicative of the value of women in those societies. Stephens (1963) reports that Murdock's World Ethnographic Sample yields the following breakdown on marriage payments:

Brideprice—260 societies
Bride service—75 societies
Dowry—24 societies
Gift or woman exchange—31 societies
No marriage payment—152 societies

This means that in 62 percent of the world's societies, a man must pay in order to marry a woman. The price is usually paid in animals, shell money, or other valuable commodities and often exceeds one's annual income. Some cultures prefer payment in service, often many years of labor to the bride's parents, or at least permit it for suitors who cannot afford to pay in goods. One famous example from the Old Testament is that of Jacob, who labored seven years for each of Laban's two daughters, Leah and Rachel.

Dowry. The dowry appears to be an inducement for a man to marry a particular woman and therefore relieve her family of the financial burden of caring for her. Although relatively rare, it is a sign of a culture that places a low value on women. Actually, the key purpose of a dowry is probably to stabilize a marriage, because it is not given to the husband but is something that the bride brings with her into the marriage. For example, in Cyprus before the time of English influence, the expected dowry was often a house. If the husband divorced his wife or mistreated her and she left him, the dowry went with her. Like modern-day wedding gifts, or the bride's trousseau, it was an investment in the marriage and intended to reduce the chances of a breakup (Balswick, 1975).

The dowry has been around for a long time. The Babylonian code of Hammurabi (1955 B.C.E.) clearly stated that the wife's property stayed with her if her husband divorced her and passed on to her children when she died. Ancient Greece and

Rome also considered the dowry to be essential in any honorable marriage (Fielding, 1942).

. . . . [R]esearch in the southern Indian state of Kerala (Billig, 1992) differentiates between the traditional dowry and an actual "groomprice." Groomprice is money paid by the bride's family directly to the husband to use as he sees fit. In the 1950s and 1960s, rapid population growth resulted in more younger women looking for husbands a few (average of seven) years older than themselves. This surplus of potential brides increased the value of husbands. Popular revulsion for the groomprice has resulted in a decrease in the age difference (now five years), women lowering their social status expectations for their husband or increasing their own education, and a government outlawing of the practice.

Sororate and Levirate. These terms refer to marriage practices designed to control remarriages after the death of the first spouse. In cultures that practice the sororate, a sister replaces a deceased wife. Assume that a man has paid a good brideprice for his wife but some time later she becomes ill and dies. He has lost his wife and the brideprice. Therefore, to make good on the original bargain, the parents who received the brideprice provide the man with a new wife. This new wife is an unmarried sister or other close relative of the first wife. Here we see how marriage is often more of an economic transaction than it is a personal relationship.

Much more widely practiced has been the levirate. Under this system, it is the husband who dies, and his wife must be married to a brother of the deceased man. There are various reasons for this practice. One is that the wife belonged to her husband as part of his property and as such would be inherited along with the other possessions by a near relative. Another is that it is presumed that women need someone to take care of them, and brothers-in-law (which is the meaning of the Latin word *levir*) should assume that responsibility. It has been reported that the levirate has been practiced by the New Caledonians, the Mongols,

the Afghans, the Abyssinians, the Hebrews, and the Hindus, as well as certain Native American and African tribes (Fielding, 1942).

The chief reason that the Hindus and Hebrews practiced the levirate was religious and had to do with the importance of having a son in the family. Hindu men needed a son to perform certain sacrifices, so if a man died before having one, a boy born to his former wife and brother would carry out those ceremonies in his name (Fielding, 1942).

For the Hebrews, it was also important that every man have a son, so that his name would not die out. There was a ritualized penalty for men who refused to marry their brother's widow and rear a son in his name (Deuteronomy 25: 7–9):

> And if the man like not to take his brother's wife, then let his brother's wife go up to the gate unto the elders, and say, My husband's brother refuseth to raise up unto his brother a name in Israel, he will not perform the duty of my husband's brother. Then the elders of his city shall call him, and speak unto him: and if he stand to it, and say, I like not to take her; Then shall his brother's wife come in to him in the presence of the elders, and loose his shoe from his foot, and spit in his face, and shall answer and say, So shall it be done unto that man that will not build up his brother's house.

The punishment for refusing to practice the levirate used to be more severe than the above-quoted ritual. In Genesis, chapter 38, we read of Judah's son Onan and how he was killed by the Lord for refusing to impregnate his dead older brother's wife. The book of Ruth in the Old Testament is also an excellent example of how the levirate worked. It is an account of how Naomi has no more sons for her daughter-in-law Ruth to marry, so she arranges for another male relative, Boaz, to take on the responsibility.

Matchmaking. There are various ways in which two young people can be brought together. Typically, the parents of both boys and girls will work out the details among themselves and then announce it to their children. The initial go-between in Turkey has been the boy's mother, who would inspect possibilities at the public baths and then give reports to her son (Tober, 1984). The popular musical *Fiddler on the Roof* is about father-arranged marriages. Often, hired go-betweens, or matchmakers, assist in making the arrangement. They might act as intermediaries between the families or suggest potential spouses. Checking for astrological or other religious signs and requirements could also be part of their job.

In the 1800s, bachelor pioneers in the American West would sometimes find a wife by ordering one from a mail-order catalog. Even today, many Asian families publish matrimonial want ads in search of a respectable spouse for their child (Tober, 1984). I recently found the following in the classified section of a Philippine newspaper:

Foreigner: video match a decent friendship marriage consultant office introducing a beautiful single educated Filipina view friendship to marriage.

Ladies: Australian European businessmen newly arrive[d] in town sincerely willing to meet decent Filipina view friendship to marriage. Ambassador Hotel suite 216.

Computer dating services in the United States, Japan, and elsewhere manifest the continued utility of professional matchmaking, even in societies in which the individuals involved make the final decisions themselves. There are also magazines designed for singles that include matrimonial or relationship want ads.

There are immigrants to Western societies who are not comfortable with love-based unions and prefer to have their marriages arranged by their parents or through a mediator. It is estimated, for instance, that up to 90 percent of the marriages in the East Indian community in Edmonton, Alberta, are to some degree arranged (Jimenez, 1992). Some ethnic Indians return to the Indian subcontinent to find a spouse, whereas others allow their parents to find a match locally for them. Some place ads in newspapers such as *India Today* or *India Abroad*, which focus on desired background characteristics such as education, religion, and age. In deference to Western customs, the young people can veto any match that does not appeal to them, and a dowry is rarely accepted.

Free-Choice Mate Selection

. . . [L]ove gradually became the principal criterion for marriage in the Western world after the Renaissance. The shift from kinship and economic motives to personal ones in mate selection led to the conclusion that the individuals themselves, rather than their parents or others, were best qualified to make the decision. In societies in which the basic family unit is nuclear, both romantic love and free mate choice are more common. This is because extended kin groups are not important enough to see marriage as needing to be group controlled.

Even though free choice is the mate selection method of the modern United States, one should not conclude that it is the most common approach in the world. In a survey of forty societies, Stephens (1963) found only five in which completely free mate choice is permitted. An additional six allowed the young people to choose their spouse, but subject to parental approval. Twelve other cultures had a mix of arranged marriages and free-choice (usually subject to approval) unions, and the final sixteen allowed only arranged marriages.

Moreover, even free choice does not mean that one can marry anyone. All societies have marital regulations. The rule of *exogamy* declares that a person must marry outside his/her group. Typically, this means that certain relatives are unavailable as marriage partners. Exogamous rules are generally the same as the incest taboos of the society, which prohibit sexual intercourse between close blood relatives. Others go beyond that, however. In classical China, two people with the same surname could not marry even if there was no kinship relation (Hutter, 1981).

The rule of *endogamy* declares that a person must marry someone who is similar to oneself in important ways, including religion, race, or ethnic group; social class; and age. These factors have been found to be related to marital compatibility and are precisely the kinds of things considered by parents in arranged marriages. One reason why the divorce rate seems to be higher in free-choice societies may be that many couples ignore endogamy issues and allow romantic love to be practically the sole consideration in mate selection. There is a tendency for marriages to be fairly homogamous, however, even in free-mate-choice societies.

A final factor is *propinquity* (geographical nearness). It is, of course, impossible to marry someone who lives so far away from you that you never meet. At another level, however, this principle refers to a human tendency to be friends with people with whom it is convenient to interact. Let us say that you leave your hometown to attend college elsewhere. You left a boyfriend or girlfriend back at home and you also meet someone new at college. All other things being equal, which one will you marry? Generally, it will be the one at school simply because it is easier.

Some Examples. Free mate choice is on the rise in China today. However, it is very different from the courtship pattern in North America. Young people gather information about each other first and check for mutual suitability before going public with their relationship. In fact, dating follows, rather than precedes, the decision to marry. Typically, the couple knows each other for well over two years before marrying. This cautious approach is paying off, as the quality of these marriages seems to be higher than that of arranged unions (Liao & Heaton, 1992).

The Igbo are a people living in present-day Nigeria (Okonjo, 1992). About 55 percent of the Igbo have their marriages arranged, while the remaining 45 percent are in free-choice unions. Most of the latter are younger, indicating a move from arranged to free choice,

which we see occurring throughout much of the world today. Regardless of type, premarital chastity is very highly valued among the Igbo.

As the Igbo move to free mate choice based on love, their various arranged practices are falling into disfavor. Customs that are quickly disappearing include woman-to-woman marriage. In this situation, an older childless woman pays the brideprice to marry a younger female, usually a cousin. A male mate is chosen for the "wife" to have children with, but they belong to the older female spouse, who has the legal role of "husband."

Another way of securing an heir is father-to-daughter marriage. If a man has no sons, he may prohibit a daughter from marrying. She has children from a male mate (not the father) but her sons are considered her father's. Women whose husbands turn out to be impotent are allowed to have a lover from whom to have children, who are considered to be the legal husband's. Other arranged practices seldom practiced anymore are the levirate and child marriages.

CRITICAL THINKING QUESTIONS

1. What four major issues influence mate choice in societies where marriages are arranged? What societal functions do the specific mechanisms of arranged marriages (such as brideprice, dowry, sororate, levirate, and matchmaking) fulfill?

2. Does marriage by free choice mean that a person can really marry *anyone*? What factors (or rules) considerably narrow the field of eligible mates in societies with free-choice mate selection?

3. What are the advantages and disadvantages of marrying for love (in free-choice societies) rather than economic or political considerations (in societies with arranged marriages)? Would marriages in North America be less likely to end in divorce if marriages were arranged?

REFERENCES

Balswick, J. 1975. The function of the dowry system in a rapidly modernizing society: *The case of Cyprus*. *International Journal of Sociology and the Family*, 5(2): 158–67.

Billig, M. 1992. The marriage squeeze and the rise of groomprice in India's Karala state. *Journal of Comparative Family Studies*, 23(2): 197–216.

Fielding, W. 1942. *Strange customs of courtship and marriage*. New York: New Home Library.

The Holy Bible. King James Version.

Hutter, M. 1981. *The changing family: Comparative perspectives*. New York: Wiley.

Jimenez, M. 1992. Many Indo-Canadians follow age-old custom. *Edmonton Journal* (July 26): B3.

Liao, C., and T. Heaton. 1992. Divorce trends and differentials in China. *Journal of Comparative Family Studies*, 23(3): 413–29.

Okonjo, K. 1992. Aspects of continuity and change in mate selection among the Igbo west of the river Niger. *Journal of Comparative Family Studies*, 23(3): 339–60.

Peters, J. 1987. Yanomamö mate selection and marriage. *Journal of Comparative Family Studies*, 18(1): 79–98.

Stephens, W. 1963. *The family in cross-cultural perspective*. New York: Holt, Rinehart & Winston.

Tober, B. 1984. *The bride: A celebration*. New York: Harry N. Abrams.

47

The Protestant Ethic and the Spirit of Capitalism

MAX WEBER

In perhaps his most well-known treatise, Max Weber argues that a major factor in the development of the capitalist economic system was the distinctive world view of early, ascetic Protestantism, especially Calvinism and Puritanism. In this excerpt from his classic analysis, Weber explains that religious ideas about work and materials initially fostered capitalism's growth; ultimately, he concludes, capitalism was able to stand on its own without religious supports.

A product of modern European civilization, studying any problem of universal history, is bound to ask himself to what combination of circumstances the fact should be attributed that in Western civilization, and in Western civilization only, cultural phenomena have appeared which (as we like to think) lie in a line of development having *universal* significance and value. . . . All over the world there have been merchants, wholesale and retail, local and engaged in foreign trade. . . .

But in modern times the Occident has developed, in addition to this, a very different form of capitalism which has appeared nowhere else: the rational capitalistic organization of (formally) free labour. Only suggestions of it are found elsewhere. Even the organization of unfree labour reached a considerable degree

of rationality only on plantations and to a very limited extent in the *Ergasteria* of antiquity. In the manors, manorial workshops, and domestic industries on estates with serf labour it was probably somewhat less developed. Even real domestic industries with free labour have definitely been proved to have existed in only a few isolated cases outside the Occident. . . .

Rational industrial organization, attuned to a regular market, and neither to political nor irrationally speculative opportunities for profit, is not, however, the only peculiarity of Western capitalism. The modern rational organization of the capitalistic enterprise would not have been possible without two other important factors in its development: the separation of business from the household, which completely dominates modern economic life, and closely connected with it, rational bookkeeping. . . .

Hence in a universal history of culture the central problem for us is not, in the last analysis, even from a purely economic viewpoint, the development of capitalistic activity as such, differing in different cultures only in form: the adventurer type, or capitalism in trade, war, politics, or administration as sources of gain. It is rather the origin of this sober bourgeois capitalism with its rational organization of free labour. Or in terms of cultural history, the problem is that of the origin of the Western bourgeois class and of its peculiarities, a problem which is certainly closely connected with that of the origin of the capitalistic organization of labour, but is not quite the same thing. For the bourgeois as a class existed prior to the development of the peculiar modern form of capitalism, though, it is true, only in the Western Hemisphere.

Now the peculiar modern Western form of capitalism has been, at first sight, strongly influenced by the development of technical possibilities. Its rationality is today essentially dependent on the calculability of the most important technical factors. But this means fundamentally that it is dependent on the peculiarities of modern science, especially the natural sciences based on mathematics and exact and rational experiment. On the other hand, the development of these sciences and of the technique resting upon them now receives important stimulation from these capitalistic interests in its practical economic application. It is true that the origin of Western science cannot be attributed to such interests. Calculation, even with decimals, and algebra have been carried on in India, where the decimal system was invented. But it was only made use of by developing capitalism in the West, while in India it led to no modern arithmetic or bookkeeping. Neither was the origin of mathematics and mechanics determined by capitalistic interests. But the *technical* utilization of scientific knowledge, so important for the living conditions of the mass of people, was certainly encouraged by economic considerations, which were extremely favourable to it in the Occident.

But this encouragement was derived from the peculiarities of the social structure of the Occident. We must hence ask, from *what* parts of that structure was it derived, since not all of them have been of equal importance?

Among those of undoubted importance are the rational structures of law and of administration. For modern rational capitalism has need, not only of the technical means of production, but of a calculable legal system and of administration in terms of formal rules. Without it adventurous and speculative trading capitalism and all sorts of politically determined capitalisms are possible, but no rational enterprise under individual initiative, with fixed capital and certainty of calculations. Such a legal system and such administration have been available for economic activity in a comparative state of legal and formalistic perfection only in the Occident. We must hence inquire where that law came from. Among other circumstances, capitalistic interests have in turn undoubtedly also helped, but by no means alone nor even principally, to prepare the way for the predominance in law and administration of a class of jurists specially trained in rational law. But these interests did not themselves create that law. Quite different forces were at work in this development. And why did not the capitalistic interests do the same in China or India? Why did not the scientific, the artistic, the political, or the economic development there enter upon that path of rationalization which is peculiar to the Occident?

For in all the above cases it is a question of the specific and peculiar rationalism of Western culture. . . . It is hence our first concern to work out and to explain genetically the special peculiarity of Occidental rationalism, and within this field that of the modern Occidental form. Every such attempt at explanation must, recognizing the fundamental importance of the economic factor, above all take account of the economic conditions. But at the same time the opposite correlation must not be left out of consideration. For though the development of economic rationalism is partly dependent on rational technique and law, it is at the same time determined by the ability and disposition of men to adopt certain types of practical rational conduct. When these types have been obstructed by spiritual obstacles, the development of rational economic conduct has also met serious inner resistance. The magical and religious forces, and the ethical ideas of duty based upon them, have in the past always been among the most important formative influences on conduct. In the studies collected here we shall be concerned with these forces.

Two older essays have been placed at the beginning which attempt, at one important point, to approach the side of the problem which is generally most difficult to grasp: the influence of certain religious ideas on the development of an economic spirit, or the *ethos* of an economic system. In this case we are dealing with the connection of the spirit of modern economic life with the rational ethics of ascetic Protestantism. Thus we treat here only one side of the causal chain....

. . . [T]hat side of English Puritanism which was derived from Calvinism gives the most consistent religious basis for the idea of the calling. . . . For the saints' everlasting rest is in the next world; on earth man must, to be certain of his state of grace, "do the works of him who sent him, as long as it is yet day." Not leisure and enjoyment, but only activity serves to increase the glory of God according to the definite manifestations of His will.

Waste of time is thus the first and in principle the deadliest of sins. The span of human life is infinitely short and precious to make sure of one's own election. Loss of time through sociability, idle talk, luxury, even more sleep than is necessary for health, six to at most eight hours, is worthy of absolute moral condemnation. It does not yet hold, with [Benjamin] Franklin, that time is money, but the proposition is true in a certain spiritual sense. It is infinitely valuable because every hour lost is lost to labour for

the glory of God. Thus inactive contemplation is also valueless, or even directly reprehensible if it is at the expense of one's daily work. . . .

[T]he same prescription is given for all sexual temptation as is used against religious doubts and a sense of moral unworthiness: "Work hard in your calling." But the most important thing was that even beyond that labour came to be considered in itself the end of life, ordained as such by God. St. Paul's "He who will not work shall not eat" holds unconditionally for everyone. Unwillingness to work is symptomatic of the lack of grace.

Here the difference from the mediæval view-point becomes quite evident. Thomas Aquinas also gave an interpretation of that statement of St. Paul. But for him labour is only necessary *naturali ratione* for the maintenance of individual and community. Where this end is achieved, the precept ceases to have any meaning. Moreover, it holds only for the race, not for every individual. It does not apply to anyone who can live without labour on his possessions, and of course contemplation, as a spiritual form of action in the Kingdom of God, takes precedence over the commandment in its literal sense. Moreover, for the popular theology of the time, the highest form of monastic productivity lay in the increase of the *Thesaurus ecclesliæ* through prayer and chant.

. . . For everyone without exception God's Providence has prepared a calling, which he should profess and in which he should labour. And this calling is not, as it was for the Lutheran, a fate to which he must submit and which he must make the best of, but God's commandment to the individual to work for the divine glory. This seemingly subtle difference had far-reaching psychological consequences, and became connected with a further development of the providential interpretation of the economic order which had begun in scholasticism.

It is true that the usefulness of a calling, and thus its favour in the sight of God, is measured primarily in moral terms, and thus in terms of the importance of the goods produced in it for the community. But a further, and, above all, in practice the most important, criterion is found in private profitableness. For if that God, whose hand the Puritan sees in all the occurrences of life, shows one of His elect a chance of profit, he must do it with a purpose. Hence the faithful Christian must follow the call by taking advantage of the opportunity. "If God show you a way in which you may lawfully get more than in another way (without wrong to your soul or to any other), if you refuse this, and choose the less gainful way, you cross one of the ends of your calling, and you refuse to be God's steward, and to accept His gifts and use them for Him when He requireth it: you may labour to be rich for God, though not for the flesh and sin."

The superior indulgence of the *seigneur* and the parvenu ostentation of the *nouveau riche* are equally detestable to asceticism. But, on the other hand, it has the highest ethical appreciation of the sober, middle-class, self-made man. "God blesseth His trade" is a stock remark about those good men who had successfully followed the divine hints. The whole power of the God of the Old Testament, who rewards His people for their obedience in this life, necessarily exercised a similar influence on the Puritan who . . . compared his own state of grace with that of the heroes of the Bible. . . .

Although we cannot here enter upon a discussion of the influence of Puritanism in all . . . directions, we should call attention to the fact that the toleration of pleasure in cultural goods, which contributed to purely aesthetic or athletic enjoyment, certainly always ran up against one characteristic limitation: They must not cost anything. Man is only a trustee of the goods which have come to him through God's grace. He must, like the servant in the parable, give an account of every penny entrusted to him, and it is at least hazardous to spend any of it for a purpose which does not serve the glory of God but only one's own enjoyment. What person, who keeps his eyes open, has not met representatives

of this viewpoint even in the present? The idea of a man's duty to his possessions, to which he subordinates himself as an obedient steward, or even as an acquisitive machine, bears with chilling weight on his life. The greater the possessions the heavier, if the ascetic attitude toward life stands the test, the feeling of responsibility for them, for holding them undiminished for the glory of God and increasing them by restless effort. The origin of this type of life also extends in certain roots, like so many aspects of the spirit of capitalism, back into the Middle Ages. But it was in the ethic of ascetic Protestantism that it first found a consistent ethical foundation. Its significance for the development of capitalism is obvious.

This worldly Protestant asceticism, as we may recapitulate up to this point, acted powerfully against the spontaneous enjoyment of possessions; it restricted consumption, especially of luxuries. On the other hand, it had the psychological effect of freeing the acquisition of goods from the inhibitions of traditionalistic ethics. It broke the bonds of the impulse of acquisition in that it not only legalized it, but (in the sense discussed) looked upon it as directly willed by God. . . .

As far as the influence of the Puritan outlook extended, under all circumstances—and this is, of course, much more important than the mere encouragement of capital accumulation—it favoured the development of a rational bourgeois economic life; it was the most important, and above all the only consistent influence in the development of that life. It stood at the cradle of the modern economic man.

To be sure, these Puritanical ideals tended to give way under excessive pressure from the temptations of wealth, as the Puritans themselves knew very well. With great regularity we find the most genuine adherents of Puritanism among the classes which were rising from a lowly status, the small bourgeois and farmers, while the *beati possidentes*, even among Quakers, are often found tending to repudiate the old ideals. It was the same fate which again and again befell the predecessor of this worldly asceticism, the monastic asceticism of the Middle Ages. In the latter case, when rational economic activity had worked out its full effects by strict regulation of conduct and limitation of consumption, the wealth accumulated either succumbed directly to the nobility, as in the time before the Reformation, or monastic discipline threatened to break down, and one of the numerous reformations became necessary.

In fact the whole history of monasticism is in a certain sense the history of a continual struggle with the problem of the secularizing influence of wealth. The same is true on a grand scale of the worldly asceticism of Puritanism. The great revival of Methodism, which preceded the expansion of English industry toward the end of the eighteenth century, may well be compared with such a monastic reform. We may hence quote here a passage from John Wesley himself which might well serve as a motto for everything which has been said above. For it shows that the leaders of these ascetic movements understood the seemingly paradoxical relationships which we have here analysed perfectly well, and in the same sense that we have given them. He wrote:

I fear, wherever riches have increased, the essence of religion has decreased in the same proportion. Therefore I do not see how it is possible, in the nature of things, for any revival of true religion to continue long. For religion must necessarily produce both industry and frugality, and these cannot but produce riches. But as riches increase, so will pride, anger, and love of the world in all its branches. How then is it possible that Methodism, that is, a religion of the heart, though it flourishes now as a green bay tree, should continue in this state? For the Methodists in every place grow diligent and frugal; consequently they increase in goods. Hence they proportionately increase in pride, in anger, in the desire of the flesh, the desire of the eyes, and the pride of life. So, although the form of religion remains, the spirit is swiftly vanishing away. Is there no way to prevent this—this continual decay of pure religion? We ought not to prevent people from being diligent and frugal; *we must exhort all Christians to gain all they can, and to save all they can; that is, in effect, to grow rich.*

As Wesley here says, the full economic effect of those great religious movements, whose significance for economic development lay above all in their ascetic educative influence, generally came only after the peak of the purely religious enthusiasm was past. Then the intensity of the search for the Kingdom of God commenced gradually to pass over into sober economic virtue; the religious roots died out slowly, giving way to utilitarian worldliness. Then, as Dowden puts it, as in *Robinson Crusoe*, the isolated economic man who carries on missionary activities on the side takes the place of the lonely spiritual search for the Kingdom of Heaven of Bunyan's pilgrim, hurrying through the marketplace of Vanity. . . .

A specifically bourgeois economic ethic had grown up. With the consciousness of standing in the fullness of God's grace and being visibly blessed by Him, the bourgeois business man, as long as he remained within the bounds of formal correctness, as long as his moral conduct was spotless and the use to which he put his wealth was not objectionable, could follow his pecuniary interests as he would and feel that he was fulfilling a duty in doing so. The power of religious asceticism provided him in addition with sober, conscientious, and unusually industrious workmen, who clung to their work as to a life purpose willed by God.

Finally, it gave him the comforting assurance that the unequal distribution of the goods of this world was a special dispensation of Divine Providence, which in these differences, as in particular grace, pursued secret ends unknown to men. . . .

One of the fundamental elements of the spirit of modern capitalism, and not only of that but of all modern culture: Rational conduct on the basis of the idea of the calling, was born—that is what this discussion has sought to demonstrate—from the spirit of Christian asceticism. . . . [T]he essential elements of the attitude which [Franklin] called the spirit of capitalism are the same as what we have just shown to be the content of the Puritan worldly asceticism, only without the religious basis, which by Franklin's time had died away. ....

Since asceticism undertook to remodel the world and to work out its ideals in the world, material goods have gained an increasing and finally an inexorable power over the lives of men as at no previous period in history. Today the spirit of religious asceticism—whether finally, who knows?—has escaped from the cage. But victorious capitalism, since it rests on mechanical foundations, needs its support no longer. The rosy blush of its laughing heir, the Enlightenment, seems also to be irretrievably fading, and the idea of duty in one's calling prowls about in our lives like the ghost of dead religious beliefs. Where the fulfilment of the calling cannot directly be related to the highest spiritual and cultural values, or when, on the other hand, it need not be felt simply as economic compulsion, the individual generally abandons the attempt to justify it at all. In the field of its highest development, in the United States, the pursuit of wealth, stripped of its religious and ethical meaning, tends to become associated with purely mundane passions, which often actually give it the character of sport.

No one knows who will live in this cage in the future, or whether at the end of this tremendous development entirely new prophets will arise, or there will be a great rebirth of old ideas and ideals, or, if neither, mechanized petrification, embellished with a sort of convulsive self-importance. For of the last stage of this cultural development, it might well be truly said: "Specialists without spirit, sensualists without heart; this nullity imagines that it has attained a level of civilization never before achieved."

But this brings us to the world of judgments of value and of faith, with which this purely historical discussion need not be burdened. ...

Here we have only attempted to trace the fact and the direction of its influence to their motives in one, though a very important point. But it would also further be necessary to investigate how Protestant Asceticism was in turn influenced in its development and its character by the totality of social conditions, especially economic. The modern man is in general, even with the best will, unable to give religious ideas a significance for culture and national character which they deserve. But it is, of course, not my aim to substitute for a one-sided materialistic an equally one-sided spiritualistic causal interpretation of culture and of history. Each is equally possible, but each, if it does not serve as the preparation, but as the conclusion of an investigation, accomplishes equally little in the interest of historical truth.

CRITICAL THINKING QUESTIONS

1. What are the distinctive characteristics of the religious orientation that Weber called the "Protestant ethic"? In what ways did they promote the development of the capitalist economic system?

2. In what respects do early Calvinists with a sense of "calling" differ from today's "workaholics"?

3. In what sense does Weber's analysis differ from the materialist orientation of Karl Marx (Reading 38), who suggested that productive forces shape the world of ideas?

48

Canada's Mythical Religious Mosaic: Some Census Findings

REGINALD W. BIBBY

Many Canadians, Bibby finds, believe that since Canada is a multicultural society, it must also feature considerable religious diversity. However, national census data suggest that Canada's "religious mosaic" is largely a myth. Bibby's research reveals that Christianity continues to enjoy a significant numerical majority in Canada, and that new religions are finding it difficult to attract new members. In fact, he suggests that Canada is characterized by an extremely narrow spectrum of religious diversity that is dominated by Catholic and Protestant "companies."

Canada historically has been a country of immigrants. Similar to the United States, much of its early population growth from the seventeenth century onward was due to the arrival of people from France and England, and increasingly from around the world. Since the 1960s, there has been a shift in the dominant origins of immigrants, with a majority now coming from Asia and other Third World countries, rather than Europe.

In the face of such cultural group diversity, Canada has taken pride in defining itself as a mosaic, a "community of communities." Such a self-definition is more than mere rhetoric. In 1971, the federal government unveiled its official policy of multiculturalism, complete with an array of programs aimed at enabling citizens of all backgrounds to participate fully in Canadian

life, and to perpetuate their national cultures to the extent they so desired. In 1988, these twin ideals were enshrined in the *Multiculturalism Act* that states the Canadian government is committed to a policy "designed to preserve and enhance the multicultural heritage of Canadians while working to achieve the equality of all Canadians."

A widely held assumption is that the cultural diversity of Canadians is translating into increasing religious diversity, as people arriving from other countries bring with them an array of different religions. Data from Canada's latest national census calls such an assumption into question.

The statistical gathering body of the Canadian government, known as *Statistics Canada*, carries out a major national census in the second year of each new decade that includes the item "What is your religion?" The question has been asked dating back to the first national census in 1871. Select runs of the 1991 census data that

Source: R. W. Bibby. 2000. "Canada's Mythical Religious Mosaic: Some Census Findings." *Journal for the Scientific Study of Religion*, 39(2), 235–39.

shed some important light on religious identification patterns among culturally diverse Canadians were made available to the author in 1996. What follows is a brief summary of key findings relating to religious identification and some of its key family- and cultural-group correlates.

RELIGIOUS IDENTIFICATION

The 1991 census found that 88% of Canadians continue to "think" that they are Catholic (46%), Protestant (36%), or adherents of Other Faiths (6%). An examination of religious identification over time shows that the proportion of the population who regard themselves as Catholics has remained fairly constant over time, while the proportion who identify themselves as Protestants has declined. The overall "Christian" total, including Eastern Orthodox, was 98% in 1871, 96% in 1931, and 84% in 1991. The remaining 16% of the populace consists primarily of those who report they have no religion (12%); this category only became a methodological possibility in 1971 through the introduction of self-enumeration. Over time, the Jewish total has remained a constant 1%, while those identifying with Other Faiths (including, in Statistics Canada's classification scheme, atheists and agnostics) has increased only marginally, from 2% to 3%.

THE ROLE OF THE FAMILY IN TRANSMITTING RELIGIOUS IDENTIFICATION

The key source of religious identification continues to be parents. People who marry partners of the same faith are inclined to pass that faith on to their children—reporting in the census that their children have the same religious identification as they do. This intergenerational pattern also holds in the case of cohabitation, as well as for the offspring of both female and male lone parents. It also is equally true in situations where parents do not identify with any religion.

Where there are exceptions to the rule, parents usually indicate that their children see themselves as having no religion. However, in the Other Faith and No Religion parental instances, some "switching" of offspring to Catholicism or Protestantism is acknowledged—2% to 4% by Other Faith and No Religion couples and, among lone parent "nones," 6% by females and 12% by males.

To the extent that identification changes, a key variable appears to be intermarriage and "intercohabitation." Catholics in particular, along with Protestants, tend to be the big winners numerically when relationships cross religious lines, while the "No Religion" category and other religious groups tend to experience significant net losses. The reasons are fairly straightforward. When people of different religions marry or cohabit, the religion of women predominates, even in the case of women who have no religious preference. Women in such relationships tend to raise their children in their own tradition, and are matched only by men when Catholic men marry Protestant women. A very important singular exception to this pattern is when women with Other Faith preferences intermarry: in such cases, they—along with Other Faith men—are inclined to raise their children in *their partner's* tradition.

The most numerous intermarriage and "intercohabitation" arrangements involve Catholic and Protestant women, who in effect "recruit" large numbers of offspring at the expense of the "No Religion" and Other Faith categories. These gains offset the frequent losses that occur when Catholic and Protestant men become involved with women who have no religious preference. Yet Catholic and Protestant men typically "add" offspring when they marry or cohabit with women who identify with other world faiths.

CULTURAL GROUP AFFINITIES

As a result of such intermarriage patterns, Christianity continues to be overwhelmingly dominant in Canada. Despite the stimulus of immigration,

TABLE 48.1 Religious Identification of Canadians, 1871–1991

	1871	1901	1931	1961	1991
Identification					
Catholic	42%	42	41	47	46
Protestant	56	56	54	49	36
Eastern Orthodox	<1	<1	1	1	2
Jewish	<1	<1	1	1	1
Other Faiths	2	2	2	1	3
No Religion	<1	<1	<1	<1	12

other major world religions are having considerable difficulty making significant numerical inroads in Canada.

The 1991 census reveals that some 65 to 75% of the affiliates of Islam, Buddhism, Hinduism, and Sikhism are immigrants, compared to about 13% in the case of both Catholics and Protestants. The census further shows that less than 2% of Canadians of British, French, German, and Italian origins *combined* are identifying with religions other than Christianity. Individuals who are identifying with Islam, Buddhism, Hinduism, and Sikhism are primarily people with Middle East and Asian cultural roots. Affiliates with European backgrounds do not exceed 3% in any of these faith instances.

In order to sustain their numbers and grow, faith groups such as these have to be able to replace their aging immigrants with offspring (birth) and resident Canadians (proselytism). To date there is little indication that such demographic developments are occurring in the numbers required.

Asian includes Middle East, South Asian, East Asian; European includes British, French, and other Western European.

For a complete listing of affiliation figures for all religious groups, broken down by province, gender, age, education, ethnicity, and language, see Statistics Canada, *Religions in Canada*, Ottawa: Science and Technology Canada, 1993. 1991 Census of Canada, Catalogue Number 93-319.

Smaller religions in the "Other Faith" category are faring even worse. For all the media hype about disenchanted and disaffiliated Canadians turning to a wide range of religious options in the last half of this century—what sociologists dub "new religions" or "para-religious groups"—the census reveals that relatively few people are actually identifying with the available alternatives. In a nation of close to 30 million people, less than 5,000 individuals are identifying with religions including New Age, Scientology, and Theosophy. Such data suggest that Canada has an extremely tight "religious market" dominated

TABLE 48.2 Religious Identification of Children* by Parental Identification and Marital Status

Parental Identification	Married Partner Same	Common-Law Partner Same	Female Lone Parent	Male Lone Parent
Catholic	99%	95	93	94
Protestant	95	87	87	85
Eastern Orthodox	98	98	82	85
Jewish	99	97	95	88
Other Faiths	94	89	86	57
No Religion	98	97	94	88

*As reported by parents for children living at home.

TABLE 48.3 Religious Identification of Children by Religious Identification of Mothers and Fathers

Religion of Mother/Father	No. of Couples	Religion of Children						Totals**
		Catholic	Protestant	Eastern Orthodox	Jewish	Other Faiths	No Religion	
Catholic/Protestant	259,130	70%	11	*	*	*	9	100
Protestant/Catholic	254,105	42	44	*	*	*	14	100
Catholic/East Orthodox	12,735	54	1	39	*	*	6	100
East Orthodox/Catholic	8,625	62	4	28	*	*	7	101
Catholic/Jewish	3,070	38	2	*	25	*	35	100
Jewish/Catholic	2,055	28	1	1	45	*	25	100
Catholic/Other Faiths	7,600	57	1	*	*	21	20	99
Other Faiths/Catholic	3,195	58	4	*	*	12	26	100
Catholic/No Religion	82,745	67	3	*	*	*	30	100
No Religion/Catholic	35,050	40	3	*	*	*	57	100
Protestant/East Orthodox	10,300	2	55	29	*	*	14	100
East Orthodox/Protestant	6,595	4	47	36	*	*	13	101
Protestant/Jewish	3,555	2	38	*	26	*	34	100
Jewish/Protestant	2,520	1	23	*	52	*	24	100
Protestant/Other Faiths	5,735	1	45	*	*	26	28	100
Other Faiths/Protestant	3,220	2	42	*	*	26	29	99
Protestant/No Religion	126,935	1	58	*	*	*	41	100
No Religion/Protestant	35,115	2	27	*	*	*	71	100
Other Faiths/No Religion	4,415	3	5	*	*	22	70	100
No Religion/Jewish	1,225	2	6	*	29	*	62	99
No Religion/Other faiths	2,365	5	4	*	*	22	70	101

*Less than 1%.
**Because of rounding on the part of Statistics Canada, some totals do not equal 100.

by Catholic and Protestant "companies." New entries find the going extremely tough.

DISCUSSION

The net result of these patterns of socialization and switching is that the vast majority of Canadians are continuing to identify with the numerically dominant Christian groups. Demographically at 82% strong, Catholics and Protestants have a large numerical advantage over other religious groups when it comes to issues of cultural maintenance and intermarriage. Even with a national policy of multiculturalism, smaller cultural and religious groups find themselves absorbing many parts of the dominant ways of life in this country. In the case of socialization and marriage, groups whose members typically comprise less than 1% of the national population usually find that their

children befriend, date, and frequently marry people from other cultural and religious groups. Apparent gains through increased immigration are neutralized by assimilation.

Numerically dominant Catholics and Protestants who marry and live with people of other religious persuasions tend to experience net gains when it comes to the religious identification of offspring. It needs to be emphasized that the key issue is not whether or not the partner "converts" to the other's faith; what is more important, numerically speaking, is how the children are raised. And here the patterns are fairly clear: the religion of the woman dominates. Given the large Catholic and Protestant numbers, the end result is that the population tends to gravitate toward Catholic and Protestant identifications.

This pattern is particularly evident when Catholics and Protestants marry people of Other Faiths, excluding Judaism. Regardless of whether the Other Faith partner is female or male, the

TABLE 48.4   Cultural Group Origins of Affiliates of Select World Religions

| Cultural Group Origin* | World Religions | | | | |
	Islam	Buddhist	Hindu	Sikh	Totals
Total - Single Origin	90%	93	90	94	91
Asian Regions	75	89	77	91	81
European	3	3	2	2	3
Other Countries	12	1	11	1	7
Total - Multiple Origins	10	7	10	6	9
Grand Total	100	100	100	100	100

*The census differentiates between "single origin" where only one national group heritage is cited, versus more than one.

inclination is for the ensuing offspring to be raised as Catholics or Protestants—or No Religion. Put bluntly, most smaller groups are losing many of their children and grandchildren to the Catholic and Protestant traditions. Alternately, they do not affiliate with any group.

It's true that there has been an increase in recent decades in the number of people arriving from countries where other world faiths are dominant. It also is true that widespread secularization has led to a decline in individual participation and organizational influence. Nonetheless, the vast majority of Canadians in the 90s continue to "think" they are Catholic or Protestant, and "think" that they are raising "Catholic" and "Protestant" children. Other world religions are having difficulty growing, due to both the tendency of their children to "defect" to Christian groups and their inability to recruit "outsiders." Even the Religion Nones are showing a net loss to the "somethings" when intermarriage and intercohabitation occur—if not immediately, then intergenerationally.

Secularization may have drastically reduced the influence that Catholic and Protestant groups have in Canada. But tradition and assimilation appear to function to keep identification with Christianity at a very high level. From the standpoint of numbers, the heralded emerging religious mosaic, so far at least, is largely a myth.

CRITICAL THINKING QUESTIONS

1. Given that Canadian law, as embodied in the *Multiculturalism Act* (1988), confirms the national support for cultural diversity, were you surprised to find out that Christian faiths continue to enjoy such a monopoly? As a sociologist, how would you explain such stability in religious faith over time?

2. With reference to the article, what influences do *intermarriage* and *intercohabitation* have on parents' decisions regarding the religious tradition in which to raise their children?

3. Bibby suggests that although secularization is diminishing the influence of religion in people's lives, religion is still identified as an important element by many of today's families. Do you see the influence of religion increasing or decreasing over the next hundred years? Why?

49

CLASSIC

CONTEMPORARY

CROSS-CULTURAL

Women and Islam

JANE I. SMITH

Many Westerners have a vague notion that women in Iran, Saudi Arabia, and other Islamic societies are subject to relentless control by men. Although there is some truth to this stereotype, a more realistic account of the relationship between Islam and gender must begin with a basic understanding of this unfamiliar religion. In this article, Jane Smith provides an overview of Islamic tenets, explores some of the variations that divide the vast Islamic world, and assesses the relative social standing of the sexes—as Muslims themselves understand it.

To attempt to talk about women in Islam is of course to venture into an area fraught with the perils of overgeneralization, oversimplification, and the almost unavoidable limitations of a Western bias. The first problem is simply one of raw numbers. There are perhaps close to half a billion Muslim women inhabiting all major areas of the world today. Is it possible to say anything that holds true for all of them, let alone for their sisters over the past fourteen centuries of Islam?

Then one must consider all the various elements that comprise the picture of Islamic womanhood. Many of these elements are directly related to the religion of Islam itself, such as past and present legal realities, roles permitted and enforced as a result of Muslim images

of women, and the variety of Islamic and hetero-Islamic rites and practices in which Islamic women have traditionally participated. Other elements contributing to the full picture of women in Islam—such as education, political rights, professional employment opportunities, and the like—have less to do with the religion per se but are still influenced by it.

The Holy Qur'ān (sometimes transliterated as "Koran") still forms the basis of prevailing family law in most areas of the Muslim world. It has always been and still is considered to be the last in a series of divine revelations from God given in the seventh century C.E. to humanity through the vehicle of his final prophet Muhammad. The Qur'ān is therefore the literal and unmitigated word of God, collected and ordered by the young Muslim community but untainted with the thoughts and interpretations of any persons, including Muhammad himself. It is obvious, then, why the regulations

Source: Reprinted by permission from *Women in World Religions* by Arvind Sharma (ed.), the State University of New York Press © 1987, State University of New York. All rights reserved.

formulated by the Qur'ān in regard to women have been adhered to with strictness and why changes in Muslim family law are coming about only very slowly in the Islamic world.

The circumstances of women in pre-Islamic Arabia are subject to a variety of interpretations. On the one hand, certain women—soothsayers, priestesses, queens, and even singular individuals—did play powerful roles in society. On the other hand, whatever the earlier realities for women in terms of marriage, divorce, and inheritance of property, it is clear that the Qur'ān did introduce very significant changes that were advantageous for women. Contemporary Muslims are fond of pointing out, quite correctly, that Islam brought legal advantages for women quite unknown in corresponding areas of the Western Christian world. What, then, does the Qur'ān say about women?

The earliest messages of the Qur'ān, and the twin themes that run through all the chapters, are of the realities of the oneness of God and the inevitability of the day of judgment. All persons, men and women, are called upon to testify to those realities. . . . Religiously speaking, then, men and women are fully equal in the eyes of God according to the Qur'ān.

Before looking at the specifics of the legal injunctions for women, it is necessary to consider two verses that have caused a great deal of consternation to Westerners. One is 2:228, which says literally that men are a step above women, and the other is 4:34, clarifying that men are the protectors of women (or are in charge of women) because God has given preference to one over the other and because men provide support for women. Perhaps because these verses have been so troublesome for non-Muslims (especially feminists), they have been subject to an enormous amount of explanation and interpretation by contemporary Muslim apologists eager to present a defense of their religion. These writers, men and women, affirm that it is precisely because men are invested with the responsibility of taking care of women, financially and otherwise, that they are

given authority over the females of their families. And that, affirm many Muslim women today, is exactly the way it should be. We will return to this perspective later, particularly in light of what a desire for liberation means—and does not mean—for many Muslim women. . . .

According to the Qur'ān, a man may marry up to four wives, so long as he is able to provide for each equally. He may marry a Muslim woman or a member of the Jewish or Christian faith, or a slave woman. A Muslim woman, however, may marry only one husband, and he must be a Muslim. Contemporary Muslim apologists are quick to point out that these restrictions are for the benefit of women, ensuring that they will not be left unprotected. In Islam, marriage is not a sacrament but a legal contract, and according to the Qur'ān a woman has clearly defined legal rights in negotiating this contract. She can dictate the terms and can receive the dowry herself. This dowry (*mahr*) she is permitted to keep and maintain as a source of personal pride and comfort.

Polygamy (or more strictly polygyny, plurality of wives) is practiced by only a small percentage of the contemporary Muslim population, and a man with more than two wives is extremely rare. Many countries are now taking steps to modify the circumstances in which a husband may take more than one wife, although only in two countries, Turkey and Tunisia, are multiple marriages actually illegal. Other countries have made such moves as requiring the husband to have the permission of the court (as in Iraq and Syria) or to get the permission of the first wife (as in Egypt), or permitting the wife to write into her marriage contract that she will not allow a cowife (as in Morocco and Lebanon). It seems reasonable to expect that other countries will make changes and modifications. It is interesting to note that while for some finances have dictated monogamy—most husbands have simply not been able to afford more than one wife—changing economic realities may again dictate that a man contemplate the possibility of having several wives to work and supply income for the family.

Muslim women traditionally have been married at an extremely young age, sometimes even before puberty. This practice is related, of course, to the historical fact that fathers and other male relatives generally have chosen the grooms themselves, despite the guarantee of the Qur'ān that marriage is a contract into which male and female enter equally. While it is true that technically a girl cannot be forced into a marriage she does not want, pressures from family and the youth of the bride often have made this prerogative difficult to exercise. Today, the right of a male member of the family to contract an engagement for a girl against her wishes has been legally revoked in most places, although it is still a common practice, especially in rural areas. . . .

In the contemporary Islamic world, divorce rates vary considerably from one country to the next. Muslim apologists insist that divorce is not nearly as common in Islamic countries as it is, for example, in the United States. This statement is generally true, although in some countries, such as Morocco, the rate is high and continues to grow. Often what is really only the breaking of the engagement contract is included in divorce statistics, skewing the measure. Many countries are now considering serious changes in divorce procedures. The simultaneous triple repudiation generally has been declared illegal, and in many countries divorce initiated by either party, the man or the woman, must take place in the court of law. Other countries add special stipulations generally favorable to the woman. It remains true, however, that men can divorce for less cause than women, and often divorces hung up in courts with male judges can prove enormously difficult for women to gain.

In accordance with Islamic law, custody of the children traditionally has gone to the father at some time between the age of seven and nine for boys and between seven and puberty for girls, depending on the legal school. This practice too is slowly changing, and in most areas women who have been divorced by their husbands are allowed to keep their sons until puberty and their daughters until they are of an age to be married.

It is considered one of the great innovations of the Qur'ān over earlier practices that women are permitted to inherit and own property. Non-Muslims have generally found great difficulty with the Qur'ānic stipulation that a woman is allowed to inherit property but that the inheritance should be only half that of a male. According to the Islamic understanding, however, the rationale is precisely that which applies to the verse saying that men are in charge of women. Because women are permitted to keep and maintain their own property without responsibility for taking care of their families financially, it is only reasonable that the male, who must spend his own earning and inheritance for the maintenance of women, should receive twice as much. . . .

According to the Qur'ān, women should not expose themselves to public view with lack of modesty. It does not say that they should be covered specifically from head to toe, nor that they should wear face veils or masks or other of the paraphernalia that has adorned many Islamic women through the ages. The Qur'ān also suggests that the wives of the Prophet Muhammad, when speaking to other men, should do so from behind a partition, again for purposes of propriety. It has been open to question whether this statement is meant to apply to all women. In the early Islamic community, these verses were exaggerated and their underlying ideas elaborated and defined in ways that led fairly quickly to a seclusion of women which seems quite at odds with what the Qur'ān intended or the Prophet wanted. When the community in Medina was established, women participated fully with men in all activities of worship and prayer. Soon they became segregated, however, to the point where an often-quoted *hadith* (no doubt spurious) attributed to Muhammad has him saying that women pray better at home than in the mosque, and best of all in their own closets. Today a number of contemporary Muslim writers are urging a return to the practices of the young Muslim community, with women no longer segregated from the mosque or relegated to certain rear or side portions as they generally have been, but participating fully in worship with men. . . .

What is popularly known as "veiling" is part of the general phenomenon of the segregation of women and yet is also distinctly apart from it. The two are increasingly seen as separate by contemporary Islamic women seeking to affirm a new identity in relation to their religion. Veils traditionally have taken a number of forms: a veil covering the face from just below the eyes down; a *chador* or *burka* covering the entire body, including the face, often with a woven screen in front through which women can see but not be seen; and a full face mask with small slits through the eyes, still worn in some areas of the Arabian Gulf. These costumes, so seemingly oppressive to Western eyes, at least have allowed women to observe without being observed, thus affording their wearers a degree of anonymity that on some occasions has proven useful.

The general movement toward unveiling had its ostensible beginning in the mid-1920s, when the Egyptian feminist Huda Sha'rawi cast off her veil after arriving in Egypt from an international meeting of women. She was followed literally and symbolically by masses of women in the succeeding years, and Egyptian women as well as those in other Middle Eastern countries made great strides in adopting Western dress. At the present time in the history of Islam, however, one finds a quite different phenomenon. Partly in reaction against Western liberation and Western ideals in general, women in many parts of the Islamic world are self-consciously adopting forms of dress by which they can identify with Islam rather than with what they now see as the imperialist West. Islamic dress, generally chosen by Muslim women themselves rather than forced upon

them by males, signals for many an identification with a way of life that they are increasingly convinced represents a more viable alternative than that offered by the West. . . .

We see, then, that while legal circumstances for women have undergone some significant changes in the past half-century, the dictates of the Qur'ān continue to be enormously influential in the molding of new laws as well as in the personal choices of Muslim men and women. . . .

I have stressed here the insistence of the Qur'ān on the religious and spiritual equality of men and women. And aside from some unfortunate *hadith* with very weak chains of authority suggesting that the majority of women will be in the Fire on the Day of Judgment because of their mental and physical inferiority, religious literature in general, when talking about human responsibility and concomitant judgment, makes women full partners with men under the divine command to live lives of integrity and righteousness. . . .

Of course, women do participate in many of the activities and duties considered incumbent on all good Muslims, but generally these practices have a somewhat different function for them than for men. Prayer for women, as we have said, is usually in the home rather than in the mosque, and does not necessarily follow the pattern of the regularized five times a day. Participation in the fast itself is normally the same as for the men (except when women are pregnant, nursing, or menstruating), but the particular joys of preparing the fast-breaking meals are for the women alone. While the husband determines the amount of money or goods to be distributed for almsgiving, another responsibility of all Muslims, it is often the wife who takes charge of the actual distribution.

The last duty incumbent on Muslims after the testimony to the oneness of God and prophethood of his apostle Muhammad, the prayer, the fast, and paying the almstax is the pilgrimage once in a lifetime to the holy city of Mecca. Women do participate in this journey, and as transportation becomes easier and the care provided for pilgrims in Saudi Arabia becomes more regularized with modernization, increasing numbers of females join the throngs which gather to circumambulate the Xaaba at Mecca each year. . . .

Saints in Islam are both male and female. One is normally recognized as a saint not by any process of canonization but because of some miraculous deed(s) performed or through a dream communication after death with a living person requesting that a shrine be erected over his or her tomb. Often a woman is favored with these dreams and after the construction of the shrine she becomes the carekeeper of the tomb, a position of some honor and responsibility. . . .

While women in the Islamic world have been segregated and secluded, and historically have been considered second-class citizens by the vast majority of males in the community, they have not been totally without power. They have been able to maintain a degree of control over their own lives and over the men with whom they live through many of the religious practices described above. The fact that they alone have the ability to bear children, the influence they continue to play in the lives of their sons, and the power they have over their sons' wives are subtle indications that there are certain checks and balances on the obvious authority invested by the Qur'ān in men. From sexuality to control of the network of communications in the family to manipulation of such external agencies as spirits and supernatural beings, women have had at their control a variety of means to exert their will over the men in their families and over their own circumstances. The subtle means of control available to women throughout the world have of course been exploited: withholding sexual favors (a questionable but often-quoted *hadith* says that if a woman refuses to sleep with her husband, the angels will curse her until the morning), doing small things to undermine a husband's honor such as embarrassing him in front of guests, indulging in various forms of gossip and social control, and the like. . . .

Until fairly recently, education for women in the Muslim world has been minimal. Girls were given the rudiments of an Islamic education, mainly a little instruction in the Qur'ān and the traditions so as to be able to recite their prayers properly. Beyond that their training was not academic but domestic. In the late nineteenth and early twentieth centuries, Islamic leaders awoke with a start to the reality that Muslims were significantly behind the West in a variety of ways, including technology and the education necessary to understand and develop it. Many of these leaders recognized that if Islamic nations were to compete successfully in the contemporary world, it had to be with the aid of a well-educated and responsible female sector. Thus, this century has seen a number of educational advances for women, and in some countries, such as Egypt, Iraq, and Kuwait, women constitute very significant numbers of the university population. Nonetheless, illiteracy in many Muslim nations continues to be high, and the gap between male and female literacy rates is even increasing in some areas. In Saudi Arabia, where at present the economic resources are certainly available, large numbers of Saudi girls are receiving a full education, though separated from boys, and are taught either by men through television transmission or by women.

In education as in most areas of life, the male understanding of women as encouraged by certain parts of the Islamic tradition continues to play an important role. The Qur'ān does state, along with the stipulation that women can inherit only half of what men inherit, that the witness (in the court of law) of one man is equal to that of two women. This unfortunately has been interpreted by some in the history of Islam to mean that women are intellectually inferior to men, unstable in their judgment, and too easily swayed by emotion. Such perspectives are certainly not shared by all but nonetheless have been influential (and in some places are increasingly so today) in making it difficult for a woman to have access to the same kinds of educational opportunities that are available to men. Certain subjects are deemed "appropriate" for a woman to study, particularly those geared to make her the best and most productive wife, mother, and female participant in the family structure.

The prevalent view, confirmed by the Qur'ān, is that women should be modest and should neither expose themselves to men nor be too much in public places, where they will be subject to men's observation or forced to interact with males not in their immediate families. This view obviously has contributed to the difficulties of receiving a full education and of securing employment outside the home. More employment opportunities are open to women today than in the past, however, and in many countries women hold high-level positions in business, government, civil service, education, and other sectors. Statistics differ greatly across the Islamic world and are difficult to assess because they often fail to take into account the rural woman who may work full time in the fields or other occupation outside the house but does not earn an independent salary. . . .

Saudi Arabia presents an interesting case study of the confrontation of Islamic ideas with contemporary reality. Women are greatly inhibited in the labor arena; because of conservative religious attitudes they must be veiled and covered, are not permitted to drive or even ride in a taxi with a strange man, and in general are unable to participate on the social and professional level with males. However, in a country in which production is both necessary and economically possible and which suffers from a lack of manpower, the use of women in the workforce or increased importation of foreign labor seem the only two (both undesirable) alternatives. Thus more Saudi women are working, and because of their right to inherit, are accumulating very substantial amounts of money. It is interesting to note the rapid rate

of construction of new banks exclusively for women in places like Jiddah and Riyadh.

The aforementioned Qur'ān verse about the witness of two women being equal to that of one man and the supporting literature attesting to female intellectual, physical (and in fact sometimes moral) inferiority have made it difficult for Muslim women to achieve equal political rights. In most Arab countries (except Saudi Arabia and certain of the Gulf States), as well as in most other parts of the Islamic world, women have now been given the vote. Centuries of passivity in the political realm, however, have made it difficult for women to take advantage of the opportunities now available to them. In some countries, such as Egypt, women are playing major political roles, but generally women politicians find little support from men or even from other women for their aspirations. This is not to underestimate the strong current in Islamic thinking which encourages the full participation of women in politics, as well as in the educational and professional fields.

Like an intricate and complex geometric pattern on a Persian rug or a frieze decorating a mosque, the practices, roles, opportunities, prescriptions, hopes, and frustrations of Islamic women are woven together in a whole. The colors are sometimes bold and striking, at other times muted and subtle. Some contemporary Muslim women are progressive and aggressive, no longer content to fit the traditionally prescribed patterns. Others are passive and accepting, not yet able to discern what new possibilities may be open to them, let alone whether or not they might want to take advantage of such opportunities. Some are Westernized as their mothers and grandmothers were and have every intention of staying that way, while others are increasingly clear in their feelings that the West does not have the answers and that Islam, particularly the Islam of the Qur'ān and the community of the Prophet Muhammad, is God's chosen way for humankind. For the latter, their dress, their relationships with their husbands and families, and their verbal assent to Islamic priorities reflect this conviction that the time has come to cease a fruitless preoccupation with things Western and to reaffirm their identity as Muslim women.

It is difficult for Western feminists to grasp exactly what the Muslim woman may mean by "liberation." For many Islamic women, the fruits of liberation in the West are too many broken marriages, women left without the security of men who will provide for them, deteriorating relations between men and women, and sexual license that appears as rank immorality. They see the Islamic system as affirmed by the Qur'ān as one in which male authority over them ensures their care and protection and provides a structure in which the family is solid, children are inculcated with lasting values, and the balance of responsibility between man and woman is one in which absolute equality is less highly prized than cooperation and complementarity.

The new Islamic woman, then, is morally and religiously conservative and affirms the absolute value of the true Islamic system for human relationships. She is intolerant of the kind of Islam in which women are subjugated and relegated to roles insignificant to the full functioning of society, and she wants to take full advantage of educational and professional opportunities. She may agree, however, that certain fields of education are more appropriate for women than others, and that certain professions are more natural to males than to females. She participates as a contributor to and decision-maker for the family, yet recognizes that in any complex relationship final authority must rest with one person. And she is content to delegate

that authority to her husband, father, or other male relative in return for the solidarity of the family structure and the support and protection that it gives her and her children.

That not all, or even most, Muslim women subscribe to this point of view is clear. And yet, at the time of this writing, it seems equally clear that if Western observers are to understand women in the contemporary Islamic world, they must appreciate a point of view that is more and more prevalent. The West is increasingly identified with imperialism, and solutions viable for women in the Islamic community are necessarily different from the kinds of solutions that many Western women seem to have chosen for themselves. For the Muslim the words of the Qur'ān are divine, and the prescriptions for the roles and rights of females, like the other messages of the holy book, are seen as part of God's divinely ordered plan for all humanity. Change will come slowly, and whatever kinds of liberation ultimately prevail will be cloaked in a garb that is—in one or another of its various aspects—essentially Islamic.

CRITICAL THINKING QUESTIONS

1. In what formal ways does Islam confer on men authority over women?

2. In what formal and informal ways does Islam give power to women to affect their own lives and those of men?

3. From a Muslim perspective, what are some of the problems with Western living and, particularly, Western feminism?

50

Education and Inequality

SAMUEL BOWLES AND HERBERT GINTIS

Education has long been held to be a means to realizing U.S. ideals of equal opportunity. As Lester Ward notes at the beginning of this selection, the promise of education is to allow "natural" abilities to win out over the "artificial" inequalities of class, race, and sex. Samuel Bowles and Herbert Gintis claim that this has happened very little in the United States. Rather, they argue, schooling has more to do with maintaining existing social hierarchy.

Universal education is the power, which is destined to overthrow every species of hierarchy. It is destined to remove all artificial inequality and leave the natural inequalities to find their true level. With the artificial inequalities of caste, rank, title, blood, birth, race, color, sex, etc., will fall nearly all the oppression, abuse, prejudice, enmity, and injustice, that humanity is now subject to.

—Lester Frank Ward, *Education*, 1872

A review of educational history hardly supports the optimistic pronouncements of liberal educational theory. The politics of education are better understood in terms of the need for social control in an unequal and rapidly changing economic order. The founders of the modern U.S. school

Source: From *Schooling in Capitalist America: Educational Reform and the Contradictions of Economic Life* by Samuel Bowles and Herbert Gintis. Copyright © 1976 by Basic Books, Inc., division of HarperCollins Publishers, pp. 347–352. Reprinted by permission of Basic Books, a member of the Perseus Book Group.

system understood that the capitalist economy produces great extremes of wealth and poverty, of social elevation and degradation. Horace Mann and other school reformers of the antebellum period knew well the seamy side of the burgeoning industrial and urban centers. "Here," wrote Henry Barnard, the first state superintendent of education in both Connecticut and Rhode Island, and later to become the first U.S. Commissioner of Education, "the wealth, enterprise and professional talent of the state are concentrated . . . but here also are poverty, ignorance, profligacy and irreligion, and the classification of society as broad and deep as ever divided the plebeian and patrician of ancient Rome."[1] They lived in a world in which, to use de Tocqueville's words, ". . . small aristocratic societies . . . are formed by some manufacturers in the midst of the immense democracy of our age [in which] . . . some men are opulent and a multitude . . . are wretchedly poor."[2] The rapid rise of the factory

305

system, particularly in New England, was celebrated by the early school reformers; yet, the alarming transition from a relatively simple rural society to a highly stratified industrial economy could not be ignored. They shared the fears that de Tocqueville had expressed following his visit to the United States in 1831:

When a workman is unceasingly and exclusively engaged in the fabrication of one thing, he ultimately does his work with singular dexterity; but at the same time he loses the general faculty of applying his mind to the direction of the work. . . . [While] the science of manufacture lowers the class of workmen, it raises the class of masters. . . . [If] ever a permanent inequality of conditions . . . again penetrates into the world, it may be predicted that this is the gate by which they will enter.[3]

While deeply committed to the emerging industrial order, the farsighted school reformers of the mid-nineteenth century understood the explosive potential of the glaring inequalities of factory life. Deploring the widening of social divisions and fearing increasing unrest, Mann, Barnard, and others proposed educational expansion and reform. In his Fifth Report as Secretary of the Massachusetts Board of Education, Horace Mann wrote:

Education, then[,] beyond all other devices of human origin, is the great equalizer of the conditions of men—the balance wheel of the social machinery. . . . It does better than to disarm the poor of their hostility toward the rich; it prevents being poor.[4]

Mann and his followers appeared to be at least as interested in disarming the poor as in preventing poverty. They saw in the spread of universal and free education a means of alleviating social distress without redistributing wealth and power or altering the broad outlines of the economic system. Education, it seems, had almost magical powers:

The main idea set forth in the creeds of some political reformers, or revolutionizers, is that some people are poor because others are rich. This idea supposed a fixed amount of property in the community . . .

and the problem presented for solution is how to transfer a portion of this property from those who are supposed to have too much to those who feel and know that they have too little. At this point, both their theory and their expectation of reform stop. But the beneficent power of education would not be exhausted, even though it should peaceably abolish all the miseries that spring from the coexistence, side by side, of enormous wealth and squalid want. It has a higher function. Beyond the power of diffusing old wealth, it has the prerogative of creating new.[5]

The early educators viewed the poor as the foreign element that they were. Mill hands were recruited throughout New England, often disrupting the small towns in which textile and other rapidly growing industries had located. Following the Irish potato famine of the 1840s, thousands of Irish workers settled in the cities and towns of the northeastern United States. Schooling was seen as a means of integrating this "uncouth and dangerous" element into the social fabric of American life. The inferiority of the foreigner was taken for granted. The editors of the influential *Massachusetts Teacher*, a leader in the educational reform movement, writing in 1851, saw ". . . the increasing influx of foreigners . . ." as a moral and social problem:

Will it, like the muddy Missouri, as it pours its waters into the clear Mississippi and contaminates the whole united mass, spread ignorance and vice, crime and disease, through our native population?

If . . . we can by any means purify this foreign people, enlighten their ignorance and bring them up to our level, we shall perform a work of true and perfect charity, blessing the giver and receiver in equal measure. . . .

With the old not much can be done; but with their children, the great remedy is *education*. The rising generation must be taught as our own children are taught. We say *must be* because in many cases this can only be accomplished by coercion.[6]

Since the mid-nineteenth century the dual objectives of educational reformers—equality of opportunity and social control—have been intermingled, the merger of these two threads sometimes so nearly complete that it becomes impossible to distinguish between the two. Schooling has been at once something done for the poor and to the poor.

The basic assumptions which underlay this commingling help explain the educational reform movement's social legacy. First, educational reformers did not question the fundamental economic institutions of capitalism: Capitalist ownership and control of the means of production and dependent wage labor were taken for granted. In fact, education was to help preserve and extend the capitalist order. The function of the school system was to accommodate workers to its most rapid possible development. Second, it was assumed that people (often classes of people or "races") are differentially equipped by nature or social origins to occupy the varied economic and social levels in the class structure. By providing equal opportunity, the school system was to elevate the masses, guiding them sensibly and fairly to the manifold political, social, and economic roles of adult life.

Jefferson's educational thought strikingly illustrates this perspective. In 1779, he proposed a two-track educational system which would prepare individuals for adulthood in one of the two classes of society: the "laboring and the learned."[7] Even children of the laboring class would qualify for leadership. Scholarships would allow ". . . those persons whom nature hath endowed with genius and virtue . . ." to ". . . be rendered by liberal education worthy to receive and able to guard the sacred deposit of the rights and liberties of their fellow citizens."[8] Such a system, Jefferson asserted, would succeed in ". . . raking a few geniuses from the rubbish."[9] Jefferson's two-tiered educational plan presents in stark relief the outlines and motivation for the stratified structure of U.S. education which has endured up to the present. At the top, there is the highly selective aristocratic tradition, the elite university training future leaders. At the base is mass education for all, dedicated to uplift and control. The two traditions have always coexisted although their

meeting point has drifted upward over the years, as mass education has spread upward from elementary school through high school, and now up to the post-high-school level.

Though schooling was consciously molded to reflect the class structure, education was seen as a means of enhancing wealth and morality, which would work to the advantage of all. Horace Mann, in his 1842 report to the State Board of Education, reproduced this comment by a Massachusetts industrialist:

The great majority always have been and probably always will be comparatively poor, while a few will possess the greatest share of this world's goods. And it is a wise provision of Providence which connects so intimately, and as I think so indissolubly, the greatest good of the many with the highest interests in the few.[10]

Much of the content of education over the past century and a half can only be construed as an unvarnished attempt to persuade the "many" to make the best of the inevitable.

The unequal contest between social control and social justice is evident in the total functioning of U.S. education. The system as it stands today provides eloquent testimony to the ability of the well-to-do to perpetuate in the name of equality of opportunity an arrangement which consistently yields to themselves the aspirations and advantages, while thwarting the aspirations and needs of the working people of the United States. However grating this judgment may sound to the ears of the undaunted optimist, it is by no means excessive in light of the massive statistical data on inequality in the United States. Let us look at the contemporary evidence.

We may begin with the basic issue of inequalities in the years of schooling. As can be seen in Figure 50.1, the number of years of schooling attained by an individual is strongly associated with parental socioeconomic status. This figure presents the estimated distribution of years of schooling attained by individuals of varying socioeconomic backgrounds. If we define socioeconomic background by a weighted sum

Figure 50.1   Educational Attainments Are Strongly Dependent on Social Background Even for People of Similar Childhood IQs

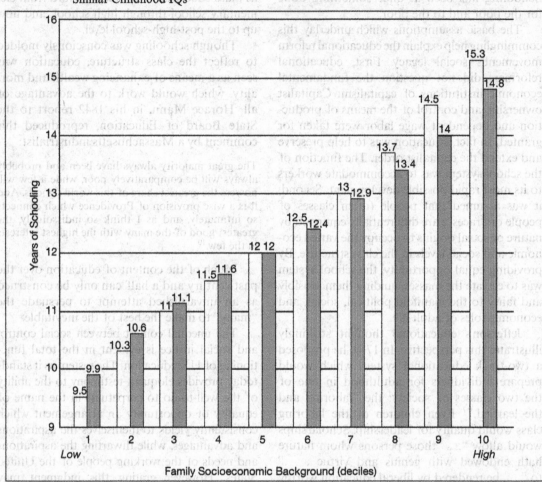

Notes: For each socioeconomic group, the left-hand bar indicates the estimated average number of years of schooling attained by all men from that group. The right-hand bar indicates the estimated average number of years of schooling attained by men with IQ scores equal to the average for the entire sample. The sample refers to "non-Negro" men of "nonfarm" backgrounds, aged 35–44 years in 1962.

Source: Samuel Bowles and Valerie Nelson, "The 'Inheritance of IQ' and the Intergenerational Transmission of Economic Inequality," *The Review of Economics and Statistics*, vol. LVI, no. 1 (Feb. 1974).

of income, occupation, and educational level of the parents, a child from the ninetieth percentile may expect, on the average, five more years of schooling than a child in the tenth percentile.[11]

. . . We have chosen a sample of white males because the most complete statistics are available for this group. Moreover, if inequality for white males can be documented, the proposition is merely strengthened when sexual and racial differences are taken into account.

Additional census data dramatize one aspect of educational inequalities: the relationship between family income and college attendance. Even among those who had graduated from high school in the early 1960s, children of families earning less than $3,000 per year were over six times as likely not to attend college as were the children of families earning over $15,000.[12] Moreover, children from less well-off families are *both* less likely to have graduated from high school and more likely to attend inexpensive, two-year community colleges rather than a four-year B.A. program if they do make it to college.[13]

Not surprisingly, the results of schooling differ greatly for children of different social backgrounds. Most easily measured, but of limited importance, are differences in scholastic achievement. If we measure the output of schooling by scores on nationally standardized achievement tests, children whose parents were themselves highly educated outperform the children of parents with less education by a wide margin. Data collected for the U.S. Office of Education Survey of Educational Opportunity reveal, for example, that among white high-school seniors, those whose parents were in the top education decile were, on the average, well over three grade levels in measured scholastic achievement ahead of those whose parents were in the bottom decile.[14]

Given these differences in scholastic achievement, inequalities in years of schooling among individuals of different social backgrounds are to be expected. Thus one might be tempted to argue that the close dependence of years of schooling attained on background displayed in the left-hand bars of Figure 50.1 is simply a reflection of unequal intellectual abilities, or that inequalities in college attendance are the consequences of differing levels of scholastic achievement in high school and do not reflect any additional social class inequalities peculiar to the process of college admission.

This view, so comforting to the admissions personnel in our elite universities, is unsupported by the data, some of which is presented in the figure. The right-hand bars of Figure 50.1 indicate that even among children with identical IQ test scores at ages six and eight, those with rich,

well-educated, high-status parents could expect a much higher level of schooling than those with less-favored origins. Indeed, the closeness of the left-hand and right-hand bars in the figure shows that only a small portion of the observed social class differences in educational attainment is related to IQ differences across social classes.[15] The dependence of education attained on background is almost as strong for individuals with the same IQ as for all individuals. Thus, while Figure 50.1 indicates that an individual in the ninetieth percentile in social class background is likely to receive five more years of education than an individual in the tenth percentile, it also indicates that he is likely to receive 4.25 more years schooling than an individual from the tenth percentile with the same IQ. Similar results are obtained when we look specifically at access to college education for students with the same measured IQ. Project Talent data indicates that for "high ability" students (top 25 percent as measured by a composite of tests of "general aptitude"), those of high socioeconomic background (top 25 percent as measured by a composite of family income, parents' education, and occupation) are nearly twice as likely to attend college than students of low socioeconomic background (bottom 25 percent). For "low ability" students (bottom 25 percent), those of high social background are more than four times as likely to attend college as are their low social background counterparts.[16]

Inequality in years of schooling is, of course, only symptomatic of broader inequalities in the educational system. Not only do less well-off children go to school for fewer years, they are treated with less attention (or more precisely, less benevolent attention) when they are there. These broader inequalities are not easily measured. Some show up in statistics on the different levels of expenditure for the education of children of different socioeconomic backgrounds. Taking account of the inequality in financial resources for each year in school and the inequality in years of schooling obtained, Jencks estimated that a child whose parents were in the top fifth of the income distribution receives roughly twice the educational resources in dollar terms as does a child whose parents are in the bottom fifth.[17]

The social class inequalities in our school system, then, are too evident to be denied. Defenders of the educational system are forced back on the assertion that things are getting better; the inequalities of the past were far worse. And, indeed, there can be no doubt that some of the inequalities of the past have been mitigated. Yet new inequalities have apparently developed to take their place, for the available historical evidence lends little support to the idea that our schools are on the road to equality of educational opportunity. For example, data from a recent U.S. Census survey reported in Spady indicate that graduation from college has become no less dependent on one's social background. This is true despite the fact that high-school graduation is becoming increasingly equal across social classes.[18] Additional data confirm this impression. The statistical association (coefficient of correlation) between parents' social status and years of education attained by individuals who completed their schooling three or four decades ago is virtually identical to the same correlation for individuals who terminated their schooling in recent years.[19] On balance, the available data suggests that the number of years of school attained by a child depends upon family background as much in the recent period as it did fifty years ago.

Thus, we have empirical reasons for doubting the egalitarian impact of schooling. . . . We conclude that U.S. education is highly unequal, the chances of attaining much or little schooling being substantially dependent on one's race and parents' economic level. Moreover, where there is a discernible trend toward a more equal educational system—as in the narrowing of the black education deficit, for example—the impact on the structure of economic opportunity is minimal at best.

CRITICAL THINKING QUESTIONS

1. Does Bowles and Gintis's description of the American education system apply to the Canadian system? How are the two systems similar? How are they different?

2. In what respects, according to Bowles and Gintis, has schooling supported the capitalist economic system? How have such supports shaped the content of the educational system?

3. What are Bowles and Gintis's conclusions about the relationship between schooling and natural ability? Between schooling and social background?

NOTES

1. H. Barnard, *Papers for the Teacher: 2nd Series* (New York: F. C. Brownell, 1866), pp. 293–310.

2. A. de Tocqueville, as quoted in Jeremy Brecher, *Strike!* (San Francisco: Straight Arrow Books, 1972), pp. xi, xii.

3. Ibid., p. 172.

4. Horace Mann as quoted in Michael Katz, ed., *School Reform Past and Present* (Boston: Little, Brown, 1971), p. 141.

5. Ibid., p. 145.

6. *The Massachusetts Teacher* (Oct., 1851), quoted in Katz, pp. 169–70.

7. D. Tyack, *Turning Points in American Educational History* (Waltham, MA: Blaisdell, 1967), p. 89.

8. Ibid., p. 10.

9. Ibid., p. 89.

10. Mann, quoted in Katz, p. 147.

11. This calculation is based on data reported in full in Samuel Bowles and Valerie Nelson, "The 'Inheritance of IQ' and the Intergenerational Transmission of Economic Inequality," *The Review of Economics and Statistics*, 56, 1 (Feb., 1974). It refers to non-Negro males from nonfarm backgrounds, aged 35–44 years. The zero-order correlation coefficient between socioeconomic background and years of schooling was estimated at 0.646. The estimated standard deviation of years of schooling was 3.02. The results for other age groups are similar.

12. These figures refer to individuals who were high-school seniors in October 1965, and who subsequently graduated from high school. College attendance refers to both two- and four-year institutions. Family

income is for the twelve months preceding October 1965. Data is drawn from U.S. Bureau of the Census, *Current Population Reports*, Series P-60, No. 183 (May, 1969).

13. For further evidence, see ibid.; and Jerome Karabel, "Community Colleges and Social Stratification," *Harvard Educational Review*, 424, 42 (Nov., 1972).

14. Calculation based on data in James S. Coleman et al., *Equality of Educational Opportunity* (Washington, D.C.: U.S. Government Printing Office, 1966), and the authors.

15. The data relating to IQ is from a 1966 survey of veterans by the National Opinion Research Center; and from N. Bayley and E. S. Schaefer, "Correlations of Maternal and Child Behaviors with the Development of Mental Ability: Data from the Berkeley Growth Study," *Monographs of Social Research in Child Development*, 29, 6 (1964).

16. Based on a large sample of U.S. high-school students as reported in John C. Flannagan and William W. Cooley, *Project Talent, One Year Follow-up Study*, Cooperative Research Project, No. 2333 (Pittsburgh: University of Pittsburgh, School of Education, 1966).

17. C. Jencks et al., *Inequality: A Reassessment of the Effects of Family and Schooling in America* (New York: Basic Books, 1972), p. 48.

18. W. L. Spady, "Educational Mobility and Access: Growth and Paradoxes," in *American Journal of Sociology*, 73, 3 (Nov. 1967); and Peter Blau and Otis D. Duncan, *The American Occupational Structure* (New York: John Wiley, 1967). More recent data support the evidence of no trend toward equality. See U.S. Bureau of Census, op. cit.

19. Ibid., Blau and Duncan.

51

Stubborn Disparities: Explaining Class Inequalities in Schooling

SCOTT DAVIES

One of the most important concepts in sociology is that of social class, in that one's background plays a major role in determining one's life chances, tastes, and even life expectancy. Many people believe that all Canadians have equal opportunities regardless of their class background. But this is not always the case. This article details how this process starts early in life and how the educational system is used to stream students according to their socio-economic background.

Canada has been transformed over this century from a predominantly rural, agricultural society to an urban, post-industrial nation. Whereas one hundred years ago most people were self-employed in family-owned farms and small businesses, today the vast majority earn their livelihood by competing in the labour market. Coinciding with these changes, the school system has expanded enormously, greatly increasing the educational attainments of Canadians. Most Canadians, regardless of social origin, earn more school credentials than did their ancestors. Indeed, Canada has more citizens attending school at its various levels—elementary, secondary, and post-secondary—than almost any other country (see Guppy and Davies 1998).

Schooling has become an increasingly important determinant of one's chances of securing a good job and a stable income, and by extension, education has become a prime arena for social competition. Schools sift and sort people into highly stratified career paths.

This raises a key question: Have all Canadians benefited equally from the expansion of the school system? Recent studies have examined trends in educational outcomes by race, gender, and social class.[1] As for race, most visible minorities, whether immigrant or Canadian-born, fare better in school than Whites, except for Aboriginal Canadians (Geschwender and Guppy 1995; Davies and Guppy 1998). Non-Aboriginal minorities, taken as a group, are less likely to drop out of high school, and are more likely to attend university. With the exception of Aboriginals, race or ethnic heritage is not a strong predictor of Canadians' educational attainment.

In terms of gender, Canadian educational trends resemble those of most other nations: an overall movement toward male-female parity (Bradley and Ramirez 1996). Whereas males still earn more advanced degrees (masters, doctorates) and continue to dominate lucrative fields of study such as computer science and engineering, females are catching up in these and other areas. Females now attend and graduate from university at higher rates than males, and are less likely to drop out of high school. Despite some lingering female disadvantages, the main trend in Canadian education, as elsewhere, is toward gender equality.

However, a very different story emerges for social class. Whether measured by high school dropout rates, standardized test scores, or university attendance rates, youth from working-class and underclass backgrounds do not fare as well as their middle- and upper-class peers. Students' class origin markedly influences their school success regardless of their race, gender, or ethnicity. Certainly, the relation between class and educational outcomes is not a perfect fit. Within every socioeconomic status (SES) category a wide range of outcomes exists, and some working-class students are very successful in school. Nevertheless, SES is the strongest and most enduring social determinant of educational attainment. Indeed, in Canada, as in most nations, socio-economic disparities in educational attainment have persisted despite decades of educational expansion and reform (see Shavit and Blossfeld 1993; Deng and Treiman 1997).

This chapter presents and evaluates sociological explanations for the persistence of these SES inequalities. While acknowledging the variation in education achievements within any SES category, I dwell on explanations of the unequal average attainments of working-class versus middle-class youth. I focus on Canada, though drawing heavily on American and British research, since socio-economic patterns of educational inequality in Canada and the United States are remarkably similar, and because much British research on the topic has influenced Canadian sociologists.[2]

HOW INEQUALITIES EMERGE: SELECTION AND CUMULATIVE DISADVANTAGE

Educational inequality is best understood as a series of dissimilar transition and survival rates between groups (see Mare 1993 for an elaboration). Schooling is laddered, with student pools becoming smaller and smaller with successive transitions. For instance, most students now finish elementary schooling and enter high school. But since approximately 20% of Canadians who enter high school fail to graduate by age 24 (Frank 1996), the pool of high school graduates is selective relative to the entering high school cohort. Since SES is an important predictor of dropping out (Gilbert et al. 1993), high school graduates have a smaller proportion of working-class students than high school entrants. In turn, another selection takes place when only some high school graduates pursue post-secondary schooling. The "survivors" of this transition are again relatively select, as the proportion of students from lower SES origins again shrinks (for Canada, see Guppy and Davies 1998; for other countries, see Shavit and Blossfeld 1993). And there is still more. In the U.S., lower SES students are less likely to attend prestigious universities, even controlling for academic ability (Davies and Guppy 1997). What causes these class disparities in educational attainment?

ECONOMIC ARGUMENTS: MONEY MATTERS

Perhaps the most elemental explanation for working-class underachievement in school focuses on how working-class families face economic constraints that impede their educational progress.

Although publicly funded, school attendance and performance requires money to pay for optional field trips, learning materials, and private tutors (e.g., piano, reading). Research shows that class background affects students' decisions about attending university, even controlling for their academic ability. This is usually interpreted as an effect of the increasingly prohibitive costs of tuition (Porter et al. 1979, Gambetta 1996, Steelman and Powell 1991). Private schools, which send the vast majority of their graduates to universities, are largely unaffordable to lower-income families. Wealthier parents are more likely to pay for additional private tutoring outside school hours (though lower-income parents would hire tutors "if they had the time and/or money" [Environics 1997]). Another economic factor is the quality of public schooling. Public schools in more affluent neighbourhoods enjoy superior resources and attract better teachers.[3] Though resource level itself does not directly produce better educational outcomes, better-funded schools produce an environment that is more conducive to educational success.

Nevertheless, economic resources—whether used for tuition, transportation, private tutors, or to avoid the need for part-time work—are not the sole factor that affects school outcomes. Countries that largely eliminated university tuition fees, such as Great Britain, France, and Australia, have class inequalities in university attendance similar to those in Canada and the U.S. This suggests that pure economic factors, while palpable, are not all-determining. There is an explanatory gap, something unexplained by economic factors. To complement economic explanations, sociologists have turned to the realm of culture.

CLASS AND FRAMES OF REFERENCE

People's economic conditions affect their sense of life options. SES origins influence their perceptions of the kinds of jobs they are likely to obtain, and the lives they are likely to lead.

Judgments about school are thus influenced by these surrounding economic conditions. In particular, this context shapes the various "push" factors providing disincentives for remaining in school, and the "pull" factors providing incentives to leave school. Working-class students confront two obvious push factors: economic constraints (as elaborated above), and their underachievement relative to middle-class children (as elaborated below). Other factors give push and pull forces extra strength and efficacy.

When explaining socio-economic disparities in education, the key factor is the gap between people's abstract values and their concrete aspirations and expectations (see Mickelson 1990). Everyone "values" education in an abstract sense. Whether through surveys, interviews, or policy statements, virtually all Canadians stress the importance they place on education. Our consumer-driven, success-striving society encourages people to pursue the "North American dream" of a prestigious, well-paying job. As a result, the number of young people wanting professional careers greatly exceeds the number of such positions that exist. Hopes for professional jobs are unrealistically high (Jacobs, Karen, and McClelland 1991).

Expressing an appreciation for education is one thing, but converting desires into reality is another. Part of this gap between expressed values and reality can be traced to factors beyond the economic realm.

"Frames of reference" refer to people's sense of desirable yet possible life options, their mental horizons that influence what they expect they can realistically attain. Immediate family and friends influence these frames greatly. We develop expectations by comparing ourselves to similar people, aligning our aspirations and efforts accordingly. These frames of reference shape our ideas of what kinds of jobs and lifestyle we want, and the role school plays in our desires.

Social class strongly influences people's frames of reference. Middle-class students have higher expectations for jobs and education than do working-class students, even controlling for differences in measured academic ability. Their higher aspirations can be attributed largely to the influence of their family and friends (Sewell and Hauser 1980; McClelland 1990).[4] These differences in frames of reference explain part of the socio-economic gap in educational success (Sewell and Hauser 1980; Jacobs, Karen, and McClelland 1991).

How does class shape these frames? In some instances, people's past experience and current social position cause them to "come to terms" with their circumstances and adjust their expectations to what is "realistic." When asked what they would like to be when they grow up, very young children often reply "police officer," "nanny," or "teacher." As they grow older, learning about the jobs of their parents' friends, these choices change. The choices change again as young people hear others encouraging or remaining mute about their occupational dreams. When confronting barriers, economic or otherwise, they often lower their original goals. Additionally, "pull factors" disproportionately entice working-class youth out of school. Especially for youth not faring well in school, domestic and employment roles act as school-leaving incentives. Relatively secure blue-collar jobs requiring few educational credentials appear as viable alternatives to schooling (Brown 1987), as do marriage plans. Even among the previously ambitious, and among the talented, early marriage reduces aspirations (Jacobs, Karen, and McClelland 1991).

PUSH FACTORS: THE STRUCTURE OF SCHOOLING

Working-class students in most countries, including Canada, are more likely than their middle-class counterparts to be streamed into less challenging, terminal programs in high school (Davies 1992; Curtis, Livingstone, and Smaller 1992). The very existence of these streaming systems, critics contend, disadvantages working-class students. These youth would fare better in a non-streamed high school environment that offered them the same curricula and expectations as other students. Being stuck in lower tracks offers these students less challenging work, and lowers their expectations and aspirations for the future. Once in different tracks, fatalistic frames of reference are reinforced, as opportunities to rise in school and learn are limited. The incentives of available jobs and/or impending domestic roles, when combined with streaming, lead these youth to perceive school as irrelevant to their future. School becomes a pointless dress rehearsal that is irrelevant to their upcoming roles.

American Catholic schools place far fewer students in lower streams, and as a result greater proportions of working-class students in these schools score well on standardized tests, graduate from high school, and attend post-secondary institutions (Lee, Bryk, and Smith 1993). Such research findings encourage the "de-streaming" movement, which seeks to abolish differential grouping and to mix students of all abilities. In the early 1990s, Ontario removed streams in grade 9, and planned eventually to phase out all streaming. However, for a variety of reasons—but largely due to teacher complaints about the practical difficulties imposed by heterogeneous ability groups—the government ended the experiment. Nevertheless, American research suggests that de-streaming could be a valid tool for easing class disparities in schooling if practical problems associated with student heterogeneity can be overcome.

Another factor shaping frames of reference, and their relation to class, is knowledge about education. Even when students from humble origins have lofty aspirations, and are academically gifted, other factors mitigate against their success. The daunting variety of choices available in modern post-secondary education, such as the distinctions between community colleges and universities, different types of degrees, the informal ranking of institutions, and the wide variety of programs available within any institution, creates an elaborate system of selection with many ports of entry. To make wise choices and maximize one's benefit, one must understand how the system operates; for example, what are the efficacious strategies for success or the informal rankings of programs and institutions? Such navigational savvy is held disproportionately by students from middle-class origins. These youth have superior information about the academic marketplace, and they are more likely to know which fields offer lucrative rewards and how to find competitive advantages. As a result, students from disadvantaged origins have a lower probability of survival in advanced stages of the education system (Davies and Guppy 1997).

MORE PUSH FACTORS: THE CULTURE OF SCHOOLING

A notable characteristic of class inequality in education is that disparities in skills, such as the ability to read, write, and reason, can be detected from the earliest days in school (Alexander, Entwisle, and Horsey 1997). Why does this occur? As has been well documented, some parents can pass on to their children non-material resources that facilitate school success. Because parental education attainment better predicts student success than parental income or class position, many sociologists have looked to the role of non-material resources in facilitating class differences in educational attainment.

More educated parents pass on to their children "human capital"—basic reading, writing, and vocabulary skills, disciplined work habits—giving their children a distinct advantage in school. More highly educated parents spend more time helping their children with school-related activities (Environics 1997), a finding that is likely a consequence of their more flexible work schedules and greater familiarity with academic matters (Lareau 1989).

Another cultural approach places less emphasis on particular skills and focuses instead on cultural tastes and aesthetics. "Cultural capital," the signature concept of French sociologist Pierre Bourdieu (Bourdieu and Passeron 1990), refers to the advantage enjoyed by students who possess sophisticated (as opposed to merely competent) conversational abilities and who have acquired a taste for literature and the arts.

In addition to the culture of the home, the culture of the classroom is also important. Many sociologists focus less on working-class culture and more on possible school cultures in order to understand class disparities. For instance, Bourdieu contends that since schools reward children who possess a certain type of cultural sophistication that is less likely to be found among the working class, schools in essence are rewarding middle-class culture. The way school is conducted—expected styles of speech, dress, and the content of the curriculum—is deemed to be largely foreign to working-class youth.

For instance, Basil Bernstein's (1973) research in East London (England) led him to postulate that middle-class children and working-class children come to school speaking different "codes"—that is, different styles of language with different grammatical rules and themes that lead to different ways of communicating. Schooling, Bernstein argued, is conducted in the more elaborate code of the middle class, putting working-class students at a distinct linguistic disadvantage. Other cultural idioms used in schools also may be class-biased. For instance, critics of standardized testing have long contended that such tests are more tests of "culture" than of cognitive ability, in that success in these tests is dependent upon having a certain cultural exposure (Contenta 1993).

Another longstanding charge of systematic bias in North American schools is that teachers, themselves middle class, hold higher expectations for middle-class students than for working-class students (see Wineburg 1987). Teachers are said to generalize, perhaps unconsciously, from the physical and social attributes of students (e.g., dress, demeanour, and speech style) to their abilities. According to this argument, teachers subtly expect well-dressed, presentable, and articulate children to be good students, and expect those with the opposite traits to be poorer students. This typecasting is also said to create a self-fulfilling prophecy. Whether via body language or the attention they give to students, teachers are said to express their expectations by treating students differently, and students are said to internalize these subtle messages. Thus, students for whom teachers have low expectations are said to eventually develop poor self-images, which in turn lead to poor academic performance.

Creating bold theories of working-class underachievement is one thing; providing convincing empirical evidence to support such theories is another. How have these theories fared over decades of sociological research?

Results are mixed, offering only qualified support. Beginning with cultural capital theory, sociologists have tested whether school outcomes are statistically correlated with various indicators of cultural capital, such as whether students have attended art galleries or museums, or whether their household provides reading material such as newspapers, magazines, and books. Findings suggest that students who regularly visit art galleries and museums achieve superior test scores (DiMaggio 1982). High school students exposed to household reading material are more likely to complete high school, attend selective universities, and enter lucrative post-secondary programs (Davies and Guppy 1997; Tanner, Davies, and O'Grady 1997). However, the link between cultural capital and class background is not exactly as Bourdieu imagines. Class background affects school success independently of cultural capital, and conversely, students with cultural capital enjoy advantages in school, independently of

SES (Aschaffenburg and Maas 1997). Not all middle-class youth participate in high-status culture—far from it—and not all lower SES children are excluded from this culture.

Bernstein's theory of language codes is less successful. His theory, while popular in the 1970s, lacks any large-scale empirical confirmation, and many researchers are highly skeptical as to whether it is applicable beyond the setting of East London in the 1960s and 1970s. Similarly, sweeping claims that working-class students are culturally alienated in schools appear to be based more on assertion than argument and detailed evidence. Examples of successful "working-class schools," where such students thrive in a culturally proletarian environment, would aid the case for these theories, but, to my knowledge, no such schools exist. In fact, research suggests that working-class student performance is raised in schools that have a more middle-class composition.

As with studies of cultural capital, research on teacher biases offers mixed findings. Proof for the famous "self-fulfilling prophecy" thesis was originally said to be provided by the famous "Pygmalion in the classroom" experiment (Rosenthal and Jacobson 1968). Rosenthal and Jacobson tested whether labelling a group of elementary students as "gifted" (when in reality they were chosen at random) would cause those children to markedly improve not only their grades but their IQ scores as well. Any improvement, the researchers reasoned, would be strong evidence of the self-fulfilling prophecy. One year later, the researchers claimed they had evidence of a strong labelling effect. The study quickly became famous and remains one of the best known in the history of educational research. Other studies quickly followed that argued that teacher typecasting was a root cause of working-class and minority underachievement in schools.

But is there clear evidence to support this claim? Few observers at the time noticed that the actual Pygmalion results were weak and uneven, and that the conclusions drawn from the data far overshot the content of the actual study, which did not directly test whether teachers negatively stereotyped working-class students. Subsequent attempts at replication have produced mixed results. Teacher expectations do not appear to consistently influence student ability.

Other types of research on teacher expectations find nuanced effects. While some conclude that teacher expectations are largely the consequence of the academic actions of students, and not vice versa (see Wineburg 1987; Farkas et al. 1990; Hurn 1993: 170–176), some suggest working-class students do endure biased treatment. Teachers from high-status origins appear to have lower expectations and give lower grades to low SES students (Alexander, Entwisle, and Thompson 1987). These students, even controlling for academic ability, are less likely to be assigned to upper tracks (Hurn 1993: 165–170). Thus, while sweeping claims that schools are culturally biased and directly "push out" able working-class students may be overstated, evidence suggests that those youth encounter some unequal treatment in schools.

SOCIAL CAPITAL AND ACTIVE CAPITAL

What might account for the complex and somewhat inconsistent effects found in research on resources and school biases? Research frequently underplays agency. The concept of cultural capital points to a potential. Parental endowments in human capital and cultural capital aid educational success, but their influence is contingent upon whether those resources are acted upon in those families. Families with impressive resources "on paper" may not spend time helping their children. Exposure to music, art galleries, and world travel may offer advantages, but only if this potential is actualized through strategic action.

Family advantages can be reinforced in different ways. Having a sizable income, for instance, can boost one's cultural capital in the form of tutoring services, attending cultural events, or travelling to exotic locales. Money allows one to take advantage of one's knowledge of the school system. Knowledge that a high LSAT score is crucial to one's chances of acceptance into law school, for example, is especially helpful if one can afford the books and study courses that can improve such scores. Conversely, families that lack advantages in some areas can compensate by excelling in other areas. For instance, many Asian immigrant parents possess little of the dominant cultural capital, few English skills, and have relatively little direct contact with teachers, yet compensate by enrolling their children in private tutoring and monitoring their children's homework at higher-than-average rates (Schneider and Coleman 1993).

"Active capital" (Looker 1994) refers to the conversion of potential resources—economic or cultural—into real educational advantage. Research shows that academic advantages are enjoyed by children whose parents more actively monitor their children's homework, spend more time with their children, and intervene positively if their children run into difficulties at school (Schneider and Coleman 1993; Lareau 1989).

What activates capital? At one level, motivation is an individual, idiosyncratic matter. Yet, sociologists know that individual effort does not occur in a social vacuum, but is embedded in broader social contexts. Relationships among students, parents, neighbouring communities, and educators can influence and channel an individual's actions. In conceptualizing these broader social effects, Coleman has referred to "social capital" as the set of collective expectations within a community that affects the goal-seeking behaviour of its members (see Coleman 1988). Communities create social capital by forging reciprocal norms of obligation among parents, youth, and schools. Such norms breed strong bonds of trust, cooperation, and mutual respect, and can channel motivation and effort. Conversely, communities with weak obligations and expectations may be less committed to their educational goals.

Differences in social capital can reinforce socio-economic disparities. Studies show that parents from lower SES categories are less active in their children's schooling (Schneider and Coleman 1993). Working-class parents are disadvantaged vis-à-vis middle-class parents by their relatively inflexible work schedules, less detailed knowledge of the school system, lesser familiarity with the social culture of teaching, and by schools that do not actively encourage parental participation (Lareau 1989; Epstein 1995).

However, these effects can be counteracted. Working-class students appear better motivated in more academically oriented schools. Researchers have found that schools with strong expectations of success raise the attainment of all children, particularly lower SES students (Willms 1986; Shouse 1996). Schools of mixed socio-economic composition benefit working-class children by exposing them to an enriched academic environment, high-status role models, and peers with high aspirations (see Hurn 1993: 168).

THEORIES OF DEEP CULTURAL DIVISIONS: DEPRIVATION AND RESISTANCE

Notions of frames of reference and forms of capital, described above, portray middle-class versus working-class families as having different outlooks and unequal resources regarding school. These cultural differences are not seen to be "deep," in the sense of reflecting profoundly dissimilar values or norms, but rather stem from their adjustments to their respective socio-economic conditions. Yet, some sociologists see much deeper cultural differences. A controversial idea that has haunted sociologists for over forty years is that working-class children are outperformed by their middle-class counterparts because of a fundamental mismatch between the cultural orientations required for school success and the culture of lower socio-economic groups. There are two versions of this thesis.

The first version, called "cultural deprivation" or "cultural deficit" theory, was popular in the 1950s and 1960s (see Hyman 1953). In this view, modern schools, as part of the societal contest for economic status and social climbing, require of the populace a set of "middle class" orientations aimed at achievement, competition, and aspiration for upward social mobility. Families from lower socio-economic strata, these theorists reasoned, desire the same material goals of income and wealth as their middle-class counterparts, but fail to embrace the attitudes or orientations needed to reach those goals. Working-class families were seen to be behind the times, mired in a pre-modern value set.

Cultural deficit theory met a barrage of criticism in the late 1960s and early 1970s. Much of this criticism consisted of moralistic charges of elitism and "blaming the victim," but there were substantive sociological criticisms as well. Perhaps the most powerful was a challenge to the claim of deep cultural divisions rooted in class. Writers such as William Ryan (1971), drawing on notions of frames of reference, passionately argued that virtually everyone in North America shares common aspirations for material wealth, but the working class adjust their expectations in response to their lower objective chances of realizing their aspirations.

The idea of deep cultural division did not vanish, however, but resurfaced in a new guise. Many sociologists in the 1970s and 1980s, influenced by Marxism, offered a novel account of deep cultural differences to explain why working-class students underperformed. In what became known as *Resistance theory* (see Davies 1995 for a review), Marxists such as Paul Willis (1977) argued that class disparities in school stem less from a working-class inability to compete, but more from their *unwillingness* to compete. This unwillingness, they argued, is rooted in a profound culture clash. Rather than sharing an orientation of status striving, Willis and his followers argued, the working class has its own defiant mores, which it forged through historic struggles with its capitalist employers. These values are said to include a preference for solidarity over competitiveness, pride in manual labour, and an antagonism to institutional authority.

Resistance theorists make two crucial inferential leaps. First, they argue that many, if not most, working-class youth are generally indifferent to school, exert little effort in classes, and participate in school deviance. Second, they argue that these anti-school subcultures have a proletarian character that, in essence, is a youthful version of factory culture. The solidarity of the shop floor is said to be mimicked by close peer relationships among teens. The pride in heavy, manual labour is said to be expressed by their disparaging of the "pencil-pushing" that pervades school work, and resentment toward the second-class status that is accorded to manual labour in schools. The antagonism to authority, as visibly expressed in workers' conflicts with factory supervisors and bosses, is transferred to student-teacher relations.

These subcultural values, in this account, lead these youth to reject school and eagerly anticipate the "real world" of employment. Simply put, working-class kids get working-class jobs by developing rebellious subcultures, thereby condemning themselves to educational failure. While acknowledging that not all working-class students engage in deviance, resistance theorists view working-class resistance to school as a prime cause of their educational underachievement.

Resistance theory has had a huge impact in sociology, but has sparked much criticism. Willis and his followers stand accused of greatly exaggerating the extent to which working-class students actually oppose school, and of offering overly romantic interpretations of school deviance. Indeed most concrete instances of "resistance"—often amounting to little more than expressions of boredom—are simply unconvincing as evidence of a deep and ideologically charged cultural division.

CONCLUSION: CHANGING SOCIETY, PERSISTING INEQUALITIES?

Class disparities in education stem from a variety of factors—unequal economic constraints, different frames of reference and endowments in various forms of capital, and some forms of bias in school. Each of these interacting factors has multiple levels of influence, from the individual, to the family, to the surrounding community, to the school. Documenting class inequalities is relatively easy, but the complexity of how class affects schooling makes convincing explanations backed by solid evidence much harder to find. Part of this difficulty stems from the fact that society and its educational institutions are constantly changing.

Schools have changed. One possible reason why recent research on school bias finds such uneven effects is that teachers and their methods have been continually altered over recent decades. While the notion of the self-fulfilling prophecy perhaps had a stronger reality thirty years ago, educators today are generally far more sensitive and alert to issues of equity and bias. Teacher colleges focus much of their training on issues of "diversity." Curricula and tests have been modified constantly in an effort to better suit a diverse student body.

Cultural configurations are shifting as well. Sociologists, more than before, doubt that social class is a primary source of cultural division in our society. Before the mid-1980s, many commonly referred to a "working-class culture" as a recognizable and coherent entity. These ideas led Resistance theorists, like the Functionalists before them, to depict a deep culture clash between working-class youth and schools. But this notion of such a distinct culture, in semi-opposition to the middle class, seems less and less plausible in North America. Most sociologists now stress instead race, ethnicity, religion, or region as more potent sources of social attachments, self-conceptions, group loyalties, and cultural conflict. Class may continue to shape frames of reference and senses of people's life options, but it is not a source of deep cultural attachment. An essential irony is that while working-class culture may have faded, class remains the key objective barrier to school success.

These culture shifts can be linked to changing economic conditions. De-industrialization is transforming the job structure that helped forge class-differentiated frames of reference. Until the mid-1980s, blue-collar jobs in resources and manufacturing that required few educational credentials attracted many working-class youth, particularly males, out of school. But the stock of such jobs is now smaller. More school leavers now encounter service-sector jobs (often requiring educational credentials, even if not high levels of skill) or the spectre of unemployment. Further, on average, women are marrying and bearing children at later ages and, perhaps as a result, female educational attainments among all classes have shot upwards. Thus, two viable alternatives that previously attracted many working-class students out of school have been recently undercut.

What impact will this change have on frames of reference and aspirations? One might expect that the weakening of these pull factors will strengthen most youth's attachments to schooling. As our society transforms itself into a "knowledge economy," lifetime learning is being hailed as the next source of educational expansion. People of all descriptions, so the argument goes, will return to school numerous times over their employment lifetimes to upgrade their skills. Will this alter the frames of reference of those who would not otherwise consider post-secondary schooling? It might, but we need to remember that educational inequality is a relational concept, not an absolute measure of attainment. Often overlooked is the fact that over the past four decades,

working-class families have substantially boosted their attainments, but inequalities have remained largely stable because the middle class has boosted equally its attainments. An understanding of inequality requires not only recognition of the barriers faced by working-class youth, but the advantages and strategies of middle-class youth. Even if working-class frames of reference change and school biases are removed—which would render working-class students more competitive—middle-class families will likely develop new strategies to keep ahead. The sharp increases in recent years in the number of families seeking private schooling and private tutoring is a likely indication of a new middle-class strategy aimed at maintaining a competitive edge in education.

CRITICAL THINKING QUESTIONS

1. What is your class background? How would you measure that? What social classes does Davies discuss? Which variables besides social class determine success in school?

2. Why do students from the middle class perform better in school than those with a working-class background? What resources are needed in order to succeed in school? How does socio-economic background affect one's career options?

3. What are the basic elements of deprivation and resistance theory? Do you think either theory (or both) provides substantial insights into why fewer people from working-class backgrounds pursue higher education? What are some shortcomings associated with these theories?

NOTES

1. Although the terms "class" and "socio-economic status" (SES) have different theoretical and empirical meanings in sociology, I use them interchangeably to refer to one's relative economic standing. Canadian trends are taken from data cited in Guppy and Davies (1998).

2. Two very important and related topics—group differences in "equity"—that is, the power to shape and influence the content and form of education, and the question of how class interacts with region, race, ethnicity, or gender—cannot be pursued here for reasons of space.

3. This tends to be a much starker phenomenon in the U.S. than in Canada. In fact, schools in neighbourhoods populated by racial minorities in urban areas like Toronto and Vancouver receive greater funds than the average.

4. The relation between frames of reference and class, like the relation between educational outcomes and class, is far from a perfect fit. Research needs to be further developed to understand why there is wide range within any class. One possibility is that low-income communities that are less tight-knit and bonded allow their members to develop expectations that are atypical of those communities (see Portes and Sensenbrenner 1993). Some low-income communities may have resources that can compensate for their class position (see Kao, Tienda, and Schneider 1996).

REFERENCES

Alexander, Karl L., Doris R. Entwisle, and Maxine S. Thompson. 1987. School performance, status relations, and the structure of sentiment: Bringing the teacher back in. *American Sociological Review*, 52(5): 665–82.

Alexander, Karl L., Doris R. Entwisle, and Carrie S. Horsey. 1997. From first grade forward: Early foundations of high school dropout. *Sociology of Education*, 70(2): 87–107.

Aschaffenburg, Karen, and Ineke Maas. 1997. Cultural and educational careers: The dynamics of social reproduction. *American Sociological Review*, 62(4): 573–87.

Bernstein, Basil (ed.). 1973. *Class, codes and control, vol. 2: Theoretical studies towards a sociology of language.* London, Boston: Routledge & Kegan Paul.

Blossfeld, Hans-Peter, and Yossi Shavit. 1993. Persisting barriers: Changes in educational opportunities in thirteen countries. In *Perpetual inequality: Changing educational attainment in thirteen countries*, eds. Yossi Shavit and Hans-Peter Blossfeld, 1–24. Boulder, CO: Westview Press.

Bourdieu, Pierre, and Jean-Claude Passeron. 1990. *Reproduction in education, society and culture*, 2nd ed. London: Sage.

Bradley, Karen, and Francisco O. Ramirez. 1996. World polity and gender parity: Women's share of higher education, 1965–1985. *Research in Sociology of Education and Socialization*, 11: 63–92.

Brown, P. 1987. *Schooling ordinary kids: Inequality, unemployment and the new vocationalism.* London: Tavistock.

Coleman, James S. 1988. Social capital in the creation of human capital. *American Journal of Sociology*, 94: s95–s120.

Contenta, Sandro. 1993. *Rituals of failure: What schools really teach.* Toronto: Between the Lines.

Curtis, Bruce, David W. Livingstone, and Harry Smaller. 1992. *Stacking the deck: The streaming of working class kids in Ontario schools.* Toronto: Our Schools/Our Selves.

Davies, Scott. 1992. In search of the culture clash: Evaluating a sociological theory of social class inequalities in education. Doctoral dissertation. Department of Sociology, University of Toronto.

———. 1995. Reproduction and resistance in Canadian high schools. An empirical examination of the Willis thesis. *British Journal of Sociology*, 46(4): 662–87.

Davies, Scott, and Neil Guppy. 1997. Fields of study, college selectivity, and student inequalities in higher education. *Social Forces*, 75(4): 1417–1138 [sic].

———. 1998. Race and Canadian education. In *The racist imagination: The sociology of racism in Canada*, ed. Vic Satzewich. Toronto: Thompson Educational Publishing.

Deng, Zhong, and Donald J. Treiman. 1997. The impact of the cultural revolution on trends in educational attainment in People's Republic of China. *American Journal of Sociology*, 103(2): 391–428.

DiMaggio, Paul. 1982. Cultural capital and school success: The impact of status culture participation on the grades of U.S. high school students. *American Sociological Review*, 47(2): 189–201.

Environics. 1997. *Focus Canada report 1997-2.* Toronto: Environics.

Epstein, Joyce L. 1995. School/family/community partnerships. *Phi Delta Kappan*, 72(5): 701–12.

Farkas, George, P. Grobe, D. Sheehan, and Y. Shuan. 1990. Cultural resources and school success: Gender, ethnicity and poverty groups within an urban school district. *American Sociological Review*, 55(1): 127–42.

Frank, Jeffrey. 1996. *After high school: The first report of the School Leavers Following-up Survey, 1995.* Ottawa: Minister of Public Works and Government Services Canada.

Gambetta, Diego. 1996. *Were they pushed or did they jump? Individual decision mechanisms in education.* Boulder, CO: Westview Press.

Geschwender, Jim, and Neil Guppy. 1995. Ethnicity, educational attainment, and earned income among Canadian-born men and women. *Canadian Ethnic Studies*, XXVII(1): 67–84.

Gilbert, Sid, Lynn Barr, Warren Clark, Matthew Blue, and Deborah Sunter. 1993. *Leaving school: Results from a national survey comparing school leavers and high school graduates 18 to 20 years of age.* Ottawa: Statistics Canada.

Guppy, Neil, and Scott Davies. 1998. *Education in Canada: Recent trends and future challenges.* Ottawa: Statistics Canada and Nelson Canada.

Hurn, Christopher J. 1993. *The limits and possibilities of schooling*, 3rd ed. Boston: Allyn and Bacon.

Hyman, Herbert H. 1953. The value systems of different classes: A social psychological contribution to the analysis of stratification. In *Class, status and power: A reader in social stratification*, eds. Reinhard Bendix and Seymour Martin Lipset, 426–42. Glencoe, IL: Free Press.

Jacobs, Jerry A., David Karen, and Katherine McClelland. 1991. The dynamics of young men's career aspirations. *Sociological Forum*, 6(4): 609–39.

Kao, Grace, Marta Tienda, and Barbara Schneider. 1996. Racial and ethnic variation in academic performance. *Research in Sociology of Education and Socialization*, 11: 263–97.

Lareau, Annette. 1989. *Home advantage: Social class and parental intervention in elementary education.* London: Falmer.

Lee, Valerie E., Anthony S. Bryk, and J. B. Smith. 1993. The organization of effective secondary schools. *Review of Research in Education*, 19:171–268.

Looker, E. Dianne. 1994. Active capital: The impact of parents on youths' educational performance and plans. *Sociology of education in Canada: Critical perspective on theory, research and practice.* Toronto: Copp Clark Longman.

Mare, Robert D. 1993. Educational stratification on observed and unobserved components of family background. In *Persistent inequality: Changing educational attainment in thirteen countries*, eds. Y. Shavit and H.P. Blossfeld, 351–76. Boulder, CO: Westview Press.

McClelland, Katherine. 1990. Cumulative disadvantage among the highly ambitious. *Sociology of Education*, 63(2): 102–21.

Mickelson, Rosalyn A. 1990. The attitude-achievement paradox among black adolescents. *Sociology of Education*, 63: 44–61.

Porter, Marion, John Porter, and Bernard Blishen. 1979. *Does money matter?* Downsview, ON: Institute for Behavioural Research.

Portes, Alejandro, and Julia Sensenbrenner. 1993. Embeddedness and immigration: Notes on the social determinants of economic action. *American Journal of Sociology*, 98(6): 1320–50.

Rosenthal, R., and L. Jacobson. 1968. *Pygmalion in the classroom.* New York: Rinehart and Winston.

Ryan, William. 1971. *Blaming the victim.* New York: Vintage.

Schneider, Barbara, and James S. Coleman. 1993. *Parents, their children, and schools.* Boulder, CO: Westview Press.

Sewell, William, and Robert Hauser. 1980. The Wisconsin longitudinal study of social and psychological factors in aspirations and achievements. *Research in Sociology of Education and Socialization*, 1: 59–99.

Shavit, Yossi, and Hans-Peter Blossfeld (eds.). 1993. *Persistent inequality: Changing educational attainment in thirteen countries.* Boulder, CO: Westview Press.

Shouse, Roger C. 1996. Academic press and sense of community: Conflict and congruence in American high schools. *Research in Sociology of Education and Socialization*, 11: 173–202.

Steelman, Lala Carr, and Brian Powell. 1991. Sponsoring the next generation: Parental willingness to pay for higher education. *American Journal of Sociology*, 96(6): 1505–29.

Tanner, Julian, Scott Davies, and Bill O'Grady. 1997. Whatever happened to yesterday's rebels? Longitudinal effects of teenage delinquency on educational and occupational attainment. Unpublished manuscript, University of Toronto.

Teachman, Jay D. 1987. Family background, educational resources, and educational attainment. *American Sociological Review*, 52: 548–57.

Willis, P. 1977. *Learning to labour.* Farnborough: Saxon House, Teakfield.

Willms, J. Douglas. 1986. Social class segregation and its relationship to pupils' examination results in Scotland. *American Sociological Review*, 51(2): 224–41.

Wineburg, Samuel S. 1987. The self-fulfillment of the self-fulfilling prophecy: A critical appraisal. *Educational Researcher*, 16(9): 28–37.

52

Japanese Mothers as the Best Teachers

KEIKO HIRAO

The Japanese government has tried to encourage fathers to share in their children's upbringing, including placing advertisements in major newspapers that read "We don't call a man a father if he doesn't participate in childcare." Nonetheless, employed mothers rather than employed fathers are the ones who leave the labour force to devote a major part of their lives to their young children's education.

. . . The intensity and the depth of involvement of many Japanese mothers in their children's education has received considerable attention (Boocock 1991; Ellington 1992; Uno 1993; White 1987). The phenomenon of the *kyōiku mama* (education mother), in which a woman devotes a major part of her life to her child's academic career, is both praised as the source of Japanese students' impressive academic success and criticized for depriving children of their free time. The description of the *kyōiku mama* phenomenon, however, has been limited by a lack of attention to how Japanese education has been privatized in the past twenty years and how the role of *kyōiku mama* has been shaped and influenced by the reality of the educational system in Japan.

Source: Keiko Hirao, "Mothers as the Best Teachers: Japanese Motherhood and Early Childhood Education." In Mary C. Brinton (Ed.), *Women's Working Lives in East Asia.* Stanford, CA: Stanford University Press, 2001, pp. 180–203.

According to a survey by the Ministry of Education, over 35 percent of schoolchildren attend *juku* (private educational institutions) that provide supplemental academic training (Ministry of Education 1994). The rate of attendance is highest among older children: in 1993, an amazing 67 percent of Japanese ninth graders were enrolled. Between 1985 and 1993 *juku* attendance increased from 17 to 24 percent for elementary school children. These *juku* statistics, however, tell only a small part of the story, which includes correspondence courses, tutoring services, and various private lessons available to children. When these services are included, 82 percent of all Japanese schoolchildren are enrolled in one or a combination of private educational programs (Ministry of Education 1994).

. . . A recent notable development in educational competition and the *kyōiku mama* phenomenon in Japan is that ever-younger children are becoming involved in educational activities outside of school. Approximately 42 percent of Japanese preschool children are enrolled in some kind of educational program outside of kindergarten and day nurseries (Ministry of Health and Welfare 1991). As Norma Field notes, childhood in contemporary Japan has become streamlined as a series of preparatory steps to productive adulthood (Field 1995), and parents—especially mothers—play a vital role as the agents of human capital investment. . . .

DATA

This [reading] is based on interviews conducted on the parenting behaviors of mothers in the Tokyo area during 1991–1992 and in Nagoya (Aichi Prefecture) in 1994–1995. The samples for the Tokyo interviews were recruited through three parenting classes sponsored by local governments and playgroup networks. The parenting classes involved approximately eighty participants in total. As I served as the coordinator/instructor, I was able to request the names of participants who were willing to cooperate in the interviews. I then added to the samples through snowball sampling methods. Twenty women from the classes were contacted for the in-depth interviews. I also utilized the discussions in the classes as a means of participant observation. Because the parenting classes were offered in the daytime, the participants were limited to full-time housewives and part-time workers. The format of the interview was mostly open-ended, with some structured questions about personal background. . . .

DEVELOPMENT OF EARLY EDUCATION PROGRAMS: AN OBSESSION WITH PRODIGIES

The educational role played by Japanese mothers starts when children are very young. Kindergartens and nursery schools expect mothers to incorporate an educational agenda

into the routine of daily life (Allison 1996). The intensity of this responsibility is illustrated by the recent development of *sōki-kyōiku*, early educational programs that are given either at home or at private, extra-school institutions. These are geared explicitly toward the development of cognitive skills in preschool children.

These programs are "extra-school" in the sense that they are independent from formal kindergartens and accredited day nurseries. Kindergartens and day nurseries operate under the auspices of the Ministry of Education and the Ministry of Health and Welfare, respectively. Because more than 93 percent of preschool children are enrolled in one or the other of these institutions, kindergartens and day nursery programs have now become comparable to formal schools. Private enterprises that provide educational services for preschoolers can be compared to the preschool version of *juku* for school-aged children. *Juku* is distinguished from extracurricular activities as it is administered outside the school system. In the same manner, early education programs function externally to the formal system of kindergarten and nursery schools.

. . . The course content offered in the extra-preschool curriculums varies widely, ranging from music lessons to reading and writing, simple mathematics to foreign languages. Some courses are purely academically oriented, some specialize in preparatory training for entrance examinations for prestigious elementary schools, and others emphasize artistic skills and music lessons. Many boast a combination of some or all of these benefits.

Kumon, a prominent *juku*, for example, invites preschoolers to work on mathematics, English, and Japanese. Founded by Toru Kumon in 1958 in Osaka as a small neighborhood *juku* for school-children, Kumon is now one of the largest *juku* establishments in Japan, with more than 18,000 branch classroom locations all over the country and a total enrollment of 1.5 million (Kumon Kyōiku Kenkyūkai 1998). . . .

During the late 1980s, Kumon expanded its programs to include the enrollment of preschoolers. In 1990, they started a correspondence course through which they delivered monthly educational kits such as videos, flash cards, and workbooks to children between the ages of two and five. In the mid-1980s, Kumon began to commend their high achievers. Among them were preschool children who could work out differential and integral calculus. These youngsters had already finished the high school level mathematics curriculum, and some of their mothers were reported to have started the program while they were pregnant.

The Association of Early Childhood Development, founded by Masaru Ibuka, the founder of Sony, states its mission as assisting in the sound development of the mother–child relationship. Its operation includes developing teaching materials, such as electronically prerecorded flash cards called "talking cards." Courses are offered to children aged 12 to 24 months old. Courses are also available to pregnant women on how to enhance the potential abilities of their unborn children. . . .

The Child Academy, founded by Makoto Shichida, offers comprehensive programs such as storytelling, flash-card learning, haiku, arts and crafts, and music. The Ishii School of Kanji Education focuses on the teaching of reading and writing Chinese characters for preschoolers, offering correspondence courses as well as instruction in classrooms. . . .

The spur for early education began in 1976 when Ibuka published a sensational book titled *Yōchien de wa Ososugiru* ("Kindergarten Is Too Late"). This book became a best-seller and was followed by a flood of publications that advocated early intervention in order to develop the cognitive and verbal skills of infants. Such publications include Shichida's *Miraculous Education for the Zero-Year-Old* (1983) and *Tips on Raising an Intelligent Baby* (1985), Mitsuishi's *Creating Prodigies* (1988), and Oshima's *Prenatal Education* (1988). The

acceleration of early education can be seen through the titles of Ibuka's successive books: *Kindergarten Is Too Late* (1976), followed by *Zero-Year-Old* (1991) and *From Embryo* (1992). We can see the shift in the messages. Kindergarten was too late in the 1970s. But in the 1990s mothers were instructed to be concerned about their children's academic achievements *from conception*.

The accelerated education in Japan parallels, to some extent, the proliferation of educational programs for preschool children in the United States. Programs with heavy educational components for prekindergarten children are also on the increase in the United States. The well-publicized "superkid" practice by Glenn Doman, *How to Teach Your Baby to Read* (1964) and *How to Multiply Your Baby's Intelligence* (1984), for example, resonates with many of the publications by Ibuka, Shichida, and Ishii. They share the common premises that children's IQ is not fixed at birth but is determined by environment and intellectual stimulation, that children's potential for learning has long been underestimated, and that intellectual growth is very rapid during early childhood. In other words, the cognitive potential of children, according to both Doman and Ishii, can be significantly boosted by early intervention programs. . . .

Once education for preschoolers proved to be a profitable business for *juku* industries, other sectors began to enter the market. For example, a company that sells underwear and other home-related products through direct-mail catalogs decided to go into the extra-preschool education business in 1992. They converted their customer list into a mailing list through which they delivered educational materials each month for children under the age of six. It is not unusual, especially in urban areas, for mothers of newborn babies to receive a direct-mail advertisement of courses offered to "enhance the academic ability" of their offspring. The early education "boom" was thus driven by the supply of these services.

Ironically, this development took place outside the public school system just as the Ministry of Education was trying to relax school schedules to remedy the excessive competition for entrance examinations. The public schools have taken to heart the criticism that excessive academic competition causes poor health among children, school violence, and bullying. Contrary to the common belief that Japanese schools are driving their students with relentless pressure for academic success, they are now shifting their emphasis to "creativity," "sociability," and "whole development" and away from rote learning. Approximately one-fourth of the time spent at Japanese schools is now devoted to nonacademic activities, such as recess and club activities (Stevenson 1992). Moreover, the Ministry of Education decided to reduce the time spent in school by seventy hours per year for elementary school students and thirty-five hours for junior high school students. The ministry also stipulates in the new curriculum guidelines that the content be cut by 30 percent, beginning in 2002.

In spite of the ministry's attempt to give children more free time and develop their creativity, the reforms have not extended to broad changes in the entrance examination system for colleges. As a result, many parents feel that school classrooms have become a place to confirm what children already know instead of a center for learning and mastering new subjects. This concern has prompted them to plan ahead out of the fear of having their children fall behind.

For example, Natsuko, who is age 36 and has three school-aged children, comments that

I was too naive when I was raising my first child. You can't believe how smart today's children are. Most first graders already know several *kanji* [Chinese characters], not to mention being able to read and write *hiragana* [the Japanese phonetic syllabary]. My daughter was the only one in the class who could not write her name. Although we are told that teachers don't expect children to have mastered these things by the time they enter school, the fact that all the other children already know them makes the slow starters fall behind.

Another problem with the educational reforms is that all schools must meet minimum standards, but private schools are not bound by the curriculum guidelines stipulated by the Ministry of Education. That is, private schools can use more advanced materials than those used in public schools. They can also allocate more hours to important subjects, such as English, which carries more weight in the college entrance exams. Given that a sizable portion of students admitted to the University of Tokyo, the most prestigious university in the Japanese educational hierarchy, come from private high schools with admission tracks tied to their own attached junior high schools, parents are reminded that educational competition starts at a very young age. Many of these schools push their curricula forward so that students can devote their entire senior year in high school to preparing for college entrance examinations. Private elementary schools are also attractive to parents who worry that their children will not fare well in the intense competition for junior high schools: many of these private institutions provide an admission track all the way up to high school. Consequently, the age for competition has been lowered, and the competition for a better school career has involved young preschool children.

Chisato is married to a computer engineer and has a three-year-old son. She is planning to send him to a private elementary school. He is attending a weekly preparatory program for the screening test. He also has to do workbook exercises at home with his mother. Chisato comments on their decision as follows:

I know it is a pity that a small boy like him has to work so hard, but it is for his own good. It is much easier to push him now than it will be later. If he can avoid the pressure of the entrance examination for junior high and high school, he can devote more time to developing his talents during the twelve years [he is in school full-time].

Kumiko, who is married to a physician, had a son just three weeks before I interviewed her. When I asked her how she felt about having a baby, she said,

I am glad Satoshi was born in April. Of course it's the best time for having a baby! The weather is nice, and I can take him outside and let him breathe fresh air. You know, oxygen is very important for brain development. Also, he will be one of the oldest in his class [the school year starts in April in Japan], and that will make him ahead of most children. Kids born in spring have better school records. I think that's why children born in April and May are overrepresented among students in the University of Tokyo.

I wish I had asked her where she got this idea about the birth month and the chance of being accepted to the University of Tokyo. When I met her a year later, she had put Satoshi in an enrichment class for infants run by one of the large *juku* establishments. She escorted Satoshi every week and joined an hour-long class with him. She commented bashfully,

Well, I don't mean to raise him as a "super kid." It's just a play group sort of program where children play with toys and listen to songs and so on. I just think it is important to let him play with other babies, because he has to know how to cooperate and socialize with his peers by the time he goes to kindergarten.

Although Kumiko's example may be an extreme case, there are three points that represent the ideas shared by many *kyōiku mama* today. First, a child has to go through keen academic competition in order to obtain a decent educational background. Second, a child's educational success depends on how much the parent puts into it. Third, the younger the child, the better the time for preparation. It is almost always the mother who is responsible for seeing to the provision of these opportunities and who is expected to be closely involved in the process. . . .

JAPANESE WOMEN IN THE COMMUNITY

While the publication trends in popular books set the tenor of public discourse on "good parenting," they also mirror what the public wants to read. The increased demands for parenting advice

reflect the social context in which adult socialization takes place for young Japanese mothers.

Adult Socialization and the Role of the Mass Media

Assuming the parental role is a totally fresh endeavor for most Japanese women, who generally become mothers without any firsthand experience of taking care of small children (given that Japanese families typically now have few children). Unlike in the United States, baby-sitting is not a socially accepted way for teenagers to earn money. So it is not unusual for a mother to start parenting with no experience in changing diapers or bathing babies. Parenting, or mothering specifically, is a performance without rehearsal.

Japanese women learn parenting from several socializing agents: parents and in-laws, friends, neighbors, older siblings, books, magazines, television programs, parenting courses sponsored by local governments, and kindergartens and daycare centers. Among these sources, the mass media is of increasing importance as a socializing agent. When asked where they obtained information on infant care, 35 percent of mothers surveyed in Tokyo named the mass media (books, magazines, and television) as the primary source of information, 34 percent named friends, and 17 percent answered kindergartens and daycare centers (Shirasa 1990). Parents and kin networks still play a major role in providing emotional support, but apparently they are somewhat secondary in the transmission of parenting knowledge.

Given the rapid pace at which childrearing practices have changed over the past decades, it is understandable that what grandmothers did thirty years ago is not often applicable to today's childrearing. For example, women in their 60s raised children when bottle-feeding was predominant; it was regarded as superior and as the "modern" way of feeding. Now the trend has reversed. Today more mothers opt for breast-feeding if it is possible (Katsuura-Cook 1991).

The arrival of parenting magazines is a rational consequence of this "information gap." They began to be published in the early 1980s and now provide detailed, up-to-date information on childrearing practices based on children's ages. Opposite to the decline in the birth rate, the circulation of parenting magazines has steadily increased. The total circulation of the major twelve parenting magazines is estimated to be as high as 2,710,000 (Shiomi 1996). Almost all of these parenting magazines contain advertisements and paid publications by companies that provide extra-preschool curricula and educational materials. No single issue appears without their advertisements and their sponsored articles on early intervention programs.

The effect of the mass media on the early education boom can be seen in a survey that showed a positive relationship between mothers' reliance on published materials for parenting know-how and their attitudes toward extra-preschool curricula. The more they are exposed to parenting information through the mass media, the more they are likely to be influenced to provide enrichment "stimulus" through extra-preschool curricula (Shirasa 1990). These mothers are also more likely to feel uneasy about their child's development if other children of the same age are more advanced in writing Chinese characters and in computations. Thus reliance on the mass media for parenting information seems to go hand in hand with the popularization of early education.

Isolation and Anxiety: Childrearing Behind Closed Doors

Another prominent aspect in the lives of Japanese mothers who stay at home full-time is their isolation with their children. Because the social spheres of Japanese men and women tend to be so distinctly separated, there are very few opportunities for full-time house-wives of salaried workers to socialize. The husband is busy with long working hours and rarely has spare time to help around the home with chores and childcare. Baby-sitters are not readily available in the neighborhood, and commercialized services are often too expensive. A mother is not qualified to have her baby enrolled in an accredited daycare center if she is not working or does not have another "legitimate" reason, such as illness. Commenting on her days with her baby, Toshiko, a full-time housewife married to a "salaryman," says: "A day, a week, and a month could easily pass without talking to any adult except for people in the market or with a salesperson who comes to our door to sell educational toys and *futon*."

In spite of the great emphasis placed on close mother–child relationships in Japanese families, literature in psychology and sociology has long ignored the situation of young mothers. The focus of attention has always been on children and on how the mother–child relationship affects the development of a child's personality, well-being, and so on. Little has been written or known about how the mother–child relationship affects mothers.

The isolation of mothers from other adult interaction is another precondition for the development of the early education boom. Ironically, extra-preschool courses provide lonely mothers with a place to meet people. Toshiko said that she decided to put her son in an enrichment program because she wanted to meet people and make friends. The "friends" she was talking about were not for her son, but for herself. Kumiko, mentioned earlier in this chapter, also said that chatting with other mothers in the waiting room while their children took classes provided a nice change of pace.

Many mothers are aware of the suffocation of lonely childrearing and many of them do try to get out of the isolation. Ochiai (1989) argues that a new type of network among mothers is emerging in urban areas in response to the lack of support from husbands and kin. They are of a spontaneous nature, usually composed of mothers who meet each other in neighborhood parks or parenting classes sponsored by the local government. These neighborhood networks provide mutual support in parenting and supplement kin networks. However, my observation is that much of what Ochiai calls "networks" tend to be exclusive, rarely involve fathers, and limit concerns to matters revolving around children.

Yoshiko used to work as a secretary at a trading company until she became pregnant. She decided to leave her job and take care of her son at home. The change in her lifestyle and the routines of a full-time housewife were "a kind of culture shock" to her. She described her days as follows:

I usually take my son to a neighborhood park in the morning so that he can play with other children. Mothers chat while children play in the sandbox. If the kids move to the swings, we move with them and chat around the swing, or slides, or whatever. Then we usually go to one of the mothers' houses, order pizza or noodles for lunch, and then chat in the afternoon while the children play in the house. When daddies are on business trips, we sometimes eat supper together. The members are the same and the topic of our conversation is the same. At first I enjoyed being with these people, but I am getting tired of it. It's so suffocating!

After several months, she decided to have her son enroll in Suzuki violin and Kumon so that she could avoid this situation.

I was getting tired of this, but did not want to be ostracized and to be left alone with my kid. Having a private lesson for him gave me a good excuse for keeping some distance from other mothers. They won't feel bad about me if I just say, "I can't join you today because I have to take my kid to a violin lesson."

Again, extra-preschool courses are meeting the demands of their patrons. They provide a place to meet other mothers—and to avoid them.

"A GOOD MOTHER" AS A STATUS: THE CULTURAL CONTRADICTIONS IN WOMEN'S ROLES

Mothers receive mixed and conflicting messages [about] labor force participation: you have to be a good mother, but childrearing will not occupy you for your entire life. On the one hand, mothers are pressed to stay home at least until their children reach the age of three. On the other hand, mothers are aware that they have to be prepared to pursue their "own lives," for their children will grow up and leave the nest. Men and women, especially those who have pursued higher education, have been exposed to contemporary cultural values that emphasize the significance of achievement. . . .

Over 80 percent of Japanese women join the labor force upon graduating from school, but more than 80 percent of these women have withdrawn from the labor force for one year or longer by the time they reach the age of 34. The probability of leaving one's job is not necessarily lower for women with higher education (Brinton 1993; Hirao 1997). That is, highly educated women are as likely to be out of the labor force as their less-educated counterparts during the prime parenting years. Moreover, the probability of coming back to the labor force after initial "retirement" is not necessarily higher for four-year university graduates (Hirao 1998). In other words, Japanese women's human capital is very much underutilized in the labor force.

The most striking thing that I noticed throughout my interviews was the frustration shared by many young mothers. "What depresses me is the social trend that gives praise to career women," said Yuko, a graduate from a prestigious four-year university. She used to work at a large department store as a sales assistant and resigned from her job when she had her second daughter.

They say it's good to be "at the top," pursue your career, and earn money. Super moms who can handle both work and family appear as attractive figures in TV dramas. I used to have self-confidence.

I was always at the top both in school and work. My grades were higher than those of my male classmates. I thought I was in a career track until I left it to take care of my kids. Now, I ask myself, "What am I doing here?" I feel trapped and left behind by the rest of the world.

Emiko, who also has two children, expresses her frustration more clearly.

I used to have everything except kids: study, work, travel, and love. I was imbued with the pleasure of achieving what I deserved. But now, I am doing nothing but raising children, feeding them, bathing them, chasing them around, and yelling at them. My speculation is that, in spite of the primacy given to mothering by childcare experts, the perceived value of childrearing is declining.

These women, particularly those with higher education, have experienced an egalitarian school environment and have internalized, to some extent, the idea that it is crucial even for women to have status in society. Upon becoming mothers, however, the role of mother becomes their primary social identity.

Ōhinata (1982) reports changes in mothers' attitudes toward the value of childcare. She compared the attitude of two cohorts of highly educated mothers, one in their 60s and the other in their 30s. Both cohorts shared the idea that childrearing is physically and emotionally demanding. A significant difference was observed, however, in how they viewed the value of childrearing. A majority (74 percent) of the older cohort agreed that childrearing is a worthwhile and wonderful job, while only 40 percent of the younger cohort shared this view. The majority (61 percent) of the younger cohort asserted that their reasons to live exist outside childrearing, while only 20 percent of the older cohort expressed this view.

The ambivalence toward parenting among young mothers is a natural consequence of changing lifestyles. Being a mother no longer necessarily provides a sense of achievement. Becoming a "good mother," however, is a different story. The ideology of the good mother has exerted a strong normative force on Japanese women during the last two decades. This is because mother and child have been seen as an inseparable pair, the mother and child relationship has been conceptualized as an extension of a mother's "self," a substantial proportion of a child's achievement is believed to result from his or her "effort" rather than from innate individual capabilities, and a child's outcomes have become more easily measurable at an early stage of childhood (e.g., school records and results in entrance examinations to prestigious elementary schools).

Mothers can learn where their child stands relative to other children at quite an early stage through various assessments. The results are thought to reflect how hard the child—and the mother—worked. When we take into account the presumably close psychological proximity between mother and child in Japan and the beliefs related to the causal link between maternal care and child outcomes, it is logical to see being a good mother as a status, one that is achievable depending on how much effort one makes.

Natsumi works part-time as a shop clerk in a confectionery store. She feels that her parenting is constantly being assessed. In her view, "'a good child' is necessary for becoming 'a good mother.'"

When I talk with other mothers, I often feel that they are evaluating each other's "worth" by the "quality" of the child. A good child is what makes you proud. It isn't your career, your achievement, or what you do as an individual. These things don't count in the world of mothers!

Tomoe, a physician's wife and the full-time mother of one daughter, described early intervention programs as "addictive."

I wasn't serious when I started sending my daughter to a *yōji kyōshitsu*. I was just curious about the program when I saw their flyer in the newspaper. After I enrolled her, however, I soon learned that such a program has an addictive power. She liked going there, and it was exciting to see how quickly and how much a child can learn. This excitement makes you feel as if it was you who took the test and scored so well. Once you feel this excitement, it is very hard to stop; you don't want to feel that you have failed in something.

The *kyōiku mama* syndrome is not an irreversible process: Tomoe began to notice that she was seeking a vicarious sense of achievement.

One day, I was telling my daughter to do her homework. She must have thought I was nagging her too much. She stared at me and said, "Mom, it's my homework, not yours. Don't talk to me like that." I realized that I was pushing her too hard and that being an extreme *kyōiku mama* can be its own form of child abuse.

CRITICAL THINKING QUESTIONS

1. The Japanese government has tried to reduce the extreme competition to enter university. Why have these efforts been largely unsuccessful?

2. How are Japanese mothers, but not fathers, socialized to be active participants in their children's early education? Also, how is the isolation of mothers one of the reasons for their involvement in the early education boom?

3. What is the cultural contradiction about gender roles that educated mothers encounter in Japanese society? Do you think Canadian mothers experience the same contradictions? Why or why not?

REFERENCES

Allison, Anne. 1996. *Permitted and prohibited desires: Mothers, comics, and censorship in Japan.* Boulder, CO: Westview Press.

Boocock, Sarane Spence. 1991. The Japanese preschool system. In *Windows on Japanese Education*, ed. Edward R. Beauchamp, 97–126. New York: Greenwood Press.

Brinton, Mary C. 1993. *Women and the economic miracle: Gender and work in postwar Japan.* Berkeley: University of California Press.

Doman, Glenn. 1964. *How to teach your baby to read.* New York: Random House.

———. 1984. *How to multiply your baby's intelligence.* New York: Doubleday.

Ellington, Lucien. 1992. *Education in the Japanese life-cycle.* Lewiston, NY: E. Mellen Press.

Field, Norma. 1995. The child as laborer and consumer: The disappearance of childhood in contemporary Japan. In *Children and the politics of culture*, ed.

Sharon Stephens, 51–78. Princeton, NJ: Princeton University Press.

Hirao, Keiko. 1997. Work histories and home investment of married Japanese women. Doctoral dissertation. University of Notre Dame, Department of Sociology.

———. 1998. Saishushoku no taiming: Kekkon/shussan taishokugo no rōdōshijō saisanyū katei no hasādo bunseki (Hazard analyses on the timing of re-entry to the labor force). Paper presented at the annual meeting of the Japanese Sociological Society, Kwansei Gakuin University, Nishinomiya, Japan.

Ibuka, Masaru. 1976. *Yōchien dewa ososugiru* (Kindergarten is too late). Tokyo: Goma Shobo.

———. 1991. *Zerosai* (Zero-year-old). Tokyo: Gomashobo.

———. 1992. *Taijikara* (From embryo). Tokyo: Tokumashobo.

Katsuura-Cook, Noriko. 1991. *Nihon no kosodate, Amerika no kosodate* (Child-rearing in Japan and the United States). Tokyo: Saiensu.

Kumon Kyōiku Kenkyōkai. 1998. *Company profiles.* Tokyo: Kumon Kyōiku Kenkyūkai.

Ministry of Education, Japan. 1994. *Survey report on Juku and other extra-school programs.* Tokyo: Author.

Ministry of Health and Welfare, Japan. 1991. *Survey on children's environment.* Tokyo: Government Printing Office.

Mitsuishi, Yukiko. 1988. *Tensaiji o tsukuru!* (Creating prodigies). Tokyo: Foyu.

Ochiai, Emiko. 1989. *Kindai kazoku to feminizumu* (Modern families and feminism). Tokyo: Keisōshobō.

Ōhinata, Masami. 1982. Hahaoya no shinriteki antei to jūsoku o motomete (For the mental stability and fulfillment of mothers). In *Ikuji noirōze* (Childrearing depression). Tokyo: Yūhikaku.

Ōshima, Kiyoshi. 1988. *Taikyō* (Prenatal education). Tokyo: Gomashobō.

Shichida, Makoto. 1983. *Kiseki ga okiru shichidashiki zerosai Kyōiku* (Miraculous education for zero-year-olds). Tokyo: Homeidō.

———. 1985. *Akachan wo kashikoku sodateru himitsu* (Tips on raising an intelligent baby). Tokyo: Nihon Keizai Shimbunsha.

Shiomi, Toshiyuki. 1996. *Yōji Kyōiku sangyō to kosodate* (Education industry and childrearing). Tokyo: Iwanami Shoten.

Shirasa, Izumi. 1990. *Sōki Kyōiku ni kansuru kahaoya no taidō* (Attitude of mothers on early education). Master's paper, University of Tokyo.

Stevenson, Harold W. 1992. Learning from Asian schools. *Scientific American,* 267 (December): 70–6.

Uno, Kathleen S. 1993. The death of "good wife, wise mother"? In *Postwar Japan as history,* ed. Andrew Gordon. Berkeley: University of California Press.

White, Merry. 1987. *The Japanese educational challenge: A commitment to children.* New York: Free Press.

53

The Social Structure of Medicine

TALCOTT PARSONS

Talcott Parsons, one of the most influential U.S. sociologists during the twentieth century, contributed greatly to the development of structural-functional analysis. In this selection, he examines the significance of health and illness within a social system, with particular attention to the social roles of physicians and patients.

A little reflection will show immediately that the problem of health is intimately involved in the functional prerequisites of the social system. . . . Certainly by almost any definition health is included in the functional needs of the individual member of the society so that from the point of view of functioning of the social system, too low a general level of health, too high an incidence of illness, is dysfunctional. This is in the first instance because illness incapacitates for the effective performance of social roles. It could of course be that this incidence was completely uncontrollable by social action, an independently given condition of social life. But insofar as it is controllable, through rational action or otherwise, it is clear that there is a functional interest of the society

Source: Reprinted with the permission of The Free Press, a Division of Simon & Schuster Adult Publishing Group, from *The Social System* by Talcott Parsons. Copyright © 1951, copyright renewed 1979 by Talcott Parsons.

in its control, broadly in the minimization of illness. As one special aspect of this, attention may be called to premature death. From a variety of points of view, the birth and rearing of a child constitute a "cost" to the society, through pregnancy, child care, socialization, formal training, and many other channels. Premature death, before the individual has had the opportunity to play out his full quota of social roles, means that only a partial "return" for this cost has been received.

All this would be true were illness purely a "natural phenomenon" in the sense that, like the vagaries of the weather, it was not, to our knowledge, reciprocally involved in the motivated interactions of human beings. In this case illness would be something which merely "happened to" people, which involved consequences which had to be dealt with and conditions which might or might not be controllable but was in no way an expression of motivated behavior.

This is in fact the case for a very important part of illness, but it has become increasingly clear, by no means for all. In a variety of ways motivational factors accessible to analysis in action terms are involved in the etiology of many illnesses, and conversely, though without exact correspondence, many conditions are open to therapeutic influence through motivational channels. To take the simplest kind of case, differential exposure, to injuries or to infection, is certainly motivated, and the role of unconscious wishes to be injured or to fall ill in such cases has been clearly demonstrated. Then there is the whole range of "psychosomatic" illness about which knowledge has been rapidly accumulating in recent years. Finally, there is the field of "mental disease," the symptoms of which occur mainly on the behavioral level. . . .

Summing up, we may say that illness is a state of disturbance in the "normal" functioning of the total human individual, including both the state of the organism as a biological system and of his personal and social adjustments. It is thus partly biologically and partly socially defined. . . .

Medical practice . . . is a "mechanism" in the social system for coping with the illnesses of its members. It involves a set of institutionalized roles. . . . The immediately relevant social structures consist in the patterning of the role of the medical practitioner himself and, though to common sense it may seem superfluous to analyze it, that of the "sick person" himself. . . .

The role of the medical practitioner belongs to the general class of "professional" roles, a subclass of the larger group of occupational roles. Caring for the sick is thus not an incidental activity of other roles—though for example mothers do a good deal of it—but has become functionally specialized as a full-time "job." This, of course, is by no means true of all societies. As an occupational role it is institutionalized about the technical content of the function which is given a high degree of primacy relative to other status-determinants. It is thus inevitable both that

incumbency of the role should be achieved and that performance criteria by standards of technical competence should be prominent. Selection for it and the context of its performance are to a high degree segregated from other bases of social status and solidarities. . . . Unlike the role of the businessman, however, it is collectivity-oriented not self-oriented.

The importance of this patterning is, in one context, strongly emphasized by its relation to the cultural tradition. One basis for the division of labor is the specialization of technical competence. The role of physician is far along the continuum of increasingly high levels of technical competence required for performance. Because of the complexity and subtlety of the knowledge and skill required and the consequent length and intensity of training, it is difficult to see how the functions could, under modern conditions, be ascribed to people occupying a prior status as one of their activities in that status, following the pattern by which, to a degree, responsibility for the health of her children is ascribed to the mother-status. There is an intrinsic connection between achieved statuses and the requirements of high technical competence. . . .

High technical competence also implies specificity of function. Such intensive devotion to expertness in matters of health and disease precludes comparable expertness in other fields. The physician is not, by virtue of his modern role, a generalized "wise man" or sage—though there is considerable folklore to that effect—but a specialist whose superiority to his fellows is confined to the specific sphere of his technical training and experience. For example, one does not expect the physician as such to have better judgment about foreign policy or tax legislation than any other comparably intelligent and well-educated citizen. There are of course elaborate subdivisions of specialization within the profession. . . . The physician is [also] expected to treat an objective problem in objective, scientifically justifiable terms. For example, whether he likes or dislikes the particular patient as a person is supposed to be irrelevant, as indeed it is to most purely objective problems of how to handle a particular disease.

. . . . The "ideology" of the profession lays great emphasis on the obligation of the physician to put the "welfare of the patient" above his personal interests, and regards "commercialism" as the most serious and insidious evil with which it has to contend. The line, therefore, is drawn primarily vis-à-vis "business." The "profit motive" is supposed to be drastically excluded from the medical world. This attitude is, of course, shared with the other professions, but it is perhaps more pronounced in the medical case than in any single one except perhaps the clergy. . . .

An increasing proportion of medical practice is now taking place in the context of organization. To a large extent this is necessitated by the technological development of medicine itself, above all the need for technical facilities beyond the reach of the individual practitioner, and the fact that treating the same case often involves the complex cooperation of several different kinds of physicians as well as of auxiliary personnel. This greatly alters the relation of the physician to the rest of the instrumental complex. He tends to be relieved of much responsibility and hence necessarily of freedom, in relation to his patients other than in his technical role. Even if a hospital executive is a physician himself, he is not in the usual sense engaged in the "practice of medicine" in performing his functions any more than the president of the Miners' Union is engaged in mining coal.

As was noted, for common sense there may be some question of whether "being sick" constitutes a social role at all—isn't it simply a state of fact, a "condition"? Things are not quite so simple as this. The test is the existence of a set of institutionalized expectations and the corresponding sentiments and sanctions.

There seem to be four aspects of the institutionalized expectation system relative to the sick role. First is the exemption from normal social role responsibilities, which of course is relative to the nature and severity of the illness. This exemption requires legitimation by and to the various alters involved and the physician often serves as a court of appeal as well as a direct legitimatizing agent. It is noteworthy that, like all institutionalized patterns, the legitimation of being sick enough to avoid obligations can not only be a right of the sick person but an obligation upon him. People are often resistant to admitting they are sick and it is not uncommon for others to tell them that they *ought* to stay in bed. The word generally has a moral connotation. It goes almost without saying that this legitimation has the social function of protection against "malingering."

The second closely related aspect is the institutionalized definition that the sick person cannot be expected by "pulling himself together" to get well by an act of decision or will. In this sense also he is exempted from responsibility— he is in a condition that must "be taken care of." His "condition" must be changed, not merely his "attitude." Of course the process of recovery may be spontaneous but while the illness lasts he can't "help it." This element in the definition of the state of illness is obviously crucial as a bridge to the acceptance of "help."

The third element is the definition of the state of being ill as itself undesirable with its obligation to want to "get well." The first two elements of legitimation of the sick role thus are conditional in a highly important sense. It is a relative legitimation so long as he is in this unfortunate state which both he and alter hope he can get out of as expeditiously as possible.

Finally, the fourth closely related element is the obligation—in proportion to the severity of the condition, of course—to seek *technically competent* help, namely, in the most usual case, that of a physician and to cooperate with him in the process of trying to get well. It is here, of course, that the role of the sick person as patient becomes articulated with that of the physician in a complementary role structure.

It is evident from the above that the role of motivational factors in illness immensely broadens the scope and increases the importance of the institutionalized role aspect of being sick. For then the problem of social control becomes much more than one of ascertaining facts and drawing lines. The privileges and exemptions of the sick role may become objects of a "secondary gain" which the patient is positively motivated, usually unconsciously, to secure or to retain. The problem, therefore, of the balance of motivations to recover becomes of first importance. In general motivational balances of great functional significance to the social system are institutionally controlled, and it should, therefore, not be surprising that this is no exception.

A few further points may be made about the specific patterning of the sick role and its relation to social structure. It is, in the first place, a "contingent" role into which anyone, regardless of his status in other respects, may come. It is, furthermore, in the type case temporary. One may say that it is in a certain sense a "negatively achieved" role, through failure to "keep well," though, of course, positive motivations also operate, which by that very token must be motivations to deviance. . . .

The orientation of the sick role vis-à-vis the physician is also defined as collectively-oriented. It is true that the patient has a very obvious self-interest in getting well in most cases, though this point may not always be so simple. But once he has called in a physician the attitude is clearly marked, that he has assumed the obligation to cooperate with that physician in what is regarded as a common task. The obverse of the physician's obligation to be guided by the welfare of the patient is the latter's obligation to "do his part" to the best of his ability. This point is clearly brought out, for example, in the attitudes of the profession toward what is called "shopping around." By that is meant the practice of a patient "checking" the advice of one physician against that of another without telling physician A that he intends to consult physician B, or if he comes back to A that he has done so or who B is. The medical view is that if the patient is not satisfied with the advice his physician gives him he may properly do one of two things. First he may request a consultation, even naming the physician he wishes called in, but in that case it is physician A not the patient who must call B in, the patient may not see B independently, and above all not without A's knowledge. The other proper recourse is to terminate the relation with A and become "B's patient." The notable fact here is that a pattern of behavior on the part not only of the physician, but also of the patient, is expected which is in sharp contrast to perfectly legitimate behavior in a commercial relationship. If he is buying a car there is no objection to the customer going to a number of dealers before making up his mind, and there is no obligation for him to inform any one dealer what others he is consulting, to say nothing of approaching the Chevrolet dealer only through the Ford dealer.

The doctor-patient relationship is thus focused on these pattern elements. The patient has a need for technical services because he doesn't—nor do his lay associates, family members, etc.—"know" what is the matter or what to do about it, nor does he control the necessary facilities. The physician is a technical expert who by special training and experience, and by an institutionally validated status, is qualified to "help" the patient in a situation institutionally defined as legitimate in a relative sense but as needing help. . . .

CRITICAL THINKING QUESTIONS

1. Does Parsons understand illness as a biological condition, that is, "something that happens to people"? What are the social elements in health and illness?

2. According to Parsons, what are the distinctive characteristics of the social role of the physician?

3. What are the major elements of "the sick role"? In what respects does Parsons view the social roles of physicians and patients as complementary? Can you see ways in which they may be in conflict?

54

Getting What We Pay For: Myths and Realities About Financing Canada's Health Care System

RAISA B. DEBER

This research illustrates how the concept of privatization is often misunderstood by conflating private delivery with private insurance. It also argues that public insurance is more equitable because it provides care for everybody regardless of health status. In contrast, private insurers prefer healthy clients and are likely to turn down potential customers who need health care the most—people who have a high risk of becoming ill or suffer from chronic conditions such as AIDS.

Canadian Medicare is, once again, under attack. Despite being wildly popular among Canadians, and internationally admired, our system of universal insurance for "medically necessary" hospital and physician services is being dismissed by critics as old-fashioned, unsustainable, economically unfeasible, and otherwise out of step with our new global times. The newspapers are full of announcements of "privatization" of hospital care in Alberta, accusations that "we already have two tier medicine" and might as well finish the job, and seemingly erudite pronouncements that we must choose between "maintaining equity" and economic good sense. Too often, however, these criticisms result from

Source: Raisa B. Deber. 2000. "Getting What We Pay For: Myths and Realities about Financing Canada's Health Care System," pp. 1–6, 8–10. Paper prepared for the Dialogue on Health Reform: Sustaining Confidence in Canada's Health Care System.

some fundamental confusions about both concepts and evidence. In consequence, they often misinterpret the actual problems with Medicare. Just as physicians cannot treat without an accurate diagnosis, healing Medicare requires that we be clear in defining our terms.

DEFINING OUR TERMS: ELEMENTS OF HEALTH CARE SYSTEMS AND THE PUBLIC-PRIVATE MIX

Although we commonly speak of a "health care system," it is important to recognize that we are usually focused more narrowly upon care for people who are (or are at risk of becoming) ill. Clearly, medical care is only one small part of what makes us healthy. As individuals, we are faced with an endless stream of admonitions to watch our diet, stop smoking, exercise more, practice safe sex, avoid recreational drug use, and, by the way, avoid stress, even when thinking about all of our unhealthy habits. As a society, we are well aware of the importance of clean air, clean water, safe foods, and being immunized against infectious diseases. We know that poverty is strongly correlated to ill health, and that an individual who must sleep on the street is unlikely to be healthy. Although we recognize the critical importance of public health or other policies outside the "health care system" toward maintaining and improving the health of the general population, and note that present-day Canadians appear to be among the healthiest and longest-lived populations in human history, this paper will deal more narrowly with medical care. There is still a need for health care services when we are sick or injured. The question this paper will focus on is how best to pay for these services.

What we will concentrate upon are the payment questions involved when an individual seeks care from hospitals, doctors, nurses, rehabilitation specialists, pharmacists, and other health care workers. We will begin by speaking of these in the language of economics. In effect, economists often view obtaining such care as a series of transactions, in which a "consumer" (often known as a "patient") "demands" services from a "provider" who in turn is paid (by someone) for the services which they provide. As we will note below, there are some conceptual differences between being a "patient" and being a "consumer," but for the time being, let us stick with the language of economics.

Using this sort of language, we can separate health care systems into three dimensions:

We will use the term *financing* to refer to the methods by which money is collected from all of those consumers, and potential consumers, of health care. Financing thus includes an array of taxes and premiums, collected from individuals and corporations, and collected by governments, insurers, and providers. Financing also includes consideration of who will be covered, and for what services.

We will use the term *delivery* to refer to all the ways in which those health care services are actually organized and delivered.

Finally, we will use the term *allocation* to refer to the variety of ways in which financing is linked to delivery. In other words, allocation refers to the way in which we choose to pay providers, and includes such topics as what incentives are inherent in the ways providers of care are paid for delivering services.

As we will see, many of the problems we have had in diagnosing the problems in our health care system have arisen from the failure to distinguish between financing and delivery. Other confusions have arisen when pathologies are diagnosed in allocation, but the suggested therapies instead deal with financing or delivery, which are working relatively well. To shift metaphors, one doesn't fix a malfunctioning appliance by breaking the parts which are already working!

Public and Private

Another set of confusions has arisen over the meaning of the terms *public* and *private*. Here, we are using the term "public" to denote "government." As we recognize, Canada has many levels of government. By "public," we can accordingly be speaking of the *federal* government in Ottawa, of the various *provincial* governments, of the series of *regional* governments and authorities within most provinces, or of *local* governments. Indeed, there has been a series of noisy battles occurring within the public sector, as provinces battle with Ottawa for more funds, and as provincial governments download some responsibilities to regions and local governments.

The term "private" is even more confusing. When we hear "private," we usually think about large *for-profit corporations*, responsible for providing a good return on investment to their shareholders. But private also encompasses *small businessmen/entrepreneurs* who do not issue stock; indeed, most Canadian physicians are private providers, running their own small businesses and making their living from the "profit." (Physicians are understandably annoyed to have their billings misrepresented as "salary"—the billings are instead their revenues, from which they must run their practices and pay their staff.) Private also includes a large *not-for-profit* sector. Some of these not-for-profit organizations, such as the Canadian Cancer Society or a local agency which delivers Meals on Wheels, rely heavily upon volunteer labour. But other not-for-profits are sizeable organizations, with paid employees. Finally, private includes *individuals* and their families. As any parent knows, most care for minor conditions is delivered privately, and never even comes in contact with the formal care delivery system.

Within the Canadian health care system, it is important to realize that almost all delivery of care is already private. Canada is not England. Under the system of "socialized medicine" found in such countries as the UK or Scandinavia, providers of health care work for some level of government and are therefore categorized as public employees. In contrast, most Canadian providers work in the private sector. This fact is often obscured because Canada has long used the rather confusing term "public hospital" to refer to private, not-for-profit institutions. To clarify the distinction, employees of "public hospitals" do not work for government, and are not civil servants. Ontario's provincial psychiatric hospitals would accordingly be classified as public delivery, because their employees are indeed part of the Ontario public service, and their management must follow civil service guidelines. In contrast, employees of the North York General Hospital report to an independent hospital board and management, and would therefore be classified as working for a private sector, not-for-profit organization. Even in the provinces which have moved toward regional authorities, the employees of these regional boards are not civil servants, and the regional management is not bound by civil service requirements.

One reason for the confusion is that our "public hospitals" do receive most of their funding from government; in 1997, just over 90% of the spending for hospital care came from public sources. However, this reliance upon public financing does not eliminate their formal organizational independence. Indeed, in that same year, physicians received 99% of their funding from the public sector, but are certainly not government employees (much as they may feel so if the paper work gets sufficiently aggravating). Political scientists are fond of attaching labels to this sort of private organization which nonetheless often acts on behalf of the public interest, and may be regulated by and funded from government. Some refer to them as "mediating structures"; others refer to them as the "third sector." Under any label, they are a critical component of Canada's health care system.

As we will see, this distinction between types of private is important in clarifying whether Ralph Klein's initiative in Alberta really represents "privatizing" hospitals. Premier Klein has introduced legislation which would permit for-profit clinics to be paid by the government for delivering insured health care services, as an alternative to giving the money to existing not-for-profit hospitals. This initiative does not represent a shift from public delivery to private delivery; instead, it is a shift from not-for-profit private to for-profit private delivery. The distinction also clarifies that privatization of funding has little to do with the need "to allow innovation in a stultified public delivery system," since, as we have just noted, most Canadian providers are already private. Instead, these debates are really about three things. First, we are often arguing about the total amount of money allocated—whether it is sufficient, and whether it is being used appropriately. Second, we may concentrate upon the nature of the incentives built into the funding allocation approach, and whether these are effective in ensuring that the services we want are being provided. Third, and critical to the debate about the Alberta initiative, we are debating the role of for-profit corporations, as opposed to not-for-profit organizations, in delivering health care in Canada.

BASIC ECONOMICS AND THE CONCEPT OF MEDICAL NECESSITY

Consider the following two scenarios:

1. You hail a taxi and ask the driver to take you to a destination across the city. You do not have enough money for the trip. Should you be taken there anyhow?

2. You have won a free all-expenses-paid week for two in a vacation spot of your choice, with the only catch being that the trip has to be taken sometime within the next twelve months. Do you accept?

In its simplest form, microeconomics deals with three components: supply, demand, and price. Price acts as the signalling factor that links supply and demand. Any self-respecting economist can plot supply and demand curves and look for their intersection. For example, if the price drops, the quantity demanded should increase; there should be a near infinite demand for free goods. Conversely, if supply is fixed and demand increases, price should rise until enough people get priced out of the market to balance the quantity supplied and this new (lower) quantity demanded at the new equilibrium price. Most people agree with the predictions which economic theory would make. For scenario 1, most would agree that the taxi driver is under no obligation to take you. If you cannot pay the cost the taxi driver wishes for the trip, you are priced out of the market for taxicabs. In turn, if you are priced out of the taxicab market, you can walk. If taxi fares get so high that there are insufficient customers, either some providers will leave the market, or prices will fall to a level with a more satisfactory balance of quantity supplied and quantity demanded. For scenario 2, most

people would be delighted to accept the free vacation.

Now consider two similar scenarios relating to health matters:

1. You come into a hospital emergency room with a ruptured appendix. You do not have enough money for the surgery. Should you be treated anyhow?

2. You have won free open heart surgery in the hospital of your choice, with the only catch being that the surgery must be performed within the next twelve months. Do you accept?

Suddenly, economic theory does not seem to apply. Most people would agree that your appendix should be treated, and would be horrified were you turned away for financial reasons. In economic terms, however, this means that we will not allow you to be priced out of the market for appendix care, or other sorts of services which you "need." Under those circumstances, we have set up a rather peculiar economic model, in which there is a "floor price" (whatever charity or the public system agrees to pay for that service) but no ceiling price. The private tier is thus free to jack up their prices as high as they wish, because anyone priced out of their market has the option of falling back into the publicly-funded tier. Indeed, providers working simultaneously within both tiers are assured that they will get at least the price which would be paid by the public tier, with the ability to collect whatever additional private charges they can as a bonus. Two disquieting consequences follow. First, under these circumstances, market forces can no longer achieve cost control; the refusal to allow people to be priced out of the market means that markets can't set a ceiling price. Second, unless the publicly-funded tier is inadequate (or at least, perceived to be inadequate), there would be no reason for "consumers" to pay extra for care. As we will note below, the myth that a privately-funded tier could strengthen the public system by "freeing up" time and resources accordingly makes no economic sense, precisely because a viable private tier depends upon eroding the publicly funded system to create a market for privately funded care.

But need has a flip side, as can be seen in considering our likely responses to scenario 2. Most people would be eager to take that free trip. However, whenever I have tested this hypothetical offer of free surgery, the main response is laughter, and then the statement, "only if I needed it." Microeconomics speaks of "demand." However, much of health care instead speaks the language of "need."

There is a category of good, often referred to as "merit goods," which most societies believe should not operate according to the laws of the market. Instead, these goods are allocated on some basis of need and merit. Need is a complex concept, and notoriously difficult to define. However, we tend to know it when we see it, at least in extreme situations. Market models are not designed to assist us in allocating resources on the basis of need. Indeed, the concept is inherently paternalistic, since "need" must be validated by some outside authority. I can tell you what I want, but we allow health professionals (or "society") to determine what I need. The term "consumer" is accordingly inappropriate when we are talking about these sorts of services. Consumers purchase what they want and can afford. Patients receive what they need. And, just as we are unwilling to deny people with a ruptured appendix care they "need," we consider it inappropriate, or even unethical, to provide most medical services if they are not needed. If a shoe store has an excess supply, they may hold a sale, and no one worries if I already have twelve pairs of similar shoes, if the shoes are unattractive, or even whether or not they fit. However, if my local hospital had surplus operating room time, it could not advertise Half-price Surgery, Today Only. We can speak of unnecessary surgery, in a way we cannot speak about unnecessary shoes. And in turn, this implies that the issue of finding the resources to pay for things that we "need" is fundamentally different from paying for things which we merely "want" or "demand."

THE NATURE OF INSURANCE

Insurance is a way to distribute risks by pooling expected costs both across time, and across a wider population. To take an arbitrary example, imagine 10,000 homes, distributed across many communities and each valued at $300,000. Now assume that, on average, one will be destroyed every year by lightning. Without insurance, most people would not be struck by lightning, and therefore would not have to replace their house, but one unlucky individual would incur a bill of $300,000. Most people would find that cost prohibitive. However, if each household paid a $40 premium, we could create a pool of $400,000. That should be enough to reimburse the unlucky individual, cover the costs of collecting the premiums, and still allow a profit for the group willing to act as the insurer. Each individual would be trading a sure loss of $40 to avoid a potential loss of $300,000. However, "on average" is not the same as "exactly." Some years, no houses would be struck. In other years, lightning might hit two or even three. If only $400,000 were collected, the pool would not be large enough to cover the losses in such years. Precisely because the number of unlucky individuals is unpredictable, the logic of insurance encourages large risk pools, so that peaks and valleys are more likely to average out to a predictable value.

However, not all houses are at equal risk. In insurance markets, this difference in risk links to two important concepts—"moral hazard," which pertains to the behaviour of those insured, and "risk selection," which pertains to the behaviour of those who are doing the insuring.

Economists use the term "moral hazard" to refer to the fact that rational individuals are more likely to buy insurance if they think they are more likely to use services. Indeed, people may even engage in risky behaviour precisely because they are insured (*e.g.*, building on a flood plain if they have flood insurance). Moral hazard in turn suggests that rational insurers are not willing to extend unlimited coverage to a population which can voluntarily decide whether they wish to purchase insurance. Some obvious examples suggest themselves. Those people wishing cosmetic surgery would be far more likely to purchase insurance which would cover such services than would the general population. Women in their 70s would not purchase additional coverage for childbirth. Similarly, those who are young and healthy may be more willing to forgo health insurance than those who already know they have a chronic disease. However, moral hazard in health care does not work in quite the same way that it does for other insurance markets. People are unlikely to abuse their health solely because they will not have to pay for the resulting care, because poor health has too many other unpleasant consequences.

The flip side of "moral hazard" is referred to as "risk selection." In this case, the rational insurer seeks to avoid those customers most likely to cost them money. Sometimes, they refuse a policy outright. Other times, they charge higher premiums. If they can, they will also seek to limit their "exposure" to claims. Just as the insurer can cap the amount payable for the destroyed house at $300,000, sellers of health insurance also try to limit the amount they must pay for claims. As one example, most dental policies sold limit the total amount that they will pay for dental work.

As Deborah Stone has noted,[1] here are two basic ways to determine insurance premiums. One approach is to charge everyone the same rate; she refers to this as employing solidarity principles. Under this type of system, often known as "community rating," those at high risk are subsidized by those at lower risk. The alternative is to employ actuarial principles, also known as risk-rating or medical underwriting. Under this model, premiums are based on expected claims. Automobile insurance works on this principle; the teenager with the sports car will pay far higher premiums than the proverbial little old lady who only drives to church on Sundays.

In general, we consider this fair. If the teenager finds insurance too expensive, she can walk or find a part-time job. Neither are we concerned if the person with a history of traffic accidents finds he cannot afford to keep driving. However, when we are talking about health care, things become a bit trickier. We are no longer as comfortable to find people priced out of the market. We are not sure whether the person with a history of cancer should pay higher premiums for health insurance. Unfortunately, any altruistic insurer who agrees to give lower rates to these high risk individuals is likely to lose their lower risk customers to less magnanimous competitors who can offer bargain rates to the healthy. As Fein has noted, the resulting spiral means that those companies willing to cover such high-risk cases usually become less and less competitive, precisely because they find themselves left with the costliest cases.[2] Solidarity-based markets are inherently unstable if competition among insurers is allowed, therefore, because competitors have an incentive to woo those at lower risk by offering them lower premiums and/or enhanced benefits (e.g., wellness programs). Without government regulation, competing insurers will employ actuarial rating, which means that high risks will eventually be priced out of the market. For example, a General Accounting Office (GAO) study of the US private insurance market found that they "virtually always denied coverage" to individuals with AIDS or heart disease; for individuals with other serious conditions, such as chronic back pain, anemia, knee injury, glaucoma, and asthma, the coverage excluded costs arising from these "pre-existing conditions." Similarly, almost all travel health insurance policies will tend to exclude pre-existing conditions and carefully examine the medical history of their prospective clients. Very few travel health insurers are willing to cover your 85-year-old mother with a cardiac condition, even though she really wants to visit Florida. In the US, insurers are increasingly seeking to avoid having to cover individuals at high risk of needing health care services; paradoxically, of course, these are precisely those who need such insurance the most. You can easily buy health insurance, as long as you are healthy and seen as likely to remain that way.

In summary, competitive insurance principles give economic incentives for insurers to limit their risk, both through defining whom they will cover, and through ensuring that liability will not be open ended. Any company not abiding by these incentives will be uncompetitive. In a competitive model, those most in need of insurance coverage are least likely to find anyone willing to insure them; if coverage is available, it is likely to be at a very high (often unaffordable) cost. Overall costs also tend to be higher, in part because fragmented payers have a diminished ability to control the costs they must pay to providers, and in part because of the additional administrative overhead introduced. (As one of many examples, providers have to deal with a myriad of insurance companies, each with different forms, rules, and regulations.) Many of these added costs fall upon employers, decreasing their economic competitiveness. For these reasons, health economists are virtually unanimous in agreeing that introducing competition in financing medically necessary care—as opposed to competition in how this care is delivered—is a bad idea. Indeed, the international evidence is clear that, when dealing with this sort of necessary care, single payer systems tend to be more economically efficient

than more pluralistic approaches to financing medically necessary services. Canadian insurers and employers agree.[3-4]

CRITICAL THINKING QUESTIONS

1. What is the difference between private insurance and private delivery, and why is this important? In your opinion, will for-profit delivery of health services solve Canada's health care woes?

2. What are some of the determinants of health that the author enumerates? Can you name some additional factors? What role do these determinants play in your own life? That is, what activities do you engage in (or reject) in order to stay healthy?

3. Explain how a private insurance system works in terms of risk (who pays the highest premiums, for example). Does such a system work for health insurance? Why or why not?

NOTES

1. Stone, D. A. 1993. The struggle for the soul of health insurance. *J. Health Polit. Policy Law*, 18(2): 287–317.

2. Fein R. 1986. *Medical care, medical costs: The search for a health insurance policy*. Cambridge, MA: Harvard University Press.

3. Deber, R. B., A. Gildiner, and P. Baranek. 1999. Why not private health insurance? Part I. Insurance made easy. *C.M.A.J.*, 161(5): 539–44.

4. Deber, R. B., A. Gildiner, and P. Baranek. 1999. Why not private health insurance? Part II. Actuarial principles meet provider dreams. *C.M.A.J.*, 161(5): 545–50.

55

Crack and Prostitution: Gender, Myths, and Experiences

PATRICIA G. ERICKSON, JENNIFER
BUTTERS, PATTI MCGILLICUDDY,
AND ASE HALLGREN

In this article, Erickson et al. report on their research into crack-using women who work in the sex trade to support their drug use. Their findings reveal the harsh realities of the streets and how socially marginalized these women are. The authors conclude that the increasing availability and use of crack have particularly serious consequences for poor women who are, or become, sex-trade workers.

Who wants to be a crack head when you think about it? Who wants to fucking stand on the corner in the fucking –18C and sell their body for a piece of rock that's going to be gone in fucking 10 minutes?

—"Jenny," age 25

The woman who sells her body for drugs is the most dependent person in the world.

—Germaine Greer, *The Whole Woman*, p. 6

This paper presents the results from in-depth interviews with 30 crack-using women also working in the sex trade to support their drug use. The gender roles perspective highlights traditional beliefs from past decades about the appeal of cocaine to women, its effects on their sexuality, and the reasons they become prostitutes.

Source: P. G. Erickson, J. Butters, P. McGillicuddy, and A. Hallgren, 2000. "Crack and Prostitution: Gender, Myths, and Experiences." *Journal of Drug Issues*, 30(4), 767–88.

INTRODUCTION

The image of the crack-using prostitute has come to epitomize the ultimate shame and sexual degradation of women, but this portrayal is merely the latest in a long series of linkages between "fallen women" and substance use (Carstairs, 1998). The drug use experience of women has long been interpreted through the lens of ingrained cultural assumptions about their "remarkable vulnerability" to addiction and their inevitable downfall once they succumb to intoxicating temptations (Fillmore, 1984). In the early decades of the past century, indulgence in alcohol, tobacco, marijuana, and heroin for pleasure or "highs" was subject to severe social disapproval, while consuming the same substances in medicinal form was acceptable (Gomberg, 1982).

In the early 1980s, the gender roles perspective articulated a broader view on substance use within the framework of women's normative role as nurturer and caregiver (Colten & Marsh, 1984). Concern about women who use alcohol or other drugs is seen as rooted in the perception that such behavior impairs the performance of their primary role; thus, they are viewed as more sick and deviant than male substance users (Marsh, 1982). Women who engage in illicit drug use are doubly deviant because they are not only breaking the law but also engaging in a predominantly male activity (Erickson & Watson, 1990). The negative sanctions applied to women who depart from mainstream standards serve as a form of social control and warning to all women to stay in their place (Rosenbaum, 1981). Like women who reject the housewife role for less traditional pursuits, women who use cocaine pose a particular threat to the gender role expectations of society.

The primary focus of this paper is the impact of crack addiction on poor women who were in, or became involved in, the sex trade. Building on the tradition of studies linking drug-using women with prostitution (Erickson & Watson, 1990), recent research has examined this latest manifestation in the crack era (Inciardi, Lockwood, & Pottieger, 1993; Maher, 1997). Maher and Daly (1996, pp. 483–484) describe how women in the street-level sex trade were affected by increased crack consumption in a New York neighborhood: "The market became flooded with novice sex workers, the going rate for sexual transactions decreased, and 'deviant' sexual expectations by dates increased, as did the levels of violence and victimization." Studies in several U.S. locales made similar observations; common practices include women repeatedly turning tricks for $5 or $10, just enough for another "rock" of crack, accepting dangerous dates, engaging in a variety of sexual practices beyond oral sex and intercourse, and servicing multiple partners in crack houses for a hit of crack (Bourgois & Dunlap, 1993; Inciardi, 1993; Pottieger & Tressell, 1999a). Like Fagan (1994), Sterk, Dolan, and Hatch (1999) contend that many of these acts go beyond conventional understandings of prostitution and constitute abusive sexual encounters.

This paper will present the results of an intensive interview study with 30 women who are heavily involved in crack use and obtain it primarily by selling or trading sex. We examine experiences in the effects of crack and the meanings of addiction for these women.

Sample and Method

Locating respondents who are engaged in activities that are both illegal and highly deviant is challenging. While studies of treatment samples have been the primary source of generalizations about illicit drug users in the past, their failure to reflect the much larger pool of unidentified users has led to more emphasis on community-based recruitment (Erickson & Alexander, 1989). Drug researchers have developed methods of locating low-profile subjects through an adaptation of qualitative and ethnographic techniques pioneered in the broader study of deviant populations (Douglas, 1972). Along with the time required to gain trust, a large element of self-selection is involved in such recruitment; cocaine use and prostitution have been studied this way (e.g., Goldstein, 1979; Erickson, Adlaf, Smart, & Murray, 1987). Since crack use is even more rare than cocaine use and lodged in groups that are quite inaccessible to random-sample household surveys, more targeted fieldwork is required.

While hidden populations of crack users have most often been studied in treatment or street samples, both approaches have strengths and limitations (Pottieger, Tressell, Surrall, Inciardi, & Chitwood, 1995). Treatment programs provide more ready access in safer settings, and their participants may be more ready to allow researchers access to their histories and experiences. They will not, however, be representative of those crack users at large on the street where ongoing use and income-generating activities are still paramount. A number of street studies of female crack users have been conducted, some utilizing large samples of several hundred women (Fagan,

1994; Pottieger & Tressler, forthcoming), others focusing on in-depth and sometimes repeated interviews with smaller samples (Maher & Daley, 1996; Sterk et al., 1999). It is clear that with empathy and persistence, researchers are able to locate women who use crack and gain the trust necessary for them to tell their stories honestly.

The site of this study was an inner-city neighborhood of Toronto known as "East Downtown," which had become notable for its street market in crack cocaine in the early 1990s. One author [Erickson] had gained some field presence and credibility in the area by undertaking some earlier collaborative research with local service-agency staff on violence in the crack trade (Erickson et al., 1996; Erickson, Butters, & German, 2000). These ongoing connections with health care providers in the area, combined with a growing concern for the impact of crack on residents and, in particular, the use of crack by some women living and working on these streets, led to this collaborative study.

Between November 1996 and February 1997, 30 women were recruited on the basis of being known heavy crack users for some years. The approach was made by a trusted local street worker who knew the women well [co-author Hallgren]. A trained person, also known and respected in the community, conducted the interviews in a local drop-in centre. The women were paid $20 and provided with food, soft drinks, and cigarettes. No names were recorded, and the identity of the women remained unknown to the research team. Most of the interviews, which took about one hour to complete, were tape recorded and transcribed, but in a few cases, at the participant's request, verbatim responses were recorded by hand. The women divulged information about many aspects of their lives related to drug use, experience with violence, and the sex trade, and appeared to be honest and open in their responses. While this particular group of women cannot be said to represent female crack users in general, it does reflect the range of characteristics and backgrounds of such women in this area of

Toronto. While a contrast to more conventional, middle-class users (Erickson, Adlaf, Smart, & Murray, 1994; Murphy & Rosenbaum, 1997), such a sample may be considered quite appropriate for providing insights into the world of the poor, female crack user.

The demographic and drug-use profile of the 30 women in our study is the following. The average age of the Toronto East Downtown sample was 31, ranging from 22 to 52 years. The majority (17) of participants were White; seven were Native Canadian, five were Black, and one was East Indian. While 27 had been pregnant and 25 had given birth, all of their children were living with relatives, had been taken into care, or were grown up. All the women interviewed lived in the area, some most of their lives, with an average time spent of seven years. While 17 women had some form of relatively stable housing such as an apartment or room, the rest were homeless, living either on the street or transiently in neighborhood shelters. Although we did not probe their educational or occupational histories in depth, very few mentioned any previous conventional jobs other than housewife, and all but one had a criminal arrest record that would have further limited employment options. All of the participants acknowledged past as well as recent or current involvement in prostitution, identifying it as their major source of income. For less than half of the women, other forms of petty crime, drug selling, and panhandling, as well as some form of welfare benefit, were additional sources of income. While we did not ask the question directly, most of the women volunteered a history of childhood or adolescent physical and/or sexual abuse.

While all the women were current crack users at the time of the interview, using it for an average of eight and one-half years (the range of time these women had been using crack was between two and 13 years), they also had a poly-drug use history. All had used cannabis, 28 had also used powder cocaine, and 27 had used numerous prescription drugs; 25 had used LSD, 14 had used speed, and 11 had used heroin. Age of first drug use was 14 years on average and ranged from eight to 26 years. Most also continued to use alcohol, marijuana, and prescription drugs in the past year and past month, with very few exclusively using crack. This profile is similar to the street samples described by Fagan (1994), Maher and Daley (1996), Sterk et al. (1999), and Pottieger and Tressler (forthcoming), with the primary demographic distinction being the higher proportion of White participants in our Canadian sample. The social disadvantage of the women in all these studies is evident, regardless of location.

In the next sections, we shall present the women's introduction to crack, their perceptions of its effects, and what they like and dislike about it.

Experience of Crack Use

The women were asked what was going on in their lives when they first were exposed to crack and what had led them to try it. Responses fell mainly in two categories. About half—16 women—identified some particularly traumatic or difficult chronic personal situations. These included the death of family members, serious illness, divorce, miscarriage, losing their children, experiencing a rape or other form of abuse, and suffering from stress, depression, or other serious mental instability. Sometimes it was a combination of things:

Three things in a row—I got raped; I came home and found my partner of 11 years in bed with my best friend; then I lost my child.

Crack's "bad press" could be an incentive to someone who was looking for escape:

I was just out of a bad, an abusive relationship. I tried to kill myself . . . I was lonely and depressed. I was watching TV one day, *COPS* or something, and saw it (crack) being done. I actually drove my car to ____ and asked for a rock. And so I started on my own.

A second set of responses referred to crack coming along when the women were already quite drug-involved; for example:

Me and my husband were both (methamphetamine) addicts. We had got arrested for dealing speed and then when I came out of jail all of a sudden this new drug was around, crack cocaine. And I went off the speed immediately and started smoking the crack.

Other women who switched their drug of choice to crack had previously been doing powder cocaine or injecting heroin. Its ready availability in their circles made crack easy to try. Finally, a third and smaller group of other responses were offered by women who simply tried it because it was around, others were doing it, or they described themselves as young and naïve.

They liked the rush, the relaxation, and the numbing effects on their emotions while still keeping them mentally alert. They could articulate many positive aspects of crack, but they also recognized its down side. Their more negative comments included that "crack wears you out," and that it made them sick, led to weight loss, and destroyed their lungs. Feelings of paranoia, depression, and memory loss were also mentioned. The worst aspect identified was coming down from a crack high, or "jonesing" as they termed it, when their supply ran out.

Are these women addicted to crack? From their own perspective, 27 of the 30 women answered that they were. Their expressions of craving and what they will do to get crack appear to substantiate their personal assessment. The question, "do you *get* all the crack you want?" produced these typical replies:

There's never enough.

The thing about crack cocaine is you never get enough.

One [hit] is too many and a thousand is never enough.

You never get all the drugs you need or want.

When asked what they do if they can't get crack, responses varied, with many women pointing out that "there's always some way to get it" if you are desperate enough:

You'll do anything to get it, that one hit on the pipe.

You want the crack so bad you'd do anything.

EXPERIENCE OF PROSTITUTION

For some women, life on the street started quite late, often after leaving an abusive relationship and having no money. "Cynthia," a 45-year-old woman with three grown children who has spent four years on the streets in Toronto East Downtown, provided this account:

Since I started crack it's been a whole different life for me. I didn't live on the street before, until I was 40 years old. I didn't start hooking until I was 40 years old. After being a wife and a mother for so many years, then all of a sudden you're into hooking and you are doing that to pay for your crack.

For others, getting involved in drug use and prostitution started at an early age. "Marlene," a 25-year-old woman who had been working in the area for the past two years, described this sequence:

I've been doing it (prostitution) since I was 16 years old, that's like what I know best. I started prostitution to support my habit for alcohol and marijuana . . . when you have so many people touching your body, I did the drugs first. I got addicted (to crack) when I was 18 and I've never stopped since that.

While some had started prostitution to support themselves, as a way to survive on the streets, or to pay for other drugs, at this stage all of these women acknowledged spending most of what they earned now on crack. These are some responses to a question asking, why do you work in the sex trade?

To support my habit . . . that's not initially why I started.

Because I don't have any other way of getting money.

I'm addicted to crack cocaine and I have no other source of income.

Central to an understanding of the sex–crack dynamic is that stopping crack use was not considered a serious option by these women. Only a minority (nine) even identified their drug use as a problem. To most, it is the solution—they continue to use because it's

what makes their lives bearable or interesting. Selling sex is the means to this end.

The sexual marketability of these women may have been reinforced by the effect of cocaine on body image and body weight. By keeping thin and subject to sexual objectification, crack-using women reflect the historical assertion that "women's social value has been inseparable from their bodies" (Brown & Jasper, 1993, p. 18). However, their subordination extended beyond simply selling sex. Some of the women recounted sexual deviations beyond what they considered normal heterosexual services for the trade (i.e., genital and oral sex), with which, nevertheless, they had complied, or been forced to perform:

I've done a lot of things for crack. Sure I've sucked a dick for crack. Sure I've been with four men one time. I had to.

In the context of street prostitution in an area with a high volume of crack consumption going on, many of the customers will also be using crack. Some of the women did sex-for-crack exchanges, what they called "freaking," in crack houses. Others serviced well-off male professionals who paid for crack and expected to get high and have sex as part of the overall transaction. This gave the women ample opportunity to observe the differential effect of crack on women and men. The Swiss psychiatrist, Hans Maier, in his 1926 treatise on cocaine addiction, believed that cocaine reduced the sexual potency of men but had this effect on women: "In women there is, without exception, an increase in both the physical and psychological components of sexual drive. There is an exaggerated sensitivity to sexual stimuli . . . [she] often makes direct sexual advance to any man who happens to be present" (Maier, 1926: tr. Kalant, 1987, p. 82). While the women in our study universally and emphatically denied that crack stimulated their own sexual arousal, they saw it affecting men quite differently:

Men get extremely horny where a lot of women don't.

Men want sex when they're on it and I can't stand it.

The women also thought that men tended to get violent on crack and that this added additional risk when sex was being traded for crack or money to male crack users, a major segment of their clientele.

Crack markets are characterized by a high degree of systemic violence (Goldstein, 1985), and prostitution is an occupation that also entails a high degree of personal risk of violence (Erickson & Watson, 1990); the combination of the two is dangerous and can be lethal. Maher and Daly (1996) noted that three of the 45 women in their study were murdered. "Sally," a 34-year-old respondent who had worked in the Toronto East Downtown for 10 years, said, "I risk my life every day," and provided some examples:

There have been fights with knives over crack, over 20 pieces in a crack house, I was almost raped because I did not want to give this guy a blowjob after he gave me a toke. . . . I had my jaw broken (by my boyfriend) when I was partying with this girl. [Why?] Because I smoked without him.

Three quarters of the women in our study reported being hurt as a result of their involvement with crack, most of them experiencing multiple incidents of violence. Nevertheless, these women acknowledge their feelings of vulnerability in their responses to the question "What is the most pressing issue to women on the street?":

There is always the fear of being beaten, robbed or killed.

Rape. It's happened to me twice this year, when I've been intoxicated.

The effects of a form of post-traumatic stress related to a history of assault and abuse may indeed contribute to the need to continue to use crack (Ledray, 1994), and the effects of abuse may become compounded for women of color (McGillicuddy, 1993). That these women survive on the street and cope as well as they do after many years of crack and other drug use reflects their ability to be streetwise and handle numerous threatening situations. Some take a certain pride or satisfaction in the various ways

their lives have evolved. "Cynthia," who came to crack later in life than most, described herself this way:

I've always been someone who liked to live dangerously, sort of on the edge. . . . I know it sounds strange for you to hear me say this, but I wouldn't change the experience that I've had, on the whole. I've learned so much.

"Rosa" described crack as a kind of catalyst:

My daughter's father was very abusive, and for some strange reason, cocaine gave me the courage to tell him to get the fuck out of my life.

Despite these assets of interpersonal skills and the excitement of the street life that clearly appeals to many of the women, their awareness of the dangers is realistic. [Two women working in the area were murdered soon after we did this study, and another was shot in a back alley in May, 2000.]

EXPERIENCE OF MOTHERHOOD

Virtually all of the women (25 of the 30) in this study are mothers. The number of children these women have had ranges from one to eight, with the majority giving birth to between one and three children; about five of them have more. In each case, none of the children are currently living with their mother but are instead being cared for by other relatives (including grandparents, aunts, fathers, sisters), have been adopted, or have been placed in foster care. In addition, some are already adults, and one woman said her daughter was on the streets.

Why are these children not with their mothers? A variety of reasons were given in response to this question. Some revolved quite clearly around issues of substance abuse:

I gave her up for adoption. She's not with me because I couldn't stop using crack. Best thing for her. I didn't want to do to her what my mother did to me, so I just figured I would just, you know, give her to Children's Aid. Then the youngest one, I went back to using and my mom took the babies and I'm still using.

My 12-year-old was taken away because I was only 14 [when she was born], my 10-year-old I sent down to my mother when she was 5, my son was born with crack in his system so the Children's Aid were involved but his grandmother took him.

[My] other daughter and son are with my little sister because of my addiction.

Many of these women recognized on their own that active mothering and cocaine use were incompatible. They were not in the position of being able to provide adequate care for their children because of their substance use—crack use in particular—and the lifestyle that went with it. They were often fortunate in having other family members available to take on the care of their children.

While these women have not given up cocaine use for the sake of their children, they have been able to make, or at least accept, the choice not to be the primary caregiver.

IMAGES OF SELF

Cooley's (1902) discussion of the "looking-glass self" suggests that self-concepts are the reflection of others' perceptions of us; in essence we are, or become, what we think others think we are. More contemporary formulations have extended this notion to a consideration of stigma (Goffman, 1963) and shame (Fossum & Mason, 1986). Since crack users and prostitutes are typically regarded with much disdain, the combination of the two identities places individuals at the extreme of stigmatization. Sometimes, external perceptions translate into self-concepts and may aid in the understanding of deviant subgroups such as the women in this study. While we did not explore this relationship in depth, we are concerned with the extent to which perceptions of others become internalized and contribute to a self-fulfilling prophecy or act as barriers to seeking help.

When the respondents in this study were asked how they felt others in their neighborhood perceived them, their vulnerability to derogatory and demeaning self-images was quite evident. Some perceptions were tied closely to crack use:

They see me as a crack-head and like a nobody. And that is true, they do, they look at me like a nobody and it really pees me off. You see me sometimes, how angry I get in that church when they start talkin' about me and putting me down 'cause they're no better than me.

Other responses identify images that revolve as much or more so around prostitution:

. . . as a drug addict, prostitute drug addict, basically that's what they think.

As a tramp. But I don't care, though, because I'm addicted to crack. I'm addicted to it, eh? I can't help myself, what they think of me 'cause whatever they think about me, I don't have time to think because my mind is just busy on the next toke.

The ability to resist such ingrained and widespread perceptions held by others poses a significant challenge to these women, and accepting the labels is perhaps the path of least resistance. However, it may also be a contributing factor to the downward spiral in which these women find themselves. If these images are internalized, then the doors to treatment and life-changing options may also be perceived as pointless. And this may in fact be one of the greatest dangers these women face.

OPTIONS FOR CHANGE?

What might make a difference in these women's lives? We asked them about their prior experience with treatment, their views on different forms of drug access, and what sorts of services they thought would be helpful to women like them. While seeking treatment had been part of the drug-use history of 22 of the women, their reasons were predominantly either to "get some rest and rehab," or to respond to some external threat, such as the loss of their children or their housing, or to reduce jail time. The short-term nature of most of these interventions and the return to life on the streets did not present a successful picture of treatment outcome.

When asked what a free supply of drugs would do to their current way of life, 23 said they would stop other illegal activities and leave the street:

Absolutely. I'm not a law breaker by choice. I much prefer not to be putting my ass on the line, so to speak.

Definitely. I wouldn't have time to do it. I'd be too busy getting high.

Not surprisingly, given that any form of cocaine maintenance has almost never been discussed even in drug-treatment or drug-policy circles, most women had not thought about such an alternative (Erickson & Cheung, 1999). For poor women, there would still be the issue of where they would get money to live. Therefore, prostitution and other illegal acts may not necessarily subside. We also asked them if they would take a "crack substitute" if one were available: 18 said they would, seven said they wouldn't, and three were undecided. The negative responses were geared mainly to not wanting to stop crack or not wishing to substitute one addictive drug for another.

The women were more expansive when offered the chance to suggest the kinds of services they would like to see offered in the community. They enumerated a number of simple needs like places to shower, do laundry, and sleep safely when they were exhausted. Most of the women, 24 of 30, also would like to see more health services geared to their needs, and many also mentioned counseling—often defined as just someone to talk to—on a 24-hour basis. These are some of the examples they elaborated:

A hotline for women, someone to offer support

Counseling to get back on track

A roof over my head 3 to 4 nights a week

A year's treatment out of the city

Somewhere to call your own

An understanding, good ear

Somewhere to go and be safe

In other words, being treated like human beings with the same needs as everyone else.

SUMMARY AND CONCLUSION

Our study of 30 crack-using prostitutes refutes the view that cocaine makes these women "sexually licentious," as was believed in earlier eras (Carstairs, 1998; Maier, 1926, in tr. Kalant, 1987). It is clear that they work in the sex trade to get money and/or crack to support their own usage when few other sources of income are available to them. Far from enjoying sex while intoxicated, they describe it as aversive. Nor was their use of crack the main impetus to a career on the streets—most were involved in both the drug and sex trades previously, but crack intensified that life and led to more dangerous and perverse sexual activities. This is similar to the conclusions of Maher and Daly (1996) and others. Nor has research on women who use crack and lead otherwise conventional lives indicated any particularly positive effect of cocaine on their sexual activities (Erickson et al., 1994). Nevertheless, it is possible that women in the lower echelon of the sex trade, many of whom have histories of early childhood and adolescent sexual and physical abuse, may be less inclined to take pleasure in sex, irrespective of cocaine use.

The other prevailing stereotype, that crack-using women are unfit mothers, was in a sense upheld by the women themselves. Most had given up their children or had them taken away, but none disputed the appropriateness of this decision. This did not mean that they had no feelings for their children—quite the opposite. We would argue that they were acting, insofar as they were able, in the best interests of their children.

The policy of legal and social suppression of crack has helped it to find ready markets in vulnerable portions of the population. Nevertheless, there is no simple answer to these women's problems, such as legalizing the supply of the drug. As they say, "you can never have enough." Unlike methadone maintenance for heroin users, there is no "cocadone" that alleviates withdrawal symptoms or provides a longer-acting substitute (Erickson & Cheung, 1999). Effective intervention strategies for problem cocaine use depend, in part, on motivation for change—noticeably absent in most of this population, who lack the stakes in conformity that provide self- and informal controls over the most excessive use-patterns (Waldorf, Reinarman, & Murphy, 1991). Moreover, these women are characterized by the poverty and lack of social support that predicts poor compliance and relapse in the management of chronic conditions generally (McLellan, Lewis, O'Brien, & Kleber, 2000). Strategies that would provide a safer environment for use of drugs, along with community outreach of health and social services, might have more individual and social benefit for such women than drug-focused policy options.

The pervasive violence and fear of violence that these women experience speaks to the importance of improving the working conditions on the street and providing safe shelters and support for these women. While they are unlikely to choose a life without crack in their present situation, some of the riskier aspects of their existence might be ameliorated by nonjudgmental approaches to meeting their basic needs. As the above discussion indicated, abstinence-oriented treatment is not a particularly appealing or an effective approach for these women. Whether a longer-term investment, geared to their lifestyle, and treating crack addiction as a chronic medical condition might produce a more favorable result remains to be tried (McLellan et al., 2000). Our participants are positively inclined to more services and support in their immediate community. These types of broad harm-reduction measures, such as housing, medical attention, and safer work conditions, might realistically focus on keeping the women alive and HIV negative rather than ending their crack addiction.

ACKNOWLEDGMENTS

This project was funded by the Drug Abuse Prevention Program of the Department of Public Health, Toronto, and facilitated by Teresa Damaso.

CRITICAL THINKING QUESTIONS

1. Review the authors' discussion of how traditional gender-role behaviours influence the public's perception of female crack-using prostitutes.

2. In the article the authors describe some of the challenges researchers face when investigating illegal-drug users. Speculate on some of the challenges researchers might confront when investigating prescription-drug use among the middle class.

3. Of the 30 women interviewed as part of this research, only 9 felt that their drug use was a *problem*; to most of the women, it was in fact a *solution*. Explain this apparent contradiction from the sociological perspective.

REFERENCES

Bourgois, P., and E. Dunlap. 1993. Exorcising sex-for-crack: An ethnographic perspective from Harlem. In *Crack pipe as pimp: An ethnographic investigation of sex-for-crack exchanges*, ed. M. Rather. New York: Lexington Books.

Brown, Catrina, and Karin Jasper. 1993. *Consuming passions: Feminist approach to weight preoccupation and eating disorders*. Toronto: Second Story Press.

Butters, J., A. Hallgren, and P. McGillicuddy. 1997. *Poor women and crack use in downtown Toronto*. Research Report.

Carstairs, C. 1998. Innocent addicts, dope fiends and nefarious traffickers: Illegal drug use in 1920s English Canada. *Journal of Canadian Studies*, 33, 145–62.

Colten, M., and J. Marsh. 1984. A sex-roles perspective on drug and alcohol use by women. In *Sex roles and psychopathology*, ed. C. Widom. New York: Plenum.

Cooley, Charles. 1902. *Human nature and the social order*. New York: Scribner.

Douglas, J. 1972. *Research on deviance*. New York: Random House.

Erickson. P., E. Adlaf, R. Smart, and G. Murray. 1994. *The steel drug: Cocaine and crack in perspective*, 2nd ed. New York: Lexington Books.

Erickson, P., and B. Alexander. 1989. Cocaine and addictive liability. *Social Pharmacology*, 3, 249–70.

Erickson, P., J. Butters, B. Fischer, E. Fehrman, D. Haans, and B. Poland. 1996. Exploring drug market violence in a more peaceable society. Appendix G in the Draft Report of the Drugs–Violence Task Force, U.S. Sentencing Commission, Washington, DC.

Erickson, P., J. Butters, and B. German. 2000. Flexing crack in Toronto: A deviant pathway for poor, homeless drug users. Paper presented at the International Conference on Deviant Pathways, Porto, Portugal, January.

Erickson. P., and Y. Cheung. 1999. Harm reduction among cocaine users: Reflections on individual intervention and community social capital. *International Journal of Drug Policy*, 10, 235–46.

Erickson, P., and V. Watson. 1990. Women, illicit drugs and crime. *Research Advances in Alcohol and Drug Problems*, 10, 859–77.

Fagan, J. 1994. Women and drugs revisited: Female participation in the cocaine economy. *Journal of Drug Issues*, 24, 179–225.

Fillmore, K. 1984. When angels fall: Women's drinking as cultural preoccupation and as reality. In *Alcohol problems in women*, eds. S. Wilsnack and L. Beckman. New York: Guilford Press.

Fossum, Merle, and Marilyn Mason. 1986. *Facing shame*. New York: Norton.

Goffman, Erving. 1963. *Stigma: Notes on the management of spoiled identity*. Englewood Cliffs, NJ: Prentice-Hall.

Goldstein, P. 1979. *Prostitution and drugs*. Lexington, MA: Lexington Books.

———. 1985. The drugs/violence nexus: A tripartite conceptual framework. *Journal of Drug Issues*, 21, 345–67.

Gomberg, E. 1982. Historical and political perspectives: Women and drug use. *Journal of Social Issues*, 38, 9–23.

Humphries, D. 1999. *Crack mothers: Pregnancy, drugs and the media*. Columbus, OH: The Ohio State University.

Inciardi, J. 1993. King rats, chicken heads, slow necks, freaks and blood suckers: A glimpse of Miami sex-for-crack market. In *Crack pipe as pimp: An ethnographic investigation of sex-for-crack exchanges*, ed. M. Ratner. New York: Lexington Books.

Kalant, O. [tr.] 1987. *Maier's cocaine addiction [Der Kokainismus 1926]*. Toronto: Addiction Research Foundation.

Ledray, Linda. 1994. *Recovery from rape*. Holt and Company, New York.

McGillicuddy, Patricia. 1993. Embodied and emboldened: Dealing with sexual violence. In *Consuming passions: Feminist approach to weight preoccupation and eating disorders*, ed. C. Brown and K. Jasper. Toronto: Second Story Press.

McLennan. A., D. Lewis, C. O'Brien, and H. Kleber. 2000. Drug dependence, a chronic mental illness: Implications for treatment, insurance and outcome evaluation. *Journal of the American Medical Association*, 284, 1689–95.

Maher, L. 1997. *Sexed work: Gender, race and resistance in a Brooklyn drug market*. Oxford: Clarendon Press.

Maher, L., and K. Daly. 1996. Women in the street-level drug economy: Continuity or change? *Criminology*, 34, 465–91.

Marsh, J. 1982. Public issues and private problems: Women and drug use. *Journal of Social Issues*, 38, 153–65.

Murphy, S., and M. Rosenbaum. 1997. Two women who used cocaine too much: Class, race, gender, crack and coke. In *Crack in America: Demon drugs and social justice*, eds. C. Reinarman and H. Levine. California: University of California Press.

Pottieger. A., and P. Tressell. Social relationships of crime-involved women cocaine users. *Journal of Psychoactive Drugs*.

———. 1999a. Dimensions of sex trading among women cocaine users. Paper presented at the Annual Meeting of the American Society of Criminology, Washington, DC, November 1998.

———. 1999b. Barriers to treatment for crime-involved cocaine-dependent women. Paper presented at the Annual Meeting of the American Sociological Association, New York, August 1996.

Pottieger, A., P. Tressell, H. Surrall, J. Inciardi, and D. Chitwood. 1995. Drug use patterns of adult crack users in street and residential treatment samples. *Journal of Psychoactive Drugs*, 27, 27–38.

Rosenbaum, M. 1981. Sex roles among deviants: The woman addict. *International Journal of the Addictions*, 16, 859–77.

Sterk, C., K. Dolan, and S. Hatch. 1999. Epidemiological indicators and ethnographic realities of female cocaine use. *Substance Use and Misuse*, 34, 2057–72.

Waldorf, D., C. Reinarman, and S. Murphy. 1991. *Cocaine changes: The experience of using and quitting*. Philadelphia: Temple University Press.

56

Disability and Genetics: Affirming the Bare Life

JAMES OVERBOE

Along with advances in medical technology come novel and challenging ethical considerations. Sociologist James Overboe writes about his experiences with cerebral palsy and raises concerns about prenatal genetic testing for this and other diseases. He is afraid that this technology will result in a kind of "genetic fundamentalism." He further expresses concern about the immense power that this type of technology gives to the medical community. Armed with this new science, medical practitioners can effectively make life-and-death decisions based on genes.

DISABLING OF THE DISABLED

Today many members of society argue for genetic testing for disabilities because they believe that the "quality of life" for both the "afflicted" individuals and their "caregivers" is diminished. Will good parenting be measured by the extent of compliance to genetic technology? If so, what are the underlying pressures for women to submit their bodies to genetic testing, and genetic diagnostics?

I would argue the disabled subject is produced in an ableist matrix. One must ask, Under what conditions does the disabled person emerge as having a "bare life," where his or her ability to achieve a "political life" is in doubt?

Source: James Overboe. 2007. "Disability and Genetics: Affirming the Bare Life (the State of Exception)." *Canadian Journal of Sociology and Anthropology*, 44(2): 219–35. The original article was extensively reorganized and edited for this book.

Or perhaps more correctly how does an ableist matrix prohibit a disabled existence from coming to fruition? By "naming" the infant "disabled," he or she is abjectified. Making the infant the "state of exception" to varying degrees paints the future not only of the infant but also of the family and the community at large as a series of problems and catastrophes that derive from the unfortunate circumstance of disability. Yet as Elliot (2001) and Skidmore (1994) argue, it is impossible to accurately predict the future "quality of life" of a disabled person. If the disabled baby is born, then the marker "disability" looms over the child's life, and is reiterated by various authorities and throughout various intervals of time to reinforce or contest this unnatural state. The naming of the disabled demarcates or places them outside normality and, in doing so, repeatedly reaffirms the norm. Thus, the binary of disability and non-disability serves to reinforce normality within our society.

Jean Bethke Elshtain (1995: 35) claims that supporters of the primacy of the "right to choice" for women have seemingly contradictory positions. On one hand, they advocate genetic testing for disabilities, while on the other they are appalled at any suggestion of testing for the sex of the foetus. Sophia Isako Wong (2002: 97) writes, "Feminists have spent ample time clarifying the distinction between biological sex (having chromosome XX or XY) and the social construction of gender." Moreover, Wong (2002: 97) asks, "Might there be an analogous distinction between trisomy 21 (having three twenty-first chromosomes instead of two) and the social construction of people with Down syndrome as disabled?" Wong (2002: 114–15) concludes:

I see no sharp line between the difficulties of being a woman in a patriarchal society and those engendered by having Down syndrome in a society focused on cognitive capacity. My intuition is that the possibilities for people with Down syndrome will increase as our society dismantles the deeply entrenched institutionalization of sexual difference. If we can move toward overcoming the Enlightenment fetishization of cognitive ability and dislodge the institutional barriers enforcing cognitive difference, perhaps we can build a society in which everyone is at home with Down syndrome.

As Wong argues, it is not simply a matter of women taking these contradictory positions in regards to genetic testing. Rather, women who are bestowed this right are being pressured into making the "correct" choice. The discourse concerning disability as it applies to the proliferation of reproductive technologies, in particular prenatal testing for detectable foetal anomalies, is not inclusive. Tremain (2006), Rapp and Ginsburg (2001), and Ettore (2001) agree that the offices of genetic counsellors, along with the overall environment, weigh the decision in favour of genetic testing. Rayna Rapp and Faye Ginsburg (2001: 538) assert that although "genetic counsellors are trained to express neutrality about the choice a pregnant woman and her partner may make around amniocentesis testing, the very essence of such technology and the offer of such tests under the terms of consumer choice are premised on the desire for normalcy and fear of unknown abnormalities."

In the following passages from the article "Miracle Kid" by Lucinda Franks, a family with a child with Fraser syndrome relate how they risk going against both normative assumptions and expert advice in order to affirm the (bare) life of their son, Max, who is living as a "state of exception."

"I don't know what this is, I just don't know," a doctor said as he put the baby into her [Max's mother's] arms. Beneath the lush head of hair, the baby's face was like a child's unfinished drawing. He had only one, unnaturally small eye, on the right side of his face. On the other side, there was a concave blankness beneath the brow. His nostrils were separated by a deep cleft, and his nasal ridge was squashed. Penelope took his curled fist and felt for fingers, but none were there [later Bernard discovered Max had fingers and toes] (Franks, 1999: 68).

Penelope and Bernard had to overcome the medical staff's negative attitude towards Max. As Penelope kept watch over Max, she noticed clusters of interns and residents came to look, and heard some of them referring to him as "it." Finally, Penelope had enough. "This 'it' is my son, and he wants to be left alone," she said. Penelope persuaded a reluctant nurse to put the child to her breast, and he began to suck vigorously. The nurse said firmly, "It's only instinct. *Any* baby will nurse [original emphasis]." Then she pointed out another nurse who was unhooking a plump baby from a ventilator and rushing out the door with him. "That baby has been on life support for months," the first nurse said, "It has been unending agony for the mother, and she's decided to end it. She's waiting in a private room so the baby can die in her arms" (Franks, 1999: 69). In comparing Max to the other baby, the nurse was placing Max in the realm of the "state of exception"—a "bare life" that was "not worth living."

This interpellation of the "bare life" that is the "state of exception" was reinforced by other medical practitioners outside the hospital. Max required various health professionals for his ongoing home-care. "The original day nurse was fired after Lulu, the babysitter, caught her washing Max's bottles in dirty dishwater. 'What's the difference? He is going to be a vegetable,' the nurse said with a shrug" (Franks, 1999: 69).

The predominant attitude towards Max epitomizes the belief that some disabled infants' existence is "not worth living." Franks (1999: 71) reports,

At a meeting to discuss Max's future, with the support of out-dated information a hospital official advised, Max's parents might be better off warehousing him for his sake and theirs. Armed with positive research on Fraser Syndrome, Penelope jumped in. "We do not intend to warehouse our son," she said icily, "There's only one option we'd like to discuss, and that is aggressive medical intervention."

Franks (1999: 77) asserts,

Max has had a profound positive effect on his mother: "The truth is that Max has made me more deeply happy than I have ever been," she explained. "He changes everyone who meets him. He changes their ideas about beauty, about worth. He has made every member of our family—immediate as well as extended—grow up and change their life view in some essential way." Max also changed the attitude of many members of the hospital staff. "We think everyone has to be perfect, physically, mentally," Dr. Flaum said, "It's easy to write people off, say, this one's so abnormal forget it. Max has reaffirmed that you cannot look at a person and know for sure he has no ability to learn and be a good member of our society."

DISABILITY AS A "BARE LIFE," WHICH IS A "STATE OF EXCEPTION"

On September 28, 1997, I was forced to look back on my own genetic makeup (as some other people perceive it) to critique the future.

Listening to the Canadian Broadcasting Corporation radio program *Cross Country Checkup* (Murphy, 1997), I heard a geneticist claim that he had "discovered" the genetic cause for cerebral palsy. Over the years, my physicians have concluded that my cerebral palsy was caused by a lack of oxygen to the brain. This new genetic explanation is a pre-cursor, and reduces

the "lack of oxygen to the brain" to a complication resulting from genetic mutations. Consequently, my body and my life are now being read through the lens of genetic fundamentalism.

Provoked, I felt compelled to respond and called the program. In my interview, I explained that the question "When should we screen for genetic defects?" devalues the experience of disability by presuming that genetic intervention is not only permissible but preferable in certain cases. In terms of so-called genetic abnormalities that may cause illness and disability, "common sense" would suggest that some intervention is not only desirable but is a societal goal. I spoke about the positive aspects of my cerebral palsy, "not in the sense of a 'gift' from which other people learn, or as God's chosen 'crippled angels,' but rather how my spasms give me great joy and how they inform my life. Any success I have is not despite my cerebral palsy but because of it!"

I also argued that these positive aspects of cerebral palsy cannot be "measured," because the ways and means of measurement are developed from the perspective that devalues cerebral palsy as an "expression of life." I spoke about the similarities between myself and Tracy Latimer, who was murdered, to forestall the invocation of a continuum of cerebral palsy with myself at the pinnacle (the poster-child for overcoming) and Tracy Latimer (symbolizing victims) shackled to the lowest rung in life and memory.

As my segment concluded, the host, Rex Murphy, thanked me for educating him as well as others. I corrected him, stating, "My intention is not to educate others but to give cerebral palsy a life-affirming presence. I explained that my life is not, and should not be, dependent upon able-bodied people understanding me or giving me their blessing." Often people who privilege an able-bodied life have demanded an explanation for my being alive. Today, by having a presence, I conveyed to the audience that no longer did I have to explain, justify, apologize for, or educate others about my cerebral palsy.

The radio segment offered me another opportunity to expose the vivaciousness of cerebral palsy as a life affirming force. Consequently, I am moving beyond the dichotomous pairing of disability and ability which restricts my vivacity.

Since I was a disembodied voice over the radio, ableist rhetoric and anger could be vented. One caller screamed, "How dare you question normality!" Others said that I should be thankful they allowed me into a regular school and I repay their generosity by making such outlandish statements. No matter what I said, the ableism was pervasive. Believing that I was too intelligent, some callers questioned my ability to comment on the lives of severely disabled people. Others maligned me for being outrageous and lacking rational thought. Paradoxically, I was either too intelligent or too stupid. Either way, the status quo which favours the body and lives of nondisabled people remains intact.

Following my segment on the radio program *Cross Country Checkup*, a mother of a disabled baby called the program. She explained how strangers would call her a "bad mother" for giving birth to a disabled child. Respondents to her segment accused her of being an irresponsible member of society for giving birth to a future "burden" on society. Like me, she was called irrational, especially after reiterating she loved her child. For the most part, respondents pathologized her decision-making abilities as well as her refusal to see the error of her ways.

The coercive nature of both public opinion and genetic counselling create an environment where the eradication of disability becomes "matter-of-fact" and "common sense," and creates a guilt-free atmosphere where the initiative to get rid of a pathology is deemed necessary. The mother who chooses to carry the defective foetus to term (by either refusing genetic testing or ignoring a positive outcome) has her status of being worthy of a "political life" questioned, especially if she does not acknowledge the error of her ways. Cautioning us about our reliance on the promise of genomics, bioethicist Dr. Robert Klitzman (2006) warns, "As we enter the new genetic age, more education is needed to help doctors, nurses, genetics counselors, patients and their families face these quandaries. We have much to learn from the Greeks: to be cautious in interpreting prognostications, to beware that genetic information, like oracles, may offer an illusion of certainty."

Researching the extermination of psychiatric patients and disabled children during the Nazi Regime, Proctor (1995: 172) writes, "Euthanasia took on less the character of a single Reich-wide 'operation' and more the character of normal hospital routine. Equally disturbing is the fact that doctors were never *ordered* [emphasis in original] to murder psychiatric patients and handicapped children. They were *empowered* [emphasis in original] to do so, and fulfilled their task without protest, often on their own initiative." In this genetic age, David Le Breton (2004: 5) asserts, "The identification of a genetic illness which is currently untreatable leads potentially to the decision to carry out a therapeutic abortion, and in this way a drift occurs, whereby medicine moves away from a therapeutic role to the project of eliminating that which it cannot treat." The Critical Art Ensemble (1998: 125) add, "To be sure, once eugenics is perceived as a means to empower the child and the parent, it loses its monstrous overtones, and becomes another part of everyday life medical procedure. Capitalism will achieve its goals of genetic ideological inscription, while at the same time realizing tremendous profits for providing the service."

(RE)AFFIRMING A DISABLED "BARE LIFE" AS AN EXPRESSION OF LIFE

Since 1997, I have become further embedded in the academic culture and my life is further read as being greatly removed from my previous existence as a cripple, as a "bare life." It is assumed that I have evolved from my earlier existence as a baby who could not communicate, sit or control any aspect of either my body or my life (what many people believe is "a life not worth living" and the epitome of "the state of exception"). I feel tremendous pressure to put on a charade and try to present myself as human and subsume my spasms. Throughout my life I have had to work to maintain my status as living a political life. Moreover, I have had to take great care not to slip back to a "bare life" (or to be perceived by others to be slipping) and returning to the "state of exception."

I am restricted by what I call "normative shadows." To varying degrees most people are restricted by "normative shadows"—a somewhat enigmatic and elusive concept—that lead to the suppression of desires that do not conform to accepted norms. Like most shadows, normative shadows cannot be grasped in a material way. They remain a feeling, a sense that one is constantly being judged according to differing criteria of normality. Like all shadows, normative shadows are elusive yet always present, simultaneously everywhere and nowhere. Yet, for those of us deemed as possible "states of exception," adhering to "normative shadows" is a necessary precondition to maintaining a "political life." A similar feeling is expressed by Neil Marcus who states, "People are always watching me . . . [ellipses in original] they're watching to see how well I do this thing. . . [ellipses in original] this thing called 'human'" (Brueggemann, 2002: 322).

Following my appearance on *Cross Country Checkup*, many people congratulated me on my strong resistance to ableism. However, I question whether resistance could create a positive space for the vivaciousness of disabled existences. Addressing the question of resistance, Linda Martin Alcoff (1999: 67) writes, "There is a kind of quest purity in the attempt to maintain only a resistance which is itself defined as a reaction to power rather than a fight for power. Resistance so circumscribed suggests a desire to inhabit a space free from criticism, responsibility, and accountability, to be always a critic never the advocate."

Simply put, I believe my disabled "expressions of life" should not defer to able-bodiedness. However, even resisting the privileging of able-bodiedness is a manner of "deference." Always "reacting against" ableism rather than "fighting for" the affirmation of my spasms left me feeling empty. When articulating positions from the dichotomy of ability and disability, I feel restricted by the incessant need to respond to the normative shadows of able-embodiment that are omnipresent in discussions and influence the parameters for the "rules of engagement" as well as the means of articulation.

CRITICAL THINKING QUESTIONS

1. What does Overboe mean by "genetic fundamentalism"? What are the dangers associated with this kind of thinking?
2. Why the comparison between abortion and genetic disease? Do you think this comparison is a fair one?
3. What point is the author meaning to make by comparing the contemporary use of genetic testing with that of eugenics in the Nazi regime? Do you agree that this is a valid point? Why or why not?

REFERENCES

Brueggemann, B. 2002. An enabling pedagogy. In *Disability studies: Enabling the humanities*, eds. S. L. Snyder, B. A. Brueggemann, and R. Garland Thompson, 317–36. New York: Modern Language Association.

Critical Art Ensemble. 1998. *Flesh machine: Cyborgs, designer babies, and new eugenic consciousness.* New York: Autonomedia.

Elliott, C. 2001. Attitudes, souls, and persons: Children with severe neurological impairments. In *Slow cures and bad philosophers: Essays on Wittgenstein, medicine and bioethics*, ed. C. Elliott, 89–102. Durham, NC: Duke University Press.

Elshtain, J. B. 1995. The new eugenics and feminist quandaries. In *Politics and the human body: Assault on dignity*, eds. J. B. Elshtain and T. Cloyd, 24–40. Nashville, TN: Vanderbilt University Press.

Ettore, B. 2000. Reproductive genetics, gender and the body: "Please Doctor, may I have a normal baby?" *Sociology*, 36(3), 403–20.

Franks, L. 1999. Miracle kid. *The New Yorker* (May): 68–77.

Klitzman, B. 2006. Genetic testing creates new versions of ancient dilemmas. *New York Times*, (Jan. 17): **http://www.nytimes.com/2006/01/17/health/17case.html.**

Le Breton, D. 2004. Genetic fundamentalism or the cult of the gene. *Body & Society*, 10(4): 1–20.

Martin, Alcoff, L. 1999. Becoming an epistemologist. In *Becomings: Explorations in time, memory, and futures*, ed. B. Gross, 55–75. Ithaca, NY: Cornell University Press.

Murphy, R. 1997. Should we screen embryos for genetic defects? *Cross Country Checkup*. Canadian Broadcasting Corporation, Radio One, (Sep. 28).

Proctor, R. N. 1995. The destruction of lives not worth living. In *Deviant bodies: Critical perspectives on difference in science and popular culture*, eds. J. Terry and J. Urla, 170–96. Indianapolis: Indiana University Press.

Rapp, R. and P. Ginsberg. 2001. Enabling disability: Rewriting kinship, reimagining citizenship. *Public Culture*, 13(3): 553–56.

Skidmore, M. 1994. Interview with Peter Gzowski. *Morningside*. CBC Radio. (Nov. 29).

Tremain, S. 2006. Reproduction freedom, self-regulation, and the government of impairment in utero. *Hypatia*, 21(1): 35–53.

Wong, S. I. 2002. At home with down syndrome and gender. *Hypatia*, 11(3): 89–117.

57

The Metropolis and Mental Life

GEORG SIMMEL

*In this, one of his best-known essays, Simmel examines what might be called the "spiritual
condition" of the modern world. His focus is the city, in which forces of modernity—
including anonymity, a detached sophistication, and a preoccupation with commercial
matters—are most clearly evident. Note that Simmel finds reason both to praise this new
world and to warn of its ability to destroy our humanity.*

The deepest problems of modern life derive from
the claim of the individual to preserve the autonomy and individuality of his existence in the face
of overwhelming social forces, of historical heritage, of external culture, and of the technique of
life. The fight with nature which primitive man
has to wage for his *bodily* existence attains in this
modern form its latest transformation. The eighteenth century called upon man to free himself of
all the historical bonds in the state and in religion,
in morals and in economics. Man's nature, originally good and common to all, should develop
unhampered. In addition to more liberty, the
nineteenth century demanded the functional
specialization of man and his work; this specialization makes one individual incomparable

to another, and each of them indispensable to
the highest possible extent. However, this specialization makes each man the more directly
dependent upon the supplementary activities of
all others. Nietzsche sees the full development
of the individual conditioned by the most ruthless struggle of individuals; socialism believes in
the suppression of all competition for the same
reason. Be that as it may, in all these positions
the same basic motive is at work: The person
resists . . . being leveled down and worn out by a
social-technological mechanism. An inquiry into
the inner meaning of specifically modern life and
its products, into the soul of the cultural body, so
to speak, must seek to solve the equation which
structures like the metropolis set up between the
individual and the superindividual contents of
life. Such an inquiry must answer the question
of how the personality accommodates itself in
the adjustments to external forces. This will be my
task today.

Source: Reprinted and abridged with the permission of
The Free Press, a Division of Simon & Schuster from *The
Sociology of Georg Simmel*, translated and edited by Kurt
H. Wolff. Copyright © 1950, copyright renewed 1978 by
The Free Press.

The psychological basis of the metropolitan type of individuality consists in the *intensification of nervous stimulation* which results from the swift and uninterrupted change of outer and inner stimuli. Man is a differentiating creature. His mind is stimulated by the difference between a momentary impression and the one which preceded it. Lasting impressions, impressions which differ only slightly from one another, impressions which take a regular and habitual course and show regular and habitual contrasts—all these use up, so to speak, less consciousness than does the rapid crowding of changing images, the sharp discontinuity in the grasp of a single glance, and the unexpectedness of onrushing impressions. These are the psychological conditions which the metropolis creates. With each crossing of the street, with the tempo and multiplicity of economic, occupational and social life, the city sets up a deep contrast with small town and rural life with reference to the sensory foundations of psychic life. The metropolis exacts from man as a discriminating creature a different amount of consciousness than does rural life. Here the rhythm of life and sensory mental imagery flows more slowly, more habitually, and more evenly. Precisely in this connection the sophisticated character of metropolitan psychic life becomes understandable—as over against small town life, which rests more upon deeply felt and emotional relationships. These latter are rooted in the more unconscious layers of the psyche and grow most readily in the steady rhythm of uninterrupted habituations. The intellect, however, has its locus in the transparent, conscious, higher layers of the psyche; it is the most adaptable of our inner forces. In order to accommodate to change and to the contrast of phenomena, the intellect does not require any shocks and inner upheavals; it is only through such upheavals that the more conservative mind could accommodate to the metropolitan rhythm of events. Thus the metropolitan type of man—which, of course, exists in a thousand individual variants—develops an organ protecting him against the threatening currents and discrepancies of his external environment which would uproot him. He reacts with his head instead of his heart. In this an increased awareness assumes the psychic prerogative. Metropolitan life, thus, underlies a heightened awareness and a predominance of intelligence in metropolitan man. The reaction to metropolitan phenomena is shifted to that organ which is least sensitive and quite remote from the depth of the personality. Intellectuality is thus seen to preserve subjective life against the overwhelming power of metropolitan life, and intellectuality branches out in many directions and is integrated with numerous discrete phenomena.

The metropolis has always been the seat of the money economy. Here the multiplicity and concentration of economic exchange gives an importance to the means of exchange which the scantiness of rural commerce would not have allowed. Money economy and the dominance of the intellect are intrinsically connected. They share a matter-of-fact attitude in dealing with men and with things; and, in this attitude, a formal justice is often coupled with an inconsiderate hardness. The intellectually sophisticated person is indifferent to all genuine individuality, because relationships and reactions result from it which cannot be exhausted with logical operations. In the same manner, the individuality of phenomena is not commensurate with the pecuniary principle. Money is concerned only with what is common to all: It asks for the exchange value, it reduces all quality and individuality to the question: How much? All intimate emotional relations between persons are founded in their individuality, whereas in rational relations man is reckoned with like a number, like an element which is in itself indifferent. Only the objective measurable achievement is of interest. Thus metropolitan man reckons with his merchants and customers, his domestic servants and often even with persons with whom he is obliged to have social intercourse. These features of intellectuality contrast with the nature of the small circle in which the inevitable knowledge of individuality as inevitably produces a warmer tone of behavior, a behavior which is beyond a mere objective balancing of service and return. In the sphere of the economic psychology of the small group it is of importance that under primitive conditions production serves the customer who orders the goods, so that the producer and the consumer are acquainted. The modern metropolis, however, is supplied almost entirely by production for the market, that is, for entirely unknown purchasers who never personally enter the producer's actual field of vision. Through this anonymity the interests of each party acquire an unmerciful matter-of-factness; and the intellectually calculating economic egoisms of both parties need not fear any deflection because of the imponderables of personal relationships. The money economy dominates the metropolis; it has displaced the last survivals of domestic production and the direct barter of goods; it minimizes, from day to day, the amount of work ordered by customers. The matter-of-fact attitude is obviously so intimately interrelated with the money economy, which is dominant in the metropolis, that nobody can say whether the intellectualistic mentality first promoted the money economy or whether the latter determined the former. The metropolitan way of life is certainly the most fertile soil for this reciprocity, a point which I shall document merely by citing the dictum of the most eminent English constitutional historian: Throughout the whole course of English history, London has never acted as England's heart but often as England's intellect and always as her moneybag!

In certain seemingly insignificant traits, which lie upon the surface of life, the same psychic currents characteristically unite. Modern mind has become more and more calculating. The calculative exactness of practical life which the money economy has brought about corresponds to the ideal of natural science: to transform the world into an arithmetic problem, to fix every part of the world by mathematical formulas. Only money economy has filled the days of so many people with weighing, calculating, with numerical determinations, with a reduction of qualitative values to quantitative ones. Through the calculative nature of money a new precision, a certainty in the definition of identities and differences, an unambiguousness in agreements and arrangements has been brought about in the relations of life-elements—just as externally this precision has been effected by the universal diffusion of pocket watches. However, the conditions of metropolitan life are at once cause and effect of this trait. The relationships and affairs of the typical metropolitan usually are so varied and complex that without the strictest punctuality in promises and services the whole structure would break down into an inextricable chaos. Above all, this necessity is brought about by the aggregation of so many people with such differentiated interests, who must integrate their relations and activities into a highly complex organism. If all clocks and watches in Berlin would suddenly go wrong in different ways, even if only by one hour, all economic life and communication of the city would be disrupted for a long time. In addition an apparently mere external factor, long distances, would make all waiting and broken appointments result in an ill-afforded waste of time. Thus, the technique of metropolitan life is unimaginable without the most punctual integration of all activities and mutual relations into a stable and impersonal time schedule. Here again the general conclusions of this entire task of reflection become obvious, namely, that from each point on the surface of existence—however closely attached to the surface alone—one may drop a sounding into the depth of the psyche so that all the most banal externalities of life finally are connected with the ultimate decisions concerning the meaning and style of life. Punctuality, calculability, exactness are forced upon life by the complexity and extension of metropolitan existence and are not only most intimately connected with its money economy and intellectualistic character. These traits must also color the contents of life and favor the exclusion of those irrational, instinctive, sovereign traits and impulses which aim at determining the mode of life from within, instead of receiving the general and precisely schematized form of life from without. . . .

The same factors which have thus coalesced into the exactness and minute precision of the form of life have coalesced into a structure of the highest impersonality; on the other hand, they have promoted a highly personal subjectivity. There is perhaps no psychic phenomenon which has been so unconditionally reserved to the metropolis as has the blasé attitude. The blasé attitude results first from the rapidly changing and closely compressed contrasting stimulations of the nerves. From this, the enhancement of metropolitan intellectuality, also, seems originally to stem. Therefore, stupid people who are not intellectually alive in the first place usually are not exactly blasé. A life in boundless pursuit of pleasure makes one blasé because it agitates the nerves to their strongest reactivity for such a long time that they finally cease to react at all. In the same way, through the rapidity and contradictoriness of their changes, more harmless impressions force such violent responses, tearing the nerves so brutally hither and thither that their last reserves of strength are spent; and if one remains in the same milieu they have no time to gather new strength. An incapacity thus emerges to react to new sensations with the appropriate energy. This constitutes that blasé attitude which, in fact, every metropolitan child shows when compared with children of quieter and less changeable milieus.

This physiological source of the metropolitan blasé attitude is joined by another source which flows from the money economy. The essence of the blasé attitude consists in the blunting of discrimination. This does not mean that the objects are not perceived, as is the case with the half-wit, but rather that the meaning and differing values of things, and thereby the things themselves, are experienced as insubstantial. They appear to the blasé person in an evenly flat and gray tone; no one object deserves preference over any other. This mood is the faithful subjective reflection of the completely internalized money economy. By being the equivalent to all the manifold things in one and the same way, money becomes the most frightful leveler. For money expresses all qualitative differences of things in terms of "how much?" Money, with all its colorlessness and indifference, becomes the common denominator of all values; irreparably it hollows out the core of things, their individuality, their specific value, and their incomparability. All things float with equal specific gravity in the constantly moving stream of money. All things lie on the same level and differ from one another only in the size of the area which they cover. In the individual case this coloration, or rather discoloration, of things through their money equivalence may be unnoticeably minute. However, through the relations of the rich to the objects to be had for money, perhaps even through the total character which the mentality of the contemporary public everywhere imparts to these objects, the exclusively pecuniary evaluation of objects has become quite considerable. The large cities, the main seats of the money exchange, bring the purchasability of things to the fore much more impressively than do smaller localities. That is why cities are also the genuine locale of the blasé attitude. In the blasé attitude the concentration of men and things stimulate the nervous system of the individual to its highest achievement so that it attains its peak. Through the mere quantitative intensification of the same conditioning factors this achievement is transformed into its opposite and appears in the peculiar adjustment of the blasé attitude. In this phenomenon the nerves find in the refusal to react to their stimulation the last possibility of accommodating to the contents and forms of metropolitan life. The self-preservation of certain personalities is brought at the price of devaluating the whole objective world, a devaluation which in the end unavoidably drags one's own personality down into a feeling of the same worthlessness.

Whereas the subject of this form of existence has to come to terms with it entirely for himself, his self-preservation in the face of the large city demands from him a no less negative behavior of a social nature. This mental attitude of metropolitans toward one another we may designate, from a formal point of view, as reserve. If so many inner reactions were responses to the continuous external contacts with innumerable people as are those in the small town, where one knows almost everybody one meets and where one has a positive relation to almost everyone, one would be completely atomized internally and come to an unimaginable psychic state. Partly this psychological fact, partly the right to distrust which men have in the face of the touch-and-go elements of metropolitan life, necessitates our reserve. As a result of this reserve we frequently do not even know by sight those who have been our neighbors for years. And it is this reserve which in the eyes of the small-town people makes us appear to be cold and heartless. Indeed, if I do not deceive myself, the inner aspect of this outer reserve is not only indifference but, more often than we are aware, it is a slight aversion, a mutual strangeness and repulsion, which will break into hatred and fight at the moment of a closer contact, however caused. The whole inner organization of such an extensive communicative life rests upon an extremely varied hierarchy of sympathies, indifferences, and aversions of the briefest as well as of the most permanent nature. The sphere of indifference in this hierarchy is not as large as might appear on the surface. Our psychic activity still responds to almost every impression of somebody else with a somewhat distinct feeling. The unconscious, fluid, and changing character of this impression seems to result in a state of indifference. Actually this indifference would be just as unnatural as the diffusion of indiscriminate mutual suggestion would be unbearable. From both these typical dangers of the metropolis, indifference and indiscriminate suggestibility, antipathy protects us. A latent antipathy and the preparatory stage of practical antagonism affect the distances and aversions without which this mode of life could not at all be led. The extent

and the mixture of this style of life, the rhythm of its emergence and disappearance, the forms in which it is satisfied—all these, with the unifying motives in the narrower sense, form the inseparable whole of the metropolitan style of life. What appears in the metropolitan style of life directly as dissociation is in reality only one of its elemental forms of socialization.

This reserve with its overtone of hidden aversion appears in turn as the form or the cloak of a more general mental phenomenon of the metropolis: It grants to the individual a kind and an amount of personal freedom which has no analogy whatsoever under other conditions. The metropolis goes back to one of the large developmental tendencies of social life as such, to one of the few tendencies for which an approximately universal formula can be discovered. The earliest phase of social formations found in historical as well as in contemporary social structures is this: a relatively small circle firmly closed against neighboring, strange, or in some way antagonistic circles. However, this circle is closely coherent and allows its individual members only a narrow field for the development of unique qualities and free, self-responsible movements. Political and kinship groups, parties and religious associations begin in this way. The self-preservation of very young associations requires the establishment of strict boundaries and a centripetal unity. Therefore they cannot allow the individual freedom and unique inner and outer development. From this stage social development proceeds at once in two different, yet corresponding, directions. To the extent to which the group grows—numerically, spatially, in significance and in content of life— to the same degree the group's direct, inner unity loosens, and the rigidity of the original demarcation against others is softened through mutual relations and connections. At the same time, the individual gains freedom of movement, far beyond the first jealous delimitation. The individual also gains a specific individuality to which the division of labor in the enlarged group gives both occasion and necessity. . . .

It is not only the immediate size of the area and the number of persons which, because of the universal historical correlation between the enlargement of the circle and the personal inner and outer freedom, has made the metropolis the locale of freedom. It is rather in transcending this visible expanse that any given city becomes the seat of cosmopolitanism. The horizon of the city expands in a manner comparable to the way in which wealth develops; a certain amount of property increases in a quasi-automatical way in ever more rapid progression. As soon as a certain limit has been passed, the economic, personal, and intellectual relations of the citizenry, the sphere of intellectual predominance of the city over its hinterland, grow as in geometrical progression. Every gain in dynamic extension becomes a step, not for an equal, but for a new and larger extension. From every thread spinning out of the city, ever new threads grow as if by themselves, just as within the city the unearned increment of ground rent, through the mere increase in communication, brings the owner automatically increasing profits. At this point, the quantitative aspect of life is transformed directly into qualitative traits of character. The sphere of life of the small town is, in the main, self-contained and autarchic. For it is the decisive nature of the metropolis that its inner life overflows by waves into a far-flung national or international area. . . .

The most profound reason, however, why the metropolis conduces to the urge for the most individual personal existence—no matter whether justified and successful—appears to me to be the following: The development of modern culture is characterized by the preponderance of what one may call the "objective spirit" over the "subjective spirit." This is to say, in language as well as in law, in the technique of production as well as in art, in science as well as in the objects of the domestic environment, there is embodied a sum of spirit. The individual in his intellectual development follows the growth of this spirit very imperfectly and at an ever increasing distance. If, for instance, we view the immense culture which

for the last hundred years has been embodied in things and in knowledge, in institutions and in comforts, and if we compare all this with the cultural progress of the individual during the same period—at least in high status groups—a frightful disproportion in growth between the two becomes evident. Indeed, at some points we notice a retrogression in the culture of the individual with reference to spirituality, delicacy, and idealism. This discrepancy results essentially from the growing division of labor. For the division of labor demands from the individual an ever more one-sided accomplishment, and the greatest advance in a one-sided pursuit only too frequently means dearth to the personality of the individual. In any case, he can cope less and less with the overgrowth of objective culture. The individual is reduced to a negligible quantity, perhaps less in his consciousness than in his practice and in the totality of his obscure emotional states that are derived from this practice. The individual has become a mere cog in an enormous organization of things and powers which tear from his hands all progress, spirituality, and value in order to transform them from their subjective form into the form of a purely objective life. It needs merely to be pointed out that the metropolis is the genuine arena of this culture which outgrows all personal life. Here in buildings and educational institutions, in the wonders and comforts of space-conquering technology, in the formations of community life, and in the visible institutions of the state, is offered such an overwhelming fullness of crystallized and impersonalized spirit that the personality, so to speak, cannot maintain itself under its impact. On the one hand, life is made infinitely easy for the personality in that stimulations, interests, uses of time, and consciousness are offered to it from all sides. They carry the person as if in a stream, and one needs hardly to swim for oneself. On the other hand, however, life is composed more and more of these impersonal contents and offerings which tend to displace the genuine personal colorations and incomparabilities. This results in the individual's summoning the utmost in uniqueness and particularization, in order to preserve his most personal core. He has to exaggerate this personal element in order to remain audible even to himself.

CRITICAL THINKING QUESTIONS

1. In what respects does the metropolis symbolize modern society?
2. What does Simmel mean by suggesting that in modern cities, people experience an "intensification of nervous stimulation"? How do we react "with our heads instead of with our hearts"?
3. What does Simmel see as the achievements of modern urban life? What does he think has been lost in the process?

58

No Place for Home

SEAN CONDON

Because of rampant drug use, the Downtown Eastside of Vancouver has received extensive national and international media attention. But the neighbourhood also houses many of Vancouver's poorest inhabitants. This reading discusses the development pressures this neighbourhood faces as land prices continue to rise in Vancouver, already Canada's most expensive housing market. With the Olympics in 2010, the struggle over housing became even more intensified as low-income housing was further threatened by tourist accommodation.

One by one, the tenants of the Burns Block hotel pour out of the building and onto the street, their belongings tucked under their arms and their faces carrying looks of shock and anger. It's a warm afternoon in March 2006, and the Vancouver Fire Department has just given the tenants crammed into the 18-unit building in Vancouver's Downtown Eastside an hour's notice to vacate their rooms. The building was condemned as a fire trap because the fire exits were blocked, the escapes screwed shut, sprinklers broken and extinguishers left untested.

Outside, the tenants are greeted by a circus of city officials trying to herd them into a nearby shelter; local news reporters rush to capture their distress; and community activists scream that city officials shut the building down unnecessarily.

Source: Sean Condon, "No Place for Home" from *This Magazine,* 40(5) March/April 2007, pp. 18–22. Copyright © 2007 Sean Condon, Reprinted by permission of the author.

Some tenants yell at the owner for allowing the building to fall into disrepair, while the owner deflects blame back onto the city for gentrifying the Downtown Eastside, Vancouver's infamous drug ghetto. As the accusations fly, most of the tenants try to come to grips with the fact that they are now homeless.

"I don't know what I'm going to do," says Alfred Melnychuk, a 53-year-old former heroin addict, with tears in his eyes. Like many of Canada's wandering youth of the early '70s, the Saskatchewan native was drawn to the Downtown Eastside for its drug scene. He was seduced by heroin and spent most of the '80s in jail for possession. Now infected with hepatitis C, he got clean four years ago and had been living in relative stability in the Burns Block for two years. "I already paid my rent yesterday and now I'm out on the street. I got no more money and no place to go."

Stretching roughly a mile along Hastings Avenue, the Downtown Eastside is one of

Vancouver's oldest neighbourhoods. Here, third-world poverty sits next to the city's main tourist area, just a short distance from the heart of downtown. Central American refugees openly sell crack cocaine, underage prostitutes sell their bodies, homeless dumpster divers sell empty bottles and cans, and crack and heroin addicts drift aimlessly outside North America's only safe-injection site. It is where alleged serial killer Robert Pickton picked up many of the prostitutes he's accused of killing on his suburban pig farm. The median household income in what is commonly referred to as Canada's poorest postal code is $12,000. More than 40 percent of the residents subsist on welfare, and they're lucky to live past 50. One of the most ethnically diverse neighbourhoods in the city, it is also home to Vancouver's largest Aboriginal community.

The Burns Block was one of 125 single room occupancy (SRO) hotels that fill the Downtown Eastside. Like many of the neighbourhood's century-old SROs, the Burns Block was a mess and a home to addicts, dealers, sex workers and mentally ill. Plagued by poverty and addiction, many of the Downtown Eastside's 16,000 residents depend on cheap hotels like the Burns Block, which account for over a third of the area's 13,000 housing units. SROs are hardly comfortable—the rooms are roughly 100 square feet and don't typically have bathrooms or kitchens, though they do often come with mice, cockroaches and bedbugs. With the average one-bedroom apartment in Vancouver going for more than $900 a month, a $325 SRO is often the only alternative for the city's low-income residents.

The century-old hotels were once used to house transient loggers and fishermen, but as drugs have permeated the area over the past two decades, these buildings have been transformed into permanent homes for the city's most desperate. Unintentionally, they have become an important stop-gap against homelessness.

After years of neglect, the Downtown Eastside is now in the middle of a major development boom and city revitalization campaign that threatens to displace thousands of its low-income residents. With the 2010 Winter Olympic Games only three years away, the city is accelerating gentrification of the notorious neighbourhood before thousands of visitors and international media arrive in Vancouver. At the same time, the city's core has run out of land, and the Downtown Eastside is being regarded as its potential new frontier.

In April 2004, Larry Beasley, Vancouver's former co-director of urban planning, gave a speech called "The Shift East" to the city's top urban developers. He announced that, despite its problems, the Downtown Eastside "will become a focus for development—beyond a shadow of a doubt." With a growing economy and relentless real estate drive across the region, suddenly the decrepit SRO hotels have become extremely valuable. The owner of the Burns Block, Nick Bahrami, purchased the hotel in 2003 for $550,000 and is now selling the empty building for a remarkable $2.5 million.

With the dual forces of pressure and potential now in full swing, SRO hotels are going down like dominos. Over the past four years, Vancouver has lost more than 800 units of low-income housing as SROs have been closed, converted, or have raised their rates beyond the $325 allocated to welfare recipients for rent. While the Downtown Eastside is in desperate need of repair, neither the city nor the province has set up a safety net to catch the residents who are being displaced by the development frenzy. As drug hotels and seedy bars give way to swanky lofts and hipster hangouts, many in the Downtown Eastside believe they are seeing the beginning of the end for its residents. Kim Kerr, the executive director of the Downtown Eastside Residents Association (DERA), an advocacy organization, says that if the city doesn't figure out how to stop the slide, the Downtown Eastside will become a neighbourhood for the affluent only.

"You will see the social services move out of the Downtown Eastside, you'll see folks thrown out on the street, and these people won't be tolerated in what will become another wealthy neighbourhood in Vancouver," Kerr says.

According to the City of Vancouver's 2005 Housing Plan for the Downtown Eastside, if SROs aren't replaced with social housing, the consequences could be tragic. "Without a policy of one-for-one replacement and comprehensive housing, health and social services, the already fragile lives of many residents would become more insecure and chaotic," the report states. "This could lead to more neighbourhood impacts through increased homelessness, substance abuse, crime, and erratic street behaviour. If housing stock is lost in this area, many low-income people would literally have no place to live, as there is little housing available elsewhere at social-assistance-level rents. SROs are the last tier of housing before homelessness."

Because of major welfare cuts by the British Columbia government five years ago, Vancouver already has a growing homelessness problem that has seen the number of people sleeping on the streets double from just over 600 in 2002 to at least 1,300 in 2005 (2,200 across Greater Vancouver). But despite the city's own blunt admission of the importance in keeping SROs open—unless they are replaced by social housing—it has embarked on an aggressive campaign to clean up the hotels that could see many of them shut down. In late 2005, the police completed a sting operation called Project Haven on three of the area's worst SROs, in which undercover officers discovered numerous cases of drug trafficking, welfare fraud and stolen goods.

The Vancouver Agreement is a seven-year-old, $20 million, multi-level governmental urban project focused on the Downtown Eastside. One of its four main priorities is to "turn problem hotels, particularly those that offer single-room-occupancy housing, into safe, clean places to live."

Former Vancouver police inspector Ken Frail, who led Project Haven, conducted a survey of 51 hotels in the area as part of the initiative. His report highlights the deplorable conditions in many of the buildings. It found that 80 percent have bedbugs, with over 2,200 fire code violations in approximately 2,700 rooms. Because of the disproportionate number of mentally ill in the neighbourhood, the buildings are also the source of hundreds of emergency calls a year. For Frail, it provides the proof that these buildings need to go.

"When I end up looking at the Downtown Eastside, I see an area frozen as an historic zone and I really think that that community is totally out of balance," he says. "It's been allowed to stagnate. A lot of the buildings are past their useful existence and I'm much more supportive of seeing an amount of development in that area."

While cleaning up SROs and providing better living conditions is a commendable goal, the plan is backfiring. David Eby, a lawyer with the Pivot Legal Society—a non-profit legal advocacy organization in the Downtown Eastside—says that since the province only gives welfare recipients $325 a month for rent (a figure that has remained frozen since 1994), SRO owners don't profit enough to provide decent accommodation. As the city cracks down, it's no longer worth it for owners to keep running the buildings as low-income residences for those who are the hardest to house.

"The Vancouver Agreement's survey of the worst hotels has put a lot of pressure on hotel owners that really aren't making any money anyway because the welfare rates are so low," says Eby, "and the problem is that it makes their business case much more difficult to justify keeping it open and that's why we've seen so many closures."

According to a recent report by Pivot called *Cracks in the Foundation*, the situation is getting desperate. A week before the Burns Block shut down, the 36-unit Pender Hotel, just a block and a half away, closed its doors. The building had fallen into disrepair a few months earlier when the fire department had stormed in looking for a crystal meth lab, knocking down most of the doors. The meth lab was never found, the doors weren't replaced and most tenants fled the dilapidated hotel. Pivot launched a lawsuit against the city, but that didn't stop the building from being sold for $1.25 million to Georgia Laine Developments, which last November also bought the Gastown hotel, of Project Haven notoriety. The company plans to turn the former drug den into a boutique hotel, and to erect a condominium on the vacant site beside it. Such conversions are becoming more frequent: Last September, the owner of the 37-unit American Hotel on Main Street kicked out its tenants and boarded up the building, with plans to turn part of the site into condominiums—despite the fact that both the province and the city deemed the evictions illegal.

In 1970 the entire city's SRO stock was 13,300 units, but the figure now sits at just over 6,000—and the number is shrinking. Pivot could find only one SRO hotel in the entire Downtown Eastside that had vacant rooms at the province's $325 welfare rate. Meanwhile, the city has been unable to keep up with the losses. The 2003 Homeless Action Plan called for the creation of 800 units of social housing, and the purchase of one SRO hotel a year. But last year Vancouver only provided funding for 155 units of social housing, and rising real estate values kept the city from buying an SRO. Pivot predicts that Vancouver's homeless rate will triple by 2010—just in time for the Olympics—unless more housing is built.

While the Olympics are often cited as the reason for the city's stratospheric real estate prices, the development fever sweeping through the Downtown Eastside has more to do with location and timing. As unbelievable as it is now, the neighbourhood was once the city's primary shopping strip. From the early 1900s to the 1980s, East Hastings hosted many of the city's top shops and restaurants. As the city shifted its focus to the western half of downtown, the neighbourhood deteriorated. By the 1980s many of the retail shops and small businesses had packed up, abandoning buildings that still sit empty. The closing of Woodward's, the neighbourhood's retail mecca, in 1993 was

the final blow. Around the same time, crack cocaine overtook heroin as the drug of choice and the area descended into chaos and HIV rates in the Downtown Eastside rose faster than anywhere else in North America.

In recent years the abandoned Woodward's building has become a symbol of the conflict between competing interests in the area. In the late 1990s, the provincial NDP government had slated the building for social housing, but when the B.C. Liberals took power in 2001, they froze spending on all new social housing projects and tried to sell Woodward's off to a private developer, prompting activists and residents to move into the building in protest.

The Woodward's squat lasted three months, and helped bring attention to the neighbourhood's housing problems, creating enough public pressure to force the Liberals to sell the building to the city instead, which revived the social housing plan. Once the Woodward's development is completed in 2009, the $280-million project will include 200 social housing units and 536 condominiums, plus Simon Fraser University's School for the Contemporary Arts, retail stores and nonprofit offices. Then-mayor Larry Campbell called Woodward's the key to kick-starting the Downtown Eastside's revitalization. Ironically, the development is responsible for kick-starting the neighbourhood's rising real estate values as well.

When the Woodward's condos went on sale last April, a massive advertising campaign told prospective buyers to "Be Bold or Move to the Suburbs." All 536 condos were sold in less than 12 hours, some going for as high as $1 million. The ripple effect has been tremendous. According to city staff, since March 2005, 13 SROs have fetched double the asking price of three years earlier. They attribute the city's inability to purchase an SRO in the neighbourhood to the Woodward's hype. Today there are "for sale" signs up and down East Hastings and the number of development permits the city has issued in the neighbourhood has more than tripled in some areas. Developers and realtors moving into the

Downtown Eastside say this is inevitable since there's no more property left downtown.

"Show me a way to have an address that close to the downtown core of a major North American city and keep property values depressed," says Bob Rennie, the realtor responsible for the Woodward's condos. Rennie says the responsibility for disappearing affordable units lies with the city for not ensuring that the neighbourhood's other developments follow the Woodward's model. Instead, the city's vision for the neighbourhood may be causing more harm than good. Last year, the city approved construction of the Carrall Street Greenway, a $5-million project to attract businesses back to the Downtown Eastside. The greenway will connect the city's popular seawall walkway with the Downtown Eastside and once it's completed, tourists will be able to stroll directly from Stanley Park into the heart of the neighbourhood. The Burns Block and the Pender Hotel sit on the Greenway's path.

The fear of eviction is beginning to sweep through the Downtown Eastside. Most of the older residents saw this show play out during Expo '86, when more than 1,000 tenants were kicked out of downtown SROs and pushed into the Downtown Eastside so the owners could fill units with tourists. The evictions were credited with at least 10 deaths from either suicide or illness. Many residents now fear a repeat of that time as the Olympics near. Not surprisingly, the Downtown Eastside has a concentration of social services to serve the drug addicted, mentally ill, or both. There is no way to know what the impact will be if people have to leave the area.

"It gives you severe depression," says Kurt Scott, a 56-year-old tenant at the Astoria Hotel, which was the third of the SROs targeted in Project Haven. "I don't know where I'd go. I can't afford $350 a month and most of the places around here are going for $385. There are a lot of people down here that have nowhere else to go. This is their home."

Down the hall from where Scott makes his coffee, his neighbour, Lori Shaw, a 49-year-old handicapped native woman, watches television while she waits for her meal to be delivered. Having lost her husband a few years ago, she threatens to put a needle to her cat and her own neck if she's forced to move.

Many people in the Downtown Eastside are beginning to get a sickening sense that time is running out on them. The Olympics are just three years away, and it would take at least that long to build a new housing project. The province, the city and VANOC have all said they will make major announcements this spring about social housing, but considering how little they have done so far, there is skepticism. Though both the federal and provincial governments are awash in billion-dollar surpluses, neither has given any indication that the money will go into housing. The next few months are critical for the Downtown Eastside and its poor residents. Without short-term plans for preventing the closure and conversion of SRO hotels and long-term solutions toward building a real Olympic housing legacy, the neighbourhood will be lost to development and many of its residents lost to the streets.

CRITICAL THINKING QUESTIONS

1. Who do you think should be responsible for housing the poor? If land prices rise, should only those who can afford it be granted shelter? Where should those unable to afford housing live? Is homelessness an option? Why or why not?

2. Do you think there is a relationship between the health of a society and how it treats its poor?

3. List some social problems that are likely to result from increased homelessness. What costs, in economic terms, are associated with this (e.g., crime, including drug-taking, takes significant financial resources to fight: police, courts, incarceration)?

59

Africville: The Life and Death of a Canadian Black Community

DONALD H. CLAIRMONT AND DENNIS
WILLIAM MAGILL

Clairmont and Magill review the effects of an urban redevelopment program that relocated 80 black families in Halifax during the 1960s. The program was intended to promote humanitarian motives, but the experience of Africville demonstrates the many problems associated with forced relocation programs.

To seek social change, without due recognition of the manifest and latent functions performed by the social organization undergoing change, is to indulge in social ritual rather than social engineering.[1]

—Robert K. Merton

Halifax, the foundation city of English-speaking Canada, experienced much change during its first two hundred years of existence. Yet the face-lift and redevelopment it has undergone since the late 1950s have effected a change as dramatic as the 1917 explosion that levelled much of the city. Stimulated by the Stephenson Report of 1957,[2] urban renewal and redevelopment have resulted in the relocation of thousands of people, the demolition of hundreds of buildings, and the construction of impressive business

Source: From Donald H. Clairmont and Dennis W. Magill. 1999. *Africville: The Life and Death of a Canadian Black Community,* Third Edition (pp. 1–19). Toronto: Canadian Scholars' Press. Reprinted by permission of Canadian Scholars' Press Inc.

and governmental complexes. The Africville relocation was part of the larger redevelopment pattern; Africville residents constituted some eight to ten percent of the people affected by approved urban renewal schemes in the city of Halifax during the relocation years.

Africville was a black community within the city of Halifax, inhabited by approximately four hundred people, comprising eighty families, many of whom were descended from settlers who had moved there over a century ago. Tucked away in a corner of the city, relatively invisible, and thought of as a "shack town," Africville was a depressed community both in physical and in socioeconomic terms. Its dwellings were located beside the city dump, and railroad tracks cut across the one dirt road leading into the area. Sewerage, lighting, and other public services were conspicuously absent. The people had little education, very low incomes, and many were underemployed. Property claims were in chaos. Only a handful of families could establish legal title; others claimed squatter rights; and still others rented. Africville, long a black mark against society, had been designated for future industrial and harbour development. Many observers reported that despite these liabilities there was a strong sense of community and that some residents expressed satisfaction with living in Africville.

In 1964 the small black ghetto of Africville began to be phased out of existence. By that time most residents of Halifax, black and white, had come to think of Africville as "the slum by the dump." Most Haligonians, including some Africville residents, did not regard the community as viable and recognized a need for planned social change. The relocation plan announced by the city of Halifax, which purported to be more than simply a real estate operation, appeared to be a response to this need. The plan emphasized humanitarian concern, included employment and education programs, and referred to the creation of new opportunities for the people of Africville. To the general public, the proposed relocation was a progressive step.

In addition to official pronouncements, there were other indications that the Africville program would be more humane and progressive than the typical North American urban relocation. Halifax city council had adopted recommendations contained in a report submitted by a noted Canadian welfare specialist experienced in urban renewal. There was much preliminary discussion of the relocation by city officials among themselves, with Africville residents, and with a "caretaker" group of black and white professionals associated with the Halifax Human Rights Advisory Committee. Relocation plans were not *ad hoc* and haphazard. City officials were required to articulate their policies well and in detail; many implications and alternatives were considered.

There were also indications in the relocation decision-making structure that the Africville program might realize its official rhetoric. A social worker was appointed by the city to take front-line responsibility for the varied aspects of the relocation and to act as liaison between the city administration and the relocatees. The social worker, who was on loan from the Nova Scotia Department of Public Welfare, had a measure of autonomy vis-à-vis the city and an independent contingency fund to meet day-to-day emergencies and opportunities with a minimum of bureaucratic delay. In negotiating the real estate aspects of relocation, the social worker brought proposed agreements before a special advisory committee consisting of aldermen and several members of the Halifax Human Rights Advisory Committee.

In terms of its rationale, public rhetoric, and organizational structure, the Africville relocation seemed worthy of study. The plan was *liberal-oriented* (that is, aimed at ending segregation and providing improved opportunities for the disadvantaged), *welfare-oriented* (that is, it hoped to coordinate employment, educational, and rehabilitative programs with the rehousing of people), and run by experts (that is, the planning, execution, and advice were provided by professionals). An examination of the Africville relocation could be expected to yield greater fundamental insight into planned social change than would a study of typical relocation programs that were accomplished by administrative fiat and stressed primarily the physical removal of persons. It seemed important to study and evaluate the Africville relocation both in its particularity and against the background of general relocation issues.

There were additional reasons for studying the Africville relocation. First, Africville was part of a trend in the 1960s for governmental initiative in relocation programs, and there was reason to expect that other tentative relocations in Nova Scotia and elsewhere would be patterned after the Africville experience. Second, Africville had attracted national and even international notice, and there was broad public interest in the relocation. Third, accounts of pre-relocation social conditions and attitudes were available. Two surveys had been conducted[3] and other material was available in city records. Finally, in 1968 the Africville relocation had already been acclaimed locally as a success. One city alderman noted:

The social significance of the Africville program is already beginning to show positive results as far as individual families are concerned. The children are performing more satisfactorily in school and they seem to take more of an interest in their new surroundings. This report is not intended to indicate that the program has been 100 percent successful; however I believe it can be said that it has been at least 75 percent, judging by the comments of the relocated families.[4]

Private communication with city officials and relocation officials in the United States and Canada brought forth praise for the organization and rhetoric of the Africville relocation.

Was the Africville relocation a success? If so, from whose perspective? To what extent? What accounted for the success or lack of it? It is hoped that answers to these and related questions will contribute to an appreciation of the Africville relocation and of relocation generally.

THE RELOCATION PHENOMENON

Relocation must be seen in the context of a general North American mobility pattern, and certain distinctive features should be noted. The most important distinction is that relocation is part of planned social change carried out, or at least approved, by public agency. The initiation of relocation, as seen by the relocatees, is usually involuntary and an immediate function of the political process. Our present concern is with relocation as it pertains to private residences, involves neighbourhoods or communities, and is a function of comprehensive programs of social change. This kind of relocation accounts for but a small measure of the mobility noted in Canada and the United States, but it was significant because it was distinctive. It was noted earlier that the Africville relocation was itself part of a much larger redevelopment project in the city of Halifax. In terms of the sweep of lifestyle change, even such large urban projects have been

dwarfed by post–Second World War Canadian relocation projects in the Arctic and in Newfoundland. In 1953, Newfoundland, with 6000 miles of coastline and approximately 1150 settlements, undertook a program to move people from the small outposts to larger viable communities which could be serviced efficiently. Between 1965 and 1970 over 3250 households were moved.[5]

As many low-income Americans and Canadians can testify, urban renewal is a prime example of forced relocation. Urban renewal legislation began in the 1940s in both countries. By 1968 approximately forty-five Canadian urban redevelopments had been initiated at a cost of 270 million dollars for 1500 cleared acres.[6] While the scope of urban renewal in Canada was quite small in the light of American experience, the Canadian program was significant enough that one can complain that there were too few Canadian studies looking into the politics, issues, and human consequences of renewal programs. To overcome this lack of knowledge and to place the Africville relocation in perspective, more comprehensive themes will be discussed in this [selection].

From a political-administrative perspective there are four relocation models: the traditional, development, liberal-welfare, and political. The Africville project is the best Canadian example of the liberal-welfare type of relocation. . . . [T]hese models vary along six dimensions: (1) ideological premises; (2) formulation of policy; (3) implementation of policy; (4) intended beneficiaries; (5) central actors and organizational units; and (6) key problems. These models are ideal types to which actual relocation programs correspond to a greater or lesser degree.

THE DEVELOPMENT MODEL

The development model was the most prevalent political-administrative approach to relocation in North America. This type of relocation was usually justified in terms of supposed benefits for the system as a whole, whether the system is society, the city, etc. It was usually initiated by order of political authorities and administered by bureaucrats; it was not anticipated that relocatees would benefit other than indirectly. The underlying ideology of the development model was system-oriented and neo-capitalist; an accurate statement of its premise in urban renewal has been offered by Wallace: "[it considers] renewal, as a public activity, to be intervention in a market and competitive system and to be justified by the need to make up for imperfections in the market mechanism that impede the adjustment process, to eliminate conditions which are economic or social liabilities."[7] In the context of contemporary urban renewal, the development model incorporated the usual city-design approach, focusing on questions of beautification, zoning, and structure,[8] and was usually intended to increase the city tax base and achieve civic pride or attract industry.

The development model can be illustrated by past urban renewal programs in Toronto. Ignoring relocatees as viable interest groups the programs operated implicitly on the basis of certain ideological premises: to correct imperfections in the social system (removal of so-called slums) and overall system development (economic growth), or both. As is the case in many Canadian cities, Toronto's past development policy was closely linked to the businesses and commercial-property industry which provided homes, apartment buildings, shopping centres, and industrial complexes. Thus the elimination of "blight areas" and construction of highrise apartment and office buildings generated an important source of urban revenue.

Referring to this policy of "dollar planning," Fraser observed:

As long as Toronto, [in 1972] like all other municipalities in Canada has to depend upon property taxes as its sole source of income, the overwhelming power of development interests in determining the direction and quality of Toronto's growth will remain unchallenged.

. . . [T]he key to a municipality's prosperity remains its rate of growth; Toronto planners have been consistently ignored by city councils that have been over

the years almost exclusively uninterested in any discussions about the quality of that development.[9]

A non-urban example of the development model of relocation has been described by John Matthiasson, in his study of the forced relocation of a band of Cree Indians in Northern Manitoba. The Cree were relocated to make way for a gigantic power project; they were not involved in the project planning and despite their displeasure "they accepted in a fatalistic manner the announcement of the relocation. They believed that the decision had been made by higher authorities, and that they had neither the right nor power to question it."[10]

The development model of relocation had its limitations. In particular, its econocentric and "undemocratic" features were criticized. The assumption that relocatees benefit indirectly from relocation was challenged, as was the premise that the system as a whole somehow redistributed fairly the benefits accruing from forcing people to move and facilitating the development of private industry. Some critics argued that if one included social-psychological factors in one's conception of costs, the relocatees could be seen as subsidizing the rest of the system. The criticism had some effect, and the liberal-welfare model became increasingly common.[11] One official explained:

In the fifteen years since [urban renewal's] inception, we have seen a progressive broadening of the concept and a strengthening of tools. We have seen, increasingly, both the need for, and realization of, rapprochement between physical and social planning, between renewal and social action. But the fully effective liaison of the two approaches has almost everywhere been frustrated by the absence of the tools to deal as effectively with the problems of human beings as with the problems of physical decay and blight.[12]

Another writer has observed,

social welfare can no longer be treated as the responsibility of private and more or less bountiful ladies and gentlemen or as the less respected branch of the social welfare community and the city government. Tied as it is to the concerns as dear to the heart of the country as economic prosperity it merits a place in the inner sanctum, particularly of planning commissions.[13]

THE LIBERAL-WELFARE MODEL

The "rediscovery" of poverty,[14] the war on poverty, the increasing pressure "from below" upon the development model, and the broadening definition of urban renewal led to the widespread emergence of the liberal-welfare-oriented approach. The liberal-welfare model, like the development model, emphasized expertise and technical knowledge in its operation and administration, and invariably was initiated by public authority. The principal difference is that the liberal-welfare model purported to benefit the relocatees primarily and directly. Under this model, welfare officials often saw themselves as "caretakers" for the relocatees; one relocation official has said, "the department of relocation is the tenants' advocate."[15] The liberal-welfare model of relocation was characterized by a host of social welfare programs supplemental to housing policies and was regarded as an opportunity for a multifaceted attack on poverty and other problems. It was this liberal-welfare model and its assumptions that shaped the rhetoric underlying the 1963–64 decision to relocate Africville.

Ideologically, the liberal-welfare model was much like the development model in that it tended to operate with a consensus model of society and posited a basic congruency between the interests of relocatees and those of society as a whole[;] it was "undemocratic" in the same sense as the development model; the low-status relocatees were accorded little attention, either as participants in the implicit political process or as contributions to specific policies or plans of action. There was an effort, however, to persuade rather than to ignore the relocatees. Criticism of the liberal-welfare model of relocation was related primarily to the ideological level. Some writers noted that liberal welfarism had become part of the establishment of contemporary North American society.[16] Its proponents were presumed to be handmaidens of strong vested interests, reconciling the disadvantaged and patching up the symptoms of social malaise. Critics pointed out that the special programs associated with the liberal-welfare model of relocation tended to be short-term and unsuccessful. The welfare rhetoric often diverted attention from the gains and benefits accruing to the middle-income and elite groups in society. The critics attacked the liberal-welfare model on the premise that the social problems to which it is ostensibly directed could be solved only through profound structural change effecting a redistribution of resources, and by providing relocatees with the consciousness and resources to restructure their own lives.

The liberal-welfare model is best illustrated by the Africville relocation. . . . The community of Africville was defined as a social problem, and relocation was regarded as an intervention strategy designed to help solve the "social and economic problems of Africville residents." The central actors in the formation and implementation of relocation policy were politicians, bureaucrats, experts, and middle-class caretakers; there was no meaningful *collective* participation by Africville residents. The relocatees were to be major beneficiaries through compensation, welfare payments, and rehabilitative retraining programs. The major problem with the relocation was that, although rooted in liberal-welfare rhetoric, it failed to achieve its manifest goals.

THE POLITICAL MODEL

The liberal-welfare model of relocation was revised and developed both as a response to criticism at the ideological level and in reaction to its lack of operational success. There was a growing interest in citizen participation in all phases of relocation; in the firmer acceptance, structurally and culturally, of the advocacy function of relocation officials; in the coordination of relocation services;

and in the provision of resources. It is difficult to assess how far this interest has been translated into fact. There appeared to be a shift in the 1970s, at least conceptually, to the political model of relocation and a frank recognition that relocation usually entailed a conflict of interest, for example, between the relocatees and the city. There was an attempt to structure the conflict by providing relocatees with resources to develop a parallel structure to that of the government. Although society and the relocatee were considered to benefit equally, this political perspective assumed that relocatees benefited both directly and indirectly; directly in terms of, say, housing and other welfare services, and indirectly by participating in the basic decision-making and the determination of their life situation. The political model of relocation was based on the premise that social problems were political problems and emphasized solutions through political action; relocation was approached primarily as a situation in which problems were solved not by the application of expertise but by the resolution of conflicting interests.

Beyond the considerable costs (the dollar cost is less hidden than in the other relocation model) and administrative difficulties entailed, there were other grounds for criticism of the political model. There was a tendency to over-emphasize the solidarity and common interests of relocatees, to exaggerate the multiplying effects of political participation in relocation,[17] and to raise serious questions about how far government could proceed or would proceed in fostering extra-parliamentary political action.

Citizen participation, a core element in the political model, was institutionalized in the United States by the community action programs of the 1964 Economic Opportunity Act. Numerous books and articles, far too many to cite, have discussed the reasons, operations, and failures of "maximum feasible participation" of the poor in the war on poverty.[18] Citizen participation was also part of the United States model city programs, which required that local residents be involved in the planning process and implementation of changes in their neighbourhoods. Contrasted with the United States, Canada has relatively few examples of related social-animation projects. The rise of "militant" citizen groups was a phenomenon which developed later in Canada. The public outcry against the community work of the Company of Young Canadians and the subsequent governmental intervention to close this organization may be an indication of the limits of this perspective. The only Canadian publication illustrating the political model of a relocation is Fraser's study of Toronto's Trefann Court. Trefann Court residents successfully fought off a development-type relocation project; subsequently, the conflict arising from different interests was recognized as an integral part of the city's social organization. Despite internal community conflict between homeowners and tenants, a number of community residents, leaning heavily on outside "resource people," developed a cohesive organization and set up a working committee (a parallel structure) to establish a conceptual scheme for community change in conjunction with the existing city bureaucracy. The Trefann Court case also pointed to a key problem in the political model, that of assessing the representativeness of any one group of citizens to speak, argue, or vote for an entire community. With the establishment of "parallel structures," many citizens grow frustrated with the tedious detail involved in committee work. In Fraser's words:

The fact that the Working Committee operated under formal rules of order, dominated by minutes, reports, rules of procedure and legislative decorum widened the gap between the committee and the community. As debates became more lengthy, detailed and technical, the meetings became harder to follow for the ordinary Trefann resident who might drop in.[19]

THE TRADITIONAL MODEL

Finally, there is the traditional model of relocation in North American society. This is a limiting type of relocation carried out under governmental auspices, for it is a form of planned social change characterized by self-help and self-direction. It is the neighbourhood or community leaders, often indigenous minority-group leaders working through indigenous social organizations, who plan and carry out the relocation, generally with official support and some resource commitment by government agencies. The traditional model entails a largely laissez-faire strategy whereby the relocatees benefit directly and technical expertise is used to advise rather than to direct. Criticism of this approach contends that, without political action, neither the available resources nor the generation of initiative can be effective in the case of low-status groups.

There are numerous examples of the traditional model of relocation. Group settlement and resettlement in various parts of Canada have been common. The relocation of Beechville, a black community on the outskirts of Halifax, is an example within the Halifax metropolitan area. Community leaders, anticipating a government attempt to relocate the residents, organized themselves into a co-operative housing association, received funds from Central Mortgage and Housing Corporation, and reorganized their community partly on their own terms. The scope available for traditional relocation models lessens as society becomes more technocratic and centralized.

CONCEPTUAL FRAMEWORK

. . . . [O]ur emphasis will be on the liberal-welfare model of planned social change and its implementation during the Africville relocation. During the analysis we focus on questions of power and exchange among the various participants of the relocation. Thus, from the perspective of power and exchange,[20] we can examine the power resources and relationships among the individual persons and groups involved in the relocation, the historical evolution of these social facts, the goals held by the different parties, and the strategies and tactics employed in establishing the terms of the relocation "contract." We can also analyse the role of outsiders, experts,

and community "leaders" and focus on questions such as the mobilization of advocacy, relocation resistances and alternatives, and the relation of rhetoric to action. It is vital in the Africville case to have a larger historical view, observing the historical exchange patterns between the city and the Africville people and tracing the implications of these patterns in making Africville "ripe for relocation" and in influencing the relocation decision-making and mechanics.

An aspect of this perspective concerns the context of negotiations and the bargaining strategies developed by the parties involved. Accordingly, attention was devoted to probing the relocatees' knowledge about the relocation; their strategies (use of lawyers, co-operation with fellow relocatees, and development of special arguments in dealing with city officials), and their perceptions of the city's goals, strategies, and resources. The relocation social worker completed a questionnaire concerning each relocated family which paid considerable attention to his negotiations with relocatees and his perception of their goals, strategies, and resources. This perspective included the concepts of rewards, costs, profits, and distributive justice. It would appear, for instance, that relocatees would have been satisfied with the relocation if rewards exceeded costs and if they thought that the city and other relocatees would not "get a better deal." Information concerning rewards, costs, sense of distributive justice, and satisfaction was obtained through the questionnaires, the interviews, and the case studies.

Despite problems in measuring each relocatee's perception of the relative profit accruing to himself or herself, other relocatees, and the city of Halifax, and problems occasioned by differences between long-term and short-term effects, this power and exchange approach is significant for the relocation literature[,] which often appears to keep aloof from the "blood and guts" of relocation transaction. Equally important, by placing the Africville relocation within a typology of relocation models, it is possible to explore the domain consensus (that is, the basic terms of reference held in common and prerequisite to any exchange) associated with the liberal-welfare approach, and especially how such domain consensus (for example, "disadvantaged communities or people have few intrinsically valuable resources and need to be guided by sympathetic experts") develops and how it sets the limits and context of bargaining and reciprocity.

RESEARCH STRATEGIES

The methods employed in this study were varied: questionnaires, in-depth interviews, historical documents, newspapers, case studies, and "bull sessions" with relocatees. A useful baseline source of data was the survey of Halifax blacks, including Africville [residents], conducted in 1959 by the Institute of Public Affairs, Dalhousie University. The original questionnaires were available for re-analysis, an important consideration since many of the data were not published and the published material contained several significant inaccuracies.[21] The 1959 survey questionnaire provided basic demographic data as well as information concerning mobility aspirations, employment, education, and social life.

The collection of data for this study began in 1968. The researchers arranged for two students from the Maritime School of Social Work to prepare twenty case studies.[22] A review of the students' case studies and field notes, guided by the perspective developed by the researchers, aided the drafting of a questionnaire. In 1968 current addresses of the relocatees were also traced and brief acquaintance interviews were conducted.

The most intensive data collection period was June to December 1969. One of the researchers (D. W. M.) conducted in-depth, tape-recorded interviews with individual people associated with the relocation decision-making and implementation: politicians, city officials, middle-class caretakers, the relocation social worker, consultants, and Africville relocatees involved in the decision-making. During these interviews

an open-ended interview guide[23] was used to explore knowledge of Africville and awareness of pre-1964 relocation attempts and also the actual relocation decision-making and mechanics. Each of the approximately two-hour interviews was transcribed and analysed for patterns. Many quotations used in this book are taken from these tape-recorded interviews.

Concurrently, the other researcher (D. H. C.), with two assistants, was meeting informally with the relocatees, individually and in "bull sessions." On the basis of these experiences and the case studies, we all drafted and pre-tested an extensive questionnaire. From September to December, 1969, the questionnaire was employed by interviewers hired and trained by the researchers. The lengthy questionnaire[24] asked about the relocatee's background characteristics: life in Africville, personal knowledge of relocation decision-making processes, relocation strategies, negotiations, costs, rewards, and post-relocation conditions. The questionnaire was given to all household heads and spouses who had lived in Africville and had received a relocation settlement of any kind. Approximately 140 persons were interviewed, several in places as far distant as Winnipeg and Toronto.

In June, 1969, the relocation social worker spent eight days answering a questionnaire[25] on the relocatees' background characteristics, his relocation bargaining with each relocatee, and his perception of the latter's rewards, costs, and strategies. Such data enabled us to analyse more precisely the relationships among parties to the relocation, for similar data from the relocatees and their perception of the relocation social worker were obtained from the relocatee questionnaire.

Two other research tactics were employed at the same time as the interviews were conducted. One of our assistants was conducting in-depth, tape-recorded interviews with black leaders in the Halifax area concerning their assessment of Africville and the implications of relocation. Another assistant was gathering historical data and interviewing selected Africville relocatees concerning the historical development of the community. Important sources of historical data were the minutes of Halifax City Council (read from 1852 to 1969), reports of the Board of Halifax School Commissioners, the Nova Scotia Public Archives, files in the Registry of Deeds, the Halifax *Mail-Star* library, and the minutes of the Halifax Human Rights Advisory Committee. In all phases of research, the Africville files in the Social Planning Department, City of Halifax were of especial value.

PHASES OF THE AFRICVILLE STUDY

The Africville Relocation Report, in addition to being an examination of relocation and planned social change and a contribution to the sparse literature on blacks in Nova Scotia, represents a fusion of research and action. The researchers did not begin the study until virtually all the Africville people had been relocated, and the research strategy resulted in the study being more than an evaluation.[26] The process of obtaining collective as well as individual responses, and of establishing a meaningful exchange with relocatees, fostered collective action from former Africville residents. Some local government officials objected to what they have referred to as the researchers' "activist" bias. The researchers maintain, however, that exchanges had to be worked out with the subjects of research as well as with the funding agencies. The liberal ethic posits informed voluntary consent as fundamental to adult social interaction; informed voluntary consent requires, in turn, meaningful exchange among the participants.

The study began in October, 1968 with a meeting of relocated Africville people. This was the first time since relocation that former residents of Africville had met collectively. This stormy meeting, called by the researchers, was a public airing of relocatee grievances and led to relocatee support of the proposed study. Subsequent talk of forming committees to press grievances with the city of Halifax was an important result of the meeting. The researchers encouraged this tendency, for the expressed grievances appeared legitimate, and the researchers considered that it would be both possible and important to tap a collective or group dimension in the relocation process as well as to study the usual social-psychological considerations.

Later in the same week, at a meeting that the researchers had arranged with city officials, relocation caretakers, and civic leaders, the researchers related the expressed grievances of the relocatees and urged remedial action. General support for the proposed study was obtained at this second meeting, and the pending reconsideration of relocation by the city's newly created Social Planning Department was crystallized.

During the winter and spring of 1969, as the present study was being planned in detail, the action-stimulus of the researchers' early efforts was bearing fruit. Social Planning Department officials were meeting with the relocatees and, as it were, planning the second phase (not initially called for) of the Africville relocation. With provincial and municipal grants totalling seventy thousand dollars, the Seaview Credit Union was organized to assist relocatees experiencing financial crises; in addition, plans were formulated to meet housing and employment needs, and special consideration was to be given to former Africville residents whose needs could be met within the city's existing welfare system. A relocatee was hired to manage the credit union and to assist with other anticipated programs.

During the main data-gathering period, the summer of 1969, and in line with a decision to obtain collective as well as individual responses, the researchers met with informed groups of Africville relocatees to discuss current and future remedial action[;] it became apparent that the so-called second phase of the relocation would be inadequate to meet the people's needs. There was little identification with the credit union and it was floundering, for many relocatees who became members were either unable or unwilling to repay loans. Other anticipated programs and action promised by the city were delayed or forgotten due to bureaucratic entanglements and to lack of organization and pressure on the part of the relocatees.

The relocatees still had legitimate grievances related to unkept promises made at the time of relocation and later. With the formation of the Africville Action Committee, a third phase of the relocation began in the fall of 1969 and winter of 1970. The task of this new committee, developed from group discussions held between the researchers and relocatees, was to effect governmental redress through organized pressure. Several position papers were developed by the Africville Action Committee and negotiations were reopened with the city of Halifax. Although numerous meetings of relocatees were held during the first half of 1970, problems within the Africville Action Committee and the absence of resource people until the fall of 1970 hindered progress. With the committee stumbling along, and the credit union and other city-sponsored projects either ineffectual or nonexistent, the relocation process appeared to have petered out. The action committee was reactivated when one of the authors (D. H. C.) returned to Halifax permanently in the fall of 1970 and groups of relocatees were subsequently reinvolved in reading and criticizing a draft of the present study and in evaluating the relocation and the remedial action taken. Since the fall of 1970, the Africville Action Committee was active. Widespread support for its claims was obtained from community organizations, subcommittees were established to deal with questions of employment, housing, and financial compensation; and city council authorized the establishment of a city negotiating team to meet with representatives of the action committee.

In 1974, at the time of publication of the first edition of this book, the Africville Action Committee, to all intents and purposes, had ceased to function. Although it could claim some credit for a special employment training program through which a number of unemployed Africville relocatees had found jobs, the action committee fell far short of its goals.

The city's lack of a positive imaginative response and the internal organizational problems of the action committee hindered other proposals. What remained in 1974 was a reorganized credit union, a modest base for further redress and group action. However, by 1999 the Seaview Credit Union was no longer in existence; it had collapsed over two decades ago. However, the community is not dead. . . . Africville still thrives in the hearts and minds of many of the relocatees. In addition, Africville still has rich symbolic value for fostering black consciousness in Nova Scotia.

POSTSCRIPT

Throughout the study, we consciously and deliberately attempted to achieve a viable fusion of research and social responsibility. The research focused on the collective responses of the group as well as on individual responses. At each stage in the study (conception, data gathering, data analysis, and preparation for publication) the collective and individual inputs that gave the study an action potential were obtained from relocatees. Drafts of appropriate chapters were sent for critical comment to officials and others involved in the relocation. The study became a stimulus to action because the normal researcher-subject exchanges could be worked out in concrete, actual terms. This was preferable to the usual research situation where, in effecting exchanges with the people being studied, the researcher typically makes vague references to the possible benefit of the study and does little or nothing to follow up implied promises of action.[27] But of course, our research strategy has its weakness too. It is difficult to feel satisfied that the kind of exchange relations that we established had productive consequences. Despite our involvement (in the early 1970s) with petitions, committee work, and attempts at rational problem solving, little redress of the inadequacies of the relocation program was achieved and the manifest goals of the liberal-welfare rhetoric of the relocation remain, in large measure, unrealized.

CRITICAL THINKING QUESTIONS

1. Review the key characteristics of the *development* and *liberal-welfare* relocation models. What are the strengths and weaknesses of each?

2. Have there been any relocation or revitalization programs in your community? If so, which relocation model appears to have provided the justification for the move? Are the people who were relocated still in the community today?

3. In your opinion, can we effectively revitalize our communities without forcing people to move? How?

NOTES

1. *Social Theory and Social Structure* (Glencoe, IL: The Free Press, 1949), p. 80.

2. Gordon Stephenson, *A Redevelopment Study of Halifax, Nova Scotia* (Halifax, NS: City of Halifax, 1957).

3. *The Condition of the Negroes of Halifax City, Nova Scotia* (Halifax: Institute of Public Affairs, Dalhousie University, 1962); and G. Brand, *Interdepartmental Committee* on *Human Rights: Survey Reports* (Halifax, NS: Nova Scotia Department of Welfare, Social Development Division, 1963).

4. Minutes of the Halifax City Council, Halifax, NS, September 14, 1967.

5. The Government of Newfoundland initiated the program in 1953. In 1965 a joint federal-provincial program was initiated under a resettlement act. In 1970 the program was placed under the direction of the Federal Department of Regional Economic Expansion. For an overview of the resettlement program, see Noel Iverson and D. Ralph Matthews, *Communities in Decline: An Examination of Household Resettlement in Newfoundland*, Newfoundland Social and Economic Studies, No. 6, (St. John's, NF: Memorial University of Newfoundland, Institute of Social and Economic Research, 1968). For a critical assessment of studies of the resettlement program, see Jim Lotz, "Resettlement and Social Change in Newfoundland," *Canadian Review of Sociology and Anthropology 8* (February, 1971): 48–59.

6. See Table 4, "Completed Redevelopment Projects" in *Urban Renewal* (Toronto: Centre for Urban and Community Studies, University of Toronto, 1968). Reprinted from *University of Toronto Law Journal*, 18, No. 3 (1968): 243.

7. David A. Wallace, "The Conceptualizing of Urban Renewal," *Urban Renewal* (Toronto: Centre for Urban and Community Studies, University of Toronto, 1968), 251.

8. An example of such a project is one reported by Thurz in southwest Washington, DC. Little was done for the relocatees, but the relocation was widely acclaimed for its futuristic redevelopment design. For a critique of this approach, see Daniel Thurz, *Where Are They Now?* Washington, D.C.: Health and Welfare Council of the National Capital Area, 1966). See also, Jane Jacobs, *The Death and Life of Great American Cities* (New York: Random House, 1961).

9. Graham Fraser, *Fighting Back: Urban Renewal in Trefann Court* (Toronto: Hakkert, 1972), p. 55.

10. John Matthiasson, "Forced Relocation: An Evaluative Case Study," paper presented at the annual meeting of the Canadian Sociology and Anthropology Association, Winnipeg, 1970.

11. In recent years some minor progressive modifications have been introduced with reference to the development model; these deal with advance notice and public hearings, relocation compensation, and the availability of housing stock. See, Robert P. Groberg, *Centralized Relocation* (Washington, D.C.: National Association of Housing and Redevelopment Officials, 1969).

12. William L. Slayton, "Poverty and Urban Renewal," quoted in Hans B. C. Spiegel, "Human Considerations in Urban Renewal," *Urban Renewal*, op. cit., 311.

13. Elizabeth Wood, "Social Welfare Planning," quoted in Spiegel, op. cit., 315.

14. For a discussion of this, see Kenneth Craig, "Sociologists and Motivating Strategies," M.A. thesis, University of Guelph, Department of Sociology, 1971.

15. Groberg, op. cit., p. 172.

16. See Alvin W. Gouldner, *The Coming Crisis of Western Sociology* (New York: Basic Books, 1970), pp. 500–02.

17. Relocation is a short-term consideration, for most services brought to bear on relocatee problems rarely extend beyond rehousing. A more general critique of the multiplying effect of citizens' involvement in relocation is given by S. M. Miller and Frank Riessman, *Social Class and Social Policy* (New York: Basic Books Inc., 1968).

18. The historical antecedents and reasons for the legislation are discussed in Daniel Moynihan, *Maximum Feasible Misunderstanding* (New York: Free Press, 1970). For an alternative interpretation, see Francis Fox Piven and Richard A. Cloward, *Regulating the Poor: The Functions of Public Welfare* (New York: Random Vintage Books, 1972), pp. 248–84. The operation of the program is discussed by Ralph M. Kramer, *Participation of the Poor: Comparative Community Case Studies* in *the War on Poverty* (Englewood Cliffs, NJ: Prentice Hall, 1969).

19. Fraser, op. cit., p. 262.

20. For a discussion of this theoretical perspective, see Peter M. Blau, *Exchange and Power in Social Life* (New York: Wiley, 1964); and George Caspar Homans, *Social Behavior: Its Elementary Forms* (New York: Harcourt, Brace and World, 1961).

21. *The Condition of the Negroes of Halifax City*, Nova Scotia, op. cit.

22. Sarah M. Beaton, "Effects of Relocation: A Study of Ten Families Relocated from Africville, Halifax, Nova Scotia," Master of Social Work Thesis, Maritime School of Social Work, Halifax, NS, 1969; and Bernard MacDougall, "Urban Relocation of Africville Residents," Master of Social Work Thesis, Maritime School of Social Work, Halifax, NS, 1969.

23. The interview guide is published in Donald H. Clairmont and Dennis W. Magill, *Africville Relocation Report* (Halifax, NS: Institute of Public Affairs, Dalhousie University, 1971), pp. A131–A135.

24. Ibid., pp. A97–A128.

25. Ibid., pp. A83–A96.

26. Some relocation studies have been carried out as part of the relocation decision-making, see William H. Key, *When People Are Forced to Move* (Topeka, KS: Menninger Foundation, 1967, mimeographed[);] others have been concurrent with the relocating of people, see Herbert J. Gans, *The Urban Villagers: Group and Class in The Life of Italian Americans* (New York: The Free Press, 1962). The present study is unique in that it fostered collective action carried out after the relocation.

27. See Craig, op. cit.

60

Let's *Reduce* Global Population!

J. KENNETH SMAIL

A familiar concern is holding the line on world population increase. But, some people are asking, has population growth already gone too far? In this selection, Kenneth Smail argues that the long-term "carrying capacity" of the planet may be only half the number of people we have now. And the time left to begin reducing population is running out fast.

The main point of this essay is simply stated. Within the next half-century, it is essential for the human species to have in place a flexible voluntary, equitable, and internationally coordinated plan to dramatically reduce world population by at least two-thirds. This process of voluntary consensus building—local, national, and global—must begin now.

The mathematical inevitability that human numbers will continue their dramatic increase over the next two generations (to perhaps 9 billion or more by the year 2050), the high probability that this numerical increase will worsen the problems that already plague humanity (economic, political, environmental, social, moral, etc.), and the growing realization that the Earth may only be able to support a global human population in

Source: The revised version of the essay, "Negative Population Growth" (Smail, 1995), revised and expanded in *Population and Environment* (Smail, 1997a) and *Politics and the Life Sciences* (Smail, 1997b). Reprinted with permission.

the 2 to 3 billion range at an "adequate to comfortable" standard of living, only reinforce this sense of urgency.

There are, however, hopeful signs. In recent years, we have finally begun to come to terms with the fact that the consequences of the twentieth century's rapid and seemingly uncontrolled population growth will soon place us—if it has not done so already—in the greatest crisis our species has yet encountered.

TEN INESCAPABLE REALITIES

In order better to appreciate the scope and ramifications of this still partly hidden crisis, I shall briefly call attention to ten essential and inescapable realities that must be fully understood and soon confronted.

First, during the present century world population will have grown from somewhere around

1.6 billion in 1900 to slightly more than 6 billion by the year 2000, an almost fourfold increase in but 100 years. This is an unprecedented numerical expansion. Throughout human history, world population growth measured over similar 100-year intervals has been virtually nonexistent or, at most, modestly incremental; it has only become markedly exponential within the last few hundred years. To illustrate this on a more easily comprehensible scale, based on the recent rate of increase of nearly 90 million per year, human population growth during the 1990s alone amounted to nearly 1 billion, an astonishing 20 percent increase in but little more than a single decade. Just by itself, this increase is equivalent to the total global population in the year 1800 and is approximately triple the estimated world population (ca. 300 million) at the height of the Roman Empire. It is a chastening thought that even moderate demographic projections suggest that this billion-per-decade rate of increase will continue well into the century, and that the current global total of 6 billion (late 1999 estimate) could easily reach 9 to 10 billion by mid-twenty-first century.

Second, even if a fully effective program of zero population growth (ZPG) were implemented immediately, by limiting human fertility to what demographers term the *replacement rate* (roughly 2.1 children per female), global population would nevertheless continue its rapid rate of expansion. In fact, demographers estimate that it would take at least two to three generations (fifty to seventy-five years) at ZPG fertility levels just to reach a point of population stability, unfortunately at numbers considerably higher than at present. This powerful *population momentum* results from the fact that an unusually high proportion (nearly one-third) of the current world population is under the age of fifteen and has not yet reproduced. Even more broad-based population profiles may be found throughout the developing world, where the under-fifteen age cohort often exceeds 40 percent and where birth rates have remained high even as mortality rates have fallen. While there are some

recent indications that fertility rates are beginning to decline, the current composite for the less-developed world—excluding China—is still nearly double (ca. 3.8) that needed for ZPG.

Third, in addition to fertility levels, it is essential to understand that population growth is also significantly affected by changes in mortality rates. In fact, demographic transition theory suggests that the earlier stages of rapid population expansion are typically fueled more by significant reductions in death rates (i.e., decreased childhood mortality and/or enhanced adult longevity) than by changes in birth rates. Nor does recent empirical data suggest that average human life expectancy has reached anywhere near its theoretical upper limit, in either the developing or developed worlds. Consequently, unless there appears a deadly pandemic, a devastating world war or a massive breakdown in public health (or a combination of all three), it is obvious that ongoing global gains in human longevity will continue to make a major contribution to world population expansion over the next half-century, regardless of whatever progress might be made in reducing fertility.

Fourth, all previous examples of significant human population expansion—and subsequent (occasionally rapid) decline—have been primarily local or, at most, regional phenomena. At the present time, given the current global rate of increase of some 220,000 people per day (more than 9,000 per hour), it is ludicrous to speak of significant empty spaces left on Earth to colonize, certainly when compared with but a century ago. And it is ridiculous to suggest that "off Earth" (extraterrestrial) migration will somehow be sufficient to siphon away excess human population, in either the near or more distant future.

Fifth, given the data and observations presented thus far, it becomes increasingly apparent that the time span available for implementing an effective program of population "control" may be quite limited, with a window of opportunity—even in the more optimistic scenarios—that may not extend much beyond the middle of the next century. As mentioned previously, most middle-of-the-road demographic projections for the year 2050—two generations from now—are in the 8 to 9 billion range. Several observations might help to bring these demographic estimates and the above-mentioned "limited" time span into somewhat better perspective:

- the year 2050 is closer to the present than the year 1950
- an infant born in 2000 will be only fifty years old in the year 2050
- a young person entering the job market in the early twenty-first century will have reached retirement age in the year 2050

These observations also make it quite clear that *those already born*—ourselves, our children, and our grandchildren—will have to confront the overwhelming impact of an additional 3 to 4 billion people.

Sixth, the Earth's long-term carrying capacity, in terms of resources, is indeed finite, despite the continuing use of economic models predicated on seemingly unlimited growth, and notwithstanding the high probability of continued scientific/technological progress. Some further terminological clarification may be useful. "Long-term" is most reasonably defined on the order of several hundred years, at least; it emphatically does not mean the five-to-fifteen-year horizon typical of much economic forecasting or political prognostication. Over this much longer time span, it thus becomes much more appropriate—perhaps even essential to civilizational survival—to define a sustainable human population size in terms of optimums rather than maximums. Further, *what "could" be supported in the short term is not necessarily what "should" be humanity's goal over the longer term.*

As far as resources are concerned, whether these be characterized as renewable or nonrenewable, it is becoming increasingly apparent that the era of inexpensive energy (derived from fossil fuels), adequate food supplies (whether plant or animal), readily available or easily extractable raw materials (from wood to minerals), plentiful fresh water, and readily accessible "open space" is rapidly coming to a close, almost certainly within the next half-century. And finally, the consequences of future scientific/technological advances—whether in terms of energy production, technological efficiency, agricultural productivity, or creation of alternative materials—are much more likely to be incremental than revolutionary, notwithstanding frequent and grandiose claims for the latter.

Seventh, rhetoric about "sustainable growth" is at best a continuing exercise in economic self-deception and at worst a politically pernicious oxymoron. Almost certainly, working toward some sort of *steady-state sustainability* is much more realistic scientifically, (probably) more attainable economically, and (perhaps) more prudent politically. Assertions that the Earth might be able to support a population of 10, 15, or even 20 billion people for an indefinite period of time at a standard of living superior to the present are not only cruelly misleading but almost certainly false. Rather, extrapolations from the work of a growing number of ecologists, demographers, and numerous others suggest the distinct possibility that *the Earth's true carrying capacity—defined simply as humans in long-term adaptive balance with their ecological setting, resource base, and each other—may already have been exceeded by a factor of two or more.*

To the best of my knowledge, no evidence contradicts this sobering—perhaps even frightening—assessment. Consequently, since at some point in the not-too-distant future the negative consequences and ecological damage stemming from the mutually reinforcing effects of excessive human reproduction and overconsumption of resources could well become irreversible, and because there is only one Earth with which to experiment, it is undoubtedly better for our species to err on the side of prudence, exercising wherever possible a cautious and careful stewardship.

Eighth, only about 20 percent of the current world population (ca. 1.2 billion people) could be said to have a *generally adequate* standard of living, defined here as a level of affluence roughly approximating that of the so-called "developed" world (Western Europe, Japan, and North America). The other 80 percent (ca. 4.8 billion), incorporating most of the inhabitants of what have been termed the "developing nations," live in conditions ranging from mild deprivation to severe deficiency. Despite well-intentioned efforts to the contrary, there is little evidence that this imbalance is going to decrease in any significant way, and a strong likelihood that it may get worse, particularly in view of the fact that more than 90 percent of all future population expansion is projected to occur in these less-developed regions of the world. In fact, there is growing concern that when this burgeoning population growth in the developing world is combined with excessive or wasteful per capita energy and resource consumption in much of the developed world, widespread environmental deterioration (systemic breakdown?) in a number of the Earth's more heavily stressed ecosystems will become increasingly likely. This is especially worrisome in regions already beset by short-sighted or counterproductive economic policies, chronic political instability, and growing social unrest, particularly when one considers that nearly all nations in the less-developed world currently have an understandable desire—not surprisingly expressed as a fundamental right—to increase their standard of living (per capita energy and resource consumption) to something approximating "first world" levels.

Ninth, to follow up on the point just made, the total impact of human numbers on the global environment is often described as the product of three basic multipliers: (1) population size; (2) per capita energy and resource consumption (affluence); and (3) technological efficiency in the production, utilization, and conservation of such energy and resources. This relationship is usually expressed by some variant of the now well-known I = PAT equation: Impact = Population × Affluence × Technology. This simple formula enables one to demonstrate much

more clearly the quantitative scope of humanity's dilemma over the next fifty to seventy-five years, particularly if the following projections are anywhere near accurate:

- human population could well *double* by the end of the twenty-first century, from our current 6 billion to perhaps 12 billion or more

- global energy and resource consumption could easily quadruple or more during the same period, particularly if (as just indicated in item 8) the less-developed nations are successful in their current efforts to significantly improve their citizens' standard of living to something approaching developed-world norms

- new technologies applied to current energy and resource inefficiencies might be successful in reducing per capita waste or effluence *by half,* or even *two-thirds,* in both the developed and developing worlds

Given these reasonable estimates, the conclusion seems inescapable that the human species' total impact on the Earth's already stressed ecosystem could easily *triple to quadruple* by the middle of the twenty-first century. This impact could be even greater if current (and future) efforts at energy and resource conservation turn out to be less successful than hoped for, or if (as seems likely) the mathematical relationship between these several multipliers is something more than simply linear. It is therefore very important to keep a close watch—for harbingers of future trends and/or problems—on current events in the growing group of nations now experiencing rapid economic development and modernization, with particular attention being given to ongoing changes in India and China, two states whose combined size represents nearly half the population of the less-developed world.

Tenth, and finally, there are two additional considerations—matters not usually factored into the I = PAT equation—that must also be taken into account in any attempt to coordinate appropriate responses to the rapidly increasing global environmental impact described in points 6 through 9. First, given current and likely ongoing scientific uncertainties about environmental limits and ecosystem resilience, not to mention the potential dangers of irreversible damage if such limits are stretched too far (i.e., a permanently reduced carrying capacity), it is extremely important to design into any future planning an adequate safety factor (or sufficient margin for error). In other words, any attempt at "guided social engineering" on the massive scale that will clearly be necessary over the next century will require at least as much attention to safety margins, internal coordination, and systems redundancy as may be found in other major engineering accomplishments—from designing airplanes to building the Channel Tunnel to landing astronauts on the moon.

In addition, such planning must consider yet another seemingly intractable problem. Because the human species not only shares the Earth—but has also co-evolved—with literally millions of other life forms, the closely related issues of wilderness conservation and biodiversity preservation must also be taken fully into account, on several different levels (pragmatic, aesthetic, and moral). In simplest terms, it has now become a matter of critical importance to ask some very basic questions about what proportion of the Earth's surface the human species has the right to exploit or transform—or, conversely, how much of the Earth's surface should be reserved for the protection and preservation of all other life forms. As many have argued, often in eloquent terms, our species will likely be more successful in confronting and resolving these questions—not to mention the other complex problems that are now crowding in upon us—*if we can collectively come to regard ourselves more as the Earth's long-term stewards than its absolute masters.*

To sum up, if the above "inescapable realities" are indeed valid, it is obvious that rational, equitable, and attainable population goals will have to be established in the very near future. It is also obvious that these goals will have to address—and in some fashion resolve—a powerful internal conflict: how to create and sustain an adequate standard of living for all the world's peoples, minimizing as much as possible the growing inequities between rich and poor, while simultaneously neither overstressing nor exceeding the Earth's longer-term carrying capacity. *I submit that these goals cannot be reached, or this conflict resolved, unless and until world population is dramatically reduced—to somewhere around 2 to 3 billion people—within the next two centuries.*

CRITICAL THINKING QUESTIONS

1. Why, according to this reading, is simply holding the line on population increase not enough?
2. What about the fact that humans share the Earth with millions of other life forms? In facing up to the problem of population increase, what responsibility do we have for other species?
3. All in all, do you agree with Smail that we must find a way to reduce global population? Why or why not?

REFERENCES

Smail, J. Kenneth. 1995. Confronting the 21st century's hidden crisis: Reducing human numbers by 80%. *NPG Forum.* Teaneck, NJ: Negative Population Growth.

———. 1997a. Averting the 21st century's demographic crisis: Can human numbers be reduced by 75%? *Population and Environment,* 18(6): 565–80.

———. 1997b. Beyond population stabilization: The case for dramatically reducing global human numbers. Roundtable: World Population Policy commentary and responses. *Politics and the Life Sciences,* 16, 2 (September, 1997): 183–236.

61

Why Humanity Faces Ultimate Catastrophe

THOMAS ROBERT MALTHUS

In this selection, from "An Essay on the Principle of Population," Thomas Robert Malthus foretells human calamity. His dire prediction is based on a single assertion: Human beings will overwhelm the earth's capacity to provide for us. Many of today's environmentalists (sometimes termed "neo-Malthusians") accept this principle and echo his early warning.

STATEMENT OF THE SUBJECT: RATIOS OF THE INCREASE OF POPULATION AND FOOD

In an inquiry concerning the improvement of society, the mode of conducting the subject which naturally presents itself is

1. To investigate the causes that have hitherto impeded the progress of mankind towards happiness
2. To examine the probability of the total or partial removal of the causes in [the] future

To enter fully into this question, and to enumerate all the causes that have hitherto influenced human improvement, would be much beyond the power of an individual. The principal object of

Source: From *On the Principle of Population*, Vol. I, by T. R. Malthus (New York: E. P. Dutton & Co., Inc., 1914; orig. 1798).

the present essay is to examine the effects of one great cause intimately united with the very nature of man; which, though it has been constantly and powerfully operating since the commencement of society, has been little noticed by the writers who have treated this subject. The facts which establish the existence of this cause have, indeed, been repeatedly stated and acknowledged; but its natural and necessary effects have been almost totally overlooked; though probably among these effects may be reckoned a very considerable portion of that vice and misery, and of that unequal distribution of the bounties of nature, which it has been the unceasing object of the enlightened philanthropist in all ages to correct.

The cause to which I allude is the constant tendency in all animated life to increase beyond the nourishment prepared for it.

It is observed by Dr. Franklin that there is no bound to the prolific nature of plants or animals but what is made by their crowding and interfering with each other's means of subsistence. Were the face of the earth, he says, vacant of other plants, it might be gradually sowed and overspread with one kind only, as for instance with fennel; and were it empty of other inhabitants, it might in a few ages be replenished from one nation only, as for instance with Englishmen.[1]

This is incontrovertibly true. Through the animal and vegetable kingdoms Nature has scattered the seeds of life abroad with the most profuse and liberal hand; but has been comparatively sparing in the room and the nourishment necessary to rear them. The germs of existence contained in this earth, if they could freely develop themselves, would fill millions of worlds in the course of a few thousand years. Necessity, that imperious, all pervading law of nature, restrains them within the prescribed bounds. The race of plants and the race of animals shrink under this great restrictive law; and man cannot by any efforts of reason escape from it.

In plants and irrational animals, the view of the subject is simple. They are all impelled by a powerful instinct to the increase of their species; and this instinct is interrupted by no doubts about providing for their offspring. Wherever therefore there is liberty, the power of increase is exerted; and the super-abundant effects are repressed afterwards by want of room and nourishment.

The effects of this check on man are more complicated. Impelled to the increase of his species by an equally powerful instinct, reason interrupts his career, and asks him whether he may not bring beings into the world for whom he cannot provide the means of support. If he attends to this natural suggestion, the restriction too frequently produces vice. If he hear it not, the human race will be constantly endeavouring to increase beyond the mean of subsistence. But as, by the law of our nature which makes food necessary to the life of man, population can never actually increase beyond the lowest nourishment capable of supporting it, a strong check on population, from the difficulty of acquiring food, must be constantly in operation. This difficulty must fall somewhere, and must necessarily be severely felt in some or other of the various forms of misery, or the fear of misery, by a large portion of mankind.

That population has this constant tendency to increase beyond the means of subsistence, and that it is kept to its necessary level by these causes, will sufficiently appear from a review of the different states of society in which man has existed. But, before we proceed to this review, the subject will, perhaps, be seen in a clearer light if we endeavour to ascertain what would be the natural increase of population if left to exert itself with perfect freedom; and what might be expected to be the rate of increase in the production of the earth under the most favourable circumstances of human industry.

It will be allowed that no country has hitherto been known where the manners were so pure and simple, and the means of subsistence so abundant, that no check whatever has existed to early marriages from the difficulty of providing for a family, and that no waste of the human species has been occasioned by vicious customs, by towns, by unhealthy occupations, or too severe labour. Consequently in no state that we have yet known has the power of population been left to exert itself with perfect freedom.

Whether the law of marriage be instituted, or not, the dictate of nature and virtue seems to be an early attachment to one woman; and where there were no impediments of any kind in the way of a union to which such an attachment would lead, and no causes of depopulation afterwards, the increase of the human species would be evidently much greater than any increase which has been hitherto known.....

It may safely be pronounced, . . . that population, when unchecked, goes on doubling itself every twenty-five years, or increases in a geometrical ratio.

The rate according to which the productions of the earth may be supposed to increase, it will not be so easy to determine. Of this, however, we may be perfectly certain, that the ratio of their increase in a limited territory must be of a totally different nature from the ratio of the increase of population. A thousand millions are just as easily doubled every twenty-five years by the power of population as a thousand. But the food to support the increase from the greater number will by no means be obtained with the same facility. Man is necessarily confined in room. When acre has been added to acre till all the fertile land is occupied, the yearly increase of food must depend upon the melioration of the land already in possession. This is a fund, which, from the nature of all soils, instead of increasing, must be gradually diminishing. But population, could it be supplied with food, would go on with unexhausted vigour; and the increase of one period would furnish the power of a greater increase the next, and this without any limit. . . .

Europe is by no means so fully peopled as it might be. In Europe there is the fairest chance that human industry may receive its best direction. The science of agriculture has been much studied in England and Scotland; and there is still a great portion of uncultivated land in these countries. Let us consider at what rate the produce of this island might be supposed to increase under circumstances the most favourable to improvement.

If it be allowed that by the best possible policy, and great encouragements to agriculture, the average produce of the island could be doubled in the first twenty-five years, it will be allowing, probably, a greater increase than could with reason be expected.

In the next twenty-five years, it is impossible to suppose that the produce could be quadrupled. It would be contrary to all our knowledge of the properties of land. The improvement of the barren parts would be a work of time and labour; and it must be evident to those who have the slightest acquaintance with agricultural subjects that, in proportion as cultivation extended, the additions that could yearly be made to the former average produce must be gradually and

regularly diminishing. That we may be the better able to compare the increase of population and food, let us make a supposition, which, without pretending to accuracy, is clearly more favourable to the power of production in the earth than any experience we have had of its qualities will warrant.

Let us suppose that the yearly additions which might be made to the former average produce, instead of decreasing, which they certainly would do, were to remain the same; and that the produce of this island might be increased every twenty-five years by a quantity equal to what it at present produces. The most enthusiastic speculator cannot suppose a greater increase than this. In a few centuries it would make every acre of land in the island like a garden.

If this supposition be applied to the whole earth, and if it be allowed that the subsistence for man which the earth affords might be increased every twenty-five years by a quantity equal to what it at present produces, this will be supposing a rate of increase much greater than we can imagine that any possible exertions of mankind could make it.

It may be fairly pronounced, therefore, that, considering the present average state of the earth, the means of subsistence, under circumstances the most favourable to human industry, could not possibly be made to increase faster than in an arithmetical ratio.

The necessary effects of these two different rates of increase, when brought together, will be very striking. Let us call the population of this island 11 millions; and suppose the present produce equal to the easy support of such a number. In the first twenty-five years the population would be 22 millions, and the food being also doubled, the means of subsistence would be equal to this increase. In the next twenty-five years, the population would be 44 millions, and the means of subsistence only equal to the support of 33 millions. In the next period the population would be 88 millions, and the means of subsistence just equal to the support of half that number. And, at the conclusion of the first century, the population would be 176 millions, and the means of subsistence only equal to the support of 55 millions, leaving a population of 121 millions totally unprovided for.

Taking the whole earth, instead of this island, emigration would of course be excluded; and, supposing the present population equal to a thousand millions, the human species would increase as the numbers, 1, 2, 4, 8, 16, 32, 64, 128, 256, and subsistence as 1, 2, 3, 4, 5, 6, 7, 8, 9. In two centuries the population would be to the means of subsistence as 256 to 9; in three centuries as 4,096 to 13, and in 2,000 years the difference would be almost incalculable. . . .

CRITICAL THINKING QUESTIONS

1. According to Malthus, at what rate does human population increase? At what rate can the earth's food supplies be increased?

2. Malthus published his essay in 1798; in the two centuries since then, has his dire prediction come to pass? Why, or why not?

3. Following Malthus's thinking, what should be the cornerstone of the world's program to protect the environment? Do you agree with his position or not?

NOTE

1. Franklin's Miscell, p. 9.

62

Fool's Paradise

RONALD WRIGHT

Global warming, deforestation, and the loss of farmland are just a few of the more press-ing contemporary environmental problems that the world faces. Will we have the foresight—and more importantly, the political will—to properly address these issues? This chapter highlights an environmental disaster of the past and considers what this might teach us about contemporary problems relating to the overconsumption of resources and the environmental degradation that this entails.

Source: Ronald Wright. 2004. In *A Short History of Progress*, pp. 55–63. Toronto: House of Anansi Press.

The greatest wonder of the ancient world is how recent it all is. No city or monument is much more than 5,000 years old. Only about seventy lifetimes, of seventy years, have been lived end to end since civilization began. Its entire run occupies a mere 0.2 per cent of the two and a half million years since our first ancestor sharpened a stone.

. . . . I outlined the rise and fall of "man the hunter" in the Old Stone Age. His very progress, his perfection of weapons and techniques, led directly to the end of hunting as a way of life (except in a few places where conditions favoured the prey). Next came the discovery of farming—likely by women—during the New Stone Age, or Neolithic period, in several parts of the world. And from that grew our experiment of civilization, which began as many independent enterprises but,

in the past few centuries, has coalesced (mainly by hostile takeover) into one big system that covers the earth.

There are signs that this experiment, like hunting, is now in danger of falling victim to its own success. I've already mentioned nuclear weapons and greenhouse gases. The big bang in the atom is obviously deadlier than the small bangs in millions of engines; but if we are unlucky or unwise, both could end civilization on its present scale. Much simpler technologies have proved fatal in the past. Sometimes the trouble lies in a particular invention or idea; but it also lies in social structure, in the way people tend to behave when squeezed together in urban civilizations, where power and wealth rise upward and the many are ruled by the few.

As I mentioned earlier, the wrecks of our failed experiments lie in deserts and jungles like fallen airliners whose flight recorders can tell us what went wrong. Archaeology is the best tool we have for looking ahead, because it provides a deep reading of the direction and momentum of our course through time: what we are, where we have come from, and therefore where we are most likely to be going.

Unlike written history, which is often highly edited, archaeology can uncover the deeds we have forgotten, or choose to forget. A realistic understanding of the past is quite a new thing, a late fruit of the Enlightenment, although people of many times have felt the tug of what the Elizabethan antiquarian William Camden called the "back-looking curiousity." Antiquity, he wrote, "hath a certaine resemblance with eternity. [It] is a sweet food of the mind."[1]

Not everyone's mind was so open in his day. A Spanish viceroy of Peru who had just seen the Inca capital high in the Andes, with its walls of giant stones fitted like gems, wrote back to his king: "I have examined the fortress that [the Incas] built . . . which shows clearly the work of the Devil . . . for it does not seem possible that the strength and skill of men could have made it."[2]

Even today, some opt for the comforts of mystification, preferring to believe that the wonders of the ancient world were built by Atlanteans, gods, or space travellers, instead of by thousands toiling in the sun. Such thinking robs our forerunners of their due, and us of their experience. Because then one can believe whatever one likes about the past—without having to confront the bones, potsherds, and inscriptions which tell us that people all over the world, time and again, have made similar advances and mistakes.

About two centuries after the Spanish invasion of Peru, a Dutch fleet in the South Seas, far to the west of Chile and below the Tropic of Capricorn, came upon a sight hardly less awesome, and even more inexplicable, than the megalithic buildings of the Andes. On Easter Day, 1722, the Dutchmen sighted an unknown island so treeless and eroded that they mistook its barren hills for dunes. They were amazed, as they drew near, to see hundreds of stone images,

some as tall as an Amsterdam house. "We could not comprehend how it was possible that these people, who are devoid of heavy thick timber [or] strong ropes, nevertheless had been able to erect such images, which were fully thirty feet high."[3] Captain Cook later confirmed the island's desolation, finding "no wood for fuel; nor any fresh water worth taking on board." He described the islanders' tiny canoes, made from scraps of driftwood stitched together like shoe leather, as the worst in the Pacific. Nature, he concluded, had "been exceedingly sparing of her favours to this spot."[4]

The great mystery of Easter Island that struck all early visitors was not just that these colossal statues stood in such a tiny and remote corner of the world, but that the stones seemed to have been put there without tackle, as if set down from the sky. The Spaniards who had credited the Devil with the splendours of Inca architecture were merely unable to recognize another culture's achievements. But even scientific observers could not, at first, account for the megaliths of Easter Island. The figures stood there mockingly, defying common sense.

We now know the answer to the riddle, and it is a chilling one. With all due respect to Captain Cook, Nature had not been unusually stingy with her favours. Pollen studies of the island's crater lakes have shown that it was once well watered and green, with rich volcanic soil supporting thick woods of the Chilean wine palm, a fine timber that can grow as big as an oak. No natural disaster had changed that: no eruption, drought, or disease. The catastrophe on Easter Island was man.

Rapa Nui, as Polynesians call the place, was settled during the fifth century A.D. by migrants from the Marquesas or the Gambiers who arrived in big catamarans stocked with their usual range of crops and animals: dogs, chickens, edible rats, sugar cane, bananas, sweet potatoes, and mulberry for making bark cloth. (Thor Heyerdahl's theory that the island was peopled from South America has not been supported by recent work, though sporadic contact between Peru and Oceania probably did take place.) Easter Island proved too cold for breadfruit and coconut palms, but it was rich in seafood: fish, seals, porpoises, turtles, and nesting seabirds. Within five or six centuries, the settlers had multiplied to about 10,000 people—a lot for sixty-four square miles. They built villages with good houses on stone footings and cleared all the best land for fields. Socially they split into clans and ranks—nobles, priests, commoners—and there may have been a paramount chief, or "king." Like Polynesians on some other islands, each clan began to honour its ancestry with impressive stone images. These were hewn from the yielding volcanic tuff of a crater and set up on platforms by the shore. As time went on, the statue cult became increasingly rivalrous and extravagant, reaching its apogee during Europe's high Middle Ages, while the Plantagenet kings ruled England.

Each generation of images grew bigger than the last, demanding more timber, rope, and manpower for hauling to the *ahu*, or altars. Trees were cut faster than they could grow, a problem worsened by the settlers' rats, who ate the seeds and saplings. By A.D. 1400, no more tree pollen is found in the annual layers of the crater lakes: the woods had been utterly destroyed by both the largest and the smallest mammal on the island.

We might think that in such a limited place, where, from the height of Terevaka, islanders could survey their whole world at a glance, steps would have been taken to halt the cutting, to protect the saplings, to replant. We might think that as trees became scarce, the erection of statues would have been curtailed, and timber reserved for essential purposes such as boatbuilding and roofing. But that is not what happened. The people who felled the last tree could see it was the last, could know with complete certainty that there would never be another. And they felled it anyway. All shade vanished from the land except the hard-edged shadows cast by the petrified ancestors, whom the people loved all the more because they made them feel less alone.

For a generation or so, there was enough old lumber to haul the great stones and still keep a few canoes seaworthy for deep water. But the day came when the last good boat was gone. The people then knew there would be little seafood and—worse—no way of escape. The word for wood, *rakau*, became the dearest in their language. Wars broke out over ancient planks and worm-eaten bits of jetsam. They ate all their dogs and nearly all the nesting birds, and the unbearable stillness of the place deepened with animal silences. There was nothing left now but the *moai*, the stone giants who had devoured the land. And still these promised the return of plenty, if only the people would keep faith and honour them with increase. But how will we take you to the altars? asked the carvers, and the *moai* answered that when the time came, they would walk there on their own. So the sound of hammering still rang from the quarries, and the crater walls came alive with hundreds of new giants, growing even bigger now they had no need of human transport. The tallest ever set on an altar is over thirty feet high and weighs eighty tons; the tallest ever *carved* is sixty-five feet long and more than *two hundred* tons, comparable to the greatest stones worked by the Incas or Egyptians. Except, of course, that it never budged an inch.

By the end there were more than a thousand *moai*, one for every ten islanders in their heyday. But the good days were gone—gone with the good earth, which had been carried away on the endless wind and washed by flash floods into the sea. The people had been seduced by a kind of progress that becomes a mania, an "ideological pathology," as some anthropologists call it. When Europeans arrived in the eighteenth century, the worst was over; they found only one or two living souls per statue, a sorry remnant, "small, lean, timid and miserable," in Cook's words.[5] Now without roof beams, many people were dwelling in caves; their only buildings were stone henhouses where they guarded this last non-human protein from one another day and night. The Europeans heard tales of how the warrior class had taken power, how the island had convulsed with burning villages, gory battles, and cannibal feasts. The one innovation of this end-period was to turn the use of obsidian (a razor-keen volcanic glass) from toolmaking to weapons.[6] Daggers and spearheads became the commonest artefacts on the island, hoarded in pits like the grenades and assault rifles kept by modern-day survivalists.

Even this was not quite the nadir. Between the Dutch visit of 1722 and Cook's fifty years later, the people again made war on each other and, for the first time, on the ancestors as well. Cook found *moai* toppled from their platforms, cracked and beheaded, the ruins littered with human bone. There is no reliable account of how or why this happened. Perhaps it started as the ultimate atrocity between enemy clans, like European nations bombing cathedrals in the Second World War. Perhaps it began with the shattering of the island's solitude by strangers in floating castles of unimaginable wealth and menace. These possessors of wood were also bringers of death and disease. Scuffles with sailors often ended with natives gunned down on the beach.

We do not know exactly what promises had been made by the demanding *moai* to the people, but it seems likely that the arrival of an outside world might have exposed certain illusions of the statue cult, replacing compulsive belief with equally compulsive disenchantment. Whatever its animus, the destruction on Rapa Nui raged for at least seventy years. Each foreign ship saw fewer upright statues, until not one giant was left standing on its altar. The work of demolition must have been extremely arduous for the few descendants of the builders. Its thoroughness and deliberation speak of something deeper than clan warfare: of a people angry at their reckless fathers, of a revolt against the dead.

The lesson that Rapa Nui holds for our world has not gone unremarked. In the epilogue to their 1992 book, *Easter Island, Earth Island*, the archaeologists Paul Bahn and John Flenley are explicit. The islanders, they write:

carried out for us the experiment of permitting unrestricted population growth, profligate use of resources, destruction of the environment and boundless confidence in their religion to take care of the future. The result was an ecological disaster leading to a population crash. . . . Do we have to repeat the experiment on [a] grand scale? . . . Is the human personality always the same as that of the person who felled the last tree?[7]

The last tree. The last mammoth. The last dodo. And soon perhaps the last fish and the last gorilla. On the basis of what police call "form," we are serial killers beyond reason. But has this always been, and must it always be, the case? Are all human systems doomed to stagger along under the mounting weight of their internal logic until it crushes them? As I have proposed, the answers—and, I think, the remedies—lie in the fates of past societies.

CRITICAL THINKING QUESTIONS

1. Wright writes that the demise of societies can be structurally determined. What does he mean by that? Can you think of some structures that will have to be changed in order to avert environmental crises in contemporary society?

2. Do you think writers like Malthus (previous reading) and Ronald Wright are too pessimistic in their analysis? History has shown Malthus to be overly negative, and his essay is often used to argue against any limitations to growth. Do you think contemporary doomsayers are likewise overly pessimistic? Will they also be proven wrong as human ingenuity averts any environmental disasters? Why or why not? Give specific examples that support your opinion.

3. Which environmental problems do you think require the most immediate attention? What are some social problems that will likely result from these environmental problems? Are you generally optimistic or pessimistic about the outcome of these problems?

NOTE

1. Quoted in Daniel, *The Idea of Prehistory*, pp. 14–15.
2. Letter of Francisco de Toledo, March 25, 1571, quoted in Luis A. Pardo, ed., *Saqsaywaman* no. 1 (July 1970): 144.
3. From *The Journal of Jacob Roggeveen*, trans. and ed. Andrew Sharp (Oxford: Clarendon Press, 1970). Quoted in Paul Bahn and John Flenley, *Easter Island, Earth Island* (London: Thames and Hudson, 1992),

p. 13, and more fully in Catherine and Michel Orliac, *Easter Island*, trans. Paul G. Bahn, (New York: Harry N. Abrams, 1995), pp. 98–99.

4. Orliac, *Easter Island*, p. 17.
5. James Cook, quoted in ibid., p. 170.
6. Ibid., p. 165.
7. Bahn and Flenley, *Easter Island*, pp. 213, 218.

63

How Many Energy Servants Are Supporting Your Lifestyle?

SARAH S. MOSKO

One of the most pressing problems contemporary global society faces today is climate change. This article provides some details about who the big energy users are, including industry.

Who do Americans blame for the 2010 Deepwater Horizon oil disaster which spewed in excess of four million barrels of crude over three months into the Gulf of Mexico and set a new record for the largest marine oil spill in history?

What do Canadians think drives the controversial Alberta tar sands operation, which has created vast land scars dotted with smokestacks, enormous sulfur piles and contaminated tailings ponds? And, who should be held accountable for the seventy-four-day-long oil spill that has devastated the livelihood of West Timor fishermen as a result of Australia's worst ever oil spill off the coast of Western Australia in 2009?

Although it's easy enough to lay blame on the collusion of governments and industry for allowing such insults to the environment, should not their frequency and enormity spur

we members of developed nations to own up to our personal roles? After all, it is ultimately our energy-intense lifestyles and attachment to fossil fuels that give our governments and the energy industry the implicit go-ahead to pursue fossil fuels at the risk of the very kind of environmental calamities we've lamented of late.

To get a grasp of the energy demand of persons living in developed nations, the United States serves as a convenient benchmark for comparison with other regions.

ENERGY TAB OF TYPICAL AMERICAN LIFESTYLE

Unless you're a physicist or energy wonk, hearing that the average yearly per capita energy consumption in the United States in 2007 was 337 million BTU probably conveys little about the typical person's energy footprint. Knowing

Source: Excerpted from NaturalLifeMagazine.com, March–April 2011, pp. 22–25. Used with permission of the author, Sarah S. Mosko.

that a BTU is an energy standard equivalent to 252 calories—about what's contained in a Snickers candy bar—is probably of little help either.

That's why Professor of Physics Richard Wolfson of Middlebury College has been giving demonstrations for the last decade that impart a real gut-level, hands-on feel for the energy it takes to support the typical American lifestyle.

His demonstration is simple but ingenious. A volunteer is asked to turn a hand crank which, through a geared system, drives an electric generator connected to two 100-watt incandescent light bulbs. The upshot is that a typical person can turn the crank fast enough to light one 100-watt light bulb, but not two. To add to the muscular feel for the effort required to turn the crank, Wolfson points out that it takes roughly the same energy output as doing deep knee bends at a rate of one per second.

The lesson is that the energy or work output of a human body is about enough to keep just a single 100-watt bulb lit. Wolfson conceptualizes this amount of energy output—100 watts—as one human "energy servant."

The question then posed is How many such energy servants does it take to power the typical American lifestyle?

Answering this requires some simple math, starting with the yearly energy consumption of 337 million BTU per capita, which is equivalent, in more familiar units, to 99 thousand kWh (kilowatt hours). Dividing this by the number of hours in a year tells us that an American typically consumes energy at an average rate of 10 kW, which is equal to 100 human energy servants (i.e., 100×100 watts).

This is Wolfson's message: The average U.S. resident enjoys a lifestyle requiring the equivalent of 100 personal energy servants cranking away 24/7.

It's obvious that a person is not drawing on 100 energy servants all the time. For instance, it takes roughly 750 energy servants just to keep a typical gasoline car traveling at a speed of 50 mph compared to, say, two energy servants to power a 40-inch television. But 100 is the number of energy servants working day and night on one's behalf when energy consumption is averaged around the clock.

HOW DO OTHER COUNTRIES COMPARE?

The high standard of living Americans enjoy only partly explains their high energy consumption. Europeans and the Japanese, for example, enjoy a comparable standard of living but use the equivalent of roughly half as many energy servants as Americans (see table on page 400). Australians trail not far behind Americans at 88 energy servants each. Canadians are the world's biggest guzzlers of energy at a whopping 124 energy servants per capita, or nearly three times the European average.

Africans, by contrast, use energy on average at an extremely low rate, equivalent to approximately four energy servants per capita. The world average is just over 20 energy servants.

Although it's easy to surmise how relatively undeveloped regions consume so little energy—like Africa, where vast swatches of people live without access to cars, electricity or basic services—it's less obvious why developed nations vary as much as they do. To approach this issue, it's necessary to first get a handle on the ways societies use energy.

By convention, the activities of a society are divided into four energy-consuming sectors: *transportation, residential, commercial/institutional,* and *industry.* The pie chart in the following page shows the relative energy consumption per sector for the world as a whole, and note that it applies equally to the average denizen of the planet. While most of us think of our home gas/oil and electric bills plus what we put into our cars' gas tanks when we contemplate the size of our energy footprint, the pie chart reveals that it is, in fact, our consumption of other material things that most adds to that footprint.

The residential sector reflects the energy to run our homes (to power lighting, appliances, and heating and cooling systems) and, at 14 percent, is the second smallest pie piece. The transportation sector covers all energy inputted to move people and goods about, be it by car, truck, train, plane, boat, or pipeline, and accounts for just over a quarter of consumed energy. As approximately half of the latter goes to shuttling people, personal transportation and running our homes together eat up roughly 30 percent of the energy humans use.

An additional seven percent goes to meeting the energy demands of commercial/institutional buildings, which make up the entire service sector of society—businesses, organizations, and institutions including schools, hospitals, correctional institutions, stores, restaurants, theaters, and the like—all of which utilize energy for lighting, temperature control systems, computers, and other appliances. Though comparatively modest, the energy that makes possible these shared facets of society is probably overlooked by most of us in reflecting on our energy footprint.

The above three sectors all pale, however, in comparison to the industry sector which accounts for over half the world's energy consumption through production of "stuff," everything from hamburgers, clothing, and computers to spacecraft, medicines, and synthetic fertilizers, plus all the factory machines that make that "stuff" . . . . essentially every manufactured or processed object you can name. The energy used at every step in production is figured in, starting with extraction of raw materials to final assembly.

And, when you figure that maybe half of the transportation sector energy goes to moving raw materials and goods about the globe, 60 percent seems a reasonable estimate of the total energy diverted to making and bringing to market all manufactured and processed goods.

A rundown of the energy-consuming steps involved in the production of a hypothetical cup of coffee, abstracted from the book *Stuff: The Secret Lives of Everyday Things* by John C. Ryan and Alan Thein Durning, drives home the point.

For a cup of coffee drunk in Seattle, Columbian coffee beans are picked from trees (planted on forest land previously cleared with chain saws) kept free of pests by application of pesticides synthesized from petroleum by-products in an energy-intensive process.

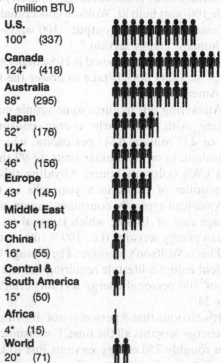

Per Capita Energy Servants*
(million BTU)

U.S. 100* (337)	
Canada 124* (418)	
Australia 88* (295)	
Japan 52* (176)	
U.K. 46* (156)	
Europe 43* (145)	
Middle East 35* (118)	
China 16* (55)	
Central & South America 15* (50)	
Africa 4* (15)	
World 20* (71)	

*Each human figure represents 10 energy servants or ~34 million BTU. International Energy Administration 2007 statistics

World Energy Consumption Sectors

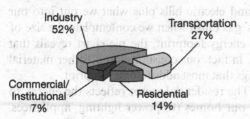

Industry 52%

Transportation 27%

Commercial/ Institutional 7%

Residential 14%

The beans are fed into diesel-powered crushers to remove the pulp before shipping to New Orleans in a freighter manufactured in Japan from Korean steel and fueled by Venezuelan oil. Iron for the steel was mined in Western Australia. Natural gas shipped in from Texas fuels the bean roaster. The beans are packaged mechanically into bags of layered polyethylene, nylon, polyester, and aluminum foil constructed from raw materials extracted and transported from abroad.

From New Orleans, the beans are lugged to Seattle by an 18-wheeler truck averaging six miles per gallon of diesel, and a smaller truck drives them to market. The paper for the wax-lined paper bags in which the coffee is sold was milled in Oregon from a local forest. The grinder and drip coffee maker the customer uses at home were assembled in China from parts made of steel, aluminum, copper, and plastic, all fashioned from raw materials from distant sites. The mug the coffee is drunk from sports the label "Made in Taiwan."

WHY CANADIANS CONSUME THE MOST ENERGY

The complexity of the energy embedded in producing just a cup of coffee should impart a feeling for the difficulty in pinpointing how energy use can differ substantially among developed nations. However, given that Canadians average nearly triple the number of energy servants per capita as Europeans, perhaps comparing the two regions on a sector-by-sector energy basis can provide a few clues.

The statistics discussed below were derived from data provided by the U.S. Energy Information Administration for 2007, in which the values for Europe are based on the 21 European countries who participate in the Organization for Economic Co-Operation and Development (OECD), a 33-member body of market democracies (including Canada and the United States) that share economic challenges.

Canada's per capita energy consumption within the residential sector in 2007 was 1.8 times that of OECD Europe, a difference not fully attributable to climate, given that both regions fall at similar latitudes. Rather, more single-person households and expanding house size, which translate into greater energy for space heating and cooling, play a big role, according to Canada's Office of Energy Efficiency (OCC), which figured the average living space in Canadian homes in 2007 at 1378 square feet, up 10 percent from 1990. The trend in Europe has been to stick with smaller homes. A London newspaper, for example, reported that the average floor space of a British new home in 2009 was just 818 square feet.

The multiplication of smaller appliances, like computers, faxes, and DVDs, and a shift to heating greater percentages of available floor space contribute additionally to growing energy use in not just the residential sector but in the commercial sector too, which weighed in at 3.6 times the per capita consumption of OECD Europe.

That Canada expends more than twice the energy per capita on transportation can be explained only in part by its size relative to European nations. Rather, Canadians have increasingly been buying gas-guzzling SUVs and minivans—40 percent of all passenger vehicle sales in 2007 according to Canada's OCC—whereas Europeans have a well-earned reputation for preferring smaller cars.

A 2007 study from the Civil Society Institute, a non-profit think tank that focuses on energy issues, identified well over 113 passenger cars being sold overseas, primarily in Europe, that averaged at least 40 miles per gallon. That the price of a gallon of gasoline in parts of Europe can be almost double that in Canada is undoubtedly a factor.

But it is Canada's industry sector, requiring three times the per capita energy of OECD Europe (and 1.7 times that of the United States), that most ratchets up its per capita consumption. Canada is invested in particularly energy-intense industries—like mining, forestry, petrochemical, pulp and paper, aluminum smelters, refining, and steel manufacturing—that drive up its energy tally.

However, there also seems to be an issue of regional mindset about energy conservation in general given that, following the energy crisis of the 1970s, western Europe has done a better job of keeping its per capita consumption in check in all four energy sectors.

BEYOND SWITCHING OUT LIGHT BULBS

So, how many energy servants do you personally have? Unfortunately, there's no simple formula to figure that out, although if you start with your nation's per capita average and then examine your personal lifestyle you should be able to come up with a fair guess at whether you fall below, at, or even above the national average. And although we're all aware by now that incandescent light bulbs are energy wasters and that switching to compact fluorescent or LED lighting can cut down on home electric bills, there's far more that we as individuals can do to trim our energy footprint. . . .

It's also helpful to get familiar with the energy demand of your home (and business) appliances. Most appliances carry a metal plate that tells the power requirement measured in watts or amps (watts = amps × volts). To figure out how much energy an appliance consumes, just multiply the power times the length of time it is in use. An easy example: one 100-watt incandescent light bulb turned on for 10 hours equals 1,000 watt hours (or 1 kilowatt hour, "kWh"). To appreciate how much energy a kilowatt hour is, consider that one gallon of gasoline is equivalent to 35 kWh of energy. One kilowatt hour would propel an auto averaging 20 mpg about 0.6 miles.

If you'd rather not do the math, here's a helpful trick to get at the relative energy demand of any given electrical appliance. First, turn off all major electrical appliances and appreciate how slowly the consumption wheel turns on your electricity meter, then compare this to how fast the wheel turns when just one appliance is turned back on. Do the same for all appliances together that run 24/7, like clocks and refrigerators, to see what your base consumption looks like.

A number of studies have been made public which quantify lifestyle changes in terms of potential energy savings. For example, University of Chicago geophysicists Gidon Eshel and Pamela Martin published a study in 2006 examining the energy Americans use for food, including agriculture, processing, and distribution. It turns out that a person eating an all-plant-based diet would consume about 10 million fewer BTU in a year than someone living on the average American diet, which derives 28 percent of calories from animal sources. Furthermore, the difference between a red meat–based and a vegetarian diet can be comparable in terms of energy consumption (and green-house gas emissions) to the difference between driving a SUV and an ultra-efficient hybrid.

The study also highlighted avoiding food waste and overeating as energy conservation strategies—44 percent of the energy inputted into U.S. food production could be saved.

Of course, installing solar electric and solar water heating systems in your home or business is an obvious means to shrink your energy footprint. And, given the huge energy invested in the making and transporting of "stuff," just buying less of it will surely put a number of the energy servants supporting you out of work. After all, there are far too few among us in the developed world not guilty of mindlessly acquiring far more than we need to live a still very comfortable life.

At its core, energy conservation is simply a state of mindfulness applied throughout our everyday lives.

CRITICAL THINKING QUESTIONS

1. The topic of global warming is a good example of the tension between agency and structure. Can we change our dependency on fossil fuels or are we so trapped within the structures of an automobile economy that there is little hope for change? What institutions or groups are against change and who is likely to support it?

2. Ceasing or slowing resource extraction for the sake of the environment would have grave consequences for the economy. Think of some examples of who would be affected by this. How would this affect different regions in Canada? What about rural versus urban regions?

3. What are some of the things that you as an individual could do in order to reduce your dependence on fossil fuels? Would it be enough for governments to encourage their citizens to reduce consumption on a voluntary basis? If not, what might motivate people to change? What kind of legislation could possibly change people's behaviour (taxes, more public transportation, etc.)?

Collective
Behaviour and
Social Movements

CLASSIC

CONTEMPORARY

CROSS-CULTURAL

64

On the Origins of Social Movements

JO FREEMAN

According to Jo Freeman, a "spark of life" sometimes transforms a group of like-minded people into a social movement. In this excerpt from her work, Freeman analyzes this process, illustrating her ideas with an account of the civil rights movement and the women's movement in the United States.

Most movements have inconspicuous beginnings. The significant elements of their origins are usually forgotten or distorted by the time a trained observer seeks to trace them out. Perhaps this is why the theoretical literature on social movements usually concentrates on causes (Gurr, 1970; Davies, 1962; Oberschall, 1973) and motivations (Toch, 1965; Cantril, 1941; Hoffer, 1951; Adorno et al., 1950), while the "spark of life" by which the "mass is to cross the threshold of organizational life" (Lowi, 1971: 41) has received scant attention. . . .

From where do the people come who make up the initial, organizing cadre of a movement? How do they come together, and how do they come to share a similar view of the world in circumstances that compel them to political action? In what

ways does the nature of the original center affect the future development of the movement?

Before answering these questions, let us first look at data on the origins of [two] social movements prominent in the sixties and seventies: civil rights . . . and women's liberation. These data identify recurrent elements involved in movement formation. The ways in which these elements interact, given a sufficient level of strain, would support the following propositions:

Proposition 1. The need for a *preexisting communications network* or infrastructure within the social base of a movement is a primary prerequisite for "spontaneous" activity. Masses alone do not form movements, however discontented they may be. Groups of previously unorganized individuals may spontaneously form into small local associations—usually along the lines of informal social networks—in response to a specific strain or crisis. If they are

Source: From *Social Movements of the Sixties and Seventies,* ed. Jo Freeman, pp. 8–13, 17–30, copyright © 1983 by Jo Freeman. Reprinted by permission.

not linked in some manner, however, the protest does not become generalized but remains a local irritant or dissolves completely. If a movement is to spread rapidly, the communications network must already exist. If only the rudiments of a network exist, movement formation requires a high input of "organizing" activity.

Proposition 2. Not just any communications network will do. It must be a network that is co-optable to the new ideas of the incipient movement. To be co-optable, it must be composed of like-minded people whose backgrounds, experiences, or location in the social structure make them receptive to the ideas of a specific new movement.

Proposition 3. Given the existence of a co-optable communications network, or at least the rudimentary development of a potential one, and a situation of strain, one or more precipitants are required. Here, two distinct patterns emerge that often overlap. In one, a crisis galvanizes the network into spontaneous action in a new direction. In the other, one or more persons begin organizing a new organization or disseminating a new idea. For spontaneous action to occur, the communications network must be well formed or the initial protest will not survive the incipient stage. If it is not well formed, organizing efforts must occur; that is, one or more persons must specifically attempt to construct a movement. To be successful, organizers must be skilled and must have a fertile field in which to work. If no communications network already exists, there must at least be emerging spontaneous groups that are acutely attuned to the issue, albeit uncoordinated. To sum up, if a co-optable communications network is already established, a crisis is all that is necessary to galvanize it. If it is rudimentary, an organizing cadre of one or more persons is necessary. Such a cadre is superfluous if the former conditions fully exist, but it is essential if they do not.

THE CIVIL RIGHTS MOVEMENT

The civil rights movement has two origins, although one contributed significantly to the other. The first can be dated from December 7, 1955, when the arrest of Rosa Parks for occupying a "white" seat on a bus stimulated both the Montgomery Bus Boycott and the formation of the Montgomery Improvement Association. The second can be dated either from February 1, 1960, when four freshmen at A & T College in Greensboro, North Carolina, sat in at a white lunch counter, or from April 15 to 17, when a conference at Shaw University in Raleigh, North Carolina, resulted in the formation of the Student Non-Violent Coordinating Committee. To understand why there were two origins one has to understand the social structure of the southern black community, as an incipient generation gap alone is inadequate to explain it.

Within this community the two most important institutions, often the only institutions, were the church and the black college. They provided the primary networks through which most southern blacks interacted and communicated with one another on a regular basis. In turn, the colleges and churches were linked in a regional communications network. These institutions were also the source of black leadership, for being a "preacher or a teacher" were the main status positions in black society. Of the two, the church was by far the more important; it touched on more people's lives and was the largest and oldest institution in the black community. Even during slavery there had been an "invisible church." After emancipation, "organized religious life became the chief means by which a structured or organized social life came into existence among the Negro masses" (Frazier, 1963: 17). Furthermore, preachers were more economically independent of white society than were teachers.

Neither of these institutions represented all the segments of black society, but the segments they did represent eventually formed the main social base for supplying civil rights activists. The church was composed of a male leadership and a largely middle-aged, lower-class female followership. The black colleges were the homes of black intellectuals and middle-class youth, male and female.

Both origins of the civil rights movement resulted in the formation of new organizations, despite the fact that at least three seemingly potential social movement organizations already existed. The wealthiest of these was the Urban League, founded in 1910. It, however, was not only largely restricted to a small portion of the black and white bourgeoisie but, until 1961, felt itself to be "essentially a social service agency" (Clark, 1966: 245).

Founded in 1909, the National Association for the Advancement of Colored People (NAACP) pursued channels of legal change until it finally persuaded the Supreme Court to abolish educational segregation in *Brown v. Board of Education*. More than any other single event, this decision created the atmosphere of rising expectations that helped precipitate the movement. The NAACP suffered from its own success, however. Having organized itself primarily to support court cases and utilize other "respectable" means, it "either was not able or did not desire to modify its program in response to new demands. It believed it should continue its important work by using those techniques it had already perfected" (Blumer, 1951: 199).

The Congress of Racial Equality, like the other two organizations, was founded in the North. It began "in 1942 as the Chicago Committee of Racial Equality, which was composed primarily of students at the University of Chicago. An offshoot of the pacifist Fellowship of Reconciliation, its leaders were middle-class intellectual reformers, less prominent and more alienated from the mainstream of American society than the founders of the NAACP. They regarded the NAACP's legalism as too gradualist and ineffective, and aimed to apply Gandhian techniques of non-violent direct action to the problem of race relations in the United States. A year later, the Chicago Committee joined with a half dozen other groups that had emerged across the country, mostly under the encouragement of the F. O. R. to form a federation known as the Congress of Racial Equality (Rudwick & Meier, 1970: 10).

CORE's activities anticipated many of the main forms of protest of the civil rights movement, and its attitudes certainly seemed to fit CORE for the role of a major civil rights organization. But though it became quite influential, at the time the movement actually began, CORE had declined almost to the point of extinction. Its failure reflects the historical reality that organizations are less likely to create social movements than be created by them. More important, CORE was poorly situated to lead a movement of southern blacks. Northern-based and composed primarily of pacifist intellectuals, it had no roots in any of the existing structures of the black community, and in the North these structures were themselves weak. CORE could be a source of ideas, but not of coordination.

The coordination of a new movement required the creation of a new organization. But that was not apparent until after the Montgomery bus boycott began. That boycott was organized through institutions already existing in the black community of Montgomery.

Rosa Parks's refusal to give up her seat on the bus to a white man was not the first time such defiance of segregation laws had occurred. There had been talk of a boycott the previous time, but after local black leaders had a congenial meeting with the city commissioners, nothing happened—on either side (King, 1958: 37–41). When Parks, a former secretary of the local NAACP, was arrested, she immediately called E. D. Nixon, at that time the president of the local chapter. He not only bailed her out but informed a few influential women in the city, most of whom were members of the Women's Political Council. After numerous phone calls between their members, it was the WPC that actually suggested the boycott, and E. D. Nixon who initially organized it (ibid.: 44–5).

The Montgomery Improvement Association (MIA) was formed at a meeting of eighteen ministers and civic leaders the Monday after Parks's conviction and a day of successful boycotting, to provide ongoing coordination. No one then suspected that coordination would be necessary for over a year, with car pools organized to provide alternative transportation for seventeen thousand riders a day. During this time the MIA grew slowly to a staff of ten in order to handle the voluminous correspondence, as well as to provide rides and keep the movement's momentum going. The organization, and the car pools, were financed by $250,000 in donations that poured in from all over the world in response to heavy press publicity about the boycott. But the organizational framework for the boycott and the MIA was the church. Most, although not all, of the officers were ministers, and Sunday meetings with congregations continued to be the main means of communicating with members of the black community and encouraging them to continue the protest.

The boycott did not end until the federal courts ruled Alabama's bus segregation laws unconstitutional late in 1956—at the same time that state courts ruled the boycott illegal. In the meantime, black leaders throughout the South had visited Montgomery, and out of the discussions came agreement to continue antisegregation protests regularly and systematically under the aegis of a new organization, the Southern Christian Leadership Conference. The NAACP could not lead the protests because, according to an SCLC pamphlet, "during the late fifties, the NAACP had been driven out of some Southern states. Its branches were outlawed as foreign corporations and its lawyers were charged with barratry, that is, persistently inciting litigation."

On January 10, 1957, over one hundred people gathered in Atlanta at a meeting called by four ministers, including Martin Luther King. Bayard Rustin drew up the "working papers." Initially called the Southern Leadership Conference on Transportation and Nonviolent Integration, the SCLC never developed a mass base even when it changed its name. It established numerous "affiliates" but did most of its work through the churches in the communities to which it sent its fieldworkers.

The church was not just the only institution available for a movement to work through; in many ways it was ideal. It performed "the central organizing function in the Negro community" (Holloway, 1969: 22), providing both access to large masses of people on a regular basis and a natural leadership. As Wyatt Tee Walker, former executive director of SCLC, commented, "The Church today is central to the movement. If a Negro's going to have a meeting, where's he going to have it? Mostly he doesn't have a Masonic lodge, and he's not going to get the public schools. And the church is the primary means of communication" (Brink & Harris, 1964: 103). Thus the church eventually came to be the center of the voter registration drives as well as many of the other activities of the civil rights movement.

Even the young men and women of SNCC had to use the church, though they had trouble doing so because, unlike most of the officers of SCLC, they were not themselves ministers and thus did not have a "fraternal" connection. Instead they tended to draw many of their resources and people from outside the particular town in which they were working by utilizing their natural organizational base, the college.

SNCC did not begin the sit-ins, but came out of them. Once begun, the idea of the sit-in spread initially by means of the mass media. But such sit-ins almost always took place in towns where there were Negro colleges, and groups on these campuses essentially organized the sit-in activities of their communities. Nonetheless, "CORE, with its long emphasis of nonviolent direct action, played an important part, once the sit-ins began, as an educational and organizing agent" (Zinn, 1964: 23). CORE had very few staff in the South, but there were enough to at least hold classes and practice sessions in nonviolence.

It was SCLC, however, that was actually responsible for the formation of SNCC; though it might well have organized itself eventually. Ella Baker, then executive secretary of SCLC, thought something should be done to coordinate the rapidly spreading sit-ins in 1960, and many members of SCLC thought it might be appropriate to organize a youth group. With SCLC money, Baker persuaded her alma mater, Shaw University, to provide facilities to contact the groups at centers of sit-in activity. Some two hundred people showed up for the meeting, decided to have no official connection with SCLC beyond a "friendly relationship," and formed the Student Non-Violent Coordinating Committee (Zinn, 1964: 32–34). It had no members, and its fieldworkers numbered two hundred at their highest point, but it was from the campuses, especially the southern black colleges, that it drew its sustenance and upon which its organizational base rested. . . . .

THE WOMEN'S LIBERATION MOVEMENT[1]

Women are not well organized. Historically tied to the family and isolated from their own kind, only in the nineteenth century did women in this country have the opportunity to develop independent associations of their own. These associations took years and years of careful organizational work to build. Eventually they formed the basis for the suffrage movement of the early twentieth century. The associations took less time to die. Today the Women's Trade Union League, the General Federation of Women's Clubs, the Women's Christian Temperance Union, not to mention the powerful National Women's Suffrage Association, are all either dead or a pale shadow of their former selves.

As of 1960, not one organization of women had the potential to become a social movement

organization, nor was there any form of "neutral" structure of interaction to provide the base for such an organization. The closest exception to the former was the National Women's Party, which has remained dedicated to feminist concerns since its inception in 1916. However, the NWP has been essentially a lobbying group for the Equal Rights Amendment since 1923. From the beginning, the NWP believed that a small group of women concentrating their efforts in the right places was more effective than a mass appeal, and so was not appalled by the fact that as late as 1969 even the majority of avowed feminists in this country had never heard of the ERA or the NWP.

The one large women's organization that might have provided a base for a social movement was the 180,000-member Federation of Business and Professional Women's Clubs. Yet, while it has steadily lobbied for legislation of importance to women, as late as "1966 BPW rejected a number of suggestions that it redefine . . . goals and tactics and become a kind of 'NAACP for women' . . . out of fear of being labeled 'feminist'" (Hole & Levine, 1971: 89).

Before any social movement could develop among women, there had to be created a structure to bring potential feminist sympathizers together. To be sure, groups such as the BPW, and institutions such as the women's colleges, might be a good source of adherents for such a movement. But they were determined not to be the source of leadership.

What happened in the 1960s was the development of two new communications networks in which women played prominent roles that allowed, even forced, an awakened interest in the old feminist ideas. As a result, the movement actually has two origins, from two different strata of society, with two different styles, orientations, values, and forms of organization. The first of these will be referred to as the "older branch" of the movement, partially because it began first and partially because it was on the older side of the "generation gap" that pervaded the sixties. Its most prominent organization is the National Organization for Women (NOW), which was also the first to be formed. The style of its organization tended to be traditional with elected officers, boards of directors, bylaws, and the other trappings of democratic procedure. Conversely, the "younger branch" consisted of innumerable small groups engaged in a variety of activities whose contact with one another was always tenuous (Freeman, 1975: 50).

The forces that led to NOW's formation were set in motion in 1961 when President Kennedy established the President's Commission on the Status of Women at the behest of Esther Petersen, then director of the Women's Bureau. Its 1963 report, *American Women*, and subsequent committee publications documented just how thoroughly women were denied many rights and opportunities. The most significant response to the activity of the President's commission was the establishment of some fifty state commissions to do similar research on a state level. The Presidential and State Commission activity laid the groundwork for the future movement in two significant ways: (1) It unearthed ample evidence of women's unequal status and in the process convinced many previously uninterested women that something should be done; (2) It created a climate of expectations that something would be done. The women of the Presidential and State Commissions who were exposed to these influences exchanged visits, correspondence, and staff, and met with one another at an annual commission convention. They were in a position to share and mutually reinforce their growing awareness and concern over women's issues. These commissions thus provided an embryonic communications network.

During this time, two other events of significance occurred. The first was the publication of Betty Friedan's *The Feminine Mystique* in 1963. A quick best seller, the book stimulated many women to question the *status quo* and some women to suggest to Friedan that an organization be formed to do something about it. The second event was the addition of "sex" to the 1964 Civil Rights Act.

Many thought the "sex" provision was a joke, and the Equal Employment Opportunity Commission treated it as one, refusing to enforce it seriously. But a rapidly growing feminist coterie within the EEOC argued that "sex" would be taken more seriously if there were "some sort of NAACP for women" to put pressure on the government.

On June 30, 1966, these three strands of incipient feminism came together, and NOW was tied from the knot. At that time, government officials running the Third National Conference of Commissions on the Status of Women, ironically titled "Targets for Action," forbade the presentation of a suggested resolution calling for the EEOC to treat sex discrimination with the same consideration as race discrimination. The officials said one government agency could not be allowed to pressure another, despite the fact that the state commissions were not federal agencies. The small group of women who desired such a resolution had met the night before in Friedan's hotel room to discuss the possibility of a civil rights organization for women. Not convinced of its need, they chose instead to propose the resolution. When conference officials vetoed it, they held a whispered conversation over lunch and agreed to form an action organization "to bring women into full participation in the mainstream of American society now, assuming all the privileges and responsibilities thereof in truly equal partnership with men." The name NOW was coined by Friedan who was at the conference doing research on a book. When word leaked out, twenty-eight women paid five dollars each to join before the day was over (Friedan, 1967: 4).

By the time the organizing conference was held the following October 29 through 30, over three hundred men and women had become charter members. It is impossible to do a breakdown on the composition of the charter membership, but one of the officers and board is possible. Such a breakdown accurately reflected NOW's origins. Friedan was president, two former EEOC commissioners were vice presidents, a representative of the United Auto Workers Women's Committee was secretary-treasurer, and there were seven past and present members of the State Commissions on the Status of Women on the twenty member board. One hundred twenty-six of the charter members were Wisconsin residents—and Wisconsin had the most active state Commission. Occupationally, the board and officers were primarily from the professions, labor, government, and communications fields. Of these, only those from labor had any experience in organizing, and they resigned a year later in a dispute over support of the Equal Rights Amendment. Instead of organizational experience, what the early NOW members had was experience in working with and in the media, and it was here that their early efforts were aimed.

As a result, NOW often gave the impression of being larger than it was. It was highly successful in getting in the press; much less successful in either bringing about concrete changes or forming an organization. Thus it was not until 1970, when the national press simultaneously did major stories on the women's liberation movement, that NOW's membership increased significantly.

In the meantime, unaware of and unknown to NOW, the EEOC, or the State Commissions, younger women began forming their own movement. Here, too, the groundwork had been laid some years before. The different social action projects of the sixties had attracted many women, who were quickly shunted into traditional roles and faced with the self-evident contradiction of working in a "freedom movement" but not being very free. No single "youth movement" activity or organization is responsible for forming the younger branch of the women's liberation movement, but together they created a "radical community" in which like-minded people continually interacted or were made aware of one another. This community

provided the necessary network of communication and its radical ideas the framework of analysis that "explained" the dismal situation in which radical women found themselves.

Papers had been circulated on women and individual temporary women's caucuses had been held as early as 1964 (see Hayden & King, 1966). But it was not until 1967 and 1968 that the groups developed a determined, if cautious, continuity and began to consciously expand themselves. At least five groups in five different cities (Chicago, Toronto, Detroit, Seattle, and Gainesville, Florida) formed spontaneously, independently of one another. They came at an auspicious moment, for 1967 was the year in which the blacks kicked the whites out of the civil rights movement, student power was discredited by SDS, and the New Left was on the wane. Only draft resistance activities were on the increase, and this movement more than any other exemplified the social inequities of the sexes. Men could resist the draft. Women could only counsel resistance.

At this point, there were few opportunities available for political work. Some women fit well into the secondary role of draft counseling. Many didn't. For years their complaints of unfair treatment had been forestalled by movement men with the dictum that those things could wait until after the Revolution. Now these political women found time on their hands, but still the men would not listen.

A typical example was the event that precipitated the formation of the Chicago group, the first independent group in this country. At the August 1967 National Conference for New Politics convention a women's caucus met for days, but was told its resolution wasn't significant enough to merit a floor discussion. By threatening to tie up the convention with procedural motions the women succeeded in having their statement tacked to the end of the agenda. It was never discussed. The chair refused to recognize any of the many women standing by the microphone, their hands straining upwards. When he instead called on someone to speak on "the forgotten American, the American Indian," five women rushed the podium to demand an explanation. But the chairman just patted one of them on the head (literally) and told her, "Cool down, little girl. We have more important things to talk about than women's problems."

The "little girl" was Shulamith Firestone, future author of *The Dialectic of Sex*, and she didn't cool down. Instead she joined with another Chicago woman she met there who had unsuccessfully tried to organize a women's group that summer, to call a meeting of the women who had halfheartedly attended those summer meetings. Telling their stories to those women, they stimulated sufficient rage to carry the group for three months, and by that time it was a permanent institution.

Another somewhat similar event occurred in Seattle the following winter. At the University of Washington, an SDS organizer was explaining to a large meeting how white college youth established rapport with the poor whites with whom they were working. "He noted that sometimes after analyzing societal ills, the men shared leisure time by 'balling a chick together.' He pointed out that such activities did much to enhance the political consciousness of the poor white youth. A woman in the audience asked, 'And what did it do for the consciousness of the chick?'" (Hole & Levine, 1971: 120). After the meeting, a handful of enraged women formed Seattle's first group.

Subsequent groups to the initial five were largely organized rather than formed spontaneously out of recent events. In particular, the Chicago group was responsible for the formation of many new groups in Chicago and in other cities. Unlike NOW, the women in the first groups had had years of experience as trained organizers. They knew how to utilize the infrastructure of the radical community, the underground press, and the free universities to disseminate women's liberation ideas. Chicago, as a center of New Left activity, had the largest number of politically conscious organizers. Many traveled widely to leftist conferences and demonstrations, and most used the opportunity to talk with other women about the new movement. In spite of public derision by radical men, or perhaps because of it, young women steadily formed new groups around the country.

ANALYSIS

From these data there appear to be four essential elements involved in movement formation: (1) the growth of a preexisting communications network that is (2) co-optable to the ideas of the new movement; (3) a series of crises that galvanize into action people involved in a co-optable network, and/or (4) subsequent organizing effort to weld the spontaneous groups together into a movement. Each of these elements needs to be examined in detail.

COMMUNICATIONS NETWORK

. . . The women's liberation movement . . . illustrates the importance of a network precisely because the conditions for a movement existed before a network came into being, but the movement didn't exist until afterward. Analysts of socioeconomic causes have concluded that the movement could have started anytime within a twenty-year period. Strain for women was as great in 1955 as in 1965 (Ferriss, 1971). What changed was the organizational situation. It was not until new networks emerged among women aware of inequities beyond local boundaries that a movement could grow past the point of occasional, spontaneous uprisings. The fact that two distinct movements, with two separate origins, developed from two networks unaware of each other is further evidence of the key role of preexisting communications networks as the fertile soil in which new movements can sprout.

References to the importance of a preexisting communications network appear frequently in case studies of social movements, though the theoretical writers were much slower to recognize their salience. According to Buck (1920: 43–4), the Grange established a degree of organization among American farmers in the nineteenth century that greatly facilitated the spread of future farmers' protests. Lipset has reported that in Saskatchewan, "the rapid acceptance of new ideas and movements . . . can be attributed mainly to the high degree of organization. . . . The role of the social structure of the western wheat belt in facilitating the rise of new movements has never been sufficiently appreciated by historians and sociologists. Repeated challenges and crises forced the western farmers to create many more community institutions (especially cooperatives and economic pressure groups) than are necessary in a more stable area. These groups in turn provided a structural basis for immediate action in critical situations. [Therefore] though it was a new radical party, the C. C. F. did not have to build up an organization from scratch" (1959: 206).

Similarly, Heberle (1951: 232) reports several findings that Nazism was most successful in small, well-integrated communities. As Lipset put it, these findings "sharply challenge the various interpretations of Nazism as the product of the growth of anomie and the general rootlessness of modern urban industrial society" (1959: 146).

Indirect evidence attesting to the essential role of formal and informal communications networks is found in diffusion theory, which emphasizes the importance of personal interaction rather than impersonal media communication in the spread of ideas (Rogers, 1962; Lionberger, 1960). This personal influence occurs through the organizational patterns of a community (Lionberger, 1960: 73). It does not occur through the mass media. The mass media may be a source of information, but they are not a key source of influence.

Their lesser importance in relation to preexisting communications networks was examined in one study on "The Failure of an Incipient Social Movement" (Jackson, Peterson, Bull, Monsen, & Richmond, 1960). In 1957 a potential tax protest movement in Los Angeles generated considerable interest and publicity for a little over a month but was dead within a year. According to the authors, this did not reflect a lack of public notice. They concluded that "mass communication alone is probably insufficient without a network of communication specifically linking those interested in the matter. . . . If a movement is to grow rapidly, it cannot rely upon its own network of communication, but must capitalize on networks already in existence" (p. 37).

A major reason it took social scientists so long to acknowledge the importance of communications networks was because the prevailing theories of the post–World War II era emphasized increasing social dislocation and anomie. Mass society theorists, as they were called, hypothesized that significant community institutions that linked individuals to governing elites were breaking down, that society was becoming a mass of isolated individuals. These individuals were seen as increasingly irresponsible and ungovernable, prone to irrational protests because they had no mediating institutions through which to pursue grievances (Kornhauser, 1959).

In emphasizing disintegrating vertical connections, mass society theorists passed lightly over the role of horizontal ones, only occasionally acknowledging that "the combination of internal contact and external isolation facilitates the work of the mass agitator" (Kornhauser, 1959: 218). This focus changed in the early seventies. Pinard's study of the Social Credit Party of Quebec (1971) severely criticized mass society theory, arguing instead that "when strains are severe and widespread a new movement is more likely to meet its early success among the more strongly integrated citizens" (Pinard, 1971: 192).

This insight was expanded by Oberschall (1973), who created a six-cell table to predict both the occurrence and type of protest. As did the mass society theorists, Oberschall said that even when there are grievances, protest will not occur outside institutional channels by those who are connected, through their own leadership or patron/client relationships, with governing elites. Among those who are segmented from such elites, the type of protest will be determined by whether there is communal, associational, or little organization. In the latter case, discontent is expressed through riots or other short-lived violent uprisings. "It is under conditions of strong . . . ties and segmentation that the possibility of the rapid spread of opposition movements on a continuous basis exists" (p. 123).

The movements we have studied would confirm Oberschall's conclusions, but not as strongly as he makes them. In all these cases a preexisting communications network was a necessary but insufficient condition for movement formation. Yet the newly formed networks among student radicals, welfare recipients, and women can hardly compare with the longstanding ties provided by the southern black churches and colleges. Their ties were tenuous and may not have survived the demise of their movements.

The importance of segmentation, or lack of connection with relevant elites, is less obvious in the sixties' movements. The higher socioeconomic status of incipient feminists and Movement leaders would imply greater access to elites than is true for blacks or welfare recipients. If Oberschall were correct, these closer connections should either have permitted easier and more rapid grievance solutions or more effective social control. They did neither. Indeed, it was the group most closely connected to decision-making elites—women of the Presidential and State Commission—who were among the earliest to see the need of a protest organization. Women of the younger branch of the movement did have their grievances against the men of the New Left effectively suppressed for several years, but even they eventually rejected this kind of elite control, even when it meant rejecting the men.

Conversely, Piven and Cloward show that the establishment of closer ties between leaders of local welfare rights groups and welfare

workers through advisory councils and community coordinators led to a curtailment of militance and the institutionalization of grievances (1977: 326–31). They also argue that the development of government-funded community programs effectively co-opted many local black movement leaders in the North and that federal channeling of black protest in the South into voter registration projects focused the movement there into traditional electoral politics (ibid.: 253). In short, the evidence about the role of segmentation in movement formation is ambiguous. The effect may be varied considerably by the nature of the political system.

CO-OPTABILITY

A recurrent theme in our studies is that not just any communications network will do. It must be one that is co-optable to the ideas of the new movement. The Business and Professional Women's (BPW) clubs were a network among women, but having rejected feminism, they could not overcome the ideological barrier to new political action until after feminism became established. . . .

On the other hand, the women on the Presidential and State Commissions and the feminist coterie of the EEOC were co-optable largely because their immersion in the facts of female status and the details of sex discrimination cases made them very conscious of the need for change. Likewise, the young women of the "radical community" lived in an atmosphere of questioning, confrontation, and change. They absorbed an ideology of "freedom" and "liberation" far more potent than any latent "antifeminism" might have been. . . .

Exactly what makes a network co-optable is harder to elucidate. Pinard (1971: 186) noted the necessity for groups to "*possess* or *develop* an ideology or simply subjective interests congruent with that of a new movement" for them to "act as mobilizing rather than restraining agents toward that movement," but did not further explore what affected the "primary group climate." More illumination is provided by the diffusion of innovation studies that point out the necessity for new ideas to fit in with already established norms for changes to happen easily. Furthermore, a social system that has as a value "innovativeness" (as the radical community did) will more rapidly adopt ideas than one that looks upon the habitual performance of traditional practices as the ideal (as most organized women's groups did in the fifties). Usually, as Lionberger (1960: 91) points out, "people act in terms of past experience and knowledge." People who have had similar experiences are likely to share similar perceptions of a situation and to mutually reinforce those perceptions as well as their subsequent interpretation. A co-optable network, then, is one whose members have had common experiences that predispose them to be receptive to the particular new ideas of the incipient movement and who are not faced with structural or ideological barriers to action. If the new movement as an "innovation" can interpret these experiences and perceptions in ways that point out channels for social action, then participation in a social movement becomes the logical thing to do.

THE ROLE OF CRISES

As our examples have illustrated, similar perceptions must be translated into action. This is often done by a crisis. For blacks in Montgomery, this was generated by Rosa Parks's refusal to give up her seat on a bus to a white man. For women who formed the older branch of the women's movement, the impetus to organize was the refusal of the EEOC to enforce the sex provision of Title VII, precipitated by the concomitant refusal of federal officials at the conference to allow a supportive resolution. For younger women there were a series of minor crises.

While not all movements are formed by such precipitating events, they are quite common as they serve to crystallize and focus discontent.

From their own experiences, directly and concretely, people feel the need for change in a situation that allows for an exchange of feelings with others, mutual validation, and a subsequent reinforcement of innovative interpretation. Perception of an immediate need for change is a major factor in predisposing people to accept new ideas (Rogers, 1962: 280). Nothing makes desire for change more acute than a crisis. Such a crisis need not be a major one; it need only embody collective discontent.

ORGANIZING EFFORTS

A crisis will only catalyze a well-formed communications network. If such networks are embryonically developed or only partially co-optable, the potentially active individuals in them must be linked together by someone. . . . . As Jackson et al. (1960: 37) stated, "Some protest may persist where the source of trouble is constantly present. But interest ordinarily cannot be maintained unless there is a welding of spontaneous groups into some stable organization." In other words, people must be organized. Social movements do not simply occur.

The role of the organizer in movement formation is another neglected aspect of the theoretical literature. There has been great concern with leadership, but the two roles are distinct and not always performed by the same individual. In the early stages of a movement, it is the organizer much more than any leader who is important, and such an individual or cadre must often operate behind the scenes. The nature and function of these two roles was most clearly evident in the Townsend old-age movement of the thirties. Townsend was the "charismatic" leader, but the movement was organized by his partner, real estate promoter Robert Clements. Townsend himself acknowledges that without Clements's help, the movement would never have gone beyond the idea stage (Holzman, 1963).

The importance of organizers is pervasive in the sixties' movements. Dr. King may have been the public spokesperson of the Montgomery Bus Boycott who caught the eye of the media, but it was E. D. Nixon who organized it. Certainly the "organizing cadre" that young women in the radical community came to be was key to the growth of that branch of the women's liberation movement, despite the fact that no "leaders" were produced (and were actively discouraged). The existence of many leaders but no organizers in the older branch of the women's liberation movement readily explains its subsequent slow development. . . .

The function of the organizer has been explored indirectly by other analysts. Rogers (1962) devotes many pages to the "change agent" who, while he does not necessarily weld a group together or "construct" a movement, does many of the same things for agricultural innovation that an organizer does for political change. Mass society theory makes frequent reference to the "agitator," though not in a truly informative way. Interest groups are often organized by single individuals and some of them evolve into social movements. Salisbury's study of farmers' organizations finds this a recurrent theme. He also discovered that "a considerable number of farm groups were subsidized by other, older, groups. . . . The Farm Bureau was organized and long sustained by subsidies, some from federal and state governments, and some by local businessmen" (Salisbury, 1969: 13).

These patterns are similar to ones we have found in the formation of social movements. Other organizations, even the government, often serve as training centers for organizers and sources of material support to aid the formation of groups and/or movements. The civil rights movement was the training ground for many an organizer of other movements. . . . The role of the government in the formation of the National Welfare Rights Organization was so significant that it would lead one to wonder if this association should be considered more of an interest group in the traditional sense than a movement "core" organization.

From all this it would appear that training as an organizer or at least as a proselytizer

or entrepreneur of some kind is a necessary background for those individuals who act as movement innovators. Even in something as seemingly spontaneous as a social movement, the professional is more valuable than the amateur.

CRITICAL THINKING QUESTIONS

1. Why has the role of communications networks in the formation of social movements only recently received the attention of researchers?
2. How do leadership roles emerge in social movements? Are "leaders" the same as "organizers"?
3. Cite some similarities and differences in the development of the civil rights movement and the women's movement.

NOTE

1. Data for this section are based on my observations while a founder and participant in the younger branch of the Chicago women's liberation movement from 1967 through 1969 and editor of the first (at that time, only) national newsletter. I was able, through extensive correspondence and interviews, to keep a record of how each group around the country started, where the organizers got the idea from, who they had talked to, what conferences were held and who attended, the political affiliations (or lack of them) of the first members, and so forth. Although I was a member of Chicago NOW, information on the origins of it and the other older branch organizations comes entirely through ex post facto interviews of the principals and examination of early papers in preparation for my dissertation on the women's liberation movement. Most of my informants requested that their contribution remain confidential.

REFERENCES

Adorno, L. W., et al. 1950. *The authoritarian personality*. New York: Harper & Row.

Blumer, H. 1951. Social movements. In *New outline of the principles of sociology*, ed. A. M. Lee. New York: Barnes and Noble.

Brink, W., and L. Harris. 1964. *The Negro revolution in America*. New York: Simon & Schuster.

Buck, S. J. 1920. *The agrarian crusade*. New Haven, Conn.: Yale University Press.

Cantril, H. 1941. *The psychology of social movements*. New York: Wiley.

Clark, K. B. 1966. The civil rights movement: Momentum and organization. *Daedalus*, Winter.

Davies, J. C. 1962. Toward a theory of revolution. *American Sociological Review*, 27(1): 5–19.

Ferriss, A. L. 1971. *Indicators of trends in the status of American women*. New York: Russell Sage Foundation.

Firestone, S. 1971. *Dialectics of sex*. New York: Morrow.

Frazier, E. F. 1963. *The Negro church in America*. New York: Schocken.

Freeman, J. 1975. *The politics of women's liberation*. New York: Longman.

Friedan, B. 1963. *The feminine mystique*. New York: Dell.

———. 1967. NOW: How it began. *Women Speaking*, April.

Gurr, T. 1970. *Why men rebel*. Princeton, N.J.: Princeton University Press.

Hayden, C., and M. King. 1966. A kind of memo. *Liberation*, April.

Heberle, R. 1951. *Social movements*. New York: Appleton-Century-Crofts.

Hoffer, E. 1951. *The true believer*. New York: Harper & Row.

Hole, J., and E. Levine. 1971. *Rebirth of feminism*. New York: Quadrangle.

Holloway, H. 1969. *The politics of the Southern Negro*. New York: Random House.

Holzman, A. 1963. *The Townsend movement: A political study*. New York: Bookman.

Jackson, M., et al. 1960. The failure of an incipient social movement. *Pacific Sociological Review*, 3(1): 40.

King, M. L., Jr. 1958. *Stride toward freedom*. New York: Harper & Row.

Kornhauser, W. 1959. *The politics of mass society*. Glencoe, Ill.: Free Press.

Lionberger, H. F. 1960. *Adoption of new ideas and practices*. Ames: Iowa State University Press.

Lipset, S. M. 1959. *Agrarian socialism*. Berkeley: University of California Press.

Lowi, T. J. 1971. *The politics of discord*. New York: Basic Books.

Oberschall, A. 1973. *Social conflict and social movements*. Englewood Cliffs, N.J.: Prentice-Hall.

Pinard, M. 1971. *The rise of a third party: A study in crisis politics*. Englewood Cliffs, N.J.: Prentice-Hall.

Piven, F. F., and R. Cloward. 1977. *Poor people's movements: Why they succeed, how they fail*. New York: Pantheon.

Rogers, E. M. 1962. *Diffusion of innovations*. New York: Free Press.

Rudwick, E., and A. Meier. 1970. Organizational structure and goal succession: A comparative analysis of the NAACP and CORE, 1964–1968. *Social Science Quarterly*, 51 (June).

Salisbury, R. H. 1969. An exchange theory of interest groups. *Midwest Journal of Political Science*, 13(1), (February).

Toch, H. 1965. *The social psychology of social movements*. Indianapolis, IN.: Bobbs-Merrill.

Zinn, H. 1964. SNCC: *The new abolitionists*. Boston: Beacon Press.

65

Suicide, Canadian Law, and Exit International's "Peaceful Pill"

RUSSEL D. OGDEN

Assisted suicide is against the law in most of the industrial world, including Canada. Opponents have organized worldwide in order to bring about a change to this legislation, which makes for an interesting example of a social movement. In this reading, criminologist Russel Ogden draws parallels between the acts of assisted suicide and suicide, which was also illegal at one time.

. . . . Whether they are prohibited, permitted, or tolerated, suicide and assisted suicide are controversial. Their legal treatment in Canada is conflicting because suicide is not a crime but it is a serious offence to assist, encourage, or counsel someone to suicide. Individuals can lawfully take their lives, but they must act independently. This legal situation has given rise to a do-it-yourself ("DIY") right-to-die movement dedicated to technologies and information to enhance the possibilities for planned and humane suicide, while limiting the legal exposure of sympathetic third parties (Martin, 2010; Ogden 2001).

My aim is to summarize the legal history of suicide in Canada and discuss the emerging social movement for DIY suicide and assistance in suicide. Exit International ("Exit"), based in Australia, is a leading organization in this

Source: Taken from *Health Law in Canada, Volume 31, Number 2*, November 2010, pp. 37–64. Used by permission of the author, Russel D. Ogden.

movement. I argue that the DIY movement is an undesirable consequence of prohibition. . . .

CANADA'S CRIMINAL CODE AND SUICIDE/ASSISTED SUICIDE

Attempted Suicide

The human obsession with fighting death has helped to turn living into an obligation (Bayatrizi, 2008). In common law, suicide was a crime of self-murder and aiding or abetting a person to suicide was equivalent to second-degree murder (Burbidge, 1890). When Canada enacted its first *Criminal Code* on July 1, 1893, suicide was not specifically forbidden by statute but attempting suicide was an indictable offence punishable with a maximum of two years imprisonment (Taschereau, 1893). In 1955 the penalty for attempting suicide was reduced to a maximum of six months imprisonment. In 1972 attempting suicide was decriminalized (Downie, 2004). A review of Canada's *Annual Report of Statistics of Criminal and Other Offences* shows that from 1876 to 1972, there were over 8600 convictions for attempted suicide, and 22 percent received jail sentences (Statistics Canada, 1872–1973).[1]

When the Canadian parliament decriminalized attempted suicide it was argued that suicide "is not a matter which requires a legal remedy, that it has its roots and its solutions in sciences outside of the law and that certainly deterrent under the legal system is unnecessary" (House of Commons Debates, 1972, p. 1699). In other words, suicide attempts would no longer be treated as criminal acts, but they would be seen as symptomatic of psychological disturbance or mental illness in need of treatment.

Assisted Suicide

Since 1893 counseling, aiding, or abetting suicide have been *Criminal Code* offences. The maximum penalty was originally life imprisonment, but in 1955 this was reduced to 14 years. Judicial sympathy for a crime that currently carries the second most severe punishment available under Canadian law is evident in a number of convictions that resulted in fines or suspended sentences (Statistics Canada, 1876–1973). The longest reported sentence is four years in an Ontario case where a husband gave his wife a loaded shotgun. The wife survived a self-inflicted wound to the belly and her husband's conviction and jail sentence were overturned on appeal (*R. v. Loomes*, 1975). The next longest sentences are two British Columbia cases that each received 42 months of jail (*R. v. Allen*, 1997; *R. v. Fraser*, 2010). Notably, *Loomes*, *Allen*, and *Fraser* all involved men accused of giving loaded shotguns to individuals who were not suffering from serious physical illness.

Only two physicians are known to have been convicted for aiding or abetting the suicides of their patients. Both received two-year sentences (*R. v. Genereux*, 1999; *R. v. Sharma*,

2007) and their professional bodies also struck them from medical practice ("Dr. Sharma," 2007; *Genereux (Re)*, 1998).

In 1993, the Supreme Court of Canada narrowly (5-4) denied a terminally ill woman's petition for a constitutional right to physician-assisted suicide (*Rodriguez v. British Columbia*, 1993). Recently, the federal parliament soundly defeated Bill C-384 (Young, 2010), a law that would have permitted voluntary euthanasia and assisted suicide (House of Commons, 2009). In contrast to parliament's position, public opinion polls show majority support for physician-assisted suicide and euthanasia (Angus Reid, 2009, 2010).

Retention of Canada's 117-year prohibition on assisted suicide is grounded in the premise that it affirms the value of life. The general counter-argument is that life includes death, and the value of life is diminished if one cannot do what one wants with it. In her dissenting opinion in *Rodriguez v. British Columbia* (1993), Justice McLachlin (now Chief Justice of the Supreme Court of Canada) observed that the law makes an arbitrary and illogical distinction between suicide and assisted suicide in that the former is legal and the latter is not.

Whether arbitrary or illogical, the effect of the law is that individuals who choose to suicide in a law-abiding manner must act to minimize the legal culpability of others. Therefore, some right-to-die proponents are backing away from legal reform agendas and are instead focusing on humane and effective DIY approaches for suicide (Battin, 2005; Côté, 2008; Docker, 2007; Humphry, 2010; Nitschke & Stewart, 2009).

THE RISE OF THE NUTECH MOVEMENT

In 1999, NuTech—new technologies for self-deliverance—was formed to promote self-empowerment through technological solutions for humane suicide (Ogden, 2001). Its principals were John Hofsess of the Right to Die Society of Canada; Derek Humphry, founder of the Hemlock Society, and Dr. Philip Nitschke, founder of Exit International (Côté, 2008; Humphry, 2008). NuTech focuses on the development of simple and non-violent suicide methods that do not require medical prescriptions. Some of the devices developed under the NuTech program use inert gas to cause death by oxygen deprivation (Ogden, 2001; Ogden & Wooten, 2002). Others methods involved carbon monoxide delivery systems (Prahlow & Doyle, 2005) and lethal barbiturates have been synthesized in home-style laboratories (Nitschke & Stewart, 2009).

Dr. Philip Nitschke entered the world stage as the first physician to legally provide euthanasia in 1996 and 1997 when Australia's Northern Territory briefly allowed the practice. Nitschke developed *Deliverance,* a software-enabled suicide machine that was used to help four people die. In 1997, the Australian federal parliament stopped the practice of euthanasia with legislation that overturned the Northern Territory *Rights of the Terminally Ill Act* (Nitschke & Stewart, 2005). *Deliverance* is now on display in the Science Museum of London (Euthanasia Machine, n.d.).

Nitschke foresaw that prohibition would paradoxically encourage research into effective suicide techniques. At NuTech's second meeting, held in Seattle, Washington, in 1999, Nitschke argued:

. . . it is [politicians'] cowardice that has provided the greatest fillip to the NuTech enterprise. Their activities have changed forever the voluntary euthanasia debate which will now move, I believe, away from legislative models towards those strategies that provide individual self empowerment.

This is a future that will cause anxiety amongst many from within the voluntary euthanasia movement and NuTech will attract considerable internal censure. In the same manner as Jack Kevorkian's activities were denounced as destructive by many supporters of voluntary euthanasia, so too will those who advocate technical solutions be criticised from within. (Nitschke, 1999, p. 7)

Nitschke has dedicated himself to fulfilling his prophecy. An array of new suicide techniques have appeared in recent years and many of the answers about how they work are available in libraries,

bookstores, and Internet sources (e.g., Humphry, 2010; Nitschke & Stewart, 2009). Medico-legal, forensic, and other scholarly journals have taken keen interest in the mechanics of these techniques and their social implications (Gallagher, Smith, & Mellen, 2003; Grellner, Anders, Tsokos, & Wilske, 2002; Harding & Wolf, 2008; Lyness & Crane, 2010; Martin, 2010; Ogden, 2010a, 2010b; Ogden, Hamilton, & Whitcher, 2010; Ogden & Wooten, 2002; Prahlow & Doyle, 2005).

The Peaceful Pill Handbook

Philip Nitschke launched the first edition of *The Peaceful Pill Handbook* (Nitschke & Stewart, 2006) at the 2006 World Federation of Right to Die Societies biannual conference, held in Toronto. Australian censors soon banned the book because it allegedly instructed on matters of crime for the manufacture, storage, possession, and importing of barbiturates, and also matters of crime for the mandatory reporting of sudden deaths (Australian Government Classification Review Board, 2007). The ban in Australia has probably helped sales since the book can be purchased in most countries through the Internet bookseller, Amazon. Indeed, the cover of the 2009 edition displays the annotations "Banned in Australia" and "Amazon Top 100 Bestseller."

The Peaceful Pill Handbook gives explicit information about several suicide methods, including hypoxia inside a plastic bag, carbon monoxide poisoning, cyanide poisoning, and overdose with certain prescription drugs. The methods are rated according to the "Exit RP Test"—a reliability and peacefulness test (Nitschke & Stewart, 2009, p. 36). Pentobarbital has the highest "reliability and peacefulness" score. This drug, in the form of barbituric acid, was first synthesized in 1864 (Mendelson, 1980) and introduced for clinical use in 1904 (López-Muñoz, Ucha-Udabe, & Alamo, 2005). Pentobarbital is a hypnotic capable of inducing sleep or coma, and in large doses it will quickly cause death from respiratory depression. A variety of barbiturates with differing properties in terms of speed of action and duration were prescribed under the trade names of Veronal, Seconal, Amytal, Pentothal and Nembutal. . . . Their hypnotic and sedative effects were so dominant commercially that fewer than a dozen other sedative-hypnotics enjoyed market success prior to 1960 (Charney, Mihic, & Harris, 2001). Before safer benzodiazepine sleeping pills started to replace barbiturates in the 1960s, prescription barbiturates were involved in more than half of drug suicides (Mendelson, 1980), including the "probable suicide" of Marilyn Monroe (López-Muñoz, Ucha-Udabe, & Alamo, 2005, p. 339). For animal euthanasia, injection of sodium pentobarbital is considered the fastest and most reliable agent (American Veterinary Medical Association, 2007). Pentobarbital is also the preferred drug for human euthanasia and assisted suicide, where permitted. For lethal purposes, the standard oral dose in the Netherlands is 9g (Kimsma, 1996), 10g in Oregon and Washington (Nitschke & Stewart, 2009), and 15g at Dignitas in Switzerland (L.A. Minelli, personal communication July 4, 2010). The maximum daily therapeutic dose is 200mg. (López-Muñoz, Ucha-Udabe & Alamo, 2005).

There are reports of suicides by pentobarbital in veterinarians and staff who have access to the drug (Clark & Jones, 1979; Cordell et al., 1986; Poklis & Hameli, 1975). In the Australian Capital Territory ("ACT"), concern has arisen that veterinarians are giving pentobarbital to animal owners. The following veterinary board statement probably has more to do with the protection of human life and professional compliance than animal care:

It has come to the notice of the Board that some veterinarians may be providing owners of animals with pentobarbitone to administer in the case of an animal with a terminal condition which does not improve with appropriate treatment.

Pentobarbitone is an extremely dangerous drug in untrained hands. The dangers to the owner or other members of the household in having pentobarbitone available are extremely serious.

The Board considers that the supply of pentobarbitone in this manner constitutes unprofessional conduct and is not to be undertaken. (ACT Veterinary Surgeons Board, 2007, p. 6)

EXIT INTERNATIONAL AND THE VANCOUVER PUBLIC LIBRARY

The Australian government's attempt to censor Dr. Nitschke has probably had the unintended effect of spreading Exit's message more widely (Jansen & Martin, 2003; Martin, 2010). Nitschke regularly promotes Exit's literature and self-help message at workshops around the world. In the autumn of 2009 Exit scheduled its first Canadian workshop, which was to be held at the Vancouver Public Library in British Columbia. However, the library reneged on a commitment to allow Exit a facility for the workshop (Bermingham, 2009). Library authorities said legal advice warned that the Exit program could contravene Canada's criminal law (Vancouver Public Library, 2009).

Exit eventually held the workshop before a packed crowd of senior citizens at a Vancouver Unitarian Church. Sales of Exit books and DVDs were brisk. As part of Exit's due diligence, attendees were required to sign an "Exit Workshop Disclaimer" verifying that they were over the age of 50 and that they would not use the workshop information "in any way to advise, counsel, assist in the act of suicide, either my own or any other person."

Veterinary pentobarbital was discussed at the workshop, complete with empty sample bottles and a video clip showing people purchasing the drug from veterinary suppliers in Mexico. Dr. Nitschke informed the audience that people had also purchased the drug in Peru, Thailand, and China. To overcome language barriers, *The Peaceful Pill Handbook* has many photographs of pentobarbital products so that foreigners need only show veterinary shopkeepers the image of the item they want to purchase.

It is impossible to know whether any of the workshop attendees actually used the DIY information to die. However, one woman who was too ill to attend the workshop later used Exit's information. . . .

DISCUSSION

Legal Considerations for the Husband and Wife

. . . [P]rovincial statutes in Canada require the reporting of suicides and other sudden deaths. British Columbia's *Coroners Act* (2007) says that a person must report the facts and circumstances of sudden deaths, including those by "self-inflicted injury," to a coroner or peace officer. The judicial interpretation of the legal requirement to report is not clear and I have not found any instances where a person has been prosecuted for failing to report a suicide. In 1994 I documented over 30 suicides and assisted suicides in a master's thesis (Ogden, 1994). The B.C. Coroner did not raise any concerns about non-reporting of death after reviewing my thesis.

A recent Ontario case raises unique issues for individuals who attend the suicide of their spouse (*R. v. Fonteece*, 2010). Mr. Peter Fonteece entered into a suicide pact with his wife, Ms. Yanisa Fonteece. Before ending her life with an overdose of an unknown type of sleep medication and alcohol, Ms. Fonteece made her husband promise that he would not intervene and that he would not end his own life until she was dead. In the three days after his wife died, Mr. Fonteece's attempts to suicide failed, and he eventually called 911. He was indicted on charges for aiding suicide and causing death by criminal negligence. The aiding suicide charge was eventually dismissed because the evidence showed that his wife died without assistance. Mr. Fonteece pled guilty for causing death by criminal negligence and he was sentenced to 105 days for the time he served before the trial, plus 12 months probation. Although it is not a crime to be present at a suicide, Canadian law prescribes a duty on spouses to provide the necessaries of life. This meant that Mr. Fonteece had a legal duty to try to rescue his wife:

Because Mr. Fonteece was the husband of Yanisa Fonteece, he had a duty in law to preserve her life by seeking medical care for her. His failure to do so represents a wanton or reckless disregard for her safety. This is the omission that is referred to in s. 219: failing to secure medical aid when he was under a duty to his spouse to provide medical care in order to preserve her life. The law does not make an exception for the expressed wishes of the spouse to end her life. (*R. v. Fonteece*, 2010, para. 13)

Canadian law establishes the right of competent adults to refuse unwanted life-preserving treatment (*Nancy B. v. Hôtel-Dieu de Québec*, 1992). Perhaps because Mr. Fonteece pled guilty, the court did not address this conflict with his wife's verbal advance directive refusing medical care: "She instructed him not to intervene and not to call for help, saying she did not want to wake up in the hospital. She made him promise that he would not commit suicide until she was past reviving" (*R. v. Fonteece*, 2010, para. 6).

When it comes to suicide, the *Fonteece* case confirms a paternal duty of one spouse to override the autonomy and self-determination of the other. In the context of the woman consuming veterinary pentobarbital in the presence of her husband, it is an open question whether his obligation to call 911 after she lost consciousness would have been anything less than futile. The massive dose brought death so swiftly that it is difficult to imagine how prompt medical care could have helped. Nonetheless, the *Fonteece* case introduces a legal nuance for spouses who plan deaths in accordance with Exit International's information:

The contest between the state's wish to preserve life and an individual's lawful right to take her own life come into sharp focus in this case. Had Ms. Fonteece not been the spouse of the accused, he would have had no legal duty to seek medical assistance for her. He would not have been subject to prosecution by the state. While the law is grounded in morality, its business is not morality. The law does not require its citizens to engage in moral behaviour; it only requires them to act according to the law. It is against that background that this court must sentence Mr. Fonteece. (*R. v. Fonteece*, 2010, para. 18) . . .

The Future of Suicide and Assisted Suicide

In less than a century, suicide in Canada has gone from being among the most serious of crimes of free will to no crime at all, reconstituted as a social problem to be addressed by "sciences outside of the law" (House of Commons Debates, 1972, p. 1699). Whether suicide should be a mental health problem subject to "prevention" is a matter of debate (Szasz, 1986).

Martin (2010) describes three general paths for the future of assisted suicide. Path 1, prohibition, is the path Canada has always followed. This path forces covert conduct. Path 2, legalization and quasilegalization, is that taken by Switzerland, Netherlands, Belgium, Luxembourg, Oregon, Washington, and Montana. This path fosters regulation and accountability (Griffiths, Weyers, & Adams, 2008). Path 3 involves the dissemination of information about techniques for peaceful death. This path is difficult to regulate and it appears to be gaining popularity. [The] report of the woman who followed Exit International's guidance to import pentobarbital and then end her life illustrates not only that the DIY advice is effective, but also that current controls of law enforcement and public health authorities are easily skirted.

I have argued elsewhere that the non-medical deathing counterculture is a direct consequence of prohibition (Ogden, 2001). In the *Rodriguez* case, Justice Sopinka said that "relaxation of the absolute prohibition takes us down 'the slippery slope'" (*Rodriguez v. British Columbia (Attorney General)*, 1993, para. 165). Absolute prohibition, however, also means an absolute lack of control. A more desirable option would be for policy makers to define situations and criteria for the regulation or legalization of assisted death so that underground activities can be limited, rather than promoted. Regulation can help to ensure society's interest that suicides occur in "appropriate" circumstances, with some assurance that it is done well and correctly, and properly documented. In the meantime, the techniques and the strategies of the DIY movement are sure to become more refined and sophisticated, thereby making it much more difficult for regulators to get the kind of "buy-in" that has been achieved in jurisdictions more permissive than Canada (Ziegler, 2009; Ziegler & Bosshard, 2007).

CRITICAL THINKING QUESTIONS

1. Do you think suicide should be legal or illegal? By the same token, do you think assisted suicide should be legal or illegal? If you answered the two questions differently, can you explain why?

2. Why are most governments in the world so reluctant to legalize euthanasia? At the same time, what explains the movement that agitates for assisted suicide?

3. Is there a danger that people might succumb to assisted suicide because they don't want to be a burden on their family? Can coercion be a problem? Is there an effective way to distinguish between a case of voluntary assisted suicide and one where coercion is involved?

NOTE

1. The figures on suicide prosecutions are based on preliminary data in a statistical project with my colleague Greg Jenion, PhD.

REFERENCES

ACT Veterinary Surgeons Board. (2007). *Standards Statement: Use and management of S8, euthanasia solutions and benzodiazepines*. Available: http://www.health.act.gov.au/c/health?a=sendfile&ft=p&fid=-1437583211&sid=.

American Veterinary Medical Association. (2007). AVMA Guidelines on euthanasia. Schaumburg, Il: AVMA. Available: http://www.avma.org/issues/animal_welfare/euthanasia.pdf.

Angus Reid. (February 15, 2010). Two thirds of Canadians express support for legalizing euthanasia (Opinion poll). Available: http://www.visioncritical.com/wp-content/uploads/2010/02/2010.02.15_Euthanasia_CAN.pdf.

———. (September 3, 2009). Britons, Canadians on the same page on legalizing euthanasia (Opinion poll). Available: http://www.visioncritical.com/2009/09/britons-canadians-on-the-same-page-on-legalizing-euthanasia.

Australian Government Classification Review Board. (February 24, 2007). *Review decision. Peaceful Pill Handbook.*

Battin, M. P. (2005). *Ending life: Ethics and the way we die.* Oxford: Oxford University Press.

Bayatrizi, Z. (2008). *Life sentences: The modern ordering of mortality.* Toronto: University of Toronto Press.

Bermingham, J. (October 26, 2009). An unholy debate: Vancouver church opens its doors to right-to-die advocate. *National Post,* p. A3.

Burbidge, G. W. (1890). *A digest of criminal law of Canada (crimes and punishments).* Toronto: Carswell.

Charney, D. S., S. J. Mihic, & R. A. Harris. (2001). Hypnotics and sedatives. In J. G. Hardman, L. E. Limbird, & A. G. Gilman (Eds.), *Goodman & Gilman's pharmacological basis of therapeutics* (pp. 399–427). New York: McGraw-Hill.

Coroners Act, SBC 2007, Chapter 15. Available: **http://www.bclaws.ca/EPLibraries/bclaws_new/document/ID/freeside/00_07015_01.**

Clark, M. A., & J. W. Jones. (1979). Suicide by intravenous injection of a veterinary euthanasia agent: Report of a case and toxicological studies. *Journal of Forensic Sciences, 24,* 762–767.

Cordell, W. H., S. C. Curry, R. B. Furbee, & D. L. Mitchell-Flynn. (1986). Veterinary euthanasia as suicide agents. *Annals of Emergency Medicine, 15,* 939–943.

Côté, R. N. (2008). *In search of gentle death: A brief history of the NuTech group.* Mount Pleasant, SC: Corinthian Books.

Docker, C. (2007). *Five last acts.* Edinburgh, Scotland: Exit.

Downie, J. (2004). *Dying justice: A case for decriminalizing euthanasia and assisted suicide in Canada.* Toronto: University of Toronto Press.

Euthanasia machine, Australia, 1995–1996. (n.d.). Available: **http://www.sciencemuseum.org.uk/broughttolife/objects/display.aspx?id=91717.**

Genereux (Re), [1998] O.C.P.S.D. No. 4.

Gallagher, K. E., D. M. Smith, & P. F. Mellon. (2003). Suicide asphyxiation by using pure helium gas: Case report, review, and discussion of the influence of the Internet. *American Journal of Forensic Medicine and Pathology, 24,* 361–363.

Grellner, W., S. Anders, M. Tsokos, & J. Wilske. (2002). Suizide mit exit bags: Umstände und besondere problemlagen bei sterbebleitungen [Suicide using exit bags: Circumstances and particular problems surrounding assisted deaths]. *Archive Fur Kriminologie, 209,* 65–75.

Griffiths, J., H. Weyers, & M. Adams. (2008). *Euthanasia and law in Europe.* Portland, OR: Hart Publishing.

Harding, B. E., & B. C. Wolf. (2008). Case report of suicide by inhalation of nitrogen gas. *American Journal of Forensic Medicine and Pathology, 29,* 235–237.

House of Commons. (2009). *Bill-C384: An Act to amend the Criminal Code (right to die with dignity).* Available: **http://www2.parl.gc.ca/HousePublications/Publication.aspx?Docid=3895681&file=4.**

House of Commons Debates, 4th Session, 28th Parliament, Vol. II (1972) (testimony of Otto Lang). Ottawa: Queen's Printer.

Humphry, D. (2008). *Good life, good death: Memoir of an investigative reporter and pro-choice advocate.* Junction City, OR: Norris Lane Press.

———. (2010). *Final exit: The practicalities of self-deliverance and assisted suicide for the dying* (3rd ed. rev.). New York: Delta.

Jansen, S. C., & B. Martin. (2003). Making censorship backfire. *Counterpoise, 7,* 5–15.

Kimsma, G. K. (1996). Euthanasia and euthanazing drugs in the Netherlands. *Journal of Pharmaceutical Care in Pain & Symptom Control, 4,* 193–210.

López-Muñoz, F., R. Ucha-Udabe, & C. Alamo. (2005). The history of barbiturates a century after their clinical introduction. *Neuropsychiatric Disease and Treatment, 1,* 329–343.

Lyness, J. R., & J. Crane. (2010). Carbon monoxide poisoning from disposable charcoal barbeques. *American Journal of Forensic Medicine and Pathology.* Advance online publication. doi:10.1097/PAF:0b013e3181d03cc7.

Martin, B. (2010). Techniques to pass on: Technology and euthanasia. *Bulletin of Science, Technology & Society, 30,* 54–59.

Mendelson, W. B. (1980). *The use and misuse of sleeping pills: A clinical guide.* New York: Plenum Medical Book Company.

Nancy B. v. Hôtel-Dieu de Québec, [1992] Q.J. No. 1, 69 C.C.C. (3d) 450.

Nitschke, P. (1999). *Self deliverance new technology conference.* Unpublished paper.

Nitschke, P., & F. Stewart. (2005). *Killing me softly: Voluntary euthanasia and the road to the peaceful pill.* Camberwell, Victoria, Australia: Penguin.

———. (2006). *The peaceful pill handbook.* Lake Tahoe, NV: Exit International U.S.

———. (2009). *The peaceful pill handbook* (Revised ed.). Bellingham, WA: Exit International U.S.

Ogden, R. D. (1994). *Euthanasia and assisted suicide in persons with Acquired Human Immunodeficiency Syndrome (AIDS) or Human Immunodeficiency Virus (HIV).* (Master's thesis, Simon Fraser University, Burnaby, B.C.).

———. (2001). Non-physician assisted suicide: The technological imperative of the deathing counter-culture. *Death Studies, 25,* 387–402.

———. (2010a). The debreather: A report on euthanasia and suicide assistance using adapted scuba technology. *Death Studies, 34,* 291–317.

———. (2010b). Observation of two suicides by helium inhalation in a prefilled environment. *American Journal of Forensic Medicine and Pathology, 31,* 156–161.

———, W. K. Hamilton, & C. Witcher. (2010). Assisted suicide by oxygen deprivation with helium at a Swiss right-to-die organization. *Journal of Medical Ethics, 36,* 174–179.

——— & R. H. Wooten. (2002). Asphyxial suicide using helium and a plastic bag. *American Journal of Forensic Medicine and Pathology, 23,* 234–237.

Poklis, A., & A. Z. Hameli. (1975). Two unusual barbiturate deaths. *Archives of Toxicology, 34,* 77–80.

Prahlow, J. A., & B. W. Doyle. (2005). A suicide using a homemade carbon monoxide "death machine." *American Journal of Forensic Medicine and Pathology, 26,* 177–180.

R. v. Allen, Vancouver, No. CC960754 (B.C.S.C.) (May 14, 1997) (Unreported).

R. v. Fonteece, [2010] O.J. No. 2020.

R. v. Fraser, Vancouver, No. 25097 (B.C.S.C.) (April 27, 2010) (Unreported).

R. v. Genereux, [1999] O.J. No. 1387, 44 O.R. (3d) 339, 136 C.C.C. (3d) 338.

R. v. Loomes, [1975] O.J. No. 1259.

R. v. Sharma, Vernon, No. 41187-1 (B.C. Prov.C.) (June 11, 2007) (Unreported).

Rodriguez v. British Columbia (AG), [1993] S.C.J. No. 94, [1993] 3 S.C.R. 519.

Sharma, Ramesh Kumar Dr. (June 11, 2007). *Disciplinary Actions of the College of Physicians and Surgeons of British Columbia.* Available: **https://www.cpsbc.ca/files/pdf/2007-06-11-sharma.pdf**.

Statistics Canada. (1876–1973). *Annual report of statistics of criminal and other offences* (Series 85–201). Ottawa: Author.

Szasz, T. (1986). The case against suicide prevention. *American Psychologist, 41,* 806–812.

Taschereau, H. E. (1893). *The Criminal Code of Canada as amended in 1893 with commentaries, annotations, precedents of indictments, etc.* Toronto: Carswell.

Vancouver Public Library. (2009). *Legal counsel advises assisted suicide workshop could contravene Criminal Code* [Press release]. Available: **http://www.vpl.vancouver.bc.ca/news/details/legal_counsel_advises_workshop_could_contravene_criminal_code**.

Young, H. (May 1, 2010). Don't fear the slippery slope. *Ottawa Citizen,* p. B.7.

Ziegler, S. J. (2009). Collaborated death: An exploration of the Swiss model of assisted suicide for its potential to enhance oversight and demedicalize the dying process. *Journal of Law, Medicine & Ethics, 37,* 318–330.

—— & G. Bosshard. (2007). Role of non-governmental organizations in physician assisted suicide. *British Medical Journal, 334,* 295–298.

66

The Disenchantment of Modern Life

MAX WEBER

In this excerpt from his speech "Science as a Vocation," delivered at Munich University in 1918, Weber claims that the rise of science has changed our way of thinking about the world. Whereas people in the past confronted a world of mystical forces, now we assume that all things yield to human comprehension. Thus, Weber concludes, the world has become "disenchanted." Notice, however, that something is lost in the process—for, unlike the churches of the past, science can provide no answer to questions about the ultimate meaning in life.

Scientific progress is a fraction, the most important fraction, of the process of intellectualization which we have been undergoing for thousands of years and which nowadays is usually judged in such an extremely negative way. Let us first clarify what this intellectualist rationalization, created by science and by scientifically oriented technology, means practically.

Does it mean that we, today, for instance, everyone sitting in this hall, have a greater knowledge of the conditions of life under which we exist than has an American Indian or a Hottentot? Hardly. Unless he is a physicist, one who rides on the streetcar has no idea how the car happened to get into motion. And he does not need to know. He is satisfied that he may "count"

Source: Excerpts from *Max Weber: Essays in Sociology* by Max Weber, edited by H. H. Gerth & C. Wright Mills, translated by H. H. Gerth & C. Wright Mills. Translation copyright © 1946, 1958 by H. H. Gerth and C. Wright Mills. Used by permission of Oxford University Press.

on the behavior of the streetcar, and he orients his conduct according to this expectation; but he knows nothing about what it takes to produce such a car so that it can move. The savage knows incomparably more about his tools. When we spend money today I bet that even if there are colleagues of political economy here in the hall, almost every one of them will hold a different answer in readiness to the question: How does it happen that one can buy something for money—sometimes more and sometimes less? The savage knows what he does in order to get his daily food and which institutions serve him in this pursuit. The increasing intellectualization and rationalization do *not*, therefore, indicate an increased and general knowledge of the conditions under which one lives.

It means something else, namely, the knowledge or belief that if one but wished one could learn it at any time. Hence, it means that principally there are no mysterious incalculable forces that come into play, but rather that one can, in principle, master all things by calculation. This means that the world is disenchanted. One need no longer have recourse to magical means in order to master or implore the spirits, as did the savage, for whom such mysterious powers existed. Technical means and calculations perform the service. This above all is what intellectualization means. . . .

Science today is a "vocation" organized in special disciplines in the service of self-clarification and knowledge of interrelated facts. It is not the gift of grace of seers and prophets dispensing sacred values and revelations, nor does it partake of the contemplation of sages and philosophers about the meaning of the universe. This, to be sure, is the inescapable condition of our historical situation. We cannot evade it so long as we remain true to ourselves. And if Tolstoi's question recurs to you: As science does not, who is to answer the question: "What shall we do, and, how shall we arrange our lives?" or, in the words used here tonight: "Which of the warring gods should we serve? Or should we serve perhaps an entirely different god, and who is he?" then one can say that only a prophet or a savior can give the answers. . . .

To the person who cannot bear the fate of the times like a man, one must say: May he rather return silently, without the usual publicity build-up of renegades, but simply and plainly. The arms of the old churches are opened widely and compassionately for him. After all, they do not make it hard for him. One way or another he has to bring his "intellectual sacrifice"—that is inevitable. If he can really do it, we shall not rebuke him. For such an intellectual sacrifice in favor of an unconditional religious devotion is ethically quite a different matter than the evasion of the plain duty of intellectual integrity,

which sets in if one lacks the courage to clarify one's own ultimate standpoint and rather facilitates this duty by feeble relative judgments. In my eyes, such religious return stands higher than the academic prophecy, which does not clearly realize that in the lecture-rooms of the university no other virtue holds but plain intellectual integrity: Integrity, however, compels us to state that for the many who today tarry for new prophets and saviors, the situation is the same as resounds in the beautiful Edomite watchman's song of the period of exile that has been included among Isaiah's oracles:

He calleth to me out of Seir, Watchman, what of the night? The watchman said, The morning cometh, and also the night: if ye will enquire, enquire ye: return, come.

The people to whom this was said has enquired and tarried for more than two millennia, and we are shaken when we realize its fate. From this we want to draw the lesson that nothing is gained by yearning and tarrying alone, and we shall act differently. We shall set to work and meet the "demands of the day," in human relations as well as in our vocation. This, however, is plain and simple, if each finds and obeys the demon who holds the fibers of his very life.

CRITICAL THINKING QUESTIONS

1. In what sense do members of a traditional society know more about their world than we do? In what sense do we know more?

2. What is "Tolstoi's question"? Why can science not answer it?

3. What does Weber see as the great burden of living in a modern society? In other words, what comforts of the past are less available to modern people?

67

Facebook: Friend or Foe?

DANIEL TROTTIER

Facebook is often seen as a neutral site for friends and acquaintances to meet and exchange information. This reading presents another, more insidious perspective on the popular social networking site.

INTRODUCTION

In comparing one kind of information leak against another, a comedian portraying Julian Assange stated, "I give you private information on corporations for free, and I'm a villain. [Facebook creator Mark] Zuckerberg gives your information to corporations, for money, and he's [Time Magazine's] Man of the Year" (SNL 2010). The real Assange had much harsher words for Facebook, calling it "the most appalling spying machine that has ever been invented" (Emmett 2011). Facebook is now synonymous with surveillance. Interpersonal, institutional, and other kinds of scrutiny take place on social media. Moreover, they interact with each other in ways that scholars and users are only beginning to understand. The full consequences of social media's

Source: Essay "Facebook: Friend or Foe?" by Dr. Daniel Trottier, used courtesy of the author.

expansion remain to be felt. Uncertain conditions of visibility are a certainty on social media.

. . . Social media are online services where users submit personal information for any number of reasons. Surveillance on social media involves numerous kinds of watchers. These include friends, family and employers, but also law enforcement agencies and those who control sites like Facebook. This paper reflects on the growth of social media services, and considers their implications for surveillance studies. It proposes a framework for understanding how social media brings together different social spheres, making a range of personal data from those spheres searchable and visible. It also considers two topics that warrant specific focus: investigative surveillance on social media, and surveillance by social media developers themselves. This approach is aligned with a science and technology studies perspective that focuses on technologies as they are taken up in society (Grint and Woolgar 1997; Nye 2006). Such a perspective highlights the design stage as well as the circumstances surrounding technological growth. Facebook is perpetually redesigning itself, and its overall trajectory remains opaque to users.

While scholars from various disciplines are studying social media, the increased visibility of personal information through services like Facebook makes them a crucial topic for surveillance studies. This perspective considers surveillance to be the focused and systematic collection of personal information (Lyon 2001). Moreover, the leak is the principal means by which information from one context migrates to other contexts. Leaks often result from malice or incompetence, but Facebook operates precisely to exchange information from one context to another. The leak becomes standard. . . .

. . . In less than six years, Facebook has accumulated over half a billion users (FB About 2011). These users share their lives with each other, including over thirty billion pieces of content per month (ibid.). Facebook was launched for university students, but its users have become demographically and culturally vast. As well, businesses, employers, and politicians now maintain a presence on the site. Official presences enable public relations and promotional efforts, but they also facilitate watching over a specific population, market, or demographic. Facebook and other social media carry a significant cultural impact. These technologies are synonymous with new media communication. Yet on first pass services like Facebook are quite unremarkable. Facebook does not perform any novel functions: its users exchange personal information and other digital media in a routine manner. Facebook's social impact can also be understated. Its users rapidly grew accustomed to sharing content with "friends," to the point that it became yet another mundane service that is embedded in social life. Facebook is remarkable in presenting itself as being very unremarkable. Social media are almost-forgettable interfaces that mediate social relations. . . .

Facebook has undergone an exponential growth in recent years, and with this growth comes the assumption that it is a de facto site for sociality. . . . Its social relevance is greatly augmented as more attention and engagement is directed towards its interface. Not only does it become the primary location to communicate with people—often in plain sight of a very broad audience—but it also becomes the first location where people are identified. Users invest their attention towards their profiles. But they also invest their reputations, as their profile comes to have a greater monopoly of their identity. Facebook's increasing control of individual identities can be compared to attempts to implement national identity cards. Identity card schemes dictate that every citizen possesses a card, and that the card becomes the frontline means to identify citizens (Lyon 2009). Yet while mandatory schemes are routinely met with resistance, Facebook's emphasis on peer relations and mutual visibility makes it a more attractive option. Moreover, social media adds a networked dimension to identity, as users are also judged by their friends' identities and content (Wills and Reeves 2009). . . .

INVESTIGATIVE SURVEILLANCE ON SOCIAL MEDIA

When a Wayne Gretzky jersey was stolen from a shop in Ottawa, it only took fifteen minutes for staff to identify one of the shoplifters on Facebook (Butler 2010). While Facebook's history is peppered with student indiscretions becoming public knowledge, police and other investigative agencies are turning to social media in order to collect information about criminal activity. Police consider social media to be part of their jurisdiction, as a source of evidence as well as a location for offences to occur. For instance, threats that are uttered online are treated as punishable offences (Protalinski 2011). Online venues are not treated as representations of real life spaces, but rather as spaces in their own right. In the United States, Department of Homeland Security officials are "friending" applicants for citizenship in order to scrutinize them (Lynch 2010). These agencies take advantage of social networks by placing themselves within a context of information sharing and personal disclosure. They also take advantage of users' so-called "narcissism" (Cheng 2010), as even people who have something to hide want to share their lives with other users.

Social media are increasingly harnessed by law enforcement and investigative agencies. These practices and tendencies also spill out in other sectors, like the investigation of insurance claims (Millan 2011) as well as divorces (Popken 2011). But this remains a critically under-theorized and understudied topic. Social media make large sections of social life visible, and investigative agencies are taking advantage of that visibility. Surveillance studies need to focus on how this visibility is being used by these agencies. This topic sheds light on contemporary investigation techniques, but it also illustrates the pathways and dynamics of contemporary social media visibility.

Police can obtain information on social media through conventional and unconventional means. Social media services have opened up official channels for police to obtain private information from their servers. These services know their value as a source of evidence for these agencies, to the extent that Facebook, Twitter, MySpace, and others have produced compliance documents (Lynch 2011) that dictate what kind of information can be obtained from warrants, court orders, and other legal procedures. When starting an investigation, it is increasingly common for police to first turn to Facebook and other social media. Not only is it a low-cost and low-risk option, but investigators also benefit from not being identified as such. Professional watchers are often personal users, and this knowledge and access are assets. A lot of information on social media can be obtained simply by logging on to these sites. When information is protected by privacy settings, investigators can use a personal profile to establish a connection with the suspect. They may pretend to be a stranger, or even a trusted friend or family member of the suspect (Zetter 2010; Kerrigan 2011). Although it is not the first time that individuals close to a suspect are used against them, social media offer novel kinds

of insight. Police can covertly monitor interaction between a suspect and their peers. This can be done with or without subpoenas, depending on the suspect's privacy settings. As well, visible social ties can themselves be informative. In the case of the stolen hockey jersey, it was the suspects' friends that gave him away, as one of these friends belonged to a Facebook fan community for the store.

Social media policing goes beyond simply gathering information about suspects. Events ranging from house parties to political protests are also made visible through social media. Not only is information about these events public by default, this information is also searchable and archived, making sites like Facebook optimal for investigations. Finally, social media are not just a new kind of watching for police. They can also make crime and criminals visible by quickly broadcasting information about subjects to a vast audience. Social media like Twitter and Facebook are employed to disseminate time-sensitive information, including AMBER Alerts (O'Connor 2011). This suggests enrolling entire social networks to report suspicious activity. A campus security director involved with this kind of initiative elaborates on its implications for surveillance practices:

I always find it very interesting that when people talk about Facebook and then the next word is security, automatically they have the George Orwell kind of 1984, Big Brother's watching. In our department, it's the exact opposite, right? We're all about sharing information. Our philosophy here is security is everybody's responsibility. Our philosophy here is giving you all the information that you need to make informed decisions about your own safety. (Daryl)

This officer positions sharing information with a population in direct contrast to watching over that population. Yet these two operate in tandem, as social media users can be both a target and an extension of a surveillance apparatus. Users not only make themselves visible in a way that augments investigative surveillance, but they also directly contribute to this watching on behalf of the investigative agencies. Social media offer multiple avenues for individuals to augment institutional scrutiny. . . .

SOCIAL MEDIA AS (META-)WATCHERS: WHAT WILL THEY DO NEXT?

Facebook's exponential growth makes it ideal for a lot of kinds of watching. These developments only underscore the urgency of looking at Facebook and other social media companies' own surveillance practices. The visibility of users on these interfaces gives the impression that they are directing the growth of social media, that the tail is wagging the dog. To be sure, the entirety of the tail is staggering, but the dog still wields control. For all the talk about coping with and taking advantage of social media, little attention is paid to its configuration. These companies are highly publicized, yet scholars and the broader public have little knowledge about Facebook's knowledge of users, as well as their intentions surrounding this knowledge. A specific type of social media surveillance, one that includes the construction and continued maintenance of a digital enclosure, is central to a scholarly understanding of social media, as well as the continued domestication of surveillance technologies.

Information on Facebook leaks from one context to another. Yet the site is designed to retain both content and users. Facebook is internally leaky, but has rigid boundaries. In this sense, it is a kind of enclosure. Mark Andrejevic refers to the digital enclosure as "an interactive realm wherein every action, interaction, and transaction generates information about itself" (2009:53). This definition suggests an infrastructure where personal information is produced and made meaningful insofar as it generates more information. The enclosure suggests a return to a kind of pre-modern sociality where everybody knows everybody else's business. Yet the presence of surveillance technology suggests new kinds of visibility. As Andrejevic suggests:

> Interactivity promises not a return to the relative lack of anonymity of village life, but rather to a state of affairs in which producers have more information about consumers than ever before, and consumers have less knowledge about and control over how this information is being used. (2007:27)

On first pass it seems that all social media users have the potential to watch over each other. But those who manage the enclosure have a privileged view of its contents. As a result, user behaviour can trigger revisions to the interface. Users may develop their own practices within an enclosure, and this can be framed as a kind of customization, or even resistance. However, the enclosure's owners can observe and either subsume or eliminate those practices. Manovich (2008) draws on de Certeau (1988) to assert that user tactics become an owner's strategies. Users may develop tactics to manage their presence on sites like Facebook, but these tactics are visible to Facebook itself. Likewise, visible protests within the enclosure and discussions about disengagement from the enclosure can be exploited to retain users. As Cohen indicates:

> Not only is surveillance the method by which Facebook aggregates user information for third-party use and specifically targets demographics for marketing purposes, but surveillance is the main strategy by which the company retains members and keeps them returning to the site. (. . .) [I]t is the unpaid labour of producer-consumers that facilitates this surveillance. (2008: 8)

The increased focus on everyday life is in itself a concerning development. Poster remarks that everyday life was formerly the remainder of institutional action and scrutiny (2004). However, the rapid onset of information and communication technologies in the domestic sphere means it is increasingly subject to commoditization and surveillance.

Treating social media as enclosures provides an important balance to perspectives that regard these services as ephemeral in use and consequence. Users do submit information with immediate and localized contexts in mind. Yet their privileging of these contexts does not diminish long-term consequences made possible by the retention of this information. There is a disjuncture between immediate use and long-term consequences of exposure in social media enclosures. People live their lives through social media, and these enclosures are the interface in relations between individuals, businesses and institutions. The mutual augmentation described here is the result of the increased co-habitation of these groups. Facebook as an enclosure retains extensive information about its users, yet little is known about what Facebook is doing with this information, or the kind of watching that it performs.

Facebook and other social media are growing, and their growth is difficult to assess. But these services follow a deliberate trajectory, even if this is only evident to its designers. Specific features are chosen instead of others, and specific purposes are privileged over others. These decisions are part of a larger vision that Facebook's developers are pursuing, and focusing on these developments will contribute to a better understanding of social media surveillance. Research on social media often treats it as sui generis, and assumes that it functions independently of human intervention. This overlooks the intentions and efforts of companies like Facebook. Moreover, this approach is troubling when talking about a platform that adopts new features on a regular basis.

Facebook is distinct from other online services in terms of the possibilities that it extends to users. Users can always upload and distribute content, and they can partially control the flow of their information, but they cannot control the interface that distributes their information. Users can report a troubling photo, or block someone from seeing their profile, but they are otherwise passive to emerging schemes for distributing information. Below are some key features that have been designed by Facebook to regulate the flow of personal information. As these become standard features of social media, we should question their inevitability, and consider alternative efforts.

1. Soliciting information from users, and enrolling friends in this effort. Facebook treats incomplete profiles as problems in need of remedy. Not only is the user faced with this concern, but their friends are also asked to provide information about the delinquent user. New users are repeatedly solicited by Facebook to provide personal information, including biographical details, social contacts, and profile pictures. Users encounter these requests when they first log on, but they also appear on their profiles as highlighted alerts. Moreover, their friends will also be asked to supply these details. These efforts guide Facebook users to obtain content from their friends. Generating personal

information on social networks rests on relations between users and their peers.

2. Restricting the outward flow of information. Facebook has long followed a "walled garden" approach. As a site of social and informational convergence, it hinders efforts to export content to other spaces. In doing so Facebook obliges users to inhabit—or dwell (DeCerteau 1988)—rather than simply visit the site. Facebook has recently augmented its messaging service in order to obviate email (Gaudin 2010), and its search feature is meant to rival Google's (Vogelstein 2009). These efforts limit not only the outward flow of information, but also the outward flow of attention by users. This produces a kind of watching based on a monopolization of social activity by one company.

3. Redirecting users towards each other as feeds. The promotion of information feeds suggests a deliberate strategy to organize and streamline the exchange of personal information. The feed represents Lash's (2006) description of information being pushed onto users. His assessment that "[t]he data find you" (ibid.: 580) can mean that relevant information is pushed onto profiled users, but it also suggests that our own personal information tracks and locates us, greatly augmenting our visibility. As stated above, this is a development that users first resisted, but have since come to treat as central to social media sociality. In that users rely heavily on these feeds, they diminish the importance of the user's construction of a profile as an identity marker, transforming self-presentation into a flow of real-time statements populated by several identities.

4. Turning personal information into advertising. On numerous occasions, Facebook has attempted to merge personal information with branded advertising (Pearlman 2007; Zuckerberg 2007; Ling 2008; Zuckerberg 2010). A comment posted about a restaurant can become an advertisement that is directed at the user's friends. Users in turn have consistently opposed these schemes. Yet Facebook continues to push this model as an inevitable feature. Social media taps into a long history of marketers exploiting personal information (Gandy 1993). Advertising schemes increasingly resemble viral marketing (Boase and Wellman 2001). Again, this suggests a dramatic lowering of the costs associated with these activities, so much so that actual user involvement in these efforts is minimized. Facebook's business strategy alters relations between consumers and producers of content (Beer and Burrows 2007). Attaching personal information to a brand or product adds contextual relevance to the latter, while making the former visible in unanticipated ways.

Social media enclosures operate through a remarkable asymmetry of visibility. User activity is made incredibly visible, while the mechanics that govern these practices are themselves hidden from view. Facebook in particular is a database, and one that contains a robust range of content. But it is also an interface for all other kinds of watching. This suggests a kind of meta-surveillance, with Facebook watching over other watchers. As Facebook itself holds all information that passes through it, any kind of watching between users is under their scrutiny. All other kinds of watching on Facebook are a matter of using Facebook, and these practices leave traces that become part of the enclosure. Even actions intended to reduce visibility, like removing content or changing privacy settings, can be recorded as a kind of information.

CONCLUDING REMARKS

Facebook and other social media increasingly regulate social life. The way they collect, archive, and disseminate personal information is noteworthy for surveillance scholars. . . . Police and other investigative agencies are developing a number of strategies to take advantage of the increased visibility of social life. Moreover, interfaces like Facebook themselves have a unique and privileged visibility and control over social media activity.

One lingering concern in the age of Facebook surveillance is the prominence of information leaks. While these were formerly a marginal but troubling occurrence, information now readily flows between social contexts. The rapid expansion of social media in a broader context of ubiquitous leaks suggests a "levelling of the hierarchy of surveillance" (Haggerty and Ericson 2000: 606), in the sense that more and more people are subject to public exposure. Yet this does not imply a democratization of visibility. Any democratizing potential is called into question when its users are entirely visible to agents whose practices remain opaque. Despite the complexity of relations and effects, it appears that new kinds of capital and control will endure through social media.

CRITICAL THINKING QUESTIONS

1. Do you feel in any way unnerved by the fact that the information on Facebook is so public? Have you ever heard of someone getting into trouble for doing something inappropriate on Facebook? (This does not have to be a crime, but something as innocent as a person misbehaving at a party.)

2. Facebook is all about impression management; that is, putting your best "face" forward. Are you careful about posting things on Facebook (e.g., a suggestive video) with the view that it might be looked at by a future employer? What are some of the other issues of concern mentioned in the reading?

3. Would you feel comfortable with having a GPS in your car or your phone that could be tracked by your parents, employer, police, or significant other? Why or why not?

REFERENCES

Andrejevic, Mark. 2007. *iSpy: Surveillance and power in the interactive era.* Lawrence, KS: University Press of Kansas.

———. 2009. Privacy, exploitation, and the digital enclosure. *Amsterdam Law Forum*, 1(4): 47–62.

Beer, David, and Roger Burrows. 2007. Sociology and, of and in Web 2.0: Some initial considerations. *Sociological Research Online*, 12(5). Available: **http://firstmonday.org/htbin/cgiwrap/bin/ojs/index.php/fm/article/view/1978/1853**. Accessed May 10, 2011.

Boase, Jeffrey, and Barry Wellman. 2001. A plague of viruses: Biological, computer and marketing. *Current Sociology*, 49(6): 39–55.

Boyd, Danah. 2008. Facebook's privacy trainwreck: Exposure, invasion, and social convergence. *Convergence: The International Journal of Research into New Media Technologies*, 14(1): 13–20.

Butler, Don. 2010. Facebook helps store owner track thief: Security video checked against business's "friends." *Ottawa Citizen*. October 31. Available: **http://www.ottawacitizen. com/technology/Facebook+helps+store+owner+track+ thief/3753823/story.html**. Accessed May 10, 2011.

Cohen, Nicole. 2008. The valorization of surveillance: Towards a political economy of Facebook. *Democratic Communiqué*, 22(1): 5–22.

Cheng, Jacqui. 2010. Govt relies on Facebook "narcissism" to spot fake marriages, fraud. *Ars Technica*. October. Available: **http://arstechnica.com/tech-policy/news/2010/10/ govt-takes-advantage-of-facebook-narcissism-to-check-on-users.ars**. Accessed May 10, 2011.

de Certeau, Michel. 1988. *The practice of everyday life*. Berkeley: University of California Press.

Emmett, Laura. 2011. "WikiLeaks revelations only tip of iceberg – Assange." *RT.com*. May 2. Available: **http:// rt.com/news/wikileaks-revelations-assange-interview**. Accessed May 10 2011.

FB About. 2011. About Facebook. Available: **http://www. facebook.com/facebook?sk=info**. Accessed May 10, 2011.

Gandy, Oscar. 1993. *The panoptic sort: A political economy of personal information*. Boulder, CO: Westview.

Gaudin, Sharon. 2010. Facebook messaging throws a blow at Google: Facebook Messages could draw users from Gmail. *Computerworld*. November 16. Available: **http:// www.computerworld.com/s/article/9196618/Facebook messaging throws a blow at Google**. Accessed May 10, 2011.

Grint, Keith, and Steve Woolgar. 1997. *The machine at work: Technology, work and organization*. Cambridge: Polity Press.

Haggerty, Kevin D., and Richard V. Ericson. 2000. The surveillant assemblage. *British Journal of Sociology*, 51(4): 605–22.

Kerrigan, Sean. 2011. US Gov. software creates "fake people" on social networks." *Examiner.com*. February 18. Available: **http://www.examiner.com/social-media-in-national/ us-gov-software-creates-fake-people-on-social-networks-to-promote-propoganda**. Accessed May 10, 2011.

Lash, Scott. 2006. Dialectic of information? A response to Taylor. *Information, Communication & Society*, 9(5): 572–81.

Ling, Benjamin. 2008. Platform: One year(ish) later. *The Facebook Blog*. July 28. Available: **http://blog.facebook.com/ blog.php?post=24577977130**. Accessed May 10, 2011.

Lyon, David. 2001. *Surveillance society: Monitoring everyday life*. Buckingham: Open University Press.

——. 2009. *Identifying citizens: ID cards as surveillance*. Cambridge: Polity Press.

Lynch, Jennifer. 2010. Applying for citizenship? U.S. Citizenship and Immigration wants to be your "friend." *Electronic Frontier Foundation*. October 12. Available: **https://www.eff.org/deeplinks/2010/10/applying-citizenship -u-s-citizenship-and**. Accessed May 10, 2011.

Lynch, Jennifer. 2011. Social media and law enforcement: Who gets what data and when? *Electronic Frontier Foundation*. January 20. Available: **https://www.eff.org/ deeplinks/2011/01/social-media-and-law-enforcement-who-gets-what**. Accessed May 10, 2011.

Manovich, Lev. 2008. *Software takes command*. Unpublished. Available: **http://lab.softwarestudies.com/2008/11/ softbook.html**. Accessed May 10, 2011.

Millan, Luis. 2011. Insurers and social media: Insurers' use of social networks impinges on privacy rights. *The Lawyers Weekly*. March 25. Available: **http://www. lawyersweekly.ca/index.php?section=article&volume= 30&number=43&article=2**. Accessed May 10, 2011.

Nye, David. 2006. *Technology matters: Questions to live with*. Cambridge, MA: The MIT Press.

O'Connor, Mary Quinn. 2011. Social-networking tools help find missing children. *FoxNews.com*. March 30. Available: **http:// www.foxnews.com/scitech/2011/03/30/social-networking -tools-help-missing-children**. Accessed May 10, 2011.

Pearlman, Leah. 2007. Facebook ads. *The Facebook Blog*. November 6. Available: **http://blog.facebook.com/blog. php?post=6972252130**. Accessed May 10, 2011.

Popken, Ben. 2011. Facebook is number one tool for divorce lawyers. *The Consumerist*. May 18. Available: **http://consumerist. com/2011/05/facebook-is-number-one-tool-for-divorce-lawyers.html**. Accessed May 28, 2011.

Poster, Mark. 2004. Consumption and digital commodities in the everyday. *Cultural Studies*, 18(2): 409–23.

Protalinski, Emil. 2011. Teenager tries to hire a hitman via Facebook, fails. *ZDNet*. February 15. Available: **http:// www.zdnet.com/blog/facebook/teenager-tries-to-hire-a-hitman-via-facebook-fails/129?tag=mantle skin;content**. Accessed May 10, 2011.

Shirky, Clay. 2008. *Here comes everybody: The power of organizing without organizations*. New York: The Penguin Press.

SNL. 2010. *Saturday night live*. Season 36, Episode 10. First aired December 18. NBC.

Vogelstein, Fred. 2009. Great Wall of Facebook: The social network's plan to dominate the internet—and keep Google out. *Wired.com*. July 17. Available: **http://www. wired.com/techbiz/it/magazine/17-07/ff facebookwall**. Accessed May 10, 2011.

Wills, David, and Stuart Reeves. 2009. Facebook as a political weapon: Information in social networks. *British Politics*, 4(2): 265–81.

Zetter, Kim. 2010. Undercover Feds on social networking sites raise questions. *Wired.com*. March 16. Available: **http://www.wired.com/threatlevel/2010/03/undercover-feds-on-facebook**. Accessed May 10, 2011.

Zuckerberg, Mark. 2007. Thoughts on Beacon. *The Facebook Blog*. December 5. Available: **http://blog.facebook. com/blog.php?post=7584397130**. Accessed May 10, 2011.

——. 2010. Building the social web together. *The Facebook Blog*. April 21. Available: **http://blog.facebook.com/blog. php?post=383404517130**. Accessed May 10, 2011.

68

The Price of Modernization: The Case of Brazil's Kaiapo Indians

MARLISE SIMONS

Among the billions of poor people throughout the Third World, few will have a chance for a better life. But this is exactly what has happened to the Kaiapo, people who live deep in Brazil's rainforest. Has affluence been the blessing that the Kaiapo imagined it would be? To at least some of their number, the modernization of the Kaiapo amounts to little more than the systematic destruction of their traditional way of life.

It is getting dark when Chief Kanhonk sits down in the yard outside his home, ready for a long evening of conversation. Night birds are calling from the bush that sparkles with fireflies. Whooping frogs make a racket by the river. No one seems worried by the squadron of bats sweeping low overhead.

It is that important moment of the day when Indians of the Amazon, who use no written language, meet to talk, pass on information, and tell stories. The night is when they recall ancestral customs, interpret dreams, and comment on changes in nature and other events of the day. But from a nearby home come the sounds of a powerful rival: A television set is screeching cartoons at a group of children. I understand now why, that morning, by way of saying hello, these naked

children of the rain forest had shouted things like "He-Man" and "Flintstones."

Three years ago, when money from the sale of gold nuggets and mahogany trees was pouring into Gorotire, Chief Kanhonk agreed to bring in television, or the "big ghost," as it is called here. A shiny satellite dish now stands on the earthen plaza like an alien sculpture, signaling that Gorotire—a small settlement of some 800 people on the Fresco River, a tributary of the Amazon—has become one of the wealthiest Indian villages in Brazil.

Yet Chief Kanhonk appears to regret his decision. "I have been saying that people must buy useful things like knives or fishing hooks," he says darkly. "Television does not fill the stomach. It only shows our children and grandchildren white people's things."

The "big ghost" is just one of the changes that have been sweeping over Gorotire, but it seems to be worrying the elders the most. Some believe it is powerful enough to rob them of their culture. Bebtopup, the oldest medicine man in the village, explains his misgivings: "The night is the time the old people teach the young people. Television has stolen the night."

When I discuss this with Eduardo Viveiros, a Brazilian anthropologist who works with a more isolated Amazonian tribe, he seems less worried. "At least they quickly understood the consequences of watching television," he says. "Many people never discover. Now Gorotire can make a choice."

It was the issue of choice that first drew me to the Kaiapo Indians of the lower Amazon Basin. They seemed to be challenging the widely held notion that forest Indians are defenseless in face of the pressures of the competitive and predatory Western world around them. Unlike most of Brazil's 230,000 Indians, they go out into the white world to defend their interests, and it is no longer unusual to see Kaiapo men—in their stunning body paint and feathered headdresses—showing up in Congress in Brasilia, the nation's capital, or lobbying by doing a war dance outside a government office. They have even bought Western gadgets to record and film their festivals.

Once the masters of immense stretches of forest and savannas, the Kaiapo were for hundreds of years among the most skillful farmers and hunters and fiercest warriors of central Brazil. They terrified other tribes with their raids. From the seventeenth to the nineteenth centuries, they not only resisted the slaving raids of the Portuguese invaders but they also attacked white traders and gold prospectors with such a vengeance that royal orders came from Portugal to destroy the Kaiapo. The white man's wrath and his diseases killed many, yet there are still close to 3,600 Kaiapo in more than a dozen different villages near the Xingu River. They have quarreled and regrouped, but their lands, several vast reservations, are more secure than those of many other tribes.

After many years of isolation in the forest, the Kaiapo now have to deal with the growing encroachments of white society. "They are going through a great transition," says Darrell Posey, an American anthropologist who has worked in Gorotire for more than a decade. "Their survival is a miracle in itself. But I worry whether they can go on making the changes on their own terms."

Colombia, Ecuador, Peru, and Venezuela—four of nine nations in the Amazon Basin, which harbors some 800,000 Indians—each have large numbers of tropical-forest Indians. But nowhere are pressures on Indian land as great as they are in Brazil. As the Amazon is opened up, developers bring in highways, settlers, cattle ranchers, mines, and hydroelectric dams. In Brazil alone, more than ninety tribes have disappeared since the beginning of this century.

The clearing of large areas of the rain forest and the fate of the Indians are also rapidly becoming an issue of international concern. Interest in the region has risen as ecological concerns, such as ozone depletion, the greenhouse effect, and other changes in the global environment become political issues. More attention is paid to scientists who are alarmed at the destruction of the rain forest—a vital flywheel in the world's climate and the nursery of at least half of the world's plant and animal species.

This has also prompted an increasing interest in the highly structured world of the forest Indians and their ancient and intricate knowledge of nature that permits them to survive in the tropical jungle without destroying it. (The Hall of South American Peoples, which includes a life-size model of a Kaiapo warrior, recently opened at the Museum of Natural History in New York City.)

As Indians find greater support among environmentalists, they also get more organized in their fight to protect their habitat. The Kaiapo held their first international congress last week in Altamira, in central Brazil, protesting government plans to build several massive dams that would flood Indian land.

In Brazil, Indian tribes occupy 10 percent of the nation's territory, although much of their land has not been demarcated. Brazil's past military regimes elevated Indian affairs to a national-security issue, because many tribes live in large areas of border land. It is official policy to integrate Indians into the larger society, and the National Indian Foundation, with its 4,900 employees, is in charge of implementing this.

In my eighteen years in Latin America, I have heard many politicians and anthropologists discuss what is usually called "the Indian problem," what to "do" about cultures that have changed little in thousands of years. One school of thought holds that the remote tribes should be kept isolated and protected until they can slowly make their own choices. Another school accepts that the Indian world is on the wane, and talks about "guiding" the Indians toward inevitable change— a process that should take several generations.

But some anthropologists and politicians, including the Brazilian government, believe in still more rapid integration. When Romeo Jucá was head of the Indian Foundation, he said that it was only right for Indians to exploit their wealth, even if it meant acculturation. "We have to be careful how fast we go," he said, "but being Indian does not mean you have to be poor."

Gerardo Reichel-Dolmatoff is one of Latin America's most respected anthropologists. He insists that the Indians are their own best guides into Western society. An Austrian-born Colombian, Reichel-Dolmatoff has worked in Colombia's forests, at the Amazon's headwaters, for almost fifty years. "We cannot choose for them," he insists. "And we cannot put them into reserves, ghettos, ashokas. They are not museum exhibits. . . . If Indians choose the negative aspects of our civilization, we cannot control that. If there is one basic truth in anthropology, it is that cultures change. Static cultures do not exist."

The Indians themselves are pleading for more protection and respect for their cultures. Conrad Gorinsky, son of a Guyana Indian mother and himself a chemist in London, recently said: "We don't want the Indians to change because we have them comfortably in the back of our mind like a kind of Shangri-La, something we can turn to even if we work ourselves to death in New York. But we are hounding and maligning them instead of recognizing them as the guardians of the forests, of the world's genetic banks, of our germ plasm and lifelines."

The aboriginal peoples we call Indians are as different from one another as, say, Europeans are. Even the most isolated groups remain separate fiefdoms with widely varying experiences, beliefs, and histories. The degree of contact they have with the outside world is just as varied.

I first met Kaiapo tribesmen three years ago in Belém, a large city at the mouth of the Amazon. I saw them again in Brasilia, the capital. In both places, they demonstrated their political skills and capacity to mobilize, showing up in large numbers to protest measures by the government. They seemed particularly adept at commanding the attention of the press. Their body paint, feathers, and other paraphernalia made them appear warlike, exotic, and photogenic.

Back in Gorotire, as it turns out, they are more "ordinary." Wearing feathers and beads, explains Kubei, a chief's son, is for special occasions. "It's our suit and tie." Besides the satellite dish, the Kaiapo also have their own small airplane. Their new wealth has also given them the luxury of hiring non-Indians to help plant new fields. But they remain ready to attack white intruders; some of the adult men have markings on their chests that record the number of outsiders they have killed.

Two roads fan out from the center of Gorotire. A new sand track leads east on a five-hour drive to the town of Redenção. The other road goes south and, in a sense, it leads into the past. Dipping into the forest, it becomes a path that meanders through open patches where the Kaiapo women grow corn, sweet potatoes, bananas, manioc. On the plain ahead, it joins an ancient trail system that once reached for hundreds of miles into northern and western Brazil.

One morning, Beptopup (medicine man, shaman, connoisseur of nature), the anthropologist

Darrell Posey (who speaks the Kaiapo language), and I wander into the bush. Beptopup walks past the plants the way you go down a street where you know everyone. Stopping, nodding, his face lighting up with happy recognition, he sometimes goes into a song—a soft, high-pitch chant for a particular plant.

He picks leaves, each one familiar, each one useful. One serves to remove body hair. Another, he says, can prevent pregnancy. The underside of one leaf is so rough it is used to sandpaper wood and file fingernails. Beptopup collects his plants in the morning, he says, because "that is when they have the most strength."

Stopping at a shrub, we look at the large circle around its stem, where nothing grows. "This and other plants have been sent to a laboratory for analysis," says Posey. "We think this one has a natural weedkiller."

Beptopup holds up a branch of what he calls the "eye of the jaguar." "This was our flashlight," he says, showing how to set it afire and swing it gently so its strong glow will light one's path.

One afternoon, when the heat has crept into everything, the women and children come back from the fields to their village. They stop and sit in a creek to escape the swirling gnats and buzzing bees. Others sit outside their homes, going about their age-old business. One woman plucks the radiant feathers of a dead macaw. Another removes her eyebrows and eyelashes, because the Kaiapo women think they are ugly. (A nurse once told me that this custom might have a hygienic origin—to ward off parasites, for instance.) Kaiapo women also deepen their foreheads by shaving the top of their head in a triangle that reaches the crown—a fearsome sight to the unaccustomed eye.

I envy a mother who is clearly enjoying herself fingerpainting her three children. She draws black designs with genipap juice. On the face and the feet she puts red dye from the "urucu," or annatto, plant; Indians say it keeps away chiggers and ticks.

Change has come to Gorotire along the other road, the one leading east to Redenção. Recent

Kaiapo history is full of "firsts," but a notable turning point came when prospectors struck gold on Gorotire land in 1980. The Kaiapo raided the camp, twenty miles from the village, but failed to drive away the trespassers. Then they made a deal.

Last fall, when I was visiting Gorotire, about 2,000 gold diggers were stripping the land to the bone farther upstream, and the River Fresco passed the village the color of mud, its water contaminated with oil and mercury. I heard no one complain about that. Gorotire gets 7 percent of the mine's profits—several pounds of gold a week.

In 1984, a lumber company completed the first road. It signed a contract with the Indian Foundation for Gorotire's mahogany (the Indians are wards of the Brazilian government). Most of the mahogany is gone now, and the government agency split the profits with the Kaiapo. Gorotire chose to spend its gold and timber profits on new water and electricity lines and rows of brick houses. Only about half of the inhabitants now live in traditional palm-frond huts.

The young Kaiapo who earn a salary as supervisors at the gold camp have bought their own gas stoves, radios, sofas, and mattresses. For the community, the four tribal chiefs ordered several boats, trucks, and a small plane that ferries people and goods among nearby Kaiapo villages.

One evening, a truck arriving from Redenção—bringing rice, sugar, bottled gas, oil for the generator—is another reminder of how fast Gorotire is adapting to a Western economy. From being a largely self-sufficient community of hunters and farmers, it is now increasingly dependent on outside goods. In Gorotire, it is clearly money, no longer disease or violence, that has become the greatest catalyst for change. Money has given the Kaiapo the means and the confidence to travel and lobby for their rights. At the same time, it is making them more vulnerable.

I have seen other villages where Indians have received large sums of money—for the passage of a railroad or a powerline, or from a mining company. Such money is usually released in installments, through banks, but its arrival has put new strains on the role of the chiefs. Money and goods have introduced a new, materialistic expression of power in societies that have been egalitarian. Among most Indians, a man's prestige has always depended not on what he acquires but on what he gives away.

In Gorotire, some of the young men complain that the chiefs are not distributing community money and goods equally, that the chiefs' relatives and favorites are getting a bigger share and more privileges.

Darrell Posey, the anthropologist, believes the greatest political change came with the road. With it, he says, "the Kaiapo chiefs lost control of which people and what goods would come in." Previously, the chiefs had been the sole distributors. They had also played the vital roles of keeping the peace and leading the ceremonies. Now, the chiefs hardly know the liturgy of the ceremonies; their main task seems to be to deal with the outside world.

The transition is also changing the role of the medicine man. Bebtopup, for example, has an arsenal of remedies for the common ailments—fevers, diarrheas, snake bites, wounds. But he and his colleagues have lost prestige because they do not know how to deal with the diseases brought to Gorotire by white men, such as the pneumonia that strikes the children and the malaria spreading from the gold miners' camp.

Anthropologists sometimes say that when outsiders visit the Indian world, they often focus on themes central not to Indians but to themselves. This might explain why I was so bothered by the garbage, the flotsam of Western civilization.

Gorotire's setting is Arcadian. It lies on a bluff overlooking the River Fresco, with views of the forests across and the mountains behind. Spring rains bring waterfalls and blossoms. But these days the village is awash with rusting cans, plastic wrappers, tapes sprung from their cassettes, discarded mattresses, and clothes. New

domestic animals such as dogs, pigs, and ducks have left a carpet of droppings. And giant rats, which suddenly appeared some years ago, seem to be everywhere; some have bitten small children.

"Indians have never had garbage that was not biodegradable," says Sandra Machado, a Brazilian researching Kaiapo farming techniques here. "No one wants to take care of it."

It is a mild moonlit evening, and in the men's house many Kaiapo are watching soccer on television. The bank of the river is a quieter place to talk.

"If you look beyond the garbage and the stone houses, this is still a strong and coherent indigenous culture," says Darrell Posey, speaking of the mixed feelings he has about a decade of developments in Gorotire. "Despite everything, the language is alive, the festivals and initiation rights are observed."

Posey says that the Kaiapo in Gorotire and in other villages continue with their age-old natural farming techniques, using plants to fix nitrogen in the soil, chunks of termite nests instead of chemical fertilizers, plant infusions to kill pests, the nests of ferocious ants to protect fruit trees from other ant predators.

Biologists often complain that there have been many studies of exotic rituals, paraphernalia, and kinships of Indians, but that Western science has paid scant attention to the Indians' use of animals and plants.

Like others working in the Amazon region, Posey worries about the gap between the old and the young. "The old chiefs are turning over decisions to the young because they can drive a truck or operate a video machine or go to the bank," he says. "But the young people don't see the relevance of learning the tribal knowledge and it's being lost."

"You can afford to lose one generation," he adds, "because grandparents do the teaching of their grandchildren. But you cannot afford to lose two generations."

Gorotire has a small Government school, designed to help Indians integrate into the national society. The teacher, who speaks only Portuguese, has started organizing annual Independence Day parades. On the blackboard is a list of patriotic holidays, including Independence Day and the Day of the Soldier. I ask the children later what a soldier is. "Something of white people," one of them says.

Chief Poropot agrees that everyone must learn Portuguese. "The language of the Kaiapo is very ancient and it will never end," he says. "But the women and the children need to learn Portuguese to defend themselves."

Defend themselves?

"If they go to shop in Redenção, they have to talk," he says. "If they get sick, they cannot tell the doctor what they have."

Thirty miles from Gorotire, in the village of Aukre, another Kaiapo tribe is choosing a different strategy for change. Its best-known member is Paiakan, thirty-seven years old, the son of Chief Tikiri.

Calm and articulate, Paiakan has been named to "keep an eye on the whites" in the state capital of Belém. He acts as a kind of roving ambassador for the Kaiapo, even though each village is autonomous. When Kaiapo interests are threatened, he sends out warnings to the communities.

Paiakan's contacts with the outside world and the many pitfalls it holds for Indians have made him more conservative, he says, more so than in the early days, in the 1970s, when he first left home to work on the Trans-Amazonian Highway. As his father's main adviser, he has insisted that Aukre remain a traditional village.

It is built in the age-old circle of mud-and-thatch huts. There is no television, running water, pigs, or piles of garbage. Paiakan and his father have also banned logging and gold digging. This appears to have saved Aukre from the consumerism—and widespread influenza and malaria—of Gorotire.

"The lumber men have come to us with their bags of money," he says. "And we know we have a lot of gold. But we do not want to bring a lot of money in. The Indian still does not know the value of white man's objects or how to treat them." Paiakan cites clothing as an example. "The Indian wears something until it is stiff with dirt, then he throws it out."

But people now want things from the "world of the whites," he continues. "Pressure from the white society is so strong, there is no wall that can stop it." It is the task of the chief to measure the change, provide explanations, he says. "If someone wants to get a radio or a tape recorder, the chiefs cannot stop it."

In Aukre, where two aging chiefs are still in charge of buying goods for the community, they say that they will not buy gadgets. "We explain we cannot buy this thing for you because we do not have the batteries you need and we cannot repair it," Paiakan says.

Of late, Paiakan has been invited abroad to campaign for the protection of the rain forest. He knows the problem only too well. Ranchers have moved almost to the reservation's doorstep, felled trees, and set massive forest fires. Because of deforestation, there have been unusual changes in the water level of the Fresco River.

"Our people are getting very disoriented," says Paiakan. "It would be as if people from another planet came to your cities and started to tear down your houses. The forest is our home." With all the destruction going on, he continues, "the breath of life is drifting up and away from us."

At the age of seventy-eight and retired from teaching at the University of California at Los Angeles, the anthropologist Gerardo Reichel-Dolmatoff lives in Bogotá, Colombia, and is still writing. After studying changes in the Amazon for five decades, he is not optimistic about the prospects for the Indians.

"In Colombia, I don't know of a single case where an aboriginal culture has found a strong adaptive mechanism," he says. "Physical survival is possible. But I have not seen the ancient values replaced by a workable value system. I wish I could be more positive. But in fifty years I have seen too many traditions being lost, too many tribes disappear."

"For 500 years we have witnessed the destruction of the Indians. Now we are witnessing the destruction of the habitat. I suggest more field work, and immediate field work, because soon it will be too late."

At a conference on ethnobiology last fall, Reichel-Dolmatoff urged scientists to insist on spreading the message that Western science has much to learn from Indians, from their well-adapted lives and deeply felt beliefs, their view that whatever man subtracts he must restore by other means.

What suggestions has he made to Indians?

"Indians have to stay in touch with their language—that is absolutely essential," he says. "It embodies their thought patterns, their values, their philosophy." Moreover, he says, talented young Indians should be given a modern academic education, but also the chance to keep in touch with their people. "They come from cultures based on extraordinary realism and imagery. They should not be forced to enter at the lowest level of our society."

One night, I ask the chiefs in Gorotire: What happens if the gold runs out? After all, most of the mahogany is already gone. Young tribesmen

have wanted to invest some of the income, and the chiefs have accepted the idea. Gorotire has bought a home in Belém for Kaiapo who travel there, as well as three houses in Redenção. There is talk of buying a farm, a curious thought, perhaps, for a community that lives on 8 million acres of land. But the Kaiapo, so they say, want it so that white farmers can grow rice for them.

And there is talk of planting new mahogany trees. Soon the conversation turns to a bird that a tribesman explains is very important. It is the bird, he says, that spreads the mahogany seeds.

CRITICAL THINKING QUESTIONS

1. What have been the short-term consequences of the Kaiapo's new wealth? What are their long-term prospects?

2. What arguments can be made in support of continued effort by the Kaiapo to economically develop their resources? What arguments can be made against doing so?

3. In what ways are other countries involved in the changes taking place in the Amazon Basin?